Deny'd to all their Numerous Sighs
& their Long Services. Let not that dull
Vertu that always opposes it self to ow
Happiness, deprive yow of a greater Pleasure, then any ~~it~~ she is able to bestow: but
if yow needs will be so squeamish & so nice to be accessary to your own Deceiving
remember that Gratitude is a Vertu too
as well as Chastity; & by so much the greater, by how much it's Contrary is more
detested. Consider Joseph, that ~~it~~ my favor
is the onely thing that can [spelling] support yow
in the Condition yow now are in the Family of my Lord, & that by Doing your
self the service I [now] beg of yow; yow will
oblige me to rivet yow so strongly to
the Dignity yow now hold, that 'twill
be out of the Power of Fortune & the
Destinys themselves to remove yow. Thorough what Throngs of Difficultys & Dangers do men pursu [Promotion] Advancement: but
when the Way to certain Greatness is ~~it~~
carpetted with Delihts, who wud not ~~this~~
pronounce him a Mad-man that shud
Decline to tread it. Sure, wud hony cure Diseases, we shud ~~think~~ [hedge] his rather in his
Braine then in his Humors, that wud procrastinate his Recovery. See how fortune our self seems to contribute to our Happiness, by befrending vs with an Opportunity so inviting to those Delights, whose Name yow must expect rather from my Blushes then my ~~words~~ [tongue]. There we will in
the fruition of each other enjoy Delihts
that the Gods themselves might envy; &
that were infinitely below what they are,
if they did as much transcend the reach
of our Expressions. Neither ought it to lessen
their Value in our Esteem, that they are censured.

a The chan-
ge of my
Affection
will ~~be~~ not
be a greater
Impossibility
then the
~~[illegible]~~ robbing of
his favor.

The Early Essays and Ethics of Robert Boyle

Edited and Annotated
With an Introduction by
John T. Harwood

Southern Illinois University Press
Carbondale and Edwardsville

Printed in the United States of America
Production supervised by Natalia Nadraga

94 93 92 91 4 3 2 1

Library of Congress Cataloging-in-Publication Data

Boyle, Robert, 1627–1691.
The early essays and ethics of Robert Boyle / edited and annotated with an introduction by John T. Harwood.
p. cm.
Includes bibliographical references and index.
1. Ethics, Modern--17th century. I. Harwood, John T. II. Title.
BJ285.B69 1991
170--dc20 90-48968
ISBN 0-8093-1522-X CIP

The paper used in this publication meets the minimum requirements of American National Standard for Information Sciences — Permanence of Paper for Printed Library Materials, ANSI Z39.48–1984.

Endpapers and Frontispiece

(*Front*) These pages are reproduced from MS 195, ff. 180^{v}-181.

(*Back*) These pages are reproduced from BP 14, ff.2^{v}-3.

(*Frontispiece*) Johann Kerseboom's portrait of Robert Boyle at the age of 62. After Boyle's death the portrait was presented to the Royal Society.

All are reproduced by kind permission of the Royal Society.

Contents

For Arthur and Nyta Harwood

Acknowledgments

I am very pleased to thank scholars and institutions for their kindness and assistance. Michael Hunter has been an invaluable source of information about the early Royal Society, and his unpublished finding list of Boyle's manuscripts at the Royal Society made my work at the Royal Society significantly easier. Robert Latham, R. E. W. Maddison, and Charles Webster kindly answered a variety of queries. Malcolm Oster shared early chapters of his dissertation and was very informative about Boyle's religious background. David Beauregard, Steven Shapin, and Michael Hunter kindly read the introductory material and offered helpful suggestions. Archie Allen, Paul Harvey, and Nancy Mace helped identify Boyle's Latin and Greek sources and provided expert translations of puzzling passages. Tom Minsker and H. D. Knoble solved the technological problems of making computers behave, and they did so with unflagging good humor, patience, and clarity. Natalia Nadraga and Carol Burns provided expert guidance in seeing this volume into print.

I am grateful to the President and Fellows of the Royal Society for permission to print manuscripts in their archives and to reproduce the Kerseboom portrait of Boyle. I am equally obliged to the librarians of the Royal Society, N. H. Robinson and Sheila Edwards, for creating such a pleasant atmosphere for research. Their staff members—Alan Clark, Nina Cohen, Sally Grover, and Keith Moore—were extremely helpful and competent in answering questions and providing information, whether I was in their Library or on the other side of the Atlantic. Likewise, I wish to thank other libraries and librarians for assistance in using their collections and for permission to reprint materials in their archives, especially the Sheffield University Library (for permission to use and quote from the Hartlib papers), the Wellcome Institute for the History of Medicine, and the British Library. Librarians at my own institution, especially Charles Mann and Sandy Stelts, were always helpful in acquiring materials and answering questions.

With support from the Institute for the Arts and Humanistic Studies at Penn State, I was able to spend a very cold January in London at an early stage of the project. My University provided a sabbatical leave in 1987-88 so that I could work with manuscripts, not microfilms. Such assistance was very welcome.

Finally, I acknowledge the unwavering encouragement of Kathryn M. Grossman, whose understanding of *ēthikē aretē* owes nothing to the *Aretology*.

31 December 1990

Abbreviations

Manuscripts at the Royal Society

Boyle Lett.	Boyle Letters
BP	Boyle Papers Volume and folio numbers for the Letters and Papers will be in *Arabic* numerals (e.g., BP 8.118-20 refers to vol. 8, ff. 118-20).

Boyle's Collected Works

BW	*The Works of the Right Honourable Robert Boyle*, ed. Thomas Birch, 6 vols. (London 1772). Individual works will be cited by the short titles listed below along with the volume and page number of this edition; the volume number will be in *Arabic* numerals.

Short Titles of Individual Works

Philaretus	*Account of Philaretus* (see Maddison)
Simple Medicines	*Advantages of the Use of Simple Medicines*
Aerial Noct.	*Aerial and Icy Noctiluca*
Aret.	*Aretology, or Ethicall Elements*
Cert. Phys. Essays	*Certain Physiological Essays*
Chr. Virtuoso	*The Christian Virtuoso*
Cont. of New Exp.	*Continuation of New Experiments Physico-Mechanical*
Things above Reason	*A Discourse of Things above Reason*
Final Causes	*Disquisition about the Final Causes of Natural Things*
Exc. of Mech. Hypoth.	*Excellency of the Mechanical Hypothesis*
Exc. of Theol.	*Excellency of Theology*
Exp. Hist. of Cold	*Experimental History of Cold*
Exp. Hist. of Colours	*Experimental History of Colours*
Exp. et Obs. Phys.	*Experimenta et Observationes Physicae*
Swearing	*Free Discourse against Customary Swearing*
Vulgar Notion	*Free Inquiry into Vulgarly receiv'd Notion of Nature*
Hist. of Air	*General History of the Air*
Languid Motion	*Great Effects of even Languid and Unheeded Motion*
Greatness of Mind	*Greatness of Mind Promoted by Christianity*
Hidden Qualities	*Hidden Qualities of the Air*
High Veneration	*High Veneration to God*
Fluidity and Firmness	*History of Fluidity and Firmness*

Blood	*Humane Blood*
Hydro. Paradoxes	*Hydrostatical Paradoxes*
Theodora	*Martyrdom of Theodora*
Mech. Qualities	*Mechanical Qualities*
Med. Hydro.	*Medicina Hydrostatica*
Med. Exp.	*Medicinal Experiments*
Min. Waters	*Mineral Waters*
Nat. Hist. of Country	*Natural History of a Country*
New Experiments	*New Experiments Physico-Mechanical, touching the Spring of the Air*
Occ. Refl.	*Occasional Reflections*
Specific Medicines	*Of the Reconcileableness of Specific Medicines to the Corpuscular Philosophy*
Orig. of Gems	*Origin and Virtues of Gems*
Orig. of Forms	*Origin of Forms and Qualities*
Porosity	*Porosity of Bodies*
Resurrection	*Possibility of the Resurrection*
Rarefaction	*Rarefaction of the Air*
Reconcileableness	*Reconcileableness of Reason and Religion*
Flame and Air	*Relation betwixt Flame and Air*
Saltness	*Saltness of the Sea*
Scep. Chym.	*Sceptical Chymist*
Seraphic Love	*Some Motives and Incentives to the Love of God*
Vitiated Sight	*Some Uncommon Observations about Vitiated Sight*
Style	*Style of the Scriptures*
Usefulness	*Usefulness of Experimental Natural Philosophy, Parts I and II*

Secondary Sources

References to multi-volume works will be indicated by volume and page number (e.g., *Anatomy* 1.30 refers to vol. 1, p. 30, of Burton's *Anatomy of Melancholy*).

Anatomy	Robert Burton, *Anatomy of Melancholy*, 3 vols. (London 1932).
Alsted	Johann Alsted, *Encyclopædia* (Herborn 1630).
Ann. of Sci.	*Annals of Science*
Arist.	Aristotle
BJHS	*British Journal for the History of Science*
BL	British Library
"Ephemerides"	Samuel Hartlib's "Ephemerides" (Sheffield University) as transcribed by G. H. Turnbull
f., ff.	fol., fols.
Fiering	Norman Fiering, *Moral Philosophy at Seventeenth-Century Harvard* (Chapel Hill 1981).

HP	Hartlib Papers, Sheffield University
Laërtius	Diogenes Laërtius, *Lives of Eminent Philosophers*, trans. R. D. Hicks, 2 vols. (Cambridge, Mass. 1925).
I Lismore	*The Lismore Papers*, ed. Alexander Grosart, first series, 5 vols. (1886).
II Lismore	*The Lismore Papers*, ed. Alexander Grosart, second series, 5 vols. (1887-88).
Maddison	R. E. W. Maddison, *The Life of the Honourable Robert Boyle, F. R. S.* (London 1969).
Nich. Eth.	Aristotle, *Nichomachean Ethics*, trans. H. Rackham (Cambridge, Mass. 1934).
Notes and Records	*Notes and Records of the Royal Society*
OED	*A New English Dictionary on Historical Principles*, ed. J. A. H. Murray (Oxford 1888-1933).
Pseud. Epidemica	Sir Thomas Browne, *Pseudodoxia Epidemica*, ed. Robin Robbins, 2 vols. (Oxford 1981).
RB	Robert Boyle
Reynolds, *Treatise*	Edward Reynolds, *A Treatise of the Passions and Faculties of the Soule of Man* (1640).
RS	Royal Society
STC	Katherine F. Pantzer et al., *A Short-title Catalogue of Books Printed in England, Scotland, & Ireland and of English Books Printed Abroad, 1475-1640*, 2nd ed. (London 1976).
Tilley	Morris Palmer Tilley, *A Dictionary of the Proverbs in England in the Sixteenth and Seventeenth Centuries* (Ann Arbor 1950). Proverbs are cited by their number in this edition (c.g, T183) and indexed under "Tilley."
Thomas, *Decline*	Keith Thomas, *Religion and the Decline of Magic* (London 1971).
Webster	Charles Webster, *The Great Instauration: Science, Medicine and Reform, 1626-1660* (London 1975).
Wilson	F. P. Wilson, *The Oxford Dictionary of English Proverbs*, 3rd ed. (Oxford 1970).
Wing	Donald Goddard Wing, *A Short-title Catalogue of Books Printed in England, Scotland, Ireland, Wales, and British America, and of English Books Printed in Other Countries, 1641-1700* 2nd ed., 3 vols. (New York 1972-88).

Introduction

> It is a happinesse to be borne and framed unto vertue, and to grow up from the seeds of nature, rather than the inoculation and forced graffes of education; yet if we are directed only by our particular Natures, and regulate our inclinations by no higher rule than that of our reasons, we are but Moralists; Divinity will still call us Heathens.
>
> Browne, *Religio Medici* ii.§2

> For Understanding rul'd not, and the Will
> Heard not her lore, both in subjection now
> To sensual Appetite, who from beneath
> Usurping over sovran Reason claim'd
> Superior sway . . .
>
> Milton, *Paradise Lost* 9.1127-31

Although Robert Boyle (1627-1691) was one of the major figures of the early Royal Society, only half of his voluminous writings focus on natural philosophy. Because he delayed the publication of most early works for several years—and sometimes for several decades—we may initially be puzzled by his intellectual development and the relationships among his texts. Aside from the extensive discussion of Boyle's participation in the so-called Invisible College, his activities and development between his return to England in 1644 and the establishment of the Royal Society have been largely ignored.[1] Such neglect is curious because so many manuscripts have survived. This volume illuminates some of his preoccupations during those years by examining his early work as a moralist.

Boyle's status as a moralist in the eighteenth century can be seen in Dr. Johnson's preface to the *Dictionary* (1755), where he defended his lexicon for making accessible the writings of Hooker, Bacon, Milton, and Boyle, propagators of knowledge and teachers of truth. Modern scholars seldom consider those authors together, so Johnson's linkage suggests how Boyle was regarded a half century after his death. His reputation in the history of science is quite secure, and no doubt the tercentenary of his death in 1991 will bring fresh appreciation

---

[1] For discussion of the Invisible College, see Charles Webster, "New Light on the Invisible College: The Social Relations of English Science in the Mid-Seventeenth Century," *Trans. Royal Hist. Soc.* 24 (1974) 19-42; Webster, *Instauration* 57-67; Maddison, "Studies in the Life of Robert Boyle, F. R. S." *Notes and Records* 18 (1963) 104-24; James R. Jacob, *Robert Boyle and the English Revolution* (New York 1977) 28-37; and Nicholas Canny, *The Upstart Earl: A Study of the Social and Mental World of Richard Boyle, First Earl of Cork 1566-1643* (Cambridge 1982) 142-43. Two unpublished dissertations also provide very useful information about Boyle's background and development: Baden Teague's *The Origins of Robert Boyle's Philosophy* (Cambridge 1971) and Malcolm Oster's *Nature, Ethics and Divinity: The Early Thought of Robert Boyle* (Oxford 1990).

of his contributions to Restoration science. What may not be noticed, however, are the connections between his natural philosophy and his moral philosophy.

It is perhaps ironic that some of Boyle's earliest writings should first be published three centuries after his death. Though numerous holographs of his early writings on moral philosophy are held by the Royal Society, few scholars have used them to explain his intellectual development. The notable exceptions are R. E. W. Maddison in his *Life of the Honourable Robert Boyle* (London 1969) and James R. Jacob in his *Robert Boyle and the English Revolution* (New York 1977). The manuscripts included in this volume were examined in the 1740s by Thomas Birch and Henry Miles, who clearly described their provenance but excluded them from the *Works* because they seemed incomplete and perhaps because the editors had already edited so much material.[2] Given the sheer quantity of these materials and the editorial difficulties they present, it is easy to see why Birch and Miles excluded these manuscripts.

The Royal Society holds more than seventy-five volumes of manuscript materials written by or associated with Robert Boyle. These materials include forty-six volumes of papers, sixteen of notebooks, and seven of correspondence. In addition, I have recently found six new volumes that shed light on Boyle's interests: five volumes of medical notebooks and a partial inventory of his library at the time of his death.[3] These materials provide an extraordinary opportunity to witness the development of Boyle's career, to explore the literary and philosophical subtexts of his scientific writings, and to observe the role of authorship in his career. Quite early in life, he began to make lists of what he had written and what he planned to write. Such lists indicate the importance of authorship in his sense of vocation and define his range of interests.

For this volume I have selected manuscripts that illustrate Boyle's persistent themes, outlooks, and methods. Some selections are essays and are classified as such in his earliest known list (e.g., "Of Time and Idleness"). Another selection, "Joseph's Mistress," is a meditation not included in *Occasional Reflections*, even though it is clearly part of those meditations; still others are either

[2] Cf. the Preface (1.iii) and the list of manuscripts (1.ccxxxvi-ccxxxviii).

[3] Boyle's medical interests are illustrated in a great number of works. MS 41 dates from 28 May 1658 and contains medical receipts from Boate, Hartlib, Dr. Willis's "receipt for me" (that is, Boyle), many of Dr. Cox's receipts (e.g., 20 August 1673) for him, and so on. The receipts reflect many persons' handwritings, suggesting that friends and relatives wrote their receipts in this volume. In the back of the volume, in the hand of his long-time amanuensis Robin Bacon, is a receipt dated 15 April 1681. In addition, I believe that four Latin medical notebooks are also in Robin Bacon's hand. (Henry Miles identified Bacon's handwriting in BL Add. MS 4229, f. 66.) MSS 25-26 and 180-81 are nearly identical in content and binding, and unlike most medical receipts, indicate their printed sources (author, title, and page number). I have not yet explored the relations between these manuscripts and Boyle's published medical receipts (BW 5.312-91). MS 23, which I have entitled Boyle's library, is included in this volume.

long essays or private sermons perhaps referred to in Table 1 as essay #21, "Of the Ethickes," or #22, "An Inquisition concerning Happynesse." Because of limitations of space, I have excluded some very passionate musings in French and English on the nature of virtue ("Diurnall Obseruations, Thoughts, and Collections," BP 44) and many other occasional writings.[4] While most early works are relatively short, MS 195, *The Aretology, or Ethicall Elements*, runs to more than 60,000 words.

These texts illustrate how Boyle's approach to moral philosophy was complemented and enriched by his understanding of natural philosophy.[5] This edition thus makes accessible the intellectual and religious origins of Boyle's most vital *themata*, which emerged at the beginning of Boyle's participation in the Invisible College, and connects Boyle's earliest ethical discourse with his later religious and philosophical writing. In historical significance these manuscripts may be compared to Newton's *Trinity Notebook*.[6] Both works disclose intellectual questions, patterns of interests, habits of mind, and, in Boyle's case, methods of expression that persisted into and perhaps shaped later writing. Taken collectively, these manuscripts shed new light on his intellectual origins and development.

In this introduction I first review the place of these manuscripts in Boyle's career as a writer. In section 2 I examine the sources and contexts of Boyle's moral philosophy, discussing the influence of Johann Alsted and of the Hartlib circle on these texts. Next I analyze the function of writing—and of writing moral philosophy—in the social milieu Boyle joined in the late 1640s. In section 4 I consider the interplay of rhetoric and ethics in his moral essays, reviewing both his dissatisfaction with contemporary ethical discourse and his efforts to solve the rhetorical problems he identified. In the final section I present the editorial policies that have shaped this volume.

---

[4] For an even more extreme form of such musings, see BP 8.118-20. Boyle began this perplexing document on 25 March 1649.

[5] Writing to Lady Ranelagh on 31 August 1649, Boyle promised to share "those moral speculations, with which [his] chemical practices have entertained [him]," indicating that he would soon complete a discourse on the theological use of natural philosophy (BW 6.49).

[6] J. E. McGuire and Martin Tamny, eds., *Certain Philosophical Questions: Newton's Trinity Notebook* (Cambridge 1983).

§1: Manuscript Evidence and the Early Career

In 1650, on his twenty-third birthday, Boyle made an inventory of his writings that reflected current interests and projects (see Table 1).[7] The longer works listed in the table pertain to moral philosophy, popular divinity, and casuistry; only nine of the twenty-six essays (#3, 4, 8-10, 13, 14, 16, and 18) are more clearly related to natural philosophy than to moral philosophy. Indeed, the balance between moral philosophy and natural philosophy at this time has a far heavier proportion of moral philosophy than in his *Works* as a whole.

While it is not possible to discern which projects were completed and which were in progress in 1650, we can safely draw several conclusions from this list and from Table 2, which summarizes the publication history of his early work. First, in addition to whatever else Boyle did between 1645 and 1660, he invested an enormous amount of time and energy in writing. Second, while some topics reflected his early interest in natural philosophy, these topics certainly did not dominate the list. To understand Boyle's development, we must recognize two facts: that he began his career as a moralist, not as a natural philosopher, and that he never lost his interest in (and need for) casuistry and popular divinity.[8] Throughout his long and varied career he found occasions to explicate natural philosophy by the principles of morality and religion (and vice-versa).

Our understanding of Boyle's intellectual origins and development has been complicated because some of the earliest writings are no longer extant. Even as a young man he burned some of his writings.[9] We further know that he

---

[7] Taken from BP 36.86. For a slightly different version of this list, see Maddison 64. This inventory, the earliest of many such lists, reveals the range of intellectual interests and writing projects. For later lists, see BP 36.20, which can be dated ca. 1657; ff. 32-35 includes published works and is dated ca. 1686; f. 59 and f. 75 are dated 7 July 1684 and list unpublished writings; ff. 122-23 (17 September 1691) lists the contents of boxes in particular rooms of Boyle's house. On f. 87, Boyle grouped his writings in five categories: theological, medical, chymical, philosophical, and miscellaneous.

[8] For a perceptive analysis of Boyle's later interest in casuistry, see Michael Hunter's "Alchemy, magic and moralism in the thought of Robert Boyle," *BJHS* 23 (1990) 387-410; for a useful summary of contemporary casuistry, see H. R. McAdoo, *The Structure of Caroline Moral Theology* (London 1949), ch. 3, and Thomas Wood, *English Casuistical Divinity during the Seventeenth Century* (London 1952). Edmund Leites has a narrower focus in *The Puritan Conscience and Modern Sexuality* (New Haven 1986) and in a collection of essays, *Conscience and Casuistry in Early Modern Europe* (Cambridge 1988).

[9] "Yet did [Philaretus] at Idle howres write some few verses both in French & Latin: & many Copys of amorous, merry, & Deuout ones in English; most of which, vncommunicated, the Day he came of Age he sacrific't to Vulcan, with a Dessein to make the rest perish by the same Fate, when they came within his Power; tho amongst them were many serious Copys, & one long one amongst the rest, against Wit Profanely or Wantonly employ'd; those two Vices being euer perfectly detested by him in others, & religiously declin'd in all his Writings" (Maddison 20-21). Later in life Boyle

Table 1. Authorship and Interests in 1650

Materials
&
Addenda

Design'd toward the Structure
& compleating of Treatises
already begun or written.
January the 25th 1649/50.

T in the Margin stands for the Treatise entituled Theodora.
DR. for Dayly Reflection.
PS. for Publicke-spiritednesse.
AR. for The Antagonist of Romances.
M.P. for My Opinion of Romances.
SS. for The Swearer Silenc't.
AP. for The Appendix to it.
S.L. for Seraphicke Loue.
CTM. for Consolation to T's Mother.
OR. for Occasionall [Meditations] Reflections.

ES. for Essays: which follow, and are signify'd by their preceding Number: viz
1. Of Time and Idlenesse. 2. Of Essays. 3. Of Naturall Philosophy and Filosofers. 4. Of Chymistry & Chymists. 5. Of Vniuersality of Opinions & of Paradoxes. 6. Of Authority in Opinions. 7. Of Antiquity & New-light. 8. Of Cold. 9. Of Atoms. 10. Of Dungs. 11. Of Good Language. 12. Of the Holy Scriptures. 13. Of the Mechanicks. 14. Of Inkes & Writings. 15. A Censure of some Preachers & Hearers of Sermons. 16. Of the Weapon salve, and occult Qualitys. 17. Of Heresies: & how little Knowledge is necessary in all Persons to Saluation. 18. Of Spotts. 19. Of true Christianity. 20. Of Reasoning & Discourse. 21. Of the Ethickes. 22. An Inquisition concerning Happynesse. 23. Of the Interpretation of Scripture. 24. Of Complaisance. 25. Of Censuring & Casuists. 26. Of the Vanity and Partiality of Fame.

was very insistent about destroying manuscripts and letters near the end of his life. "Whatever Papers be found of mine relateing to Theodora," he ordered, should "be burnt without fail" (BP 36.116). On ff. 122-23 he indicated where he kept particular manuscripts: on 17 September 1691, for instance, he kept a

---

resumed *writing* poetry: see MS 186 for a poem that served as an inventory of his writings (f. 16); for a more serious poem on faith and philosophy, MS 187, f. 147^v. BP 42 contains a small miscellany of seventeenth-century poems by such poets as Herrick and Carew as well as a comedy in French, *La Philosophe Duppé*, which was set in London.

Table 2. Publication of Boyle's Early Writings

Date of Composition	First Publication	Title
1645-47	1991	*The Aretology*
1646-49	1665	*Occasional Reflections*
1646	1991	"The Dayly Reflection"
1647-48	1655	"An invitation to a free and generous communication of secrets"
1647-49	1991	*Of Vice*, *Of Piety*, *Of Valour*, and other essays
1648	1659	*Seraphic Love*
1648	1695	*Free Discourse Against Swearing*
1649-50	1744	"An Account of Philaretus"
1649-52	1661	*Style of the Scriptures*
1649	1687	*Martyrdom of Theodora*
1650-53	1957	"Of ye Atomicall Philosophy," "Propositions on Sense, Reason, and Authority," and "The Requisites of a Good Hypothesis"
1651-1661	1954	"Reflections on the Experiments vulgarly alledged to evince the 4 Peripatetique Elements." These reflections are an early version of *The Sceptical Chymist* (1661).
1652-58	1663	*The Usefulness of Experimental Natural Philosophy*, pt. 1

Theodora manuscript in his bedroom. Since no manuscript of *Theodora* or its second part has survived, I assume that Boyle's wishes were executed. Similar instructions seem to have affected the survival of other documents, including Boyle's diary and his correspondence with Hartlib.[10]

Boyle's correspondence with Hartlib disappeared at two different times and from two different places. The Hartlib Papers at Sheffield University include only two scraps of writings in Boyle's hand, one an undated medical receipt for treating "feavers or the Ague" (HP 65/14). Since Birch printed almost eighty letters between Boyle and Hartlib, Hartlib must have had a large amount of correspondence at his death. It seems odd that none of their letters or copies have survived among Hartlib's papers. Clearly, these documents were carefully sifted, probably at Boyle's request and possibly by his friend John Worthington,

---

[10] In the "Dayly Reflection," he told Lady Ranelagh that he had invented "a kind of written Diary, to preserue Choicer obseruations and Collections from Vanishing," a diary that would "auoid the Inconuenience of Bulke without incurring that of Confusednesse" (BP 7.280^{v}). This diary has not survived. A small portion from the second part of *Theodora* was printed in *Occ. Refl.* 2.455-56.

who was the first to organize Hartlib's papers and extensive correspondence.[11] It is unfortunate that the Hartlib Papers do not include this correspondence. Even more regrettably, a similar pattern exists at the Royal Society.

We know that some correspondence between Boyle and Hartlib survived at least to the mid-eighteenth century, when Miles transcribed and Birch reviewed it for inclusion in Boyle's *Works*. An undated agreement between them stipulated that "when Mr. Miles shall have transcrib'd such of the Letters to Mr. Boyle as he thinks proper, they [will] be reviewed [by Birch] in order for publication" (BL Add. MS 4229, f. 79). Since Birch did not review Miles's selection of manuscripts, his scrutiny of letters may suggest concern about their content. Birch printed seven letters between Boyle and Hartlib for the years 1647-50; not one holograph or copy has survived at the Royal Society. For the 1650s, Birch printed more than seventy letters; not a single MS or copy has survived. (In the Birch edition, their correspondence terminated abruptly in 1659, though Hartlib lived until 1662 and his correspondence with Lady Ranelagh continued through 1660.) It is not clear what happened to the letters after they were transcribed. For no other early correspondent is the record so meager or the pattern so consistent. Because of this lacuna, the survival of Boyle's early ethical writings is all the more valuable.

As Table 2 indicates, Boyle spent the late 1640s writing a broad range of texts.[12] The connections between the ethical and scientific writings are intriguing for at least two reasons. Both interests coexisted throughout his life; and both encouraged him to move from private analysis and reflection to written communication. As Boyle would have known, *communication* and *community* are

---

[11] Maddison's list of Boyle's correspondence makes it easy to determine which letters in Birch still survive and thus whether factors other than chance may be involved (see "A Tentative Index of the Correspondence of the Honourable Robert Boyle, F. R. S.," *Notes and Records* 13 [1958] 128-201); see also J. J. O'Brien, "Samuel Hartlib's Influence on Robert Boyle's Scientific Development. Part I: The Stalbridge Period" and "Part II: Boyle in Oxford," *Ann. of Sci.* 21 (1965) 1-14 and 257-76. Maddison does not discuss two lengthy manuscripts by Michael Sendivogius, BP 31 and BP 34. As transcribed by Hartlib's son-in-law, Frederick Clodius, these letters were written between 1 February 1646 and 28 January 1647 and described a secret philosophical society. Boyle's connection with these MSS is not clear, though it would be surprising if Hartlib or Clodius did not share them with Boyle. Sendivogius, a German alchemist, died in 1646. For Hartlib's support of the Rosicrucians, see his letter to Oldenburg in *The Correspondence of Henry Oldenburg*, ed. A. Rupert Hall and Marie Boas Hall, 9 vols. (Madison 1965-) 1.195-97. Maddison discusses Boyle and secret societies in "The Life of Robert Boyle: Addenda," *Ann. of Sci.* 45 (1988) 193-95, and Webster examines Hartlib's connection to secret societies in *Samuel Hartlib and the Advancement of Learning* (Cambridge 1970) 31. For Boyle's alleged connection to a secret society, see the breathless narrative by Michael Baignet, Richard Leigh, and Henry Lincoln, *The Holy Blood and the Holy Grail* (London 1982) 133-34 and 453-55. The authors report that a manuscript, now missing, listed both Boyle and Newton as Grand Masters of the Prieuré de Sion.

[12] For discussion of this period in Boyle's life and the dating of these MSS, see Maddison 57-88, Teague 24-42, and Jacob 43-82.

related etymologically; work that did not serve the needs of a community was suspect.[13] Comments on literary and rhetorical theory persisted throughout his career, perhaps most interestingly in the scientific writings of the 1660s and 1670s. When considered as a subtext within his scientific discourse, Boyle's notions about the rhetoric of scientific communication deserve far more prominence, say, than those of Thomas Sprat. Sprat's *History of the Royal Society* (1667), an idealized portrait of the discourse community it claimed to describe, was written by someone who was quite innocent of actual experiments.[14] For Boyle, experimentation and communication were always related. With the possible exception of Descartes, no seventeenth-century scientist was more self-conscious about the importance of audience and style in discourse.[15] No member of the early Royal Society pursued a wider range of rhetorical forms. Certainly, the *Robert Boyle, Fellow of the Royal Society* (as his title pages designate him after 1664), was not the same Robert Boyle who composed an astonishing variety of works in the late 1640s and early 1650s as he moved precociously and privately among Samuel Hartlib's circle of reformers and experimentalists. One of the figures most admired in that circle was the German theologian Johann Alsted, the major source of Boyle's ethical writings.

---

[13] For another view, see "Of Publicke-spiritedness" (BP 36.62).

[14] Brian Vickers has demolished Richard Foster Jones's view of Sprat in "The Royal Society and English Prose Style: A Reassessment" in *Rhetoric and the Pursuit of Truth*: *Language Change in the Seventeenth and Eighteenth Centuries* (Los Angeles 1985) 3-76; see also his *English Science, Bacon to Newton* (Cambridge 1987) 11-18 and *In Defense of Rhetoric* (Oxford 1988); Michael Hunter's "Latitudinarianism and the 'Ideology' of the Early Royal Society: Thomas Sprat's *History of the Royal Society* (1667) Reconsidered," in *Establishing the New Science*: *The Experience of the Early Royal Society* (Woodbridge 1989); Tony Davies, "The Ark in Flames: Science, Language and Education in Seventeenth-century England," in Andrew E. Benjamin, ed., *The Figural and the Literal* (Manchester 1987) 83-102; and Robert Markley, "Objectivity as Ideology: Boyle, Newton and the Languages of Science," *Genre* 16 (1983) 355-72.

[15] For analyses of scientists as writers, see esp. Steven Shapin, "Pump and Circumstance: Robert Boyle's Literary Technology," *Social Studies of Science*, 14 (1984) 481-520 and Jan V. Golinski, "Robert Boyle: Scepticism and Authority in Seventeenth-century Chemical Discourse," in Benjamin, *The Figural and the Literal*, 58-81. Other useful studies include Charles Bazerman, *Shaping Written Knowledge* (Madison 1988); Gillian Beer, *Darwin's Plots* (London 1983); Clifford Geertz, *Works and Lives*: *The Anthropologist as Author* (Stanford 1988); Owen Hannaway, *The Chemists and the Word* (Baltimore 1975); Patrick J. Mahony, *Freud as a Writer* (New Haven 1987); and Jonathan Rée, *Philosophical Tales* (London 1988).

§2: Sources and Contexts of Boyle's Ethics

It is both tempting and misleading to view the Interregnum Boyle in the light of his later accomplishments and the agenda of the Royal Society. I have found nothing about his childhood or adolescence that indicated a special interest in or aptitude for natural philosophy. The writings in this volume defined his early interests as the reform of moral philosophy and the pursuit of godliness.

Perhaps the point is so obvious that its significance should be restated. The Restoration Boyle was a public figure prominently associated with the image and mission of the Royal Society; this figure was acutely conscious of his role in articulating and promoting its aims. He was both a prominent symbol of the Society and one of its primary proselytes. His private correspondence with Henry Oldenburg, Robert Hooke, and John Beale often touched on the status of the Society and, more broadly, the prestige of the New Philosophy and his own role in the Society. We are very familiar with *this* Robert Boyle. The Interregnum Boyle was a far more shadowy figure, a fledgling experimentalist working first in moral philosophy and then in natural philosophy, actively seeking a theory of communication adequate for both subjects. Nothing was inevitable about the direction or pace of his development.

Modern historians have advanced quite different arguments about the major influences on his intellectual origins. For Webster, Boyle matured within the scientific and social framework of the Hartlib circle, members of which also included prominent Anglo-Irish figures. For Jacob, Boyle wrote in response to an "aristocratic ethic," his outlook being shaped most formatively by the loss of his Irish estates. More recently, Canny has argued for the primary influence of Anglo-Irish culture, though supporting Webster's position and rejecting Jacob's. Canny argues that the Earl of Cork and Hartlib had important similarities in their outlook on the world:

> [If] one is to seek for the basic cast of mind of the young Robert Boyle . . . then one is closer to the truth in accepting the mental outlook of his father, rather than that of the Hartlib Circle, as the original die. That such was the original is further confirmed when we take account of the striking similarity in the outlook of the children that are best known to us—Robert, Catherine, Roger and Mary—a similarity that cannot be attributed to their all having come under the influence of the Hartlib circle.
>
> Canny 148

I find the positions of Webster and Canny plausible and easily reconciled; Jacob's analysis is far more problematic because his thesis is broader than his evidence warrants. In addition, he does not adequately recognize the extent to which Boyle's outlook was grounded in Christian humanism. But for all three positions, the ethical writings provide important information.

Boyle's sources would have been familar to educated young men of his generation. We know from letters to his father what subjects he and his brothers studied at Eton and in Geneva under the tutelage of Isaac Marcombes, including daily discussion of Calvin's *Institutes*.[16] He would have been familiar with the most important ideas of the ancients—Aristotle, Plutarch, Seneca, and Cicero—though it is difficult to know how much firsthand knowledge he had of their texts. As both Margo Todd and John Morgan demonstrate, the classics of pagan moral philosophy were transmitted in various ways in godly schools and households: translations, commentaries, compendia, encyclopedias, meditations, and sermons, sometimes with citations of the sources and often without.[17] But the central text was *always* Scripture itself. Todd's description of Christian humanists accurately describes Boyle's approach to his sources as well as his own educational program after his return to England in 1644:

> An overriding biblicism may be regarded . . . as a defining characteristic of Christian humanists. It was their regard for the Scriptures which guided their extra-biblical pursuits: their perception of a biblical concern for individual morality attracted them to the Roman Stoics; the need to understand the Bible contextually drew them to the study of ancient history; the need for a purified text of the Scriptures impelled them to pursue knowledge of Greek and Hebrew and of classical grammar and rhetoric.
>
> Todd 23

Given Boyle's abiding concern with biblicism and personal piety, I question Jacob's claim about the role of an "aristocratic ethic" (47-48). Nothing in Boyle's ethics was not also found in Alsted and contemporary Christian humanists like Hartlib and Dury.[18]

My notes indicate quotations, allusions, and references to classical authors, but in most cases Boyle could have derived his quotations from a single source: Johann Alsted's *Encyclopædia* (Herborn 1630). This massive work runs to almost 3.5 million words, approximately the size of Boyle's *Works*, and fills

---

[16] See Maddison (ch. 1-2) and Teague (ch. 1-2) as well as Boyle's own account in *Philaretus;* for Calvin, see *II Lismore* 4.100-01. In the library at Eton College are four books with Boyle's signature in them: Cicero's *Epistolae Familiares* (1550), Aristotle's *Ethica* (1584), *Politica* and *Oeconomica* (1587), and two books of Biblical commentaries (1623) by a Spanish theologian, Joannis Treminius. Robert Birley notes that the books probably belonged to Boyle's tutor, John Harrison, in "Robert Boyle at Eton," *Notes and Records* 14 (1959) 191. In the flyleaves of the Treminius volume and the *Ethica*, Boyle had scribbled "I Robert Boyle doe say Albert Morton is a brave boy."

[17] Todd, *Christian Humanism and the Puritan Social Order* (Cambridge 1987), ch. 2-3; and Morgan, *Godly Learning*: *Puritan Attitudes towards Reason, Learning, and Education, 1560-1640* (Cambridge 1986), ch. 2. See also Robert Hoopes, *Right Reason in the English Renaissance* (Cambridge, Mass. 1962).

[18] For useful background, see H. R. McAdoo; Richard Westfall, *Science and Religion in Seventeenth-Century England* (New Haven 1958); and Eugene M. Klaaren, *Religious Origins of Modern Science* (Grand Rapids 1977). Klaaren pays particular attention to Boyle's voluntarism, an important aspect of his moral philosophy and religious outlook.

about 2,500 pages.[19] Alsted has not been previously mentioned in relation to Boyle, though Webster touches on his millenarian works (Webster 5, 8, et passim).[20] Alsted is discussed neither by Jacob nor Maddison. Though I have found no references to Alsted in Birch's edition, Boyle mentioned him by name in the *Aretology* (f. 188v), noting the date for Aristotle's death. But debts to Alsted go much deeper than this, and the absence of direct references should not be surprising. Encyclopedias have always been more used than cited.

Who was Johann Alsted (1588-1638)? One of many seventeenth-century polymaths, he was professor of philosophy and theology at Herborn. An ardent Protestant, he wrote works on mathematics, physics, music, casuistry, rhetoric, logic, philosophy, and Scriptural interpretation. His apocalyptic writings were translated into English in the 1640s. In the preface to one work, *The Beloved City, or The Saints Reign on Earth a Thousand Yeares* (1643), the translator identified him as a divinity professor at the University of Leyden (vii). In book 24 of his *Encyclopædia*, Alsted sought to harmonize ethics, economics, politics, and schooling and thereby to strengthen the church, state, and home. Like Comenius (who was his student) and Hartlib, he wanted to reform Protestant society by reforming its schools.[21] A paramount concern in this great scheme was moral education. So when Boyle analyzed the "Inborn Seeds of Vertu that by Nature we bring along with vs into the World; out of which being cherished and improued by Precepts and Education, Vertu is afterwards by it's causes Excited and produced" (*Aret.* f. 95v), he addressed a problem of keen interest to Hartlib and Dury. Unlike the millenarian sects, Webster has argued in *Samuel Hartlib and the Advancement of Learning* (Cambridge 1970), Hartlib's circle regarded

> piety and learning [as] integrally related manifestations of the regenerate intellect. This ascetic-religious ideal provided the underlying motivation for their utopian writings

---

[19] In his "Ephemerides" for 1648, Hartlib recorded that "Alsted's son brought his fathers Encyclopaedia revised corrected and much enlarged to Herborne to the Earles there where it lyes deposited till it can bee printed." The work was reprinted in 1649. Boyle owned at least four books by Alsted: *Synopsis theologiæ . . . locorum communium theologicorum* (Frankfurt 1630); *Compendium lexici philosphici grammatica Latina* (Herborn 1613); *Definitiones theologicæ* (Frankfurt 1626); and *Methodus sacrosanctæ theologiæ* (Frankfurt 1614). The *Encyclopædia* was not listed in Boyle's library, perhaps because it was housed in a room not included in Warr's inventory. I suspect, though, that it was purchased from Boyle's estate by John Warr the Younger, for it was listed on p. 4 of Warr's sale catalogue (15 May 1717): *A Catalogue of Mr. John Warre, Secretary to the Honourable Robert Boyle, Esq: deceas'd, and of another Gentleman* (BL shelfmark 821.e.4[8]). As with Boyle's sale catalogue, which also mixed his volumes with those of someone else, one cannot be certain who owned which books. The British Library owns John Evelyn's copy of Alsted's *Encyclopædia* (shelfmark Eve.c.6).

[20] A brief biography is presented in Percival R. Cole, *A Neglected Educator: Johann Heinrich Alsted* (Sydney 1910). Like Hartlib, Alsted warrants far more scholarly attention.

[21] Boyle's library included at least seven books by Comenius.

> and philanthropic projects. They operated under a deep sense of religious obligation, convinced that their aims were sanctioned by Providence as appropriate to the penultimate stages of history.
>
> Webster 3

If moral education was the goal, Alsted provided a method that Boyle found attractive and believed would be effective.

For a precocious teenager who was not at university, Alsted provided access to an enormous world of learning not otherwise available in Stalbridge or even in London. Besides offering a survey of ethics that was thoroughly Protestant, Alsted also demonstrated an approach to rhetoric that Boyle found attractive.[22] The absence of persuasion was one of Boyle's major objections to the contemporary teaching of ethics:[23]

> I think it very Necessary, that men shud be Tauht, not only How they may be Vertuus, but also [How] <Why.> And that our Ethicks shud [not only direct vs by Precepts, but Persuade vs by Incentiues. teach] <instruct> vs, not only how to make <court> loue to Vertu, but why we shud be in Loue with her.
>
> *Aret.* f. 193

Since such incitement to virtue is not found in Aristotle or in the Scholastic ethics, Boyle's concern with persuasion, not just instruction, is noteworthy. Alsted offered almost equal portions of instruction and persuasion.

Alsted knew what his readers needed: sound doctrine, an erudite commonplace book, and many aids to expression. Quite methodically, he surveyed the content and then provided an elaborate florilegium to enrich the reader's own store of memorable language (and commonplace book). Every topic bristled with sententiae, dicta, hieroglyphs, enigmas, similitudes, exemplars, and emblems, in most cases indicating his sources.[24] When we consider how Boyle revised his manuscripts and drew on his commonplace book, we see the impact of Alsted's florilegium and its rhetorical approach.

In book 21 Alsted presented his redaction of ethics, acknowledging fully his debts not only to patristic writers and pagan philosophers but also to

---

[22] For an excellent analysis of Alsted's approach to rhetoric, see Debora K. Shuger, *Sacred Rhetoric: The Christian Grand Style in the English Renaissance* (Princeton 1988), ch. 2.

[23] The significance of the brackets and braces in quotations from Boyle's MSS is explained in the section on editorial policies below.

[24] John Ray and Francis Willoughby, as Keith Thomas observes, were the first English naturalists to reject the emblematic tradition in natural history (*Man and the Natural World: Changing Attitudes in England 1500-1800* [London 1983] 67). In 1678 Ray noted his exclusion of "hieroglyphics, emblems, morals, fables, presages or aught else appertaining to divinity, ethics, grammar or any sort of human learning" and promised to include "only what properly relates to natural history." Boyle actively contributed to both the emblematic and the non-emblematic traditions.

Melanchthon, Luther, and other contemporary Protestants. He divided his *Ethics* into thirty-three chapters, some of which Boyle followed quite closely. In Table 3 I have translated Alsted's chapter titles into English so that we can compare them more easily with Boyle's chapters in MS 192 and with the materials printed in this volume. Even without an exhaustive comparison of the two writers, I find that Boyle cited at least fifty times either Alsted's own words or his sources: the citations are most frequent for Alsted's first eight chapters. My figure excludes such other references as Alsted's chronology. Several examples should illustrate Boyle's methods of dealing both with Alsted and with other sources, ancient and modern.

First, we should compare the chapters included in MS 192, the draft that preceded the *Aretology*, with Alsted's arrangement of material. Table 4 indicates just how closely the source was followed: in book 3, the four chapters strikingly resemble Alsted's first five chapters; in addition, the first chapter of book 2 corresponds to Alsted's second chapter. The debt to Alsted is quite evident, even if we compared only these particular chapter titles. But we also see that Boyle wrote essays on topics to which Alsted devoted a chapter: for example, complaisance (essay #24 in Table 1) corresponds to chapter 21 in Alsted; Boyle's essays on piety, valor, and sin, two of which are included in this volume, likewise follow his principal source. In the light of these parallels, I see three different ways in which Boyle used Alsted. He sometimes translated Alsted verbatim, sometimes freely adapted the concepts or images, and sometimes retained the structures but supplied additional (or different) illustrative examples.

In the *Aretology*, for instance, Boyle translated Alsted's metaphoric description of virtue:

Lex naturæ est fundamentum in templo virtutis, Synteresis est compages conclavium, Conscientia tectum. Nam lex naturæ sustentat hanc domum; synteresis ornat & conservat, non secus atq; conclave servat res varias; conscientia tempestates vitiorum arcet, si sit integra, si vulnerata & cauteriata, admittit non aliter atq; tectum corruptum pluvias. Itaque lex naturæ habenda est pro voce Dei. Alsted 1248-49	In the Temple of Vertu (says one very wel) the Law of Nature is the Foundation, Synteresis, the Chambers, and Conscience the Roofe; For the First sustains it: the Second adorns and vpholds it; and the Thurd; as when it is kept in repaire, keepes out the Storms of Vices and vnruly Passions; so if it be [let] suffer'd to fall to Delapidations, lets them in. f. 116^{v}

While this translation is both accurate and graceful, two other features are even more notable. In MS 192, Boyle had written that "the Will is the Foundation of Actions, Sincerity the Walls and Constancy the Roofe. The first begins them; the second polishes them, and the last perfects them." In his first draft Boyle altered Alsted's concepts while retaining his architectural metaphor. The revision in the

Table 3. Alsted's Chapters

Ch.	Page	Title	Ch.	Page	Title
1	1235	Of moral happiness	15	1283	Of the desire for getting a thing honestly
2	1241	Of the subject of moral philosophy	16	1284	Of parsimony
3	1244	Of the causes and effects of moral virtue	17	1285	Of fortitude
			18	1291	Of human kindness
4	1251	Of the subjects and collateral circumstances of moral virtue	19	1292	Of refinement of manner
			20	1295	Of particular justice
5	1254	Of those things related and opposed to moral virtue	21	1301	Of complaisance
			22	1303	Of generosity
			23	1307	Of gentleness
6	1255	Of prudence	24	1310	Of humility
7	1260	Of universal justice	25	1312	Of harmony
8	1264	Of piety	26	1319	Of truthfulness
9	1267	Of temperance	27	1325	Of the pleasantness of speech
10	1273	Of watchfulness			
11	1274	Of selfishness or self-love	28	1327	Of silence
			29	1330	Of seriousness
12	1275	Of moderation	30	1331	Of civility
13	1279	Of assiduity	31	1335	Of modesty
14	1282	Of a sufficiency	32	1336	Of moral action
			33	1339	Of particular ethics

Aretology restored Alsted's terms: the Law of Nature is the foundation, Synteresis the chambers, and Conscience the roof. Always fascinated by powerful metaphors, he experimented with Alsted's by testing its suitability to other arguments.

A second important feature of Boyle's use of sources is that he seldom named an author whom he quoted or paraphrased, consistently preferring general labels—"as one witty person says" or "as one says wisely." In the example above, Boyle was freely translating Alsted's text, not adapting it as he had in the previous draft, and he did not identify the author. This practice has complicated the identification of his sources, both when he is drawing on contemporary English writers and especially when he is translating from other languages. (He later stressed the importance of citing sources in natural philosophy in *Cert. Phys. Essays* 1.313; in *Reconcileableness* 4.156, he discussed the rhetoric of citations.) But to say that Alsted was Boyle's primary source is hardly the full story.

Table 4. Boyle's Chapters in MS 192, *Ethicall Elements*

Book		I	Book		III
Ch.	1	That there is a Felicity.	Ch.	1	Of the Deffinition of Moral Vertu.
Ch.	2	Of False Felicitys.	Ch.	2	Of The Causes and Effects of Morall Vertu.
Ch.	3	Of the tru Felicity and the Degrees Thereof.	Ch.	3	Of the Subjects and Adjuncts of Morall Vertu.
Book		II	Ch.	4	Of the things Allied and Contrary to Morall Vertu.
Ch.	1	Of the Subject of Morall Philosophy in Generall.			
Ch.	2	Of the Will.			
Ch.	3	Of The Sensitiue Appetite, and the Passions thereof.			

No seventeenth-century work on ethics could ignore Aristotle's *Nichomachean Ethics*, however eager an author might have been to distance himself from Aristotle and the Schoolmen. My notes to this edition indicate where Boyle's argument is tied most closely to the *Nichomachean Ethics*, thus recognizing the preeminence of Aristotle even among those, like Alsted, who wished to reform the teaching of ethics. But my citations of Aristotle should not suggest that Boyle followed Aristotle directly. Unlike Aristotle and Cicero, for instance, Boyle did not discuss friendship (cf. *Nichomachean Ethics* VIII-IX), emphasizing instead the dangers of bad company and the importance of good companions—namely, reason and conscience. If Cicero wanted to prepare his readers for the duties of Roman citizenship, Boyle prepared himself (and his readers) for spiritual warfare.

Alsted fully acknowledged his debt not only to Aristotle but to many other pagan authors, especially Plato, Epicurus, Pythagoras, and Plutarch among the Greeks and Cicero, Horace, Juvenal, and Seneca among the Romans. Unlike Boyle, Alsted included many specific references to the church fathers and to St. Augustine, whose commentary on the pagans (e.g., the commentary on Varro in *De civitate Dei*) was widely quoted by many Protestant reformers. Among these reformers, Alsted most often mentioned Melanchthon, Luther, and Calvin, but Erasmus was also quoted copiously. (Boyle's library included Melanchthon's *Loci communes rerum theologicarum* [Wittenberg 1535], five works by Luther, five by Calvin, and ten by Erasmus.) Even if Alsted was the primary source, Boyle was still drawing on the intellectual resources and spiritual outlook of Protestant humanism.

When we examine an earlier draft of the *Aretology*, the *Ethicall Elements* (MS 192), we see some interesting traces of Alsted's outlook and structure but also some significant alterations. In discussing heroic virtue, Alsted identified exemplars: in government were Moses, Joshua, Samson, Cyrus, Alexander the Great, Julius Caesar, Constantine, and Charlemagne; in arts were Plato, Aristotle, Aquinas, Pico Mirandola, Erasmus, and Melanchthon; in religion were the apostles and martyrs; in mechanics were Archimedes and Albrecht Dürer (Alsted 1252). In comparing Boyle's list, we should notice both what is similar and what has been added:

> But heere is [no] to be noted that thes Heroicke Spirits are not excited euery Yeare: but perhaps one or 2 in [ag] an age: when it pleases God to [re] reforme Arts [or and Gouernments] or Mores: or make some great reuolution /change and &c/ in Commonwealths. Thus [did D] were [Da] Moses, [D] Sampson, and Dauid reformers of [the Common] Isræl: and thus in euery Science God has raised vp certain Heroicke Spirits, to be the lihts and Paterns /Ornaments thereof/ As in Philosophy, Plato, Aristotle, Aquinas, Mirandula, [Scalige] and the like: in Physicke, [Vi] Asculapius, Hippocrates, Galen, Paracelsus, and the like: in Iurisprudence, Iustinian, Vlpian, Gratian, &c. In the [Me] Astronomy Hipparchus, Ptolemy, Alfonsus (the King) Copernicus, Tycho Brahe, Galilæus and others; in Geometry Euclide and Archimedes: in the Mechanickes, Archimedes, Albert Durer, and Steuin: in Nauigation, Columbus, Americus Vesputius, Drake, Cauendish, [V] Oliuer van der Nort: and many others, whom for breuity sake I omit. where it is to be observed that no [Disc] Science or Discipline has beene adorned with so many Heros, as Moral Philosophy: for shee can claime almost all the Heros of the World for her owne: and as they [ador] embellish her, she makes them.
>
> MS 192, ff. 123-24

After following Alsted very carefully for the first half of this passage, Boyle freely added his own list of heroic figures for categories that Alsted had ignored: astronomy, geometry, mechanics, and navigation. In the corresponding section of the *Aretology*, he sharpened the focus considerably by omitting the modern exemplars: "Thus we may say Salomon was endow'd with an Heroick Prudence, Ezechias with an Heroick Piety, Dauid with an Heroick Valor, Iohn the Baptist with an heroic Temperament, Aristides with an Heroick Iustice; and Christ with all Vertus in a heroicall Degree" (f. 153^{v}). The earlier draft illustrated the possibility of achieving heroic virtue through quite different vocations and stressed the rarity of such spirits in any age; the revision emphasized the centrality of moral virtue and omitted the exemplars. Boyle's interest in heroic virtue—what it was and how to attain it—surfaced in many later works.[25] Since this important theme had its first expression in the *Aretology*, we should recognize both Alsted's influence and Boyle's originality.

If Boyle derived from Alsted the basic concepts and structure of his

---

[25] He praised heroic wits in the commonwealth of learning (*Cert. Phys. Essays* 1.308), argued that only transcendent wits were worthy of writing theology (*Style* 2.309), and wrote *Theodora* as a meditation on the patterns of heroic virtue (*Theodora* 5.260). For other reflections on heroic virtue, see *Greatness of Mind* 5.557; *Theodora* 5.301; and *Occ. Refl.* 2.398.

argument, he added his own material and supplemented the presentation with striking illustrations, sayings, and metaphors gleaned from others. What shaped his presentation was the desire to have an impact, not to impress with the breadth of his reading. Boyle's other sources, both contemporaries and the ancients, tell us a great deal about what he was reading and what he found memorable.

Except for Alsted, I have found no specific debts to other Renaissance works on ethics. Modern works were also widely available and were of interest to Dury, Hartlib, and Benjamin Worsley, a close friend of Boyle. On 11 May 1649, for example, Dury wrote to Worsley from Amsterdam, praising Johannes Crellius's new work on ethics.[26]

> Concerning Morality there is nothing i think so becoming a man, nothing so lamentably wanting in Christianity, nothing lesse or worse thought in the Vniuersity. I confesse i thinke with your friend Epictetus and Antoninus to bee of all other the marrow to whom you may return this information That Crellius hath collected all the comands and precepts al most in Scriptur that concern the doing of any moral duty or abstaining from any moral evil, and hath handled them and compiled them under an Ethica Christiana, wch booke truly is much pleasure. It is come out lately and for feare of offence and prejudice going under the name of Cyrillus. There are many Copies of them sent into Engl.
>
> Boyle Lett. 7.1^{v}

As Boyle probably knew, Dury had anonymously translated Crellius's *Vindication of Liberty of Religion* in 1646. Among the modern ethics available to Boyle were Lambert Daneau's *Ethices Christianae* (1577); Theophilus Golius's *Epitome Doctrinae Moralis* (1592); Eustache de Saint-Paul's *Ethica* (1609); Franco Burgersdyck's *Idea Philosophia Tum Moralis, Tum Naturalis* (1631); William Pemble's *A Summe of Moral Philosophy* (1632); Joannis Magirus's *Corona virtutum moralium* (1632); and Adrian Heereboord's *Collegium Ethica* (1648), whose work appeared after Boyle began his *Aretology*. There is no evidence that Boyle read or owned any of these works (though he possessed a 1658 edition of Heereboord's *Logic*); nor does he refer to any of them in his printed works.[27]

Like Alsted, these moralists sought to explain the workings of the reason, will, and understanding and provided an overview of the passions. Boyle could also draw on the insights of moral psychology and practical divinity, both of

---

[26] This letter and the next one in the volume, neither of which Birch printed, has very interesting references to Boyle, Petty, Wilkins, and Worsley. Worsley's sale catalogue indicated that he had collected a large number of Socinian tracts, many written by Crellius. By 1666 John Beale feared that the Socinians' rhetorical skills were as formidable as the Jesuits' (6.413).

[27] William Pemble is mentioned in *Origin of Forms* 3.9, but the reference merely placed him in a list of ten modern writers opposed to Aristotle's physics. There is no reference to Pemble's *Summe*.

which approached the moralist's problems from other perspectives. Because so many writers treated the same topics, identification of particular sources is difficult, but Boyle has left some intriguing clues in his discussion of several topics.

Every contemporary moralist had to discuss the passions, but there was little consensus about their number, nature, operation, and control.[28] Boyle's taxonomy of the passions was hardly original, but his language suggests that he might have had a particular source, Thomas Wright's *Passions of the Minde* (1601). After listing the passions, Boyle illustrated how each worked by presenting the fable of the wolf and the sheep.[29]

> Ffirst, the Woulfe conceiuing the flesh of the Sheepe, as Good, Loueth it: then, being Absent, desires to eate it: and hauing gotten it, Delighteth in it. The Sheepe (on the contrarie) conceiuing the Woulfe vnder the Notion of euill, Hates him: seeing him comming fflyes him: and feeling herselfe seized by him, Griues to become his prey. But now (to come to the Inuading Appetite) suppose the Woulfe see the Sheepe guarded with the Sheapeard and his Doggs: yet thinking the Enterprise, tho Difficult yet ffeasable, hee erects himselfe with hope: whereupon neglecting and despising the guardians of the flocke with a great deale of Boldnes and Courage hee falls vpon it. But being in the first onsett pinched by a Mastiue; inflam'd with Angre, hee seeks to reuenge himselfe vpon the Dogge: but Hee is soe well seconded by his companions, that the Woulfe, findinge more resistance then hee expected, begins to ffeare the euent of the busines. Whereupon hee is soe furiously assalted and pressed by the Sheapeard, that after a little Hope had made him maintaine the fray a while longer; thinking the victorie impossible; seased with Dispaire, hee betakes himselfe to his heeles and runns away.
>
> *Aret.* ff. 71-71^{v}

The ultimate source of this taxonomy is Aquinas (*Summa Theologica* I.2.q26.a.I), which Wright cited, but who conceived the allegory? Boyle's language is so similar to Wright's that even a brief quotation suggests a specific debt:

> First, the woolfe loueth the flesh of the sheepe, then hee desireth to haue it, thirdly, hee reioyceth in his prey when he hath gotten it: Contrariwise, the sheepe hateth the woolfe, as an euill thing in himselfe, and thereupon detesteth him as hurtful to hirselfe; and finally, if the wolfe seize vpon hir; she paineth and grieueth to becom his prey: thus wee haue loue, desire, delight, hatred, abhomination, griefe, or heauvinesse, the six passions of our coueting appetite. . . . [But] in fine, receiuing more blowes of the sheepeheard, more wounds of the dogges, awearied with fighting, fearing his life, thinking the enterprise impossible, oppressed with the passion of Desperation,

---

[28] For an exemplary study of this bewildering topic, see Anthony Levi, *French Moralists: The Theory of the Passions, 1585-1649* (Oxford 1964); for a broader overview, see H. M. Gardiner et al., *Feeling and Emotion: A History of Theories* (New York 1937), ch. 5.

[29] This passage has been transcribed by an amanuensis, and its spelling is very different from Boyle's.

> resolueth himselfe, that his heeles are a surer defence, than his teeth, and so runneth away.
>
> Wright 41-44

Boyle probably knew Aquinas only through Wright or other contemporary writers who drew on the same traditions; there is no reference to or quotation of Aquinas in his published works. Boyle was not interested in the unresolved debates about the number of the passions; he was interested in controlling his own passions and helping his readers control theirs. And in that task, figurative language as powerful as Wright's was a potent resource.

If Boyle derived his basic structure from Alsted, he gathered many of his most striking passages from English authors ranging from poets to divines. As with Alsted, his debts were chiefly unattributed quotation and paraphrase. We should consider how he borrowed from Henry Hammond's *Of a Late, or, a Death-Bed Repentance* (1645) in "Of Sin," for the borrowing represents a common pattern. Enumerating a list of reasons not to postpone repentance, Boyle combined paraphrase and direct quotation:

> That to repent vpon one's Deth-bed is a Resolution not to begin to liue well til we haue no more [of] <make an End> to liue at all, and extreamely vnreasonable that the last Minit of our Life, shud be the first (Minit of our Living wel) whereof the very Foundation is contrary to the Performance; and (as one has it wittily) the Condition of all a man's Good life, a Presumtion that he shal not liue. Sure tis very Ridiculus for a man to resolue to liue well vpon no other Consideration but because the Time is com when he thinks he shal dy.
>
> "Of Sin" f. 31

> 1. That it is at that time most *improper* and out of season, very unreasonable that the *end* of the *life* should be the *first* minute of *living well* . . . 2. That it is a *ridiculous* thing, for a man to resolve to *live* well upon no other consideration, but because the time is come when he thinkes he shall *dye* . . .
>
> Hammond 27

There can be no doubt that Hammond was the "witty" source. Since Boyle quoted Browne's *Religio Medici* (1642) several times in the "Dayly Reflection," we can speculate about Browne's appeal. I suspect that Boyle was intrigued by Browne's blend of psychological and religious introspection as well as by Browne's rhetorical sophistication. These sources disclose some of what Boyle read during the 1640s and suggest how he read these authors.

Direct quotations illustrate his knowledge of seventeenth-century English poetry and practical divinity. He must have been very fond of George Herbert's verse: he quoted "The Church-Porch" four times in the *Aretology*, though never mentioning its author by name. Herbert was "a religious Poet of ours"; Edmund Waller, a friend of Boyle's family, was "our English poet" and was not otherwise identified, though he quoted the same lines in the *Aretology* that he also would repeat in *Style* 2.299.

Quotations are one thing, but echoes are another. When Boyle wrote that virtue was "somwhat a Coy mistress, and perhaps wil be very shy of accepting of the leauings of that Strumpet, Vice" (*Aret.* f. 188), his language was very reminiscent of George Wither's *Faire-Virtue, The Mistresse of Phil'Arete* (1622), which featured poems on such topics as "Of Man," "Of Ambition," and "Inconstancie." Just as Boyle used the persona of Philaretus in his autobiography as well as in *Occasional Reflections*, Wither frequently employed the persona of Phil'arete as he wrote about the passions—love, lust, envy, choler, jealousy, covetousness, and ambition. Wither also depicted Phil'arete in *The Shepheards Hunting* (1622), a dialogue on ethical subjects. (The resemblance between "Phil'arete" and "Philaretus" has not, I believe, been previously mentioned.) While I have found no direct quotations of Wither's poetry in Boyle's published or unpublished works, I would not be surprised if Boyle had read him. But a similarity is not a source.

Because Renaissance writers were so fond of commonplaces, proverbs, and sententiae, the sources of many images cannot be conclusively traced. So when Boyle noted that the "Life of the Wicked like the Flame of a Candle" expires "in a snuffe /stink/ whereas that of the Vertuus, like the Flame in Iuniper, leaues a Perfume <behind it> after the Extinction" (*Aret.* f. 213), he invoked a proverbial image.[30] He used the same image in "Of Sin" and variants of it in many other works (e.g., *Resurrection* 4.202). But a more literary treatment existed, for example, in Francis Quarles's poem "On the Hypocrite," which was included in *Divine Fancies* (1632):

> He's like a Christmas Candle, whose good name
> Crowns his faire actions with a glorious flame;
> Burnes cleare and bright, and leaves no ground for doubt
> To question, but he stinks at going out;
> When Death puffs out his Flame, the snuff will tell
> If he were Wax, or Tallow, by the smell.

Was Boyle's image derived from Quarles, or was it simply an analogue derived from proverbial lore? I cannot be certain. Similar topics (e.g., "bosom-sins") invited similar figurative language, and a single florilegium on hypocrisy (cf. Alsted 1253), whether in Latin or in English, could underlie Boyle's images of hypocrisy in *Occasional Reflections* 2.393-94; *High Veneration* 5.143; *Theodora* 5.276 and 285; *Christian Virtuoso* 5.526; and *Swearing* 6.15. But we can

[30] Morris Palmer Tilley, *A Dictionary of the Proverbs in England in the Sixteenth and Seventeenth Centuries* (Ann Arbor 1950). This proverb is C49. Proverbs are hereafter cited by their number in this edition.

hardly ignore other contemporary writers who covered the same material and invoked similar language. Daniel Dyke's *Mystery of Selfe-Deceiving* (1615) and William Fenner's *Treatise of the Affections; or, the Soules Pulse* (1641) went through many editions and offered very detailed analyses of hypocrisy. Likewise, many works of casuistical divinity anatomized quite common spiritual states. In the absence of specific debts, such works are probably best considered as part of the context for his ethics rather than as sources.

What were Boyle's debts to pagan philosophers? Translations of and commentaries on Aristotle's *Ethics* were very numerous because of Aristotle's secure place in the Scholastic curriculum, but I have identified no edition that Boyle used.[31] The most important source for Boyle's discussion of pagan philosophy was Diogenes Laërtius's *Lives of the Eminent Philosophers*. We know that he read this racy collection of potted biographies and anecdotes (BW 1.355), but I cannot determine which works of pagan philosophy Boyle had carefully read before beginning the *Aretology*.[32] His most densely allusive passage occurred at the beginning of "Of Piety," where within three paragraphs he quoted Plato three times in a Latin translation, Cicero three times, and Seneca once. While most of his citations were little more than tags, a few illustrate how he reshaped ancient texts to fit his argument.

For example, at the beginning of "Of Piety," Boyle quoted a lengthy sentence from Seneca's *Epistulae Morales*. While he usually translated his Latin quotations, he did not translate this marginal insertion:

> Primus deorum Cultus est, Deos credere; de inde reddere illis majestatem suam; reddere bonitatem; scire illos esse qui præsident; qui vniuersaui suâ temperant, qui humani generis tutelam gerunt.

> The first way to worship the gods is to believe in the gods; the next to acknowledge their majesty, to acknowledge their goodness without which there is no majesty. Also, to know that they are supreme commanders in the universe, controlling all things by their power and acting as guardians of the human race.

As presented, Seneca's views were quite unexceptionable, but interestingly, Boyle silently omitted the conclusion of Seneca's sentence: "even though [the

---

[31] Thomas Hobbes's contempt for the *Nichomachean Ethics* is well known. Aubrey recorded that to Hobbes "Aristotle was the worst Teacher that ever was, the worst Politician and Ethick—a Countrey-fellow that could live in the World would be as good: but his *Rhetorique* and *Discourse of Animals* was rare." Luther considered the *Ethics* an affront to God's will and the Christian virtues (Fiering 10).

[32] Jacob claims that "Boyle steeped himself in ethical theories before setting out to write his own" (55), but he has misunderstood the reference to Epicurus (56) and has misread "mentions" as "intentions" because the writing by the amanuensis is difficult to read. I have found no evidence that Boyle's knowledge extended much beyond Alsted and Laërtius.

gods] are sometimes unmindful of the individual."[33] Considering Boyle's emphasis on Providence throughout this volume and his career, it is understandable for him to revise Seneca to make or preserve his point.

In the same essay, his references to Seneca's *De Providentia* and Cicero's *De Natura Deorum* helped to support notions of Providence elaborated not only in the *Aretology* (cf. bk. 2, ch. 4) but in many other works as well.[34] Recognizing the importance of this theme in Boyle's outlook, we see how he both acknowledged and revised the writings of Seneca, the Christian Stoic, with a rigorously orthodox Christianity. We should also recognize that Hartlib's associates shared this concern. In Hartlib Papers 26/8/1 is Dury's proposal, "A Designe for Registring of Illustrious Providences," which described a way to determine whether an incident of special providence had occurred and, if so, how it should be registered for others' benefit. Likewise, Boyle considered how to "read" reliably the decrees of Providence in *Occasional Reflections* (2.418-19) and in many later works; in *Philaretus* alone, he mentioned more than a half-dozen incidents.

Even though Boyle owned Ficino's translation of Plato (1548), I find no evidence that his knowledge of Plato was much deeper than the summaries in Laërtius and Alsted. Under Marcombes's tutelage, he may have read extensively among the Roman moralists; certainly, the citations of Cicero are far more numerous than of any other ancient philosopher. But firsthand knowledge of Greek philosophy cannot be documented. Boyle's understanding of pagan philosophy is an important issue, for every Christian writer on ethics faced the problem of reconciling pagan moral philosophy and Christianity.[35] His solution was quite simple: he cited pagan positions and then either corrected or supported them with Scripture. His biblicism sometimes relied very heavily on his concordance. (In the "Dayly Reflection," for instance, *consider* was clearly the keyword [f. 276] and generated sixteen quotations, an exceptionally large number.) He dutifully cited the positions of the Stoics, Epicureans, and Peripatetics, but one would never conclude that any contemporaries were seriously interested in these philosophies or in modern refinements of them.[36]

---

[33] Seneca, *Epistulae Morales* 95.50.1-2, trans. Richard M. Gummere (Cambridge, Mass. 1925).

[34] Besides the many references in *Philaretus*, see his letter to Lady Ranelagh (1.xxxvi); *Life of Richard Boyle* (1.vii); *Seraphic Love* (1.290); *Occ. Refl.* (2.418-19); *Vulgar Notion* (5.197, 211, 213, and 251); *Theodora* (5.256, 270, and 279); *Final Causes* (5.427); and *Chr. Virtuoso* (5.519-21, 534).

[35] For an excellent review of how Boyle's contemporaries used pagan philosophers, see Fiering, ch. 1 and 4; William T. Costello, *The Scholastic Curriculum at Early Seventeenth-Century Cambridge* (Cambridge, Mass. 1958); and Levi. For Boyle's assessment of pagan philosophers, see *Style* 2.285, where he also offered some observations on Aristotle's *Nichomachean Ethics*.

[36] Browne's discussions in *Religio Medici* were equally perfunctory (e.g., i.§55). But many contemporaries *were* interested in the content and implications of pagan philosophies, perhaps most prominently the Cambridge Platonists. For discussion of the influence of Stoicism on Renaissance humanism, see Todd 27-30 and her article, "Seneca and the Protestant Mind: The Influence of Stoi-

If the pagans were cited perfunctorily, Scripture was cited abundantly. The index lists several pages of scriptural citations, and when we compare these citations to the pattern for Boyle's career, we find remarkable consistency.[37] As with his classical citations, the scriptural patterns are noteworthy. He quoted from or referred to the Old Testament slightly more often than to the New Testament, with Psalms and Proverbs accounting for one-third of the Old Testament references. Matthew was the most heavily cited book, being quoted or cited four times more often than either John or Luke. And in Matthew, Boyle referred five times to the parable of the talents (Matthew 25:14-30). For someone who was discovering his vocation, this parable was a crucial text.

Just as Boyle did not engage extensively with pagan philosophers, he also avoided most of the intellectual quarrels that exercised seventeenth-century divines. I do not assume that Boyle read every book in his library or that he agreed with the views of every author he read; nor can I tell when he acquired individual volumes. But if we look not just at individual works but at kinds of works in his library, we clearly see his interest in theology and moral psychology.

Lucas Osiander's *A Manuell or Briefe Volume of Controversies of Religion* (1606) would have provided an overview of theological debates, but Boyle also owned five collections of theological commonplaces; about a dozen catechisms, all except one published before 1650; five marrows of divinity, one of them (Edward Fisher's *The Marrow of Modern Divinity* [1646]) presented as a dialogue among Evangelista, Nomista, Antinomista, and Neophytus); and a voluminous treatise by Boyle's friend, Archbishop Ussher (*A Body of Divinitie* [1645]). He also owned two editions of Zacharias Ursinus's *Summe of the Christian Religion*, several cases of conscience and guides to a good conscience (for example, William Lyford's *Principles of Faith and Good Conscience* [1642]); and numerous works on spirituality, including Juan de Valdés's *Divine Considerations* (1646). His library included seven works by William Ames as well as William Perkins's *Works* (1613, 1616) and John Jewel's *Works* (1609). As this

---

cism on Puritan Ethics," *Archive für Reformationsgeschichte* 74 (1983) 182-99. For broader discussions, see Leontine Zanta, *La renaissance du stoicisme au XVIe siecle* (Paris 1914); J. L. Saunders, *J. Lipsius: the Philosophy of Renaissance Stoicism* (New York 1955); and Richard H. Popkin, *The History of Scepticism from Erasmus to Descartes*, rev. ed (New York 1964). For Epicureanism, see Lynn Sumida Joy, *Gassendi the Atomist: Advocate of History in an Age of Science* (Cambridge 1987). Thomas Traherne's *Christian Ethicks* (1675) illustrates the impact of the Cambridge Platonists on ideas derived from Scholasticism. Traherne's major source was Eustache's *Ethica*. For a modern edition of this work, see Carol L. Marks and George Robert Guffey, eds., *Christian Ethicks* (Ithaca 1968).

[37] See Teague 243-47 for scriptural citations in the *Works*. In Boyle's *oeuvres*, Biblical citations averaged 1.06 occurrences per page of the Bible, with Genesis, Psalms, Matthew, and Romans most frequently (Teague 71).

list suggests, his holdings included a broad spectrum of works by Anglicans, Presbyterians, and Puritans and thus reflects an early commitment to latitudinarian principles.[38]

These divines were represented by a wide variety of religious works, not just theological tomes. Works of popular divinity stressed the removal of scruples, doubts, or moral objections and featured such rhetorical tactics as pointed questions to the reader, catechetical dialogues about doctrine or behavior, or a highly repetitive structure of doctrine-reasons-use. These rhetorical structures evidently left their mark on Boyle's patterns of expression. Since he was especially eager to anticipate and answer objections, we should note that these tactics were prominent features of such works as John Preston's *Life Eternall or, a Treatise of the Divine Essence and Attributes* (1631) and *A Liveles Life*: *or, Mans Spirituall Death in Sinne* (1633); Robert Harris's *Way to True Happiness* (1632); and Henry Scudder's *Christians Dayly Walke* (1637). But we should also include *The Saints Dayly Exercise*, Robert Bolton's *General Directions for a Comfortable Walking with God* (1638), John Owen's *Display of Arminianisme* (1643), and John Saltmarsh's *Free Grace* (1646). William Fenner's *Treatise of the Affections* (1642) offered exceptionally vivid psychological portraits of spiritual states, a topic of keen interest in "Doctrine of Thinking" and "Dayly Reflection." While such works provided part of the context for Boyle's ethics, I do not consider them as sources except where I have found direct borrowings.

Given the number of religious volumes, we might have expected Boyle to address the great debates about free will vs. determinism—Augustine and Pelagius, Luther and Erasmus, the Calvinists and the Arminians, the supporters and opponents of William Laud—that agitated so many controversialists during the 1640s. He did not. Was it odd that he ignored the issues of free will and predestination and did not wrestle with the problem of justification or that his views of the passions and the workings of conscience were not more original?[39] His silence is less puzzling when we understand his view of controversy. The Erasmian pursuit of consensus in these early texts is consistent with his later rejection of "needless" controversy.[40] His intention was to avoid dogmatism and to seek consensus, not to win debater's points. In concluding his discussion of pleasure and pain, for example, he noted that

---

[38] For a broad view of latitudinarianism, see Frederic Bradford Burnham, *The Latitudinariam Background to the Royal Society, 1647-1667*, unpublished diss. (Johns Hopkins 1970); see also Michael Hunter's exemplary study, "Latitudinarianism."

[39] Oster argues convincingly that Boyle wrestled with the problem of justification in "The 'Beame of Diuinity': Animal Suffering in the Early Thought of Robert Boyle," *BJHS* 22 (1989) 151-80. For interesting information about Newton's approach to his conscience, see Westfall, "Short-writing and the State of Newton's Conscience," *Notes and Records* 18 (1963) 10-16.

[40] For other statements of this principle, see *Vulgar Notion* 5.174; *Scep. Chym.* 1.466; and *Orig. of Forms* 3.6.

> To this Doctrine of Pleasure and Paine diuers other Questions miht <indeed> haue been added but being of the Nature of those Crawfishes that afford far more to Pick then to Eat; I wil leaue their Discussion to those that haue a mind to be rid of their time; only aduertising the Reader, that hauing deliuered this Doctrine more out of the Opinion of others then my owne; I do not pretend to maintain it against all commers; [but] and if any man will correct it with [illeg.] a more probable Doctrine he may do it vnresistedly for me; who am neuer so concerted of my owne liht, but that I will willingly be content to put out my candle at the Rising of the Sun.
>
> *Aret.* f. 91^{v}

Modesty and freedom from dogmatism were salient traits in his later writings (cf. *Scep. Chym.* 1.463 and *Chr. Virtuoso* 5.536), but such tolerance was first established in these ethical writings. In mid 1648, in fact, he told Lady Ranelagh that he had completed an essay on toleration (6.45), a remarkable fact in the light of his anxieties about the sects.[41]

His approach and tone were significantly influenced by the outlook and activities of Hartlib and Dury. In his "Dayly Reflection," for example, Boyle argued against both dogmatism and uncharitable zeal in terms that echo many works associated with Hartlib's circle.

> And surely he that shall impartially and vnbyass'tly [ex] consider, how vast /large/ a Portion of Knowledge is yet Problematicke, [cannot but find it vnreasonable in most thin] how little of Truth we are groundedly and thoroughly [convinc't of] <satisfy'd> our selues, and how much lesse of it we are able clearly and vndeniably to demonstrate vnto others, will think the Points not few in which 'twere very vnreasonable to passe harsh Censure vpon all Dissenters. It has often been obseru'd, that they haue the most of Fierceness in their Opinions that haue [fewest] <the least of> Argument for them.
>
> "Dayly Reflection" f. 284

Among the major points of Jacobus Acontius's *Satans Stratagems, or the devils Cabinet-Council Discovered* (1648), an anonymous translation sponsored by Hartlib but involving contributions by Dury and Thomas Goodwin, were the need to avoid unnecessary controversy (18) and the importance of gentleness in dealing with opponents. The translator noted that in "every Controversy [there is] a double Combate, between us and our dissenting opposite, and between us and *Sathan*" (35, italics reversed). To fall into rancor was to fall into Satan's snare; a safer tactic was moderation.[42]

Boyle worried intensely about such snares, some of which are listed among the "remoras of truth" in Table 5. For each remora (laziness, dulness, misuse of means, and prejudice) he noted the cause(s). The removal of these impediments was just as important in moral philosophy as in natural philosophy; indeed, the

---

[41] No essay by this title has survived, nor is "Of Divinity" listed in Table 1.

[42] For the importance of manners in disputation, see Steven Shapin and Simon Schaffer, *Leviathan and the Air-Pump: Hobbes, Boyle, and the Experimental Life* (Princeton 1985) 72-76.

Table 5. Remoras of Truth

1. Lazinesse. cau's by
    1. Vnderualuing of Truth
    2. Apprehension of it's Difficulty.
    3. Feare to find it, as crossing our &c.
    4. Beleefe of hauing it already.
2. Dulnesse. which is either Incorrigible: being so by Nature: or Corrigible: proceeding from
    1. Lasinesse.
    2. want of meanes.
    3. Credulity.
    4. Incredulity.
3. Neglect or Misapplication of the Meanes which are
    1. Method.
    2. Illumination (attain'd by Prayer)
    3. Reading.
    4. Meditation.
    5. Obseruation [6] (vnder which, Tryals and Experiments)
    6. Conuersation (either by Discourse or Letters.) The Handmaid of all these is Repetition. or chewing of the Cud.
4. Prepossessions against the
    1. man. that he is either, <singular> Ignorant, Vitius, Contemtible, hereticall, of such a Time Place, or Parentage. or thine Enemy. A conceit of our owne infallibility.
    2. Thing. that is either. New. <[singular]> or Old. or Extrauagant to our Former receiued Customes [or] Opinions, or Interests. Or coms from hated Persons. or from Persons very much belou'd or of very great Autority.
    3. The meanes. Either in the Method, or the stile, or the Bulk or Number of the Discourses. Or the Vsing Violence in obtruding opinions vpon vnwilling receauers.

BP 14.24

six steps to truth—method, illumination (attained through prayer), reading, meditation, observation, and conversation—were equally applicable to ethics and natural philosophy.[43] Such irenicism, a strong quality of the Hartlib circle, marks an important continuity between Boyle's early outlook and his opposition to the "vanity of dogmatizing" after the Restoration.[44]

---

43 This selection, taken from BP 14.24, probably represented a planning document—the "heads" of an argument—for an essay. It is written not as sentences but as a series of points. See "Of Publicke-spiritedness" (BP 36.62) for another such list.

44 In Table 1, note "Of Censuring & Casuists."

Despite Boyle's personal modesty, his friends were aware of his aptitude for meditation and his success in transforming private observations and reflections into public discourse. In 1653, for example, William Petty strongly praised his ability to reason clearly from evidence and to communicate persuasively his conclusions. We should note that the praise is for Boyle's *method.*

> What a faculty have you, of making every thing you see an argument of some useful conclusion or other! How much are you practised in the method of clear and scientifical reasoning! How well do you understand the true use and signification of words, whereby to register and compute your own conceptions! So well are you accomplished in all these particulars, that I safely persuade myself, but, that you modestly think every scribbler wiser than yourself, that you can draw more knowledge and satisfaction from two hours of your own meditation, than from twelve hours endurance of other men's loquacity.
>
> BW 6.138

Through his reading, writing, and participating in the social network of Lady Ranelagh's household, Boyle developed ethical positions that he never substantially altered and that were extended and elaborated in a wide range of works published after the Restoration. Within this social and intellectual milieu he constructed a philosophy of life committed to intellectual enquiry, personal piety, and public service. Central to that life were the discovery and communication of truth and the ardent promotion of moral excellence. As I show in the next section, the *Aretology* and his moral essays emerged from his dissatisfaction with the teaching of moral philosophy and from his passionate desire to promote social reform by improving the teaching of ethics.

§3: Ethics and the Quest for Virtue

Boyle's quest for virtue was quite typical of the social circle in which he lived. Like Dury, he showed far more interest in the common good—in ethics, casuistry, practical divinity, and communication—than in systematic theology. We recall that in his *Motion Tending to the Publick Good* (1642), Dury proposed to create professorships of practical divinity at Gresham College as well as at Oxford and Cambridge. Todd argues that the "ultimate goal of the work ethic, for protestants as for their Catholic humanist mentors, was the common weal. . . . William Perkins might have been quoting Starkey or Elyot when he defined a legitimate vocation as one 'ordained and imposed on man by God, *for the common good.*' Christians 'may not live idly . . . and give ourselves to riot and gaming, but labour to serve God and our country, in some profitable course of life'" (148).[45] Thomas Wood defines this outlook as casuistical divinity, the

[45] Boyle also pursued this theme in an unfinished MS, "The Gentleman" (BP 37.160-163 and

advocates of which encouraged

> detailed and systematic interpretation of all that is implied in [the] Pauline epitome of Christian living. They were concerned with every conceivable aspect of that life, whether public or private, whether personal or social, which should issue from Christian faith and worship. They conceived their task as one of intensive and extensive moral education. It was their aim to educate the individual conscience in the way of holiness, and to educate the social conscience in the way of justice.
>
> Wood x

Examples of this outlook abound: consider his discussion of sumptuousness (*Occl. Ref.* 2.445), the distinction between what is lawful and what is sinful (2.405), the analysis of oaths (*Swearing* 6.13), the justification of lawlessness (*Theodora* 5.284-85), the judge's legal reasoning (5.278), the obligations of gratitude (5.279), and the grounds for suicide (5.267-69).[46] His casuistical divinity was grounded in the ethical writings.

McAdoo observes that because the Caroline moralists based their casuistry on "Scripture and reason instead of upon authorities, canon law and the confessional" (79), the education and exercise of the individual conscience was an important component of Christian liberty. So when Boyle asked "Whether Euil may be don that Good may come of it?" (*Aret.* f. 100), he modified a commonplace ("Never do evil that good may come of it," Tilley E203) by casting the question as a case of conscience. His "case" thus rehearsed many of the arguments found in contemporary casuistry: he responded to criticisms of his own position; anticipated arguments, scruples, and doubts; and reasoned carefully about the assumptions, applications, and implications of his position. Indeed, in godly households, ethics invited such reasoning:

> This Doctrine of Willingness and Constraint is very vsefully deliuered in the Ethickes; because they greatly vary the Nature and Condition of our Action; and teach vs to judge cleerly of many Particular Cases, wherein otherwise, we shud but grope after the Truth.
>
> *Aret.* f. 109

His background in casuistry is clearly indicated in this treatment of motivation and shaped his approach to many kinds of questions as well.

In his "Dayly Reflection" (f. 279), for instance, his casuistical reasoning may help to explain his later position on oaths. We know that in 1680, when Boyle declined the presidency of the Royal Society, he wrote to Hooke about his

---

169). I believe that Jacob attaches far too much weight to this fragment and ignores the larger weight and more systematic arguments of the *Aretology* and other writings in this volume.

[46] In Table 1, note the essays "Of Reasoning & Discourse" and "Of Censuring & Casuists," either of which could be comments on casuistry.

"great (and perhaps peculiar) tenderness in point of oaths" (BW 1.cxix). The younger Boyle wondered whether he should take an oath about daily meditation and answered his own questioned thus: "To Assigne <consecrate> dayly such and <or> so much time to Meditation or the like deuout Employments, by /with/ the solemne engagement of an Oath; That as I dare not Condemne it as vnlawfull, so I cannot commend /approue/ it as Conuenient" (f. 279). About the same time, in his essay on *Swearing*, he discussed the circumstances in which relating another's oaths was not just lawful but necessary (6.13). Clearly, his anxiety about oaths in 1680 resumed a line of reasoning (what Boyle might call "self-conversation") begun forty years earlier. If he would not approve a private oath to help regulate his own meditation, one could imagine his scruples about taking a public oath as the president of the Royal Society.[47]

From other sources we know that his practice of casuistry played a significant role in his private life. Peter Pett and John Evelyn, two longtime friends, recalled that Boyle would spend Sunday afternoons pondering moral issues with friends and catechizing his family, a crucial activity in godly households.[48] His financial support for Robert Sanderson, author of *De Obligatione Conscientiæ Prælectiones Decem* (1660), is well known.[49] Likewise, his support for the translation and publication of religious works extended throughout his life; his conception and endowment of the Boyle lectures is simply one final expression of this outlook. He believed in the efficacy of such moral reasoning, and it is clear what he hoped to accomplish by supporting others' writings. But why did he devote so much time on an ethics at the outset of his career?

Writing an ethics served at least five purposes. First, it enabled him to clarify and articulate his moral foundations. The act of writing tested, reflected, and reinforced his preoccupation with a central core of ethical problems. Moreover, it provided him with a document that he could revise into other, shorter essays on more limited topics. In "Of Sin," for example, he identified ten antidotes and then refuted a dozen common self-deceptions about sin; these twelve self-deceptions were very similar in style and content to the fourteen pleas for sin refuted in *Swearing* 6.4-20. To state it another way, Boyle assembled an armory of arguments against moral laxity and then used those arguments against a specific sin, swearing. His list rehearsed many of the common strategies presented in many works of casuistical divinity. By gathering and sifting these arguments, he addressed questions that he found most compelling and perhaps most useful for himself and others.

Second, his early writings offered a chance to test different rhetorical

---

47 See also Hunter, "Alchemy" 392-93.

48 For Pett's recollections, see BL Add. MS. 4229, f. 39^{v}; for Evelyn's, see E. S. de Beer, *The Diary of John Evelyn* (Oxford 1955) 3.160.

49 BW 1.lix-lx. Sanderson dedicated this work to him.

strategies. Boyle was not writing merely for himself; he referred to his "Reader" more than a dozen times in this volume. As I argue in the next section, he believed in the power of written communication; if written well, an ethics and other works of popular divinity would promote moral reform. (As he was to discover, the rhetorical problems were far more complicated than he had expected.) Third, writing on moral issues, especially with an emphasis on the reform of education, helped to establish his role in the Hartlib circle. We should recall that Philaretus has very specific remarks about the pedagogical manner of his tutor, Marcombes (Maddison 22), and his headmaster at Eton, John Harrison (Maddison 9-15); how Boyle had been educated was important to him and provided him with principles and examples to affirm or to reject.[50] While Boyle was still in Geneva, Lady Ranelagh was actively supporting Dury and Hartlib, so much so that it was common for Hartlib's mail to be delivered to her home or to Sir John Clotworthy's.[51] It was not inevitable that Boyle would play any role in that group, much less the role that developed. Quite literally, he composed a role for himself through what he could contribute to its aims. Several of the young men associated with Hartlib—one thinks immediately of John Hall, John Milton, Benjamin Worsley, and William Petty—shared Boyle's diverse interests, but their lives, careers, and patterns of authorship took very different directions. Through these early writings, I would argue, Boyle found a vocation, a concept crucial to the moral life.[52]

Fourth, writing on ethical topics was a discipline that encouraged the reflection and self-scrutiny essential to morality. Boyle was highly self-conscious about moral reasoning and scrupulous about his own moral life.

---

[50] Canny observes that "despite Cork's belief that a man's aptitude and temperament were formed from birth he clearly thought that education determined the formation of character. It was, seemingly, in this belief that he set his mind to design an educational programme intended to equip each child to fulfil the social role that his own material success had made possible for them" (120-21). I have found no evidence to support Canny's claim that each child's education was tailored to suit him or her.

[51] See HP 3/2/112, a letter from Dorothy Moore Dury to Hartlib (10 April 1645), which was to be left with "Lady Ranalaugh or Sir John Clotworthy in Queene Street next the Queen Statu London." Webster's analysis of Lady Ranelagh's role is excellent (64ff). A large number of her letters and papers (e.g., her questions about a kingless polity in HP 26/13) are extant among the Hartlib Papers, a sharp contrast with the fate of Boyle's correspondence and papers.

[52] The index lists the large number of references to "calling" or "vocation," but they are especially numerous in Boyle's discussion of education (*Aret.* bk. 2, ch. 4). In HP 3/3/45 Dury commiserated with Hartlib (27 October 1646) about the difficulties that Hartlib's son had encountered in finding a trade. In later life, what did Boyle consider his vocation? In *Exc. of Theol.* he posed the interesting problem of making physics a "secondary" subject after having written many works to promote its study (4.35); in *Vulgar Notion* he explained why he never made divinity, philosophy, or physic his profession (5.160); in *Chr. Virtuoso* 5.509, he stressed the importance of his being a layman and a Christian virtuoso, probably the most succinct definition of his vocation.

As Michael Hunter has shown, his preoccupation with moral questions worried him even late in life, when he sought the counsel of several bishops as he reflected on moral choices made decades earlier (Hunter, "Alchemy"). Finally, writing consumed a great deal of time and energy. Unlike his brothers and many other young men in the 1640s, Boyle avoided the military life, marriage, and the university. He was understandably apprehensive about idleness. Closely related to this anxiety was his fear of an uncontrolled imagination. Writing on moral topics helped to discipline his imagination; and like all habits, writing about virtue became a habitude. "Now since a Habitude is acquired by the frequent rëiteration of Action of the same kind," Boyle noted in the *Aretology*, it followed that whoever "wud be Vertuus must diligently exercice himself in the Operations of Vertu" (f. 125). Writing about virtue became an operation of Virtue.

Through authorship, I would argue, Boyle found a vocation. As he was aware, the political perturbations of the 1640s offered a special opportunity to pursue not just virtue but heroic virtue:

> Heroical Men ar more frequently <obseru'd> (for the most part) in Common-welths then in Monarchys; not that they ar more frequently born there; but partly because that in [Common] Republickes the way to honor and preferment lys more open to desert, which is a quickning Spur and a great incitement to Noble Spirits; and Partly too, because the lesser Inequality of Men's Conditions in Common-welths, renders these Heroick Spirits more conspicuus: which in Monarchys wud be swallow'd by the Glory of the King or Princes; to whom for the most part ar attributed the most Glorius Action of their Subjects.
>
> *Aret.* ff. 156-56^{v}

Such political commentary is not found in Aristotle's brief discussion of heroic virtue (Nich. Eth. VII.i.1), though it is a strong feature in Alsted's account of the Reformation. Boyle's numerous comments on heroic virtue, like his discussion of piety, indicate his interest not only in private virtue but also in its public enactment.[53] Because *Philaretus* abounds with biographical details, we can easily see that many of the recurrent issues and problems presented in the *Aretology* emerged from Boyle's experience. Many of these topics reflect his views of education in general and moral education in particular.

Boyle developed these ideas in a lengthy addition to the *Aretology*. An educated person, he argued, has been

---

[53] For a very different concept of heroic virtue, see Sir William Temple's "Of Heroic Virtue," first published in *Miscellanea, the Second Part* (1692). Like Boyle, Temple was the author of romances and some early moral essays; unlike Boyle, he was very sympathetic to Epicureanism and scepticism. His account of heroic virtue stressed non-Christian exemplars. Boyle and Temple were neighbors in Pall Mall for several years (Maddison 133).

> 1. Seasonably (or Betimes) instructed, in the 2. Doctrine of Vertu; 3. Engaged (and persuaded) to it by Solid Reasons, and conuincing Arguments; 4. Stir'd up and excited to it by Good Examples; 5. Maintain'd and warm'd in the Loue of it by Good company: 6. Excited to Goodnes by Emulation <Praise> and Reward, and deterred from Vice by fit Correction. 7. heihtned in it by Generous Ends and Aims; and after all this tauht to know his Proficiency or Vnproficiency therein. 8. Settled in an honest Vocation. 9. Refresht with Lawfull Recreations, and 10. tauht to conuerse with himselfe.
>
> *Aret.* ff. 122^{v}-23

The first seven traits describe ways to pursue moral virtue; the last three characterize aspects of the virtuous life. For him, the dangers of miseducation and the value of true education can hardly be overstated.

Nothing in Boyle's formal education had prepared him for a traumatic religious conversion. His graphic account of the experience and its aftermath is enriched by references to, not descriptions of, temptations, hideous thoughts, religious doubts, even notions of suicide (Maddison 32-36). This malaise lasted for several months.[54] What finally rescued him, he recalled ten years later, was his *groundedness* in religion: knowing what he believed and why he believed it. Essential to the moral life was knowing how to deal with objections to one's beliefs and practices, whether these objections were raised by other people, Satan, or one's own lingering doubts.[55] Thus, Philaretus

> deriu'd from this Anxiety the Aduantage of Groundednesse in his Religion: for the Perplexity his doubts created oblig'd him (to remoue them) to be seriously inquisitiue of the Truth of the very fundamentals of Christianyty: & to peruse what both Turkes, & Jewes, & the cheefe Sects of Christians cud alledge for their seuerall opinions: that so tho he beleeu'd more then he could comprehend, he might not beleeue more then he cud proue; & not owe the stedfastnesse of his Fayth to so poore a Cause as the Ignorance of what might be obiected against it. . . . [There] is nothing worse taken vp vpon Trust then Religion, in which he deserues not to meet with the True one that cares not to examine whither or no it be soe.
>
> Maddison 35-36

Since his concern with answering objections was not limited to moral philosophy, his early work in ethics gave him practice at dealing with challenging doubts and objections. He thus achieved groundedness on topics he considered central to moral virtue even as he recognized that certainty was not possible on

---

[54] His description of his conversion and subsequent spiritual crisis should be understood within the framework of many such accounts printed in the 1640s. For a valuable overview, see Nigel Smith, *Perfection Proclaimed: Language and Literature in English Radical Religion, 1640-1660* (Oxford 1989).

[55] Boyle develops this point in his "Dayly Reflection" (f. 283^{v}). In 1691, Burnet diagnosed the cause of Boyle's religious doubts as "depressions or weaknesses of the Animal Spirits oftentimes proceeding from the want of Nourishment or Free Air or Exercise, or pleaseing Circumstances, &c" (Hunter, "Alchemy" 410).

all topics. Quite simply, one needed to learn lines of reasoning that were morally most secure. Consider a few examples from later works.

In the *Sceptical Chymist*, Boyle confronted each speaker with a wide spectrum of objections and evaluated each speaker's success in addressing those objections. Carneades, for example, had a significant advantage by holding the negative, for

> if among all the instances he brings to invalidate the vulgar doctrine of those he disputes with, any one be irrefragable, that alone is sufficient to overthrow a doctrine, which universally asserts what he opposes.
>
> *Scep. Chym.* 1.461

Boyle organized *Style* around his responses to criticism of Scripture (2.256); in *Reconcileableness* he maintained that some unanswered objections were not fatal (4.174), a concession not altogether comforting since it implied that other unanswered objections might be. Such examples could be multiplied easily without altering the point: Boyle was extremely sensitive to argument and persuasion and very apprehensive that otherwise solid positions could be overthrown by an objection, either unanticipated or unanswerable.[56] When we examine Boyle's revisions of these ethical writings, we see him constantly posing new questions, objections, and arguments and then trying to discover ways to answer, resolve, or refute the new points. His responses led him to experiment with a variety of rhetorical forms.

Rhetorical experimentation encouraged him to investigate the dynamics of persuasion, that is, the connection between textual features and readers' responses. He assumed that if texts were constructed properly, they would achieve their author's intentions and would educate the reader's judgment. He argued that to

> kno the Tru Nature and Causes of things, dos very much clarify and refine the Iudgment; and teaches vs to set a tru Valu and æstimate vpon things, according to their essentiall worth: and not to [rate] prize them by the rates of the vulgar; who in <most> matters that Concern tru Vertu and Knoledg, shud haue their Scorn and Admiration inuerted, to haue them plac't aright.
>
> *Aret.* ff. 192^{v}-93

Knowledge of causality was important both in natural philosophy and religion.[57] Boyle assumed that causality could be understood in the physical world and that

---

[56] For further examples, see the *Life of Boyle* 1.cxlvii; *Vulgar Notion* 5.161; *Orig. of Gems* 3.552-54; and *Reconcileableness* 4.174.

[57] See esp. *Final Causes* 5.392-444, but see also Barbara Donagan, "Providence, Chance and Explanation: Some Paradoxical Aspects of Puritan Views of Causation," *Journal of Religious History* 11 (1980-81) 385-403.

equally knowable principles could explain the operations in the mental world. Hence, he was interested both in the causes and the effects of thoughts and deeds, images and memories. At stake was the piety crucial to his religious convictions and to the life of virtue.

The focus on piety is a prominent feature of many early writings. In *Theodora*, for example, the description of Didymus's piety is probably a self-description. Didymus was someone

> in whom divine grace had produced so early a piety, that he was a well grown Christian, before he was come to be a full grown man. And judging the most flourishing time of his age to be, for that reason, the fittest to be devoted to the most worthy of objects; he was enabled to suppress the heats of youth, and despise the vanities of the world, even while that usually ungoverned age made the former most impetuous, and gave the latter the great endearment of novelty.
>
> *Theodora* 5.306

Seraphic Love was part of a larger design to inculcate piety and reverence for Scripture (*Style* 2.248); *Occasional Reflections* illustrated how "to convert the meanest things to the noblest uses, and make whatever one pleases subservient to piety, by skilfully imploying even slight and unpromising occasions, to represent her, with the advantages of a varied and surprizing dress, whereby you may procure that virtue lovers, and your selves friends" (2.460).[58] In Boyle's understanding of spirituality, piety was jeopardized by its contrary, raving.

Raving, which was triggered by visual images evoked through reading, scenery, or memory, meant several things to Boyle. First, it was a mental text—specifically, a play or romance, his codewords for dangerous or uncontrollable thoughts. Second, raving could be resisted, if not overcome, by prudent discipline of one's mental and spiritual life. Third, resistance was not easy, for once the habit was acquired, control was difficult and relapse easy. Finally, uncontrolled raving dramatized the need for moral education. In this recurrent theme we can see a very personal struggle. In the "Doctrine of Thinking," for example, he identified a personal temptation and strongly warned of its power: "But he that will not yet beleeue the Strange Efficacy of pursued Thoughts, which way soeuer they apply themselues; let him but consider our newfashiond Plays and our Modern Romances" (f. 8). Boyle spoke from experience. As a child he was very fond of reading ancient and modern romances—Honoré d'Urfeé's *L'Astrea*,

---

[58] In 1664 Boyle corresponded with John Eliot about the translation into an Indian language of Lewis Bayly's *The Practice of Piety* (BW 6.510), one of Cork's favorite books (Canny 27-28). Comenius translated the work into Czech. Besides the Bible and an account of a witchcraft trial, Cork was known to have Perkins's *Cases of Conscience*, *The Practice of Piety*, manuscript sermons by Archbishop Ussher, sermons by Dr. Downham, and "four manuscript books of religion bound up in quarto" (Canny 27-28).

Amadis de Gaule, and Quintus Curtius's *History of Alexander* (Maddison 17, 28, and 31). He was so engrossed by Quintus Curtius, Robin Bacon told Burnet, that he once missed his coach.[59] Missing a coach was trivial compared to losing his virtue. Because Boyle viewed spiritual states as analogous to texts, he often described moral issues in literary terms. If we understand his framework, we can more readily understand the interconnectedness of reading, writing, and piety.

In *Philaretus*, Boyle depicted the dangerous causal connection between raving, literature, and melancholy. Literature relieved melancholy but fed raving. For example, reading *Amadis de Gaule* and other "Fabulous and wandring Storys" unsettled his thoughts, for

> meeting in him with a restlesse Fancy, then made more susceptible of any Impressions by an vnemploy'd Pensiuenesse; they accustom'd his Thoughts to such a Habitude of Rauing, that he has scarce euer been their quiet Master since, but they would take all occasions to steale away, & go a gadding to Obiects then vnseasonable & impertinent.
>
> Maddison 17

When he later went to a Carthusian monastery, even more dangerous raving led to profound religious doubts.[60] Throughout his "Doctrine of Thinking," he treated thoughts both as texts and as acts: each had subjects, themes, and audiences. He observed that "the most remarkable Vanity in the Text . . . of our Thoughts; is, when we [make] <faine> a supposition [of a] and then in our Thoughts descant vpon it . . ." (f. 17). Perhaps the only positive use of "raving" occurred when he was musing about the definitions of nature (*Vulgar Notion* 5.175). In all other cases, it led by association to twin dangers, atheism and lust.

In "Dayly Reflection," Boyle made even more explicit the parallel between thoughts, experiences, and texts:

> For in effect, Experience Consists, not in the multitude of years but in that of Obseruations, . . . Thus this Admirable Examen makes <renders> a man <become> both the Teacher, the Scholler and the Booke of his owne selfe.
>
> "Dayly Reflection" f. 272^{v}

Framing the issue in terms of student, teacher, and book, he invoked the master trope of textuality. To state it another way, Boyle persistently viewed both objects and concepts as texts: the universe was a text; the self was a text; the

---

[59] BL Add. MS 4229, f. 66. For his love of Quintus Curtius at Eton, see Maddison 15. He owned a 1633 copy, and references to Alexander abound, with six references in this volume alone.

[60] Burton noted that Carthusian friars were especially vulnerable to religious melancholy (*Anatomy* 1.220, 245-46).

[60] See, for example, *Occ. Refl.* (2.427); *Chr. Virtuoso* (5.514 and 534); and the writings in this volume.

mind was a text. But roles were fluid, not fixed. The mind was a repository for texts, the texts themselves, and the author of the texts. From this trope emerged a recurrent pair of related metaphors, reading and writing.[61] Literally and figuratively, one wrote his own life.

Like Browne and Bacon, Boyle divided knowledge into two books, Scripture and the World, and he sought strategies for reading and writing about the word and works of God.[62] I am not sure whether Boyle had read much of Bacon by 1650; he certainly had read Browne, who often invoked the metaphor of world as text: "Thus there are two bookes from whence I collect my Divinity; besides that written one of God, another of his servant Nature, that universall and publik Manuscript, that lies expans'd unto the eyes of all; those that never saw him in the one, have discovered him in the other" (*Religio Medici* i.§16).[63] Because God was the author of Scripture, Boyle needed to become a better reader of the Word, to read it without the distortion of others' translations. Hence, he learned several ancient languages during the late 1640s and early 1650s: Chaldee, Syriac, and Hebrew. Likewise, God's other book, Creation, required a similar investment in interpretive skills—in this case, observation and experimentation—if one wished to understand the author. The text of nature, as he called it, was "God's stenography" (*Usefulness* 2.63) or hieroglyphics (*Occ. Refl.* 2.349).[64] But who would teach him how to read Creation, how to read "lectures of ethicks or divinity" from the text of Creation (*Occ. Refl.* 2.336)? Part of Boyle's originality was to confront that question directly and to seek strategies of interpretation appropriate to the task. For him, *reading* the Word and the World posed related problems of interpretation and, in a sense, textual analysis. *Writing* about the Word and the World carried similar problems and responsibilities and required comparable rhetorical sensitivity.

What kind of life (or book) would Boyle write for himself if he could not control his raving? Certainly, he could not expect to achieve piety, nor could he educate others. If the dangerous effects of raving were known, what were its causes? Boyle traced his habit of raving to his boyhood. He confessed that

---

[61] For remarks on the metaphor of reading, see *Style* (2.258, 260, 262, 264, 269, 276, 277, 279, 289, 297, and 321); *Exc. of Theology* (4.17); *Chr. Virtuoso* (6.773, 796); and *Occ. Refl.* (2.326, 349, 387, and 408-10). This list is far from exhaustive.

[62] Boyle once discussed three books—the Book of Nature, the Book of Scripture, and the Book of Conscience (BP 8.123-39)—but he did not use this division elsewhere. For Francis Bacon's discussion of the "Two Books," see *The Advancement of Learning* I.iii.

[63] Beginning with Sprat's *History*, traditional historiography has accorded Bacon the predominant influence on the outlook of the early Royal Society, but the early Boyle is more influenced by Browne than Bacon. Taken collectively, Boyle's references to Bacon are mildly critical, for Bacon was not an experimentalist—precisely the same criticism also made of Pascal. For such criticism, see *Fluidity and Firmness* 1.417; *Usefulness* 3.404; *Exc. of Theol.* 4.17; and *Exp. Hist. of Cold* 2.472.

[64] For similar views, see *Usefulness* 2.19-20 and *Occ. Refl.* 2.340.

Philaretus

> would very often steale away from all Company, & spend 4 or 5 howres alone in the fields, to [walk] about, & thinke at Random; making his delighted Imagination the busy Scene, where some Romance or other was dayly acted: which tho imputed to his Melancholy, was in effect but an vsuall Excursion of his yet vntam'd Habitude of Rauing; a Custome . . . much more easily contracted, then Depos'd.
>
> Maddison 24

He admitted that he had seen some plays of Machiavelli in Italy (*Occ. Refl.* 2.213), but he was not sad that the London theatres had been closed. In fact he worried far less about the physical theatre than the theatre of his own imagination. So that Boyle could "ever afterwards devote his thoughts with the greater purity to the Divine Life and Love, and the glories of the divine holyness," Pett recalled, he "totally forbore reading bookes of poetry and never saw any Play, nor read either Play or Romance; no not so much as those writ by his ingenious brother the Earle of Orrery, as I have reason to believe."[65] For him, the most dangerous theatres were psychological and were entered either through raving or through the reading of romances.

> For my part (Dear Sister) I must confesse that when in my solitary retirements I do sometimes deuest myselfe of all sublunary Relations; and with abstracted thoughts looke <behold> on the Intrigue and Passages of the world, with the same temper <eyes> that I haue don on Playes, (I meane only to [deli] please and to informe my selfe, without being otherwise concern'd either in the miscarriages of Actors or the Euents of things;) I little misse /I do not much regret the Absence of/ Blacfryars. . . .
>
> "Dayly Reflection" f. 276^{v}

Strongly opposed to the reading of romances, Boyle wrote or had planned to write at least two essays against the genre (for "The Antagonist of Romances" and "My Opinion of Romances," see Table 1).[66] We should recall Cork's opposition to his children's reading of plays and romances, a position vigorously

---

[65] BL Add. MS 4229, f. 39. One of his few books of modern poetry was a translation into heroic couplets of Edmund Spenser's *Faerie Queene*: *Spencer redivivus* (1687). The only work by Orrery was *A treatise of the art of warr* (1677). Since Orrery's plays were among the most important "heroic plays" on the Restoration stage, it would be interesting to know if the brothers ever discussed the concept of heroic virtue vital to Boyle's ethics and Orrery's drama. Martin Butler analyzes the conflicts in the Boyle family about the theatre, especially after Frank's marriage to Elizabeth Killigrew, who had urged Mary Rich to see plays (*Theatre and Crisis* [Cambridge 1984] 116-17).

[66] See *Style* 2.313, but if these essays have survived, I have not seen them. For Mary Boyle's excessive love of plays and romances, see Sara Heller Mendelson, *The Mental World of Stuart Women: Three Studies* (Brighton 1987) 80. Also relevant is Marcombes's letter to Boyle's father (*II Lismore* 3.281), which described not only the boys' reading but bad moral habits—drinking, borrowing, and lying—learned at Eton.

endorsed by Marcombes. Boyle's anxieties about romances and plays thus exemplify two larger issues—the proper use of leisure time and the proper control of the imagination—to be addressed in moral education.

Even as a child Boyle seemed unusually serious. At Eton he took "noe pleasure in playing with boyes nor running abrood," Robert Carew reported to Cork (*II Lismore* 3.243). In early manhood he engaged in gaming only to hasten recovery from illness.

> Durst I venture to alleadg [my own] any Actions of mine for Examples to others; I wud tell the Reader, that eu'n whilst I was not conuinc't of the vnlawfulnesse of Play; /Dicing/ The Consideration of it's affinity to Idleness made me [I] still refrain['d] to vse <practice> it, but when I was vnder the Fisitians hands; so that I vs'd Gaming but as other sick Persons vse Posset drinke, To make <helpe> my Fisick <to> work the better.
>
> "Of Time and Idleness" (f.16)

Cork's sensitivity to such social and moral issues can be glimpsed from the tone of Lewis Boyle's letter to him (27 December 1638):[67]

> As concerning my reading of Romancyes & playbooks, I neuer (thanks be to God) haue been much inclined vnto them before your Lordships commands to ye contrary, But since, I doe most faithfully protest vnto your Honor, that I haue not as much as look'd on Romancy, Playbooke, or any Pamphets of that kind.
>
> *II Lismore* 3.277-78

Even if Lewis avoided romances and plays, Philaretus recorded that his favorite recreation in Geneva was reading French romances (Maddison 31).[68] Hence, Boyle knew from personal experience how powerfully romances stirred him:

> But he that will not yet beleeue the Strange Efficacy of pursued Thoughts, which way soeuer they apply themselues; let him but consider our newfashiond Plays and our Modern Romances: <that> what perfection they haue been capable to giue so meane[r] and barren a Theame as Loue; and if Rauing can fly so high, to how lofty a Pitch Meditation may soare, and I am confident he shall meet no other Remedy [of] <to cure> his vnbeleefe.
>
> "Doctrine of Thinking" f. 8.

---

[67] For Cork's use of gambling to gain social acceptance, see Canny 73-74.

[68] Boyle owned at least two romances: Mateo Aleman's *The rogue, or the life of Guzman de Allafarache* (1622) and Richard Head's *The English rogue* (1680), the opening pages of which describe the outbreak of the rebellion in Ireland. We might also include John Bunyan's *Pilgrim's Progress* and a version of Edmund Spenser's *Faerie Queene* (*Spencer redivivus* 1687). There is no evidence that he owned or read either of Orrery's works of fiction: *Parthenissa* (1654-69) and *English Adventures* (1676). Samuel Johnson considered *Theodora* the first work "to employ the ornaments of romance in the decoration of religion" (*Life of Johnson*, ed. R. W. Chapman [Oxford 1953] 222).

His fond childhood memories of romances and his equally forceful rejection of the genre signify an increased consciousness of the moral life and the importance of moral education. His experimentation with fictional forms (as in "Joseph's Mistress," which presented the seducer's arguments with no rebuttal) and intense moral conflicts (as in *Theodora*) channeled an old passion into an activity that was safer for him and potentially beneficial to others.

If Boyle has accurately characterized his fear of raving and idleness, then we can see how responsive he was to the pleasures of the imagination.[69] One way to discipline it was to develop a formalized method of channelling thoughts into meditations and observations into reflections, ensuring that morally correct interpretations were drawn from experience. Through meditation on experience and the mediation of written language, he gained both insight and control, allowing him to focus his reading and writing on topics of immediate concern to himself and his circle of friends and family. At the same time he was revising the *Aretology*, he also pursued a new interest, natural philosophy. In both areas, he sought to remove the "remoras of truth," and in both areas he faced two related problems. Who was his audience? And what would be the most effective way to persuade his readers?

§4: Ethics and Rhetoric in the 1640s

As he worked on the *Aretology* in 1646, Boyle summarized his aims and progress in a letter to Isaac Marcombes, his former tutor:

> The *Ethics* hath been a study, wherein I have of late been very conversant, and desirous to call them from the brain down into the breast, and from the school to the house. I have endeavoured to make it not only a lanthorn, but a guide, in a just, though a brief treatise, that I am writing of it; having already with much trouble in some sixteen chapters travelled through the most difficult part of it, and that wherein I saw others deficient, I believe I shall leave the rest to be compleated by those, who enjoy more leisure.
>
> BW 1.xxxiv

The title page of MS 195 states "begun at Stalbridge" in 1645, but the meaning of "begun" is not clear. Did Boyle mean that the project—his *Ethics*—was begun in 1645, or did he mean that he began the revised draft in 1645? Neither manuscript has sufficiently precise internal references to allow exact dating, but

---

[69] If idleness was one danger, its opposite was also a possible snare. In "Dayly Reflection," Boyle noted that "It has euer been one of the greatest and most successfull Policys of the old Tempter (as I show in [my] a Treatise, Of the Strategems of the Deuill) by keeping in a perpetuall /continuall/ Hurrey, so to [diu] busy our Cares <thouhts> about the Accessary /Incidents/ of Life, as to diuert vs wholly from the Thoughts of the Bisnes /Errand/ of our Liues, or at least to put of /defer/ those Thoughts so long, till at last they serue rather to beget Despaire then Amendment" (f. 275).

I suspect that the revised draft, MS 195, occupied much of his attention between 1646, when he settled at Stalbridge, and 1647, when his friendship with Benjamin Worsley and others in the Hartlib circle encouraged his interests in natural philosophy and diverted him from moral philosophy. His reference to "16 chapters" is puzzling, for the *Aretology* has only ten chapters—two in the first book and eight in book two; its earlier draft, MS 192, had ten chapters spread over three books (see Table 4). Since neither had sixteen chapters, what did his reference mean?

Several possibilities exist. First, Boyle might have envisioned the *Aretology* as a work that included the ten extant chapters plus the three essays in MS 196 ("Of Sin," "Of Piety," and "Of Valour"). Those topics followed Alsted's order quite closely and continued the argument of the *Aretology*. And if he considered the long essay on education as a separate chapter (now included in book 2, ch. 4 of the *Aretology*), then we are closer to sixteen chapters. A second possibility is that he had worked his way through sixteen chapters of Alsted, with the original intention of providing a redaction of all thirty-three chapters. (His citations, however, reflect greatest reliance on Alsted's first eight chapters.) More likely, "sixteen chapters" referred to the original ten chapters of MS 192 and some combination of his revision in MS 195. Most important, however, is what he hoped to achieve in his texts and how he thought skillful rhetoric could enhance the teaching of ethics. On these two topics he offered illuminating comments about the *Aretology* in his private correspondence and in the manuscripts themselves.

Boyle mentioned the *Aretology* in five letters written between 1646 and 1653, addressing Lady Ranelagh (30 March 1646); Marcombes (22 October 1646); a brother, probably Broghill (4 April 1647); Hartlib (8 April 1647); and John Mallet (1653).[70] To each correspondent he emphasized a different aspect of the project. In a lengthy letter to Lady Ranelagh, he mentioned only that his progress was slow, complaining twice about his distaste for making and receiving social visits. To Marcombes, as we have seen, he described his status in somewhat more detail.

In the third reference to his ethics, Boyle drew directly on the contents of his work. He chided his brother (probably Broghill) for delaying repentance. "I am content . . . to Procrastinate this Theame," Boyle wrote, "till I shew <yow> at large in some Discourses of my Ethickes, both the Reasons and Grounds of my Advice. . . . I iudg'd it necessary to premise this Patterne of Counsell . . . to the whole Peece yow shall find in my Ethickes."[71] Dramatizing the evasions and seductions of self-deception was a popular topic in practical divinity, a genre in which Boyle was especially interested and which he thought would be

---

[70] BW 1.xxx, 1.xxxiv, Boyle Lett. 1.137, 1.xxxviii-xxxix, and BL Add. MS 32093 respectively.

[71] Boyle Lett. 1.138^{v}. This letter was not printed by Birch.

beneficial to his brother. In 1648 Hartlib published a translation of Jacobus Acontius's *Satanæ Strategemata* as *Satans Stratagems, or the devils Cabinet-Council Discovered*, a project for which Dury and Thomas Goodwin were responsible (Webster 34). In an epistle (9 February 1647) included in the volume, Goodwin observed that "He that will the Iudgment win, / With th' *Affections* must begin" (italics reversed). But how would one win the Judgment? And how should one begin with the Affections? The answers were not obvious.

In a fourth reference to the *Aretology*, he confided to Hartlib that his opinions "both about the nature and the teaching of virtue, will doubtless appear as paradoxical to others, as they seem probable to" Boyle (BW 1.xxxiv).[72] Why did he consider his views about virtue and the teaching of virtue paradoxical? At first glance, the claim is puzzling, for nothing in his texts contradicts the tenets of orthodox Christianity. His remark makes sense, though, if we consider the literary milieu in which Boyle found himself, especially the relationship between Hartlib, Boyle, and John Hall (1627-56). We recall that Hall sought Boyle's patronage for a book of poems, *Emblems with Elegant Figures* (1647). Boyle politely avoided the role of patron but was careful not to offend Hartlib, who served as intermediary and perhaps as mentor to both young men.[73] Though Boyle praised Hall's discernment and remarked on his precocity, I do not know whether he was aware that Hall was born in Lismore in 1627, making them the same age.[74] Boyle's comments make most sense when we recognize how differently Hall and Boyle approached the *teaching* of virtue.

By 1647, Hall was already the author of a collection of essays, *Horæ Vacivæ*, and a volume of poetry. Boyle was struggling with the *Aretology*. These two young authors, both in active correspondence with Hartlib and Worsley, offer an interesting contrast in outlook and method. Their approach to the

---

[72] We should recall that in Table 1, the fifth essay was "Of Vniuersality of Opinions & of Paradoxes." The epigraph to "Doctrine of Thinking" is not in Boyle's hand but reads: "I wud rather [ex] perplex then Instruct most those I heere desire to informe."

[73] Hall eagerly sought Hartlib's assistance. On 21 December 1646 Hall promised Hartlib 100 copies of his forthcoming volume of poetry, and he expressed the desire to meet John Milton, the "author of that excellent discourse of Education [Hartlib was] pleased to impart" (HP 60/14/5). (Like Milton and William Petty, Hall would also write a proposal to reform education: *An Humble Motion to the Parliament . . . Concerning the Advancement of Learning* [1649]). Hartlib seemed to have a high regard for Hall's intellectual judgment and literary gifts, for in early 1647 Worsley, Hall, and Hartlib corresponded about "whether the Scriptures be an adequate Iudge in physicall controversies" (HP 36/6/1-3). (For Boyle's later views of this topic, see *Vulgar Notion* 5.174). Hall's correspondence with Hartlib and Boyle is well summarized in G. H. Turnbull, "John Hall's Letters to Samuel Hartlib," *RES* n.s. 4, 15 (1953) 221-33. Hall later translated two works by Johann Valentin Andreae for Hartlib and translated Longinus's *On the Sublime* into English (1652).

[74] Boyle showed an awareness of Hall's youth when he observed that Hall had "September in his judgment, whilst we can scarce find April upon his chin" (1.xl); for remarks about his own beardless chin, see "Dayly Reflection" (f. 272^v) and *Occ. Refl.* 2.366.

teaching of virtue and the image of the author were radically different, and so Boyle's methods might seem "paradoxical" to Hartlib. Hall's essays focused on topics often addressed in the *Aretology* and other works listed in Table 1. His volume offered a literary approach to fourteen subjects: Of Opinion, Of Time, Of Felicity, Of Preaching, Of Fame, Of Studies, Of Company, Of Friends, Of Dissimulation, Of Recreations, Of Warre, Of Religion, Of Rewards, and Of Fables. Several of these topics have the same titles as Boyle's essays listed in Table 1, but the authors approached the topics with a different sense of audience and purpose. "Of Felicity," the third essay in *Horæ Vacivæ*, was a very literary treatment of standard *topoi;* it did not promote moral edification. We may be sure that Boyle would never have chosen a title like "empty hours" or "idle hours"; nor would he have attempted to address such an important topic in so few words. If Boyle and Hall differed in purpose, they differed even more sharply in the image of the author projected in their writings.

Hall's volumes of essays and poetry emphasized the author's precocity and extolled his literary genius. The frontispiece of *Horæ Vacivæ*, a plate by William Marshall, depicted Hall at age nineteen, and the volume was adorned with commendatory epistles, one by the dramatist James Shirley.[75] The contrast between Hall's self-promotion and Boyle's modesty—his earliest publication was anonymous—could hardly be greater. Far from promoting moral reform, Hall's writings were merely literary exercises, public opportunities to display rhetorical finesse and court patronage. If the traditional moralists offered solid doctrine but no incitements to virtue, Hall offered rhetorical display and predictable platitudes. Boyle's method, by comparison, *was* paradoxical.

Boyle's final reference to his ethics occurred in a letter to John Mallet in 1653, where Boyle again described his method as paradoxical:

> as for the giddy Multitudes here in England I confesse my Apprehensions are very sad, that amonst too many, this Multiplicy of Religions will end in none at all; for to say that they will quit Christ for Epicurus, would scarce expresse the worst of my Feares. . . . I hope one Day to show yow a couple of Discourses the one Philosophicall concerning Felicity, the other Theologicall, concerning Libertinisme, wherein I hope my Paradoxes on both those Subjects, will not appeare improbable Vntruths.
>
> BL Add. MS 32093 f. 293^{v}

Clearly, Boyle thought his approach was paradoxical, but it is much easier to see

[75] In the Kerseboom portrait painted late in his life, Boyle pointed toward his printed works, directing attention away from the person and toward his texts. An earlier portrait by William Faithorne prominently featured his scientific instruments. Despite the modesty of these iconographic gestures, Boyle was interested in how he was portrayed: see his correspondence with Hooke about the Faithorne engraving (BW 6.488ff). For Beale's advice about managing his fame, see BW 1.cxxxi, 6.374, 447, and 451. Boyle reflected on the perils of fame in *Exc. of Theol.* 4.53 and 57-58.

what made it rhetorical. The failure of traditional moral philosophy to be persuasive was, in fact, his chief criticism of ancient and modern ethics.

Boyle presented his most sustained criticism of ethics in *Style* 2.287-90, but he peppered his early works, including the *Aretology*, with briefer criticisms and objections to contemporary practices. His central objection was not to doctrine but to rhetoric. "It is a mistake to think," he wrote,

> that a large system of ethicks, dissected according to the nice prescriptions, of logick, and methodically replenished with definitions, divisions, distinctions, and syllogisms, is requisite or sufficient to make men virtuous. *Too many of our moralists write, as if they thought virtue could be taught as easily, and much in the same way, as grammar; and leaving our rational motives to virtue, and determents from vice, with other things, that have a genuine influence on the minds and manners of men,* they fall to wrangle about the titles and precedencies of the parts of ethical philosophy, and things extrinsecal enough to vice and virtue; they spend more time in asserting their method, than the prerogatives of virtue above vice; they seem more sollicitous, how to order their chapters than their readers actions; and are more industrious to impress their doctrine on our memories than our affections, and teach us better to dispute of our passions than with them.
>
> *Style* 2.287 (emphasis added)

Why was moral virtue not being achieved? Quite simply, ethics was more successfully taught in the school than in the home; it could be mastered in the brain without affecting the breast, to paraphrase Boyle's letter to Marcombes (BW 1.xxxiv). The understanding was strengthened while the will remained untouched (*Swearing* 6.3). We do not need to decide whether this criticism was accurate or whether he solved the rhetorical problems he diagnosed. We should, however, observe how he defined the problem of communication and experimented with strategies for solving it.

When I mention Boyle's theory of rhetoric, I refer not to a treatise by that title but to his knowledge and practice of the arts of communication.[76] During his stay in Geneva, Philaretus studied "both Rhethoricke & Logicke, whose Elements (not the Expositions) Philaretus wrote out with his owne hand; tho afterwards he esteem'd both those Arts (as they are vulgarly handled) not only vnseasonably taught, but obnoxious to those (other) Inconveniences & guilty of those Defects, he dos fully particularize in his Essays" (Maddison 30). Throughout his career Boyle used the prefaces of many major works to reflect not only on the circumstances of composition but also on his particular rhetorical strategy. Such rhetorical self-consciousness is a major feature of the early

[76] For a useful survey of the training in logic and rhetoric that would have been found at Eton and perhaps under the tutelage of Isaac Marcombes as well, see Wilbur Samuel Howell, *Logic and Rhetoric in England, 1500-1700* (Princeton 1956). For Boyle's opinions of Cicero and Isocrates, cf. *Occ. Refl.* 2.239-40.

writings.

The parts of rhetorical theory, Boyle noted, include "embellishments of our conceptions and . . . the congruity of them to our design and method, and the suitable accommodation of them to the various circumstances considerable in the matter, the speaker, and the hearers" (*Style* 2.301). Nothing in this definition of rhetoric was original: sources could be found in Aristotle, Cicero, or Quintilian and their Renaissance successors. More notable is the meta-commentary on rhetorical issues in so many works, where he reflected on the particular applications and implications of rhetorical theory. Thus, when he apologized for writing the bare truth in *New Experiments* (1.117)—that is, "without allowing it any of those advantages that method, style, and decent embellishments, are wont to confer on the composures they are employed to adorn"—he was *not* criticizing such strategies as being inherently unsuitable for natural philosophy. He was acknowledging only that he had not had enough time to polish the work.[77]

We have noted the quantity of his early writings in the first two tables, but we should consider also their rhetorical diversity. Between 1645 and 1655, he pursued a wide range of experiments and observations in natural philosophy, drawing later on this work in his *Usefulness* and *Sceptical Chymist.* He also wrote an ambitious work of popular divinity (*Seraphic Love*), an original analysis of style (*Style of the Scriptures*), an influential collection of private meditations (*Occasional Reflections*), and a religious romance (*Theodora*). Boyle's primary purpose in these works was not to provide information; it was to persuade. He sought to influence the manners and minds of the readers.

His first publication, "Invitation to a free and generous Communication . . . from Philaretus to Empericus," appeared anonymously in a volume edited by Samuel Hartlib in 1655.[78] Even if the point of this epistolary essay was to

---

[77] Boyle's concern with *method* (both of experimentation and of expression) is an important element in his later writing. Regarding his method of composing the *Hist. of Air*, he noted that "in that first draught he followed my Lord *Bacon*'s advice, not to be over-curious or nice in making the first set of heads, but to take them as they occur. But now that thus much comes to be published, which perhaps may serve to some men as a common place for the history of the air, the titles have been a little more increased, or methodized, to which any one may add as he finds occasion" (5.610). For other comments on method, see *New Experiments and Observations . . . Cold* 2.469 and *Reconcileableness* 4.153. As we have seen above, in 1653 Petty praised Boyle's method of using experiments and meditation (6.138). In 1666 Beale urged Boyle to *methodize* his unpublished papers (6.404-08), and RB wrote to Oldenburg about his method of writing natural history (6.216).

[78] See Margaret Rowbottom, "The Earliest Published Writings of Robert Boyle," *Ann. of Sci.* 6 (1950) 376-89. He used the pseudonym or variants of Philaretus in other later writings as well (cf. *Occ. Refl.* 2.460); and he sometimes referred both to an "I" and a Philaretus in the same discourse (*Occ. Refl.* 2.426). His fondness for such pious nicknames is further seen in his dedication of *Occ. Refl.* to Lady Ranelagh, whom he addressed as Sophronia, thus associating her with the Greek word for temperance (*sōphrosunē*) or wisdom (*phronēsis*) or both. After the publication of *Style*, Boyle received a letter addressed to Aretaphilus (BW 1.lxx), apparently a variant of Philaretus. In HP

persuade people to share their medical receipts, the more general problem for Boyle was how to *communicate* his argument persuasively. Before he could communicate anything of importance in moral philosophy or in natural philosophy, he needed to make himself a writer.

Boyle often remarked that *how* he wrote had an important effect on *what* he communicated, regardless of the form of the text. John Christie emphasizes the importance of recognizing textual strategies in all discourse, a point that Boyle would have heartily supported:

> Conventional scientific and philosophical reading tends strongly towards discrimination by content. However, to focus on content at the expense of expression introduces another and comparable form of blindness, for the work of the expressive mode, language, will tend to go unglimpsed unless matched by an active reading constantly aware of the textual tactic and strategy which written language always and inevitably embodies.
>
> *The Figural and the Literal* 2-3.

Indeed, given the range of his *oeuvres*—which take the form of letters, dialogues, reports, descriptions, sermons, meditations, and oratory—it is by no means certain that he would accept the dichotomy between "rhetorical" and "philosophical" writing. I therefore disagree with Brian Vickers, who assumes that because Boyle wrote *New Experiments Physico-Mechanical* in the form of a letter, he "had not yet moved from the 'literary' to the 'scientific' mode" (*English Science* 46). I do not think that the categories were so firmly determined. Boyle would continue to experiment with rhetorical forms because he was not certain about the best way to persuade his intended audience.[79] Putting aside his formulaic litanies that his manuscript was not ready for the printer or that the printer or his amanuensis had been careless, Boyle often addressed the literary subtexts that affected seventeenth-century readers and writers of the New Philosophy. Let me examine some of those subtexts.

First, Boyle had an acute sense of the need to accommodate his material to the readers of his moral philosophy. He went to even greater lengths to create an audience for his natural philosophy.[80] If a writer's audience is always a fiction,

---

17/7/1 is a letter from George Starkey (30 May 1651) in which he referred to himself as Philalethâ Philopono Hermetica Schola Chemiatrâ.

[79] For other approaches to this issue, see James Paradis, "Montaigne, Boyle, and the Essay of Experience" in George Levine, ed., *One Culture*: *Essays in Science and Literature* (Madison 1987) 59-91 and J. Paul Hunter's "Robert Boyle and the Epistemology of the Novel," *Eighteenth-Century Fiction* 2 (July 1990) 275-81.

[80] Cf. remarks about shaping material to different kinds of audiences in *Style* 2.274. In *Cert. Phys. Essays*, Boyle justified both his style (1.304) and his selection of *essays* as his form (1.300). See also Robert Markley, "Robert Boyle on Language: Some Considerations Touching the Style of the Holy Scriptures," *Studies in Eighteenth-Century Culture* 14 (1985) 159-71.

as Walter Ong has argued, then what kind of fictional audience did Boyle invent?[81] The question is important because strategies of accommodation are shaped by assumptions about readers—their knowledge, outlook, and interests. He made quite similar assumptions about both fictional audiences. For natural philosophy, his readers were defined as potential experimentalists whose lives would be sharply improved by pursuing what Shapin and Schaffer call "the experimental life."[82] His nephew Richard Jones, who had been tutored in logic by John Milton, chaperoned on the Continent by Henry Oldenburg, and addressed as "Pyrophilus" in several works by Boyle, thus represented a fictionalized "Every Reader." As such, his fictional attributes are important. Pyrophilus belonged to "this sort of virtuosi" among the nobility and gentry who were disgusted by what the schools taught about "forms, and generation, and corruption," a reaction that was "usual among ingenious readers" (*Orig. of Forms* 3.5). Boyle's rhetorical task was to show such readers precisely what the experimental life involved while depicting its rewards in such a way that gentlemen would want to embrace it.

If the readers of the New Philosophy knew almost nothing about experiments, then the readers of his moral essays knew too little about virtue, what it was, how to achieve it, and why it mattered. To make his readers lovers of virtue (=*philaretus*), he wrote about moral excellence: *ēthikē aretē* were Aristotle's words for moral excellence. His task in moral philosophy was as lofty as the challenge of persuading readers to share their medical receipts or gentlemen to pursue the experimental life. More important, he would argue that the experimental life, properly understood, contributed to the moral life.

Boyle's rhetorical aims remained remarkably constant throughout his career. The Interregnum Boyle wrote an *Aretology* to promote moral excellence; the older Boyle published an account of how Christianity promoted "greatness of mind," basing his argument not on "the opinions of the injudicious vulgar, but the judicious estimates of reason, improved by philosophy, and enlightened by natural theology" (*Greatness of Mind* 5.551).[83] About 1650 Boyle projected a work entitled "The Christian Gentleman"; the older Boyle published *The Christian Virtuoso*. To educate Christian Virtuosos, he illustrated how virtuous persons "read" the world, Scripture, and their own interior life,

---

[81] Ong, "The Writer's Audience is Always a Fiction," *PMLA* 90 (1975) 9-21.

[82] *Leviathan*, ch. 2. J. Paul Hunter attributes to Boyle an important role in creating an audience for fiction ("Robert Boyle and the Epistemology of the Novel"), a remarkable irony given Boyle's profound ambivalence about fictional forms.

[83] One has greatness of mind if he "uses his utmost moral diligence to find out what are the best things he can do, and then, without being deterred by dangers, or discouraged by difficulties, does resolutely and steadily pursue them, as far as his ability and opportunites will serve; and this out of an internal principle of love of God and man, and with a sincere aim to glorify the one, and benefit the other" (*Greatness of Mind* 5.552).

forestalling objections and rejecting their usual evasions for loving virtue less than it deserves.[84]

If his social standing would help to persuade others to write occasional meditations, it also would encourage gentlemen to do experiments.[85] That, at least, was the fictive audience to whom he wrote. For these experimentalists, Boyle provided extensive details and "circumstantial witnessing."[86] His early career found him reading and writing about both moral philosophy and natural philosophy, thereby addressing kinds of readers who were far more closely related in 1650 than they are today. While his actual practice needs to be studied much more carefully than it has been, we should also attend to his own statements about the arts of discourse.

Boyle defended his style of scientific writing as one driven by the needs of novice experimentalists.[87]

> But besides the unintentional deficiencies of my style, I have knowingly and purposely transgressed the laws of oratory in one particular, namely, in making sometimes my periods or parentheses over-long: for when I could not within the compass of a regular period comprise what I thought requisite to be delivered at once, I chose rather to neglect the precepts of rhetoricians, than the mention of those things, which I thought pertinent to my subject, and useful to you, my reader.
>
> *Cert. Phys. Essays* 1.305

For rhetorical reasons he demonstrated how he made reflections and experiments, how he extracted significance from them, how he integrated personal experience and biblicism. In each mode, eyewitness testimony was crucial to his *ethos*, his credibility. And in each mode, he assumed that his audience would be responsive both to evidence and to style. Boyle believed that style was crucial to the acceptance of content, regardless of subject or genre, and his works are embroidered with observations about style. Most crucial to his own literary practice were figurative language, proverbs, and chiasmus.

Figurative language was important because powerful metaphors made a

---

[84] Boyle described how he read books of devotion (*Style* 2.289) and Scripture (2.276 and 321). Beale wrote to Boyle about how people read Boyle's writing (6.429); see also *Occ. Refl.* 2.434 and 449. Boyle was acutely aware of the importance of illustrations in helping his audience *read* natural philosophy: for discussions with Beale, Hooke, and Oldenburg, see 2.738, 3.178, 3.430, 6.178, 393, 404, 490, and 499-501.

[85] *Occ. Refl.* 2.326. For a particularly well-documented account of the Protestant meditative tradition and Boyle's place in it, see Barbara K. Lewalski, *Protestant Poetics and the Seventeenth-Century Religious Lyric* (Princeton 1979) 151-63; see also Isabel G. MacCaffrey, "The Meditation Example," *ELH* 32 (1965) 388-407.

[86] I have conflated two concepts from Shapin and Schaffer: "circumstantial report" and "virtual witnessing" (60-65). For valuable comments on the importance of eyewitness testimony, cf. *Scep. Chym.* 1.486 and *Style* 2.314.

[87] See esp. *Exp. Hist. of Cold* 2.471; *Med. Hydro.* 5.454; and *Final Causes* 5.393.

lasting impression on the memory. They were aids to seeing and remembering.[88] Those "truths and notions, that are dressed up in apt similitudes, pertinently applied, are wont to make durable impressions on that faculty [memory]" (*Occ. Refl.* 2.333).[89] Boyle's fascination with metaphoric language must have been shared by his contemporaries. For example, in John Preston's *Saints Dayly Exercise* (1631), an enormously popular work, similes were noted in the margins. Boyle's exposure to natural philosophy offered him a powerful new vocabulary, one in which objects were worthy of study in themselves and as part of a richly symbolic universe of meaning. Natural philosophy provided new occasions for pushing literal details into figurative meanings.

In his essay "Of Sin," for example, Boyle insisted first on the literal meaning of soap and then evoked its figurative meaning. "Repentance is the Soap of the Soule that scoures out all it's Spots," he wrote, using a traditional figure. But repentance was also like an invaluable powder he had tried, one "that is both a Purge and an Antidote, both Curing Diseases already contracted and arming vs against future." (There is no way to identify this remarkable powder, but Hartlib's "Ephemerides" [1649] contains at least a dozen comments on Lady Kent's powder, with several references to the views of Boyle and Lady Ranelagh.)[90] Yet Boyle pushed the image even further, simultaneously extending both its literal meaning and its figurative potential by enriching the circumstantial details:

> But it's Vtilitys (both great and Numerus) ar extream liuely Emblem'd by an admirable liquor a great Filosofer lately show'd me the Experiment of; whereof a few drops instil'd into a great vessel of the most stinking water that runs in the kennell, not onely frees it presently from all <[offensiue]> [ill] il tast and smell, and so restores it to it's

---

88 The standard work on memory systems is Frances A. Yates, *The Art of Memory* (Chicago 1966). Hartlib had given Caleb Morley's manuscript on memory to John Beale, a topic discussed at length in a letter to Boyle in 1660 (6.330-39), but to transcribe it required a missing key.

89 Similar comments are found in *Style* 2.299-305 and many other places. For Boyle's discussion of the signatures of plants, see the *Aret.* f. 123^{v}. Vickers praises Boyle's use of metaphors (*English Science* 15).

90 Elizabeth Grey, Countess of Kent, wrote *A Choice Manual of Rare and Select Secrets*, an extremely popular collection of medical receipts. Boyle owned the second edition (1653) of a work that saw nineteen editions. Boyle's early interest in medicine, both literally and figuratively, became a life-long interest; by 1653, Petty considered Boyle a hypochondriac (6.138). For other aspects of this interest, we should consider Lady Ranelagh's medical MSS as well: at the Wellcome Institute, MS 1340 is listed as Lady Ranelagh's household and medical receipts (cf. #53, "Of roses my brother Robert Boyls way"); BL Sloane MS 1367 contains another collection of her choice receipts (ff. 1-95), many in her own hand. Ff. 81-83 list her abbreviations (which she called "Our Abbreviations"), and she also includes an index. She often identifies who gave her the receipt. For Lady Ranelagh's role in freely disseminating Boyle's medical compounds, see Antonia Fraser, *The Weaker Vessel* (London 1984) 133. A broader examination of the social dimensions of contemporary medical practices is offered in Lucinda McCray Beier, *Sufferers and Healers: the Experience of Illness in Seventeenth-Century England* (London 1987).

> [illeg.] former Purity and Clearnes; but secures it for euer from future corruption; and not onely so, but frees those very lees that carri'd that Putrefaction, From all offensiue Sent.
>
> "Of Sin" ff. 33-33^{v}

Boyle moved from soap to powder to an "admirable liquor," capping the movement by calling it an emblem.[91] As he stated elsewhere, metaphors were to the mind what microscopes were to the eye.[92]

The oscillation between literal and figurative is not only an important aspect of Boyle's sense of style but a link between his moral philosophy and his natural philosophy. His account of the "admirable liquor [of] a great Filosofer" illustrates his way of addressing two frames of reference. But who was this great philosopher that so affected him? Between 1645 and 1648 Hartlib received several enquiries and reports on this topic, notably a letter from Benjamin Worsley (8 May 1648).[93]

> The Cure of stincking water, I now know and without an injunction or sacrament of secrecy, having found it out myselfe, by Mr. Borrells favour in giving me leave first to taste it, and after upon a suspition to make a proof or 2 of it myselfe in his chamber. It being a liquor which I as well know as I did Urine, as sone as I had proved it though I esteeme of it not halfe so much (as I do Urine) now I have It. It being as noxious to be taken inwardly as the other is noysome.
>
> Hartlib Papers 71/15/1-2

On the basis of this letter to Hartlib and others from Boyle to Worsley (BW 6.40-41), I suspect that Worsley was the "great Filosofer." More important, however, is Boyle's use of natural philosophy to talk about spiritual states. Or as he claimed, "This <Emblem> . . . dos sufficiently apply itself." The repetition of *emblem* cannot be accidental. Precisely the same argument explains his reference to furnaces in "Of Piety" (f. 39^{v}), to chemical knowledge in *Seraphic Love* (1.258), and to lodestones in many works.[94] Boyle demonstrated in these early writings an interest in natural philosophy as a source of figurative language and an incitement to piety. Clearly, he found similitudes powerful and hoped that

---

[91] A child liked to look at emblems and the flourishes of a Greek or Hebrew Bible, Boyle noted, but when he learned to read, the pleasures were even greater (*Seraphic Love* 1.283).

[92] *Chr. Virtuoso* 5.511-12. Dealing primarily with Descartes and Newton, Colin Turbayne's argument about metaphor and science also applies to Boyle (*The Myth of Metaphor* [Columbia, S.C. 1970]).

[93] I am grateful to R. E. W. Maddison for pointing out Boyle's later reference to this experiment or to a very similar one in *Spec. Medicines* 5.93.

[94] For the lodestone as religious symbol, see the *Aret.* f. 180; *Seraphic Love* 1.274; *Reconcileableness* 4.177, 179; and "Dayly Reflection" f. 272; for its interest to natural philosophers, see *Usefulness* 2.10; *Continuation of New Exp.* 3.238; *Exp. et Obs. Phys.* 5.569-75; and *Languid Motion* 5.11.

they would be as memorable for readers as they were for him. At the same time, he knew that reading only for similitudes was as dangerous as hearing sermons only as oratory (*Occ. Refl.* 2.449).

Boyle's early experimentation with metaphor in moral philosophy should be linked with his later use of metaphor in natural philosophy. The "mechanical philosophy" and the "corpuscularian hypothesis" are both deeply implicated in and dependent on figurative language. Part of Boyle's task in the New Philosophy was to find the best possible metaphors for unobservable subjects (Turbayne 96). Writers of meditations, Boyle observed,

> may have the satisfaction of making almost the whole world a great *Conclave Mnemonicum*, and a well furnished *Promptuary*, for the service of piety and virtue, and may almost under every creature and occurrence lay an ambuscade against sin and idleness.
> *Occ. Refl.* 2.334

He was particularly eager to find a language adequate for analyzing and celebrating the natural world, in part because such figures always permitted a range of meanings and applications. But his central assumption was that they *affected* an audience as they affected him.

The interest in heroic virtue, as I have noted above, emerged in the *Aretology* and persisted throughout his career. In *Greatness of Mind* (5.558), for instance, his aim "was to make impressions on an illustrious person, not by dry precepts, or languid discourses, but by exciting him to heroic virtue, by the noblest patterns and ideas, and the most moving incentives, he could propose."[95] But however potent metaphors might be, a successful writer needed other strategies as well. To achieve his lofty aims, Boyle experimented with a variety of rhetorical techniques. His patterns of revision disclose textual features that he found most attractive. Among them is the use of proverbs.

Proverbs were an important dimension of these early texts. He was especially responsive to *sententiae*, whether in Latin, English, or French. Like his use of Psalms and Proverbs, they reflected, in Dr. Johnson's words, truths too important to be new. Proverbs were the common property of Boyle's age, and writers as diverse as Bacon, Milton, and Browne drew freely and creatively on traditional expressions and the received wisdom encoded in them. When Sir Thomas Browne drafted his thoughts about ethics in *Christian Morals*, first published in 1716 but written during the 1670s, he mixed pious exhortation with proverbs, Biblical allusions, and his distinctive imagery. Unlike Boyle, he did not offer a closely reasoned argument; he assumed that the eloquence of his sententiae would be sufficient. Boyle's fondness for certain proverbs is demonstrated by his repeated use of them—or variants of them—in many works. Both

---

[95] For an illuminating discussion, see Shuger, ch. 5.

his arguments and his proverbial expressions are repeated in later writings. The sheer number of proverbs reflected Boyle's confidence in the wisdom and memorability of such utterances. If metaphors were aids to vision, proverbs were aids to memory. Both were important inducements to readers like Boyle.

Finally, we should recognize Boyle's favorite rhetorical scheme, chiasmus. Literally meaning "crossing," chiasmus acquires its power by balancing and contrasting its paired elements, binding them mnemonically as the pattern unfolds. Once heard or read, a chiasmus is easily remembered, as Boyle's fondness for them suggests. He frequently exmployed this scheme at the end of paragraphs, and a few examples should illustrate this practice:

> They that haue the most Objects for their Passion, haue the lest Passion for any Object.
>
> The Sin of Custom, came from the Custom of Sin.
>
> They ar such Good Teachers and such bad Liuers, that they Confute their Doctrine by their Practice, and Condemn their Practice by their Doctrine.
>
> Yow wil quickly find that tis not because <we find> Goodness [is] so Difficult that we go faintly on; but 'tis because we go so faintly on that we find it so Difficult.
>
> For woful Experience tels vs, that many Times, those Actions, which hauing once don in the transport of our Passion, we cannot vndoo, vndoo vs.
>
> And Ignorance is neuer the true Cause of a Fault, when a fault is the cause of that Ignorance.

In more than a few cases, he indulged his taste for chiasmus with his habit of unattributed borrowing: "(with the Words of an Excellent Modern Author) in a Word, the Plesure of the Body is but the Body of Plesure; but the Deliht of the Soule is the Soule of Deliht" (*Aret.* f. 215^{v}). Chiasmus was especially critical at the end of paragraphs or other divisions, where he wished to achieve closure and heighten emotional impact. Rather frequently, in fact, he added a chiasmus in marginal insertions. If chiasmus did not alter the argument, it did elevate its tone and make the passage more memorable. Attention to his revisions tells us a great deal about how he read his own texts and those of other writers. For Boyle, reading and writing were analogous acts and, if done properly, could be aids to virtue. By observing how he revised his texts, we see how he critiqued his own performance. His deletions, additions, and insertions provide additional information about his understanding of his audience and his discourse.

When we consider his revisions—the massive number of interlinear and marginal insertions, deletions, and provisional alterations of words or phrases—we see an author who was usually more attentive to surface detail than to broader rhetorical issues. (There are, of course, substantial exceptions to this generalization: the addition of his "treatise" on education in the *Aretology* makes this draft substantially longer and more complex than MS 192.) He was much more likely to add material than to delete it and quite commonly replaced a short phrase with several sentences.

In this volume Boyle made about 2,000 deletions and about 1,300 interlinear additions. For the 500 marginal insertions—usually on the same page of the manuscript but sometimes signaled from several pages later—Boyle used about one-third simply to indicate a Biblical source or to insert a short phrase. The other two-thirds were occasions either to depart from his main point—he was a highly digressive author—or to provide further support for his argument, usually by anticipating and refuting objections.

What Boyle added to and suppressed from his text provides an interesting commentary upon his drafts. Always reluctant to make political statements after the Restoration, Boyle's caution is clear even in the 1640s as we can see in the political example deleted from his discussion of voluntary and involuntary actions.

> The Mixt or Inuoluntary Actions are those to whose Production, partly constraint and partly the Will concurre. Which arriues, when a man is Induc't to do any thing or to leaue it vndon; either by the Hope to obtaine thereby a Greater Good, or to Euite a greater Euill. As when a Marchant is forc'd to cast his goods ouerboord into the Sea, to auoid Shipwrack; or a man suffers his Arm to be cut of to saue his Body: [*or when a Prince vnjustly confiscates a Subjects Goods to benefit the Common-welth.*]
>
> *Aret.* f. 98^{v} (emphasis added)

Boyle had used the shipwreck example earlier in the text, perhaps deriving it from Aristotle (Nich. Eth. III.i.4-5), but the reference to an unjust prince was found neither in Aristotle nor Alsted. There were, of course, countless comments about unjust princes in the 1640s, and Boyle certainly heard some of them. I doubt that this deletion was made for stylistic reasons. Such deletions provide insights into Boyle's self-censorship as well as his literary judgment.

An insatiable reviser, he was often indecisive both about individual words and sentence structure. Often he left several alternative expressions on the same line without indicating his final choice. Despite his frequent complaints about sloppy amanuenses and careless printers, his composing habits indicate great difficulty in completing final drafts. He was always sensitive to additional counterarguments and curious about the effect of choosing one word or phrase rather than another. An even more worrisome problem, though, was the fear of an unanswerable objection. He correctly observed that some arguments based on experimentation were exceptionally dangerous:

> There are some arguments, which being clearly built upon sense, or evident experiments, need borrow no assistance from the refutation of any of the proposers or approvers and may, I think, be fitly enough compared to arrows shot out of a cross-bow, and bullets shot out of a gun, which have the same strength, and pierce equally, whether they be discharged by a child, or a strong man.
>
> *Reconcileableness* 4.156

No amount of stylistic revision could protect his argument from such attack whether he was writing about natural philosophy or moral philosophy.[96] For Boyle, the stakes were very high. His early commitment to the frustrations of authorship reflected his affection for what he wrote about and for those whom he addressed. If he accomplished nothing else in the 1640s, he discovered that authorship was a vocation that perfectly suited his outlook and aptitudes.

§5: Editorial Policies

An editor of seventeenth-century manuscripts can produce quite different kinds of texts. A "diplomatic" edition has the primary advantage of fidelity to the manuscript; it is a typeset equivalent of a facsimile and thus preserves all textual features, even if some features (deletions, overwriting, insertions, inconsistent punctuation, and stray marks) may render interpretation more difficult. A modernized edition eliminates many of these features by imposing the stylistic conventions of the editor's age. Birch's "modern" version of the letters and manuscripts makes Boyle seem like a writer of the mid-eighteenth century; Birch silently modernized the printed works as well, establishing an edition that has far more textual authority than it warrants. M. A. Stewart's modern edition of some philosophical works is exceptionally candid about his emendations and the basis for them.[97] Because I have chosen to present an old-spelling edition of these early manuscripts, I should explain briefly my textual policies.

Though I admire the editorial practices of J. E. McGuire and Martin Tamny in presenting both a "diplomatic" and a fully modernized version of Newton's *Certain Philosophical Questions* (Cambridge 1983), their procedure would hardly work for Boyle. First, Newton's *Trinity Notebook* (Add. 3996) is a unique holograph. As a commonplace book, it reflects Newton's early thoughts about ethics, rhetoric, and logic as well as questions of natural philosophy. It is clear that Newton was not writing for publication. But there is only one copy of it, and the revisions, while numerous and interesting, are relatively easy to present. The editors' "expanded" edition presents in modern English Newton's sometimes cryptic entries. While McGuire and Tamny have successfully addressed the challenges of Newton's manuscript, Boyle poses other difficulties.

---

[96] Johnson misattributed the quotation to Bacon (*Life of Johnson* 1283).

[97] M. A. Stewart, ed. *Selected Philosophical Papers of Robert Boyle* (Manchester 1979) xxiv-xxxi. Stewart notes that "Boyle scholarship is at present dominated by the use of the verbally corrupt 1772 edition of the Collected Works, . . . which has acquired an authority it never deserved, partly because commentators have mistaken the eighteenth-century archaism of its typography, spelling and punctuation for the authentic convention of a century before, and partly because they have been over-ready to take nonsense for period quaintness" (viii). The forthcoming edition of Boyle's printed works, which will be edited by Michael Hunter and Edward B. Davis, should provide scholars with trustworthy texts.

First, the *Aretology* (MS 195) is about three times longer than an earlier draft, *Ethicall Elements* (MS 192), but many passages in MS 195 indicate "revision in progress" (for example, two or more versions of the same sentence with no indication of a final choice). Second, MS 195 sometimes follows the original very closely, sometimes adds to or deletes from it rather minor passages, and sometimes departs significantly from it. Several of the the major omissions contain quite interesting material. (As I mention above, for example, Boyle's ranking of his contemporaries' scientific achievements is included in MS 192 but omitted in the revision.) Without presuming to be Boyle's co-author, the modern editor is still faced with making choices among various versions of some passages. Third, both manuscripts are filled with the usual abbreviations, inconsistencies, and stylistic conventions characteristic of seventeenth-century manuscripts in general and of Boyle in particular. Maddison's diplomatic transcription of the "Philaretus" autobiography (2-45) relies on a complex sequence of editorial signals and illustrates some of Boyle's most persistent traits: frequent revisions, usually stylistic rather than substantive, in the form of overwritings, interlineations, and deletions; frequent insertions of words or phrases without indication of the words or phrases to be deleted; inadvertent repetition or omission of words or letters; and illegible words or doubtful readings. Birch had simplified the textual problems by silently editing the MS into conformity with eighteenth-century conventions.

In this old-spelling edition, I preserve as much as possible Boyle's spelling, punctuation, and capitalization. His inconsistencies are not, I believe, likely to obscure his meaning. In the textual notes, I identify by page and line number passages that I have emended. Where clarity requires minor changes, I identify the original form along with my emendation. In several places I have altered paragraphing for the sake of clarity. I have silently provided the correct spacing between words that have been run together, and I have expanded all abbreviations except for "&" and "&c". For example, Boyle usually abbreviated felicity as "felz" or even "fz"; he has similar abbreviations for frequently used words ("D S"="Dear Sister"). A few abbreviations were used only once and in contexts where their meaning was unclear. I have not preserved all of the overwriting, as when Boyle changed the case of a letter. He was sometimes very careless with parentheses, and I have provided the missing parenthesis where the grammar, syntax, or style requires it. Again, the textual notes indicate my emendations.

Through these editorial policies, I hope to provide a visually simple representation of complicated texts. I have used three special symbols: words in [straight brackets] indicate Boyle's deletions; words in <angle brackets> indicate his interlineations; and words set off by ↑an up-arrow and a down-arrow↓ indicate insertions either from the margin of the current page or from elsewhere in the manuscript. If the insertion comes from another page, I indicate the source in the textual notes.

Boyle often provided a marginal insertion but failed to indicate where on the page (or on another page) it should be placed. In most cases I have placed this insertion about where it is found on the page unless the grammar or syntax of the insertion clearly indicates a more plausible place. Boyle has marked six passages in these manuscripts with insertions within insertions; thus, the insertion ends not with one down-arrow but two.↓↓ Where Boyle made an insertion or interlineation but failed to eliminate the original (e.g., re<peat>act indicates that he originally wrote "react" but then wrote "peat" above "act"), I list both words in the textual notes but provide only the later choice in the text itself.

Finally, I have also preserved what I presume are Boyle's editorial marks. For instance, in "Of Time and Idleness" (BP 14.16), he wrote contemptuously about

> [h]unting, Hawking, shooting, and all other Recreations whatsoeuer, when their Immoderate °Length or ^{O} Frequency, makes them too Prodigall of Time. A Fault Epidemicall in those men, <(honorable Butchers! <caterers>)> that wast the greatest part of their owne Lifes in shortning that of a <harmlesse> Partridge or a Deere.

He added to this heavily revised passage a curious set of editorial marks: a small superscript "°" before "Length" and a larger superscript "o" before "Frequency." What do such marks mean? Frankly, I am not certain, but Boyle used such marks in six passages printed in this volume. Likewise, he included a brief marginal insertion in shorthand that I have been unable to translate (*Aret.* 183).

I have used footnotes sparingly, usually to indicate Boyle's sources or to identify parallels with other texts written in the 1640s or much later. Where he has drawn on proverbs, I have cited the source in Tilley's edition. Because of the influence of Aristotle's *Nichomachean Ethics* not just on Alsted but on Boyle's contemporaries, I have also indicated similarities and differences between Boyle's views and Aristotle's.

Finally, although all dates are Old Style, I follow the modern convention of beginning the new year on 1 January. Unless otherwise stated, the place of publication is London.

The Early Essays and Ethics of Robert Boyle

The
ARETOLOGY
or
Ethicall Elements
of
Robert Boyle.

Begun
At Stalbridge,
The   of
1 6 4 5.

That's the tru Good that makes the owner so.

|f. 52|

ARETOLOGY.
Liber Primus
which treteth of
FELICITY.

Chapter I.

That there is a Felicity

That Supreame Degree of Humane Happiness that we commonly call Felicity; is a thing, that all men, by seeking, confess to Be.[1] Which opinion, the following reasons, sufficiently confirm. 1. Whatsoeuer we do, is don for sum End. That End once obtained, ceases to be an End, and becoms but a Meanes to a Further End; and this yet to a |f. 52v| Farther: So that, Ne detur Progressus in Infinitum, lest we shud make an Endles Progresse or Graduation, and there be no Ending in these Ends;[2] we must necessarily at last com to and stop at, that Last End, which is nothing else but our Souuerin Good, or Felicity. 2. God and Nature had don something in vaine, by imprinting naturally in man the Desire of a Felicity he cud neuer com to enjoy. 3. Since there are diuers Goods desired only for the sake of others, as Riches for Conueniency, Fisic for Helth, and the like, it argues that there must be som Good desirable only for it self; and all other Goods but in order to that; and this very Good is what we term Felicity. 4. As there ar diuers particular Ends of man, considered in some certain State of life; as King, Physitian, Shoomaker, |f. 53| Or the like; so is there one Generall and vniuersall End of man, not as any of these, but as Man; and that End is Felicity. Where it is to be obserued, that to this End, all humane Axions tend; either [Truly] <directly,> as those of Vertu; or by Accident, as Eating, Drinking, and the like; or according to the Opinion of the Doer; as all Euil ones; which, tho Bad, he still apprehends as Good for him. 5. And certinly the Condition of man, wud render him of all other Cretures the most miserable, if he were only subiect to vn-happines, without being capable of Felicity.

---

[1] The title page is found on an unnumbered leaf at the front of MS 195. Ff. 12-46 present in a slightly different form the material found in the two chapters of book 1 and the first two chapters of book 2. Ff. 46-51 are blank.

[2] Alsted 1236 and Nich. Eth. I.ii.1.

Chapter II.

Of False Felicitys

I. Now altho[u] all men agree that there is a Souuerain Good, and consent, for the most in the establishing |f. 53v| It's principall Attributes, as that it is Supreame, Sufficient, Contenting, and the like; yet in the Application of these Propertys there is so great a Dissonance, that Varro the Filosofer in his time, recned vp no lesse then 288 dissenting Opinions of Felicity.[1] The Causes of which Diuersity may be, 1. The Blindness of our Iudgments in Discerning the true Attributes of Happines; and the Deprauednes of our Affections in applying them. 2. The [Desi] Ambition of contradicting others, with the Vanity of acquiring Fame, by the Erection of New Sects.[2] 3. An Enuius Persuasion that others are happier then vs: which once we argue, that since that Happiness consists not in any of those Goods that we enioy in common with them; we must needs place Felicity in that Good which |f. 54| they Possess, and we Want. Whereas not only that Perswasion is often False, and the Goods we enuy far from Felicity; but for the most part also, when we enuy one that is truly happy; we do it for diuers Goods in whose Possession he excels vs; as Riches, Honor, Vertu, Helth, and the like, and so are very apt to mistake in the Discerning which of those Goods is the true Felicity.

II. Notwithstanding this great diuersity of Opinions concerning Happiness; they may al be conueniently reduc't to 5 Principal, whereon all the rest haue their Dependance. For according to the Seueral humors of men, and the Diuers Courses of life, that they affect: som place it in the Erthly and obuius Goods; either of the Body, as Plesure, Helth, Buty, and the like; or of Fortune, namely, Riches; or of Opinion, |f. 54v| to wit, Honor: others in the more inward and solid Goods of the Mind; either Theoreticall, namely, Knoledg; or Practicall, to wit, Vertu.[3]

III. The Epicureans place man's Happines in the Plesures of the Body; which, tho, being the Opinion of a Beast rather then of a man, it wud not deserue the Confutation;[4] yet, since too too many in these Dregs of Time, tho their

---

[1] Alsted 1239. The major discussion of Varro's views is Augustine's *City of God* XIX.1. Varro's work has not survived.

[2] In a letter to Francis Tallents (February 1647), RB noted that the sects had returned with a vengeance from Amsterdam (1.xxxiv).

[3] A standard refutation of heathen philosophies—those of the Epicureans, Stoics, Peripatetics, and others—is Aquinas's *Summa Contra Gentiles* III.i.xxv-xl.

[4] Cf. Epicurus's letter to Menecæus in Laërtius's *Life of Epicurus* 10.28, where Epicurus placed felicity not in the senses but in good health. In his later career RB expressed horror at 'Epicurean'

Words detest it, owne it in their Axions; Remember that, 1. It is a happines not only common with vs as to the beasts butt euen where they may goo beyonde man: being both more capable of them and free from that shame and |f. 55| remorse of conscience which like thornes doo euer accompany the roses of vnlawfull pleasure,[5] 2. they are common to good men, and ill; and ar neither causes, signes, nor effects of goodnes. 3. they are neither certine, nor durable, but dye either before the possessor or with him; being like medlars noo sooner ripe then rotten.[6] 4. Those that are [past past] past haue not satisfied; neither will those that are to come being the same satisfie; besides that pleasures are like wine, and as this by drinking, soo they by enioying dimminish. 5. The pleasures of the body can not satisfy the nobler parte of man the soule. 6. And lastly, that for the greatest <pleasures> of the body man seeks darke and secret places. Now as one sayes very well, Apage |f. 55v| felicitatem quæ latebras Quærit. Foh vpon solitude that is faine to seeke corners.[7]

↑Neither is it a Sufficient Argument for this sensuall Opinion, to say, that, That is the Souuerain Good, that all Animals together Desire: now all Animals both Reasonable and Vnresonable desire and deliht in the Plesures of the Body: which therefore [are Feli] in their Enjoyment giue Felicity. For, |f. 61| 1. the Very being desired by all Animals argues it not to be Felicity; since that is a Good proper to Man, and incommunicable to Beasts. 2. Tis tru, that there is something in Man that is Naturally desirous of Sensual Deliht, namely, the Sensitiue Appetite; but that being but the Ignobler part of the Soule, and comming short of Reason; it were absurd to place the souuerain Good in an Inferior Faculty. 3. Besides that the Diuines deny this Procliuity to Sensuality, to be Naturall and inb[red]born to man in his first Creation; wherein the Sensitiue Appetit was wholly subiect to the Command of Reson, as that was conformable to the Image <Will> of God; but meerly by the Fall of our first Parents, which vitiated our Nature, and oftentimes subiects the Braine to the Belly.

IV. This oppinnion is commonly fathered vpon Epicurus followed by Eudorus before Christ, and Cerinthus, and Mahomett [illeg.] after Christ but Epicurus himselfe is excused by Seneca and others, and Laertius in his life mentions a certin Epistle of his to one Menecœus,[8] wherein expounding himselfe,

---

atomism and chance (*Final Causes* 5.428) and associated the Epicureans with such enemies of religion as Hobbes (*Reconcileableness* 4.166). For an excellent analysis of Pierre Gassendi's role in disseminating 'Epicureanism,' see Lynn S. Joy, *Gassendi the Anatomist: Advocate of History in an Age of Science* (Cambridge 1987).

[5] Cf. Tilley R182, "No Rose without a thorn." The proverb is also used in bk. 2, ch. 4.

[6] Cf. R133, "Soon ripe, soon rotten" or M863, "Medlars are never ripe till they be rotten."

[7] A variant of "truth seeks no corners" (T587) or the Latin tag, "veritas non querit angulos." Cf. Frances Quarles's "On Corner-sinnes" in *Divine Fancies* (1632). RB used the same proverb in "Of Sin."

[8] Cf. Laërtius, 10.28. Jacob has misunderstood the reference to Epicurus (Jacob 56).

hee seems to place felicetie not in the pleasure of the maw, and senses, but in that of a helthfull body, and to <the> calmnes of a mind vntrubled with Passions, which oppinnion tho it bee not altogether true, that pleasure being but a consequent of happiness and not happiness it selfe, yet dos far more sauor of a Philosopher |f. 56| then the other.↓

V. To this Opinion ar theirs to be reduced that place Happiness in the other Goods of the Body; namely, Strength, Buty, and Helth. But tru Felicity consists not in the First. For 1. It is out of our Power to acquire. 2. Loosable by Age, Sicness, Deth and the like. 3. It perfectionates the noble part of man, the mind: but is a Good confin'd to the Body. 4. It is common both to Good and Bad, and wherein euen diuers Bests excell the King[s] of Animals, man: which sure, were Strength, Felicity, they shud neuer do. &c. Neither in the Second, For, 1. It is out of our Power. 2. Peculiar to the Body. 3. Transitory and short-liu'd. 4. Oftentimes hurtfull to the Owners, (as to Thamar, Lucretia, Cleopatra, and others, who had been [less] more |f. 56v| Happy, had they bin less Faire) by occassionning Pride, Luxury, Rapes, and other Inconueniences.[9] 5. To all which ad; that is esteemed handsom, in one cuntry, is oftentimes thought vgly in another: as in Ethiopya they esteem a cole-blac face with broad flapping lips, marks of comliness; whereas they paint the Deuill, white: and in a great part of the Est-Indys, to haue red teeth, blood-hound eares, and brests hanging downe as low as the waist, are Characters of Buty.[10] Nor in the third, For, 1. Out of our Power. 2. Easily loosable, and subiect to a thousand mischances. 3. Often times a fomentor of Vice and Mischeefe. 4. And not onely common with vs to Brutes, but wherein for the most part they exceede vs. &c.

VI. The miser makes his happines consist in riches, and such other goods of fortune but 1. they doo not fill, |f. 57| or satiate the appetite, butt like hott waters rather encrease a mans thirst, then Quench itt. 2. Theire possession is incertin but theire losse (at last) most certine. 3. They are common to good and bad: and not onely cannot better their owners; but very often if they find them not bad make them soo. 4. They concerne not the Soule at all: but may consist, with the greatest misery of the body, sikness, and of the mind vice. 5. They are not desired for themselues; but for something els: and are only good when they are parted from. 6. They proceed for the most parte from others pouerty; and soo some cannot bee happie, but by others misery. To wit, wee may add the testimony of most rich men themselues; who in this poynte as most experienced are most to bee beleeued.[11] |f. 57v|

VII. The Politician and the Souldier places his felicitie in honor and

[9] For the rape of Thamar (or Tamar), see 2 Sam. 13.

[10] For similar remarks on Ethiopians' notions of beauty and the whiteness of their devils, cf. Browne's *Pseud. Epidemica* 1.520-21; the first edition appeared in 1646.

[11] This attitude toward wealth is modified later in the *Aret.* (e.g., bk. 2, ch. 4).

renowne. But first honor is often gotten by ill men and that to for euill axions. 2. It depends vpon other mens Iudgments, being a good without either lock or key: and soe 3. may bee gott without the meritt, and lost without our fault; soe that many bad men haue it, when many good men goe without it. 4. It betters neither the body, the mind, nor the fortune. 5. If it bee bad it is not to be esteemed: and if good, it is butt the Shadow of virtue, which <is> by consequent the worthyer of the two. 6. Lastly it can doe a man noe good att all after Deth, for in heauen it is needlesse: and in hell bootles.

VIII. Allied to this, is the Opinion |f. 58| Of Diuers Princes and Great-men of these very times; whose Practice makes their Felicity consist in Power, Command, Nobility, and Outward Greatness:[12] Which is a Happiness, 1. Without vs. 2. That betters not: but rather oftentimes Corrupts ↑By facilitating our way to Sin, and remouing the apprehension of Punishment.↓ 3. Common to Good and Euill. 4. That is Incertin of a Continuance, but Certin of an End. 5. Wherein all cannot be Happy, and the Felicity of Som shud be grounded vpon the Misery of others. 6. That to be kept carefully is very Trublesom, and otherwise, Dangerous. Besides that Princes ar commonly the last to kno the Truth, being faine to heare with other people's Eares, and see with their Eys: their Axions are more ey'd and censur'd: their Faults more notorius: their very marryages and Frendships (the sweetest and freest of outward goods) made, rather for Interest then Affection; In Sum; if a Prince be Good, he is his People's Slaue; if Bad, they are his Feare. His condition being like the hihest trees in Forests, |f. 58v| Most subiect to Agitation.[13]

IX. The Speculators and diuers Filosofers place happiness in Contemplatiue Knowledge, and in the Vnderstanding of a certin Encyclopedia that comprehends all Arts and Sciences.[14] But 1. Knowledg is common both to Good and Euill. 2. When Knowledg is arriued at the hihest Degree of Perfection, then a Singular Property of it is to kno it self to be Imperfect. 3. Knowledg is commonly but a Spy of Misery; it shos vs that we ar in the Way of Infelicity; but cannot sho vs how to get out on't: and, like Lihtning in a Tempest, serues but to discouer what Pickle we are in. 4. Our Knoledg is like our Siht, but of a very short reach; and leaues far more beyond it then on this side of it: and this they that kno most, kno best: for we kno so Little, and that Little so Imperfectly; that we may very well confess with that Filosofer, that Maxima pars eorum quæ sci-

---

[12] It is not clear to what extent RB's points were direct political commentary.

[13] At his execution in 1641, Wentworth said, "Put not your trust in princes." RB was painfully aware of the political maneuvering that affected England, Ireland, and Scotland; members of his family had played and were playing major roles.

[14] The reference is probably to Alsted's *Encyclopædia* (1630). RB referred to Alsted by name in the *Aret.* (bk. 2, ch. 4).

mus, est minima pars eorum quæ nescim.[15] |f. 59| The Greatest part of what we kno, is but the lest Part of what we Ignore. 5. Knoledge often brings but Trouble and Vexation to it's Owners; leauing them far more douts then it resolues; according to that of the Wise-man (Eccles. 1, 18.) For in much wisdom is much greef: and he that increseth Knoledg, increseth Sorro. It cannot but Greeue a Knowing man to see the Irregularitys that lawless Power acts agenst Iustice and Reson: and to see Wisdom despized without being able, either to help it self, or remedy these Disorders. 6. [Kno] Lastly, Knoledg has, Generatio Longa, Fruitio Breuis; tho A long Generation, yet but A short Fruition: it is so long in the Purchasing, that it seldome coms to the Enjoying. For we lern with labor, and by Peece-meal; and since, (as Hippocrates has it) Vita breuis, Ars longa,[16] one half of a man's life is spent to instruct the other. Nay, for the most part, our Knoledg is like the Staires of a Scaffold, at whose |f. 59v| Top, we find our Death. Yet so far indeed Knoledge may go, that tho it be not Happiness it self, yet it may serue vs to discouer it, and sho vs the way to attain it. But how far Contemplation conduces to Felicity, the ensuing Chapter will instruct vs.

X. Somthing of kin to this Opinion seems to be that of Plato, who plac't Happiness in the Contemplation of Ideas.[17] But there is such an ambiguity in that Word, that what he ment by it, is more difficult to kno then Materiall. Most esteem, that by Idea he meant a certin common Form or Abstract Essence, subsisting out of God; from which all other singular things receaue their Being, and vpon whose Moddel they are created. In this sence Aristotle denys, not only that there is any such Idea; but that |f. 60| granting ther wer, our Felicity shud consist in their Contemplation.[18] For our Happines dos not [illeg.] consist in naked Speculations, [but] but in the Exercice of those Axions that are <naturally> within the reach of our owne Pow'r. But the Platonicians themselues expound their master otherwise; and diuers Moderns affirm, that it is cleer both out of his own Ritings, and his life in Laërtius that he plac'd happines in the Vision or Fruition of God;[19] to which thos Vertus that can heere be acquired, he esteem'd Meanes enlihtning our Vnderstanding and Purging our Will, that so we may the better and more easily contemplate God and be vnited to him. And this Vision and Fruition of God, he cals <an> Idea; which [our mind] we shud always contemplate that we may be always Happy. And in this Sence, Plato's Opinion, and

---

[15] Cf. N276, "I know nothing except that I know nothing" or what Laërtius attributed to Socrates (2.5.16). A similar quotation was used in the *Scep. Chym.* 1.464.

[16] Hippocrates, *Aphorisms* 1.1, is often cited as the source of this common tag.

[17] Cf. Alsted 1239, where he reviewed the standard authorities, including Plato and Aquinas.

[18] Nich. Eth. I.vi.1-16.

[19] Cf. Laërtius, III.76; among the works of the Cambridge Platonists, we should note Ralph Cudworth's sermon preached before the House of Commons (31 March 1647) and Benjamin Whichcote's sermons, which date from the mid-1630s. RB owned Ficino's translation of Plato (Lyons 1548).

the Christian Truth, shake hands together.[20] |f. 60v|

XI. Thus what most men want or Fancy most, that they make their Felicity; and so esteeme it, til, hauing obtain'd it, they find the Vanity of their Desires in the Emptines of their Enjoyments. For all these Imaginary Felicitys, ar either, not truly Good; or not in our own Power, or not so always. This made all those, that seem'd born to be the ornaments of Mankind, to seek their Happines in a Hiher Region; being taut by Experience, that Those only ar (Felicitating) Goods that make their owners so.[21]

[20] The harmony of Platonic philosophy and Christian theology was a central tenet of the Cambridge Platonists.

[21] Cf. the epigraph for this volume: "That's the tru Good that makes the owner so."

|f. 64|

ARETOLOGY
The Second Booke
which Treateh Of Vertu.
The First Part.
Euidencing The Nature of Vertu in generall.

Chapter I.

Of the End and Matter of Moral Vertu

I. Hauing thus discouered the Cuntry wherein the Pallace of Felicity is seated; let vs now consider the Way that leads men to it, namely Vertu: for to the Pallace of Felicity the only hih-way is Vertu.

Now as there is a [double] <two-fold> Faculty in the Reasonable Soule that being subiect to Vices and Imperfections, stands in Need |f. 64v| of a Bettering; so is there a twofold Vertu appointed for the Perfectionating of that two-fold Faculty; namely, Intellectual, that Illuminates the Vnderstanding; and Morall, that Regulates the Will.[1] But Because Contemplatiue Vertus can challeng but an Indirect and Relatiue tractation in [their Discourse] Doctrine of Morality; therefore disposing of them in the Reare [in] of this Discourse, we will presently fall vpon the handling of Morall Vertu.

II. And because we then beleeue our selues to haue a cleere notion of any thing, when we kno it by it's causes; that Doctrine dos <heer> iustly claim a Precedency; that treats of the 4 Causes of Vertu; namely Finall, <namely, Felicity> Materiall, Efficient, and Formall:[2] whereof the First hauing been sufficiently vnfolded in the foregoing Booke; resignes it's interest heere; and giues vs leaue to proceed to a Distinct consideration of the other three. |f. 65|

Now because Vertu, being a Habitude, cannot haue riht to a Matter properly so called, (that being peculiar to Bodily Substances,) therefore the Filosofers <haue> attributed <vn>to it, somthing that holds the Place of Matter, and Analogically resembles it; namely the Subiect of Moral Vertu, to wit, the Soule;

---

[1] For an excellent survey of the background to this moral psychology, see Robert Hoopes, *Right Reason in the English Renaissance* (Cambridge, Mass. 1962) and Norman Fiering, *Moral Philosophy at Seventeenth-Century Harvard* (Chapel Hill 1981).

[2] RB's approach was characteristic of Scholastic training in logic and rhetoric that would have been found at Eton and perhaps under the tutelage of Isaac Marcombes as well. For useful background, see Wilbur Samuel Howell, *Logic and Rhetoric in England, 1500-1700* (Princeton 1956).

and it's Object, namely, the Passions of the Mind.[3] As for the First; since to treat of the Soule, is the Proper of the Naturalist, not the Moralist; we refer the Reader that desires a full Knoledg of that Subiect, to the Books of Naturall Filosofers, (and the Morall Introductory præfixed to this Treatise)[4] contenting our selues for the Present [to tuch at 2 Necessary questions that concern the Matter] with [The First shall be whether the Vnderstanding commands the Will, or the Will the Vnderstanding. To which I answer, that, When things are as they shud be, the Will dos neuer any thing but according to the |f. 65v| Counsel and Directions of the Vnderstanding: but taking things as generally they ar; it is answer'd, that both Command, and both Obey in a diuers respect; yet so that the Vnderstanding seems to haue som Preeminence aboue the Will] a Necessary Question; namely whether the Subiect of Moral Vertu be the Resonable or the Sensitiue Appetite; that is, whether Iustice, Courage, Liberality, and the like; be seated in the Will, or in the Affections.[5] To which they answer, that it is Primarily and Radically (as they term it) seated in the Will: for 1. Since the Passions of the Mind in their own Nature are neither Goo nor Euill; but acquire all their Goodness from that Moderation which they receaue from the Conduct of the Will; it iustly argues, that the Will it self must first be season'd with those Vertus, whose |f. 66| Influences so worke vpon the Affections. 2. Since Iustice and Vertu, whereby we imitate the Axions of God, is a Trace or Relique of his Image; it seems far more conuenient to lodg that lineament of the Image of God in that Faculty of man wherein that Imag[in]e dos consist, then in that which we haue common with the Beasts. 3. Besides that if Vertu did primarily reside in the Sensitiue Appetite; then, when [our] the Soules are diuorced from the Body, Iustice and Vertu shud be altogether diuorced from the Soule; since the Habitudes and Functions of the Sensitiue Faculty suruiue not the Body. Yet for all this we cannot deny, but by the Influence of the Vertus of the Will, the [A] Sensitiue Appetite may not acquire good Inclinations and laudable Habitudes: and so may be called Vertuus by Participation: as in the Art of Riding the Great Horse, the Habitude of Horsmanship |f. 66v| is indeed principally in the Rider; but yet may be in som sort said to be in the Hors, in Respect of his being Drest (as [we call] <they term> it) and his Obedience <rediness> in answering the Motions of the Rider.[6]

IV. Now to come to the Doctrine of the Passions of the Mind, we must kno

---

[3] For analysis of the passions in Renaissance ethics, see Anthony Levi, S. J., *French Moralists: The Theory of the Passions, 1585-1649* (Oxford 1964) and Fiering (ch. 4). For a more literary treatment, see Lily Bess Campbell, *Shakespeare's Tragic Heroes, Slaves of Passion* (1930).

[4] For a useful survey, see H. M. Gardiner et al., *Feeling and Emotion: A History of Theories* (New York 1937), ch. 5.

[5] For discussion of contemporary views of the will and the intellect, see Fiering, ch. 3.

[6] For RB's readiness to ride the great horse in Geneva, see Maddison 31.

that their Consideration, as they ar Facultys or Qualitys of the Soule, together with their Fisicall Causes, and Effects vpon the Body; properly belongs to the Naturall Filosofer: so that the Moralist only handles them, as they ar the Object of Moral Vertu; and ar by it's Gouernans redusible to conformity with reason.[7] And that these Affections are the Obiect of Morall Vertu, is euident, in that the principall office of Vertu is to regulate the Passions of the Mind, and make them conformable to the laws of Moderation. |f. 67|

These Passions are properly called by a General Name, Affections; becaus they variusly affect the Mind with Loue, Anger, Feare, and the like. Their Seat is the Sensitiue Appetite; as appeares, by their being Familiar to Beasts. And that they ar to be found in Bests; may be proued (against the Stoicks) because 1. Dayly Experience, which witnesses that they Fear, Hate, Loue, and the like. 2. They ar endowed with the Sensitiue Soule and it's requisites; in which Number, ar the Affections. 3. Because they ar Necessary to the Preseruation of their Nature, which wud be extremely dull and Sluggish in it's owne Conseruation, had they not Passions to excite them. But yet there may be som difference obserued betwixt the Passions of Beasts, and those of Men: for Beast's Affections ar not reducible to the Meane of Vertu: but then on the |f. 67v| Other Side; Beasts haue both fewer Passions and Plesures; (as wanting, for the most Part, the Delights of the Ey, the Eare, and the Smell; and being not subiect to Zeale, Shame, and som other Affections)[8] and ar generally more moderate in them; being content to Satisfy Nature, that is content with a little: whereas Man has Glory, Auarice, Conscience, and the like to affect him, and his concupiscences hauing once ouerflown the Bankes of Reason; ar like a Fire blowne vp by the Feuel of their Enjoyments into a greater Flame. Besides these, there are certin Analogicall Passions also in the Reasonable Soule; ↑for al those Passions whose Object is a Spiritual and Eternal Good or Euill, tho they also affect the Sensitiue Appetite, haue their cheef seat in the Will of the Reasonable Soule;↓ as we may see in the Nature of the Angels, who wanting the Sensitiue <Appetite> ar yet touched with somthing like Loue, [H] Zeale, Feare, Anger, and the like, as the Scriptures teach vs.[9]

↑Where it is to be obserued, that man's being subiect to more Affections then Beasts, is not because in him there ar (as some suppose) Affections of a twofold kind; the one in the Will, and the other in the Sensitiue Appetite: but

[7] This topic is extensively discussed in William Fenner's *A Treatise of the Affections* (1642), a book that RB owned, but similar material was also found in Edward Reynolds, *A Treatise of the Passions and Faculties of the Soule of Man* (1640) and many other seventeenth-century works. Reynolds, Bishop of Norwich, copiously illustrated his material with quotations from classical authors.

[8] Gardiner reviewed briefly the wide range of Renaissance discussions of this topic (119ff).

[9] RB's view was a commonplace (cf. Fiering 273-74), but it helps to explain his fascination with the nature and operation of angels, a topic he frequently discussed (cf. 1.274, 4.9, 4.19, 4.73, 4.159, 4.407, 5.142-43, 5.146, 5.148, 5.295, 5.422, 5.510, 6.684-86, and 6.773).

because som ar stirred vp meerly by the Iudgment of the Sensit<iue>; and <Fa> others by Reason through the Mediation of the Senses (mediante sensu). For Reason in her self conceiues many Plesures and Paines, to whose Desire or auersation it excites the Sensitiue Appetite by the Ministry of the Fancy. Now these last kind of Affections ar peculiar to Man: the others, that arise from the Senses alone, are to be found also in Beasts.↓ |f. 68|

It is frequently enquired why Youth is more subiect to the Transports of their Passions, then men of riper Age.[10] To which it may be answered, that it is, 1. Because the Humors of their Bodys (Blood and Choler) ar then most feruent and at their [g] heiht: and the Humors haue a great Influence vpon the Sensiue[11] Appetite in the Exciting of Passions. 2. Because the first Yeeres of a man's life, ignoring the Vse and Dictates of Reson; is wholly gouerned by the Fancy and Sensitiue Appetites: so that, when the Young man coms to attain an Aage, that is Ripe for the Vse of Reason; the Imagination accustomed to command, and to stirr vp the Sensitiue Appetit; wud stil continue his vsurped Power; and reiects the Counsells of Reason, as of an vp-start Souuerin. 3. Besides that Youth has not yet attain'd Experience enuf to kno, the Inconueniences that wait vpon a Senseless Obedience to Sensuall Appetites. |f. 68v|

Now the same Sensitiue Appetite, as it has Reference to an Object Good or Euil considered in themselues, and without the Circumstances of Danger or Difficulty is termed by the Filosofers Appetis Concupiscibilis, the Coueting or Desiring Appetite: but when the same Sensitiue Appetite has Relation to a Good or Euill that has som Circumstance of Danger or Difficulty annexed to it; then it acquires the Name of Appetitus Irascibilis, the Impugning or Inuading Appetite: tho som think this Appetit vnfitly termed by the Filosofers, Irascibilis;[12] because oftentimes the Passions of this Appetite ar Excited, (as hope, Fear, and Boldnes) without the Spur of Choler: specially when the Difficulty arises, not from blocks laid in the way by men; but from the Nature of the Thing. And thus the Sensitiue Appetite, is, by the Circumstances of it's Obiects, distributed into two others; which we will |f. 69| heereafter call the Coueting and the Inuading Appetite.

This Sensitiue Appetite is the Proper Seat of the Affections, which by som [thus] defined to be Motions of the Sensitiue Appetite, arising from the Imagination of some Good or Euill, to auoid what is thout Euill [and] or Inconuenient; and obtaine what is iudged Good and Pleasant. These Affections the Stoicks tauht to consist in Opinion; but falsly; for 1. They differ in Definition. 2. The Seat of Opinion is in the Braine; of the Affections in the Hart. 3. An Opinion [can n] may be conceiued in the Mind without any motion of the hart; but not an Affection: for Ioy proceeds from an exciting and kindly dilation of the Spirits in

[10] Nich. Eth. VII.xiv.6.

[11] "Sensive" is synonymous with "sensitive" (*OED*).

[12] For discussion of this topic, see Fiering 82-83 and Gardiner 119-48.

the Hart; greefe contracts the Hart, and Feare the Sinews; which ar Reall Motions and no Opinions. Yet for all this it cannot be deny'd; but that the Affections [often] ar moued, often Cheefly, somtimes Only, by Opinion. |f. 69v| For vpon the Iudgment, whither Tru or False, of the Obiect in the Esteematiue Faculty, depends the Commotion of the Affections. Whence we may easyly discern the Cause of their so frequent Blindness and Irregularity.

The Number and Distribution of the Affections is much controuerted [by] amongst Moral Authors; a greate part of whos Treatises vpon this Subiect [ar] consist in the Confuting of one another.[13] But we will for the present be content to make vse of the most receiued [Diui] Opinion; which (tho perhaps none of the Exactest) is not inconuenient for our present purpose: and thus marshals our Affections. The Passions of the Mind receaue their Diuision from the seuerall References they haue vnto their Obiects: which is principally the Good, and Secondarily the Euil of things. And [first] (to begin with the [Impugning] <Coueting> Appetite) if the Obiect be considered barely in it's own Nature, as Good or Euill, that is, Conuenient or Disconuenient |f. 70| to the Faculty; without including any circumstance of distance from, or Vnion to, the Subiect; in this case it produces, if the Obiect be Good, Loue; if Bad, Hatred: which are the 2 Radical and Fundamentall Passions of all the rest. Secondly, if the Object be considered as absent (or distant) from the Subject (in regard of reall Vnion) then the Passions are; in respect of Good, Desire: in respect of Euil, Fliht [and] or Abhomination. And, Thirdly; if the Obiect be considered as present, (by a reall Contract, or Vnion with the Faculty) then it worketh, if it be Good, Deliht; if Euill, Greef or Sorro. Againe (to com now to the Inuading Appetite) as the Object beareth of with it the Circumstances of Difficulty and Danger; it may be considered; either as exceeding the Naturall Strength of the Power; which implyes; in respect of Good an Impossibility to be attained, and so works, Despaire; and in respect of Euill an |f. 70v| Improbability of being auoided, and so works, Feare: or Secondly, it is considered as not exceeding the Strength of the Power, (at least with those Aids it calleth in;) in which regard, Good being presented as Attainable, produces Hope; and Euil presented either as Auoidable if it be future, [and] so worketh Boldness to breake thorou it; or as requitable, if it be past produces Anger to reuenge it. And thus we haue 6 Passions in the Coueting Appetite, and 5 in the Inuading: which some, not inconueniently, thus diuide. In the Coueting Appetite, say they, the Object is either Good, which considered abstractiuely in it's owne Nature, works Loue; if Absent, Desire; and if present, Deliht: or Euil; which considered <nakedly> in it self, produces Hatred; if absent; Fliht; and if present, Sorrow. And as for the Inuading Appetit; is either Good; which if one thinkes he can obtaine, produces Hope; if not, Despaire: or Euill, which if it be

[13] Levi, Fiering, and Gardiner provide an exhaustive list of such discussions.

absent and one apprehends and flys it, breeds Feare; if one is confident to |f. 71| Ouercome it, Boldness: and if Euill be present, Anger. That is, the Impugning appetite, towards <a> future Good, is stirred vp to Hope or Despaire; towards Future Euils, to Fear or Boldness; and towards the Present Euil, it is moued to Anger; but towards the Present it is <not> touched by any Passion; as finding there no Difficulty nor Resistance.

Now all these Passions are not vnfitly explaned in the familiar Example of the Woulfe and the Sheepe.[14] Ffirst, the Woulfe conceiuing the flesh of the Sheepe, as Good, Loueth it: then, being Absent, desires to eate it: and hauing gotten it, Delighteth in it. The Sheepe (on the contrarie) conceiuing the Woulfe vnder the Notion of euill, Hates him: seeing him comming fflyes him: and feeling herselfe seized by him, Griues to become his prey. But now (to come to the Inuading Appetite) suppose the Woulfe see the Sheepe |f. 71v| guarded with the Sheapeard and his Doggs: yet thinking the Enterprise, tho Difficult yet ffeasable, hee erects himselfe with hope: whereupon neglecting and despising the guardians of the flocke with a great deale of Boldnes and Courage hee falls vpon it. But being in the first onsett pinched by a Mastiue; inflam'd with Angre, hee seeks to reuenge himselfe vpon the Dogge: but Hee is soe well seconded by his companions, that # the Woulfe, findinge more resistance then hee expected, begins to ffeare the euent of the busines. Whereupon hee is soe furiously assalted and pressed by the Sheapeard, that after a little Hope had made him maintaine the fray a while longer; thinking the victorie impossible; seased with Dispaire, hee betakes himselfe to his heeles and runns away.

But before we com to the Particulari<zi>ng of Passions; it |f. 72| wil not be amiss to compose a Noble Difference betwixt the Peripateticks and the Stoickes; whereof the first, esteeming the Affections of the Mind neither morally Good nor Euill in their owne Nature [but] and therefor wer to be moderated by the Prescripts of Reason: whereas the Latter esteeming them intrinsecally euill, and as the Working of the Sea, that serue but to cast vp mire, and toss the Ship of Reason; wud haue them vtterly rooted out: and reduce the Wise-man to such a Sencelesness (by them called Apathy or Affectlesnes) as shud make him vncapable of Ioy, vnmou'd with Feare, not touch't with Pitty; and finally so much a man, as not to be an Animall. Diuers there are that not improbably esteem, that there is heere but a strife about the [Name] <Word>, whilst they agree in the Thing: for the Aristotelicians |f. 72v| do not allow the Cherishing of Passions so far as to enable them to discompose the Mind; and either inuite or Force men out of the [Ways] <Paths> of Vertu: neither do the Stoicks deny but that the Wise

[14] Cf. T. W. [Thomas Wright], *The Passions of the Minde* (1601), which was aimed at physicians of the soul (sig. B3v) and discussed concupiscible (coveting) and irascible (invading) appetites in language remarkably similar to RB's (35-44). Wright attributed his discussion to Aquinas, *Summa Theologica*, I.2.q26.a.I, as he noted on p. 217, but I have not found the material in that location.

Book Two, Chapter One

man may be subjected to the First commotions and Sudden Transports of Passion; but only they wud haue his mind settled in that Immoueable Constancy, that no impulsions of the Sensitiue Appetite shud be able to make wander from the Dictates of Reason. So that the Difference heer seems to be but Nominally, the Peripateticks [vnder] meaning Passions, and the Stoicks, Perturbations.

But howsoeuer since this Opinion of the Stoicks is vsually taken in the most rigid Sence, and in that Sence too has a multitude of Patrons: it will be worth while to disproue it, with these following reasons.[15] Namely because 1. ther ar som Passions, as Pitty towards the Afflicted, Naturall Affection to Father and Mother and the like; that euery where pass current for Good with the Stamp of Generall Approbation. |f. 73| 2. Affections [were] ar Naturall to man; and so born with him, that he can as soone deuest himself of the being an Animal, as exempt himself from the Commotion of his Appetites. Whose <not> being intrinsically euill appeares also; in that Adam was subiect to his Passions before his Fall. 3. Christ himself greeued for the Deth of Lazarus, [Ioh] Iohn 11. had Compassion on the fasting Multitudes, Matt, 15. loued St Iohn: and the like. 4. Eu'n God dos entitle himself to Loue, Anger, Mercy, and diuers other Passions, in the holy Scripture: which, tho spoken after the manner of men, (as the Diuines say very well, that Affectus tribuuntur Deo propter similitudinem Effectus: we father Affects vpon God, by reason of the likeness their Effects haue to ours)[16] wud certinly neuer be attributed to that Supreame Goodness, were they Essentially Euill. 5. Many affections ar eu'n commanded by God, [M] both in Mat, 5. and in diuers other Places of the Scripture. 6. Lastly, |f. 73v| Passions ↑(so they mistake not their tru Objects, and exceed not their du Mesure.)↓ ar not only necessary to the conseruation of our Nature; but also, if wel made vse of, Excellent Instruments for the Bettering of Moral Vertu; whose motions wud be extreamely dull and languishing, were they not, [quickned and] as it were, enliuen'd by these Sprihtly Passions, stirring vp the Spirits and quickning the Fancy. Thus we see Anger and Shame, the Whetstones of Courage; Loue and Compassion the Exciters of Bounty; Feare the Sharpner of Industry, and caution against [In] Rashnesse and Indiscretion: as also Hope the Anchor of Patience that keepes her from that Shipwrac in the midst of the Tempestuus frownes of aduerse Fortune.[17] Wherefor since Passions ar of so Excellent an Vse, when well employ'd; let vs rather labor their reducing when they rebell, and their Moderation then

---

[15] Cf. Todd, *Christian Humanism and the Puritan Social Order* (Cambridge 1987), ch. 2.

[16] RB owned Thomas Jackson, *A Treatise of the Divine Essence and Attributes* (1628) and John Preston, *Life Eternall or, a Treatise of the Divine Essence and Attributes* (1631), but discussion of divine attributes was a common feature of many theological works.

[17] Cf. Alsted 1243, "Ira vocatur cos fortitudinis & animi nervus, cujus intentione & laxatione impetus gubernatur." RB also referred to anger as the whetstone of courage in *Occ. Refl.* 2.407. All of these symbols are traditional. This passage also follows very closely Reynolds, *Treatise* 59.

their Extirpation: (as when a Picke is warpt, we Striue to Straiten it not to break it.) Yet with this Caution that we neuer let the Passions rise hih enuf to ouercast the Serenity of the Mind with sudden Clouds: |f. 74| for Passions to the Ship of Vertu ar like the Wind: if it blowes not at all, the Ship lys Wind-bound and rids no way: if it swel the Sailes with a Gentle Gale, the Ship is carried on finely: but if it once [g] blo boisterous, and gro Tempestuus; it drownes it. Truly, he spoke not amisse, that cal'd this Blockish Stupidity of the Stoicks; an Opinion, which, while it goes about to giue vnto man an absolute Gouernment ouer him self, leaueth scarce any thing in him, which he may command and gouern. (Not vnlike those Tyrants, who to [command] acquire an absolute comand ouer their Subjects, destroy those Subjects that they are to command.)[18] I wud therefor haue the Good man somtimes tuch't <mou'd> with <moderate> Passions, not transported with lawless Perturbations: and enioy a Tranquillity of Mind proceeding, not from a Stoicall Benummedness, but a Vertuus Calmness: the true Temper of the Wise-man consisting; not in the being Without Passions, but in the being Aboue them. |f. 74v|

To com now to the [Particular] handling of these Affections in Particular; we wil onely hint their Natures by their Deffinitions; and so proceed.

First therefore, Loue is a Passion whereby the Mind desires to be vnited to the thing loued, and made (as it were) one with it. Whither the Good of it's Obiect be either Laudable (or honestum), Profitable, [and] or Delihtful.

Commonly they make a twofold Loue: for when the Passion is bounded with the Object and looks not to a further End, it is called Amor amicitiæ, a loue of Affection; but when the Inclination affects the Obiect but in reference to a farther End; then they term it Amor Concupiscentiæ, a loue of Interest. After the first manner we loue our Selues, <namely> for our Selues; after the Second we loue meat and Drink; to wit, in order to our own Conseruation. Loue is also distributed into Gratuitus, such as ↑that of↓ Fathers to their Children; and mercenary, such as that of |f. 75| Seruants to their Masters: this loues for a reward; and that [fi] seeks it's reward in louing. But in Generall, there is a threefold Loue: of Actions, as when we affect the Actions of Vertu; of things, as when we Loue our Mony, our horses or our Bookes; and of Persons; as when we loue our Mistrisses; which last kind of Loue, if it be Mutuall, is stiled, Frendship.[19]

Hate or Hatred is an Affection of the Coueting Appetite flowing from an Auersion of that Appetit against an Obiect iudg'd Euill or Inconuenient. (Now both in Loue and Hatred; <and the rest of these Passions,> no matter whether the Object be really Good or Euill, or whether only it seem so; for both moue alike.)

---

[18] See Reynolds, *Treatise* 47; for criticism of the Stoics, see Fiering 75.

[19] One of the most important differences between this work and the Nich. Eth. is that Arist. included a very long discussion of friendship (bk. 8-9). This is one of RB's few references to friendship.

Desire is an Affection of the Coueting appetite, inciting it to the acquisition of that Good which it wants, and is iudged conuenient. (This Passion differs from Loue; in that it is 1. commonly more feruent and vehement. 2. It presupposes |f. 75v| Loue; for we neuer [Loue] Desire but what we loue; tho we often loue what we do not Desire, as those things we enioy alredy. For, 3. Desire stil presupposes the Absence of the thing desired: and so becoms but an Vnenjoy'd loue, as loue but an Enjoy'd Desire.)

Fliht or Abhomination is an auersion of the Coueting appetite, whereby it is incited to shun an Absent Euill.

Ioy or Deliht is a sweet Acquiescence of the Coueting Appetite in the presence or Fruition of an Object iudged Good and Conuenient. (This is the Passion wherewith we hug, and, as it were, embrace, the possessed Good. Neither is it much materiall whether the beloued Obiect be present or Absent: so it be certainly ours: for conceiuing it vnder the Notion of Present, we anticipate our fruition: as the Saints on Erth Possess heu'n before they Enter it.)

Greef <or Sorrow> is an Affection, |f. 76| whereby the Sensitiue Appetite, is troubled and Dejected by the Sense and feeling of a present Euill. (Whither the Euill be really present in the Place, or but apprehensiuely to the Imagination.)

This Greefe, if it be for a past fault, is cal'd Repentance. If to see another enjoy a Good we think him vnworthy of, it is term'd Nemesis. If it be inueterate and Habitual, it festers into Melancholy: if it reduce the Soul to such Streihts that it seems to haue depriu'd it of all means to escape, we stile it Anxiety or Angustia. And if it surprize the Soule with such a Violence as seizes on and benums the members of the [M] Body, obstructing their functions, we term it, Accedia or Astonishment. Now in Ioy ther is a Diffusion of the Spirits from the hart to the outward Members; and in ↑Greef↓ a [contr] retreat of them from |f. 76v| the outward Members to contract themselues into the hart: so that it has somtimes happened, that Sudden and Immoderate fits of Ioy and Greefe, the latter by an ouergreat crouding and compression of the Spirits into the hart, has made them throng and stifle themselues to Deth; and the latter by an vniuersall sally of the Vitall Spirits from the hart in to the outworcks of the body, has giuen the Enemy, Deth, opportunity, to take an vnresisted Possession, of that Emty Castle; and so both of them have been guilty of thos sudden and vntimely Fates, whereof Historys ar not barren in Examples.[20]

To com now to the Passions of the Inuading Appetite, Despaire or Desperation is an Affection of the [Ira] Inuading Appetite, whereby it is depriued of all hope of acquiring the desired Good, and so leaues of the Pursuite of it, as of a thing impossible to be attained. |f. 77| And if this Good be the Souuerin Good,

---

[20] Cf. *Philaretus* (Maddison 32-33), *Occ. Refl.* (2.377, 379, 437), and *Exp. et Obs. Phys.* (5.585). The topic was extensively illustrated in Bacon's "Of Death."

this Despaire is one of the Cheefest Ingredients of the hihest vnhappiness: and in this Despaire the Diuines, for the most part, esteeme the greatest of hell-fire to consist. Som few oppose to this Despaire, Assurance, when is certin of the getting the desired Good; but that seems inconueniently to be rank't amongst Passions, since it is destitute of Emotion.

Feare is a Passion of the Inuading Appetite, whereby it is kept in an [doutfull] anxius and perplexed Expectation of a thretning Euil, or the losse of som Good, which is iudged Difficult to be auoided. (It differs somthing from Fliht, in that Fliht absolutely respects an Absent Euill to shun it; but feare lookes vpon the absent Euill, as somthing that must com.)

Hope is a Passion of the Inuading Appetite, where by it is kept in a doutfull Expectation of a future Good, which, tho Difficult, is thouht Possible and Probable to be attained. For as ther is no Fear but [mixed] mingled with som |f. 77v| Hope; so is there no Hope without the admixtion of som Feare. Either of these Passions being somewhat doubtfull and Suspensiue, tho leaning more to one side then the other. For we neither Hope what we kno will com to pass; as that the Sun wil rise to morro morning: [as that if we put our hand into the Fire, it wil burn it:] nor apprehend what we are sure is vnauoidable; as, the Deuils fear not that Hel they ar sure they cannot escape. 'Tis tru, it seems that Louers often hope for the Rising of the Sun: but 'tis not so much a Hope that it wil rise, as a Desire that it may rise quickly. (The Certinty of a thing changing the Hope of it into Expectation.) And the Deuils, it seems, ar apprehensiue of the Torments of Hell which they cannot auoid: but indeed they fear but the time of the Beginning of those tortures, and their Degree, which they yet ignore. And generally, in all such cases, tis not the Thing it self, but som doutful Circumstance of the thing that is hop't for, or apprehended.

Hope is commonly by the Diuines made a Vertu; which if we take the precize [mes] Signification |f. 78| of the Word, it cannot be; Hope being a Passion, not a Habitude, and seated, in the Appetite, not in the Will. But (says a Diuine to excuse it) As when a Horsman's Name is Vnknown, we vse to signify him by the Shape and Colour of his horse: so when a Vertu is destitute of a Name, we commonly giue it that of the Passion that it rules and Moderates.[21] And thus we call that Vertu, Hope, that eleuats, and, as it were, screws it vp from Erth to heu'n.

By the like improper Expression, the whole Body of [prac] Piety and practical Religion is entitled the Feare; wherein we vnderstand not the Passion, Fear: but all that inward Reuerence and Obedience, that men vse to giue outwardly to those they fear.

Feare is opposed to Hope as it's Contrary; but Despaire is opposed to Hope as it's Priuation.

---

[21] Source unknown.

Boldness, or Confidence, is a Motion of the Impugning Appetite, against an imminent Euil, which, tho difficult to be [oue] auoided, is conquerable.

Anger, or Wrath, is a Passion of the Inuading Appetite, |f. 78v| whereby we ar [mo] incited and moued to reueng and punish that which [ha] we think to haue don vs any harm or Iniury. (This Passion, when it is in a hih Degree, is termed Rage or Fury; [illeg.] when for the cause of God, Zeale. [Whereof Dauid, Fineas, and many others are examples in the Scripture.

Al the other Passions are leasht together, and go by Paires; whereof one is contrary to the other: but Anger marches alone, and has no opposite; for not to be Angry is no Passion.

Neither dos it preiudice our Description of Anger to say that Children ar oftentimes angry with their Parents, on whom, for all that, they do not desire to reueng themselues: for they think it a kind of Punishment, to manifest by their Silence, Absence, or som such other mild way, that they ar displeased.] ↑Such as was Phineas his act in washing the Israëlite's whoredom with his blood; and our blessed Sauiors, in driuing out of the Temple, those that made the very Innocent Doues guilty of it's Profanation.↓[22]

{And heere we must in Generall Obserue, that the Passions of the Coueting precede those of the Inuading Appetite, for those (as Loue and Hate;) are often |f. 79| stirred vp without these: but these neuer moued without those: for (For Example) we neuer Hope nor Feare, but what we loue, hate, or Desire. In return whereof, this latter Appetite, helps much the former: for when the Coueting Appetite desires that which it cannot haue without difficulty, then in coms the Inuading Appetite, and remoues the Obstacles, and resists the hindrances. Now in Beasts the Fancy or Imagination[s] sways the Scepter, and absolutely [stirs] moues and gouerns these Affections: but in Man, Reson dos, or shud, command, and oftentimes corrects or Disapproues the Iudgment of the Fancy, which considers only what is Plesant or Conuenient, not what is [Iust] Resonable or Honest.}

The other Passions hitherto treated of, go by Paires hand in |f. 79v| hand: whereof one is stirred vp by Good and the other by Euill. But Anger marches alone: because the Inuading Appetit against the Present Euill is moued with Anger, but against present Good it is not stirred vp by any Passion, because therein it finds no difficulty of resistance; without which the Impugning Appetite lyes still: and, not to be Angry, is not a Passion.

Now the Passions hither to treted of, are, as it were, Elementall Passions, [out of] <by> whose diuers mixture are compounded seuerall other Passions, which it were needless and Endless to particularize, but by a general Title, they ar stiled Mixt Passions or Affections. Thus Loue to the thing we want, and Greef

[22] For Phineas, see Num. 25:6-9; for the money-changers, see Matt. 21:12.

that another has it, breeds Enuy; Loue to the thing we haue, and hating the communication of it to another, Iealousy; and the mixture of a kind of Loue to the Party, and Sorrow for his Sufferings, make a compound Passion cal'd Pitty. |f. 80|

But lest we shud stir vp the Readers Passion[s] with a too tedius Discours of Passions; we will fring this Pathology (for so is the Doctrine of Affections stiled) with a few practical Obseruations, disgested into these 2 Rules.

Where the First shal be, that the Frequency, lastingness, and Degree, and all other materiall Circumstances of any Passion, ouht to be grounded on, and, regulated by, the Nature of it's object; and not by the priuate Humor, Custom, Habit, Complexion, Preiudice, or other like qualifications of the Party affected. To see a Soft-natur'd man insensible of some petty Indignity; [&c] or a fyri-spirited man inflamed with a more vehement and [las] during Passion vpon the Sense of som mor notable Iniury reflecting vpon his honesty or good name; is not in either of thes, any great matter of Commendation; because tho the Nature of the Object did in both warrant the quality of the Passion; yet in |f. 80v| those Persons, they both proceeded more out of their owne Natures and humors then the serious consideration of the Natures of the Iniurys themselues; by which (only) the Passion is to be regulated.

The Second Rule shal be to Take heed, when any violent fit of Passion, (specially those violent ones of Loue, Hatred, Feare and Desire) is vpon thee, of making any Resolution or doing any act of greate concernment, that can be Safely differred till a more calm temper of thy mind: and aboue all, take heed of doing irreuocable acts in thine Anger. Such as the making of Voues that cannot be recal'd; or the reuealing of Secrets, which makes a man a Bankrupt for Society for euer: and in generall all those things that once don ar euer don, and like the Persian decrees, can neuer be reuers'd nor repeal'd.[23] For my part I esteeme this Precept one of the vsefullest in all Morality, and the breach of it, frequently, one of the most dangerous. For woful Experience tels vs, that many |f. 81| Times, those Actions, which hauing once don in the transport of our Passion, we cannot vndoo, vndoo vs.

↑Ther is therefor 3 Principal Particulars wherein we <may be> faulty concerning our Passions: namely, The Object; the Degree, and the Continuance. In the Object [we may sin] (which, with the Circumstances that attend it, holds (commonly) the Place of Cause of our |f. 84v| Passions) we may sin, in placing our Affections vpon a wrong Object, [lo] Ioying for what we shud greeue, Fearing what we shud Hope for, louing what we shud hate, and the like. As when a man reioyces in a good man's Fall, or is sorry for <his neibor's> another's [conuersion;] happiness; or apprehends [that] his owne Conuersion which he shud

[23] See Dan. 6:8 and 15.

desire, or else [hating] detesting the Vertuus, dotes vpon the Profane. In the Degree or Mesure of our Passions, we may be faulty, not only by neglecting or inuerting that <Subordination> Gradation of our Affections, which the Worth of their Objects dos require; as when we loue our Frends better then the Truth, or our Purses then our Consciences; but also when we loue a fit object immoderately, or it begets in vs too violent a Passion. For the Affection ouht always to beare a Proportion to the tru Estimation of it's Object as to vs: and therefore, that excessiue Passion that Louers beare [and] to their Mistresses, and do so vainly brag of, is iustly condemnable. And generally, All Passions, like Meat and Fisic, when they once com to be operatiue /hot or Cold/ in the Fourth Degree, degenerate into Poyson.[24] And lastly: [and] we may be to blame in the Continuance of our Passion, when it [remaines] lasts too long for the Subject, or admits of no alteration vpon the Change of the Object: as when a man showres down teares too long for his Deceased Friend, or a frantic Louer continues yet to court <and embrace> the brethless carcas of his deceased Mistres. Tho this last kind of failing be easily reducible to one of the first 2: the changing of the Object with the Continuance of the Affection, making vs to place that ↑Affection, either vpon an vndue Object, or in too hih <vehement> a Degree.↓↓

But because the wholsom aduice this Precept giues vs, is often frustrated by the tumultuary onsets and sudden surprisals of [D] vnruly Passions; we will therefore fortify our Reason against them with this Morall Pentagone.

The first Bulwark therefore shall be to Suppress the First Motions and [Sup] Resist the very Risings of Disorderly Affections. The gretest things, haue, for the most part, Small beginnings; and then they ar easy to be subdu'd; which if they be not; we shal not perhaps be able to Cut down that Tree, that we miht haue hinder'd to grow.[25] It is therefore <very> Good to haue an Ey vpon all the First commotions of the Mind; and Appease the Sedition before it get Hed: lest if we Will not, when we Can, we cannot when we will.

The Second is carefully to auoid the Occasions of those Passions we ar most inclin'd to. For Occasion is a mute Invitation and a liuely Spur to the Appetite.[26] Since according to the Axiome, |f. 81v| Objecta mouent Sensum; the Objects moue the Senses, and they the Appetite:[27] Presence stirs vp more liuely, Absence moues more faintly; because the Idea of the Object stirs it far more coldly then the Object it selfe.

---

[24] In medieval natural philosophy "the fourth degree" referred to the "successive stages of intensity of elementary qualities of bodies (heat and cold, moisture and dryness)" (*OED*).

[25] Cf. T442, "A great torch may be lighted at a little candle" or S714, "Of a little spark a great fire."

[26] Cf. I37, "Who would do Ill never wants Occasion" or O8 "He that takes away the occasion takes away the Offence."

[27] Alsted 1244.

The third is, To weih and consider wel the tru Worth and Value both of things, and of one's self; and to ponder the Inconueniences that arise, from the vnruly rule of vnbridled Passions. For the first, Sure [if] <did> we know the true Price of things, we wud neuer set so hih a rate vpon vs as we do. For the Second; If with a Noble Pride we wud but consider, what a Portion of Diuinity God has bestow'd vpon vs; we shud be asham'd to see that part which we haue as man, Reason, be ouer-ruled by that that we haue as Beasts, Fancy: and the Image of God to be marshal'd in the Reare, when that of the Beast commands the Van. Truly if it bee a greate Shame, for a King to be vnbenowned by his owne subiects; it shud bee a very greate one for vs, to lose by our baseness the command of our affections: since |f. 82| that was but Fortunes guift, this, natures: that may bee lost by her inconstancie that gave itt; this only by his vnworthiness that might and did not keepe it.[28] What a Shame is it for the Mistress reason to bee commanded by her seruants, the affections. Tis less shame to be born a Slaue, then, (by a man's own Baseness,) to becom one. He is more then a King that is one of himself: as being Commander, both of the Epitome of the World, and of him for whom the World was made; As he (on the contrary) is but a royall Slaue, that commanding abroad, Obeys at home: and as much as there he domineers ouer others, heer lets his Passions lord it ouer him.[29] And as for the 3rd, there ar very few to whom their own feelings may not read Lectures of the Disorders that wait vpon the transports of disorderly passions: to which I will only adde, That Passions, as they ar Excellent Seruants, |f. 82v| so they ar Very bad Masters; and, like Fire and Water, can neuer be Kings but they must be Tyrants.[30]

The fourth Remedy is Delay; whilst we do not absolutely reject the Motions of our Passions, but onely Defer, and put of their Execution: whilst in the mean time Reason has leisure to recollect it self; and diuers things may interuene, that may make the Passion [at] first Languish, and then Vanish. For Generally Time (almost) euer fauors Truth and Reason; whereas Violence and Wrong ar cheefly befrended by Celerity. And Passions, for the most part, like the ancient Gaules, spend all their Fury in the First onset: and the Brunt of that Shoc being once sustained, like snow-bals in hot wether, they melt in the

[28] While the trope of reason as king is familiar, it had a special resonance in the mid-1640s. Charles I spent a night at Stalbridge on 8 October 1644, though there is no evidence that RB was in attendance (Maddison 61).

[29] Levi and Fiering summarize a bewildering array of opinions about the passions, their taxonomy, foundations, influence, and so on: "the seat of the passions could be in the body, soul, mind, or heart; and to achieve the good life the passions could be moderated, eradicated, stimulated, or overcome; their number was 3, 4, 7, 12, 15, or uncountable" (Fiering 149). For some of RB's perspective, cf. *Swearing* 6.13.

[30] Cf. F253, "Fire and water are good servants but bad masters," a proverb repeated in "Of Sin"; Reynolds used the same proverb of servants/masters and wind/waves in his *Treatise* 46.

Running. They ar ouercom at last if they do not ouercom at first.

The Last Remedy of Passion is by Passion it self; which is don, either by Curing a |f. 83| Passion with it's Contrary, as excessiue Loue with Hatred; and so driuing out one Nayle with another:[31] or els by Distraction; when to allay and remit the Violence of one Passion, we admit of som further Perturbations from others, and so distract the forces of the Former.[32] As when in Baths, when the Water is too hot, by the admixture of cold water, we reduce it to a lukewarm temper: ↑or a Merchant casts away his ware out of the Ship, lest himself shud be cast away in it.↓[33] Sometimes also when a Passion is too reflexiue vpon it self; it is very good to scatter and diuert it by Communication; as wee see greef lihtned by laying a Part of the Burden vpon other men's shoulders. And somtimes too, the [same effect is wrought] vehemency of a passion is allaid by extending on diuers objects (so they be not absolutely subordinate one to another.) For thus the Riuer of Passion, when it is cut into many lesser Streames, runs Weaker and Shallower.[34] The |f. 83v| Multiplicity of the Object must needs distract and weaken the Affection; as those ar obserued not to be the greatest Louers, that ar the most Amorous; and generally, They that haue the most Objects for their Passion, haue the lest Passion for any Object.

This Doctrine of the Affections, has been by Aristotle and the [most] greater part of the Moralists, either wholly neglected, [and] or very lamely and confusedly deliuer'd vs: so that it both [mor] needs and deserues a Reformation. I wish som Body wud begin it that wer able to perfect it. And sure it is of more Importance then most [People] Men imagine: for the Passions ar the Materials in the Wel ordering and contriuing whereof consists Vertu's Architecture: (whence som haue defin'd it, Affectus ratione temperatus, a Passion moderated by Reason.)[35] and the Sensitiue Appetite, is an vnruly Courser, in whose wel riding and managing, (cheefly) consists Vertu's Horsmanship.[36]

---

[31] Cf. F277, "One fire drives out another," L538, "One love drives out another," or P457, "One poison expels another."

[32] In the margin RB wrote, "Heere Place Saul's Example." David used music to distract Saul when Saul was obsessed by an evil spirit (1 Sam. 16:14-23).

[33] Cf. Nich. Eth. III.i.4-5 and *Reconcileableness* 4.186.

[34] Cf. R139, "A river running into many brooks becomes shallow."

[35] Cf. Alsted 1243. For other uses of the metaphor, cf. the soul as architect of its mansion (*Vulgar Notion* 5.241) and God as architect (2.312, 3.54, 4.38, 5.139, 5.195, and 5.203). RB used the "Temple of Vertu" in bk. 2, ch. 4, and he stressed the *architecture* of thought in his "Doctrine of Thinking" below.

[36] The image of the passions or appetites as a horse is a commonplace derived from Plato's *Phaedrus*. Like other moralists, RB often invoked this image.

|f. 85|

Chapter II.

Of Plesure and Paine

That Plesure and Paine ar to be treated of in the Ethickes, appeares both by the Generall consent of the Moralists themselues; and also because that [in] as in <our> Passions, so in Plesure and Paine, there is a certin Mediocrity to be obserued; neither ouht the Baits of Plesure entice vs out of the Paths of Vertu, nor the Stings of Paine deter vs from their pursuit. Besides that this Doctine fals within our consideration, in regard that Plesure is an indiuiduall concomitant of Felicity; and Plesure and Paine, ar Affections, (or Adjuncts) of the Passions of the Mind.

Now the [Words] <Terms> of Plesure and Paine, haue principally a twofold Signification. For sometimes they ar taken for those things that cause or occasion Plesure and Paine; as we count Wine and Women among the Plesures of the Body; because there flows a Plesure from their Fruition: and in this Sence it is [many] that many |f. 85v| Constitute Plesure and Paine the [f] Object of the Ethickes, namely, the Passions and all other things that produce Pleasure and Pain: and sometimes againe they ar taken in the proper Signification, for the Affections that accompany[s] and follo[s] the Motions of the Mind, [which] and ar not indeed themselues Affections, but concomitants and Adjuncts of the Affections.[1]

In this latter Sense, Pleasure is commonly described to be, The End or Accessary Perfection of a Perfect Operation. Others (more Intelligibly) define it in general to be, [A signe of a Perfect Operation in an Animal, wherein the Faculty ↑(or meets with)↓ is applied to a very good and proportionable Obiect.] ↑The Sign of a Perfect Operation in [an] Animals; arising from the Faculty's [perception of an] Good and proportionable perception of an Excellent Object.↓ Whence it follows; [that Plesure it self is neither Naturall Faculty, Habitude, nor Operation.] We may without so much adoo cal it, A sudden Complacency of the Faculty arising from the Vn-hindred performance of it's Operation. Where note, that it is termed Sudden in regard of the quickness of it's Resultancy; for no sooner is the Operation perfected, but the Plesure begins. |f. 86| From hence it follows, that Plesure flows not immediatly, either from the Natural Faculty, or from the Habitude; but from that Faculty's or Habitude's Operation. And by Consequent, that Plesure is neither the Operation, nor the Faculty, nor the

[1] Cf. Nich. Eth. VII.xii.2ff.

Habitude it selfe; but a certin Perfection that is joyned with the Operation, and compleats it; and that as an End, which tho not principally intended by the Agent; yet inseparably accompanys that Perfect Action that is intended by the Agent as the Beauty (say they) is a perfecting Signe and Affection of Helth and a flourishing Age.

Now as Plesur giues an outward Perfection to the Action so it presupposes an Inward Perfection in the Action, from which (Perfection) it flows: as Paine (on the other side) accompanys an Imperfect Action. Now that is cal'd a Perfect Axion, that proceeds from a very wel dispozed and vnhindred Faculty, and the |f. 86v| Object it tends to in it's kind most excellent. Thus we feel a Plesure in the Act of Seeing; when, [the Ey is vn-offended, the Siht not hindred, and the thing we look vpon, Faire,] both the Faculty of seeing is neither offended nor hindred; and the thing we looke vpon, is Faire.

The Imperfect Action, from which flowes Paine, is That which proceeds [either] from a [Vitiated or hindered] Faculty, which is either Vitiated or hindred; or which tends to an Object vnsuitable to the Faculty. So we feel a Paine in the Act of Seeing, when either our Eys ar sore, or we look vpon an Obscœne and Horrid Spectacle.

By the foregoing Doctrine we may gather, that Plesure requires a Proportion betwixt the Object and the Faculty that is to perceiue it: which (Proportion) being once taken away, the Plesur ceases, and Pain succeeds it. <From> [W]hence we may gather the Reason why our <bodily> Plesures ar not perpetuall; but the Continuance of those things that at first pleased, at last tyres vs out |f. 87| and vexes vs: Namely because we ar not able to bear out and go thorou with a continued Operation: for the Spirits, [by] whose Assistance /Seruice/ we [performed] ↑necessarily↓ vsed in the plying of our Operations, being exhausted and consumed; and so the Proportion of the Faculty to the Object, changed, we are weary, and the Minds attention is slackned and allay'd; and so, the Plesure, at first languishes and gros tedius; then, when it once cloys vs, it altogether ceases; and at last goes out in Paine. From hence we may likewise collect the Reason why Trafit sua quem voluptas,[2] why men are so peculiar in their likings, so that oftentimes what pleases one, displeases another: namely, because there is a great Variety in the Constitutions of men's Facultys, each of which requires a[n] proportionable Object; and one [can] Object cannot be suitable ↑and conuenient↓ to them all.

Now Plesures ar distinguished according to the Distribution of the Functions they wait vpon. For Euery Action is accompanyed by a certin |f. 87v| Peculiar and Familiar Pleasure that furthers and promotes it. As we see those (cæteris paribus) learn best Geometry, Music, or any other Science that learn it with most

[2] Virgil, *Eclogues* 2.65. RB repeated the tag eight paragraphs later.

Book Two, Chapter Two

Pleasure. And generally, Those Operations ar the most exactly performed, that most please the Agent in the Doing.

[Now since those things must needs be specifically Different, that ar the proper [illeg.] Propertys of things that ar specifically different;]

Now Plesure, according to the Distribution of it's Subjects, is commonly diuided into the Plesure of the Mind and that of the Body. Which Diuision som confirm, because (say they) the Plesures of the Mind and those of the Body, when in a hih degree, ar hindrances to the Perception of each other. |f. 88|

The Plesur of the Mind is proper to the mind, and [results] is so peculiar to the Soule, that the Body tasts not (properly) of it. The Plesures of the Body fall vnder the Perception of the Senses; and ar so enjoyed by the Mind that they affect also the Body; namely, the Senses, which appertaine to the Body.

[Now] There is a Double Plesure of the Mind: Contemplatiue and Practick. The First consists in the quiet and vndisturbed Contemplation of hih and noble Objects, and in a peacefull Meditation of Sublime and heu'nly things: whereby men becom the Priuy Counsellors of Nature, and conscius of all her Secrets.[3] The Latter [pe flowes] waits vpon the Possession of those Diuine qualitys that make vp the Image of the Creator, and an vn-interrupted practice of Iustice, Temperance, Courage, and the Chorus of those other reall Graces, that tho |f. 88v| the World neglect them, can reward themselues.

The Senses of the Body ar ansuerable in Number to the Senses, that perceiue them. For som belong to the Siht, others to the Hearing, others to the Sent; and so [to] in the rest of the Senses. Of these, the Beasts enjoy those that belong to the Senses of Tast and Tuch, (or Feeling:) the others they ar little or not at all sensible of, except by accident; namely, as the Plesures, renew the memory of, or incite the Imagination[s] to, the Plesure of the Tast and Feeling. Thus when the Wolf is delihted with the [illeg.] Bleating of a Sheep, tis not for any pleasure he takes in the Sound; but because that Noise stirs vp his Appetite to Desire and Hope for to eat the flesh of the Sheep; and perhaps feeds his Memory with the past Pleasure he has formerly had in the Eating of Sheepe. |f. 89|

Where by the Way it will not be vn-necessary to obserue the Difference betwixt Plesur and Paine, and Ioy and Greefe: whereof those are attributable also to the Body; these are peculiar to the Mind. Ioy and Greef ar Affections of the Sensitiue Appetite, and ar seated there: but Plesur and Paine [are also] reside in the outward and Inward Senses, and are their Affections. Besides, the Vnderstanding hath also it's Delihts.

Plesure is again by a Second distribution diuided into Naturall and

[3] This is RB's earliest linkage of natural philosophy and religion. For other views of contemplation and meditation, see *Occ. Refl.* (2.338, 2.443); *Exc. of Theol.* (4.27, 29); *Things above Reason* (4.446); and *Chr. Virtuoso* (6.717); for an overview, see Norman Pettit, *The Heart Prepared: Grace and Conversion in Puritan Spiritual Life* (New Haven 1966).

common, and Proper and aduentitius. The Former is that which all Animals naturally and promiscuusly desire and perceiue; in the vse of Meat, Drink, Venus, and all other Plesures necessary to the conseruation of the Animal, both in himself, and his Kind. The Proper is that Peculiar Plesure, that the Animal takes in this or that kind of Nurrishment or Venus; which he finds most delihtfull to his Fancy |f. 89v| And Appetite. And of this Plesure it is said that Trahit sua quem qua voluptas.[4] ↑Lastly, Plesur is diuided into Syncere [and] Pure, and Impure or Mixt: the First is without any admixture of Paine, the Second participates of it.↓

Now according to the laws of Contrarys, Paine, (it's opposite) admits of the same Distribution that Plesure has, and, [it] like it, may be diuided, First into the Paine of the Body and that of the Mind; [and] Secondly into the Paine that is Common to all Animals, and that which is Proper to Som: and Lastly in that Paine which is Pure, and that which is Mixt.

Now since Plesure is an Affection that accompanys Operations, it seems [it] that it shud be [illeg.] iudg'd of by the Operations from which it flowes; wherefor, since of Actions som ar Good, som Bad, and som Indifferent; so of Plesures; som ar to be esteemed Good and lawfull, som Bad and vnlawfull; and others, of a middle kind of Nature betwixt both.

That all Plesur is not Euil, appeares, in that there is a kind of Plesure that inseparably accompanys Felicity and the Actions of Vertu. |f. 90| Besides that Plesur is a Good desired [for it selfe] of naturally of all Animalls; and that for it self; for we ask not a man why he had rather be delihted then pained, no mor then we ask him why he had rather be Happy then Miserable. To which ad, that if Paine be an Euill; it's contrary, Plesure must needs be a Good; and that God himself enjoys a Plesur as infinite as his Essence. Againe, That all Plesures ar Good is an Opinion that is thouht to want a Patron to Defend it. So that the Question now remaining is, whither <or no> the [Ple] moderate Plesures of the Body be vtterly to be rejected as Euill; [as the Planicians seem to maintain all Plesur to be Euill.] For all these the Platonitians <opinion> seem'd to condemn; [for] as we [do] <condemne> their Opinion. For God placed Adam in a Paradice of Plesure; and often promises it as a reward of Piety: besides, that God has seasoned and as it were sweetned all the Necessary actions of our life with a certin Pleasure that is thereby shown to be necessary to the Conseruation of our |f. 90v| Nature. And truly if we conceiue Paine vnder the Notion of Euill, I kno not why we shud not apprehend it's contrary, Plesure, vnder that of Good. Neither kno I why, [since that] Plesur that is the Signe and concomitant of a perfect Operation, shud be euill it self. Besides that al men esteeme Vertu, with Plesure to boot a greater good then Single Vertu. But, that which has rendred the Name of Plesure Odious, is, that Custom has restrain'd [it] ↑the Signification of that

[4] RB used the same tag from Virgil earlier in this chapter.

word↓ to the vnbridled Lusts and immoderate Pleasures of the Body, which can neuer be sufficently railed at. And indeed 'tis no great maruel if men commonly by the Word Pleasure, vnderstand that which is lawless and excessiue, since the most part of men <neither> kno nor follow, any other, Deliht.

Now the Pleasures of the Mind iustly challenge a Preeminence [before] <ouer> those of the Body: [for] cheefly for these Reasons. 1. Because like Vertu and Felicity, they admit of no excess; specially when they flow from perfect Habitudes. 2. Because they ar far Lastinger then the Plesures of the Body. 3. Because they ar Pure and Syncere without admixture of Paine. 4. And because they reside in a Subiect far more Noble and Excellent: for the Seat of Spirituall |f. 91| Plesures, is the Vnderstanding; of Bodily, the Senses. Yet for all this the Latter ar generally more delihted in and Desir'd, Because 1. They ar more Known and Notorius. 2. They ar born and brouht vp with vs, where as [illeg.] we are not capable of the others till a certin Age. 3. Most men ignore tru Pleasures; and want judgment to discern them. 4. In the greater part of Men the Sensitiue Faculty is the Predominant Faculty,and so those Plesures ar thought the best that most deliht the Senses. 5. The Deuil and our own natiue Corruption disturbe vs <oftentimes> in the Fruition of the Intellectuall Plesures; but further vs [V] in the Pursuit and Enjoyment of Sensuall Delihts. 6. And lastly because these are necessary to the Conseruation both of the Indiuiduall and the kind; and besides remedy diuers naturall inconueniences.

To this Doctrine of Pleasure and Paine diuers other Questions miht <indeed> haue been added but being of the Nature of those Crawfishes that afford far more to Pick then to Eat; I wil leaue their Discussion to those that haue a mind to be rid of their time; only aduertising the Reader, that hauing deliuered this Doctrine |f. 91^{v}| more out of the Opinion of others then my owne; I do not pretend to maintain it against all commers; [but] and if any man will correct it with [illeg.] ↑a more probable Doctrine↓ he may do it vnresistedly for me; who am neuer so concerted of my owne liht, but that I will willingly be content to put out my candle at the Rising of the Sun.[5]

5 RB also stressed the importance of avoiding dogmatism in *Scep. Chymist* 1.463 and *Chr. Virtuoso* 5.536. Cf. S988, "To set forth the Sun with a Candle." The comparison of human reason and the candle was often used by the Cambridge Platonists (Patrides 11-13).

Book Two, Chapter Two

|f. 93|

Chapter III.

Of Moral Actions

Hauing in the foregoing Chapter discoursed of the Final and Materiall Causes of Moral Vertu; we wil now proceed, to the handling of the Efficient Cause, which is either Ministerial, ([handled] <treated of> in the ensuing Chapter,) or Principall, namely, Morall Actions reduc'd to [the] Mediocrity. Whose Doctrine we wil therefore the more accurately deliuer, because it is not onely very vsefull and Necessary in the Ethickes; but has also a great Influence vpon the Whole Body of Ciuil Filosophy.[1]

The Fisitians, according to that celebrated Saying of their Master Galen, Mores animi sequuntur Temperamentum Corporis, The Customes of the Mind |f. 93v| Follo the Temperament of the Body; wud haue the Vertus and Vices of the Soule depend vpon the Temper and Proportion of the Humors of the Body.[2] Drawing their Argument from Experience: for we see that they in whom Choler abounds, are generally Hasty, and Firy Spirits; in whom Melancholy prædominates, Sad, Pensiue, and Ingenius; and so of the rest of the Humors. But altho we do not deny but that such a disproportionate Proportion of humors, as wholly vitiates the Necessary Instruments of the Soule, dos, as it were, Enforce certin Axions and Customes vpon the Mind; as we see that Choler hihly inflamed driues a man into Fury, and the Excesse of Melancholy into Frenzy and Madness: yet we affirm, that a Naturall Temper, such as is generally to be found in most men's Bodys, |f. 94| Tho indeed it be capable to Incline a man to such and such Passions or Habitudes; yet it dos not Necessarily and (as it were) forcibly produce them: but those Inclinations may be very wel altered and corrected by a contrary Institution. For, 1. Experience furnishes vs with many Examples of men Chast, Valiant, [D] Actiue, and the like, whose Temperament promis't no such matter, but rather the quite contrary; witnes the Famous Story of the Fisiognomist and Socrates.[3] 2. The Naturall Temper is (almost) vnalterable; but the Customs and Habitudes of men ar subiect to frequent Vicissitudes. 3. And we

---

[1] Cf. Alsted on mediocrity ("Virtutis forma est mediocritas" 1245), a topic extensively discussed in Nich. Eth. II.ii.6ff.

[2] Alsted 1249. When RB quoted this tag (D381) again in the next chapter, he called it "more famous than true."

[3] Alsted summarized Zopyrus's judgment about the physiognomy of Socrates, arguing for the merits of the "philosophia practica." Quoting Melanchthon, Alsted noted, "Bonus Physicus facit bonum Ethicum" (1236).

haue our Temperament from Nature, but not our Vertus, (as it shal be heereafter prou'd.)

The Stoicks they wud haue Vertu naturall to the Soule of Man, and he born with it; but Vices they wud haue in the Mind prӕternally, or |f. 94v| Besides Nature; namely, when men Deuiate from their Natural Goodnes; either seduc't by ill Examples, or corrupted by Euil Customes. And so they wud haue Liuing according to Nature, and Liuing Virtuously to be one and the same thing.[4] But falsly: For 1. That which is Inborn and Naturall can by no contrary accustomance be taken away; as the flinging of a Stone 1000 times vpwards wil neuer take away it's heuiness, and make it tend vpwards:[5] but we see the Habitudes of Men change frequently from Good into Bad, and from Bad into Good againe. 2. If a Faculty be Natural to a Man (in est à Naturâ) then it is perfectly in him at the very Beginning, and so produces it's Axions, but is not produc'd by them, as the Faculty or Power of Seeing, Heering, and the like; But Vertus ar not Perfect from the Beginning; but ar little by |f. 95| Little acquir'd and improued by Axions. 3. Lastly, If Vertu were connaturall to Man, then all, or at lest the greatest part of, Men shud be Vertuus; as most men are endowed with the Facultys of Seeing, Tasting, Smelling, and the like: whereas we see but few men Vertuus, and Children, if let alone, are more prone to Euill then Good. But how far Nature is conducible to Vertu, we shall see hereafter.

We wil therefor constitute a Three-fold <Efficient> cause of Vertu. The first is Almihty God, who by the Efficacious Operation and Concourse of his Holy Spirit, purges our Soules from the Drosse of their Naturall Corruption; and Endowes them with those [heu'nly V] tru and reall Vertus, that ar too heu'nly to proceed but from so Diuine an Author. (But this we resigne to the Diuines to treat of.) The Second is Certin [natural] <natiue> Principles of Goodness, and |f. 95v| Inborn Seeds of Vertu that by Nature we bring along with vs into the World; out of which being cherished and improued by Precepts and Education, Vertu is afterwards by it's causes Excited and produced.[6] The last and maine cause is assuefaction[7] and Exercice: for as a Rider by Practicing to ride, gets the Habitude of Horsmanship, and a Painter by frequent drawing and limming the Art of Painting; so by the frequent Practice and Reiteration of Vertuus Actions, is acquired the Habitude of Vertu.[8] And that this Accustomance to and Practice of Morall Actions, is the Principal Ciuil Efficient Cause of Morall Vertu, may

---

[4] For Laërtius's discussion of the Stoics, see his life of Zeno (7.1-160). For later views of Stoics, Epicureans, and Peripateticks, see *Reconcileableness* 4.166.

[5] Cf. Nich. Eth. II.i.2.

[6] RB focussed his own material in the *Aret.* on this topic. In bk. 10 of the Nich. Eth. Arist. stressed the connection between education and politics.

[7] The *OED* notes a 1644 usage by Kenelm Digby as the first occurrence of "assuefaction," the act or process of accustoming.

[8] Arist.'s examples were learning to build houses or to play the harp (Nich. Eth. II.i.4).

Book Two, Chapter Three

appeare because otherwise, why shud Lawgiuers propose Rewards to such as giue themselues to the Practice of Vertu, and inflict Punishments on them that ar giuen ouer to the Exercice of Vice?[9] For certinly if either Vertus or Vices were Natural to vs, the [one] <first> were needless, or the latter, Unjust. But of this we need no other [Witness] argument then Experience it selfe, which witnesses, that by doing |f. 96| (For Example) Iust or Valiant Actions, we ar made (or become) Iust or Valiant Men.

But heare we ar met with by an Objection wel worth the Answering, namely, He that [dos] operates Iustly and Valiantly is already Iust and Valiant; and therefore by doing Iust and Valiant Actions is not made so. To which the Moralists answer by distinguishing the Actions of Vertu into Precedent, which go before the Acquisition of the Habitude of Vertu; and Subsequent, which flow from the Habitude of Vertu already acquir'd. The Actions that Precede the Habitude of Vertu ar don indeed by the Man, but not as their principall and Primary cause; (namely Knoing, Willing, and Constant) but either by the Desire of Praise or Reward; or the Feare of Infamy or Punishment; or by Imitation, or by another's Persuasion or Command, or the like: As we see those that lern to be Smiths, or any other Handycraft, exercice and produce diuers acts of the Art, before they com to be Artists, and by these Operations little by little, [co] acquire the Art or Habitude it selfe. But those Axions of Vertu that |f. 96v| Follow the Habitude, not only ar don by the Man, but flow from him as the principall and Primary Cause; and that not according to another's Modell, but according to the Idea he himself has conceiue'd in his Mind. By the First kind of Axions the Habitude is Produc'd; by the Second it is Euidenc't and Confirm'd. Now the Difference betwixt these 2 kinds of Actions is, cheefly, in that 1. The Former ar more Perfect and more conformable to the Exact rule of Reason, from which the latter do somwhat Decline; which Imperfection tho, is little by little by Assuefaction corrected. 2. The Former Actions ar more Difficult, and laborius (because of the greater Reluctancy of the Appetite) then the latter. 3. The Antecedent Actions of Vertu ar [mor] <less> Constant and vn-interrupted then the Subsequent. 4. And lastly, the [Former] Preceding Actions ar seldom vnaccompany'd with Trouble and Paine, whereas the [Subse] Following ar don merrily and Performed with Plesure. Which Difference is easily obseruable in the Example of 2 men the One Temperant and the other |f. 97| Continent: Both [abstaine] do the same thing, in abstaining from vnlawfull Plesures; but the Latter, because he has not yet acquired the Habitude of Vertu, dos it not without Trouble and Difficulty, because of the reluctation of the Passions; which the Former hauing tamed and Subdu'd; dos it with Ease, and Plesure.[10] To be short; the Actions flow from the Habitude of Vertu differ not from those that produce

[9] Cf. Nich. Eth. III.v.7.

[10] For continence, see Nich. Eth. VII.iif.

it in Kind (in Specie) but only in Degree and Perfection. Where the Reader is to take notice that is the Preceding Axions of Vertu (and not the Subsequent) that we heer call Morall Actions, and com now to treat of, as of the principall Efficient Cause of Morall Vertu.

For the More Distinct handling of these Humane Actions, we will Consider in them First their Kinds, and then their Principles.

Morall Actions are commonly diuided into Willing (or Free) and Constrain'd (or Forc'd), Spontaneum and Inuitum. The Latter shal be first treated of to illustrate the Former, tho it belong to this Place |f. 97v| But Reductiuely (as the Schoolmen speake) and as it is the Contrary of the Free-wil Action.[11] And heere the Reader is to obserue, that this Discourse is not intended of all Free and Forc't Axions generally (in which Sense Brutes, [and] and Inanimates ar said to do Axions Willingly or Constrainedly;) but only of those that ar produc'd by a Man quatenus a man.

The Constrain'd Action is that which proceeds from an outward Principle (or Cause) and is don agenst the Inclination of the Agent. There is therefor a double Kind of constrained Actions; the one acted [throu] by Violence, and the other throu Ignorance. He that vnderstands these 2 ways wel, may easily conceiue how one may Act freely and willingly.

The Vn-willing Actions by constraint ar, when the Cause or Principle of the Action is out of the Agent; so that he that Dos or Suffers, contributes nothing to the Doing or Sufering. |f. 98| (As when a Storm Driues a Pilote with his ship to split vpon the Rockes.) Wherefore that an Action may be cal'd truly forc'd or Violenc'd, 2 things ar required; the One that the Cause of the Action or Passion be with ↑(or out of)↓ out him that acts or Suffers; and the Other that the thing Acting or Suffering haue no Inclination nor Intention to that Action or Passion. For (By Example) if a man fling down a Stone from the Top of a Tower; tho the Cause of this motion be without the Stone; yet this Falling is not properly to be called Violenc't; because the Stone had an inward Inclination and propension to it.[12]

Now these Violenc't Actions are againe subdiuded into Meer and Mixt.

The Meerly [vio] or simply Violent is that whose cause is purely and only force, and is properly cal'd [st] Violenc't: As if a man shud take my hand, and in spite of my teeth make me strike my Father with it.[13] Yet <is> |f. 98v| This Kind of [Action] <Coaction> altogether vncapable to Violence the Will; which is [vncapable] impossible to be forc't either to approue of or dislike but what it pleases it selfe: As for the outward Action, it is not Mine, but His that dos it; and

---

[11] For voluntary and involuntary actions, see Nich. Eth. III.i-v and V.viii-ix and xi.

[12] RB's example suggested more familiarity with Arist.'s mechanics than with Galileo's or Kepler's. RB was in Florence when Galileo died (Maddison 39).

[13] The same example was used in Nich. Eth. V.viii.3-4.

makes vse of my hand as an Instrument to do a thing my Wil disapproues.

The Mixt or Inuoluntary Actions are those to whose Production, partly constraint and partly the Will concurre. Which arriues, when a man is Induc't to do any thing or to leaue it vndon; either by the Hope to obtaine thereby a Greater Good, or to Euite a greater Euill. As when a Marchant is forc'd to cast his goods ouerboord into the Sea, to auoid Shipwrack; or a man suffers his Arm to be cut of to saue his Body: [or when a Prince vnjustly confiscates a Subjects Goods to benefit the Common-welth.][14] Or when a man drinkes a bitter Potion vpon the Hope thereby to recouer his helth.

These Kind of Actions, |f. 99| If yow consider the Cause that moues them, which is External; seem <indeed> to be Constrain'd: but if yow reflect vpon the Inward and Immediate Cause, yow shal find them to participate more of Willing Actions then Constrain'd: For the Will being a While held in Suspence, and, (as it were) in Equilibrium, at last enclines to suffer one of the Inconueniences; to decline a greater Euill, or obtaine a greater good. For without this Consent of the Will, the Outward Members wud neuer (For Example) cast the Marchandize into the Sea. Wherefore this Kind of Action do not vndeserue som Praise if they ar Good; nor som Shame, if Euill; and therefore their Circumstances ar heer diligently to be pondered, and the Action iudged accordingly.

It is heer not Vselesly enquired, How far forth it is lawfull for a man to Act, out of the Hope of a greater Good, or Feare of a greater Euill? To which it is answered, First that |f. 99v| There is a two-fold [Goo] Euil (and by consequent a double good opposed to it) the one Greeuous, and the other Sinfull; the one Suffering and the other Gilty: as when a Robber is executed for killing a man vpon the hih-way; the Murder is the Sinfull Euil, and the Hanging the Greeuous. This premised we answer, 1. That betwixt 2 Goods of the same kind (namely both Pleasant, Profitable, or Vertuus,) the greatest is to be chosen; and betwixt 2 Greeuous Euils, the Least; according to that general Dictate of Prudence, betwixt 2 Euils the lest is to be chosen.[15] 2. That if 2 Sinfull Euils be presented, a man ouht to chuse Neither, but reject both. For Sin is committable vpon no Conditions; neither can a man be forc't to elect either, since the Will, that is the Seate of Vertu and Vice can be constrain'd but that it may refuse both. ↑Tho most men mis-apply the Saying of 2 Euils the Lest is to be chozen, which tho ment but of Greeuous Euils, they stretch to sinfull, and giue themselues leaue to commit [a Sin] one Sin to auoid another.↓ 3. That if of 2 Euils, the one Greeuous, and the other Sinfull, one cannot be auoided, the greatest Greeuous Euil is to be

[14] RB had used the shipwreck example above (Nich. Eth. III.i.4-5), but the reference to a prince's unjust seizure of goods—a reference that RB then deleted—is found neither in Arist. nor Alsted. Alsted noted, "Qui peccat contra conscientiam, ædificat ad gehannen" (1249).

[15] For discussion of prudence, see Nich. Eth. VI.v-xiii; for the choice between evils, see V.iii.16.

chozen before the lest Sinfull. Heere the most part of |f. 100| Moralists ar of Opinion, that of 2 Euils of Punishment, both vndeserued, and of which one cannot be auoided; a Vertuus man shud not chuse the Least, but reject both; lest (say they) he draw vpon himself the Suspition of Deseruing that Punishment that he chooses. But [for my] this Opinion is by me suspected of too much Suspition: for besides that it is not necessary, no nor vsuall that men shud be suspected of deseruing euery Euil that they cannot auoid; [besides that, I say, it seems very Inconuenient [for] out of the Apprehension of anothers groundless <vndue> Suspition to transgress <of one of> the most general and Fundamental Maximes of all Prudence, which is of 2 greeuous Euils to choose that which is lest Euill.] ↑(as If I shud be thouht to merit Robbing meerly because a theefe vpon the hih way [illeg.] constraines me to deliuer <part with> either my life or my Purse.) Besides that I say, I shud be afeard that to [at] transgress one of the fundamental laws of Prudence for feare of another['] [gro] man's groundless Suspition, were like the better in effect, then to be com a Fool for fear of being <causelesly> thouht a Knaue.↓ But the most important difficulty of all remains yet behind, which is, Whether Euil may be don that Good may come of it?[16] To which I answer, that A greeuous Euil may be admitted, if it conduce to the |f. 100v| Acquisition of som great Good; as when a man takes loathsom Fisic to recouer his Helth, or mortifys the Flesh to quicken and Viuafy the Spirit; but a Sinfull Euill is neuer to be commited, that the Greatest and most Vertuus Good whatsoeuer may follow of it. Because 1. It is absolutely condemned by the Holy Ghost, Rom# #.[17] 2. What is Euil intrinsecally and in it's own Nature can by no Circumstances be made Good. 3. Euil is not a Fit and proper meanes to produce Good, which is not truly Good, if it be not so as wel in [his] it's Causes as in it Self. 4. The Euil yow commit is always certin, but the Good that shud ensue it, (for the most part,) incertin: so that yow ar sure to do Euill, without being certin to do Good. (But this whole Section is by som not inconueniently referred to the Doctrine of Prudence.)[18]

There arises heere a |f. 101| Second Question, namely, Whither those Actions that a man dos, seduc't by Plesure, be to be esteem'd Constrain'd or no? Since Plesure seems to [illeg.] haue a stronger Influence vpon a man's Actions then Violence it self. To this it is Answered, that These kind of Actions ar rather Willing then Constrain'd; For Nature made the Will the Mistress of the Affections, not their Seruant; and if the Will enslaues it self to the Sensitiue Appetite, 'tis it's owne fault, that is willing to [obey] <serue> where it may command. The

[16] RB modified the commonplace, "Never do evil that good may come of it" (E203), by continuing his moral reasoning. For a broad overview, see McAdoo, *The Structure of Caroline Moral Theology* (London 1949).

[17] RB omitted the reference, which is probably Rom. 3:5-8.

[18] Cf. Alsted's sixth chapter, "De Prudentiâ" (1255-1260).

Book Two, Chapter Three

like may be said of those Actions that seem to be forc't from vs by great Promises and Terrible Thretnings: [to] which to excuse tis in vaine that we pretend Necessity; since, the Souuerain and greatest Necessity of all (for a man) is to be Vertuus.

Now to com to the vnwilling Actions throu Ignorance we must know, [illeg.] |f. 101v| [An Action proceeding from an Agent, that [without his Fault] is Ignorant of som Circumstances belonging to the Action. This premised, It is demanded, Whither or no, and How Far, Ignorance can excuse a committed Fault? To giue a Satisfactory Answer to this Question, we must kno,]

First, that it is one thing to Sin Ignorantly, and another to Sin by Ignorance.[19] That there is a double Ignorance, the one of the Riht, and the other of the Fact.

The Ignorance of those things that ar, of Common Riht, and those things that one is oblig'd to kno, dos not render an Action Inuoluntary; nor excuse a Fault commited by it: as if a man vpon a Priuate grudge murder his Enemy; or a Citizen transgress the publish't Lawes of the Common-welth; 'twil not serue the Turne to say they did it [by] throuh Ignorance of those Laws that prohibit such kind |f. 102| of Action: for they ouht to haue, and, (had they vsed that Diligence they shud) miht haue knowne them.

The Ignorance of the Fact, or rather of the Circumstances of [illeg.] it; is, when a man ignores, either the Kind or the Circumstances of the Fact. As if a man shooting at a Deere, the Arrow glancing shud kill his Father. These kind of Actions ar to be esteemed Inuoluntary, as being caused meerly by Ignorance: and therefore ar excused both by God and man if qualify'd with these 3 necessary Conditions; namely, that they be 1. Occasion'd throu pure and dissembl'd Ignorance. 2. And that Ignorance to be Vn-affected, and not drawn vpon our selues by our own Negligence. 3. And lastly follow'd by Sorrow and Repentance, after the Knoledge of the Fault. For if Repentance follow not such a kind of Action, it cannot be iudged meerly Inuoluntary; since, tho the Will did go before the [Will] Act, |f. 102v| yet after it is don it approues it by not disliking it. As if (to make vse of our Former Example) a man shooting at a Stag, chance to kill a man, and finds it his Father, the Greef he instantly conceiues vpon it, sho's the Act to be inuoluntary; but if comming to see what he had don, he finds that he has kild his Enemy, the Ioy he conceiues at the [Act] Chance, shos the Action <not> to be <in>Voluntary; because, tho the Will anteceded not the Fact, yet it accompany'd the Discouery of it; and he is beleeu'd to [desire] be willing that the thing be don, that is glad when it is don.[20]

[19] Cf. Nich. Eth. III.i.13-19 and III.v.8. RB's examples and analysis of five kinds of ignorance differed from Arist.'s, especially in his emphasis on repentance in the following paragraph. "Ignorance" is also discussed at length in "Of Sin" below.

[20] McAdoo notes that both Jeremy Taylor and John Bramhall used a similar example, one that

[Now Ignorance is [illeg.] thorou Ignorance of [illeg.] whither the thing has been so done]

By the Ignorance of the Fact we ignore whither a thing has been (so) don; and by that of Riht, whither it shud be don. Yet [no often] <it happens som> times the Ignorance of the Fact, occasions the Ignorance of Riht; as he that ignores whither Christ has been Crucify'd for vs or no, must by consequent |f. 103| Ignore, whither he is to be beleeu'd in or no.

Now Ignorance is also diuers other ways diuided; as 1. Into Simple Ignorance, such as is to be found in Children and Mad-men; and Malitius Ignorance, that Knowing the Truth, will yet with specious Reasons, seeme to ignore the Truth, and oppose it. 2. Into Curable, when he that Ignores, may lern the Truth if he will; and Incurable, as that of a Blind-born man, who is incapable of knoing the Difference of Coulors. 3. Into Vniversall and Particular: and so a man that knos the Vniversall Maximes of Riht and Wrong, may yet commit a Fault in applying them to particulars. As one that knos that To Steale, is vn-lawfull, may yet ignore, that to Clip money is a Theft:[21] so one that knos that Incests ar forbidden, may yet ignore that to marry one's Neece is an Incest. 4. Into Willing and Vn-willing. He is voluntarily Ignorant, that wil not learn, but auoids and declines the Occasions of being tauht for feare of obliging himself to lead a life answerable to his Knoledge. |f. 103v| To this Kind of Ignorance is to be reduced the Rash and Negligent Ignorance; as it wud be in him that shud fling stones [into] out of the Window into the Street, and hauing hurt the By-passers, answer, that He did not kno that those stones wud meet with any Body. 5. Lastly there is an Ignorance of those things that [w] one is bound to know; as the Laws of God, and the Fundamental known Laws of one's own Cuntry; and an Ignorance of those things that one is not oblig'd to know; as of the Motions of the Stars, and the Particular Statutes of a Forrein cuntry. Now the Simple Ignorance, the Irremediable Ignorance, the Particular Ignorance, the Inuoluntary Ignorance, and the Ignorance of what one is not obliged to know; seem to make the Action Vn-willing and to excuse it; but the other Ignorances, ar held, not only not to excuse the Fault; but in many Cases, instead of Diminishing it, to Augment it. |f. 104|

Where it is also to be obserued that all these Kinds of Ignorance, whither they be excusable or not; hinder any Action don throu them, to be truly Vertuus: and therefor, tis enuf that they can obtaine Pardon without aspiring to deserue Prayse.

There arises heer a Considerable Question, whither or no those Actions ar to be esteemed properly don throu Ignorance, that a man dos when he is transported with a fit of Anger, or when he is Drunke, since in those Cases, a man's Mind is so ouer-clowded with Wine, and Choler, that he knos not what he dos,

came from Aquinas (*The Structure of Caroline Moral Theology* 47 and 57).

[21] Such theft was common in the seventeenth century.

Book Two, Chapter Three

and is sorry for it afterwards?[22] To which they answer, that it is one thing to commit a Fault Ignorantly, and another to commit it by Ignorance. He is said to Sin By Ignorance, to whom Ignorance is the Impulsiue [illeg.] cause (or Motiue) of the Euil he has don, which he wud not haue don, had he known it. As when a Vertuus man [illeg.] marrys his owne Sister, that he knos not to be his Sister. |f. 104| But he is said to do a thing Ignorantly, (or Ignoringly) that while he dos it, ignores indeed what he dos; but yet so, that the <principall> Cause of the Action is not his Ignorance, but som other thing. As when Lot had to do with his 2 dauters; he did it indeed Ignoringly, but not by Ignorance; for the fault proceeded not from his Ignorance, but his Drunkenness; which occasion'd his Ignorance.[23] This premised; we answer to the Question, that those Kind of Action ar not to be esteemed Inuoluntary; because they ar don meerly Ignorantly and not by Ignorance; which is heer but a Concomitant of ↑the Principall Causes,↓ Anger or Drunkenness; which being in our Power to moderate or Auoid, renders the Action Voluntary; or (at least) don by an Ignorance, which hauing vn-necessarily drawn vpon our selues, makes vs guilty of all the Euils [th] it produces; since according to the Maxime of the Logicians, Causa causa, est etiam causa Causati; That which is the Cause of any thing, is the Cause of that also, where of that thing is Cause.[24] |f. 105|

Commonly indeed men are more Easily induc't to forgiue those Iniurys that haue been don them out of Passion or Drunkenness, then when one is in a Sober and settled Temper of Mind: because in Choler and Wine men's Iniurys looke less as if they were intended to offend; and ar commonly more repented of afterwards. But if we consider the Offences then giu'n as Publick; then Aristotle with the most of the Moralists, wud haue such People doubly punish't; first, (to omit the Ill Example they giue) for the Drunkenness it self, and then for the Fault they commit by it.[25] But it were not amiss to distinguish Drunkenness, [A] Choler, and their like, into Habituall and Actuall: the Actions that proceed from the Actual, (specially if the Motiue that occasion'd it be potent and Violent) seem to deserue som kind of Excuse, for the fore-alleadged Reasons: but <in> those that proceed from Customary Drunkenness, (and the like) the Drunkenness seem rather to Aggrauate the |f. 105[v]| Faults then Diminish it; partly for Aristotle's Reason's, as because that Custom, that produces the Euill, was first produc't by it.[26] And generally we are to obserue, that tho towards men, those Faults that we do out of an ill-contracted Custom, if [they illeg.] we endeuor to Preuent their Doing and repent their Being don; seem to deserue som kind of Pitty and

[22] Cf. Nich. Eth. III.v.8, 15.

[23] Gen. 19:30-38.

[24] Alsted 450.

[25] For references to Pittacus's severe sentence, see Nich. Eth. III.v.8 or the *Rhetoric* II.xxv.7.

[26] Cf. Nich. Eth. III.v.10-12. RB discussed the power of custom in "Of Sin."

Extenuation: yet ↑if we consider them in↓ themselues, the Case stands otherwise, For The Vse of Sinning lessens not the Guilt; and The Sin of Custom, came from the Custom of Sin.

Thus far of Inuoluntary Actions; by which we may easily comprehend the Nature of Willing Actions, which are those [illeg.] whose Principle or cause is in the Agent himself, and he too knoing all the Circumstances of the Fact, or Action. Now the Principle or Cause of the Action is then said to be in the Agent; when ↑there is↓ no out ward Violence to constraine him, but he acts according to the Command of his Will, guided by the |f. 106| Dictates of his Reason.

Thus much of the Kinds of Moral Actions; now let vs proceed to the Principles of Voluntary Actions, which are two-fold; First an Act of the Vnderstanding, namely, Consultation; and Secondly an Act of the Will, which is againe Double, to wit Simple (or Meere) which is particularly called Volitio; or restrain'd and Determinated, which is called, Election.

Consultation is a Ratiocination, (or Discoursiue enquiry) of the meanes [to] by which the Proposed End may be obtained.[27] Wherefore the things that fall vnder Deliberation, ar the Means that wee think conducible to obtaine the proposed End; but not the End, as End; because that belongs to the Volition, and in all Consultations is to be presuppoz'd. Now Deliberation is to be vsed only in Bisnesses, 1. Doubtfull and somwhat Incertain. 2. That concern our selues. For tho we oftentimes consult of the Bisnesses of our Frends and Clients, yet it is because |f. 106v| Interessing our selues in them; we be[e]leeue to be concern'd in their Affaires. 3. And in those things where the Reason and Power of Man is able to do something, and worke som alteration. For no man deliberates of those things that ar aboue the reach of his Reason and Power to worke vpon: as ar things Past, Necessary, ↑Meerly Natural,↓ Impossible, and the like. As (For Example) no man will Deliberate whither [Au] Cesar be Ded or No; or whither the Sun wil rise to morrow or no: ↑or whether he [must] shud drink vp the Sea or no,↓ or whether he must euer Dy or no, and the like. Now Dout differs from Deliberation in that Dout is the Gender, and Deliberation the Species; besides that we often dout of those things that concern vs not, and ar out of the reach of our Power: as whether the Earth moues or stands stil, and whither the [M] Sun be of a Firy Constitution, or warms only by his motion: and a world of other things, that com not into Deliberation.[28] There is no Deliberation without som Dout, but there are |f. 107| many Douts without Deliberation.[29] But the Art of

---

[27] For discussion of deliberation, see Nich. Eth. III.iii.1-20.

[28] RB's examples of scholastic topics that did not warrant deliberation differed sharply from Arist.'s (III.iii.3-9): "nobody deliberates about things eternal, such as the order of the universe, or the incommensurability of the diagonal and the side of a square . . . [or] solstices and the sunrise . . . [or] droughts and rains."

[29] Barbara J. Shapiro reviews the changing notions of probability and the grounds of persuasion

Consulting being one of the Dutys of Prudence, [illeg.] requires to be marshal'd vnder that Vertu, whereunto I refer the Reader.

Volition, (or Willingness, or, the Act of Willing) is an Appetition of a Tru or [Apparent] Seeming Good with Reason. [Where it is to be obserued, that as there is a two-fold Good that is the Object of the Will, and one Reall, and the other only Apparent: so there is a two-fold Reason, that apprehends each its seuerall Good; the one Riht, that embraces the Tru Good, the other Seduc't, that approues that which is only Specius.] Of this Volition an inseparable Affection is Liberum Arbitrium, or man's Free-will; which [is by som described to be, A Power or Faculty of the Soule (tho others wil haue it a Modus of the Will)] (leauing the Many [of] other Significations of the Word, [ne] as needless to our purpose) we heere take to be that Power or Faculty, whereby it may at Plesure, Will or Nill, [dis] |f. 107v| Approue or Dislike, Prosecute or Decline the thing Proposed.[30] Wherefore, to skip ouer those Endless, (and oftentimes vseles) disputes, that the Diuines and Schoolmen shouel vp vpon this Subject; we wil onely [illeg.] heere set down the most Christian and Rationall Opinion; which is, that tho in Spirituall and [Theologicall] ↑Supernaturall↓ Matters, the Will be not indifferent to Good and Euill, but (not withstanding its Liberty) cannot but Sin (1 Cor. 2; and 2 Cor. 3,5.) yet in the Exercice of Ciuill Vertus, [of] (and Œconomicall Arts) a man out of his owne Free-wil may giue himself either to Vertu or Vice, and approue or disapproue the thing proposed, as himself pleases: and by consequent that it is naturally in his Power to be Virtuus or Vitius as himself will. And that the Will of man is altogether Free in Outward and Ciuil Bisnesses, may easily be proued, 1. By Experience, which [euidences] witnesses that we can (For Example) Drink or not Drink too much; giue away |f. 108| Or not giue away our mony, and the like. 2. Because Liberty is an Inseparable affection of the Will, and cannot be taken away without destroying the very Nature of the Will it selfe, and make it of a Will, a Nill. 3. And because otherwise in Vaine or iniust were all Laws, Reward's, Punishments, Præcepts, Prayers, Exhortations, and the like. This Liberum Arbitrium belongs to the Intellect as the Fountaine, Principle and Director of it; but to the Will as the Party that makes vse of it and puts it in Practice. Or, as the Schoolmen speake, it is Radically in the Vnderstanding, but Formally in the Will.[31]

Election, or Choice, is a Premeditated Appetition of those things that ar in our Power to do. Tho this Choice be very neere of kin to Volition, yet in this they differ, that Volition principally regards the End; Election is busied about

---

in *Probability and Certainty in Seventeenth-Century England* (Princeton 1983).

[30] Cf. Alsted 1248.

[31] For the debate about whether virtue was located in the will (as Ames contended) or the practical intellect (as Perkins argued), see Fiering 61. RB owned a substantial collection of works by both authors.

the Meanes: Election is cheefly employ'd about those means that concern vs, and ar in our Power, whereas the Will oftentimes regards those things that neither |f. 108v| Concern vs, nor ar in our Power. The Will tends to a certin [log] End; but the Election is a choise amongst diuers thinges. Tis tru, that after an Election amongst diuers meanes, the chozen meanes become the Object of the Will; but not as means, but as Ends. For Example, War is chozen as the fittest means to acquire a Kingdom: but after one has once resolu'd and concluded for War, then War is considered as the End, and [and] meanes and helps ar souht for to make the Warr.

There is also a greate deale of Difference betwixt Election and Opinion; For the End of the One is Good, of the other, Truth: againe, the Subiect of Opinion is all things, that of Election only what is in our Power. Besides that by our Election of Good or Euil we ar termed Good or Euil our selues; but not so by our Opinion; for no man will beleeue another wise or Valiant meerly because he thinkes himself to be so. |f. 109| Lastly, tho there be an Inseparable Coherence betwixt Consultation and Election; yet they differ, 1. In the Subject, that [being] belonging more to the Vnderstanding; This, to the Will. 2. In the Object; that being about things doutfull and Incertin; this of things esteemed Certin because of the Preceding Consultation. Wherefore 3. That, in order of Time Precedes, this, followes.

This Doctrine of Willingness and Constraint is very vsefully deliuered in the Ethickes; because they greatly vary the Nature and Condition of our Action; and teach vs to judge cleerly of many Particular Cases, wherein otherwise, we shud but grope after the Truth.[32]

[32] RB's interest in casuistry is indicated in this discussion of motivation.

Book Two, Chapter Three

|f. 112|

Chapter IIII.

Of the les Principal Efficients of Moral Vertu

The les Principal [or] Efficient Causes of, or Subsidiary Helps to Morall Vertu, are branched into 2 sorts: Naturall and Acquisite. And the Former of these 2 belong, either to the Body or to the Mind.

That Natiue secundary Cause that belongs to the Body, is, a Good Temperament, or, a Helthfull, exact, and wel-proportion'd constitution of the 4 Humors. (Whereby the Body is enabled readyly to execute all those functions that ar required of it.) And this certainly is no contemptible help to Moral Vertu. For how much the [m] giddiness of the Spirits and the |f. 112v| Corruption of the Humors dos vitiate and depraue the functions of the Soule, the dayly experience of Frantick men's Actions may abundantly informe vs. And tho that receiued Axion of Galen, Mores animi sequuntur Temperamentum Corporis;[1] if precisely taken, be far more Famouse then True: [yet cer] (as has been already demonstrated) yet certainly; since the Soule, tho not in Being, yet in Acting, depends much vpon the Organes of the Body; we must be forced to allow, that the Harmony of the Humors, and the Purity of the Blood (which makes the Spirits cleere, actiue, and firm) are Helps to Vertu not to be contemned.[2] Now the Best Constitution is held to be a Sanguine Temper Bordering vpon Melancholy: being a fit Mixture of the two Extreames.[3] |f. 113| Hence we may see how ayry is the Doctrine of the Magititians about the Power they attribute to Pretious Stones and other Naturall things to confer such and such Vertus: For those but Dispose the Body and these but Incline the Mind.[4]

As for the Mind, there ar also in it certin natiue and inborn Seeds and Principles of Vertu; whereof some are to be found generally in all men, others onely in Vertuus Dispositions. And of the first sort, som Moralists not vnfitly reckon

---

[1] Alsted 1249.

[2] For a contemporary review of the humors, see Reynolds, *Treatise* (1640), ch. 1.

[3] Cf. Alsted, "Hîc excellit temperamentum sanguineum melancholico proximum: quia sanguis lætitiam parit, quam moderata melancholia temperat" (1249). Arist. maintained that the best philosophers, statesmen, poets, and artists had melancholic temperaments (*Problemata* XXX.1). The *locus classicus* for this topic is Robert Burton's *Anatomy of Melancholy* (1621); RB owned a 1676 edition, but there were many earlier editions.

[4] For acute analysis of sympathetic magic, see Thomas, *Decline*, ch. 7-9. In Table 1, note essay #16. Of the Weapon-salve, and occult Qualitys. Also relevant is Michael Hunter's "Alchemy, magic and moralism in the thought of Robert Boyle," *BJHS* 23 (1990) 387-410.

vp three, viz, the Law of Nature, Synteresis, and Conscience.[5]

The Law of Nature is that Naturall Liht of Knowledg or that inborn Law of God, that he lites in euery mans heart, showing vs the Difference between Good and Euill. |f. 113v| Out of which flow Ius Naturæ and Ius gentium: (of which more in another Place.)[6]

Synteresis (say they) is that which inclines and fits vs to giue assent to those Practical Principles, that the Law of Nature holds forth and comprehends.

Conscience is that applying Faculty of the Mind, which Excuses or Condemnes: and therefor may be termed A Sens of God's Iudgment of our Actions. Or a Coppy (or Counterpart) of th<ose> Records which God keeps in heu'n of euery man's Doings.[7]

The Rudiments of the Law of Nature ar in our Harts, but the Lineaments ar in the ten Commandements. That is the Embrio whereof this is the Child.[8] ↑This made the Apostle say of the Gentiles, that they had The Work of the Law ritten in their Hearts.↓[9] For the Liht of Nature and meere humane Reason tels euery man that There is a God, whom (by consequent) we ar bound, |f. 114| Both to Loue and Adore: As also that we ought to Loue our Neibor's as our Selues: when the Pagan Emperor Seuerus his Motto was, Quod tibi fieri non vis, alteri ne feceris.[10] Now these 2 ar the Summary of the Decalogue, as Christ himselfe teaches, Matthew 22.[11] And this Cicero cals very fitly, Non scripta, sed nata Lex.[12] But because th[e]is Vniversall Malice and Wickedness of men, did continually endeauour, not onely to Forget, but euen to efface and blot out this Law of Nature; therefore the Wisdom of God thouht it expedient, to preuent that Designe, and both Ratify and Expound that Law of Nature in the Decalogue: which is a Commentary vpon that, as all the Laws in the World ar but Commentarys vpon this. |f. 115|

For both the Law of Nature is the Epitome of the Decalogue, (as we haue showne already) and in the Decalogue, each Syllable is so Big with Sence, that out of it the Iewish Doctors haue collected the 612 Laws of Moses: and their

---

[5] Fiering has an excellent discussion of these concepts as used by Perkins and Ames (52-62).

[6] In *Style* 2.291, RB stated that the light of nature and the Gospels contained all things necessary for salvation.

[7] Cf. Alsted 1249. "Lex naturæ & synteresis formant propositionem in syllogismo practico, conscientia assumtionem & conclusionem."

[8] Cf. Alsted 1249, "Lex naturæ in corde hominis est quoad rudimenta, in Decalogo quoad lineamenta."

[9] Romans 2:15.

[10] Anon., *Scriptores Historiæ Augustæ* 1.18.51.8.1.

[11] Matt. 22:34-40.

[12] Alsted quoted generously (1250) from Cicero's *Pro Milone* 10.3-5, though the quotation was also found in Cicero's *Orator* 165.4. See also Fiering (60) for similar statements by Bacon, Ames, Reynolds, and others.

Rabbies do affirm that on euery Word of the Commandements dos depend those Myriads of Sentences.[13]

The Synteresis can neuer be thorouly [exiced from] <Extinguished in> the Soule of Man; tho somtimes the Clouds of Impetuous Affections, and the long Custom of sinning do for a Time eclipse it: but for all these [fits of] Lethargick fits, it neuer Dyes in man but with him.

As for the Conscience, there's no[w] body that (in som measure) knos not what it is, tho euery one be not able to expresse it. Now a man's Conscience is |f. 115v| Such, as ar his Actions. Whence arises that vsual Distinction of Conscience into Good or Euill; that waiting vpon a Vertuus Life, this is a Vitius. (I meane not euery particular Action but the Whole Current of the Life.) And as a Bad Conscience is a Mouing hell, so is a Good one, a Perpetual Feast, and a Heu'n vpon Erth.[14]

After euery moral Action follows an Inward Syllogism; wherein the Law of Nature and the Synteresis make the Major, and the Conscience the Minor and the Conclusion: and this Syllogism, is, (as the Conscience it self) either Absoluing or Condemning; i.e. pronouncing, Not-guilty, or Guilty. For Example, After the Chast Iosef had refused the adulterous Embraces of his lustfull Mistress;[15] the Law of Nature instantly says within him, |f. 116| Whosoueur dos refraine from committing Adultery (specially if sollicited thereunto by the Allurements of aduantage, and the Terror of Threatnings) in doing so, dos wel: to which Principle the Synteresis assenting; the Conscience makes this Assumption; Atqui I haue don so; and from thence draws this Conclusion, Ergo, I haue don Well: and from this [Conclusion] Iudgment of the Conscience follows a Secret and vnspeakable Ioy and Satisfaction. Contrarywise; In the Bisnes of Dauid and Bathsheba,[16] his Law of Nature and Synteresis, say thus; Whosoeuer committeth Adultery, (and Murder,) sinneth: whence his Conscience argues thus, Atqui I haue done so: Ergo I haue sinned. And from this Definitiue Sentence |f. 116v| Of the Conscience, proceeded that vnparalleld Sorrow and Anxiety of Mind, which we find so feelingly exprest in the Booke of Salms.

In the Temple of Vertu (says one very wel) the Law of Nature is the Foundation, Synteresis, the Chambers, and Conscience the Roofe; For the First sustains it: the Second adorns and vpholds it; and the Thurd; as when it is kept in repaire, keepes out the Storms of Vices and vnruly Passions; so if it be [let]

---

[13] Alsted 1249; in *Style*, RB mentioned that the Jews reduced "the whole law to 613 precepts, affirmative and negative, according to the number of the letters of the decalogue" (2.290).

[14] H408 and M969.

[15] Gen. 39:1-18. Cf. RB's meditation on "Joseph's Mistress" below. This example was also found in Alsted.

[16] 2 Sam. 11:1-26.

↑suffer'd to↓ fall to Delapidations, lets them in.[17]

Those Natural Principles of Vertu that ar more Peculiar; ar certin Inclining Seeds or Dispositions vnto such and such Vertus, which ar not without distinction bestowed vpon all men; but appropriated to certin |f. 117| Ingenuus Natures [and] or Dispositions. And that there is [no] such a Diuersity of Inclinations, needs no other Witness then Experience, which dayly shos vs, that to som Nature has been so liberall of her Endowments that they ar Born Vertuus, or at least become so, they scarce know how themselues: whereas others com into the World with such potent Inclinations to Vice, that their whole Life seems but a Continuall Warfare against their irregular dispositions; and they ar faine to toyle and sweat for the acquiring of those Vertus, that the others attaine to with Plesure and Ease. These Dispositions flow (for the most part) from the Temperament of the Body, and the Aspects of the Starres; and in their possession, [d] the tru Naturall Nobility dos (cheefly) consist.[18] |f. 117v|

Now of these Steps to or Principles of Morall Vertu, there may be as many as ther <ar> Vertus themselues to which they do incline vs. Authors diuie and reckon them euery one as best pleases himselfe. But the most Notable [do som] ↑(besides those treated of in Ch. the 7.)↓[19] are these that follow: whereof som haue relation to our Selues, and som to others. [Of]

Of the First sort ar, 1. Natural Abstinence, consisting in a certin Contempt or Disregard of bodily Plesures, which may be somtimes obserued in Children themselues. 2. The Thirst of Prayse and Glory. Such as was conspicuus in Themistocles, who being before a deboyst young man, and beginning to consume whole nihts in walking the Streets; asked the Reason of it, answered, that the Trophees of Miltiades wud not suffer him to sleepe.[20] [4] 3. Patience or Tolerancy Naturall, bordering vpon Obstinacy; |f. 118| whereby men do manfully vndergo labours and Difficultys, and beare out constantly afflictions and

---

[17] Cf. Alsted 1248-49 for RB's source of this image.

[18] While RB was dismissive about "mercenary astrologers" below (bk. 2, ch. 6) and in his later career rejected judiciary astrology (*Languid Motion* 5.51), he did not question the premises of astrology for explaining human personality. Far from being sceptical, he wanted to investigate how physico-astrological effects operate, as was shown in his correspondence with Hartlib. Hartlib wrote that "Mr. *Worsley* is expecting still some engagement upon his physico-astrological letter: but except I have an account from *Oxford* upon the fore-said letter, I am forbidden farther communications" (6.97). RB's letter to Hartlib (5.638-45) about astrology was perhaps this response, thus dating it about 1657 or 1658. See also *Cert. Phys. Essays* 1.346. For helpful modern perspectives, see Patrick Curry, ed. *Astrology, Science and Society: Historical Essays* (Woodbridge 1987) and Michael Hunter and Annabel Gregory, eds., *An Astrological Diary of the Seventeenth Century: Samuel Jeake of Rye, 1652-1699* (Oxford 1988). At the birth of each child Cork carefully recorded the astrological sign.

[19] In that chapter RB discussed the degrees of moral virtue, including half-virtues and heroic virtue.

[20] See Plutarch, *Life of Themistocles*. Miltiades was regarded as a great tyrant.

Crosses. [5] 4. Stoutness of Mind against Dangers and Difficultys. Of the Second sort are 1. Natural Equity, louing to giue euery one his due, and hating to see anyone wronged or Defrauded. Which I haue seen bud forth in diuerse in the very Infancy of their Age. 2. Communicatiueness of Nature, scorning to hord things vp, and apt to bestow them where one likes.[21] 3. Mercyfullness of Disposition, whereby a man ↑is easily wrouht vpon to forgiue repented of Iniurys and↓ dos not insult ouer another's misery, but is apt to haue a compassionate feeling of it, and to releeue. 4. Faithfulnes, in [st] keeping ones word, and sticking close to one's Frend; and 5. Secrecy in keeping another's counsel. 6. Naturall Courtesy or Humanity, consisting in an Esiness of Accesse |f. 118^{v}| and an Obliging Behauior. These ar the principal Demy-Vertus, which ar therefore cal'd Naturall, because they ar born with vs, and ar discernable in Children themselues. Their Contrary Dispositions ar termed Semi-Vices.

It is a Quære not vn-worthy the Resoluing, whither man be naturally enclin'd to Vertu or else to Vice. To which 'tis answered.

1. That if we speake of Theological Vertus, Man, that to Ciuil Vertu has no mor weiht then a Fether, to Diuine is as liht as Ayre: and he that in the former is but Purblind, in the Latter has no Eyes at all. (But this Discourse reapes the Diuine's haruest.)

2. But in Relation to Morall or meerly Ciuill Vertus; that which ([under] til better information) I conceiue most probable, (to waue the tedious and intricate |f. 119| Disputations of the Schoolmen) is this.[22] That man being composed of 2 principall Ingredients, the Rational Part, and the Animall; the former whereof is that Spirituall soule, which makes him Companion to the Angels; and the Latter, that Body, and all that he holds in common with the Beasts: either of these Parts is [incli] naturally inclin'able to that good, which (in som sort) is answerable to it's owne nature: the Soule to Truth and Vertu; and the Body to Bodily Delights. Now because it happens for the most part, that those sensuall [Delihts] Plesures that the Outward man affects (or at least[s] in that degree that it affects them) straying [out] beyond [of] the [Bounds] limits of reason, do so wrap vp their Vitiusnes in their Pleasantness, that a man can not swallow downe this Bait, without taking in also that hooke; therefore it |f. 119^{v}| Fals out, that while the Propensity of the Animall Part, determined to those Plesures that ar twisted together in one Cord with Vice; pursuing a seeming Good, it settles, (By

---

[21] In 1647-48 RB wrote "An invitation to a free and generous communication of secrets," which Hartlib published in 1655 as part of his *Chymical, Medicinal and Chyurgical Adresses* (1655). (M.E. Rowbottom first noted this publication in "The Earliest Published Writing of Robert Boyle," *Ann. of Sci.* 6 [1950] 376-89.) On 3 July 1649 RB wrote an essay to Hartlib on communicativeness (Boyle Lett. 6.3) which covered much of the same ground; for the heads of an essay on public-spiritedness, see BP 36.62.

[22] This explanation is typical of Scholastic ethics. Cf. Fiering, 81-2, where he analyzes Eustache's response to the question "whether vice is contrary to nature."

Accident) in most things, vpon a Reall Euill. And thus the Reasonable part of man is naturally inclin'd to Good; and the Animal, naturally, (tho by accident) set vpon Euill. But because in the most part of men the Pusillanimity of the Reasonable part, giues leaue (as it were) to the vnruly Affections, to snath out of it's hand that Scepter of Power whereby Nature had enabled it to keepe them in aw; and that Sensible Plesures do most sensibly affect vs, (it being far more easy to [illeg.] debase the [An] Reasonable Part then to sublime the Animall) it happens that in most men, the |f. 120| Inclination to Vertu is les potent then the Propensity to Vice. Tho in sundry Persons, the [Stren] Natural Cleernes and Strength of their Reason, Good Education, or the Diuine Assistance, do ouersway the Bent of the Affections, and make a man les inclinable to Euil then to Good.[23]

THE Acquired Secondary Causes of Morall Vertu, are all Generally included in this one Word of Education; whereof [our] the Scope our Dessein not giuing vs leaue for the present to make a large Discourse (which we intend, God willing, in a Particular Treatise) we will now be content summarily to deliuer the Motiues to it, and the Manner of it.[24] |f. 120v|

For the First, The Motiues ar obuius and, better knowne then taken notice of: To which miht be vsefully added the [Consideration] Meditation of these and the like places of Scripture.[25] But to the vulgar Inducements (which for this time I must skip ouer) I shal desire the Reader to ad, these 2 Important, and, (for the most part) vnheeded Considerations.

The First shall be, That man, as we haue partly seen before, coms into the World without any proper Inclination either to Vertu or Vice (I meane Ciuil, not Theological) but only with this Principle, that he seeks a Good. And so, as either Vertu or Vice is made appeare Good or Euil vnto him, he either embraces, or rejects it. Now most men, (as we haue already declar'd) being |f. 121| in the Infancy of their Age inclined, Naturally (tho by accident) to those sensuall Pleasures that ar Vitius; it happens, that if either these <Euill> Inclinations be seconded by <an> euill Nurture; or Reason be not excited, directed and

---

[23] This view of human nature is very different from the emphasis on human depravity found in Calvin's *Institutes*, a work in which Marcombes daily tutored RB (*II Lismore* 4.100-01).

[24] In the lengthy insertion that follows, RB presented material not included in MS 192. He sketched his notions of education, emphasizing the "Motives and Manner" of education. His treatise should thus be read in the light of other works on the *reform* of education associated with the Hartlib and Comenius circle. The most famous work is John Milton's *Of Education* (1644), which was dedicated to Hartlib; but John Hall contributed *An Humble Motion to the Parliament . . . Concerning the Advancement of Learning* (1649), and William Petty provided *The Advice of W. P. to Mr. Samuel Hartlib. For the Advancement . . . of Learning* (1648). Webster's *Instauration*, ch. 3, is an invaluable guide to the reformers' plans; see also Charles Webster, ed. *Samuel Hartlib and the Advancement of Learning* (Cambridge 1970). Milton briefly tutored Lady Ranelagh's children and, like Hartlib, ran a small school.

[25] Cf. "Dayly Reflection" and *Occ. Refl.* for examples.

strengthned by Education, and the Children, as they ar capable, made to vnderstand, that the tru Good consists not in these transitory plesures of the Body, but in the Vertuus Contentments of the Mind;[26] otherwise, I say, it happens for the most part that the Animall part being then in it's greatest vigor, <heiht> and the sensuall appetites then most vnmanageable, whereas the Reasonable faculty, either not at all, or but very faintly exercises it's functions; |f. 121v| that the Sensual Part dos either by and enticing the rationall, draw it to comply or to a concurrence with it self in the Opinion of Good: or else when Reason, now com to maturity, wud slip it's neck out of the Yoake; the Affections (pleading prescription) haue so long and so perfectly enthralled it, and ar so habituated to domineere, that it is vnable to shake of that Yoake, whereof it miht easily haue impeach't the putting on.

The Second shall be, that such as we breed our Children, such must we expect our Magistrates, our Ministers, nay Our All, when they com to be men. It being a Vanity to looke for Pepins from that Stock whereon we neuer graffed but Crabs.[27] Wherefore |f. 122| Lycurgus amongs the Lacedemonians did very wisely ordaine, that a matter of so Publique a Concernment, shud be entrusted to the Care of the Publique Magistrate: thinking it an egregious peece of folly to be so carefull of the Goods of the men and so neglectful of making the men Good; and esteeming it (perhaps) no great peece of Iustice to hang those for stealing that were neuer whipt for Pilfering.[28]

The Same Lycurgus tauht his Spartans the Power of Education by this pretty deuice. He had 2 whelps of the same Sire and Bitch to be bred, the one in the Kitchin and the other in the Kennel to hunt; Which being one day produc't both together before the People; and hauing |f. 122v| commanded Meat to be set before them, and a Hare also to be let loose; the Hunting-dog presently fals a running after the Hare, and the Kitchin-Cur fals as greedily to his Vittles. Lo, says Lycurgus then, do yow not see how vnlike these 2 whelps (to whom Nature gaue the same Inclinations) ar made by their vnlike Educations: and how much Education conduces more to Vertu, then very Nature.[29]

Now as for the Manners of Education, [as much] ↑so far forth↓ as will serue our present purpose (for the full and Exact handling of it properly belongs to the Œconomicks) we wil (breefly) include it in these 10 particulars. Namely that a man be 1. Seasonably (or Betimes) instructed, in the 2. Doctrine of Vertu; 3. Engaged (and persuaded) to it by Solid Reasons, and conuincing Arguments; 4. Stir'd up and excited to it by Good Examples; 5. Maintain'd and warm'd |f.

[26] Cf. the epigraph to this volume: "That's the tru Good that makes the owner so." RB owned such works as Jeremiah Burroughes's *The Rare Jewel of Christian Contentment* (1649).

[27] Cf. C788.

[28] Source unknown.

[29] Plutarch, *Moralia* 3B ("The Education of Children") and 225F ("Sayings of the Spartans").

123| in the Loue of it by Good company: 6. ↑Excited to Goodnes by Emulation <Praise> and Reward, and deterred from Vice by fit Correction.↓ 7. heihtned in it by Generous Ends and Aims; [illeg.] and after all this tauht to know his Proficiency or Vnproficiency therein. ↑8. Settled in an honest Vocation. 9. Refresht with Lawfull Recreations, and 10. tauht to conuerse with himselfe.↓[30] And at either of these we will tuch in their Order; And,

I.

For the First. That Education shud begin Erly or Betimes, is very Necessary: Children being like Corrall, which newly pul'd out of the Sea, dos easily receiue any Impression; but being once let alone in the Aire, dos so harden, <with time> that it becoms capable of none but what Nature giues it.[31] What Iustice is it to expect a Crop from that Field in the Haruest, that we neuer tooke the Paines to sow in the Spring.[32] Sure, Education has little less power to dispose men to Vertu or Vice then Nature: and more men becom Bad or Good that ar Bred so, then that ar Born so.[33] |f. 187|

And it is generally obserued, that the Greatest Spirits if vncultiuated by Education, proue the Worst: as the Richest Soiles, if one lets them ly fallow, ar most fruitful in Weeds and Thistles.[34] Men of Great Parts, being always, either very Good or Extreamly Bad; like those Spirits that were neuer clothed with Bodys, either Angels, or Deuils. Heerein truly, most men ar very Faulty, who not only suffer, but euen Welcom and applaud the first Essays of Sin in their Children and allow them to do any thing whilst they ar Little, neuer considering, that the Sin grows with the Child, and when It coms to be a Man, that coms to be a Vice. Whereas indeed, Euil in Children shud be nip't in the very Bud; for they that wil Laf at their Children's Faults, shal haue occasion to Weepe for their Vices. Wise Solomon tels vs, (Pro. 22,15) that Foolishnes is bound in the Hart of a Child; but the Rod of correction shal driue it far from him[h]. Wherefore says he |f. 187v| (Pro. 19,18) Chasten thy Son while there is hope, and let not thy Soul spare for his Crying. For, (Pro. 29,15) The Rod and Reproue giue Wisdom: but a Child left to himself bringeth his Mother to shame. Wherefor says he again (Pro. 13,24) He that spareth his Rod, hateth his Son; but he that loueth him, chastneth him betimes. For indeed, tis somewhat of the latest, to begin to oppose Sin,

---

[30] RB also explored these themes in "Dayly Reflection" and "Doctrine of Thinking."

[31] Browne summarized modern views of coral in *Pseud. Epidemica* 1.134-35 . For RB's later references to coral, see *Fluidity and Firmness* 1.435, *Occ. Refl.* 2.455, and *Orig. of Forms* 3.59.

[32] Gal. 6:7.

[33] RB wrote in the margin, "(Turn onward til yow com to this Marke)." His discussion of moral education runs from ff. 187-231.

[34] This proverb (C668) can be traced to Plato's *Republic* VI.6. RB used it again in this work (bk. 2, ch. 6) and in *Occ. Refl.* 2.394.

when Faults by Indulgence ar hardned into Vices, and Vices by Custome ar turned into Manners. And it was not without Resons that one said, that He that wil not vse the Rod on his Child, his Child shal be vsed as a Rod on him.[35] ↑And tho Children, as long as they ar Children, be not capable of exercising the perfect operations of Vertu; yet it is very good to vse them to those Axions wherein Vertu (Materially) dos consist. For the Heathen Poet cud tel vs to this Purpose, Quo semel est and, that is, New Vessels do the odor long retaine of the first liquor that they do containe.↓[36] It seems most Parents ar afeard their Children shud be Vertuus too soone; and think the Lees of a man's Life good enuf for God. [illeg.] As if God were bound to accept of the Dry Bones, when the Diuel has suckt out all the Marrow. But I'm sure Solomon teaches them an other Lesson, when he bids them (Ecc. 12,1.) Remember now thy Creator in the Days of thy Youth, |f. 188| while the Euil days com not, nor the Yeers draw Nih; when thou shalt say, I haue no Pleasure in them. And, (Pro. 22,6) Train vp a Child in the Way he shud go, and when he is old, he wil not depart from it. What a happy thing is it, when Parents, like Hannah, (1. Sam. 1,11,) giue their Children vnto the Lord, All the Days of their Liues, and dedicate them to God from the very Womb! When a man's <Conscience> can say to his God, as Good Obadiah sayd to the Profet (1 Kings, 18,12) I thy Seruant feare the Lord from my Youth; and can [say] <speake> truly of the Commandements [as] <what> the Young man said Boastingly (Matt, 19,20) All these things haue I kept from my Youth. God always required in his Sacrifices, the First Fruits, the First born, and Lambs without blemish, to sho vs how much he [illeg.] affected [illeg.] the First fruits of our Yeares, and perfectest part our Age, and how much he expected that the Best master shud be first serued. Vertu is somwhat a Coy mistress, and perhaps wil be very shy of accepting of the leauings of that Strumpet, Vice: And for my Part, I must confess, that I thinke it but a very Bad Symptom, then only to |f. 188v| Thinke of going to God, when one is ready to go out of the World, and to make Religion, our Refuge, not our Choice.

II.

For the Second. It is douted, whether or no Vertu can be tauht, and Lerning do Conduce to the Practice of Vertu?[37] To which it is answered. 1. That a man may very wel be Vertuus, without the Knoledg of that Science we call <the> Ethickes, or Morals. For it is very possible for a man to extract and practice the

---

[35] Cf. R153, "He has made a rod for his own tail" and F122, "He that corrects not small faults cannot control great ones."

[36] Horace, *Epistolae* 1.2.69.

[37] Arist. considered young men unsuitable for studying ethics (Nich. Eth. I.iii.5); Alsted disagreed (1349).

Rules of Wel liuing, out of the Liht of his owne Reason, and the obseruation of other men's Actions. And indeed, History dos witness, that there were many famous Heros and men Eminently Vertuus, ↑(as all the Patriarcks and almost all the Prophets and Worthys of the Old Testament.)↓ before euer there were any Books of Ethicks writ in the World. (Aristotle, who, according to Alstedius, dy'ed about the Year of the World 3618, being the first Noted compiler of the Ethickes into a Body of Doctrine.)[38] And for these latter Times Experience testifys the same: |f. 189| many in <these> our days being [very w excellently wel vers't in] ↑intimately familiar with↓ the Practise of Vertu, who ar vtterly vnacquainted with it's Definition.

2. The Doctrine of Vertu alone dos not suffice to make a man Vertuus. <For> All the Definitions, Precepts, and Disputations in the World, can but instruct the Vnderstanding how to operate in Vertu; but cannot compell the Will and the Affections, to chuse and embrace it.[39] It being no Vnusuall Matter, for the Vnderstanding to submit to the Acknowledgment of that Truth, against which [the W] neuertheles the Wil and the Affections maintaine a Rebellion. Wherefore we see so many of your great learned men, that haue whole Oceans of Science, but scarce Drops of Conscience: who ar such Good Teachers and such bad Liuers, that they Confute their Doctrine by their Practice, and Condemn their Practice by their Doctrine. And indeed I haue always obserued, that those men, that haue [the] great Natural parts, and but little Morall, (I meane an Exquisite |f. 189v| Knoledg in a Knaue's keeping) proue the Dangerousest men in the World; whilst they make vse of that blazing Flame of their Reason, not to guide them in the Paths of Vertu, but to liht them to their Lusts. And that [Lea] Knoledg that shud be the Fisitian, is but the Katerer of their Appetites. Methinkes, these famous Good Moralists and bad men, that haue so much of Vertu in their Tongs that they haue none of it in their Harts; ar iust like the old Chalden Astrologers, who grew hoare-headed in the Contemplation of the Heuens; and spend their whole time in writing, disputing and Discoursing of them, and yet wer always depriued of their Enjoyment.[40] But what my Opinion is concerning the Doctrine of Vertu, I haue elswhere already deliuered; I wil onely now ad; that As a man may haue the exactest Notions in the World, of the [Nat] Essence, Definition, qualitys, and Effects of Fire; and yet be benummed with Cold; so a man may be |f. 190| extreamely knoing, in the Nature, Definition, Causes, Propertys, and Effects of Vertu; and yet for all those sublime Notions, ly wallowing in the Mire of sensual <swinish> Vices.

3. That the Knoledg of the Ethics, (I mean Ethicks Iudiciusly and Practically written,) is, tho not absolutely Necessary, yet extreamely helpefull, to the

[38] Alsted 2151.

[39] Cf. S475, "Compelled Sins are no Sins."

[40] For a similar example, see Nich. Eth. VI.vii.5-6.

Practice of Vertu. For how shall a man be able to decline Vitius, and exercice the Action of Vertu; without the tru Knoledg of those things, wherein the Nature of Vice and Vertu dos consist? And since the more a thing affects the Vnderstanding, the deeper impression it makes in the Will and the Affections; and since that the Loue of Good and the Hatred of Euil, ar as it were, the 2 Arms, wherewith we embrace Vertu, and thrust away Vice: how [sh] can we do either of them in that Degree that we shud, without the tru Knoledg both of Good and Euil? Man is not led by Instinct, like Beasts: the [Intellect] Vnderstanding must go before with a |f. 190v| Lantern, and then the Will, (that neuer moues, but to what is known) treads the Way it sees.[41] Tho the Intellect is not able to compel the Will, yet is it very powerful in persuading it. And the greater liht the Vnderstanding giues the Will, the better is the Will able to discern the Louelines of Vertu and the Deformity of Vice: and by consequent the More it is brouht to affect the one and detest the other. For when the Vnderstanding is enlihtned by the Knoledg of Truth, it inflames the Will with the Loue of Goodnes:[42] (so neer an Alliance [is] there is betwixt these 2 Perfections.) Hence Diuinity ↑by some,↓ has been not vnfitly termed, an Affectiue Science: because tho it reach to Contemplation, <it> ends in Practice, the Consideration of the Glory of God, kindling in vs a Zeale vnto it. Now altho we do not deny, <but> that, as we haue said before, the Knoledg of Vertu, may be had without that of the Ethickes; yet certinly it is very seldom attained, either so fully or so Exactly, and neuer so |f. 191| [soo] Quickly and so easily, without it as with it. For besides, that it discouers vnto vs, where the Pallace of Felicity is seated; and presents vs with the Doctrine of Morall Actions (deliuered in the foregoing Chapter) 2 Points, concerning which Mistakes ar very incident, to those that haue not refined their Reason by Discourse; it ransacks the very Cabinets of Reason and Time, to vnty for vs the knots of Intricate Disputations, and resolue vs of the Truth, in all doutfull Questions; to [furnish vs with a Treasury of the Pithy Apothegmes, and] chalke vs out the Paths we shud tread with <the most> excellent Precepts, and quicken vs therein with [heroick] the most noble Examples. In sum: A wel pen'd Ethick, is a Iudicius extract, in order to [Moral] Vertu, of all, that the Wisest men haue said, and the best men haue Done.

4. That [Learning] <Knoledge> (euen |f. 191v| in those Contemplatiue Sciences, as the Physics, Metafisics, and Mathematickes) dos greatly conduce to the

[41] RB wrote Marcombes in 1646 that his *Ethics* was to be "not only a lanthorn, but a guide" (1.xxxiv).

[42] In *Usefulness* 2.5, some of which was written about the same time as his moral essays, RB noted Pythagoras's saying that "there are two things, which most ennoble man, and make him resemble the gods; *to know the truth*, and *to do good*. For, *Pyrophilus*, that diviner part of man, the soul, which alone is capable of wearing the glorious image of its author, being endowed with two chief faculties, the understanding and the will; the former is blest and perfectionated by knowledge, and the latter's loveliest and most improving property is goodness."

Practice of Vertu.[43] For tho it happen oftentimes, as we haue already intimated, that those that haue (in the vulgar opinion) the best heads, haue the worst harts; yet this arriues, not through the Fault of the Lerning, but by the fault of the Man, who being vitiusly [en] disposed himself, makes vse of a thing, in it's owne Nature Good, ↑(or at least Indifferent)↓ to a Bad End. An Inconuenience incident to the most excellent things: since the Worst (and most [Dangerus] <Pernitius>) Abuse, is that of the best things. Now the Furtherance that Lerning affords to Vertu ar principally 4. ↑(To omit the many Similitudes and Comparisons, and, if youle pardon the Word, <frase> Allegories in things and Real Parables, that it presents vs withall.)↓[44] For 1. It instructs vs in many things, whose Knoledg is to the Ethickes, if not Necessary, at lest vsefull: as the Doctrine of Principles, Causes, and Ends; that |f. 192v| Of the Soule with it's Faculty and Immortality, and the like. 2. It withdraws and diuerts our thouhts oftentimes from Erthly and sensuall Objects, and so deliuers vs from many occasions of Sinning, and especially from Idlenes.[45] 3. In the contemplation both of Naturall and Supernaturall things, we meet with many Incentiues to Vertu, and Dissuasiues from Vice. How can a man that has the lest spark of Goodnes in him, consider the Infinitely good and infinitely Perfect Nature of God, without being enflam'd with a Desire of being like him?[46] How can he consider that no les Boundless then vndeserued Bounty of the Great Creator, without feeling in himself the Baits and motions of Gratitude? How can he consider the vast Immensity of the heu'nly Orbs, without lafing at the meane Ambition, of our Lofty Statesmen, that can part with their Assurances of all this to purchase an |f. 192v| Inconsiderable share of a Molehill? And [W] how (lastly) can he consider the Ruf Draughts and Images of Vertu in the Very Brutes, without a Noble Scorn, that he shud make himself inferiour to them by his Actions, that God made so much superior to them by his Birth; and that while all the Creatures vnanimously conspire, to attaine in their particular Conditions, the End of their Creation; man alone, shud striue to frustrate his by his Actions, and be the onely [peece out of order in this goodly and regular a frame of the World] ↑iarring Voice to spoile the Harmonius Concert of so [many wel tun'd Cretures;] numerous a Set of wel-tun'd Creatures;↓ making vse of his Reason, to becom the more vnresonable? 4. To kno the Tru Nature and Causes of things, dos very much clarify and refine the Iudgment; and teaches vs to set a tru Valu and æstimate

[43] Two decades later, Sprat offered similar arguments about the moral and social benefits of experiments in his *History of the Royal Society* (1667) 329-78.

[44] Such rhetorical ornaments were a staple in Alsted, as is the "Treasury of the Pithy Apothegmes" to which RB referred above.

[45] See "Of Time and Idleness" for extensive discussion of this point.

[46] RB developed this argument at much greater length in *Seraphic Love* (1659), which was written ca. 1648.

vpon things, according to their essentiall worth: and not to [rate] prize them by the rates of the vulgar; who in <most> matters that |f. 193| Concern tru Vertu and Knoledg, shud haue their Scorn and Admiration inuerted, to haue them plac't aright.

III.

For the Third. I think it very Necessary, that men shud be Tauht, not only How they may be Vertuus, but also [How] <Why.> And that our Ethicks shud [not only direct vs by Precepts, but Persuade vs by Incentiues. teach] <instruct> vs, not only how to make <court> loue to Vertu, but why we shud be in Loue with her.[47] For Man (at lest such as we suppose heere to Instruct) being a Reasonable Creature, must [ha] by that Reason be wrouht vpon: Neither wil the Wil be induc't to embrace a Quality so distastfull to the Appetite, til the Vnderstanding haue iudg'd it extreamely desirable. And it is the Prerogatiue of Perfect things (such as is Vertu) that the Better they ar knowne, the better they ar belou'd. Besides, there is such a |f. 193[v]| Principle of opposition in the Nature of most men; that, for those that haue no autority ouer them; to command them to do such a thing and not to Persuade them, is the next way to persuade them not to do the thing yow command them. Wherefor eu'n God himself, tho his very Commandments [ar] <shud be> sufficient Reasons for, and Motiues to, our Obedience; yet ↑gratiusly↓ accomodating himself to the Frailty and Weaknes of our Nature, dos not vnfrequently giue vs Reasons for that Will of his, which is it self the Supream Reason of all things and dos persuade vs, exhort vs, nay and intreate vs oftentimes that we wud be <pleas'd to be> happy. And, indeed, I haue obserued, that the Derth of truly Vertuus men, which has been in all Ages so much lamen<te>d by those that were so, may in a great Mesure be imputed to this Derth of Inducements.[48] For whilst the Inconueniences only of Vertu ar obuius, |f. 194| and not the Prerogatiues; tis no wonder if most men refuse to marry that Lady, where the Expences must be great, and the Dowry Nothing <small>. But amongst those themselues, to whom a better Nature has giuen more Fauorable Dispositions to Goodness: we see the greter part by much; that thinking Vertu indeed to be a louely Quality, will readily embrace it, and part with many little Pleasures and Profits for it's sake: and wil so long entertaine a Frendship with it, as no powerfull Interest of their owne opposes it. But if once it com in Competition with a Predominant Passion or Temtation; as the Apprehension of Deth or Dishonor; the thirst of Greatness or Reuenge, and the like; then instantly [they desert] the Ways of Vertu <ar deserted:> (principally)

[47] Since such incitement to virtue is not found in Arist. or in the Scholastic ethics, RB's concern with persuasion, not just instruction, is noteworthy.

[48] The full title of *Seraphic Love* was *Some Motives and Incentives to the Love of God.*

because, tho they ar presauded that vertu indeed is a [Noble] very great Good; yet they ar not [th] fully and thorouly conuinc'd in their Iudgments, |f. 194v| that it is so Great and so transcendent a Good, that all other[s] goods that [can] com in to competition with it ar to be slihted for it. The Vnderstanding Merchant that meets with this Perle (Matt. 13,45,46) wil sell all that he has to buy it. But lest I shud my self be guilty of that Defectiuenes this way, that to almost all our Moralists may iustly be imputed, I wil select out of the [Multitude,] ↑whole quiver↓ som choise Prerogatiues, as so many Loue-shafts, to enflame our Harts, and a vehement and Pure Affection to this Queen of Qualitys: as, namely, because 1. It is the Proper and peculiar Good of Man, as man. [For euen Mountaines may haue a Being, and Iewels, and Mines; Plants haue a life, Beauty, and Groth; Animals Beasts, may haue lon Comlines, long life, agility, Sense, and Sensual delihts.] ↑Other goods ar common with him to the Creatures: Is he Faire? so is a Peacock, Strong? so is a Lyon, Nimble? so is a Hare, helthfull? so is a Serpent; long-liu'd? so is a Rauen; wel-cloth'd? so is a Sable? Fear'd? so is a Wolf; [a sweet-si] wel-voic't? so is a Nihting-gale, a great Drinker? so is a Fish; plunged in sensuall Delihts? so is a Hog; and so [forth] along.↓ But man alone that is [only] capable of Reason, is alone capable of Vertu. |f. 195| Wherefore as much as Man is more excellent then any other Creture, so much [if the] dos the Good that he enjoys as Man, transcend that, which, [as any] by the riht of being any other Creture he can enioy. And as we do not esteem an armor so much for the silken laces, the Curius Caruings, and the Radiant gildings; ↑(which ar but accidental enrichments)↓ as for the Lihtness, fitness, and strength, which ar the qualitys that it has as Armour; so ouht we not so much to esteeme a man by how richly he weares, how daintily he fares; and how much he receiues; which ar but ornamental accomplishments; but by how much he knows and how wel he liues, which ar the reall Perfections of the reasonable Creature, as it is a reasonable Creature.

2. It is a Good, that lys in euery man's Power to attaine. There ar many Goods, that tho desirable, that ar so hih seated, that they affect vs with no other Passion then that of Greefe for being vnable to com neere them; |f. 195v| always exciting our Hunger, but neuer [stirring] satisfying our Appetite. [And others, there are, that like the Fruit of cert] But Vertu is a Good within our Reach; nay, within our Selues. Do but desire to be Vertuus, and thou art half way on thy Iourney; go but on to what thou desirest, and thou art at thy Iourney's End.[49] Wherefor, me thinks, that as we do far more affect those Children that we kno to be our owne, then any that Chance or Strangers can bestow vpon vs; so we shud set a much hiher Value vpon this Good, that we ar only for to our selues, then vpon any other Goods that either Fortune or Nature can present vs withall.

[49] This phrase is repeated a few pages later as well as in “Of Sin.”

3. And of which without our own Fault we cannot be depriued. When we part with <a> Good[s]; the greater that the Pleasure was, we receau'd in the Enjoying it; the greater is the greefe we resent for the loosing it. [B] And when we kno, that we may be depriu'd of that Good, we kno |f. 196| not how soone, and must be so at last; we anticipate our Sorrow by our Feare and loos a great part of the Plesure, before we lose the Possesion. But Vertu is a Structure that he only that built it can destroy: it being seated in the Will, which is as much Priuiledg'd from Compulsion, as the Soul is from Deth.[50]

4. It is the most Louely Quality in the World. As being the Beauty of the Soul, and one of the Noblest Lineaments of the Image of <that> God in Man; who being Infinitely louely because of his Perfections; has bestow'd a greater measure of louelines vpon those, whom he has enrich't with a greater [Measure] <share> of his Perfections. And certinly, so louely, and so attractiue is the Nature of Vertu that it forces admiration in it's very Enemys; and [m] constraines, eu'n those that hate it to respect it. This is the Reason, that makes all men (eu'n the Worst) desirous to Bee, or at least to Seem Vertuus. And those very Hypocrites, whose Passions or Interests wil not giue them leaue to Be Vertuus; |f. 196| ar Industrius to cuzen the World and themselues with the being thought so.[51] And indeed, if we will seriously consider it, we may obserue, that when the Wicked slander the Vertuus; they neuer slander the Action as Vertuus in it self; but always vnder[st] the Notion of being opposite to som Vertu or another, either Real in it self, or by them for it's likeness to som Vertu, esteem'd so. Thereby expressing, both the Hate they beare to the Person, and the Inward respect (that; in spiht of their teeths,) they ar forced to beare to Vertu.

5. It is one of the most Honorable Qualitys that can be. For Honor being but the Shaddow of Vertu; he that possesses the Body, shall either enjoy that Shaddo, or not Need it.[52] The Vertuus will always giue commendations to meritt: and from others, ‘tis more prayse then to haue it, to haue deseru'd it. An ancient Filosofer desired once an Orator to plead his Cause for him; which he did with so superlatiue Commendations of his Client, that the Iudges gaue Sentence in his fauor. Whereupon the Orator |f. 197| vpraidingly asking the Filosofer, what good all his Vertu did him in that Extremity? [was answered,] Why says he, It did me this Good, that [all the Commendations your <Eloquence> cud give me, that made true] my Vertu verify'd all the Commendations your Elo-

[50] This point is also made in bk. 2, ch. 3.

[51] For other references to hypocrites, cf. *Occ. Refl.* 2.393-94, *High Veneration* 5.143, *Chr. Virtuoso* 5.526, and *Swearing* 6.15.

[52] Cf. P541, “Praise is the shadow of virtue”; in *The Marrow of Theology*, Ames wrote that all men have “a certain inclination to dimly known good” and the “shadows of virtue are approved and cultivated by all” (I.x.26).

quence cud giue it. /me./[53]

6. It is the most vseful and Profitable Quality in the World, both to Particular men, and also to the Commonwealth. The Former. For Diligence [reaches] furthers Vertus in the getting of riches; [and] Liberality teaches vs how to spend them; and Patience how to liue contentedly without them, Ciuility acquires vs Frends; Iustice, exemts vs from Enemys; but if any wil be so malitius as to offend vs, Courage makes vs, either conquer our Enemys, or ouercom their Victory with our Constancy. Valor and Wisdom gain vs esteem; Temperance [m] keepes both the Body and the Mind in helth; Prudence seasons all our Actions with Discretion, and Piety draws down a Blessing vpon them from aboue. The Latter. For take away [all] |f. 197v| the Exercice of Moral Vertus; and yow take away the Foundation and Cornerstones from the Fabrick of the common-welth. Who knos not that Iustice and Valor ar the 2 Pillars of a State, the one ruling the Subjects amongst themselues at hom, and the other defending them from Enemys abroad. Wherefore in all wel-gouerned Kingdomes of the World, Rewards haue been proposed to Vertu, and Punishments ordained against [Vice] Offenders. Nay such is the Essential Necessity of these 2 qualitys to the Maintenance of a State, that euen those Pyrates and other Rogues; that seem to haue sent an open Defiance to Vertu; without some measure of these 2 cannot possibly subsist. For indeed, Take away (altogether) Iustice and Valor; and the Assemblys of men, will be turned into Herds and Droues of reasonable Beasts. So Necessary a Quality is Vertu, that euen Vice it selfe cannot [(] long (be able to) subsist with out it. |f. 198|

7. It is the most Rauishing and Contenting quality that man is capable of. For otherwise, why shud so many famous, impartiall, and Iudicious men, in all ages, and in all Countrys; trample all other kind of Contentments vnder foot, when they once came to dispute the Precedency with this? And Reason it self dos manifestly concur. For the Exercice of Vertu either is it self, or at least dos immediately produce, the Supreamest Good in the World, namely, Felicity. And certinly, those that ar so ambitious of bringing forth the Actions of Vertu; cannot chuse but take a very great deal of Pleasure, both in the Doing, and in the hauing don them. ↑According to that of the Wiseman, Pro. 21,15. It is Ioy to the Iust to do Iudgment.↓ And if Pleasure (as it is vsually described) be but the Consequent of a Perfect operation; how greate a Pleasure may we conclude that to be, that waits vpon so perfect an Operation, of the Noblest part of Man, the Soule? |f. 198v| He that wears a Good Conscience carrys the Elysian Fields about him; and is there entertained with continuall Feasts;[54] which ar as much more sauory then those of the Palate /World/ as the Soule is more Excellent then the Body. <And> since all men confess the Torments of the Conscience, to be of all euils

[53] Source unknown.
[54] Cf. H408.

the most [Delihtfull] <intolerable>: why we shud we not allow, the Embraces of the Conscience to be of al Plesures the most Delihtfull? But he that neuer felt this, is no more capable to conceiue of it ariht, then he is to haue a tru Notion of the Sweetness of Hony, that neuer tasted it.

8. [Because] All those Heros and Filosofers that seem to be born for the Ornament of Mankind, haue euer esteemed it the Cheefest Good. And certinly that so many Sages, and Worthys, [of] that did so differ in their Ages, Cuntrys, Humors, Fortunes, Religions, and Interest, shud |f. 199| neuertheles al of them concur, in giuing their Vote for the Præeminency of this Quality, is me thinks, a [Witness,] Testimony aboue Exception. [And] <For> if the Autority of one single Wise man beares so great a Stroke in the crediting of an Opinion: what shud not the Consent of such a Croud of Sages do, whose Cuncurrence remoues the Suspition of Error, whilst their Mutuall Enmity exempts them from that of Compliance?

9. It is the Principal End of man's Creation. For God hauing made the World to communicate his Goodness and manifest his Glory to his Creatures. But man he made (morally <humanely> speaking,) to the End, that he [glorify] by a Vertuus life glorifying his maker heere; his maker may without iniury to his Iustice, Glorify him heereafter. Besides, that <one of> the Principall Ends that God propos'd himself in the Creation, being his owne Glory; and man being no way more able to glorify his Maker, then by a Vertuus Life |f. 199[v]| and holy Conuersation, it must necessarily follow, that this Exercice of Vertu [wa] is one of the Principal Ends of man's Creation. (Which being by the sole Power of Nature vtterly vnable to do, in that mesure of Perfection that God in his Law required of vs; the Apostle speaking our Sauior Iesus Christ, tels vs (Titus the 2,14) that he Gaue himself for vs, that he miht redeem vs from all iniquity; and purify vnto himself a Peculiar People, zealous of good Workes.

10. It most of all likens vs to God, and (as it were) allyes vs to the Diuine Nature. For God being vnimitable by vs in the [Or] Infiniteness of his Power, and the Vnsearcheableness of his Wisdom, has onely propos'd himself our Pattern in the Goodness of his Nature. Which, as it is more conceiuable by our apprehensions and more proportionable to our Abilitys, so it is more beneficiall to vs in the Practice. ↑And this the Lord himself teaches vs, when he says so often, not, be yow great for I am Great, or Infinit, for I am infinit, but Be ye Holy for I am holy.↓[55] Wherefore <also> our Sauior Christ [is] when (Matt. 11.29.) he bids them lern of him: he |f. 200| says not For I haue created [al] the World out of Nothing by Omnipotence, and rule all things as I list by my Prouidence: but he says, Lern of me, for I am meek, and lowly in hart. Not that I wud conclude an Identity betwixt those Infinite Perfections of Almihty God, and

[55] Lev. 11:44 or 19:2.

those Vertus of our that represent them; (since they ar only Qualitys in vs, but essentiall to him) but only, that since God is an Essence transcendently both Pure and Good, the more we haue <approach> in vs of <to> that Purity and Goodness, the greater is the resemblance, (or rather the less is the Dissimilitude) betwixt ours <us> and the Diuine Nature.[56]

11. It is of all Qualitys the most acceptable vnto God. Not only for other Reasons, but also <for this;> because it is the [on] Principal, if not the onely, return we can make vnto him for all his vnspeakable Benefits. So that we must <shud> needs be ambitious of the Sirname of Vertuus, were it but meerly to auoid the Brand of being Ingratefull. For as when |f. 200v| any Body has very hihly obliged vs, we ar industrius to discouer what he loues, and what he hates; that by practising the one and Declining the other we may manifest our thankfulness to the obliging Party in both: so shud we deal with Almihty God: and to express our Gratitude to him, vtterly detest those Vices which we kno he so infinitely abhors; and cheerfully embracing those Vertus which cannot chuse but (extreamely) please him, since they ar, both the Images of his (own) Perfections, and the Fruits of our Obedience to his Commands. And therefore our Redeemer himself, (Iohn 14.15) tels vs, If ye loue me, keepe my commandements: [arguing] Charact<e>ring by the Integrity of our Obedience, the Sincerity of our Loue.

12. And Lastly. It is of all qualitys the most Felicitating, both in order |f. 201| to this Life, and that which is to com. Vertu being the onely Doore /Gate/ that giues entrance into the Pallace of Felicity, and the onely |thing| that, if I may so speake, giues vs liuery and Seisin of Happines.[57] This I hope is euident, by what alredy has been discoursed. And certinly (not to repeat other reasons) if God be infinitely happy, because he is infinitely Perfect; the greater mesure of those Perfections we Possess, the greater Portion <Degree> of Felicity, we must necessarily enjoy. And thus much for this Life: but for the next; in comparison of which our Present happines is but the Ernest of a Greater; the very Heathen themselues, thinking it vnjust to terminate that man's happiness with Deth, whose Vertu as well as his Soule was Immortall, cud fain to Elizian Fields, the Poets Paradice, where the vnfetterd Soules of worthy men, did [enioy a] eu'n glut themselus with Pleasures, not les lasting then they were extreame. |f. 201v| But for vs, Christians, that ar tauht by a Diuiner Master in a better School, We according to his Promise look for new heu'ns and a New Erth, wherein dwelleth Rihteusness (<2.> Pet. 3.13) where the Father of Mercys and God of all Comfort ↑2. Cor. 1.3. a. Psal. 16.11. b. Ier. 31.13. c. Psal. 36.8. d. Reu. 7.15,16,17. e. 2 Cor. 3.18.↓ in whose Presence is Fulnes of Ioy, and at whose riht hand there ar

[56] RB elaborated on this argument in many passages of *Seraphic Love*, *Greatness of Mind*, *Theodora*, and *Chr. Virtuoso*.

[57] Seisin is "possession as of a freehold" (*OED*).

Book Two, Chapter Four

Pleasures for euermore, <a.> shall turn their mourning into Ioy, <b.> and satisfy them abundantly with the fatness of his house, and make them drink of the riuers of his Pleasures. <c.> They shall [hunger no more, nor thirst] be before the Throne of God, and serue him day and niht in his Temple; and he that sitteth on the Throne shall dwell among them. They shal hunger no more, neither thirst any more; neither shall the Sun liht on them nor any heat. For the Lamb which is in the midst of the Throne shall feed them, and shall lead them |f. 202| vnto liuing Fountains of waters, and God shall wipe away all Tears from their Eys. <d.> And so We all with open Face, beholding, as in a Glass, the Glory of the Lord, ar changed into the same Image from Glory to Glory, euen as by the Spirit of the Lord. <e.> I cud extreamely enlarge my self vpon Euery one of these 11 Prerogatiues: but <<fearing to haue transgress'd> <been too much falty> to much that way already>> I am rounded in the Eare to conclude with saying, that since Vertu is a Quality <Good> so Noble, so Attainable, so Permanent, so Louely, so Honorable, so Profitable, so Contenting, so nobly Presidented, so much man's End, so Diuine, so Gratefull vnto God, and so Felicitating ↑(of vnto man);↓ and the most of all these in the Superlatiue Degree: why shud we not, hauing found such an inestimable Treasure of [ha] Felicity in the Field of Vertu, do as the discreet Merchant spoken of Matt. 13.44. did in [that] <his> case, go and sell all that we haue with Ioy, and go and |f. 202v| Buy that Field. For in this Case the Greatest Prodigality is the Greatest Thrift, Vertu being of the Nature of those Purchases, that can neuer be, either too far fetcht or too Deerly bouht.

But Stay. [As] Before I make a further Progress in the Doctrine of Education, I [m] find my self necessitated to rid out of the way diuers objections, framed against the Desirableness of Vertu; grounded vpon som nconveniences that ar said necessarily to wait vpon her. They ar all reducible to 8 heds. <gener.> It being alleadged against the Excellency of Vertu, that

1. It is a very Difficult Quality both to acquire and to keepe. To which I answer, 1. It is confest so. But what is there of Excellent [but] that is not so too? Difficilia qua Pulchra.[58] Opposition fences about whatsouer deserues a Value aboue the common rate of things. And the Kernell of |f. 203| Excellency, is not to be com by without breaking the shell of Difficulty. 2. Since Toyle and Labor is euery where necessary, [where] how can it possibly be more vsefully employ'd then in the Acquisition of so transcendent a Good, that did we swim to it, throuh a lake of our owne sweat or a Riuer of our owne Blood, it wud yet deserue the Purchase. For we vse not to esteem Paines so much by the Degree of the Labor as by the Proportion it beares to the Good it obtaines. Thus what we shud think a Toylsom Trouble to gaine but an ordinary Fortune, we [sh] <w>ud think but an Easy purchase of the Treasures of Crœsus. And therefore, Gen.

[58] The Latin tag was a commonplace; cf. T181, "Excellence is difficult."

29:20, tho Iacob serued Laban 7 Yeares for his Mistres Rachel, yet the text tels vs that that apprentiship of yeares Seemed vnto him but a few days for the Loue he had to her. 3. Do but consider what a deale of Labor, deluded Mortals spend on Worldly trifles. Throu what Tempestuous Seas, boisterous gusts, and Vninhabitable Deserts dos the gaping Merchant[h] [pursue] hunt after a few poore lumps of Yellow Erth. |f. 203v| How many Climats dos the glutton ransac to make himself the <a> more refined Beast? What a Carbonado dos the Sojer make of his Body, for 5 or 6 poore pence a day, and through what a groue of Pikes and Swords, dos the Commander pursue the vnsatisfying glory of an Empty Name! And shal not Reason haue vpon our Axions, as great an Influence as Folly has vpon theirs. 4. ↑We must not only look vpon the ruggedness of the way, but also cast an eye vpon the Pleasantness of the Iourneys End. 5. I'm sure Our Savior tels vs, Matt. 11,30. that his Yoake is Easy, and his Burden liht. And the Wisest of Mortals ↑discoursing of the Propertys of Diuine Wisdom, Pro. 3.17. that Her ways ar Ways of pleasantness and al her Paths ar peace.↓↓ Neither is the Acquisition of Vertu such an impossible peece of Bisness as most men ar pleaz'd to beleeue it.

The [Di] Imagination of the Difficulty is more difficult to surmount then the very Difficulty it selfe. We wud faine flatter our selues into a Beleefe that we haue strong inclinations to Vertu: and father our owne Bacwardness to climbe, vpon the steepness of Vertu in the ascent. Do but resolue to run the Venture of it once, |f. 204| and yow wil quickly find that tis not because <we find> Goodness [is] so Difficult that we go faintly on; but 'tis because we go so faintly on that we find it so Difficult. I kno not what others thinke on't, but for my part I haue been long of that opinion, that Many men miht haue gon to heu'n with half the Paines they take to go to hell. ↑Do but dare to begin: he that sets forwards is half [on] to his Iourney's End, and Vertu, like a Stone falling downwards the farther it moues, the less resistance it findes.[59] Besides that in [those] the Difficult Axions of Vertu, the Labor vanishes as soon as the thing /work/ is don, and leaues the onely <continent> Pleasure to suruiue (it.)↓

2. It is a very Dangerous Quality. To which I answer, 1. By denying it to be so. For Iustice, Liberality, Ciuility, and Temperance blast the very occasions of enmity in the Bud: Prudence teaches vs to decline the Strokes of those that cannot [be] justly be auoided; and Valour enables vs to surmount their oppostions. ↑Wisdom and Vertu ar the safest Passport to carry a man thorouh al human Chances and Calamitys. And therefor it has bin [usually] truly obserued, that whom Fortune has a minde to ruine, she first uses to deceiue or rob of this

[59] For the Scholastic roots of this belief, see Marshall Clagett, *The Science of Mechanics in the Middle Ages* (Madison 1961) 542ff; see also Alsted 685-88. RB later drew on the work of Galileo and other contemporaries: cf. *Usefulness* (3.431, 460-61), *Exc. of Mech. Hypoth.* (4.71), and *Chr. Virtuoso* (5.527).

(sacred) Protection.[60] 2. Tho Vertu dos indeed somtimes engage men into Dangers, yet it is not of it's owne Nature but meerly by accident. For were all men Vertuus, it were the safest, profitablest, and most happy Quality in all the World. A thing that wil very wel deserue our most serious consideration, |f. 204v| Vnto which it wil most euidently appeare. So that it is not because som men ar Vertuus that they ar [in] <Subject> to Danger; but because all men ar not so too. 3. As there is a Deuil to malice Vertu, so there is a Prouidence to protect it.[61] ↑Length of Days is in the Scripture frequently promised to the Godly.↓ Behold, (sayth Dauid) The Ey of the Lord is vpon them that feare him; vpon them that hope in his Mercy; to deliuer their Soul from Deth, and to keepe them aliue in famine. (Psal. 33,18,19.) The Wicked, (says he,) plotteth against the iust and gnasheth vpon him with his Teeth; the Lord shal laf at him, for he seeth that his day is comming, The wicked haue drawn out the sword, and haue bent the Bow to cast down the poor and needy; and to slay such as be of vpriht conuersation, Their sword shal enter into their own hart, and their Bows shal be broken. Psal. 37. 12,13,14,15. For, saith the same Dauid, (Ps. 34,19.) Many ar the Afflictions of the Rihteous, but the Lord deliuereth him out of them all. So that we ouht to haue an Ey, not only vpon the <sharpness of the> Sword that strikes vs, but also vpon the hardness of the Sheeld that defends vs. 4. How many Diseases do [s own In] |f. 205| we swallow downe thorou our Throates; how many Dangers ar attendants vpon our Auarice, and what terrible fals dos our Ambition giue vs; from all which Vertu giues [vs] ↑her followers <votarys>↓ an Excmption? And certinly the Historys of all Aages will inform vs, that where Vertu, like Saul has kild her Thousands, Vertu, like Dauid, has [kild] <murder'd> her Ten-thousands. It being but an ordinary Spectacle to see a Tyrant swim to his graue in a riuer of his owne Blood.[62]

3. It is a Quality disesteemed by the most part, both of the greatest, and of thc knowingest men. This Objection staggers many, whose wayting popular Iudgment makes the Greater part, and the Better conuertible. But 1. We must not only [how many there be of this opinion, but who they ar that hold it.] ↑consider what men say, but also vpon what Principles they speak↓ it. For a Drunkard to condemn Sobriety is no [wonder] <scandall>; because therein he but complys with his Nature; but when a man that is that way inclin'd protests against

[60] A variant of the proverb, "Whom the gods would destroy they first make mad."

[61] A persistent theme in *Philaretus* was RB's providential escape from danger and illness: RB "would professe that in the Passages of his Life he had obseru'd so gratious & so peculiar a Conduct of Prouidence, that he should be equally blind & vngratefull, shud he not both Discerne & Acknowledge it" (Maddison 16). RB's father had insisted on the same perspective (*Life of Richard Boyle* 1.vii), his motto being "God's providence is [his] inheritance." See also *Seraphic Love* (1.290), *Occ. Refl.* (2.418, 419), and "Of Sin" below. Documenting such acts of providence fascinated Dury and Hartlib. Canny analyzes Cork's view of providence (28ff) in some detail.

[62] Cf. S474, "Who swims in Sin (Vice) shall sink in sorrow."

Drunkenness, he is far the sooner to be beleeu'd; because therein, he opposes his appetite. 2. There is scarce any of these Notoriusly vitius that ar not asham'd to owne a disregard of Vertu or an Esteem of Vice as they ar in themselues: but |f. 205^{v}| when once their own particular faults ar prest home vpon them: being persons whom their Parts or Places make very tender of their Repution, and beleeue it a less shame <disgrace> to defend then to forsake an Error; they pump their Wits to find out Euasions to whatsoeuer is objected against them; and ar very industrius to make people beleeue, the Progeny of their Humors to be the [Effects] Off-spring of their Iudgment.[63] Which truth [may very eui] <this Symtom dos> euidently [appeare] <bewray> in that, none ar more inuectiue then they against those Vices with which neither themselues, nor those they loue or depend on, remaine vninfected. 3. It is very possible that a man may be [otherwi] very Intelligent in other Matters, and yet an ignorant Nouice in Morality; and so as Incompetent a Iudge of the Excellency of Vertu or Vice, almost as a blind man wud be which were the fairer Colour of Carnation or gowne.

Tis no wonder now to find men that ar Trauellers abroad to be strangers at home, neither is it a Prodigy, to find |f. 206| a man nowadays, [bett] far better acquainted with the Nature of Heu'n then the Way to go to it. 4. It is [b] not only possible but Frequent, to see a man haue a great deale of the Liht of Truth in his Vnderstanding, without the least Degree of the heat of Vertu in his Affections, [being] like an ouergrown Toad, that has a Iewel in his head, and Poyson in his hart.[64] ↑As a man may haue a most exquisite knoledg where in the Nature of Riches dos consist, and in what Mines and Places they ar to be found and yet be all this while pinched himselue, with the pressing necessitys of a Penurius Indigence.↓[65] So that I shud no more wonder to see a great Scholler a bad liuer, then to see a quick-sihted Child, that has excellent Eys to discern which is the best

---

63 In a letter to a brother (18 April 1647) not printed by Birch, RB promised to send his *Ethics* in order to show how to refute the evasions of conscience (Boyle Lett. 1.137-38): "No, no; tis nothing to be in a Good Religion, if in that Religion yow be not Good: for your Religion's being Good, if yow be not so too; that makes yow by so much the Worse, by how much greater your obligation and opportunitys haue been to grow Better" (f. 137). RB then argued against against delayed repentance: "I am content . . . to Procrastinate this Theame, till I shew <yow> at large in some Discourses of my Ethickes, both the Reasons and Grounds of my Advice. . . . I iudg'd it necessary to premise this Patterne of Counsell . . . to the whole Peece yow shall find in my Ethickes." The recipient was probably Broghill.

64 T360; Browne offered a learned discussion in *Pseud. Epidemica* 1.210-13, but see also Shakespeare, *As You Like It*, ii.1.12: "Sweet are the uses of adversity, / Which, like the toad, ugly and venemous, / Wears yet a precious jewel in his head."

65 An accurate account of the economic fortunes of the Boyle family after the outbreak of the Civil War (see *II Lismore* 5.22 for the Cork's financial collapse). After the outbreak of the rebellion in Ireland, Philaretus regarded Lismore Castle only as "an Instance & a Lecture, of the Instability of that Happinesse, that is built upon the incertin Possession of such fleeting Goods, as it selfe was" (Maddison 3).

way, carryed away ouer hedg and ditch by the hed strong[ness] <fury> of [his] <an vnruly> horse. Specially since St. Paul himself cud haue occasion to complaine Rom. 7.15 For [that which I do, I allow not.] what I wud, that do I not; but what I hate, that do I: and againe verse the 19. For the Good that I wud I do not: but the Euil [that] <which> I wud not, that I do. 5. That most of our grand<ees> [men] ar <so> apt to discountenance Vertu, is but little to be regarded: for [that] the Splendor of their greatness has no faculty at all of enlihtning their Vnderstandings: and that they ar more enclinable to vice then other men, proceeds meerly from that the Superfluitys of their Condition, and the Throngs of Flatterers |f. 206v| that continually beseedg them afford them stronger Temptations to Wickedness, then they do to other men. 7. Neither ar we bound to beleeue all thes Macchiavillians to be such Incomparable Politicians as they ar generally giuen out for. Our own times will be able to afford both recent and very pregnant Examples, that for the most part this <so> admired Subtility is [a] but a cunning way of vndoing themselues, at the last: and many by their heaping Projects vpon Proiects haue made and climbd a Ladder, at the top of which, when they thouht to haue seated themselues vpon a Throne, they haue <but> found themselues vpon a Scaffold.[66] 8. But the Critical moment to iudge securely of men's opinions in this particular is the houre of Deth, when Conscience wil speake, and Dissimulation is bootless. And then the most [intimite] <darling> fauourites of the Diuel, wil exclaime with wicked Balaam, Num. 23.10. Let me dy the Death of the Rihteous, and let my last End be like his. So that what our |f. 207| English Poet, said <about the choice> of the Mistresses of his Affections, we may very wel <in this case> apply to those of our opinions, that

> Tis not her <that> first we loue
> But whom Dying we approue.[67]

4. It is a Dul and Melancholick quality. This Objection I must confess did a long while more puzzle me to answer then all the rest besides. For certinly the mopish retiredness of the greatest part of the religius, I can no way either Deny or Approue: it being extremely iniurius To themselues, vpon whom they pul

---

[66] For the same point in similar language, see "Of Sin." This example perhaps commented on the fall of Thomas Wentworth, a particularly vexing adversary of the Earl of Corke, but it obviously has wider application. In "Of Great Place," Bacon observed that "All Rising to *Great Place*, is by a winding Staire," but the image was a commonplace.

[67] Edmund Waller, "An Apology for Having Loved Before," ll. 11-12. RB used this quote elsewhere (*Style* 2.301) and also quoted Waller's verse in *Occ. Refl.* 2.443. Waller, a friend of the family (see the letter from John Beale to RB, 6.325), irritated Lady Ranelagh with his gallantry (6.521). He was perhaps the target of the anecdotal sayings attributed to Lady Ranelagh in the moral essays below.

down such an vnnecessary drooping.[68] To Vertu; vpon whom they bring such a needless scandall: as if one cud not be wedded to her without being diuorc't from all ioy and Recreation. And lastly, to others: whom they discourage from their setting forth, and retard in their Progress in the Ways of Vertu: from whom their very faces friht suitors at their first addresses; as indeed, Who that were not deeply enamored, wud be ambitius of the Seruice of that Mistress, whose Fauorites bewray by their lookes the Discontentedness |f. 207v| of their Minds: (looking as if they were shortly to go into, or newly coming out of a Graue?) But to wipe of this Aspersion, consider, 1. Sullenness is no Property of Vertu <in> it self, and therefor not Necessary to the Vertuus. For certinly Vertu being the most Felicitating and contenting Quality in the World, (as has been already proued) cannot necessarily depriue vs of so great a Signe and Effect of it as is Ioy. Neither dos God at all require it at our hands. That Father of Mercys did neuer vndertake to abridg his Children of their Innocent Pleasures. And indeed, if such Priuiledges belong to any, who can haue [more] <a Better> title to them, then the Children of the Kingdom, the Religious. And Christ himself, that is neuer read to haue laft, grac't a Feast (of Ioy) with the very Maidenhed of his Miracles, Iohn. 2.11.[69] But the plaine truth is that many out of a needless Peeuishness, turn Theeues to themselues, whom they causlesly |f. 208| abridg of those lawful Priviledges whereof God has allowd them the Enjoyment. [The Wisest of Mortals speaking of solid Wisdom tels vs] The Kingly Profet, Ps. 32.10,11. tels vs that Many Sorrows shal be to the Wicked, but he that trusteth in the Lord, mercy shall compasse him about. And in the following verses he bids vs, Be glad in the Lord and reioyce ye Rihteus, and shout for ioy all ye that ar vpriht in hart. It is the Precept of the Apostle, 1. Thess. 5.16. Reioyce euermore. Who also tels vs, Gal. 5,22. that the Fruit of the Spirit is Loue, Ioy, Peace, &c. and Romans, 14,17, that The Kingdom of God is not meat and drink, but Rihteusness, and Peace, and Ioy in the Holy Ghost. ↑And De. 28. 47, 48 God dos threaten his People to punish with Sorrow and Misery, the want or neglect of <Ioy and> Gladness. And indeed↓ the whole book of God is eu'n crouded with Passages to this purpose. For, Liht is sown for the Riteus, and Gladness for the vpriht in hart. Ps. 98.11. 2. Men oftentimes in the Vertuus mistake seriousness, and employednes of Mind for Melancholy humors, ↑as if the hart cud not be merry within without hanging out the flag of lafter at the Mouth.↓[70] When alas,

[68] Such "drooping" was a common satiric target, as can be seen in William P. Holden, *Anti-Puritan Satire, 1572-1642* (New Haven 1954), but in "Of Piety" (f. 55v), RB decried profane persons who teased the pious with the label of "Puritan." Cork used "Puritan" as a term of opprobrium, convincing Mary Boyle to be "set against being a puritan" (see Canny 34-35 and Sara Heller Mendelson, *The Mental World of Stuart Women*: *Three Studies* [Brighton 1987] 80).

[69] Browne also discussed whether Christ ever laughed (*Pseud. Epidemica* 1.588-89).

[70] Epictetus had advised against careless laughter: "Do not laugh much, often, or unrestrainedly" (*Enchiridion* 33.4); for Alsted's advice on the regulation of conversation, including laugh-

tis onely that the Mind of man taken vp with [e] <the> Fruition of a Solid and most satisfying Ioy, disdaines to be diuerted from the Contemplation of so great a Happiness, by these worthless trifles, <obiects> that tickle the Spleene of deluded mortals, and begets their mirth. |f. 208v| An Excesse of Sorrow may be oftentimes consistent with lafter; <(which is but, Ioy from the teeth outward)> but not so with Solid Ioy; which argues, that the latter much more participates of the Nature of tru Gladness then Mirth it self. Little Ioys like Brookes and Torrents find a Tong, when the great ones, like the deepest Riuers, ar silent; <speechless> [making vp with] <spirl[y]ing in> the profundity of their Streames, what they want in the Loudness of their Murmure.[71] 3. The Faut then is not in the Thing but in the Men; and ouht the more to reflect vpon Vertu it self, then an Astronomer's wilful gazing himself blind by stedfast looking vpon the mid-day Sun ouht to be imputed as an Inconuenience to his Art. 4. ↑The grand occasiones of the Vertuus Melancholy, is their sadnes for their Sins: which Sorrow, tho it eclipse our Ioy for a /the/ time, dos reuiue it againe afterwards; making vs glad, not that we haue Sinned, but that we haue Repented. Then when the repenting<ant Sorro> Greefe of the Godliest distils it selfe into Teares, The Dauhter destroyes the Mother, and the Tearres that that kind of Sorro produces, drownes that very sorro that produc'd them.↓[72] 5. The Vertuus ar melancholy, not because they ar Vertuus, but because they ar not Vertuus enuf. Which euidences that their Sadness is grounded, not vpon the Fruition, but the Want of Vertu. And their Melancholy proceeds, not from that they haue so much of Goodness, but from that they haue no more.

5. It is a Discountenanced |f. 209| Quality, and which the very Vertuus themselues, ar ashamed to owne in Company. To which I answer that, 1. This scoffing is not tru of all the Vertus, but only of Sobriety, Chastity, and perhaps one or two more besides.[73] 2. 'Tis men's own Cowardice that they will suffer themselues to be laft out of their goodness. For did they but <dare to> cloth Vertu with that Confidence that the Vitius do Profaneness, theyr <boldness> miht easy<ly> make as arrant a sneake of Vice, as the Wicked's Impudence dos now of Vertu. There is such a Majesty in Goodness, that one resolued looke of it, dashes Vice, (if it be not altogether Brazen fac't) quite out of countenance. I haue often seen and not seldom try'd, that the bare Presence of a Notoriusly Vertuus Person, has hinder'd a whole Company of licentius Gallants from those ryotous [Cour] Axions which otherwise they intended to perform. And indeed in

---

ter, see 1331-35. The high number of Biblical citations is unusual, suggesting both RB's sense of urgency as well as the difficulty of making this point on strictly logical grounds.

71 Cf. W123.

72 The final section of Burton's *Anatomy* dealt with religious melancholy: causes, symptoms, cures, and so on. But many clerics also analyzed the dynamics of repentance.

73 RB stressed this point in "Of Piety," but see also *Style* 2.303-04.

this kind of Contention of Precedency, I haue euer obserued that to begin first is mainly materiall, the Victory commonly taking part with that side that has the Courage to giue the first onset. If Vertu sneakes, tis no wonder if the Vitius gro Impudent; but if we do <once> but begin to censure their Follys, there is such a self- |f. 209v| Consciusnes in Vice, as wil easily enable vs, to make them asham'd that wud otherwise haue made vs so. 3. Consider who [that] they are that make a lafing stock of Vertu; namely, [such as] <Persons so wicked, that they> ar not contented to disapproue Vertu in themselues, but endeauor also to discountenance it in others. And therfore the Kingly Profet, in that Gradation that he makes of Sins, Ps. 1.1. Places these Deriders at the vpper end of the Bord, and makes the Chaire of the Scorners, the Very Throne of [Imp] Vngodliness. And so Foolish, that to disgrace Vertu they take the onely way that in that Condition is left them to exalt it; and that is for them to discommend it. Were not he then a pretty Merchant, think you, that shud be asham'd of his Wine, meerly because it disrelishes to a few diseased Palates, when himself and all the world besides ar convinced of it's Excellency? 4. Consider also what Younglings in Vertu they ar that this Scar-crow dos deterre. For indeed it seems, that none but Children in Vertu can be frihted from their Happinesse |f. 210| By such Bugbeares as this. For why shud not Vertu stamp as great a Confidence vpon my Brow, as Vice vpon anothers; and I be more asham'd of a good Action, then he of a Bad one. ↑And indeed who wud not scruple to become a Suitor to that Mistress, whos very Seruants ar asham'd to own her?↓ In any Good Action that must needs be Bad that opposes it: And to abstaine from Vertu for feare of other's censure, is to make one's self a Foole for feare of being thout so. As I haue often at great men's Tables seen Cuntry peole laft at for rising with hunger, for feare of being censur'd of vn-mannerliness in satisfying their Appetite. I wud desire such lenharted People to [reade ouer] <consider> Matt. 10.33. And to remember, that tru Shame consists, not so much in the Euill of other men's opinions as in that of our Axions. Wherefor to blush at <a> Vertuus and not to change Countenance at a Vitius Axion ar almost equally condemnable. And shame (in these matters) always argues a Fault; which if it finds not, it makes, and <or> which, if it proceeds not from, it produces.

6. It is an Impouerishing <beggerly> Quality. To which I answer, that 1. |f. 210v| Pouerty in it's own Nature, is no necessary attendant on Vertu. As it permits vs not ↑the hunger of↓ an vnsatiable Rapine, so it secures vs from the flux of a [bottomless] <shoreless> Prodigality. Tis tru, that it is vsually longer in building vp a fortune then is Couetousness, but that Fortune, tho slowly, is both more [surely but] certin in the building, and more [secure] <lasting> when it is built. Whereas [F] Estates like Fruits, that ar so quickly ripe ar vsually seen to be

as suddenly rotten.[74] 2. Vertu prohibits but vnlawfull gaines: which ar so far from contributing to our [W] Riches; that Ill-got mony like a [rotten /cored/ sheepe, corr infects the whole [W] flock of our wel acquired welth] ↑canker'd member spreads the Infection ouer other the whole sound body of our wel acquired Wealth,↓ and Couetous men (as one says very wel) doing nothing but torment themselues to get that, for the getting of which they shal be tormented. 3. If it shud chance either to debar vs from any iust Profit, or occasion the losse of any thing that is iustly our own: the Welth that it giues vs, dos most abboundantly recompence that that it takes from vs. For ↑Vertu is so [gre] excellent and necessary a Good, that tis by her that all [outward] external aduantages [ar made so] <become goods> is not more vnto vs. For tho it be very Tru that God made them Good in themselues, yet tis Vertu that makes them so to vs.↓ What pray yow is the End for which we desire Riches, but Contentment; which if Vertu can afford vs in the Absence of our Riches; why shud we not |f. 211| beleeue that we may be welthy enuf without them? ↑He that had so [preeminent] much Experiencye both of Abundance and want; can tel vs, Ps. 37.16. that A little that the rihteus man hath is better then the riches of many wicked. And he that knew how to be abased, and also how to abound, (Ph. 4.12.) can assure vs 1. Tim 6.6. that Goodliness with Contentment is great gain.↓ Certinly the Riches Vertu can bestow vpon vs, do as much [a] excell those which for her sake can be taken /rauish't/ from vs, as the End is better then the Meanes. What is a little white and Yellow Erth, ↑and those meane hapines they can procure vs;↓ to those illustrius and Noble Endowments of the Mind, the Iewels of <moral> Vertus set in the Gold of <resened> Knoledg; to a Soule that [f] can embrace prosperity without Dotage, and [welcome] endure Pouerty without [Misery] /Deiectedness/ and [can] needs not to feare the eating rust or Pilfering Theefe, or the vnexpected Treachery of an vnfaithful Seruant:[75] whose principal Riches, neither the Wind can blow away, nor the Waues drowne, nor the Fire melt; but he can swim with his Treasure out of a [spr] Shipwracke[d]; and saue it from the Flames of a sacked Citty. All these Riches, being, not Fortune's Goods, but his, which as they ar aboue her power to giue, so they ar beyond it to take away. Let not therefore the feare of Pouerty discourage thee from treading the gainfull Paths of Vertu; since she will be sure to make thee ↑[happy,] rich either to thy contentment or in it;↓ either contented with Riches or Rich in thy Content. |f. 211v|

[74] RB used the same proverb about medlars above (bk. 1, ch. 2), "no sooner ripe then rotten." The speed with which Cork amassed his fortune was often remarked: his enemies saw it as evidence of corruption and he saw it as the work of providence. Canny analyzes in great detail both positive and negative assessments of Cork (ch. 2-3).

[75] Cf. Luke 6:19-21. An especially painful example of such treachery was the failure of William Perkins to send £250 to Marcombes in 1642; for RB's letter to his father, see *II Lismore* 5.114-15; for Cork's letter to Perkins, see *II Lismore* 5.117-18. In October 1646, RB complained to Marcombes about Tom Murray's dishonesty (1.xxxiii).

Book Two, Chapter Four

7. It is a mihty obstacle [to w] both to honor and to Greatness. To which I answer; that, 1. I do confess it proues so now and then: but tis ↑meerly by Accident since↓ vnder such Persons, as hating to see the same man both Good and great together; make Wickedness the onely Ladder to Preferment. And in such a case, it argues a noble greatness of the Mind, to disdain to grow great. Besides that it is a greater Glory to haue deserued without reward then to be rewarded without Desert. And as for the Infamy which miht be apprehended from such Persons, it is very little to be feared, since their Discommendation is no Disprayse: for they whose Axions speake so ill of themselues, wil scarce be beleeued when their Tongs speake ill of others. 2. How many Worthys has Vertu lifted vp to the very Pinacle of [Fo] Renown and Greatness. The Historys of all Ages ar Crowded with the Examples of this Truth. For eu'n Vertu as Wel as Fortune has her Trumpets and her Crownes, which somtimes she bestows vpon her Fauorites. And indeed it is generally obserued, that Great built vpon |f. 212| Vice, like a Top-heauy Tree, where the Branches ar too great <bigg> for the Roots, dos easily becom a Windfall: whereas that greatness whose Foundation is Vertu; as it is perhaps longer in building, so it is by far more difficult to be pulled down. Besides that a Crown got without Wickedness, may be lost without Misery: whereas those that trample vpon their Honesty to rayse their Fortunes, seldome meet with fals, but they break their Necks. 3. A Dram of Honor from wise and Good men, is worth a pound of it from any body else.[76] And therefore the Ancients wisely so contriu'd it, that a man cud not enter into the Temple of Honor, but the passing thorough that of Vertu. For certinly, If Honor be more in the Honoring, then in the Honored Party, that Esteem wherein it consists, must needs admit of a very great Alteration from the Degree of worth of him that giues it. And therefore it has bin said, that he onely can giue tru Commendations that deserues them. But most men do vsually <deceiue themselues> mistakeing Fame for Honor: And think that to consist in being tost |f. 212v| to and fro in a great many men's mouth's; which indeed consists in the good opinion that good men haue of our good Actions.[77] And therefore it is that these men ar desirous of a Fame rather Great then Good; and ar so ambitious of an empty Name, that rather then not be Famous they wil be infamous. As if all those were inthron'd in men's opinions that ar frequent in their mouthes; and [of] that Iudas, Nero, Satan, and thousands others, whom tho we talke of much, we esteem but very little. Wherefor if tru honor do not so much consist in the Esteem of other men,

---

[76] A conflation of various proverbial expressions (e.g., M998, "Mischief comes by the pounds and goes by the ounces"), but see also D582 and O85-O87.

[77] For fame as the shadow of virtue, see *Occ. Refl.* 2.405; for a later and quite personal view of the inconveniences of fame, see *Exc. of Theol.* 4.53 and 57-58. John Beale frequently raised the question of RB's fame and its proper management (e.g., 6.374, 447, and 451). RB's essay, "Of the Vanity and Partiality of Fame," which he mentioned in BP 36.86, is not extant.

as in those Actions of ours that ar the Ground of that Esteeme, we may safely conclude, that it is one of the Prerogatiues of Vertu to haue tru honor in her onely gift. And truly, if we wil but go to the Cost to try it, our own Experience wil quickly teach vs, that There is no Honor to that, that a man's owne wel-informed Conscience giues him; Neither dos this Fame that waits on Vertuus actions, transcend that which is procured by Vitius ones or Greatness, only in the Deseruedness of it, but also in the Enduring. |f. 213| For the Rihteus shall be in Euerlasting Remembrance, Ps. 112.6. and the memory of the Iust is blessed, but the Name of the Wicked shall rot. Pr. 10.7. Vertu being alone capable to priuiledg our memorys from the graue, and riuet [our Honors] <them> [vn]to Immortaliity. [And] The Fame of [Bad men] the Wicked either [ex] dys with the Man or Suruiues but to his Infamy. And all these Mausolean monuments of Vitius Greatness, do but perpetuate the Author's Infamy; either becomming a prey to the Iron Iawes of deuoring Time;[78] or if they scape them, remaining, the Monuments indeed of his Wickedness, <Vanity> and <tho> but the Sepulchers of his Reputation. But Vertu, caruing /hewing/ vs Monuments (or rather Shrines) in the [Im] neuer-dying Soules of worthy Men; makes our Memorys as Dethless as their Receptacles ar Immortall. The Life of the Wicked like the Flame of a Candle going out in a snuffe /stink/ whereas that of the Vertuus, like the Flame in Iuniper, leaues a Perfume <behind it> after the Extinction.[79]

8. And Lastly. It is a Quality that debars vs from and abridges vs of, our Plesures. To which I answer, that 1. It abridges vs of no lawful Delihts; and the restraint of <from> those |f. 213v| that ar not Lawfull, can with no more Iustice occasion a Disrelish of Vertu; then the Fisitians denying his Patient the Wine he thirsts after in the heat of his burning fit, can iustly bring a Disrepute vpon him. 2. It rather changes, then depriues vs of our Plesures. It but diuerts the Soule from these sensuall trifles, to fix it vpon more Noble and refined Obiects. The Drunkard he takes Pleasure in being ouercom with Wine, but Vertu makes him take a greater in ouercomming it. The Miser, his deliht is in hourding vp mony; but Vertu shos him a way to find as great a one in the spending it. The Gallant he makes it his Plesure to frolicke it in good Company; but Vertu teaches him how to meet with good Company when he is alone, and so of the rest. Thus Vertu by an aduantagious Exchange for vs, serues her followers as the <silly> Indians do our Mariners, giuing them for Beads and Whistles and Gugawes, pre-

---

[78] In Dan. 7:7 one of the beasts has iron teeth, but cf. T326, "Time devours all things," or Edmund Waller's "Upon His Majesties Repairing of St. Paul's" (1645), l. 34, for similar imagery.

[79] RB used the same comparison, derived from a proverb (C49), in "Of Sin" and variants of it in many other works (e.g., *Resurrection* 4.202). The stink of a candle could make women miscarry (3.687 and 5.201), RB noted, but some pregnant women liked its smell (4.44). The image was a commonplace.

cius wares and substantiall meat.[80] 3. The Plesures that it giues vs do incomparably transcend those that it takes away from vs. For first it is both truly and generally obseru'd; that Sinfull Pleasures ar far greater in the Conceit then in the Enjoyment; |f. 214| whereas Vertuus Plesures on the Contrary ar found to be sweeter in the Inioyment then they were in the Conceit. [A] The Diuel cunningly in the Former showing vs only what is fit to allure, but hiding the Shame, remorse, Emptiness, and all other Inconueniences that wait vpon so [faire] <promising> an outside: and in the latter amplyfying onely those Difficultys that may discourage vs, and clouding all those [Excell] Prerogatiues that ar attendant on them. So that what is vsually said in the Prouerbe that the French ar Wiser then they [ar] <seem,> and the Spaniards seem wiser then they ar;[81] may not vnfitly be applyed to the contrary Delihts of Vice and Vertu; namely that the former seem greater then they ar, and the latter ar greater then they seem. ↑And indeed, the Pleasures of the World ar very much beholding to the Clarity /Fauor/ of our Imaginations, for the Esteem that we ar pleas'd to make of their sweetness: /Happiness/ which certinly is to be found far greater in the Pen [of] /Fancy/ of a Poet then in (the Reality of) the Things themselues.↓ Againe, In sensual Plesures a man is for the most part forc'd to go [out of himself; and to go] abroad (if I may so speake) to fetch in external Objects to furnish out his Delihts. The Miser must haue his Bags, the Glutton his Dishes, the Drunkard his good-Company, and the wencher his Courtisane to satisfy their Appetites: and all this must they go seek for out of themselues: |f. 214v| whereas the Vertuus man finds [all th] (the cloth laid always at home and) all this within himself: and carrys his [Bo] Daintys, his Company, his Treasure, and his Mistres, always about him in his Breast. Besides. Fleshly Plesures ar of a fading Nature; and perish in th'injoying; and like a beautifull flower, /rose/ wither in our very hands, eu'n whilst we ar admiring and commending them.[82] They ar Subject to a Thousand Casualtys throu the Inconstancy of Fortune, and if for all that they leaue not vs, we shal be necessitated to leaue them by the certinty of Deth. And then, their Presence was not more welcom then their Absence wil be greeuous. But, Vertu, is aboue the Reach of Fortune and Priuiledg'd from the Dominion of Time. Lastly. Vitius Pleasures ar like Riuers that discharge themselues into the Sea, sweet at the Spring, but salt at the Mouth;[83] whereas those of Vertu ar like a Cup of Beere and Sugar, which is euer the Sweeter, the neerer yow come to the Bottom. ↑And

---

[80] For a similar illustration, see *Swearing* 6.25.

[81] Bacon used the same proverb in "Of Seeming Wise."

[82] A common trope in *carpe diem* poetry: cf. the first stanza of Robert Herrick's "To the Virgins, to make much of Time." For later attacks on transient pleasures, see *Reconcileableness* 4.185 and *Chr. Virtuoso* 6.791.

[83] For a similar image, cf. "Dayly Reflection" f. 282v; for RB's explanation of this phenomenon, see "Saltness of the Sea" (3.764-81).

<Or> as a religious Poet of ours has pithily exprest it

> If thou do Ill, the Ioy Fades, not the Paines:
> If Wel, the Paines doe Fade, the Ioy remaines.↓[84]

Remorse of Conscience is <oftentimes> a Shrewd thorn in [the] <our> sides, eu'n in the very Act and heiht of our sinful Delihts.[85] For Generally, [any] whatsouer it be that |f. 215| Crimes acquire vs, is like a peece of meat that a Dog snatch't out of a boyling Pot, whereby he so scalded his Chops [in] with the snatching it, that it [def] frustrates him of the Pleasure he hop't for in the Eating it. But when once <the> vnrelenting Archer coms to stare thee in the Face, and thy Conscience, (which, as one wittily obserues then vses to speake loudest, when men grow speechless)[86] wil no longer be put of; but sets thy Sins in order before thee; then all thy past Plesures wil become thy present Sorrows, and (without timely Repentance,) thy future torments; which wil be both Intolerable and Interminable; and wil neuer, either remit of their Degree, or draw neerer to their End. Then [our] we haue no such Paines, as our former Plesures; and 'tis a Deth for vs to thinke vpon our past liues. This same Sin is a Viper <Serpent> that has his Poyson in it's Tayle:[87] and indeed it is the vsual Stratagem of the Deuil to flatter vs into security with the Concealment of our Vices, til by presenting them all in a Body to our expiring Eys, he can friht vs into Despaire.[88] |f. 215v| [On the] The Vertuus man on the other side, [in] at the End of his Days finds but the Beginning of his Happiness: and that there is no Prospect in the whole world, like that which from a man's Deth-bed looks bac vpon a wel-acted Life: when a man can walk bac againe to his Cradle, without being frihted in the way by any Sinful Enormitys of his Life. This Inward Release of the Conscience giues <strokes> a man <with> a [Ioy that] <Peace of Mind as> alone [can] is

---

[84] George Herbert, *The Temple* (1633, first ed.), "The Church-Porch," ll. 461-62. This poem was clearly a favorite of RB's, for he quoted it four times in the *Aret*. The concluding stanza is representative of this poem, though not the larger collection in which it appeared: "In brief, acquit thee bravely; play the man. / Look not on pleasures as they come, but go. Deferre not the least vertue: lifes poor span / Make not an ell by trifling in thy wo. / If thou do ill; the joy fades, not the pains: / If well; the pain doth fade, the joy remains." For this famous concluding couplet, F. E. Hutchinson noted the many classical authors who described the brevity of pleasure and the persistence of shame (*The Works of George Herbert* [Oxford 1941] 483-84).

[85] This proverb is also used in bk. 1, ch. 2.

[86] The horrors of a guilty conscience were richly described by many contemporary writers.

[87] S858, "The sting is in the tail" or S859, "There is a sting in the tail of all unlawful pleasures." For RB's experimental work with vipers, see *Usefulness* 2.85-89 and *Simple Medicines* 5.126. In the former experiment, RB paid a man to have a viper bite him, so that RB could test a remedy.

[88] Dramatizing the evasions and seductions of self-deception was especially popular in works of practical divinity. In 1648 Hartlib published a translation of Jacobus Acontius's *Satanæ Strategemata* as *Satans Stratagems, or the devils Cabinet-Council Discovered*.

able to more then Counteruaile all the Pleasures whereof Vertu can abridge vs: a Ioy so transcendent that it is far better felt then express't; and which like the new name written in the white Stone, Reuel. 2.17, none can [sufficiently] <fully> kno as he that has <receaueth> it. The Notional taste of it's sweetness being nothing to the Experimental tast thereof. To conclude ↑(with the Words of an Excellent Modern Author) in a Word, the Plesure of the Body is but the Body of Plesure; but the Deliht of the Soule is the Soule of Deliht.↓[89]

(But of <about> most of these Particular Points, the Reader, may, God willing, receaue further satisfaction heereafter in their due Places.) |f. 216|

IV.

For the Fourth. It is generally obserued, that al those that ar lest led by Reason, ar most led by Example. Which if it be true, who can dout how great an Influence the Examples of others must necessarily haue vpon the Axions of Children: who like Apes, acting more by Imitation then Reason, and being very apt to do whatsouer they see don, may be easily molded into almost any Form <that> their Instructors please. And certinly most men ar more powerfully if wrouht vpon by Examples <those liuing laws> then <by ded> Precepts: because those barely chalk vs out the Way; these do not onely that, but quicken vs in it: partly by Emulation, and partly by the Remouall of that <usual> objection of Difficulty with which we ar apt to stop the Mouths of our Consciences.[90] Besides, that men giue far more Credit to our Axions then our Words, and take nothing so much Notice of what we say as of what we do. Where for it is very requisite that our Youth shud haue such an Instructor, as shal not onely point him out, but lead himself the Way that he shud go. For he that teaches wel and liues ill, puls down more with his hands then he builds vp with his Tong: Men being very inclinable to beleeue, that if [he spoke what he means, he wud] |f. 216v| his Words were suitable to his opinions; his actions wud neuer be so vnsuitable to his Words. But aboue all Domestick Examples ar heer both most necessary and most to be regarded: not onely for their frequency (tho that be very

[89] Source unknown.

[90] The persuasive power of examples is a recurrent theme. In *Theodora* 5.257, RB observed that devotional writing would render virtue amiable and recommend piety "to . . . readers, that are much more affected by shining examples, and pathetical expressions, than by dry precepts, and grave discourses." For the danger of bad examples, see *Greatness of Mind* 5.559. But even in natural philosophy, RB later wrote, most "readers, to whom we would give good impressions of the study of nature, . . . will probably be more wrought upon by the variety of examples, and easy experiments, than by the deepest notions, and the neatest hypotheses" (*Usefulness* 3.395). The proverb lore associated with examples was also very rich: I65, "Infants' manners are molded more by the example of parents than by stars at their nativity"; E213, "Examples teach more than precepts"; P561, "He preaches well that lives well."

considerable) but also for that in all Actions, the Autority of the Person giues autority to the Example. And Children ar very apt to persuade themselues, that it is a kind of proud vndutifulness, to aspire to be better men then their Fathers. ↑Thus we see that <even> whole Kingdoms vse to coppy after the Example of the Princes Practice, and [ar] do far more carefully conform themselues to his Life then to his Laws.↓ Whence it happens for the most part, that the Sins of Parents ar the Parents of Sins; as the Vertus of the Teachers ar the Teachers of Vertu: And, as one says very wel, A father that whipping his Child for swearing, swore himself in the whipping him, did more harm by his Example then Good by his Correction. Tho indeed it be but a sheepish <kind of> obsequiusness to follo rather men's bad Examples then their good Precepts: as if I shud not rather beleeue /take part with/ men's rectify'd reasons then their depraued Affections: or he cud not haue a good Ey that has but lame feet. For my part I shud desire to lern Vertu of one that cud teach me better the Practice |f. 217| of it then the Definition.[91] But if that Happines be deny'd me, I [shal] <wud> do in my Enquiry after the ways of Vertu, as we vse to do about <that of> the hih-ways that lead from one Place to another; where if we meet a fellow that profers to conduct vs, we ask not how good a man he is, but how good a Guide. And since there is scarce any man (in this Life) so compleatly wicked, but that there is som thing of good in him, nor <any> so perfectly Vertuus, that his Practice is a full and adequate Pattern of Perfection, it wil be no vnprofitable aduice, not to [esteem] <value /rate/> too [much] <precicely> the Example by the Person, nor by ones self altogether to the Examples of one or a few [Persons:] <men, tho neuer so excellent,> confining ones haruest to one onely Field, as if an Alms were to be refused, because it is a gowty hand that holds it forth. But like the Bee, <to> suck Hony out of euery Example, and to gather a flower tho it gro but in a Ditch, and trample vpon a Weed, tho [w] <we find> it spring<ing> in a Garden.

V.

For the Fifth. If Good Examples (as we haue seen already) be such great[ly] furtherers to Youth in<to> the Acquisition of Vertu; I think it will not be douted, but that Good Company dos also greatly conduce thereunto: being nothing else but as it were a continuall |f. 217v| Chaine or Succession of Examples; which tho perhaps they affect vs not so much as others do for the time, yet

[91] Cf. *Philaretus's* description of Marcombes, whose "practicall Sentiments . . . in Diuinity were most of them very sound; & if he were giu'n to any Vice himselfe, he was carefull by sharply condemning it, to render it vninfectious; being industrious, whatsoeuer he were himselfe, to make his Charges, Vertuous" (Maddison 22). His only vice being choler (Maddison 22), he was perhaps the Frenchman whom RB cured of choler (*Swearing* 6.20-21).

supplying with their frequency what they want in their force, they do by insensible Degrees work the mind to a (kind of) Conformity [wi] /to/ those we conuerse with.[92] For not onely Loue makes vs desirous to resemble those that we [loue] /affect/ but most men (and youth especially) being asham'd to be heteroclites /Sep/ from the rest of the Company; it happens that amongst good Companions Vertu comming to be in Fashion, Vice, out of a self-guiltines is easily dash't out of Countenance, and may be forgot by Discontinuance: which how considerable an aduantage it affords, is not easy to be beleeued. ↑The siht of others falling heartily to their Vittles awakens our Stomacks /Appetite/.↓ Eu'n Saul himselfe cud profecy when amongst the Profets, 1 Sam. 10.10 and 19.20 &c. Good companions, like Princes in a Defensiue Leage, defend each other from the Attempts of the Common Enemy; no good motion amongst them goes out for want of cherishing, [n]or [lys hid] <droopes> for want of exciting: for like fire-brands put <set> together they enflame each other with the Loue of Vertu. Neither ar the Aduantages of good Company restrained to the Mind only, but redound also to the |f. 218| Benefit of our Reputation, by the Good opinion it acquires vs amongst the better sort of People, of our Fortune by preseruing that from [the] Dissipation by riotous Courses; and of our Bodys, by abridging them of Intemperant excesses. Besides that the Society of the Godly oftentimes, makes vs either Sharers in their Blessings, as Iacob's did Laban, and Iosefs Potiphar; or auerts Iudgments from vs, as ten rihteus Persons wud haue sau'd <eu'n> beastly Sodomites from that fiery Deluge,[93] [or] and St. Paul's Company preseru'd all those that were with him ↑in the Ship↓ from the Merciless Fury of the Waues, Acts. 27.24. To be short, Euery man is expensiue of that Quality that is Prædominant in him, and labours to assimilate others to himselfe. And [euery] there is no man that has not in him both Good and Bad, either of which Encreses as it finds it like, or declines as it meets with it's contrary. Thus Peter that denyed Christ amongst the Iewes, <Priests> confessed him amongst the Apostles. Wherefore it is very requisite that our Youth be [con] bred vp amongst honest Companions; and, if it may be, amongst such that ar (or at least som of them) better and wiser then |f. 218v| themselues; that they may haue always som thing to lern, and be less subiect to ouer-weening. Tis but a mean kind of Pride to striue to be always the best man of the Company; and to be ambitious to be euer the best man of the Company is [the next way] <a ready way> to becom the Worst. Not that I wud haue him gro the worst man in the Company he keeps, but

[92] Many books in RB's library stressed the danger of bad company: cf. Henry Scudder, *The Christians Dayly Walke* (1637) 214ff. RB made similar points in a letter to the anonymous Count in 1647 (1.xliii), *Occ. Refl.* 2.420-23, and *Greatness of Mind* 5.559. The store of proverbs is very rich: T87, "Tell me with whom whou goest an will tell thee what thou doest"; M536, "Keep not ill men company lest you increase the number"; or C570, "It is better to be alone than in bad company."

[93] See Gen. 24:29-31:55, 39:1-18, and 18:32; see also "Joseph's Mistress" below.

that I wud haue him endevor to keepe Company with such men as may be better then himselfe. Gold (says one) carried vsually in the same Pocket amongst syluer, looses both of it's Colour and Weiht. And so do men by the Frequent hanting of Inferior Company. I wil conclude with this Caution: that howsoeuer a Constant breeding amongst Vertuus Company, haue al the Aduantages that we haue spoken of; yet it wil not be amiss now and then vpon occasion to let our Youth haue a taste [of] /Siht/ of Euill; that he may thereby lern to detest it.[94] For if Young men ar neuer permitted the Siht of Bad Company, they ar apt to Imagine to themselues a Sweetness in it, that wil fal short in their Triall, and restrained Nature gros more Violent: Indeed, if we cud passe the World without |f. 219| Meeting Vice, this kind of Practice were [needless:] <necessary> but since that is a Happinesss not to be expected here, it is little less Necessary, [to] for our Vertuus Youth to haue som Knoledg of the Ways and Stratagems of Vitius men: then it is for the Logician to lern the Doctrine of Sophismes, or the Fisitian that of Diseases. As the skilfull Pilot, we see, knos as well the Rocks, and Coasts, and Shelues and quicksands; as the safest Harbors or securest Channels.

It is <not> therefor [good] <amisse> vpon occasion to let our Youth haue a siht of the Riotous Courses of Euil Company, that when his occasions <necessarily> lead him to their conuersation, he may not be a Nouice amongst them, nor vtterly vnacquainted with their Tricks and Delusions: which has been often obserued to haue been the ruine of hopeful Youths. Prouided always, that our Youth haue with him, some body to antidote him against the Infection of wicked acquaintance, and to teach him to make a Good vse of Bad /Euil/ Company; as indeed it may be made of the worst. For since we haue not only Vertuus Actions to Imitate but Vitius to auoid; as the Examples of Good men furnish with Presidents for the former, so those of Bad men, ar our best Instructors concerning the latter. |f. 219v| Certinly, Companyons ar like Book's; out of the very worst somthing of Good may be pick't:[95] and there is [scarce any] not any cheaper, nor

[94] Recalling visits to Florentine bordellos in 1641 or 1642, RB noted that he would "sometimes scruple, in his Gouernor's Company, to visit the famousest Bordellos; whither resorting out of bare Curiosity, he retain'd there an vnblemish't Chastity, & still return'd thence as honest as he went thither. Professing that he neuer found any such sermons against them, as they were against themselues. The Impudent Nakedness of vice, clothing it with a Difformity, Description cannot reach, & the worst of Epithetes cannot but flatter" (Maddison 40). In *Swearing* 6.15, RB recounted that he "was much taken with an *Italian* gentleman, who spying a friend of his peep out his head from behind the door of a *Bordello*, to see if he might retire undiscovered; 'Come forth, come forth, cries he; you need not be ashamed to leave that sluttish place; but you should have been ashamed to have entered it.'" Cf. W531, "To the wise it is no shame to enter a bawdy house, but not to know the way out on it."

[95] This commonplace may be derived from Pliny the Younger, *Epistolae* III.5: "No book is so bad but benefit may be derived from some part." In his *Areopagitica* (1644), Milton could not praise a fugitive and cloistered virtue. Pepys's attitude toward the uses of wicked books makes an interest-

scarce any better way to lern the Detestation of Vice, then [to read] out [out] of other's Vitius Actions to read Lectures of the Contrary Vertu[u]s.[96] ↑Wise men lern mor by fools, then fools by Wise men: for Wisdom can make vse of Folly, but not folly of Wisdom.↓ For Vice is such a lothsom Complexion, that [illeg.] meerly to see it naked, is to any ingenuus mind, a sufficient motiue to detest it.[97] The Vgliness of Sin in other's teches vs it's Deformity in our selues; and it is but a Vanity to beleeue, that others find not Vices [as] to be as misbecomming in [ot] vs; as we do in them. So that at the last /worst/ we can at least make this vse of the [be] worst Company; [either] to lern, either to abandon those falts that we haue, or to auoid those that we may fal <illeg.> into: making it serue, either as [a Purge] <Fisic> to [cure] <remedy> past Faults; <sins> or an Antidote to preuent Future. But by the way it wil be very vsefull to take Notice, that of all other Vitius companions those ar the most Dangerus, (especially to Youth,) that haue both great Parts, and, little, or less gross and |f. 220| remarkable Vices. For whilst we admire the Persons, and that wit wherwith they Excuse their Faults, ↑(which ar not scandalous /palpable/ enuf to carry <bear> with themselues their owne Condemnation)↓ we are easily persuaded that those Fauts /Errors, or Failings/ of theirs ar the Issue of their Iudgments, which ar indeed but the Of-spring of their ([Irreg] vnruly) affections. Whereas Gros, heinous, and Palpable Sinners, (as we haue already insinuated) ar Sermons against themselues, and like vgly (sluttish) <pocky> Whores, becom their own Antidotes. [/antidotes agenst themselues./] ↑And for one [wel] not wel rooted in Vertu to conuerse <frequently> with Profane Wits; [is] in hope to lern wit by their Company; is to go in to an Infected howse to fetch <look for> out a [Iewell] [gau] gaudy Sute of Clothes: where the Danger is far greater then the Aduantage.↓[98]

---

ing contrast (February 8-9, 1669).

[96] Cf. *Occ. Refl.* 2.336, where RB argued that meditation could make "the world vocal, by furnishing every creature, and almost every occurrence, with a tongue to entertain him with, and [could] make the little accidents of his life, and the very flowers of his garden, read him lectures of ethicks or divinity." Browne noted that the heathens "knew better how to joyne and reade these mysticall letters [of nature], than wee Christians, who cast a more carelesse eye on these common Hieroglyphicks, and disdain to suck Divinity from the flowers of nature" *Religio Medici*, ed. L. C. Martin (Oxford 1964) ii.§16, p.15.

[97] In *Phaedrus* 250D, Plato argued that to see beauty would lead to a love of wisdom. Cicero quoted this point in *De Officiis* 1.15.

[98] An early instance of the danger of the "Wits" to moral judgment and behavior. RB's long poem "against Wit Profanely or Wantonly employ'd" has not survived (Maddison 21).

Book Two, Chapter Four

VI.

For the Sixth. Vertu grows Dul without the Spurs of Honor and Reward: ↑and Vice gros hedstrong without the Curbs Of Feare and Punishment.↓ And the Pöet tels vs that Honos alit Artes: Commendations water Knoledge.[99] It wil be therefore very vseful to prayse [before our] in the Presence of our Youth som of his Companions for som Quality that he either wants, or possesses but in a more remiss Degree: and so to kindle Emulation betwixt them, which is commonly hottest amongst Equals, and to which Youth is [commonly] <usually> very Inclinable.[100] Prouided always that there be a great Deale of Care had to hinder this Emulation from degenerating into Enuy: which differs from Emulation, in that This makes vs desirous to imitate and Excell men's Qualitys; whereas that causes <us> to hate |f. 220v| or maligne their Persons. It is also very good, if our Youth be of an Ingenuus Disposition, to commend him for his very Endeuors, tho they fall short of the Desired Effect; and in the Presence of others to praise him for some good quality that he has yet but imperfectly attained: for that wil <oftentimes> work very strange effects, and make him striue to excell himself, and be extreamely industrious in the acquisition of that quality that he is commended for; lest he shud frustrate that expectation that he belieues men haue conceiued of him.[101] Neither has experience found it fruitless to [giue] cherish with pretty recompenses the first Essays, or master-peeces of deseruing Youth: and what to others is giuen as a Due, to giue to them <him> as a Reward. But if all this will not [d] incite our Youth to the Loue of Vertu; at lest let Chastisement deter him from the Practice of Vice: and this Chastisement ouht to be Seasonable, Reasonable, and Suitable to the Faut and Person. [For] Of the First of these Propertys we haue said somthing already, to which I wil only now ad; that the Correction ouht almost to ouertake the Fault before it haue hardened him and, (as it were) erth't it self in him; and tauht him to excuse one fault with a<nother> greater. |f. 221| And that a Twig wil easily whip that fault out of a Child, that a Cudgel will scarcely be able to beat out of him when hee's once grown a man. For the Second, the Correction to be Reasonable must be don calmly, and without Anger; that it may appeare [that yow ch] that yow whip not the Boy but the Sin, and punish, not the Iniury but the Offence. For he that chastises [in] <with> Passion, commonly chastizes without Reason, and teaches the Youth to hate rather his [Master] <Teacher> then his Faut. Besides, to be

---

99 Cicero, *Tusculan Disputations* 1.4.5. It is not clear why RB attributed this tag to a poet.

100 RB's head master at Eton, John Harrison, "would sometimes commend others before [RB] to rowze his Emulation, & oftentimes giue him Commendations before others, to engage his Endeauors to deserue them" (Maddison 14-15).

101 RB reported that in the presence of others, Marcombes was "always very Ciuill to his Pupills; apt to Eclipse their Failings, & sett off their Good qualitys to the best aduantage" (Maddison 22).

Reasonable it must be accompany'd with Instruction: and an endeauor to make the Corrected party more sorrowful for his Faut then for his Punishment; and sensible that yow giue his Correction, not to Passion but Iustice, and not to a reuengful Appetite in your self, but a Desire of his Good and amendment. [And for the Last.] To beat people without teaching them is to vse them worse then Dogs. Instruction must be first premised; and then Correction put it home. Instruction without any Correction makes vs impudently bold; and Correction without instruction makes vs slauishly fearfull.

And for the third. The Punishment must not exceed the Fault; nor equal it; if it be waited on by Contrition; it being a kind of Iniustice to giue him his full measure of Correction, who has |f. 221v| already inflicted (a great) part of it vpon himself by his Repentance. As for the Persons of them that offend; Stubborn Natures must be tamed with sharp Corrections; and the Remedy answer the Disease: but soft <fine> and Noble Dispositions ar better wrouht vpon by threatnings and Shame; and to som Natures; tis a sufficient punishment to [let] <make> them kno that they haue deseru'd it. Whens arises that Custom (tho how iust, may be question'd) receiued in diuers places, not to whip the Children of Princes and greate men, but som of their Fauorite Companions in their stead; that they may see in what others suffer for them [illeg.] what themselues haue deserued; and their owne faults in other's Punishments.[102] But here we ar carefully to take heed neuer to put any Youth to so open and great a Shame, that may banish shame out of him heereafter, and exempt him from the Feare of a greater; for [by too strait pinching /curbing/ him to break that principal Curbe] ↑that yow may beat him with the raines, to pul ouer /of of/ his head the Principal Bridle↓ that restraines the Wicked from the most [abhominable offences] <licentius villanyes>; and has prou'd the [ruine] <undoing> of many a Youth that had not perhaps otherwise prou'd <half> so incorrigible. And heer I cannot but take notice of a preposterous c[o]ustom [gen] too commonly receiued amongst the vulgar of our Teachers, |f. 222| whereby they wil more and sooner correct a Youth for his Faults in matter of Lerning, then those that he commits agenst Vertu: sooner for breaking of the head of Priscian, (as they vse to speake) then for so doing to that of Socrates; sooner for a Solecism then a Sin, and for speaking Fals, then for speaking Falsly. As if [to be a good Gra] it were more important or more in our Power to be a Good Grammarian then a good man; and to trangress <forget> the Rules of Lilly /Gramer/ a greater [faut] <crime,> then to violate the Lawes of God.[103]

---

[102] In his *Church-History of Britain* (1655), Thomas Fuller mentioned that Mungo Murray served as whipping boy for Charles I.

[103] "Breaking the head of Priscian" meant violating a rule of grammar, Priscian being a Roman grammarian (c. 500); William Lily (or Lilly) was the author of a famous grammar that saw many editions and imitations after 1567. RB owned a 1679 edition of Lily, but many other grammars in

VII.

For the Seuenth. By Heroic Ends I mean our Resolution and Endeauor to attaine an Eminency in Vertu; and as St. Peter bids vs to grow in Grace 2. Pet. 3.18. and not stint our selues too quickly in Vertu, by saying, so much is a Competency for me of Goodness, and so far I wil go, and not a step further. ↑See Matt. 5,48. 1 Cor. 1,10. and 14,20. and 13,10. Eph. 6,13. Ph. 3,15. Coloss, 1.28. 1 Pet. 1,13.↓ We ar but il marksmen at Goodness, and always vndershoot the White /mark/ and therefor to hit it, we must be careful to take our aime aboue it. He shal seldom obtaine to be Good that endeuors not to be very good; nor a common Vertu that [st] labors not for an excellent one. Certinly, a kind of |f. 222v| Lethargy /Drowsines/ of the Mind has been a Disease long Epidemicall to the World: and there is a world of barren parts /land/ yet in the Soules of men that containe rich mines in them, and wud easily admit of a Further improuement. And that Beame of Diuinity (that rather wants the vse of it's strength <Power> then strength to vse) makes many things Difficult or Impossible, meerly by it's beleeuing them to his own Strength and how to vse it) miht not vndertake and go thorouh with? But of this more heereafter. Let vs for the present take notice, that one of the maine causes why men ar vniversally so Defectiue in Goodness, is because they ar too Abject <drooping> in their Ends and [then it is no wo] fix their Hercules'es Pillars too neere;[104] and then it is no <great> wonder if he dos not shoot hih that aimes low. Wherefor it wil be requisite to infuse into the mind of our Youth [Gal] Gallant /honest/ and Noble resolutions; and to propose to his Imitation the [fairest] <most compleate> Patterns of Vertu to coppy out. For certinly, As he that shoots at the Sun, shoots hiher then he that means but a Tree; /stone/ so most commonly he that aimes at Perfection in Vertu; coms neerer to it, then he that intends but a Mediocrity. |f. 223| It is also good to make men sensible with all, that it is their Duty, in case they find themselues inabled, not only to arriue at, but euen to go beyond their Presidents. For to what End were these Greater Abilitys bestowed vpon vs, but that our Vertus shud be answerable to our Parts. He that had [10] <5> Talents, <and> brouht in to his Lord [10] <5> Talents of Improuement; which he is no more thanked for then he that hauing but 2 improu'd those 2 to four, Matt. 25. For vnto whomsoeuer, (says our Sauior) much is giuen, of him shal be much required.[105] Luk. 12.48. The Pallace of Vertu had for euer ly'n vnbuilt, if euery man had stay'd til som body else had layd the first stone. And sure if all [we] the

---

his library were derived from Lily: cf. Thomas Granger, *Syntagma Grammaticum, or an Easie, and Methodicall Explanation of Lillies Grammar* (1616).

[104] The Pillars of Hercules were the two promontories at the Strait of Gibraltar.

[105] This is the first of five references in this volume to the parable of the talents.

World has been infected with this same lazy Opinion; he that first began to walk <creepe> in the Paths of Vertu; had confin'd the Actiuity of all his Successours to that Snaile-like Pace, and hindred them from running to Felicity. And [the] Mankind had been to this day depriued of all those Heroick Examples that haue eterniz'd the Glory of their Authors, and render'd Antiquity the Wonder <Admiration> of succeeding Ages. But to auoid diuers Misprisions that may be made of this Doctrine, we shal need a double Caution. The First is, that this gretness of aimes is always to be vnderstood, in proportion to men's |f. 223v| Abilitys and Condition; so that he that according to the Parts and meanes that he is endow'd with dos aim at a proportionable degree of Vertu, performs that which in this place we require. Where it is neuertheless [di] worthy to be obserued, that there being as it were 2 ranks of Vertus; the one consisting principally in Doing, and to whose Eminency outward meanes ar necessary, as Liberality, Courage and the like; and the other cheefly in abstaining, ↑in declining Vices,↓ and for which [we are princi] outward helps ar not so requisite, as Temperance, Patience, and the like: it is in euery man's Power to attaine an [good] <Eminent> Degree of these latter; but not so of the Former. As it is not in euery man to imitate the Mu<ag>nificence and Magnamimity of Alexander,[106] but any man may (if he wil all the Endeuor that he may) imitate the Temperance and Patience of Socrates; and auoid the Lust and Cruelty of detestable Nero. For it is far more easy to decline men's Vices then to imitate their Vertus. And therefor it has been truly said that none but Heros shud vnderstake to repeate the Actions of Heros; and that they ar proposed to [common] <ordinary> men, not to Imitate, but to admire.[107] The Second Caution is, |f. 224| That when we haue to do with [abiect] <meane> or [stubbor] Vicius Natures, or else with great Persons that cannot endure to be opposed; [that] it were indiscreet to press them to too strict a preciceness at the beginning; for when they beleeue that they shal neuer hold vp to the Top of the Hill, they wil be apt to refuse to climb vp a foot: and [those] we must be content to make them a little Good, whom we ar vnable to make better: besides that when we haue once got them on a little way in the Paths of Vertu; we may the more easily work vpon them more, and invite them to a further Progress: as we see in sic Persons; we may make them by little and little drink of and retaine that Potion, which shud we powre down into their Stomakes at one drauht, they wud cast vp euery drop againe. The Neglect of this Caution I am confident has occasioned the Ruine of many, whom the indiscreet seuerity of Som of the Vertuus has frihted from Goodnes in their very first adresses to it. So that what an Italian Statesmen says of Princes, ↑in matter of Gouernment

---

[106] One of RB's favorite books at Eton was the life of Alexander by Quintus Curtius Rufus (Maddison 15); RB owned a 1633 edition. Once while travelling, RB stopped at an inn and was so engrossed in reading Quintus Curtius that the coach left without him (BL Add. MS 4229, f. 66).

[107] Heroic virtue is discussed at length in bk. 2, ch. 7.

/Policy/↓ may be very wel applyed ↑in an absolute sence↓ to multitudes of other Persons; namely that Those who too seuerely restrain them within certin narrow limits, dishearten, not instruct them: whence it oftentimes ensues, that hauing broken those narrow bounds; and thereby thinking that they haue transgressed |f. 224v| the Lawes of a Good Prince, they becom hedlong as bad as who is worst.[108]

VIII.

For the Eighth. That it is very requisite (if not absolutely necessary) to settle our Youth, of what Degree or Quality soeuer, in a fit Vocation, may appeare, because 1. A Conuenient ciuil Calling is a[n] souueraigne Preseruatiue agenst Idleness, (that mother of Vices) and an excellent preuention [against] <of> a world of Idle, Mclancholick and exorbitant thouhts, and vn-warrantable Actions.[109] 2. Diligence in a lawfull Calling is either Necessary or vsefull for a comfortable Prouision of Erthly Necessarys and Conueniencys; God's Blessing vpon this Diligence being his vsual way to enrich his Seruants with temporal blessings; and the Apostle tels vs that if we prouide not for our Family, we ar worse then Infidels.[110] 1 Tim. 5,8. 3. He is but an vseless wastful Droane, and vnworthy of the Benefits of Humane Society; whose endeauors in som honest particular Calling, do not som way or other Cooperate (and contribute) to the Good of the Common-welth. |f. 225| 4. An honest Calling is an Academy <School> of Vertu; and giues occasion both to acquire those Good qualitys that we want and Exercice and improue those that we possess. 5. The Command [(or rat] is vniuersal to Adam and his whole Posterity Gen. 3,19. In the Sweate of thy Face shalt thou eat bread, til thou return vnto the Ground; either by Labor of Body, or Toyle of Mind, or both. Wherefor no greatnes can iustly plead an

---

[108] I have not found a source for this view. RB referred to Machiavelli five times in *Style* (2.296, 309, 312-13, and 315), but other possibilities include the writings of RB's grandfather, Sir Geoffrey Fenton. Fenton translated a number of books (some of Cork's proudest possessions) on political and moral topics: *A Forme of Christian Pollicie* (1574) dealt with moral and political principles of Christian government; *Golden Epistles* (1575) contained a "varietie of discourse both morall, philosophicall, and divine"; *The History of Guicciardin* (1579) was a translation of a history of the wars in Italy. For a discussion of the latter, see Canny 28.

[109] I13, "Idleness is the mother of vices." For a similar discussion and similar examples, see Burton, *Anatomy* 1.242-44 and "Of Time and Idleness." Robert Bolton stressed the importance of an honest calling in *General Directions for a Comfortable Walking with God* (1638) 48-50.

[110] When RB's father sought to recall RB and Frank after the outbreak of the rebellion, he wrote to Marcombes (9 March 1641): "But as I am compelled in my age to doe, soe must they in their yonger yeares commend themselues, and the raiseing of their estates, to gods blessing and their owne good fortunes, and soe with your assistance dispose of themselues, either the one way or the other, as they may hereafter worke out a fortune for themselues, for I am no longer able to giue them exhibition. But yf they serue God, and be carefull and discreet in their carriadge, God will bless and prouide for them, as hitherto he hath done for me . . ." (*II Lismore* 5.22).

Exemption from a Vocation: which eu'n Adam had in the glory of his Innocency, Gen. 2.15. Neither ar riches giuen vs meerly to enjoy but [also] to Vse; there being no reason that because a man is Steward of a great family, he shud [hau] cast of all care of Administration: since to whom most is giuen, of him shal be most required.[111] Of the 2 Brothers that shar'd the World betwixt them the one was a Plow-man, and the other a Shepheard.[112] And Examples ar frequent in Scripture of those whom neither Nobility, nor Welth, nor Grace, hindred from Labor in a ciuil calling. ↑See (also) Ps. 128,2. Pr. 10,4. and 12,11 and 13,4. and 20,4. and 28,19. and 31,27. Eccles. 5,12. Eph. 4,28. 1. Thess. 3,10,12. Iob. 5,7.↓ Amongst the Romans euery man was to weare in the Streets the Badg of that Profession that he liu'd by: (If that law were transplanted |f. 225v| hither, I'm afeard our Streets wud hardly be ouer-[thron] <crowded>:)[113] and amongst them too, rustick Labors <haue> Christen'd many Noble Familys: neither is the Example obscure of that Famous Dictator, who from putting his Oxen vnder the Yoake, was [ele] chosen to bring his Cuntry's enemys vnder the Yoake: which <peece of> seruice he had no sooner performed, then he cheerfully returned to his Old employment agen.[114] Since then a <som> Vocation is necessary, it wil be very expedient that our Youth fal to it betimes; both for the facility of his Lerning, which is greater then, than at other times: and for to auoid that Idleness, which miht otherwise endanger him: for many, hauing too long thout it too erly to begin at last com too think it too late, and make it their Vocation to haue none: these had rather beg then work, and make their Tongs, not their hands, to feed their Mouths. But against these sturdy beggers it is wisely ordain'd by the Laws of China, that they shud be <soundly> punish't that needlesly beg an Alms; and they no les punisht that ar such fools as to giue it them.[115] Now this Particular Vocation, to be fit /good/ ouht to haue these 2 Propertys, namely, that it be, both Lawfull and Conuenient. 1. For the First of these; |f. 226| If the Calling be not lawful, we can neither labor in it with Comfort; nor expect God's blessing vpon our Labors.

Tis a sad Case when a man is bred vp to such a Profession, that he must of Force be vndon either in this World or in the next: And those Sins ar very

[111] Luke 12:48.

[112] Gen. 4:1-25.

[113] Style and ornamentation of togas signalled social status and some social roles (e.g., of senators), as RB would have learned from Cicero and Livy. For a helpful description of "masterless men," see Christopher Hill, *The World Turned Upside Down* (Harmondsworth 1972), ch. 3, and A. L. Beier, *Masterless Men: the Vagrancy Problem in England, 1560-1640* (London 1985). Webster discusses the proposals of the Hartlib circle for employing the poor (361-69).

[114] The reference is to Cincinnatus.

[115] On indiscriminate almsgiving, see Todd, *Christian Humanism*, 137-38 and 164-65. RB could have learned about the laws of China from Alvaro Semmedo's *History of China* (1642), for he twice referred to this book in *Usefulness* 2.104 and 161.

seldom banish't that can plead Necessity for their Stay: Interest and Necessity being obserued to be of all <other> Diuels the 2 hardest to be cast out. Wherefor we must be sure, that the Generall and Particular Callings do not clash together: a Care that in som men's Opinion belongs to the Magistrate, as being his Duty to suffer <tolerate> no dishonest Professions in the Common-welth: for it seems to them a kind of Injustice that he shud be punish't for being a Knaue in his Profession, that is a Knaue by his Profession.

2. To com to the Second. The Conueniency of a Calling consists in a double Fitness /suitableness/ the one to the Disposition, and the other to the Condition of the Party. As for the Former, the Calling shud be such (if it may be) to which the Party is naturally fit and inclined; or at lest such as for which he has no violent auersion: for men seldom arriue at any degree of excellency in that which they vndertake against their Nature[s] and Wils; (as hauing a double difficulty to surmount, that of the thing it self; and that |f. 226v| of their (own) auersion:) whereas a Natural Inclination to any thing is vsually accompany'd by an aptness /fitness/ to it; and dos extreamely facilitate the way to a Perfection in it.[116] Wherefore in som common-welths anciently, and yet to this day in som of the Estern parts, it is the care of a Publicke Magistrate wel skil'd in those Bisnesses, to sift out Children's Dispositions, and fit them with Callings answerable thereunto. And the Ancient Egyptians were so scrupulous in this Particular; that their Custom (tho in many <some> things not commendable) [was,] when any man had a mind to settle his Son in som certin Trade, was; to leade him thorough all the Streets of the Towne, that hauing seen all the Trades that were there practic'd /exercic'd/ he may make choice of that to which his Nature most inclin'd him.[117] ↑We must not therefore send a soft contemplatiue Nature to the Warres; nor one that delihts but in Drums and Trumpets and Armes and Blood, to the Vniversity and so forth.↓ But this Doctrine must be taken with this Prouiso: that in the Children of mean and Needy Persons, the Inclination must not be so much [loo] considered as the Necessity: and generally; if the Auersion of the Party against a Calling in all other Particulars conuenient, be but little; it is not much to be regarded; as that which by Reason and Custom, will in time be easily surmounted.[118] |f. 227|

As for the Latter. The Profession must be suitable /answerable/ to the Condition of the Person; being neither too much aboue it; nor so abiect as to dishonor [it] (or preiudice) it. For euery man is not bound to labor with his hands: there is a Sweat of the Braines, perhaps no less Toylsom then the Sweat of the

[116] Canny observes that "despite Cork's belief that a man's aptitude and temperament were formed from birth he clearly thought that education determined the formation of character" (120-21).

[117] Burton noted a similar example (*Anatomy* 2.70). For an overview of Puritan and Anglican views of vocation and work, see Todd, ch. 5.

[118] Cf. Webster, ed. *Samuel Hartlib and the Advancement of Learning* (Cambridge 1970).

Brow: and the Seueral Necessitys and conuenyences of man require seueral [Prof] Vocations to remedy /supply/ or attaine them. A great man may employ himself, either in Embassys abroad, Magistracys at home, Commanding the Field /warres/, making of Books, ordering his houshold, improuing his Fortune or his Mind; or in acquiring those things that ar necessary or conducible to [the acq] these, and make that his Calling. While a Gentleman; (to calm that Tempest this Doctrine has rais'd amongst them) [When is in any lawfull <honest> way doing Good to himself, his is emp] busying himself in any lawfull Employment that tends to the Good, of himself, his Family, others, or the Commonwelth, he may be (fauorably) thouht <beleeued> to be diligent /to embrace/ in his Profession. |f. 227v| But when a Gentleman ↑(of which pray God we haue not too many:)↓ that may (if he will) be an vseful Instrument of the Publick Good; shal spend his whole stock of <precius> time in Carding, Dicing, Hunting, reuelling, Seeing of Plays, Reading of Romances, Powdring his haire, Staring vpon looking-glasses, courting of Ladys that he means not to marry (not to mention what is worse) ↑and in Sum make Vacation his only Vocation:↓[119] he must haue a Stronger Charity then Iudgment, that beleeues that God and Nature intended onely this for that man's Calling. Neither wil it be vn-vsefull for him now and then to auoid Idleness <and exercice the Body> to do som Work or other with his hands; a Doctrine that I haue diuers times (by Digging, sawing of Wood, and such other ways) practised my self; tho I miht perhaps haue had as great a share of these [(aforenamed)] needles Recreations, as another.[120] I remember that while I liued in Italy, I obserued that the Greatest Nobility there did exercice Merchandize by their Seruants and Factors;[121] and wud laf <smile> at ours for letting vast summs of mony ly [in] rusting in their Coffers; whilst by keeping Ships at Sea (or a hundred other ways) they miht lay |f. 228| it out to the great benefit both of themselues, and the Common-welth: neither did they esteem it a less shame /discredit/ (if there were any) for our Noble men to b<u>y and Sel Land, and Horses themselues; then for them to do it in<to> Silkes, and Sattins, and other [Mer] precius Merchandizes by Proxy. I cud tel yow too of diuers <som> of the Turkish Emperors, who thouht it no disparagement to their greatness, at spare houres to exercice som handicraft or another;[122] and of that great

---

[119] In his *Holy State* (1642), Fuller described the "Degenerous Gentleman" as one whose "*Vacation is his vocation* . . . But they who count calling a prison, shall at last make a prison their calling" (413).

[120] "Of Time and Idleness" included a similar example.

[121] RB observed that Venice, "where the greate Concourse of forreine Nations numerously resorting thither for Trade or Nobler Bisnesse, presents the senses with a no lesse Pleasing then constant Variety" (Maddison 38).

[122] In "Of Time and Idleness," RB referred to this passage. Burton noted that "The Turks enjoin all men whatsoever, of what degree, to be of some trade or other, the Grand Seignoir himself is not excused. 'In our memory' (saith Sabellicus) 'Mahomet the Turk, he that conquered Greece, at that

and Wise Moorish King <Iafur> Almansor, who conquer'd Spaine, and by his Vertu added many other Prouinces to his hereditary Dominions /Kingdomes/ that he did not disdaine ↑at his leasure time,↓ not onely to make coats of maile with his own hands, but also to take the Paines to becom excellent therein.[123]

IX.

For the Ninth. We shal discourse of Recreations, God willing, more fully in a more due and Conuenient Place: content for the Present to take Notice, that [Recr] moderate Recreations, that ar |f. 228[v]| vseful to all men, ar Necessary to Youth <and men>. Too much Study and attention of [mind,] <their Spirits> instead of Sharpning, duls and blunts [their Spirits] <the Mind.> ↑The Soules of young men like the Bodys of young beasts, by being put vpon hard work <labor> too betimes <erly,> loosing of their Strength, and being hindered in their Growth and↓ Youthfull Capacitys, like Corn-Fields, sown too thic, bear the less Crop: and their Memorys, like Purses, cram'd too ful (so that the Purstrings cannot shut) instead of holding more then ordinary, let all fal /run/ out. Wel natur'd Youths, like Colts, shud be vsd gently, til they ar wel back't and fit to carry burdens: and it were no hard nor vseles bisness to vse them (especially the Children of great men) so, as they may thinke their very Study a Recreation: as I remember I was vs'd /seru'd/ som yeeres ago <since> by a discreet Tutor. /School-master./[124] And indeed I haue euer obseru'd <it> to be very dangerous, to set Youths too great taskes, and giue him but <too> little Recreation: for (to omit that those to whom the lawfull ways of Pleasure ar abrid'g, will oftentimes find out /make vse of/ those that ar vnlawfull) <both> those that ar Cloy'd with Study during /in/ their Youth do vsually loath and abstaine from it <altogether> when they |f. 229| com to be of Age: and also those (whom restraint has made vn-acquainted with pleasures, and) who haue been <too> long kept fasting from recreations in their Minority, when they once com to vse their owne liberty, and

---

very time when he heard ambassadors of other princes, did either carve or cut wodden spoons, or frame something upon a table.' This present Sultan makes notches for bows" (*Anatomy* 2.70).

[123] A possible source is Robert Ashley, *Almansor The Learned and Victorious King that conquered Spaine* (1627), a source of John Dryden's heroic plays, *The Conquest of Granada*, parts 1 and 2 (1671, 1672). RB also cited this example in "Of Time and Idleness" below. In Sir William Temple's "Of Heroic Virtue," first published in *Miscellanea, the Second Part* (1692), Almansor is also mentioned.

[124] See RB's description of his education at Eton, where John Harrison, the head master, having noticed "some aptnesse & much Willingnesse in [RB] to learne; resolu'd to improue them both by all the gentlest wayes of Encouragement. . . [He] was carefull to instruct him in such an affable, kind, & gentle way, that he easily preuail'd with him to consider /affect/ Studying not so much as a Duty of Obedience to his Superiors /Parents/ but as the Way to purchase for himselfe a most delightsome & invaluable Good" (Maddison 9-15)

haue full [meales] <dishes or Tables> set before them [vsually] most commonly surfet vpon <of> them.[125]

X.

As for the Tenth and Last. Our Proficiency or vn-proficiency in <toward> the attainment of Vertu, is to be knowne by Self-examination and certin Symptomes. A tru and searching Self-examination is a very difficult peece of Bisnes: because therein Partiality or Self-loue dos vsually widen our Vertus, and either hide or lessen our Faults; and the Soule, like the Ey, that sees other things directly sees it self but by reflection. This kind of Examen, may be either Yearly, Monthly, Weekly, or Dayly, which last, as most profitable, I haue [tr] already treated of in a little Discourse by it selfe:[126] the Sum where of is, That euery Euening, Morning, or any other most conuenient time of the Day, [we] |f. 229^{v}| that shal be found most conuenient, we shud recollect our selues and consider 1. What we haue learn't that [fore] Day that we knew not before, 2. What Good we haue don that Day: and 3. What Euil (either Ciuil moral or Spirituall) we haue committed the foregoing Day: meditating vpon all these with their most materiall Circumstances, and making vpon them what Reflection the things shall require and Deserue. Now as for the Symtomes or Tokens we made mention of; a man may conclude /argue, or guess/ his Proficiency in Vertu, if 1. [If] We find the Contrary Vices either wholly or greatly abated and subdued in vs. As we may argue that we haue profited in Liberality, if we find in our selues less Gaping after another's Goods, or feel our selues less affected with accidental Losses. 2. We find a greater calmness of <in> our Affections; For Vertu being the Moderatress of our Passions; their orderly quietness /Moderation/ must needs argue her Dominion ouer them: as we may conclude a[n acquisition of] <growth in> Valor, from the <more> faint assaults of our feares [giues] in great or sudden Dangers. This |f. 230| makes many reckon vp amongst the Symptomes of acquired Vertu; Chast and vntroubled Dreames: because it argues, wel regulated Affections, when the horse gos on his way /behaues himself/ quietly, tho his Rider be asleepe. 3. We feel in our selues a vehement thirst after a further Degree in <of> Vertu: without which thirst many beleeue that there can be no tru Loue of Vertu. 4. We approach neerer and neerer to the Approued Examples of the [best] most Vertuus men. 5. We siht more and more those [the] Inconueniences that attend on Vertu; and can vnder Value [those] <any> thing[s] when <that> [they] <it> coms in competition with it: and can draw [mo] Instructions out of euery [thing] /Object/ we meet with all, making all <accidents and>

[125] In 1653 Petty worried that RB would damage his health by reading too much (6.138).

[126] Cf. "Dayly Reflection"; in BP 35.172-73, RB called the work "Dayly REFLECTOR" and dedicated it to Lady Ranelagh.

Book Two, Chapter Four

occasions [and occasions] serue vs for arguments or the augment of Vertu.[127] ↑This is called Heu'nly mindedness.↓[128] 6. We can with greater Ease and Deliht exercice the Operations of Vertu: for in it, as in Trades, those that haue profited and ar skilfull, find a greater Pleasure and Facility in their Work[es]<ing.> ↑Vsus promptos facit.↓[129] 7. If our Loue to Vertu do more and more disengage it self from by-respects and fix vpon Vertu it self, and for her owne sake: for like Oyle, if she be tru, she must needs always swim at the Top.[130] Vertu |f. 231| is too louely a [W] Mistress to be courted but for <the sake of> her Waiting-women['s] (Honor, Safety, Reward.) [sakes] Neither will she euer be truly and entirely his, that seeks an End rather beyond her Selfe.[131]

Admonition.

Thus far of Education in order to the Ethicks: wherein I haue been the more prolix /full/ partly because of the vsfulness of the Argument, /Theame/ and partly to supply the negligence and Defects of others therein. More particular, and perhaps more profitable Rules miht be giuen [abou] concerning Education considered in it selfe: som of which we may perchance one Day venture to publish to the World.[132] What has been already deliuered is enuf to manifest /display/ the extrem faultiness of most Parents in this Particular; too many of whom one may too iustly apply that witty (tho wicked) Reply of a Gentleman of my acquaintance, who being rated by his Mother for Disobedience and amongst other things reproach't how much he was beholding /obliged/ to her for bringing him into the World, in a great Fury made her, this Answer, (By god, Madam) I am not beholding to you at all, For yow got me but for your Pleasure and brouht me forth for your Ease.[133] |f. 123ᵛ|

---

[127] Petty praised RB's use of meditation in 1653 and mentioned, perhaps hyperbolically, that RB meditated for two hours (BW 6.138); from her conversion in 1647 to the end of her life, RB's sister Mary meditated for two hours each day (Mendelson 94-95). For a broader perspective, Mary's own account is useful: T. C. Croker, ed. *Some Specialities in the Life of Mary, Countess of Warwick* (1848).

[128] In "Dayly Reflection" RB defined heavenly-mindedness as a "certin exquisite Temper and Disposition of Soule, which some haue (aptly enuf) Christn'd Heu'nly-mindednesse. For the faythfull Practise of this Reflection dos very much facilitate Repentance, by making it ouertake Faults, before Custom and Neglect has hatch't them into Vices: and allowes them not the least Pretence to the Title of Prescription" (f. 271ᵛ).

[129] Cf. U22, "Once a use and ever a custom."

[130] T568, "Truth and oil are ever above." RB used this proverb both in bk. 2, ch. 6, and in *Cert. Phys. Essays* 1.349.

[131] V81, "Virtue is its own reward."

[132] As far as I know, RB never published such a work.

[133] RB repeated this anecdote in BP 38.202, where it was dated 12 February 1647. Who was the source of this anecdote? Tom Killigrew is a plausible candidate: cf. Marcombes's complaint to

But to auoid the Mistakes that may arise from the Diuers Significations of the Word, Vertu: we must know that there is a fourefold kind of Vertu. The first is Naturall, as we say the Vertus of precius Stones, ↑and herbs,↓ the Vertu of a Dog, namely Fidelity; the Vertu of Rheubarbe, to purge the Ill humors, and of Dictamum, to cloze vp Wounds.[134] Breefly, they call Natural Vertu, any Quality or Perfection whereby an Irrationall Creature is able to do any thing of Good, profitable, or Commendable. (To this kind som refer the Vertus of Angels, others to the next.) The Second is Infused Vertu as Faith, Hope, Charity, Profesy, ↑the gift of Tongs, and Miracles,↓ and the like, proceeding, not from Accustomance, but from God. The Third is Intellectuall Vertu, as Prudence, Wisdom, Art, and the like. The Fourth and last is Morall Vertu, of which onely in this Place we intend to treate.

Cork about Killigrew (20 December 1641). Marcombes did not "loue profaine & irreligious discourses, and . . . [he] can not approue one that speakes ill of his o[w]ne mother and of all [Killigrew's] friends and that playes ye foole allways through ye streets Like a Scoole Boy, hauing allwayes his mouthe full of whoores and such discourses, and braging often of his getting mony from this or ye other merchant without any good intention to pay" (*II Lismore* 4.235). A very full summary of Killigrew's personality and later career in the theatre can be found in Philip H. Highfill et. al., *A Biographical Dictionary of Actors, Actresses, Musicians, Dancers, Managers & Other Stage Personnel in London, 1660-1800* (Carbondale 1973-), vol. 9. The MS now returns to f. 123^v without any formal transition.

[134] The virtues of rhubarb have been well known, wrote Browne, since Hippocrates (*Pseud. Epidemica* 1.363); "dictamum" is an obsolete form of dittany, "a plant famous for its medicinal qualities" (*OED*). Hartlib's "Ephemerides" (1648) contained many comments on the distinctive signatures of plants, referring to the works of Oswald Croll, Heinrich Noll, Paracelsus, and Helmont. RB's examples mixed different kinds of virtues, but the last two reflect RB's interest in acquiring and understanding medical receipts. Both Shaw and Birch praised RB's judicious assessment of the "specific virtue of the Peruvian bark, . . . *ens veneris*, *osteocolla*, the *ens primum* of balm, *Butler*'s stone, the sympathetic powder, the weapon salve, the alkahest of *Paracelsus*, the *virgula divina*, the transmutation of metals, projection, or the philosopher's stone" (1.cxlvii). For RB's spiritual pain over several items on this list, see Hunter, "Alchemy."

|f. 124|

Chapter V.

Of the Definition of Morall Vertu

Hauing in the Former Chapters discoursed of the Final, Materiall, and Efficient Causes of Moral Vertu; our order dos now require that we shoud proceed to the handling of it's Formal Cause or Nature; which may be best [illeg.] <discernd in> it's Definition.[1]

Now the Moralists in their Ethicall Treatises deliuer sundry Definitions of Morall Vertu: but they, differing for the most part rather in [Lang] the Expressions then the meaning, [ar] their Substance is Contained in the vulgar Definition attributed to Aristotle; which, because generally receau'd, we will not for the present decline to make vse of. The Sence is to this Purpose, that Perfect Morall Vertu (for the Imperfect is handled elsewhere) |f. 124v| Is an Electiue Habitude consisting in the Mediocrity that is referenc't to vs; and that as a man truly Prudent shud determine it.[2] This Definition taken in Peeces and considered in particular, will giue vs a true account of the Nature of Morall Vertu. It presents vs with 5 Obseruables: namely, that 1. It is a Habitude; 2. That this Habitude is Electiue. 3. That this Habitude consists in Mediocrity. 4. That this mediocrity must be in regard of vs. 5. And lastly, that the Rule of this Mediocrity is the Determination of a truly Wiseman. At each of these we will tuch breefly and in order; and

I. For the First. That Vertu is a Habitude may appeare; because that all confessing it to be a Quality it is none of the 3 other kinds of Quality. Not a natural Faculty; as has been already proued: not a Passible |f. 125| Quality or Passion; because Vertu is employ'd in the commanding and regulating the Affections; which ar often Euill, whereas Vertu is always Good: nor an externall Figure; as being but the Affection of a Corporeall thing. Wherefore it remaines that it must be a Habitude. Which is also confirmed, because we see, that as the Art of Dancing (For Example) is gotten by the frequent Practice of dancing Courantos, Brawles, Sarabands, and the like;[3] and all other Habitudes ar acquired by the Rëiteration of those Operations that ar proper to that Habitude; so the Habitude of Vertu is produc't by the constant rëiteration of [V] Honest Actions.

---

[1] Cf. Alsted 1248.

[2] Nich. Eth. II.vi.15.

[3] Although Marcombes considered the dancing master exceptionally good (*II Lismore* 4.103), RB heartily disliked dancing (Maddison 31).

Now since a Habitude is acquired by the frequent rëiteration of Action of the same kind; it follows, that he that wud be Vertuus must diligently exercice himself in the Operations of Vertu: but the Number of these Actions, that [are] is requisite to form a Habitude, [illeg.] |f. 125v| is left vndetermined; because it wholly depends vpon the Intensity of the Action and som other qualifications not reducible to certin Rules. Only in Generall we may obserue, that the more vehement (or intense) and vn-intermitted the Actions ar, the fewer of them wil serue the turne: insomuch that som ar of Opinion, that one Action may be so superlatiuely Vertuus, as alone to produce a Vertu; the Intensity of the Degree, recompensing the Scantness of the Number.[4] From this Vertu's being a Habitude it follows; that in Vertu, from a Single Act to the Habitude, the Consequence is not good. Thus was Dauid no Tyrant tho he causelesly slauter'd Vriah,[5] nor Cambises a Iust Prince, tho he once did an Exemplary peece of Iustice vpon a notoriusly bribe-catching Iudge, whom hauing caused to be flead, he had the Tribunall, wherein the Son succeeded him, couered with the Father's skin, motto'd with this Warning, Lern to iudge iustly.[6] |f. 126| These are in both but Actions by the By; that ar inconsiderable in comparison of the Contrary Habitudes. These Solitary kind of Action do no more qualify the Doers Vertuus or Vitius; then a Bungler's making one compleate Character, or a Good [men] Penman's mis-shaping one Letter, qualify them Good or Euil Writers.

II. This Habitude is termed Electiue, partly to difference it from the Habitudes of the Body, and ↑Moral Vertu↓ from Intellectuall Vertue; and partly to distinguish the Action of Vertu from all Actions, Ignorant, Constrain'd, Rash, Naturall and Accidentall.

III. This Habitude is said to Consist in Mediocrity, or in the Middle or meane betwixt 2 contrary Vices; as by the Enumeration or Induction of euery Vertu in particular may easily appeare. Besides, that, since euery thing, (as a Circle,) has but one middle or meane (the Center) but many extreames; it wud follow, that concerning the same thing there [shud] were |f. 126v| Many Vertus and but one Vice, the contrary whereof is manifestly true.[7] And certinly if Passions and humane Actions ar blamed when they ar faulty in either of the Extreames of Excess or Defect; those that ar limited with the Bounds of Mediocrity ar to be esteemed commendable and Vertuus. If Extreames destroy the Nature of Vertu, we may conclude it to consist in the Meane. And this Mediocrity is by the Filsofers constituted the Form of Vertu, (namely the Analogicall, for being a Quality it is capable of no other.)[8] ↑And this is cleerly intimated by

[4] Cf. Alsted 1246-47.
[5] 2 Sam. 11:3-26.
[6] Alsted 1246.
[7] Nich. Eth. II.vi.13.
[8] Alsted 1245; Nich. Eth. II.ii.6ff.

God himself, who Deut. 5,32. commands his People Not to turn aside to the Riht hand or to the Left.↓ ↑The Pythagoreans indeed held Vertu to consist in the Extreame: which, as it is interpreted, [thwarts] destroys not this [Opinion:] Assertion. For then both the contrary Vices ar ranked in one of the Extreames, namely, Opposition to riht reason; and Vertu holds the Place of the other Extreame, namely Conformity thereunto. And so Vertu comming vnder the Notion of Good, and both the Vices together vnder that of Euill, becom opposite Extreames one to another: whose Middle is Innocency (or Indifferency.) And Vertu which is the Middle of them separated[y] is their Contrary extreame if ioyn'd <united> together.↓ |f. 127[v]|

↑There is also a Double Medium, the one Positiue which they call the Meane of Participation; because it participates and results from the Coniunction of the 2 opposite Extreames; as Lukewarmness is betwixt (extreame) Heat and Cold; or [the] Gray between Blac and White, being as it were the mixture of them both: The other Medium they term Priuatiue, <usually> or Meane of Negation: which participates of neither of the Contrarys, but becoms their Middle by auoiding /declining/ both: as a man that has <both> his eys shut is the meane of Negation betwixt [a] the man that sees and him that is blind; and indifferent actions are in the same kind of Middle betwixt [Vertu] Good ones and Bad ones, being neither the one nor the tother /Good nor Bad./ The Filsofers generally make Vertu to consist /place Vertu/ [in] not in the Former but in the Latter of these 2 Middles. Tho som ar pleas'd (perhaps not improbably) to make Vertu, formally (as they speake) or as a Commendable [Qualit] Habitude to consist indeed in the Middle of Negation: but Effectiuely (as they term it) in that of Participation. As Liberality in it self participates neither of Auarice nor Profuseness: but the Liberal man in the Distribution of his Mony, (seems to) imitates Partly the Prodigal [by] in giuing enuf; and partly the Miser, in not giuing any more <then euf.> But the best on't is, that these Nicetys ar more intricate then Materiall.↓[9]

IV. This Middle is said to be (quoad nos,) in regard of vs, or referenc'd to vs. Which that we may the better vnderstand; we must know, that there is a twofold Middle where in the Meane of Vertu may be souht. The One is the Middle in regard of the things as [a] the Centre is the Middle of the Circle, and 6 is the Middle between 4 and 8. The other is the Middle in respect of |f. 127| the Persons, that is, of Vertus. As in Matter of giuing Almes; he that giues according to his own Ability, and the want (and desert) of the Beggar, he obserues the Middle in respect of the Persons; auoiding on the one side Niggardliness, and on the Other, Profusion: ↑and this Middle is properly called Mediocrity.↓ For the better Declaration of this the Moralists do generally heer deliuer the Doctrine of the

[9] For detailed analysis of the virtues, the vices of excess and deficiency, and the difficulty of achieving the mean, see Nich. Eth. II.vii-IV.

2 Middles, Arithmeticall and Geometricall, correspondent to the Meane referred to the Thing, and the Mean referred to Vertus.

The Meane Arithmeticall is that which is Equidistant from both the Extreames; as between 2 and 8 the Middle Arithmeticall is 5, because it is 3 less then 8, and more then 2. So beween 4 and 8 the Middle Arithmeticall is 6, as being the Half of the 2 Extremes (4 and 8) exceeding the one iust as much as it is exceeded by the other. The Meane Geometricall, properly, the Middle of Proportion, is that Wherein, |f. 128| Such is the <ratio, or> Proportion of the lesser Extreame to the Medium, as of the Middle to the Greater Extreame.[10] Thus betweene 2 and 8, the Geometrical meane is not 5, but 4. For as 2 is iust half 4, so 4 is iust half 8. And so between 16 and 4, the Me<a>ne Arithmeticall is 10, (as equally distant from either of the Extreames) but the Geometricall is 8. For as 4 is to 8, so is 8 to 16: (that is, the Proportion is Double.)

Now the Filosofers constitute not the Nature of Vertu in the Arithmeticall Meane, but in the Geometricall: for the Arithmeticall meane is invariable and Equi-distant from the Extreames: but the Geometricall Middle dos som times approach more to the lesser Extreame, and som times to the Greater; and so dos Vertu; which, according to the Diuersity of the Circumstances, is somtimes neere to the Vice in Excess, and somtimes to that in Defect. [illeg.]

And for the Discouery |f. 128v| which of the 2 Vitius Extreames has the least repugnancy to the Nature of the Vertu; the Rule seems to be, that We must diligently consider the Principall Act of each Vertu: for if that Act do cheefly consist in the Doing or operating any thing; then, Generally, the Vice that is in the Excess of that Action is more like to the Vertu, then that which is in the Defect. For tho that Vice and the Vertu differ in the Manner and degree of that Action, yet they agree in the Substance because to Ouer-doo is to Doo howsoeuer. And thus we see Prodigality to be liker Liberality then Couetousness is; and Rashness liker Courage, then Cowardice. But if the Principal Act (or duty) of the Vertu be placed in Abstaining: then that Vice (generally) that Sins in the Defect, is less vnlike the Vertu, then that which is faulty in the Excesse: For the like Reason Whence to ouer-Abstaine from the Vse of Women (tho lawfull) is neerer of kin to Chastity then Whoring is: and too [illeg.] spare a Diett, |f. 129| Les vnlike Temperance, then Gluttony or Drunkenness.

Now because as it is hard to hit at first dash the Center of a Circle, so it is difficult to keepe one's self so in the Middle, as not to encline to either of the Extreames: besides the Particular Precepts that euery Vertu giues to find the Mediocrity that belongs to it; we will heere deliuer 3 generall Aduices to find out this Mediocrity in Generall.[11] The First is, to Decline most that Extremity

---

[10] Nich. Eth. II.vi.5-8; Alsted (1245-46) cites Melanchthon.

[11] Cf. Nich. Eth. II.ix.1-6. RB followed Arist. closely for the first point but not for the next two, where Arist.'s rules are "to notice what are the errors to which we are ourselves most prone . . . and

whereunto we ar most Inclin'd: ↑(and which by consequent promises vs most Plesure)↓ and leane a little to the Contrary Extreame. As for Example, the Miser may wisely go a little beyond the Bounds of Liberality, and [illeg.] <aduance> into the Confines of Prodigality. For it is in Euill Habitudes as in Crooked Stickes; [illeg.] to make them straiht, yow must bend them the Contrary way. For between 2 contrary Crookeds the Meane will be Streight. The Second is, To decline ↑(cæteris paribus)↓ that extreame most, that is most repugnant to Vertu. As to fly Cowardize more then Temerity, as more remote from Valor. |f. 129v| The Third and last is, that Since the Vehemency of any Passion darkens the Ey of the Iudgment; we shud in euery [co] Action of Concernment, stay till those Clouds be ouerblowne, that we may the better afterwards discern the Mediocrity we Desire.

V. Lastly, it is said that this Mediocrity must be As a prudent man wud determine it. [For illeg.] For, since because of the great multitude and variety of Circumstances, it is a very hard thing to find out this Geometricall Middle amongst them all: therefore dos Aristotle adde, that this Mediocrity so difficult to be proportionable to all the Circumstances; shud not be [estimated] <defined> by the Fancys and opinions of the Vulgar, or any such like way; but [illeg.] <determined> by the Iudgment of a Prudent Man.[12] Which Iudgment may be had 3 ways: Either by the Counsels and Opinions of |f. 130| the Wise-men themselues that liue amongst vs: Or by their Examples: Or by their Writings and Discourses of Vertu. But it seems that Aristotle had don far better to haue determin'd this Mediocrity According to the Prescription or dictates, of Rihtly informed Reason. For 1. All men ar men, and the Wisest men as well as the best hound ar som times at a Faut. 2. In many particular and sudden cases and affaires, neither the Directions nor the Examples of the Prudent ar possibly to be had. 3. And lastly, the most famous men for Prudence, <do> themselues dissent [a] (and not seldome) about the very Essentials of [illeg.] Vertu. Thus, Aristotle approu'd Priuate Reuenge, which Plato condemn'd.[13] And Cato held it a Point of Courage not to suruiue the Liberty of the Common-welth, which Cicero deny'd.[14] We therefor constitute the tru Rule of Morall Vertu to be [a] the rihtly-informed Reason: |f. 130v| And make it's Form to consist in it's Congruency or Agreeableness ↑of our Actions↓ there vnto. (As the Form of Vice in it's Repugnancy vnto it.) But because all the Parts and Facultys of the Soule haue been greatly vitiated by the Fall of our first Parents; and yet those very wise and

---

then we must drag ourselves awy in the opposite direction" and to be "most of all on our guard against pleasure." RB conflated Arist.'s points with two points of his own.

[12] Cf. Nich. Eth. VI.v-xiii; Alsted 1245 ("Virtutis forma est mediocritas").

[13] Cf. Nich. Eth. V.v.3 and *Rhetoric* I.ix.24.

[14] Cf. Cicero, *Ad Atticum* 1.18.7 and 2.1.8. RB echoes wide-spread criticism of the ancients' moral relativism (Fiering 95-96).

prudent men that Aristotle heer [illeg.] speakes of, haue, (for the most part) ignor'd that Corruption: it has hapned, that both they, and all those also that steer their Action by base Naturall Reason haue, by the following of so Blind a Guide, mistaken Vice for Vertu, and Vertu for Vice. Wherefore, to speake like Christians, we must (with the Diuines,) constitute the Law of God to be the tru and Perfect Rule and Pattern of Vertu: and establish the Form of Vertu in it's Conformity or conueniency thereunto, as that of Vice, in it's Discrepancy from it, or Vnsuitableness to it. |f. 131| And because the Law of God insisting cheefly vpon Generals, dos not oftentimes descend to Circumstances and Particulars; therefore for our Instruction in such [illeg.] Particular occurrences and Singular Cases, we must furnish our selues with and imitate such Doings and Saying of holy men, as are proposed and Commended vnto vs in the Holy Scripture. As also those commendable Precepts and Example of the Vertuus Heathen, ↑as far forth, as↓ [so] they [be] <ar> not repugnant to the Law of God.[15]

Thus far of the Definition of Vertu; which to euidence the better, we will illustrate it by 2 or 3 questions that concern the Nature of Vertu in Generall, reseruing the Controuersys for their proper Places.

The First Question is, Whither all Declining from the Meane of Vertu be Vitious? To which the Moralist's Answer is not amisse, That all Declension of the Meane has indeed a Smack of Vitiusness;[16] |f. 131^{v}| But if it be petty, it is inconsiderable in comparison of the Good of the Action, by which it is so couered and Swallow'd vp, that either it appeares not at all, or at least depriues not the Action of all Commendation.

The Second is, Whither the 2 [ext] opposite extreames or contrary Vices ar more repugnant one to another, then to the intermiddle Vertu?[17] To which som Moralists not vnfitly answer, That if we consider the Degrees of the Affections in whose Mediocrity Vertu dos consist; then one of the Contrary Vices will be more opposite to the other contrary Vice, then to the middle Vertu. Thus there being a hiher degree of Anger and Boldness in Rashness then in Valor; it follows that Cowardliness is more repugnant to Temerity then to Courage, (as being in a Degree more distant from it.) But if we consider this Contrariety of Vertu and |f. 132| Vice, absolutely, and in it's owne Nature, that is, as they ar bare Qualitys; then [the] either of the Extreames is [illeg.] <lesse> repugnant to it's opposite Extreame, then to the Middle Vertu. As Cowardice is more contrary to Courage then to Temerity. For all Vertu [illeg.] fals vnder the Notion of Good; all Vice vnder that of Euill: so that [Vertu] 2 contrary Vices, tho they [illeg.] differ from <one> another in the Species, yet they agree in the Gender; (namely, Vice;) whereas the Particular Vice differs from the Particular Vertu,

---

[15] See Dury's letter to Worsley (11 May 1649) "concerning Morality" (Boyle Lett. 7.1^{v}).

[16] This discussion is vaguely related to Nich. Eth. II.ix.7-9.

[17] Cf. Nich. Eth. II.viii.1-8.

not onely in the Kind, but in the Genus also.

The third is, Whether or no there be such a [illeg.] necessary linking together or Concatenation of all Vertus; that he, that has (truly) one, has necessarily all the rest; and he that has not all, has None? This Question is not without Difficulty to be resolu'd: there being very weity reasons alleadged on both Sides:[18] but the most rationall |f. 132v| Opinion seems to be this. [First,] That there is a Vertu Perfect or rather Compleate; which in all Occasions whatsoeuer is constant to the tru Mediocrity of Vertu, without sweruing from it. And there is a Vertu Imperfect or Incompleat; which is indeed for the Maine generally Virtuus; but then vpon [illeg.] som particular occasions, wil a little resent of humane Fragility, by admitting som little mixture of Vice; which tho so insensible that it destroys not the Nature of the Vertu, yet is able a little to taint and contaminate it. And of this kind ar most Vertus that ar actually to be found [in] amongst men. This premised, we answer, that of Imperfect Vertus, such as are vsually to be found amongst men, one may very well possess one (or som) without the others. For 1. [illeg.] History and Experience abundantly testify, that diuers haue bin, (For Example) Iust that were Cowards, and Valiant that were Drunkards. 2. Since Nature and Assuefaction ar the Efficient |f. 133| Causes of Vertu; and many ar naturally enclin'd and accustomed to one Vertu (as Liberality) that ar not so to another, we must conclude, that one Vertu may be acquired without the Acquisition of the others. 3. And certinly if there were no true Vertu but that that is join'd to and [illeg.] consociated with all the other Vertus; then we may go looke for tru Vertu in another world; for (as the Poet has it) No man wants Vices; he is best that has but the least.[19] But of those Vertus that we haue termed Perfect and Compleat, it seems that no man can haue One truly that possesses them not All. For in the Perfect Habitude of any Vertu it is required that one may exercice the Functions and operations of that Vertu, Constantly and without any <inward> Impeachment: which [cannot be don as long as Vertu is joyned with reall Vices] ↑is inconsistent with that Vertu's Fellowship with tru Vices:↓ for (By Example) Couetusnes hinders the Exercice of Valor; Frihtfulness the Action of Iustice; Drunkenness those of Prudence, and the like. Besides that the Scripture manifestly requires a perfect Concatenation |f. 133v| Of all Vertus that any miht be tru Vertus. For St. Iohn teaches vs (1. Iohn, 3.) that he that loues God cannot hate his Neibour: and St. Iude tels vs (cap. 2,26)[20] that As the Body without the Spirit is, Ded, so Faith without Works is ded also: and (verse the 10 of the same Chapter) that Whosoeuer shall keepe the whole Law, and yet offend in one Point he is guilty of all. For the Confirmation [of]

[18] Laërtius reviewed these arguments in his *Life of Zeno* 7.125: "[The Stoics] hold that the virtues involve one another, and that the possessor of one is the possessor of all."

[19] Source unknown.

[20] The reference is to the epistle of James, not Jude.

whereof we will add, that many [are generally esteemed to excell in one kind of Vertu without the others] qualitys pass generally for tru Vertus, that indeed ar but the Images and Shadows of [illeg.] tru Vertus (such<y> was Alexanders Courage, Lucretia's Chastyty, and diuers others) as we shall manifest heereafter. Whereas on the other side it may somtimes happen, that one Vertu may indeed be more conspicuus in a man, either because he giues himself more to it; or has greater <meanes and> conueniencys to practice it, or stronger incitements to the Exercice of it: and yet it will not follow that this man is depriu'd of the other Vertus, |f. 134| tho he possess them more obscurely and in a more remisse Degree.

|f. 135|

Chapter VI.

Of the Properties of Morall Vertu

The Propertys of Moral Vertu (which distinguish the Tru from the Bastard) ar principally 3, Syncerity, Integrity, and Perseuerance: tho I ignore not that in other authors these Termes ar vsed; rather as the Names of Vertus themselues then those of the Affections of Vertu.[1]

Now each of these Propertys is Two-fold; Generall and Particular: the former extends it self to all Vertus (and Vices) vniversally; the latter is restrained to euery Vertu in particular, and reaches to all the Parts of that Vertu, and all the Vices opposite thereunto. As (For Example) there is a Generall Integrity which makes vs embrace all Vertus and detest all Vices; and there is a particular Integrity in Valor, which makes vs embrace not onely the Doing, but also the Suffering part of it; and in Chastity; which makes vs detest, not onely Sodomy and Incest; but also bare Wenching, and Lasciuius Discourse. The like may be said of the other 2 Propertys (and the rest of the Vertus;) but we wil treate of these Affections now onely in the Generall, because that sufficiently |f. 135v| Includes their Doctrine in the Particular, [But] applying <only> what is said of Vertus and Vices in General, to the Parts of euery particular Vertu, and it's opposing Vices.

Integrity (therefore) is that Property of Vertu, that makes vs Embrace all Vertus, and detest all Vices without any exception or reserue.[2] Which Description branches this Property into 2 Parts; the one obliging vs to the Acquisition of euery Vertu; and the other to an Enmity against euery Vice.

For the First. We do not thereby vnderstand that a perfect Acquisition of all Vertus is absolutely necessary: since there ar Degrees both in their Necessity and Excellence. But only this, that the Good man ouht to <desire and> endeauor the Acquisition of euery Vertu in som [D] competent [M] Degree or Mesure; and not (as many do) stint himself by saying, so many Vertus wil I acquire, or so many Parts of such and such a Vertu; but the rest I [wi] am resolued not to meddle with. This latter kind of Integrity (I say) is to be laboured for /studied/ because 1. He that loues Vertu as Vertu (and tis so that it ouht to be loued) must

---

[1] This chapter does not follow Arist., but with its emphasis on biblicism and self-scrutiny, it follows rather closely some parts of "Dayly Reflection."

[2] In this chapter RB signalled his organization by writing the topics—integrity, sincerity, and perseverance—in letters approximately 4X larger than usual. In "Dayly Reflection," he discussed integrity, sincerity, and humility.

loue euery Vertu: (it being |f. 136| a no les Tru then vseful Maxime, that if any thing has a Property meerly because of any quality, whatsoeuer [has] <possesses> that Quality must also haue the Property also:[3] as if a Circle, as a Circle be round; then euery Circle is round: and if a man, as man, is a reasonable Animal, then we may safely conclude that euery man is a reasonable Animal.) 2. The same God that commanded one Vertu, commanded all: and therefore in the Præface to the Commandements it is said, That God spake ALL these Words: ↑And Deut, 27,26, He sayth, Cursed be he that confirmeth not [al the wor] ALL the Words of this Law to do them:↓ and Integrity and Sincerity is vsually in the Scriptures honored with the Glorius Title of a Perfect hart:[4] wherefore not to care for the acquiring of euery Vertu, is a shrewd sign of hollownes, and that indeed thou carest for none [beyond] but for thy own Ends: for if really out of God's command thou embracest this Vertu; why dost thou not also as wel embrace the rest, that ar equally by him commanded; certinly, he that [in] resolues to walk according to Conscience, and declines Integrity, is either a Foole or a Knaue; A Foole, for doing so much, or a Knaue for doing no more.

Integrity is the Silken thred that runs throu the Chaine /neclace/ |f. 136^{v}| of those Orient Perles we call Vertus, and couples <ankers> them together: once cut that String, and yow endanger the spoiling of the whole Chaine. And in the Body of Vertu, as in that of man, all the Parts ar so necessary and ioyned together with <in> so exact a Symmetry; that [none can be Des] (as there is none Superfluus /or redountant/) so there can be none Defectiue /wanting/ with a notable /great/ Deformity or <and> Inconuenience. 3. There is [not] <scarce> (in my poore opinion) a more senceless generation of People in the whole world then that of these Semy-good men. For they ar sharers in all the Miserys of the Vertuus, without participating of their aduantages; which arise not from a bare Acquaintance, but from an Entire Frendship and familiar Intimacy with her. They neither ar smil'd vpon by Astrea nor ly with Venus: hauing too little of Goodness to make them tast of the Sweets of Vertu, and feast themselues with the Delihts of a peaceful Conscience: and too much to suffer them to plunge themselues vnrestrainedly into the bewitching Pleasures of the World. Vertu is like a most excellent Potion; a few spoonfuls wil but augment the Paine, whereas if one drink it all, it wil cure the Disease. And in a Word, [these] <such> a motley-minded man

[3] A maxim in logic.

[4] Cf. Gen 20:5, 1 Kin. 9:4, and Ps. 78:72.

Has but enuf of Vertu to controule
His Plesures; not enuf to saue his Soule.[5]

|f. 137|

For the Second. There ar (principally) 3 kinds of Sins, that hinder the Practice of this second member /Part/ of Integrity; namely, Secret Sins, Little Sins, and Darling Sins.[6] ↑And the greater Number of these to concur, the more difficult is that Sin's Ejection.↓ 1.) First therefore, there ar many whom meere Shame or Feare of Punishment wil not suffer to commit gross and remarquable Villanys; but if they can once draw the Curtin of Secrecy ouer their Vices; they care not how vgly themselues are, so they do not appeare so: this is frequent especially in [Contemp] <Speculatiue> Wickedness, as when men murder their Neibors with their Thouhts, and commit Adultery [wi] in their Imaginations.[7] But methinks they shud consider, that 1. Vice is to be hated <principally> for it's owne vgliness /toadishnes/ and not for the Punishment that attends it: [for] and he that declines it otherwise not hates the Vice, but feares the Consequence. If we respect those we loue, remember that whensoeuer thou sinnest a man stands by; and no matter who sees it not, if thy selfe sees it. ↑And Conscience like an Owle, can see in the Darke, and has Whips for Secret as wel as for open <public> Faults.↓ 2. To God all things ar naked, and no Darkness can [sh] cloud thee from the [searchin] penetrancy of his Siht: that inaccessible Liht brings liht along with him wheresoeuer he coms <is>; and by his vbiquity he is euerywhere. Thou canst not enjoy thy Mistress so [priuately] <secretly> but the Aire must of Necessity be made priuy to the Offence; if then thou canst not |f. 137v| Shun the Presence of a Creature, how canst thou hope to fly /escape/ the omnipresence of the Creator. 3. It were a Senceless thing, because there is not a [Swarm] croud /throng/ of gazers on, to dare to commit a Crime so it be in the Presence of the Iudge, the Accuser, the <a> Witness, and the Hangman: and yet this is thy case in the most priuate Sin, which can neuer be don so secretly, as

[5] Source unknown.

[6] A popular topic in contemporary religious discourse. In this section RB employed material used in other works—"Dayly Reflection," "Of Sin," and *Swearing*—and stressed the *evasions* by which sins were rationalized. Cf. "Dayly Reflection": "And in effect, 'tis more happy to be [cred] resented then Easy to be credited /beleeu'd/ how much the Dayly appeareance before the Tribunall of our owne Conscience alone, dos contribute to the Establishment <and Encrease> of Syncerity. For these <many> Secret Sins, that like Screetchowles [fre] affect the Darke; and loue not to appeare where they may be seene, seldome frequent those Soules, where they are vsually expos'd vnto the Ey of Conscience: and banish themselues from those Places where they perceiue themselues to be taken notice of. [And then] This <pious> Practise makes vs contract a Habitude of Paying a iust Reuerence to our selues: and then this Habitude makes vs lesse Feare to haue Witnesses of our Actions, then to do Actions that need <to> feare a Witnesse" (BP/7, f. 270).

[7] Cf. Matt. 5:28 and "Doctrine of Thinking."

not to be euident /apparent/ to God, the Deuill, and thy owne Conscience. No matter who ignores it if these kno it. For the Conscience (alone, says one) is more then 1000 witnesses, and God more than a 1000 Consciences.[8] 4. Secret Sins ar at last the most Seuerely Punish'd: as indeed it is but Reason that God shud punish those Sins most, that none but himself can punish: for otherwise the assurance of Impunity wud abandon the World to all kind of Secret Licentiusnes. ↑Our Sauior tels vs Matt, 10, 26. That, there is nothing couered that shal not be reuealed; nor hid that shal not be known. And certinly when things do once com to a Discouery, the Secrecy of the Sin wil [cond] ad to the Greatnes /openness/ of the Shame: as we see in Dauid himself, who sinning but in Secret, was publikely and exemplarily punished before al Israel and before the Sun.↓[9] And ([as] <what> one says [uery wel speaking of Gluttons)] ↑excellently concerning Gluttons, may be very fitly applyed to these retired /[se] priuate/ Sinners, that↓ As those Offences ar counted the Greatest, which cannot be punished by a Cunstable, a Iustice, or Iudge of the Assize; but ar reserved immediately to be punished by the King himselfe: so Gluttons must needs be Sinners in a hih Degree, who ar not censurable by any Erthly King, but ar referred to be judged at God's tribunal alone. 2. Secondly, There ar many others (I had almost said Al men) that wil not indeed choke their Consciences with enormous /vnnatural/ |f. 138| Crimes, but yet do not scruple at the Swallowing down Petty Sins, as they ar pleazed to call them. But I wud desire these also to consider, that, 1. No Sin is little, but Comparatiuely. As a Dwarf is a man, so euery Sin [is] (tho neuer so little) is a Sin still: and therefore the Apostle tels vs, Rom. 6,23, that The Wages of Sin (without Distinction of Small or Great) is Death.[10] ↑Or admit the Act be smal, yet the Circumstances may make it Deadly.↓ Wherefor if Hel be the Prison <Abode, or Habitation> of Sinners, the most that [illeg.] these Petty sinners can expect, is but a [more] <Less> <in>tolerable Dungeon: and I'm aferd they'l find the Cup of God's wrath bitter enuf, tho they drinke (it) not (of) to the very Lees /Bottom./ 2. Small Sins ar oftentimes no less dangerous then great ones, because of their Multitude and vndiscernedness. A [li] pocket-pistol may serue the turn to kil a man, as wel as the greatest Canon; [a Dagger /Penkife,] and is it euident that the wounds of a rapier ar far more dangerous <mortall> then those of a Sword. ↑And who knos not that the very Pric of a Thorn neglected, (specially if it be poyson'd) may fester into a Gangrene.↓ Raine that fals in smallest Drops

---

[8] Many of RB's figurative expressions are found in Alsted 1249. "Hæc est occultum quidem, sed magnum flagellum; est carnifex, mille testes, vermis rodens, equuleus perpetuus, infernus horribilis, monitor surdo verbere aurem vellicans. Et, quod mirabile est, conscientia est tribunal Dei in homine, est actor, rea, judex, scriba, & testis."

[9] 2 Sam. 12:1-22.

[10] RB added the words in parentheses.

makes the Erth more Durty then that which fals in hard Showers.[11] Were we but as carefull of our Soules as we ar of our Bodys, we wud <we be as careful to> auoid [as wel] the lest Sins in the one, as we ar to the lest Swatches in the other. 3. Little Sins ar Wedges that make way for the Driuing in of Greater. Giue but the Old Serpent leaue to put in his head, and Ile warrant heel quickly wriggle in his Body. The Prouerb can |f. 138v| Teach vs, that Giue the Deuil an Inch and hee'l take an Ell.[12] Great Theeues (says one) vse to put in little Boys at the Windows of the houses they intend to rob; that they once got in may let in the rest: and so Satan [gets] thrusts in little Sins into our Soules first that they may afterwards open the Doore for <to the> greater. 4. These Petty Sins, tho they Profit least, ar oftentimes no less seuerely punish't then the greate<r>st. As we see that God commanded them to be put to Deth that did but gather Stics vpon the Sabbath Day:[13] for the easyer the Law is to be kept, the greater is the Punishment due to it's Breach. /illeg./ As one of our Poets has it very well,

> The cheapest Sins most deerly punisht are
> Because to shun them also is so cheap.[14]

There is nothing in the whole World worth the Sinning for. (Matt 16.26) But to sel our Soules for trifling Sins, argues not only a Wicked, but a Base and Meane Spirit. Sure wud I part with mine, it shud be to circle my Temple with a Diadem, or to enjoy the Embraces of a Buty capable to seduce a Saint: ↑and I wud scorn to do wrong vnder the taking away of a Citty;↓ in that of Cesar's Humor[s]; who said, Aut non violandum Ius, aut regni causâ violandum: Iustice is not to be trampled vpon at all, or (but) when ‘tis to rayse [our selues] <us> /step vp/ into a Throne.[15] Certinly it argues a greater Basenes /illeg. to Vice/ to steale a Penny then to steale a Pound; and therefor our Sauior tels vs, that |f. 139| He that is vnjust in the least, is vniust also in much:[16] For in all these <kind of> things, we must not consider so much the Weiht of the Thing, as the Autority of the Commander.

3.) Thirdly. There ar many, and eu'n amongst the best men themselues, that tho they ar content to part with their other Sins: yet wil still allow himself one fauorite Vice or another, <from> which he will by no meanes admit of a Diuorce. And this is vsually that which 1. Thyne owne Conscience vpon any

---

[11] D617.

[12] I49.

[13] Num. 15:32-36. RB inadvertently omitted the reference, though leaving space for it.

[14] Herbert, “The Church-Porch” (ll. 67-68).

[15] Suetonius, *De Vita Caesarum* 1.30.5 or Cicero, *De Officiis* 3.82.17-18. RB used a variant of the anecdote in *Swearing* 6.26.

[16] Luke 16:10.

dangerous Sickness, great Danger, or sudden Affriht; of it's own accord seizes vpon and endites thee of.[17] 2. Thy truest Friends (and especially a Powerfull and searching Minister) do the most often check thee, [for. 3.] and thy Enemys principally Diffame thee, for. 3. Thou art the most frequently and greeuously punished for; [in] euen in the Interpretation and guilty acknoledgment of thine owne Conscience. 4. Dos most of all hinder thy Totall and vnreserued resignation to God and Vertu: and which on the Contrary vpon any [great] <solemn> Vow of Reformation, or to scape out of any great Danger, thou dost engage thy self to abandon, with the greatest Confidence that that wil proue an expiatory Sacrifice to appease God's Anger. 5. Thou art most Carefull to hide, most feareful it shud be tuc't vpon (specially by a thundring and searching Minister) and most Industrius, to Nullify, Shift of, Extenuate, or Excuse. 6. Thou art of'nest tempted to, committest with most Deliht, hast lest power to resist, [and most po] most takes vp thy Thouhts, |f. 139^{v}| and has most power to diuert thee from Vertuus Actions, and religius Dutys. 7. Is (usually) the Epidemicall Sin of thy Age, Condition, Cuntry, Company, or Profession.

But this very Bosome-deuill must not be harbored in the Good man's Brest,[18] [For, 1.] Because, 1. Al Sin, as Sin is Detestable, neither can thy affecting it, devest it of it's Euill. And therefore all Vices ouht to be tolerated, or none: for the same Reason /excuses/ that thou canst plead for the retention of that Sin that is thy Darling; another may alleadg for keeping of any other Vice that is his. ↑Wel said a famous Schoolman, that Al Sins ar coupled together,[19] tho not in regard of Conuersion to Temporal Good, (for some aim at Pleasure, some at Profit, and som at honor. &c) yet in regard of auersion from Eternal Good; (that is God) So that he that lookes but toward one Sin, is as much auerted and turned back from God, as if he looked to all.↓ 2. That very thing that most men make an Argument for it's Retaining, shud be an Inducement of it's Banishment; namely, that it is but one; For certinly his Loue to Vertu must be very Cold that wil not afford to part with one Single Plesure /vice/ for her Sake. And he's a Fool in parting with so many, or a Knaue /Vitius/ in parting with no more.[20] ↑To tel God </Vertu/> that thou art willing enuf to renounce all thy former /other/ Sins; but thy [minion and] Predominant corruption thou wilt by no meanes be drawn to part with; is as if [her] a Wife shud tel her Husband, that for her other Louers (that she car'd not much for) she was content to disclaime them all; but one

[17] RB covered some of the same material in "Dayly Reflection" (f. 269). Cf. the description of Philaretus's conversion in the summer of 1640 (Maddison 32) and his sister Mary's conversion in 1647 (Mendelson 80-82).

[18] See, for example, such poems as "On bosome-sinnes" in Francis Quarles, *Divine Fancies* (1632) or V68, "To nourish a viper in one's bosom."

[19] Source unknown.

[20] RB used the same fool/knave distinction on f. 139^{v} above.

adored Minion she was resolued by no meanes to discard, but wud make a Partner with him, both in her Bed, and in her hart. As little reason as the Wife's Excuse has to her Husband, has thine to God /Vertu./↓ 3. It is a Vanity (and a misconceit that I haue obseru'd to haue bin the Ruine of a world of people /men/) to beleeue that ↑so chaste a Matron as↓ Vertu wil euer be bound to dwel (Felicitatingly) in that Hart, where the Strumpet Vice is permitted to keep a Lodging. It has euer been the Deuils Policy to diuide the hart of man, and [as] demand but one part of it for himself, leauing the other to God, who he knos scorns, /disdains/ to be a sharer with him, and therefore if he be permitted to haue any part at all, God will haue none at all. The Diuel says of the Soule, as the pretended Mother did of the Child, ↑1 Kings 3,26.↓ Let it be neither mine nor thine but Diuide it. But the True |f. 140| Mother wil rather let the Supposed haue it whole, then be contented <consent to> with so vnjust a Partition. 4. ↑This one darling Vice may proue as ruinous [and des] to the Soule as a Swarm and↓ One beloued Sin is able to keep Possession of [thy Soule] <it> for the Deuil /Vice/ as wel as a [Thousand] whole Regiment; and he wil bind thee as fast with one such Chaine as with a 1000 others.[21] One neglected Leake is enuf to sinke the greatest Ship.[22] St. Iames tels vs, Iames 2.10. that Whosoeuer shal keepe the whole law and yet offend in one Point (namely entertaine any one known Sin with allowance and Deliht, and not resolue and striue against it) he is guilty of all.[23] And why shud it not be as Iust with God to destroy a man for one cherished habituall Sin, as for a Prince to put him to Deth for one Actual Murder? If a man receaue a [hu] wound in any one of the Vitals, it is sufficient to dispatch him tho all the other Parts of his Body remaine vn-hurt. No matter whither the Fouler catch the Bird by the head, or by the Foot, or by the Wing: [if] so he catch her by any Part she is sure his owne.[24] We may raise the Wals of a Towne round about as hih as the Third Region <Sunne and> of the Aire: if we leaue but one Breach open, 'tis enuf for the Enemy to com in at, and occasion the Loss of the Towne. ↑Alleadge not that it is Difficult: for to pay but with Indifferent Sins or Vices one [cares] <sets> not much [for,] by, for [the Loue] sake [of] Vertus, is scarce thankworthy; but for the Loue of Vertu to beare thy Darling Sin out of thy Bosome to make her roome, is an Action that wil riuet thee eternally to her fauor. The Sacrifice being still more precius, [illeg.] /acceptable/ the more precius is the thing that is sacrificed.↓ To Conclude, As to the [helth of ful] <free> and Perfect helth of the Body, it is requisite, [that] not onely

---

[21] The image can be found in the *Book of Common Prayer*: cf. the collect "O God, whose nature is ever to have mercy and to forgive, receive our humble petitions; and though we be tied and bound with the chain of our sins . . ."

[22] Cf. Thomas Fuller, *Holy State* (1642): "Many little leaks may sink a ship" (20).

[23] RB also used this quote on f. 133^{v} above.

[24] For the devil as fowler, see *Occ. Refl.* 2.446.

that it be free from the Plage, the Small-Pox, the Stone, the Convulsion, and the Dropsy; but also there is necessary |f. 140v| a full Immunity from all /euery/ Diseases whatsoeuer: so is the Mind in a Sound and Perfect state /helth/ barely for the being free of Pride, Ambition, [Couet] Lust, Couetusness and the like, but then onely, when it is exempt from all fostered Vices without Exception. One cherish't Vice being as capable to ruine the Soule, as one Disease to kill the Body.

Syncerity is [a] that Affection of Vertu that makes all it's Actions be don willingly, and for a Riht End.[25]

I hope we shal need no other Inducement to this Quality then to consider, that this is that Distinguishing Property of Vertu that differences the True from the False, or the Reall from the Apparent: And [as it were the Soule /Life/ of Vertu is Actions that distinguish the Body from the Carcass. /Cadauer./] the only thing that stamps vpon the Action of Vertu a Character of Happines. /Sacrednes/ And certinly Syncerity is of all things that which has the cheefe regard to in our Performances. And therefore in the Sum of the Law deliuered by our Sauior (Matt 22.) We ar commanded not onely to [Serue] <loue> the Lord our God; but to [serue] <loue> him with all our hart. And therefore (Pr. 23.26) It is said, My son, giue me thine hart. ↑And Prou. 3,1. Let thine hart keep my Commandements.↓ And (1. Kings, 8.61) Let your hart therefore be |f. 141| Perfect with the Lord your God: and (1. Cron. 22.19) Set your hart and Soule to seek of the Lord. And againe [(1 K 2.4)] (Ier. 4.14) Wash thine hart from Wickedness that thou mayest be saued. ↑And indeed this Lesson may be very easily read in the Scripture; that God, dos not put our Grace /Vertus/ in the Ballance to see if they be weiht; but rubs them vpon the tuchstone to try whether they be tru.↓ [And the [Spectacles] Perspectiue-glas that wil help vs to a siht of the (invisible) Deity /Diuinity/] And hence it is, that [with out the] ↑where there is no↓ Truth of Vertu (Sincerity) there is neuer any Truth of Consolation. Performances without Syncerity being but the Carcases of Vertu; which hauing no tru Life in themselues, can impart no tru heat to the Soule. And the bare Shel of Vertu, in aduersity, is the Shadow of a Bouh [illeg.] vpon the Water; which while the Drowning man thinkes to saue himself by catching; fils his hands but with Aire, and proues no impediment to his Sinking. For God himself tels vs (1 Sam. 16.7.) that The Lord Looketh vpon the hart. And (Ps. 66.18) it is said, that, If I regard iniquity in my hart the Lord wil not heare me. And Dauid (Ps. 15,2.) Opens the gates of the heu'nly Ierusalem to him only, that speaketh the Truth in his hart. And Christ himself, (Matt, 5,8) [entailes happines vpon] <makes> Sincerity, when he says, Blessed ar the the Pure in hart, for they shall see God; And Dauid (Ps. 7.10) entailes God's Protection <deliuerance> vpon the Vpriht in hart.

[25] "Syncerity" is written in letters 4X usual size.

Now the Marks or Tokens of this Syncerity, are many,[26] As, 1. The Desire and endeauor of Growth, [in] and that in all Vertus and all their Parts. |f. 169| ↑↑The Declining of all Vices, tho neuer so Little, Secret, or Darling. 3. Goodness in Priuate. 4. Goodnes in bad Times. 5. The Loue of Goodness in others. 6. The Willingness to be, and Patience in the being, reprou'd. 7. A Daring and Desire to look into the Strictest and most refined Patternes and Precepts of a Vertuus Life. 8. And the Louing Vertu more for it's selfe, then for any Good that may accrue to one thereby. But because [diuers] the truth (of) diuers of these Symtomes dos perhaps neuer com to an Actuall Triall: [we must] the way must be, seriously to examine our Selues, and catechize our selues, about all those Points that are likely to hinder our total obedience to the Dictates of Vertu; and if thereupon, we find our selues fully resolu'd to adhere vnto Vertu [not] beyond all by-respects, and notwithstanding all opposition: then certainly we may from that resolution make a strong Presumption of our Sincerity. Prouided, always, that we duly weih the Difficultys before we vndertake the Enterprize, and consider the Price as wel as the Purchase: for many that are Wolues in their Resolutions proue Sheepe in their Practice, because they look't only vpon the |f. 169v| Sweetnes they shal tast in the Enjoyment; without considering the Difficultys they must ouercom in the Acquisition. As the Humorous Sick man resolues to take that Fisick before it is brouht him, which hauing by the tast found loathsom, he wil rather Dy then swallow; because in the first temper he considers it meerly vnder the Notion of bringing helth, and in the latter, [of] vnder that of being bitter.[27]

We shal therefore constitute 2 maine acts of Syncerity; Vnfeignedness of Intention and Endeauor to perform syncerely a man's whole Duty; and a Rectitude of Ends; whereby a man, in the Actions of Vertu, aimes principally at Vertu her self; (of which more heercafter.) ↑For, as to the First, the very hethens themselues took it for an Ill Omen, when the Sacrifice wanted a hart;[28] and for the Second, as the [Noblest] ↑richest↓ of Metals, Gold, may ↑(by the Goldsmiths wil)↓ be formed /mould/ into Vessels for the most nasty and Sluttish vses; so the noblest of Actions, (I meane those materially good) may by the Ignoble Ends to which they ar directed; becom <debased into> things meane, contemtible, nay and shamefull to.↓

The onely opposite to Syncerity is Hippocrisy; ([that] real Equivocation,) which is, A Simulation of Moral Vertu; or, if yow wil, the Putting on of a seeming Vertu, for the more easy attainment of a man's owne By-Ends.[29]

---

[26] For Alsted's florilgeium on sincerity, see 1253.

[27] Cf. RB's medical anecdotes from his days at Eton (Maddison 16, 18).

[28] Cicero reviewed an extensive literature on auspices and divination, including references to such sacrifices, in *De Divinatione* 2.78ff.

[29] For Alsted's florilegium on hypocrisy in the church, see 1253, but see also *Occ. Refl.*

This Vice is so Epidemicall that it <here> wil need no very strong faith to beleeue that of the Profet, Ier. 17,9. The hart is deceitfull aboue all things |f. 170| and desperately wicked; who can kno it? Now altho in [direct] the particular the kinds of hypocrites, may be made as numerous, as are the Indirect Ends they aime at or Deceitfull (deceiuing) Principles, they go vpon; yet for Breuity sake we will reduce vnto these generall heads; therefore, 1. Som there ar that put on Vertu to gaine an Esteeme amongst the Religious, (who vse to consider more a man's Graces then his Parts;) which amongst vitius persons, the meanness of their Abilitys giues them little hope to obtaine. 2. Som there ar that do it to deceiue the Religius and others more neatly and vnsuspectedly; who, as our Sauior says, Mat. 23.14, Deuour Widdows houses, and for a Pretence make long Prayer; and to whom Religion serues for a Stalking horse, to deceiue the Simple with. 3. Others there ar that do it for By-Respects, as hope of aduancement or aduantage from som Godly Kinsman /Parent/ or Religious great one: and these People ar Vertus mercenarys, that serue but for their Pay. ↑And such people commonly thro of their Vertu in the Enjoyment of their Desires; as Trauellers do their Boots when they ar arriued at their Inne. As is prettily tauht vs by the Story of that Abbot of Glastenbury &c.↓[30] 4. Others there |f. 170v| are that do it out of meere Hope or Feare of Reward or Punishment in this Life or the Next: the [M] World is commonly beholdyng to the Magistrate for these Peoples Vertu; and their honesty [is rath] (howeuer in this corrupted Age so magnifyed for it's rarity) is rather Innocence then Vertu; and themselues rather good Subiects then Good men. 5. Others there ar that do it because they haue been bred vp to it, and Religion is in Request in their Age, Cuntry, Family, or Company: |f. 171| ↑these kind of People ar not properly Vertuus, but in the fashin; and their Vertu has much more in it of the Ape then of the man. 6. Others there are, that seem Religious because the Shamefastnes of their Nature bridles their Corruption; and makes their Vices, like the Owle, aferd <abhor> to be lookt <seen> vpon: such People indeed ar [fa] not Vertuus; but only they ar asham'd <dare not> to own the being otherwise. 7. Others again there be <and those many> that put on Vertu out of an affectation of Singularity and contradicting; which study not so much to be good as to be Cross: and som of these People there be, that put on a Catonian and Satirical humor, on purpose to haue their mouthes stopt with som preferment: like som Curs that bark, not to discouer /friht away/ the Theefe, but to procure /get/ the Sop. 8. Others <finally> there ar, [fi] that pretend to Vertu, to gaine an Vniversall and Promiscuus Applause from all sorts of People. And this kind of Hyppocrisy I haue obserued to be very epidemical amongst those,

---

2.393-34; *High Veneration* 5.143; *Theodora* 5.276 and 285; *Chr. Virtuoso* 5.526; and *Swearing* 6.15. Daniel Dyke's *The Mystery of Selfe-Deceiving* (1615) and William Fenner's *A Treatise of the Affections; or, the Soules Pulse* (1641) went through many editions.

[30] Source unknown.

that in other things were Inriched |f. 171v| with the choisest Endowments. These People weare [Vertu] <Good> [not as] as som of our gallants do their slash't suites; not as a Garment /clothing/ but an Ornament; and value Vertu but as a boate that may land them at applause.↓

↑Now these ar the most vsual Symptoms of a Dissembler, 1. Extolling his own Goodness: as Mountebanks boast more the Excellency of their Receits, then the most able Fisitians. 2. Heauy censuring of others for liht Faults. 3. Strayning (as our Sauior has it) at a Gnat, and Swallowing a Camell.[31] 4. Shrinking in the time of Persecution; which is the tru fire, that tryes whither thy Loue to Vertu be disinterest <or> for Ends. And indeed Sultry Wether is the best to discouer painted faces in. 5. The vnequal beating of his Pulse in matters of Piety; Strong and quick in matters that ar gaz'd on; but weake /faint/ and dul in priuate Actions. When a man vses Religion like his Cloake, which he weares whilst he is abroad, but puts /thros/ of when he coms home. 6. The making Vertu a thing rather Notional then Practicall. 7. And the bearing too glorious an outside /sho/ of Religion: as we see gilt cups more glittering then those of massiue gold; and indeed they may wel afford to make an ↑aduantageous sho of their↓ Merchandise /ware/ that haue nothing in the Ware-house, all in the Shop.↓ |f. 171v|

But I shal desire al these to consider, 1. That there is nothing in the world more Inconsistent with Vertu then Hippocrisy: A man may be a Drunkard, or a Miser, or a Wencher, and yet in the Generall be a Vertuus man; but Vertu and hippocrisy cud neuer yet be brouht to dwel together in the self-same brest. For Vertu residing in the Will, and being in [outward] <externall> Actions but as they ar the Emanations of that Will, it is euident, that <in> the Hippocrite, the Wil being not Vertuus, the Actions can lay but an vnjust claime to so glorius a Title. And indeed, Hippocrisy, not only taints the rinds, but rots the very Core of Vertu. 2. How meane and disingenuus a Vice it is; for [those that glo] not only tis a Vice, that those that practice most ar asham'd to owne: but those very brazen- |f. 172| faces, that glory in their Shame, and will euen brag of whoring, drinking, Swearing, and the blackest villanyes; wil be angry to be but suspected of Hyppocrisy. And indeed, If hyppocrisy be iustifiable, why dare not men owne it; and if it be not, how dare they practize it. Sure where the Syncerely vertuus man, is like the Kings Dauter, Ps. 45,13. All glorius Within; the Hippocrite is like a great man's cushion /of state/ cast with fine Satin /veluet/ and rich embrodery, but stuft with, Feathers, hay, or som such trash; or, as [the ho] our Sauior diuinely has it, Matt, 23,27, like a Whited Sepulcher, whose outside weares the liuery of Innocence, but the within is nothing els but Rottenness and Stench. 3. That there is no Sin more Dangerous; ↑the Hippocrite↓ being so far from admitting a Remedy, that he will neuer aknoledg his Disease. And this

[31] Matt. 23:24.

will moreouer appeare partly from that Terrible Obseruation of our Diuines, that [From Gen] the Bible, from Genesis to the Reuelation, affords vs no |f. 172v| President of a Hippocrites Repentance; and partly because, that as many tell lys so long and so confidently, that at last they ar brouht to beleeue them themselues; so many, by an inveterate Hippocrisy haue so habituated themselues to a shew of Godlines, that at last they beleeue themselues really possest on't; and dy Hyppocrites, conceal'd, not only to the World but themselues. And indeed it is but iust, that those that haue endeauored to deceiue God and others so long, shud deceiue themselues at last. 4. That the Punishment of the Hippocrite is, or shal be ansuerable to his Crimes. For eu'n in this world, how many Plesures must he loose, and how many [Troubles] <Inconueniences> must he run into, to keep on the maske, whose fall wud vndo him. And in the next he has smal Reason to expect better entertainment; if he remember that he must there be punish't as an Impostor, [that] <a> counterfait that gaue himself out for one |f. 173| of the King of heu'ns Children: and that our Sauior Matt. 24,51. dos make the Lord, in <full turn principall> reueng of <all the> [mis] Crimes of his oppressiue steward, to appoint him his Portion with the hyppocrites; to whom it seems thereby that there belongs a double share of Torments. <[Shame]>

And sure, If the best things corrupted proue the Worst, what Flames wil be thout hot enuf for them that turn Vertu it self into a Crime.[32] A Hippocrite has but iust Religion enuf <in him> to condemn him; and render him inexcusable, in that he did so much and did no more. And [his Coun] the Seemingness /Shaddo/ of his Goodnes wil ad to the Reality of his Torments /Euill./

Now the 2 legs vpon which this same painted Colossus stands, ar, Desire of Aduantage /reward/ and Desire of Applause; no man pretending Religion, but either for <to get a> Recompence, or to win esteeme. But for these, I shal desire the reader to consider. 1. That all seeking for honor or aduantage by Vertu [is] <seems> not absolutely condemnable: for since we [usually] allow most things in the World more |f. 174| Ends /vses/ then One, I know not why we shud giue Vertu leaue only to Content vs and not also make vs great [and] <or> honorable. The Filosofers tel vs that Subordinate Ends destroy not one another. And sure since it is vnlawful to acquire Riches and honor by forbidden /vnlawful/ meanes, it will not be vnlawful to pursue /seek for/ them by those that ar vertuus /worthy/: Besides that the Scripture in many places bayting Vertu with heu'ns Prosperity, dos not obscurely intimate, that it is lawful for vs to desire /endeuor/ What it is Iust with God to Promise. 2. Neither dos it seem that tho in the General a man be rihtly Principled in the Ends of his Axions, yet in euery particular Axion he is bound to look at Vertu or Happines as the Principal End of that Axion: as the Soldier is not oblig'd to think vpon the Peace of the Kingdome he

[32] RB used the same proverb in bk. 2, ch. 4.

fihts for, in euery particular thrust he makes, or blow he wards: ↑and the Temperatest man in the World tho in the general he eates to liue, yet in the particular, (laying that consideration aside) he eates to satisfy his hunger.↓ so that to syncerity it seems to suffice, that a man be in a |f. 174v| tru and willing readiness to all Vertus Performances; and wud go thorouh with euery Particular Duty, tho there were an Absence of those Secondary Ends he aymes at in it; and tho he found in their Roomes their contrary Discouragements. So that Syncerity seems to allow men to haue an Ey /squint/ at their own Iust, [Ends] tho Inferior Ends; and challenges indeed a Pre-eminency, [aboue,] but without excluding the rest; content to be the Principal tho /if/ not the Sole Ingredient of Vertuus Actions; [So] And so it seems to consist not in a Total Immixednes, but in a due Subordination /ranking/ marshalling/ of [illeg.] Ends. 3. That tho in Vertuus Actions we may haue Ends besides Vertu; yet we must haue none beyond it. For if we value any thing aboue Vertu, and that thing chance to come into Competition with Vertu, we must necessarily desert the one to adhere to the other. No no, Vertu like oyle in Water, is neuer truly [w] but when it swims vpon the top:[33] |f. 175| she disdains to dwel any where, where she is not queene, and wil neuer truly tye her self to him, that courts her for her Dowry, not for her Selfe. [No] Honor and Reward shud be the Attendants /consequences/ not the Ends of Vertuus Actions; they shud be the fruits /prizes/ of the Victory, not the Motiues to the Warr. 4. That tis a Folly to be Vertuus for Honor or Reward; when he that is so gets but them, whereas he that loues Goodnes for it self, gets both them and Vertu to boot. Heer what God says vnto Salomon, (2 Chron, 1,10 and 11) Because this was in thine hart, and thou hast not asked Riches and — .[34] And our Sauior tels vs, (Matt. 6,33) But seek ye first the Kingdom of God and his Rihteusnesse; and all these things shall be added vnto you. And this is an Argument that wil deserue a very serius consideration. 5. As for Aduantage or Reward; those that pursue it by Hyppocrisy do often misse their marke; either by som rash or casual discouery of their Deceit /craft/ or else by the iust Iudgment of God, who takes pleasure to |f. 175v| deceiue them (in their hope) that endeauor to deceiue him: Whence Iob tels vs (Iob 8,13) that the Hypocrite's hope shall perish. ↑And indeed their Reward had need to be very great on Erth, since Matt. 6,1 dashes them out of all hope of receiuing any in heauen.↓ Besides [that] it seemes very vnhandsom to employ the Noblest qualitys of the Soule, to [obtaine] <serue> the meanest of Ends: which makes me fancy them like the <our som> [Fu]

[33] Cf. T568, "Truth and oil are ever above," a tag also used in bk. 2, ch. 4.

[34] RB's hiatus probably indicated that he intended an additional Biblical citation. The connection between virtue and riches is vividly made in this passage, particularly in 2 Chron. 1:12: "wisdom and knowledge is granted unto thee; and I will give thee riches, and wealth, and honor, such as none of the kings have had that have been before thee, neither shall there any after thee have the like."

Mercenary Astrologers, that ar conuersant with heu'n, but to get a little mony vpon Erth.[35] 6. That as for Applause or Esteem I wud haue yow remember; that Commendations ar no such euidence of worth; since they ar neither paid to good Actions always, or to them only. That if the Cause set a value vpon the Prayse, that of a man's owne Conscience shud be rated <income> aboue all the rest;[36] as that which is paid but to merit; and is not subject to Inconstancy; whereas all those Commendations [men haue] ar as little auaileable to whom Conscience giues the ly; as it is to the Sicke[ne] man to haue thousands [illeg.] extoll his Cooking well, while he feeles in the meane time the swift |f. 176| and successiue returns of Frost and Dog-dayes (domineering) in his Veines. That these vndeserued Prayses ar real Blames: for whilst men prayse yow for [illeg.] quality yow want, they tacitly censure yow for [that] the want of that Quality: and while they commend what yow seeme, they condemn what yow are. And that (lastly) it is no very great Policy to part with heu'n for a little <blast of> empty Aire (our Sauior, Matt 6,2, [tell] to cut of <hope of> Hippocrites to get a Reward, telling them that they Haue it) nor much greater Happiness, to be Commended where yow ar not, and Tormented where yow are.

Perseuerance or Constancy is that Property of Vertu, where by the Vertuus ar enabled to persist in the ways of Vertu to the very End, (and that without any frequent and considerable Interruptions.) notwithstanding all Discouragements and Oppositions.[37]

This Property therefore has 2 principal branches: |f. 176v| By the One it resists and surmounts all the Difficultys laid in our way, by [the En] outward Discouragements, the Endeuors of the Deuill, and the Peruersnes of our own Nature: and by the Other, it keepes vs in a Constant, and almost euen Tenor of Goodness, not suffring Vertu to be arrested in it's Progresse; nor frequently and considerably put to the worst by any Temptation or Sin. For tru Perseverance like a Good horse must not only carry a man at last to his Iourneys End; but must before not to stumble or be resty by the Way.[38]

Now we may be incited to Perseverance if we wil but consider, 1. That Constancy is a quality so noble, that eu'n when it degenerates into Obstinasy, it is not lookt vpon but as somthing of Gallant: That great Vertu we so admire in the Ancients, was for the most part but a downriht and blunt Constancy.[39] It steels the brest against all the treacherous bac-blos of |f. 177| fickl Fortun. It emboldns a man to bid defiance to all oppositions; and throu their vtmost

---

[35] For fees charged by contemporary astrologers, see Thomas, *Decline* 381-82.

[36] Cf. *Greatness of Mind* 5.554.

[37] "Perseverance" is written in letters 4X usual size.

[38] "Resty" is an obsolete form of "restive" (*OED*).

[39] For other remarks on constancy, see RB's letter in 1647 (1.xliii); *Seraphic Love* 1.274; *Theodora* 5.298; and *Greatness of Mind* 5.560.

violences cuts [it] him out a way to his Happines. [The Vnst] Nothing is more vnalterable then God's Decrees, or more vn-vary'd then the Motions of the Spheares. The Good Angels ar confirmed in Good; and the wisest men most constant in their Resolues; and in Sum, the Perfectest things [ar] lest subject to change; (Instability proceeding from the Defect of /weknes/ Iudgment.) Whereas our Inferior and Ignobler World, is the Stage whereon Inconstancy (perpetually) acts her part in a 1000 varius postures;[40] and we see women, and young men, and fooles; whom ar thouht to haue less of Iudgment, ar [much] vsually incinable to be fickle; and in this Sens, a Wise man pronounc't, that Mutability is the Badg of Imperfection.[41] ↑Look but how long the wrangling Lawyer or greedy Merchant ar in the Prosecution of their Suits and Traffic: and shud we be les [resolued] /constant/ in the Pursuit of [happ] Felicity then they in that of an Inferior Good?↓ 2. That Constancy is the onely quality that puts vs in actuall Possession of the Cheefest of Goods, Felicity: and therefor one prettily |f. 178| cals it that Golden Clasp ↑(since happines is the concomitant of Vertu)↓ that joynes Grace and Glory together:[42] and indeed it is the Excellence /Vertu/ vpon which our Sauior himself entayles the Crowne; (Reu. 2,10) Be thou faithfull vnto Deth, and I wil giue thee a Crowne of Life. ↑[Perseuerans is the Image of Eternity and that only which with Eternity is rewarded.]↓ How much therefor ouht we to court this Quality that only has the Priuiledg to Crown vs. 3. That without this Quality the Attainment of Felicity is Impossible: for he must be alwayes Good, that wil be alwayes happy. Finis coronot opus:[43] and Tho we vse to say, He [is] <has don> half[-way] that has [wel] begun, yet in this Case we may as truly say, He has don nothing that dos not End. For tho yow set forth neuer so well, yet if yow tire before yow com to your Iourneyes End, yow shal neuer get thither: [and he is as wel drown'd that faints but a stone's cast, as he that faints a furlong <[lcague]> from the Shore.] So that me thinks, that he that (in his Age) [grows weary of the Paths of Vertu; is like] |f. 178v| desists from his commenced Course of Vertu, is not vnlike the Foolish Plowman, who hauing taken a great deal of Paines [in the Winter to [pl] manure and im] all the rest of the Yeare to Manure, Plow, harrow and Sow his ground; out of a little lasines in the haruest /Autumn/ for feare of the heat and toyle of the reaping, looses all the fruits of his Labour, and the benefit of his haruest.

Now there ar [4] <5> principal Impediments (besides those mention'd in

[40] Cf. Alsted 1253 for a florilegium on inconstancy. The metaphor of life as a stage play was a commonplace, one found in *Seraphic Love* 1.289 and *High Veneration* 5.143.

[41] Cf. M1336, "Mutability is the badge of infirmity." In *Vulgar Notion* 5.187, RB rejected the idea of the heavenly immutability.

[42] Cf. William Perkins, *A Golden Chaine; or the Description of Theologie* (1591). RB owned two vols. of Perkins' *Works* (1613 and 1616).

[43] E116.

the Chapter) of our Perseverance in Vertu; viz, the Apprehension of it's Difficulty or Impossibility; Violent Temptations; Lasting Temptations; [and] Relapses, and Remissions.[44]

1. To the First of these we haue already elsewhere giuen a Sufficient Answer. To which we wil now only adde, 1. That tho the Oppositions of Vertu [ma] present themselues al at ons to the <our> Imagination, yet they do not so in <to> our Tryall. For the Past and the Future ouht not to friht vs; those ↑in the Present↓ being already vanquist /gon/ |f. 179| and these being yet to come. And therfore we must not consider all the Difficulty of Vertu together, because they assault vs not all together; but to a part of them we haue a part of Time allow'd vs for their /our/ resistance. So that I see no reason why he that has already ouercom past difficulty, shud not dare to resist the Present, and hope to surmount the Future. 2. That since tis the Will only that giues any thing a sweet or bitter relish (as to the Soule) if we can incline <compose> our Wills to the Desire of that which other men think harsh, why shud those Difficultys be a Terror to vs. What delihts one man's Palat is vnsauory, /distastful/ to anothers. We see greatbellyd women can ↑with neglect of the most exquisite banquets↓ desire eu'n with longing and eat <with deliht> Snakes, or Magots, or Charcoale and such like other trash, as wud turn the Stomack of a very Sea-man;[45] and shal [an] not an Incorruptible Soule haue as great a Power to sway the Appetite to Liking or dislike as the corrupted Stomacke. If we can once bring the wil to like of Trouble for Vertus sake, the Difficultys wil thenceforth remaine so but in Name, |f. 179v| for Willingnes sweetens the bitterest Pills; and whoeuer wants not that, Difficultys, tho neuer so harsh in themselues, wil be plesant to him. See a pressing Instance of it in our Great men, that wil oftentimes leaue Plenty and Prosperity at home, and crosse the Seas to seek out Dangers and Opposition, which they wil cheerfully and with deliht go on vpon for the Purchase of an Emty Title, or the honor to be tak'd of.[46] Tennis, which our Gallants make a Recreation, is much more Toylsom then what <many> others make their Worke;[47] and yet those deliht in the one and these detest the other; because we do [illeg.] this out of necessity, and the other out of choice.

2. For the Second, It wil be fit to consider, 1. That Nullum Violantum Durabile,[48] These sudden /boysterous/ Gusts quickly spend themselues with their

---

[44] These topics are also treated in "Of Sin" and *Swearing*.

[45] The same example is used in *Swearing* 6.26 and *Vulgar Notion* 5.237.

[46] RB's reference to "Great men" was probably a general statement. But the purchase of titles was an accusation often made by the enemies of RB's father (Canny, ch. 2). RB referred twice to "empty titles" in this work.

[47] At Geneva RB's recreations "were sometimes Maill, Tennis (a Sport he euer passionately lou'd;) & aboue all the Reading of Romances" (Maddison 31). RB used tennis to illustrate a scientific point in *Of the . . . Nature of Cold* 3.744-45.

[48] Alsted 1236; N321, "Nothing violent can be permanent."

own Violence: and loose in their Lastingnes what abounds in their Force. Wherefor do but hold out a little longer, and the Enemy must of necessity raise the seege; do but keep your ground a while, and y'ar Victorious. 2. |f. 180| That We ar very apt to think our Temptations greater then they ar; to excuse our Frailty if we fall: but certinly both our Dangers and our Temptations ow the[ir] best part of their greatnes oftentimes to our owne feares. Be but resolu'd and thou makes the greatest Temptations little; for they, (like Dangers) take their Denomination from the Proports they haue, to the Resistance they find. 3. That A Gallant man when he finds himself assaulted by a Great /fierce/ Temptation, ↑instead of being discouraged,↓ shud <thankfully> say like Alexander when he went to fiht with Porus the Indian King /Giant/ At last I haue met with an Enemy worthy of my Self.[49] A woman may kil a Child, but 'tis for Dauids to ouercom Goliaths. And since the Difficulty of the Atcheeument is the greatest ornament of the Triumph; the more Powerful the Enemy, the more Glorius the Victory. ↑To ouercom ordinary Temptations is Comendable but to ouercom <subdue> Gyant-like Temptations is Glorious.↓ 4. That it wil greatly conduce to remember, that There wil be more Pleasure in the Victory ouer the Temptation, then in the Enjoyment of the Sin. ↑Specially this Conquest, that [being] dos not only [illeg.] manifest our strength but augment it. For as those winds /gusts/ that ouerthrow Trees, root them the Deeper, so repuls't Temptations strengthen and confirm the mind. ↑(Tis the Symtom of a Gallant resoluednes of mind, when the Soule in Vertu of Perseuerance breakes thorou with an Euennes of Mind the Temptations of Prosperity and Terror /Rigors/ of Aduersity which bloc vp it's Passage to Felicity and neuer lays downe armes til the final /total/ Conclusion of the War; like the Needle in the Compasse, that in the fury of the greatest Tempests remains stil fixt vpon /tru[50] to/ it's former North.)↓↓ |f. 180v|

For the Third; take notice, 1. That Temptations in this life cannot possibly be auoided, and to go out of the reach of Temtation is to go out of the World. Wherefor since yow cannot fly them, ouer com them: neither ar they without their benefits, and those great ones, as I cud esily sho yow if this wer a fit plas for their Inuentory. And a Temptation like Samson's Lyon, tho difficult to be kild is ful of hony /swetnes/ when ded.[51] Besides that Temptations ar necessary to the Triumf of your Vertu; for how wil it be crown'd if it fiht not; and how can it fiht if it want an Enemy? ↑Ther was neuer any famous Saint in the World, that was not beholding to Temptations both for his Happines and for his Glory.↓

---

[49] RB's fascination with Alexander has been mentioned above (cf. *Aret*. bk. 2, ch. 4.).

[50] RB used the lodestone extensively both as a religious symbol (*Seraphic Love* 1.274; *Reconcileableness* 4.177 and 179; and "Dayly Reflection" f. 272) and as a topic for natural philosophers: *Usefulness* 2.10; *Continuation of New Exp*. 3.238; *Exp. et Obs. Phys*. 5.569-75; and *Languid Motion* 5.11.

[51] Judges 14:8-9.

Book Two, Chapter Six

2. That lingring Temptations leaue of all other the lest excuse to the Sinner; whilest they giue him leasure to arm himself cap a Pé, and put his Reason into all the Postures of Defence. ↑And it is les disgraceful to be snapt vp by Surprize, then to be beaten [in] /ouercom/ in the open Field.↓ Consider therefor what thou art about to do; remember that 'tis thy Soule thou fihtst for and that, The Title to a Kingdom's <Empire> but a Trifle vnto this. 3. That we shud Compare not the Trouble of the Resistance with the Sweetnes of the Sin; but the Plesure /glory/ of the Victory |f. 181| with the Sorro /Repentance/ for the fault. Certinly there is a Ioy in the Victory of a Temptation that only the Inhabitants of the Spheres, and louers in their Mistresses Embraces can imagine. <kno> 4. [That] ↑Look not only vpon the Power of him that assailes [but vpo] also vpon the Omnipotence of him that has promised to rescue. Heb. 13,5. I wil neuer leaue thee nor forsake thee. See Ephes. 6,10,11,12. Iames. 1,2. 5. Why shud the Deuil be more constant <intent> for <to> thy ruine, then thou thyself for thy Preseruation. 6.↓ That 'tis Madnes to think to be rid of a Temptation by consenting to it; for that's the next way to haue it a perpetuall Retainer. The Deuil, like a Begger being always importuning those that vse to giue him /not to deny 'im/ And like a Dog, seldom troubling thos howses where he [is] constantly receiues the welcom of a Cudgil. /Whip/ And without question euery act of Sin inclines vs to the Repetition of it self, and weakens our Resistance agenst it; as we shal proue hereafter. The Oracle therfor that I wud vpon this Subject comend vnto thee, is that which Experience has tauht my self, namely that Temptations ar more Easily Subdu'd then satisfy'd.

4. For the Fourth. Relapses may be consider'd vnder a Double Notion, either befor a man has fallen into them, or after.[52] |f. 181v|

Vnder the Former Notion these Considerations wil not be vnuseful. [Ty] 1. That as in Diseases, so in Vices, Relapses ar extreamely Dangerous. ↑Water once heated and againe expoz'd to the Cold, contracts a more Intense Degree of that quality then it had before.↓[53] Our Sauior tels vs in the 12 of Mat. that when the Vnclean Spirit[s] after his Departure out of, makes a re-entry in to the Soule of man; he brings along with him a whole family of Deuils; and makes the last State of that man much wors then the first.[54] The like is repeated by St Peter, (2 Pet. 2,20, [21]) who ads this Reason in the self-same Place, For it had been better &c. And therefore in the Ensuing Verse he rakes kennels and hogs-tyes to find comparisons odius enuf for their Crime.[55] And /for/ indeed Relapsing is but

[52] For similar discussions of relapses, cf. *Occ. Refl.* 2.381 and *Swearing* 6.18. The topic was extensively treated in contemporary works of popular divinity.

[53] RB was fascinated by experiments involving heat and cold: see esp. *Exp. Hist. of Cold* 2.508-659, where he tested Arist.'s claim that heated water froze faster than unheated water (2.638).

[54] Matt. 12:43-45.

[55] Cf. 2 Pet. 2:22: "But it is happened unto them according to the true proverb, The dog is

a practical kind of Apostasy. 2. Weih the Pleasur of the Sin with the Reluctancy [that] of Consciens that precedes consent, with the Emtiness and Disturbedness of the [Deliht] <Plesure> /Enjoyment/ and the Repentance that attends it; and then consider whither the Deliht of the Victory be not greater then that of the Offence. <Sin> |f. 182|

Truly I cannot but wonder, that those that haue had so much Conscience as to repent a Sin, shud haue so little Reason as deliberately to recommit it. For they kno (tho they wil not giue themselues leaue to remember /consider/ that the sweetnes of the Plesure in committing it, counteruailes not the bitternes of the Sorrow [in] in repenting it: [besides that the Sting of Conscience wil not suf] and the Plesur is not only fading and momentary; but that [in the very act of Enjoyment, the St] Sting of Conscience will not suffer [it] ↑the very act of enjoyment↓ to pas vn-molested.[56] 3. Why canst thou not by the sam means /ways/ that thou hast held out hitherto, hold out stil. /hereafter/ Temptation grows easyer by a customary resistance, and Custom, that ouercoms Nature, wil resist Temptation. How chance thou, that were able to begin, art not able to perseuere? Since the beginnings (of things) ar the most difficult, why wilt thou to auoid a little trouble in resisting, by a frequent relapsing, put [the] thy self to the great truble of a perpetual beginning? |f. 182v|

4. Lastly, yow must not only a Poet's Precept,

> Look not on Plesures as they Come but Goe.[57]

But remember but to looke on Sin when yow ar ready to commit with the same Ey that yow wil look vpon it after /as soon as euer/ yow haue committed it and yow ar safe. [In a word, Behaue thy self Gallantly, Play the man, think thou hearest Christ saying (Matt, 24,13) He that shall endure vnto the End, the same shal be saued; remember that thy past /former/ Resistance is (but) [an Engagement] engages thee vnto a future; otherwise, All that thou hast don wil but serue to condemn thee for doing no more.]

Touching Relapses vnder the Second Notion, ther ar 2 things that wil deserue our Notice; 1. That since so great a Disgrace has befallen thee, lern to be more humble in the Estimation of thy own abilitys; more watchfull and circumspect |f. 183| in standing vpon thy Guard; and more Prudent and cautelus by obseruing the occasioners of thy fall. 2. Since what is don is past recalling, lern at lest to redeem thy fault, and by a noble kind of Reuenge; make thy past Sin a Promoter of thy future Vertu: and thus shalt thou extract [Eu] Good out of Euill,

---

turned to his own vomit again; and the sow that was washed to her wallowing in the mire."

[56] RB had used this image earlier: S858, "The sting is in the tail" or S859, "There is a sting in the tail of all unlawful pleasures."

[57] Herbert, "Church-Porch," l. 457; cf. P414, "Pleasure and joy soon come and soon go."

like Valiant Sojers that being by their Enemys beaten vpon their knees, rise vp more stout and furius then before. ↑Many had neuer seen themselues Victorius, if they had not (first) felt themselues wounded and the greatest ar not without such Skarres; be not therefor so much trubled with thy foyle as zealous to repay it with a more succesfull Combat.↓[58]

5. For the Last. I heere vnderstand by Intermissions, Som (Voluntary) Interruptions of the Actions of Vertu; and abatements <cooling> of our feruor towards it; tho without the Purpose of a Totall falling of. /Desuetude/ Now that these ar not to be giuen way to may easily appeare. 1. Because that if your Loue to Vertu be rihtly grounded, it must be be built vpon the Dictates of your Reason which in this case ouht to weih /balance/ all the Inconueniences that may |f. 183v| attend it: and if so, Why haue yow not the same Reason to continue to be good that thou had to begin? As [Vertu] <Happines> is the Inseparable Companion of Vertu; so dos the Degree of the one correspond to the /answer the/ Degree of the other: and therfor he that wud not feel a Diminution in /of/ his Happines must admit of None in his Vertu. Sure me thinks the greatest Good, Felicity, shud not be pursued with smal Desires; but the Intensity of the Affection shud be proportion to the Excellence of the Object. 2. Such Remissions haue oftentimes proued extreamely dangerus: (as [those] <after> sweating men ar aptest to take cold.) and occasion'd that Detestable Neutrality (Reu. 3,16) which in the Laodicean Angel our Sauiors Stomack cud by no meanes disgest. And indeed it is easy to obserue, that the Slacning of one's former feruor, dos oftentimes (if not cause a Total Apostasy to Vice) lead to /End in/ a meer <Form of> |f. 184| Hippocrisy [or Em] and by insensible Degrees stealing away the Soule of Vertuus Action (a Riht Intention) left them but the liueless Carcasses of Performances. And vpon this ground it is, that it has bin truly noted that those for the most par't that haue set out (in the Course of Vertu) with a full Career, haue tyr'd before they cam half way to their Iourney's End; like Comets that make an admired Blaze at first, but presently after go out in snuffe. So it wil be wisdom not to enter into to great a Strictness of Vertu at the Beginning, lest finding thy self vnable to keep all those Precepts thou be discouraged from keeping any. But rather to follow that Poets Aduice who bids thee

[58] Much of the martial imagery had Biblical origins, but RB owned Erasmus's *Enchiridion militis Christiani* (Leiden 1641), a widely read exemplification of such imagery.

Book Two, Chapter Six

— Therfor set forth so
As all the Day thou maist hold out to go.[59]

And imitate our Oraters who [illeg.] vse an Humble Voice at the Beginning, but raise it in the Progress: and our Iockys, who put not their horses to their gretest speed till they com neer the Post. |f. 184v| Whereas they tyre by the way that spend that in the beginning of the Course, that wel manag'd shud /miht/ carry them on to the very end. And certinly this Euil is so much the more Dangerous, by how much the les it is (to be) perceiu'd: for like the Consumtion of Vertu /its Soul/ it steales vpon it by vnfelt approaches; and is seldom known to be a Disease, til it be almost beyond the help /reach/ of a Remedy; and ↑like the stone thrown into the Water that neuer stops til it coms to the very bottome.↓ And therfor we see many men's liues like the Nebuchad-nezzar's Image (in the 2nd of Dan.) whose Golden Head degenerated thorou Siluer Brest, Brassy thyhs, and [wo] Iron Legges into feet of Clay.[60] And remember, Pray, that our Sauior, after a Liberal Encomium of the Efesian Angel, makes it a sufficient cause of quarrel with him, that he had left his first Loue, (Reu. 2,4.) and that in the Ways of Vertu, wher we striue agenst the Stream, he that endeauors not a Progres, is easily beaten /born, hurry'd/ back to a Regress. 3. The Remissions, that we commonly yeeld to for Ease, |f. 185| do indeed, but put vs to a further Trouble: by necessitating vs to such frequent Beginnnings; which in these Matters ar euer held the most Difficult. ↑Thc safest and most vsual way to happines is by Walking or running in the Paths /Ways/ of Vertu, and not by Iumping.↓ It is much easyer to keep a Stone rowling, then to moue /stir/ it at first: [illeg.] to keepe it in Motion then to giue it a Motion; and when one is <hot> running, to stand stil dos by contracting a stifness, indispoze vs to the Continuance of our Course.[61] Disdainc therefor these Interruptions, and be not Discouraged; For if it was in thy Power to do that which is more Difficult, to begin, it wil be much more to do what is les, to continue; and thou wilt find it les trouble to perseuere once then begin often. 4. Lastly, Consider that tis not a Good beginning only, or a Fit or 2 perhaps of Vertu that wil serue the Turn, For, says one, in the Way to heu'n there is nothing don while ther remaines any thing vndon,[62] |f. 185v| A man may be as wel drown'd within a Stone's Cast as a furlong /Legue/ of the Shore;[63] and Perseuerance is the Image of Eternity, and the only Quality which is rewarded. St

[59] Herbert, "Church-Porch" ll. 185-6, slightly misquoted: "therefore set out so, / As all the day thou mayst hold out to go."

[60] Dan. 2:31-35.

[61] The first two examples are taken from classical mechanics, the last from personal experience. RB's ideas about and experiments with motion—in large objects, fluid bodies, and invisible bodies—appeared in many later writings.

[62] Source unknown.

[63] RB used this comparison on f. 178 but then deleted it.

Paul brands Changelings with Folly, (Gal. 3.3.) when he askes the Galatians, Are Ye so foolish? hauing begun in the Spirit ar ye now made perfect by the Flesh? (And) Haue ye suffered so many things in vaine? To conclude, [b] Behaue thy self gallantly; Play the man, Think thou euer hearest the Eccho of those Words /that Promise/ of Christ's (Mat. 24,13) He that shall endure vnto the End, the same shal be saued: and remember that thy past Good Actions engage thee vnto future; otherwise, All that thou hast don wil but serue to condemn thee for doing no more.

|f. 144|

Chapter VII.

Of the Degrees of Moral Vertu, where of Half-Vertus and Heroick Vertu

There are 3 Degrees of Morall Vertu, the Disposition, the Perfection, and the Excellency.[1] The first initiates vs into Vertu; the Second posseses vs of it's Nature; the last Sublimes vs in the Degree. The first is termed a Half-Vertu; the second a (Full Vertu, or) Vertu, absolutely, and the third a (perfect, or) Heroicke Vertu. Of which, hauing already discoursed of the Middle most, it remaines that we say somthing of the other two: and so treat of the Imperfection and Perfection of Moral Vertu.

But the Opinion of the Stoickes nips our whole Treatise in the very Bud, by denying [all] any Degrees in Vertu; and affirming that he that has any vertu truly has it perfectly, and he that possesses it not [truly] Perfectly dos not possess [illeg.] it truly. They making Vertu to be as a Mathematicall Line, that has no latitude or bredth at all, but consists (as it is termed) In indiuisibili.[2] |f. 144v| Which Opinion is by the Moralists generally rejected, Because 1. Vertu, (as being a Habitude) is a Quality: and it is the [illeg.] common condition of all qualitys to admit Magis and minus (as they speake,) that is a Greater or more intense, and Lesser, or more remiss Degree.[3] As Heat (For Example) is Greater in the Hart, lesser in the Arms; and more vehement in the Fire then in a Stone. 2. Vnanswerable Experience witnesses that not onely one man [m] has attain'd a hiher Degree in a Vertu then another, but that oftentimes one and the same man may <somtimes> dayly improue himself and be a greater proficient in som particular Vertu; and somtimes againe decline and slacken in it. 3. Diuers Actions, as admitting a greater Difficulty in the Nature of the Thing it self, and meeting also with a far greater opposition in the Nature of the Doer, require a Stronger Vertu then others that want that Difficulty and those Temtations. ↑4. Because they ar opposed to vnequall Vices, (as shal be proued hereafter.)↓ 5. St Paul himself tels vs, (1. Cor. 13.) that Vertu in this present life, [w] is more Imperfect then twill be in |f. 145| The Life to come.[4]

One Objection indeed is to be taken out of the Way, which seems to euince

---

[1] Cf. Nich. Eth. VII.i.

[2] Cf. Alsted 1246. For RB's refutation of the Stoics' view of the passions, see *Occ. Refl.* 2.406-8.

[3] Cf. Alsted 1246.

[4] 1 Cor. 13:10.

the Contrary of our Opinion, which is, that If Vertu can admit of More and Less, it follows that that arriues, because it is (complicated and) mixed with it's contrary Vice; which were absurd. To which they answer, First by denying a little mixture of Vice with Vertu to be absurd. For Vertu is not in this life to be found so syncere and so pure, but that it has yet somthing of Vice adherent to it, more or less according to the Proficiency a man has made in the Vertu. Yet this, or any petty declining from the Meane is not to be termed Vice, but Vertu; because this is the prædominant quality; and, according to the Rule of the Logicians, A maiori parti fit denominatio.[5] The Title follows the more considerable part. Iust as in Water, tho Warm Water, because it has not so thorouly driuen away the Cold, is not altogether so hot as |f. 145v| Boyling water; is neuertheless called, not Cold, but Hot; because Heat is the commanding quality, and is there found in a far hiher degree then Cold. Secondly, they [illeg.] deny the Consequence; for the admitting of More and less in Vertu proceeds not from it's participation of Vice, but from that it's Form ↑(like health in the Body)↓ <not> consisting in an Individual Point (as they call it,) but has in it a certin latitude; within the limits whereof, there may be a More or Less precize Mediocrity, that is, a greater and lesser degree of Vertu. Thus Vertu in Adam, tho before his Fall it was tru and vncontaminated with the admixture of any Vice; yet was it less intense, and in a lower degree then the Vertus of Christ and the holy Angels.[6]

Hauing thus warranted the lawfulnes of our Diuision, we wil now begin with these Imperfect Vertus, commonly termed Semi-vertus; which are, certin |f. 146| Dispositions to and Rudiments of Vertu; which ar indeed commendable in themselues, but haue not yet fully attain'd to that Completness and Degree of Good, [wh] that is necessary to the Constitution of the Tru Forme of Vertu.

Now these Half-Vertus ar two-fold, Naturall or Acquired.

The Naturall ar certin commendable Affections that incline a man to [illeg.] ciuill Vertus, and ar as it were the Sparks and Seeds thereof. [Of] These, tho they may be diuersly diuided, ar not inconueniently reduced to [Ob] Plyableness or Obedience and <Shame or> Shamefastnesse; whereof the one renders a man instructable in all Good, and the other with-holds him, at least from the practice of enorm Euils. And that there is <generally> such seeds of Vertu in the Nature of man, which God has left there as reliques of his Image, euen after the Fall, to distinguish the Societys of men from Assemblys of Beasts; may be proued, partly by dayly Experience, which shos vs that som men ar more prone to Iustice, others more enclin'd to Valor; som giuen to Contemplatiue Sciences; |f. 146v| Others born to the Mechanick Arts; and partly out of that place in the 2nd to the Rom. <14 and> 15, where St Paul speaking of the Gentiles sayth that

---

[5] A tag from logic (cf. Alsted 411).

[6] Moralists debated the status of the affections and understanding in Adam and Eve before the Fall. For Fenner's discussion, see 60ff.

Book Two, Chapter Seven

they haue the Work of the Law written in their Harts; and that they Do by Nature, the things contained in the Law.[7]

Now Pliableness of the Mind or Obediency is a riht Affection of the Mind whereby it is willing to <enquire of others,> receiue and follow those Precepts and Instructions of Vertu which it finds agreable to Reason, tho be not yet in possession of the Habitudes of those Vertus to which it is exhorted. And this Counsellableness of the Mind is the Maine Disposition, by whose Improuement the Habitudes of all the other Vertus ar acquired. For next to the Hauing Wisdom in one's selfe, is the Willingness to Lern it from another. But heerin these 2 extremes ar carefully to be auoided; the one is a certin Waxiness or Easiness of Nature, whereby one is prone to receiue <all kind of> [illeg.] impressions, without examining whither they be reasonable or no; and the other is a kind of Obstinacy, whereby a man |f. 147| is giuen to leaue vnsouht and reiect the Instructions and Aduice of others, be it neuer so wholesom.[8] He that is faulty in the First of these, is like to purse vp much Copper vnder the Notion of Gold; and he that is faulty in the Latter, to neglect much Gold vnder the Notion of Copper.

Shamefac'tnes is a commendable Affection of the Mind, whereby a man feares the Shame or Infamy that proceeds from known <dis-honest> [illeg.] or vnseemly Acts, and is asham'd of them, if he has chanc't to commit them. This Affection, tho as a Subordinate it may be reduced to the Passion of Feare, yet in 2 things it differs from it; the one, in that Feare arises from the Apprehension of Danger, Shamefac'tness out of that of other's Disesteem or Reprehension; the other, in that Feare for the most part, clothes the Cheeke in a white, Shame in a Scarlet, liuery.[9] Now since Shamefac'tness dos but auert men from Vitius and vndecent Axions, not for the Sin but for the Shame; it follows, that it is not properly to be cal'd a Vertu (in it selfe.) Tho indeed it be not vnfitly |f. 147v| termed a Vertu by Accident; partly because it withholds men from the commission of Shameful and vndecent Actions (I meane of those that ar [illeg.] notoriusly condemned;) and partly because it is a Signe of hauing repented the doing them. And certinly this Affection is a very strong Bridle to curbe in those Natures that ar not al together vn-natural, tho not from all secret and common Faults, yet at least from engaging themselues into those Enormous and Notorius Crimes, [illeg.] <that they were> otherwise enclinable enuf to run themselues hedlong into. Wherefore it ouht carefully to be excited and improued in Young-men, to whom it [mo] seems most properly to belong, since they onely (almost) ar capable of that Liuery of Vertu, or, as (Socrates cal'd it,) that Purple of Vertu, the Blush.[10] Not that ↑(as som wud haue it)↓ we wud quite exclude from it, [the]

[7] Rom. 2:14-15.

[8] Cf. Nich. Eth. VII.ix.2-3.

[9] For this color imagery, cf. Nich. Eth. IV.ix.2.

[10] The quote is attributed to Diogenes the Cynic in Laërtius, *Life of Diogenes* 7.54. The quota-

Those that are Vertuus, especially when growne to be Men: for tho the Generall of their Life be Good, yet are there none in this World to be found so faultless, but that they oftentimes slip into those Actions that giue them cause enuf to be |f. 148| ashamed; and make them blush, tho not in their Cheekes, yet at least in their Reason.[11] This Affection has 2 Extreames; the One in Excess, and that is an Ouerbashfulness or certin kind of Womanish Shamefac'tness, when men ar asham'd of that, that is neither Dishonest nor mis-becoming; as ther ar many that ar asham'd to look a stranger in the Face, and wil blush as soone as euer they ar look't vpon by a Stranger: and this [sh] Bashfulness is reprehensible, and is cured by frequent conuersing with vnknown Persons; being occasion'd but by the Want of vn-wonted Company; whence Trauellers, and Soldiers, and Courtiers ar so little troubled with it. The extream in Defect is Impudence, or [illeg.] Brazen-frontedness; when a man commits the most shameful Actions without being the least jot asham'd; being deterred from heinous Crimes, neither by the Fear of God, nor the Shame of Men. Of this kind of Shame was ment the Common Saying, Perijt est, cui Pudor perijt; he is lost that has lost his Shame.[12] That is, He that murder's his Shame burys himself in it's Graue. |f. 148v|

Now com we to those Semi-vertus, that ar acquired (as Perfect Vertus ar) by Institution and Exercice; which ar those, that ar bounded indeed with the limits of Mediocrity; but find a Difficulty and truble to obserue it; because that the Affections obey not yet the Prescripts of Reason without som [illeg.] ↑Resistance↓ and Reluctancy. And this Reluctancy is the maine thing that differences them from perfect vertus; wherein, not onely (as heere) the Reason prescribes what is iust; but the Affections also, as far more thorouly tam'd, do readily obey the Commands of that Reason.

Now there may be as many Semi-vertus constituted as there are Morall Vertus in all; because euery kind of Vertu dos admit of that [Com] Struggling betwixt our Reason and our Affections, that makes the Distinction between Half and Full Vertus. But not to dissent from [the common Custom of the Moralists, and] Aristotle, and the Moralists, we will not inconueniently reduce them to 2 heds, Continency and Tolerancy; whereof the first moderates, (tho imperfectly) |f. 149| the Coueting; and this, the Inuading Appetite. To which 2 Vices are ↑opposed, Incontinency and Softnesse.↓[13]

Continency is often taken for Temperance it self; but heer we only mean

---

tion is also found in *Usefulness* 2.174, where RB considered the physiology of blushing; see also *Specific Medicines* 5.99.

[11] Cf. the treatment of modesty in Nich. Eth. IV.ix.1-8.

[12] Cf. M1033, "She that loses her Modesty . . . has nothing else worth losing" or S271, "Past shame, past amendment (shame once found is lost)."

[13] For discussion of self-restraint, see Nich. Eth. VII.i-x; for continency, see III.x.8-xii. Contemporary moralists covered similar points.

by it, a certin Step or Disproportion to Temperance, or those other Vertus that ar busied in the regulating of the Coueting Appetite. For there is a twofold Continency and Incontinency, the one absolutely so called; which obserues a Mediocrity, ↑or Immoderation↓ in the necessary Pleasures belonging to the Body, namely Meat, Drinke, and Women. The other is continency In part, which is employ'd about those Pleasures that ar not necessary, nor belong not to the Body, such as those that arise from Mony, Honor, and the other Objects of the Coueting Appetite. He that keepes or keepes not a Moderation in those necessary Plesures, is said to be continent or Incontinent simply, without any other adjection: but he that obserues or obserues not a Mediocrity in these latter kind of Plesures, is said to be Continent or Incontinent in (matter of) Mony, Honor, or any other the like Object about which |f. 149v| his Continency is employed. Absolute Continency is a Degree to Temperance as Continency in part <is a Step> to Liberality, Modesty, and other Vertus. Our Discourse shal onely reach <Absolute> Continency and Incontinency; since from the Knowledg thereof, the Doctrine of the Continencys and Incontinencys in part may be easily deduced. That Continency therefor that is absolutely so termed, is a Semi-vertu, whereby a man [illeg.] containes himself within the Limits of Mediocrity in the Desire and Fruition of those Pleasures that concern the Tuch and Tast; tho it be with som Difficulty and Striuing. And heerein it differs from Temperance; for tho both of them haue the same Plesures for their Object; and neither of them [illeg.] <will> for the loue of any bodily Pleasure, be enticed to violate the Prescripts of Reason: yet the Temperate man he performs his Operations without any considerable reluctancy of his Appetite; whereas the Continent he must Struggle with his |f. 150| Passions, and Fiht for the Victory before he gets it. In short, the Temperate Man he Commands his Appetite, the Continent, he must Force it; being faine to tame his rebellious Affections, whereas the other has no rebellius affections to tame. The one being a King of his Affexions, the other a Conqueror.

The Extreame that opposes Continency in Excess, belongs to the Doctrine of Temperance, where also it is treated of. The Extreame in Defect gos vnder the Name of Incontinency, which is, a Semi-vice, Whereby a man is ↑by his Cupiditys↓ carried away [by] to vnlawful Pleasures, tho not without som reluctancy of the Reason.

The same Rapport or Analogy that we haue said to be betweene the Temperate man and the Continent, may be also obserued to be between the Intemperant man and the Incontinent; for the former prosecutes vnlawfull Pleasures because he esteems them Good and Desirable; whereas the Incontinent judges them to be euill, but yet ↑the strength of↓ his Cupiditys [illeg.] in spite of the Reluctancy of his Reason, |f. 150v| is enueagled to embrace them. So that here is the Difference, they both (indeed) follow vnlawful Plesures; but the one pursues (after) them, the other is drawne by them. According to that common Saying,

—Video meliora, proboque, Deteriora sequor— .[14]

Hence the Moralists conclude, that Incontinency is a lesser Ill then Intemperance, 1. Because the Intemperant sins Electiuely and Willing, ↑his very Reason being (as it were) vitiated, and conspiring with his disorderly Affections,↓ the Incontinent, (almost) vn-willingly, or, at least, grudgingly. 2. Because the Intemperant by reason of the long accustomance of Sinning is more obstinate in his Course, whereas the Incontinent is commonly <more> penitent after he has don a fault; and therefor the more easy to be reclaim'd of the two. 3. Because the Sin of the Intemperant being Habituall, seems to be without intermission; whereas the Incontinent has good and faultless Interualls, or Pauses; wherein he repents the [Eu] faults he committed in the bad ones. |f. 151| Hence Aristotle cals the Incontinent man, not Bad, but Half-bad.[15] Yet is not this Incontinency so triuial an Euil, but that it is inconsistent with perfect Prudence. For he that is truly Prudent, must be truly good; which the Incontinent, as such, is not. Besides that to perfect prudence is necessary both a cleare Iudgment, and an vndisturbed [illeg.] <Action>; but in an Incontinent, his turbulent Affections, (oftentimes) both Cloud his Reason, and vitiate his Practice.[16]

Now the Difference betwixt the Continent man and the Incontinent, consists; not in the rectitude of their Iudgments; for both judge the same thing of Pleasures; but in the Strength and Constancy of their Reasons; which in the Continent ar so [strong] <vigorus> that [they ar] <it is> able to resist the Onset of his Cupiditys, and subdue them, whereas in the Incontinent it is so weake, that it is for the most part Tyred out or Ouercome by them. |f. 151v| But tho in this indeed the Continent man agrees with the Obstinate, that they both persist firmly in their Purpose: yet in this they differ, that the Obstinate man is constant to whatsoeuer purpose, the Continent but to a Commendable purpose: the Continent wil readily giue way to Reason, but wil by no means suffer himself to be led away by his Cupiditys; whereas the Obstinate man he wil not be tractable to any reason that contradicts his, tho neuer so apparent; but yet wil (for the most part) easily let himself be led aside by his Affections.[17]

Heere it is enquired, whither or no <when> the Incontinent commits a Fault, he dos it knowingly or Ignoringly? To which the Moralists answer, that he dos it, partly knowingly and partly Ignoringly.[18] For absolutely, and while he considers those Pleasures wherein he sins barely in themselues, he is able to giue a riht estimate of them: but when it comes to those particular |f. 152| Cases,

[14] RB did not translate Medea's famous line from Ovid's *Metamorphoses* 7.20—"I see the better and approve it, but I follow the worse"—but left space for a translation.

[15] Nich. Eth. VII.ix.3.

[16] Cf. Nich. Eth. VI.v-xiii for a lengthy analysis of prudence.

[17] Cf. Nich. Eth. VII.ii.7.

[18] Cf. Nich. Eth. VII.ii.1ff.

wherein he sins; then those Plesures, which he Absolutely dislik'd; Comparing [wit] them with all the Circumstances ↑that present themselues at that time when he sins;↓ he now embraces; because the Strength of his Cupiditys darkens and offuskes his Iudgment; and hinders him to apply his generall Notions to these particular cases. Which misprision of his Iudgment ouht only to be vnderstood, of the Time whilst he actually Sins: for it [dos] often happens, that presently both before and after the committing of the fault; he iudges ariht of those Pleasures wherein he Sinned, not only in general, but also in particular. From this Estimate arises his Repentance.

There is a two-fold Incontinency, Surprizednes (or Precipitancy) and Infirmity. The former is that whereby a man is suddenly as it were Transported by some Vehement Affection to som misbecomming Action, before he has had time to think or deliberate vpon it. |f. 152v| The Latter is that whereby, a man hauing resolued to resist the Assaults of his Affections; and hauing for a while repelled them; yet at last, tyr'd out and weary'd with their Importunity, besides (tho not against) his will, lets himself be ouercom by them. And this latter is thouht to be more blamable then the other, because in this, a man has leasure to Fortify himself against the onsets of his rebellius Passions; whereas, in the other, a man wants time to recollect himself; and is ouercom by his Enemy, (almost) before he knew that there was an Enemy to ouercom him.[19]

Tolerancy is a Demy-vertu, whereby a man, in the sense and sufferance, of paines, difficultys, and Troubles for honestys sake, obserues a Mediocrity; [that is strugled with and resisted by the Appetite.] tho not |f. 153| without a certin struggling and Combat of the Mind.

It differs from Courage as Continency dos from Temperance; for as Continency containes with struggling <and paine,> so Tolerancy suffers with struggling <and paine>: whereas Temperance and Valor, do these things, not onely with readiness, but also with Pleasure. ↑Where it is (by the way) to be obserued that that Continency, Tolerancy, and Obediency that ar prescribed and [set forth] held forth in the Scripture ar deseruedly ranked amongst the most perfect hih, and Difficult Vertus of a Christian. (But their handling belongs to the Diuine.)↓

The Excess of Tolerancy is treated of in the Doctrine of Courage. The Defect is a certin Softness or Tenderness, whereby men either not vndertake, or not go thorou, with those things, that they iudge ouht to be vndertaken and gon thorou with: but for a little Paines [illeg.] or petty Inconueniences, suffer themselues to be deterred therefrom. And this Softness is either Voluntary (by a man's owne fault) or [illeg.] <Naturall,> proceeding, from the Nation, as in times past amongst the Persians;[20] or the Age, as in Children; or the Sex, as in |f. 153v| Women; or, lastly, from Diseases, and the like.

[19] Cf. Nich. Eth. VII.vi.1.
[20] Cf. Nich. Eth. VII.vii.4-6.

Thus far of Semi-vertus, which are a Degree [be] of this Side of Moral Vertu; now we must proceed to that which is a Degree beyond it; namely, Heroicke Vertu; which is nothing but Moral or Intellectuall Vertu in the Superlatiue Degree; or, Moral Vertu compleate and perfect, accompany'd with a certin Splendor or Eminency.[21] Thus to [fiht for one's cuntry] render one's Life for the Defence of one's Cuntry is an Act of Courage, but to do it, as Camillus [did] ↑is said to do,↓ for one's ingratefull and iniurius Cuntry, is an Act of Heroick Courage.[22] Thus to abstaine from the forbidden pleasures of Women, is an Act of Chastity; but to choose Misery with Chastity rather then Preferment with Pleasure and to embrace (for Vertu's sake) a [Pri] Dungeon rather a Mistris, as Iosef did, is an Effect of Heroick Vertu.[23] ↑Thus we may say Salomon was endow'd with an Heroick Prudence, Ezechias with an Heroick Piety, Dauid with an Heroick Valor, [illeg.] Iohn the Baptist with an heroic Temperament, Aristides with an Heroick Iustice; and Christ with all Vertus in a heroicall Degree.↓[24] |f. 154|

Now tho in euery Vertu (both Intellectuall and Morall) this Perfection or Heroick Vertu miht be obserued; (since there is in euery Vertu a [Hi] Supreame Degree; and that is the thing that constitutes Heroick Vertu;) yet it is far more obseruable <and resplendent> in Iustice, Liberality, and Courage; because the 2 former ar more beneficial to others and of more frequent vse; and the latter is employ'd in matters of great Difficulty and Moment, and that make a great Noise in the World. Wherefor of these cheefly is the ensuing Discourse to be vnderstood.

There are [illeg.] <Three> principal Characters and Dutys of Heroick Vertu. 1. An Extraordinary Impulsion (or excitement) or, as it were, a Diuine rapture. Such an Inward and extraordinary Vocation was in the Apostles, Wiclef, Calvin and Luther when they vndertooke the Reformation of Religion. 2. An invincible Constancy, whereby God dos so confirm the harts of the Heros in their Purposes; that no Difficultys nor Dangers, (be |f. 154v| they neuer go great) ar capable to make them desist from the Pursuite of their Enterprises. And 3. This Constancy is accompany'd, or rather Crowned with an (almost) Incredible Successe; not onely for the greatness of it, but also for the shortness of the Time wherein it was obtained.[25]

These Heroick Vertus do not (as som wud haue it) differ from common Vertus, in the Kind, but only in the Degree. For neither their Objects nor their

---

21 Arist. said very little about heroic virtue, but cf. Nich. Eth. VII.i.1.

22 Arist. used Hector's bravery as his example; RB's example came from Roman history. The legend of Camillus, who saved Rome after the Gallic invasion, was greatly exaggerated by later writers (e.g., Livy, 5.51ff).

23 Gen. 39:1-18. Cf. "Joseph's Mistress" and *Theodora*.

24 For Alsted's list, cf. 1252.

25 Alsted noted the same three requirements: "impetus extraordinarius sive raptus divinus, constantia summa, felicitas incredibilis" (1252).

Ends (which ar the things by which Vertus ar specifically distinguish't) do specifically differ. Besides that their Definitions differ not in Essentials. And in[deed,] effect, ‘tis but with Iustice, Courage, and the like, that all our Heros make such a glittering. Yet [there is a foure-fold Difference obserued by the Moralists betwixt Heros, or those that ar endowed with Heroicke, and them that ar gifted but with ordinary Vertu.] this Heroick is obserued to differ from Common Vertu, 1. In |f. 155| the Efficient Cause. For tho God indeed as the [gen] Cause of Causes, and most general Cause of all, do also concurre in the Production of ordinary Vertu, yet in Heroick Vertu there is a more speciall and Immediate Concourse of the Diuine Vertu; which the Diuines cal Auxilium Speciale, or, a Particular Helpe, without which it is thouht, that amongst the very Heathen themselues, none euer attained to any Heroick quality. The most Sublime and rationall amongst the [An] Gentile Filosofers, acknowledged this Truth, which occasion'd Cicero to say, Nemo Vir magnus sine afflatu Diuino.[26] For whensoeuer it pleases God to worke som greate Reformation in Sciences or Arts, or [to] som [illeg.] notable change in Kingdoms or Common-welths; or generally, any extraordinary Alteration in the state of humane things; he dos for the most part excite Heroick Spirits, which he makes his Instruments to effect it. Thus he excited Cyrus to free the People of Israel from the Babylonish Captiuity, and Attila King of the Huns, to punish the vnbounded Wickedness of the Roman Emperors.[27] Wherefore Heroick Spirits |f. 155v| are very Rare, as ar the Occasions for which they ar excited. 2. In the Subject; for Common Vertu is admissible into any Kind of Spirits; [but] and is therefore frequent: but Heroick Vertu requires Heroick Spirits; men (commonly) whose Temperament is, as it were, a Quintessence: hauing the Same analogy to the 4 Temperaments, that Heuen has to the 4 Elements. 3. In the Degree. For common Vertu refin'd or rather Sublim'd to the Supream Degree, becoms Heroicke. Whence arises the Greatnes of it's Lustre, and that Admiration that it begets in the Minds of the Beholders. 4. And lastly, in the Celerity of the Success, or the quickness of effectuating it's Purposes: which in Heroick Vertu is admirable, and seems incredible; whereas in Common Vertu, the best Desseins ar often times, either altogether vnsuccesfull, or do but, as it were, Crawle to their Accomplishment. And hence we may gather why Heroick Vertu is called also Diuine, to wit, Partly because it proceeds more Immediatly from God, and partly because it dos more approachingly liken a man to him.[28] |f. 156|

But heere it is to be obseru'd, that tho Magnificence and Magnanimity

[26] Cicero, *De Natura Deorum* 2.66, 67; Alsted 1250; and Jam. 1:17. RB uses the same quote in “Doctrine of Thoughts” below.

[27] For Cyrus, see 2 Chron. 36:22 and Ezra 1:1-4; Alsted called Attila, “Flagellum dei” (1252) .

[28] For later commentary on heroic virtue and heroic wits, see *Cert. Phys. Essays* 1.308; *Style* 2.309; *Exc. of Theol.* 4.28; and *Greatness of Mind* 5.550.

consist in a certin Greatness, yet it is not in Heroick [Vertu] Greatness.[29] For that kind of Greatness is necessary to the <very> Constitution and Essence of those Vertus, in what Persons soeuer ar endowed with them; but that Greatness that we call Heroicall, may be wanting to any Vertu, without destroying or abolishing the Essence or Integrity of that Vertu.

This Heroick Vertu in a diuers respect may be termed ↑both↓ a Mediocrity and an Eminency. That in regard of the 2 Vitius Extreames of which it consists in the Middle; This in regard of Common Vertu, which it excells in Degree.

These Heroical Men ar more frequently <obseru'd> (for the most part) in Common-welths then in Monarchys; not that they ar more frequently born there; but partly because that in [Common] Republickes the way to honor and preferment lys more open to desert, which is a quickning Spur and a great incitement to Noble Spirits; and |f. 156v| Partly too, because the lesser Inequality of Men's Conditions in Common-welths, renders these Heroick Spirits more conspicuus: which in Monarchys wud be swallow'd by the Glory of the King or Princes; to whom for the most part ar attributed the most Glorius Action of their Subjects.[30] Whence it was obserued, that after [the Emperor had once brouht] the Roman Liberty ↑had once bowed it's neck to the Yoake of the Emperours,↓ [under their Yoake] there was in Rome, both fewer Heros, and those too less taken Notice of.

Tho this Vertu be far more rare amongst women then amongst men, because the Edg of their Spirit is turned, and their minds debased by their Education; yet are they not wholly to be excluded from it; witnes the Blessed Virgin Mary, Debora, Iudith, Semiramis, Queen Elisabeth of England, and diuers others.[31] And truly it were too great an Iniury to that pleasing Sex, to Womanize [Minds] ↑Spirits↓ as wel as their Bodys; and to thinke that there |f. 157| cud not be a Masculine Vertu in a Feminine Name. The Principles and Beginnings of this Vertu, ar to be found in Children, witness the Heroick Transports of Dauid, Cyrus, Cato, Alexander, and others: but the Ripeness and Perfection of it is not obseruable till their riper Yeares.

Tho Noble Familys, by reason of their Domestick Examples, Vndistractedness for want of Necessarys, and other Furtherances, may (generally) entitle themselues to a greater Number of Hero's then others can. Yet haue they not made it, so much their Property, but that men of meane and Ignoble houses may haue a iust title to it; if they can make Desert their Plea. For surely Heroick Vertu was and is the tru Fountaine of true Nobility; and 'tis that, not the Herald's <moth-eaten> Bookes nor the Vulgar's empty Titles, that ennobles a Family.[32]

---

[29] For "magnificence," see Nich. Eth. IV.ii.1-22; for "greatness of soul," see Nich. Eth. IV.iii.1-38. *Greatness of Mind* 5.550-62 is RB's most sustained discussion of these topics.

[30] This political commentary is not found in Arist.

[31] Alsted also mentioned several of these women (1252).

[32] Cf. Juvenal, "Virtue alone is true nobility" (Sat. 8.20). RB discussed this topic further in

To this Heroick Vertu is opposed the Souueraine Degree |f. 157v| Of Vice, cal'd [Brutishnes] <Diuelishnes,> or Brutality ↑which is an Eminency of Vice↓ whereby a man, [illeg.] hauing shaken of the Yoake of Reason, striuing to put out the Naturall liht of his Conscience, and deuesting himself of all humane Affections; giues [hi] himself vp to wallow hog-like in the mire of his vnlawfull Pleasures; and to commit such horrid Crimes, (without Shame or remorse) as other men's very Nature wud abhor, and which abase him beneath the Condition of a man, and make him, (if I may so speake) A reasonable Beast.[33]

And as Heroick Vertu eleuates a man somthing aboue a man, so Brutality depresses him below a man, (I was about to say) below a Beast. For not only it dos neither Follow nor loue Vertu, but euen Hates it and Scornes it.

This Diuelishness is either destitute of Reason, or conjoyned <and accompany'd> with it. |f. 158| The Former is either simply destitute, as in Madmen, or but partly, as in those in whom, som Disease has caused an extraordinary and exorbitant Intemperancy of the Humors; as also in those whom their Custom from the very Cradle has beastiz'd, as the Cannibals;[34] and in those also that ar transported with an vn-measurable thirst of Reuenge, such as the Poëts describe in Medea, Progne, and Atreus.[35] The latter arises from a Monstruous Peruersity, or an inueterate Wickednes turned into Nature; such as was in Nero, Heliogabalis, Andronicus, and such other Monsters of Mankind; and this is far worse then any common Vice. The latter of these is directly, the former but indirectly and in part, opposed to Heroick Vertu. The former requires rather the Fisitian then the Filosofer; the latter Requires indeed the [Counsels] <Aduice> and Paines of the Moralist, but very seldom (or neuer) Requites them.

"The Gentleman" (BP 37.160-63 and 169), the first sentence of which reads: "Tho I ignore not that the true Seat of Nobility is much more properly establish't in the Mind then in the Blood; & that many enioy that Ornament in a very high Degree, that neuer brought it into the World with them; yet the very First Attribute /Condition/ I shall require in the gentleman I am to discourse of, must be, that he be Born one." This is the second reference in the *Aret.* to "empty titles."

[33] Cf. Nich. Eth. VII.v.1ff.

[34] Cf. Nich. Eth. VII.v.2.

[35] These famous legends can be found in many classical sources, each story having the element of cannibalism.

Chapter VIII.

Vertus Contrarys

|f. 160|

Hauing thus taken a View of Vertu as it is in it selfe, and as it is considered in it's Propertys and Degrees; we wil now illustrate it with the Doctrine of it's Opposites: which fal [illeg.] <within> the Cognizance of the Moralist, vnder the Notion of Vertus Contrarys: and he treats of Vices, by the same riht that Fisicians treat of Diseases, and Logicians of Fallacys.

There is a two-fold Contrary to Morall Vertu; [the Simulation of] <a Counterfet> Morall Vertu, and, Morall Vice; or, Seeming Vertu, and Reall Vice.

[The Simulation or Feigning of Moral Vertu, is that Quality, whereby a man puts on a Seeming Vertu to deceiue others.] ↑For (as one says very wel) For all the Seueral Gems [in] of Vertu; Vice has Counterfet Stons wherewith she guls the Ignorant.↓[1] And by Seeming Vertus I heere vnderstand, Certin splendid and less obserued Vices, opposed to other Vices more generally taken Notice of and Condemn'd, which therefore the Ignorant Vulgar mistake for Reall Vertus. As, how often dos Profuseness pas for Liberality; and Rashness vsurp the Title of Courage? [illeg.] The Reason seems to be, Because the Vulgar, ignoring |f. 160v| In what the tru Nature of Vertu dos consist, conceiue it meerly vnder the Notion of something opposite to Vice; and so finding these Specious Vices more opposite then true Vertus to those other Vices, that ar most obvius to their notice; is very Apt to mistake them for those Vertus, that ar contrary to the Vertus they oppose. And certinly Vice, considered barely in it's owne Nature, is branded with so perfect a Deformity, that the veryest Reprobates wud abhor it. Wherefore Vice, since in it's owne Nakednes all wud loath it; dos often steale vpon vs and inveagle our Affections vnder the borrow'd Dress and Resemblance of Vertu; or else varnishes itself ouer with som kind of Conueniency. And vnder one of these 2 Notions, it often deceaues vs and we court it. According to that of the Poet,

---

[1] RB discussed dissembling at length in bk. 2, ch. 6, and often referred to the distinction between true and counterfeit coins in later works: *Cert. Phys. Essays* 1.308; *Experiments and Notes . . . Chymical Principles* 1.591; *Vulgar Notion* 5.159; *Chr. Virtuoso* 5.538; and *Swearing* 6.9.

Fallit nos Vitium specie virtutis and vmbrâ
Vice often dos deceiue our Eys
In Vertu's Shadow and Disguize.[2]

Hence arises that [M] Saying, that [illeg.] That is the most Dangerous Euil, that is likest Good and is not it.[3] And hence also may the Question be resolued, Which |f. 161| Of the 2 be the worser Vice, that which is most Difform and repugnant to the Vertu, or that which is liker to it? To which it is answered, that the first is the Greater, as more Distant from the Vertu; but the Second is the more Dangerous, as more easily deceiuing vs. [But of this Contrary enuf Already.]

But that those Actions that are truly Vertuus, may be distinguished from them that ar so but in show, we wil Character the former with these Prerogatiues. As 1. That [illeg.] he that dos the Action knos it to be Good. For Ignorance was Neuer the true Mother of true Vertu. 2. That it be don for a good End. For he that dos a Good Action without a Good End, may do Good, but not Well. A Good End is the Glory of God, and the Exercice of Vertu. Other Ends indeed may concurre; but not as Principals, but as accessarys. 3. That it be don by Good meanes. To defend a Good cause by Ill meanes, and tel a Ly to defend the Truth, dos vitiate the best Intents. And a Good ill acquired ceazes to be a Good. 4. With Cheerfulness [illeg.] Readiness, and Plesure. 5. And lastly, with Constancy; |f. 161v| For when [illeg.] men desist from doing Good; they seem to repent the hauing don it; and their former Actions condemne their Latter. These Single Sallys of Good, ar rather Occasionall good Action, then Vertuus. Hence we may discouer the Difference betwixt a Good Action and a Vertuus Action. For in euery Action there are 2 things to be considered; the Materiall and the Formall part thereof. The first alone may make an Action Good, but the Second is also necessary to make it Vertuus. The Materiall [Act] Part is the thing don; as to giue Almes; the Formal Part is the [thing] End, Manner, Measure, and other Circumstances of the Doing it. Thus to giue Almes to the Poore is Materially Good; but if it be don Farisaically, to be seen of Men, it is not Vertuus. Thus in a iust War, to fiht in the Defence of one's Cuntry, is Good: but to fiht principally for [Ho] Reputation or Booty; or to get a Victory by the breach of an Oath, is Blameable.[4] But of this First Contrary of Moral Vertu, enuf already.

The Other Opposite to Moral Vertu is Morall Vice, which is an Electiue Habitude |f. 162| Consisting in that Immediocrity that is repugnant to the Determination of a truly Wise man. This Habitude (as Vertu's Opposite,) is, like it,

---

[2] Juvenal, *Satires* 14.109; Alsted 1254.

[3] Source unknown.

[4] RB's emphasis on motivation, not just actions, is typical of contemporary works of practical piety and casuistry.

seated in the Will. It consists in Immediocrity; for tho indeed there may be a Middle in Vices themselues, yet it is not that Middle of Reason that we call Mediocrity. For Mediocrity is the tru rule and square of Good, and that Middle that perfect Prudence ordaines to be embrac't.[5] Propertys that can neuer be applyed to that Middle perhaps may be found in Vices.

Now Vice, (say the Moralists) is opposed to Vertu, both Contrarily, as a Good Habitude or Action is opposed to a Bad one; and Priuatiuely (as they vse to call it,) in that Vertu as a Habitude is opposed to Vertu as a Priuation.

Vertu consisting in the Meane, there may be a straying or receding from that Meane two manner of Ways; to wit, Either in Ouer-passing it, or in Comming short of it. Whence arises that ordinary Diuision of Vertu into Excess and Defect; or Vice Exceeding, and Vice Deficient. |f. 162^{v}| The First is that whereby a man recedes from the meane to too much and the Second that whereby one declines from the Meane to too Little. They ar commonly called the Extreames (or Opposites) of Vertu. For euery Vertu has 2 opposite Vices, the one sinning in the Excess, and the other in the Want or Defect: [illeg.] whereof the First Dos, More; or Abstains, Less, then the Vertu: the latter, Dos, Less; or Abstains, More, then the Vertu. Thus to Liberality is opposed, in Excess, Profuseness; in Defect, Auarice. And thus the Extreame of Chastity, is, in Defect, Icyness; in Excess, Wenching. And according to the diuerse Qualifications of the Meane, it happens, that [now] <somtimes> it approaches neerer to the Excess, and somtimes to the Defect; as we haue seen already.

But here it is diligently to be obserued, that tho indeed for the Generall all Vices ar reducible to Excess or Defect; yet in the Particular there are Infinite diuers Degrees |f. 163| In this Excess or Deficiency. And as from one Place to another there is but one direct Way; but there may be a world of By-ways; so in Vertu there is but one true Meane; but there is a World of seuerall Extreames; more or Less Euil, as they decline more or less from the Meane. Truth and Vertu being single and onely, whereas Falshood, and, (as Pythagoras [being] wud haue it) Vice, being Infinite.[6] [Thus if betweene 30 and 40 ounces ↑of meate↓ be the stint of Mediocrity for Alexander to eat in a Day; not onely 41 ounces wil be too much, but also 45, 50, 60, 200, and so in infinitum: and not only 29 wil be two little, but 25, 20, 10, 2, and so in infinitum, wil be also too Little.][7] Thus if 10 lb be the stint of Mediocrity for Aristotle to giue Diogenes; not onely [illeg.] <11> pound, but also 17, 18, 20, 30, 100, and so in infinitum will be too much to giue him: and on the other side, not onely 9 lb, but also 8, 7, 5, 4, 2, and so in infinitum will be too Little. Where it is further also carefully to be obserued, |f. 163^{v}| that Since in an Action a man may be faulty, not only in Exceeding the due

[5] Cf. Nich. Eth. II.vi.15-20.

[6] Nich. Eth. II.vi.14.

[7] Cf. Nich. Eth. II.vi.6-7; Alsted 1245.

Measure, or comming Short of it; but also in the [illeg.] doing of it ↑for a wrong or Sinister End,↓ in a misbecomming Manner, at an vnseasonable time, in an vnfit Place; and by sinning in diuers other Circumstances: therefore, not onely the Excess or Defect in the Measure; but also any other material and important Circumstance or qualification, <if Bad,> is capable to vitiate the Action, and constitute a Vice opposite to that Vertu against which it sins. As, in our former Example, [illeg.] Aristotle miht not onely haue been faulty in giuing Diogenes more or less then 10 peeces; but also in the giuing it him, that [h] it may be return'd againe with Vsury, or out of Importunity; or with reproaching [illeg.] <words> and with the gesture of one that refuses; or in the Market-place for Ostentation, and diuers other ways. A thing, which if the Moralists had well taken notice of; they had (perhaps) [deliuered] <giuen> vs a more full and exact account of Vices, then hitherto they haue don. |f. 164|

To these [it] we will adde this other Obseruation, that, as there are <always> seuerall Vices opposite to one Vertu; so there is somtimes One Vice opposite to seuerall Vertus, tho to the one more directly then to the other. So [Drunkeness] Temerity is Directly (or principally) opposed to [Temperance] <Courage,> Indirectly to Prudence. Drunkenness is opposed both to Temperance and Taciturnity; and Auarice is contrary both to Liberality and Iustice.

But if the Paradox of the Stoicks [be] <were> receuable, all this Discours of the Degrees of Vice, miht wel haue bin spared: for they admitt of no such Degrees in Vice, making them all equall.[8] Which opinion we can by no meanes [of] admit of. Because 1. There is no Deflexion from a meane, but admits of Degrees: wherefore since the Nature of Vice, consists in the Declining from the Meane; we must needs confess that the Degrees of Vice are correspondent to these Degrees of Deflection. 2. Vice, (being a Habitude) is a Quality; and euery Kind of quality admits degrees of Intensity and Remisness. 3. Vices ar the Contrarys of vnequall Vertus. 4. All Lawgiuers and Laws ↑and God himself in the Political Lawes of the Iewes,↓ make the Punishments of faults vnequall, which yet they |f. 164v| Proportion to the Fauts themselues. 5. Our Sauior tels vs in Express terms, (Mat, 10,15) that those of Sodom and Gomorrha shal be more tolerably treated at the Day of Iudgment, then those that shall refuse to be receaue his Apostles. ↑And therefore our Sauior Christ himselfe in many Places (as Matt, 7,4,5) compares som sins for their (comparatiue) littleness to [Beames] <Motes,> others for their gretnes and enormity to Beames.↓ And truly I cud neuer conceaue, how the giuing a man a box o'the Ear in one's Anger was as greate a Sin as to kil him in one's Anger: or the [Murdering of ones Father but an equall Crime with the Murdering of a Stranger.] ↑giuing away but of a shilling too much, an equall Prodigality with the giuing away of a man's whole Estate.↓

[8] For a convenient source of Stoics' arguments, see Laërtius, *Life of Zeno* 7.125-28.

For sure the Circumstances, which are the things that qualify our Actions, ar very Different in seueral Sins. The Argument of the Stoicks was, that to Sin was to decline from Mediocrity: wherefore, whether a man declines much or little from the Meane, he equally recedes from the Definition of Vertu. As a man that fals from the Bank into the Riuer, is as wel drowned if he be drown'd [if] neere [it] ↑the Brink↓ as if he drow'nd far from it. But as for the Argument, it is euident that it proues only that no Vice is a Vertu; which no Body denys; not that all Vices |f. 165| are equally Vices, which is the Question[s]. It proues that all Vices ar as wel Vices, but not they ar as Much Vices one as another. As for the Simile, it is not put ariht. For they shud haue demonstrated that he was equally deepe in the Water that was vp but to the Ancle, with him that was vp to the chin, or ouer head and eares; which is absurd. In their Simile he that is drown'd is drown'd by the Water, which is supposed to be as deepe neere the Brink as any where else; the Contrary whereof in the Nature of Vice, we haue already demonstrated.

Tho all the Moral Vertus may be as it were link't together in one Chaine; yet it is not so in Vices. For Vertus not onely ar not contrary one to another, but by their consort [for] help and compleat one another: whereas Vices being repugnant, not onely to Vertu, but among themselues; (as Auarice to Prodigality) [illeg.] the Contrary Vices cannot dwel together at the same time in the same Subject. So that it seems that a man cannot at once possess aboue half of the whole Number of Vices. ↑Howeuer Euil is very fruitful, and one Sin begets another; as Gluttony, Wenching; Lust, Impudency; Auarice, Theft; and many Vices, Lying.↓ Where note, that one may pass from one |f. 165^{v}| Contrary Vice to another, without passing by the Intermiddle Vertu; as From Cowardice to Rashness without passing by Courage, and from Profuseness to Auarice without passing by Liberality. This Experience witnesses; [illeg.] neither is it contradicted by the Common Maxime that says, There is no Passage, from one Extreame to the Other, without passing by the Middle; for that Maxime was calculated for Natural Filosofy; not for Moral; (wherein [men] now and then men skip ouer the Middle) tho in som sences it may be applied to this also.

Sin, Vice, and Vitiosity ar commonly confounded and promiscuusly taken one for the other: but some there be that more subtilly distinguish them; making Sin an Euill Act, as to be Drunk; Vice, an Euil Habitude, as Drunkenness; and Vitiosity, the Quintessence of Vice, or Vice so inveterate that tis Naturaliz'd. A Fault they make a little Sin, or a Sin wherein a principall |f. 166| Ingredient is Ignorance, or Carelesness. And sure there must go more Sins then one to build vp a Vice: for Vice, (as being Vertu's Contrary) is a Habitude, which is not acquired but by the Reiteration of Action. Neither can one Vitius Action make a

[8] RB used this trope earlier in this book, though applying it very differently.

man Morally Vitius. As Noah, tho once Drunke, was yet no Drunkard, because it was agenst his Custome.[9] But how many of these Sins ar required to make vp a Vice, we cannot determine: for that depends, cheefly, vpon the Intensity of the Act[ion,] and the Procliuity of our Nature to it; which, the greater they are, the fewer Actions ar required; the lesser, the More. Where it is not vnfit to be obserued, that as in [Vertu the] Good the Habitude is more Excellent then the Action, so in Bad, the Action is les Euil then the Habitude. As the once Actual Drunkenness of Noah, was not so great an Euill as the Habitual Drunkenness of Alexander the Great. To which we wil ad this Obseruation, that whereas in Moral Matters it is less Ill to sin Ignoringly, in the Intellectuall Vertus it is [a] a less Fault to erre |f. 166^{v}| Knoingly then thorou Ignorance.[10]

Now as <the Habitude of> Vice is acquired by the Rëiteration of Vitius Actions; so to Breake it of is required, not onely a Discontinuance of Sin, or a [sin] bare Cessation from the Exercice of it's Acts; but also a contrary Habitude. For one (By Example) that loues to Ouer-drinke, may be Not-drunke, (as when he wakes first in the Morning) and yet be still a Drunkard: because he (dos but intermitt the Acts, and yet) retaines stil the Habitude of Drunkeness; which to leaue indeed, he must diligently endeauor the Acquisition of that of Sobriety.

Now the Causes of Vice (which I wil now but reckon vp) are 1. ↑Inconsideration the Cheefest of al.↓ Ignorance and Error in the Vnderstanding, 2. Peruersenes and Deprauedness in the Will, 3. Vnruliness in the Affections, 4. An Euil Temperament of the Body, and 5. The Temptations and suggestions of the Diuell.

The Principall Occasioners (which we will be content only to name) are, 1. Euil Examples. ↑specially of the Great ones and the learned.↓ 2. Bad Company. 3. Opportunity of Sinning. 4. Prosperity lulling vs asleepe in Security; 5. Aduersity, almost |f. 167| necessitating vs to Euil Courses. 6. Prejudices against the Vertuus, and the ways of Vertu. 7. Feare and shamefac'tness of the ways of Goodness. [and] 8. Self-Interests. 9. Hope of Long Life [or] <and> failing trust trust in god's Mercy at the last. 10. The want of som Discreet and resolute Frend to tel vs freely and Seasonably of our faults; and bring the [Ethic] Precepts of Vertu home to vs by particular Application. The Remedys of all which are scatteringly deliuered here and there about the Booke. Som there ar that deduce all the Causes of ↑knoing Sin and↓ Wilful Vice from these 2 polluted Fountaines, <Springs> Pride in the Mind and Lust in the Body. But certinly the bitter Root out of which all these Sinfull /vitius/ branches grow; is much rather the Louing the Creature [aboue] <more then> the Creator, or if yow wil, the not louing God aboue all things: which to the Attentiue considerer wil appeare the Tru

[9] Gen. 9:20-21; Alsted used a different set of examples (1246-47) to distinguish between single acts and a habitude.

[10] RB discussed some of the same material in bk. 2, ch. 3.

Fountaine of all wilful and knowne Vices. For if a man lou'd God aboue all things (as being incomparably the Excellentest Object, he dos more then Deserue the Supreamest Degree of our Loue) sure he wud neuer dishonor his Nature by <fals or> needless [of per] Oaths; nor be Avaritius when he knos the Expence of his Mony wil do God Seruice; nor suffer the feare of Death to friht him out of the Paths that his |f. 167v| maker delihts in: and generally we neuer wittingly commit a Sin, but [for] when [we prefer] in our [Affect] Esteem we prefer our Honor, Plesure, Profit, or som such other thing, to the Loue of our Creator. And <in a word> if we did truly and really loue God aboue all things, we cud not but be extreamly industrius to learn the Knoledg of what dos /will/ please him: and with no less a Care and Diligence, practice that which we haue discouered to be acceptable vnto him; and auoid <decline> whatsoeuer we haue found /or, find/ disagreable <odius> /repugnant/ to his Nature. So that <ernestly> to endeauor an vnderualuing of our selues (and the World) and to bring our selues to loue God in the Superlatiue /hihest/ Degree, is <one of> the readyest way that I kno of to the Declining of all knowne Vice and the attainment of (a) Perfection in Vertu.

Of Sin

|f. 4|

1. Sin is a Quality most vnworthy of a Man; for his Excellency (as that which discriminates him from Inferior Creatures) consisting in the Vse of Reason; and to live Vertuusly being nothing else then to live according to riht Reason and vitiusly, to live contrary thereunto;[1] it wil needs follow, that Vice [that V] must of all things be the most vnworthy of a man, which puls down the Man to set vp the beast within him. And in Effect, Sin is Nothing els that the doing somthing contrary to /against/ the Dignity of a man's Essence. And therefor it is one of the greatest Suttletys of the Tempter [to] and of the Occasioners of men's wickedness, to present Sin vnto vs, barely vnder the Notion of somthing that is Displeasing to God; and neuer vnder that of being vnworthy of and Destructiue to our selues.[2] Because the looking on Sin meerly as somthing of Dishonorable to God, dos not arm vs with that <half that> height of <that> hatred against it, which we wud [entertaine, if we lo consist] |f. 4v| Al of vs conceiue, did we (but) consider it as somthing of extreamely injurius to our Selves; Whereas indeed we ar the Partys most offended by it; God being so, cheefly but because it renders vs vnfit for him to convers with and vncapable of the reception of those ouerflowings of Goodnesse /mercy/ that he created vs to communicate vnto vs: but we being really degraded of that (Character of) Dignity [ha] which the Diuine Image (Piety and Reason) had stamt vpon vs; and our Natures debased /sunk down/ into the abhor'd <slauish> Condition of Brutes and Diuels.[3] 2. It is a Quality extreamely offensiue to God. First, as it is contrary to the holines of his Nature: then as it denys him the [Glory] <Seruice> he requires, and (actually dishonoring him) robs him of the Glory he deserues: next as it renders a man vn-capable of the Effusions of his Bounty; and lastly as it is a Deflection <from him> to his Enemy the Deuil, or the Workmanship of his hands, /his Seruants/ the |f. 5| Creatures. Which made a Diuine of ours Say, that Sin was A Practical Blasphemy to /agenst/ all the Attributes of God. ↑Shal we deliht in that, that hinders God to deliht in vs?↓ And that Sin is in effect of all other things the most Displeasing vnto God, is hence manifest, that [God,] Sin is the only <sole>

---

[1] The next two essays or sermons, "Of Sin" and "Of Piety," are taken from MS 196. Ff. 1-3 are blank. RB did not provide a title, but the topic is clearly "Of Sin" and continues the discussion of "virtue's contraries" with which the *Aret.* concluded. RB also discussed right reason in the *Aret.* (bk. 2, ch. 5). I have not included the third essay, "Of Valour," because it is very fragmentary and very incomplete.

[2] RB was keenly interested in collecting Satan's arguments and in developing responses to them: cf. the *Aret.* (bk. 2, ch. 4). In "Dayly Reflection" (BP 7.275), RB referred to his treatise, "Of the Strategems of the Deuill," a work that has not survived.

[3] For a later view of the rational soul and the image of God, cf. *Chr. Virtuoso* 6.751 and 775.

Object of his hatred; he neuer detesting any of his Creatures (as in themselues good, because of his own making) but by reason of that Sin which he sees inherent in; and for which we see him oftentimes punish euen those that he is pleased to honor with the Glorius Title of his Frends, after so rigorous /seuere/ a manner. ↑All his Creatures God refused not to own, but Sin he neuer wud, as no Creature of his making but when the Deuil (says one wittily) wud be counterfeting God,[4] and take vpon him to be a maker, he brouht forth Sin; other Creatures he cud make none: and therefore, so much as a man sins, so much he recedes from ↑the Primum Ens and[5] so much he is made a Creturc of the Diuell.↓↓

[3.] And it is not inobseruable that the very hethens cud beleeue that a Good man may be Poore, and Diseased, and an Exile &c, and yet be acceptable to the Gods; but not possibly Vitius without incurring their Displesure. /Hatred/ 3. Sin of all others is the Greatest Euill. First as separating between vs and the fruition of the greatest Good, next, as being the most contrary of things to the most Wise and best of Beings /Essences/ God: [then] (as has been shewed already.) |f. 5v| Then as Simply and Vniuersally Euill, all Euill, and no, nor Neuer Good, ↑after as not prejudicing only the Body or fortune or such other les Essentiall Goods but seizing on and corrupting the very [Soul of man] noblest part of man, the Soul.↓ And lastly as the Ground and fountaine of all other Euils. Wickednes was the first founder of hell, and the Apostle tels vs, [that] (Rom 5,12) that Sin was the bringer in of Deth into the World. [And] Which made one say that cud we rip vp the Womb of Sin as Nero did his Mothers, we shud find it [Good bi] not onely big, but redy to be deliuered of all kind of Euils.[6] And certinly we [must] may very wel beleeue that God accounts Sin to be the Greatest of Euils, since he employes other Euils as Fisic (either) to Preuent Sin or to cure it. And sure God is to good /wise/ a Fisician to make the Fisic wors then the Disease. 4. It is of all others the most odious [Shamefull and infamous] quality. Why hate we the Deuil but because of his Wickedness. For sure his Essence wud otherwise be rather the object of our Enuy then our Hatred. Tis a thing we detest eu'n where it prejudices vs not as in Iudas, Herod, Nero, and millions of others whom |f. 6| We neuer receiu'd any Iniury from, nor fear it in the Future. There being certin Iustice and Noblenes in man's Nature, that condemnes Vice presently, when an immunity from Self-respecte giues it the /a/ freedom to act. And truly it is extreamely Obseruable, that the <very> Wickeddst men (if the matter be narrowly pry'd into,) when they accuse their greatest Enemys, raile at them vnder the Notion of [th] being guilty of som Vitious quality or other, which yet perhaps they wil [cherish] <excuse> and cherish in themselues. A

[4] Source unknown.

[5] "Primum ens" is the prime matter, a concept from medieval philosophy. For RB's discussion of the primum ens in contemporary natural philosophy, cf. *Usefulness* 2.147-49.

[6] Cf. Alsted 1239.

notable /noble/ Euidence, that All men hate Sin as sin, tho som perchance may loue it as their owne. 5. Vice is a quality very shameful and Infamous. Witnes that the Wicked, Owle-like, vse to seek Corners and fly the liht:[7] that they rank those they wud discredit, vnder the Colors of Vice. That so many [cover] <seek to hide> their Vices with the Disguise of hypocrisy, so many endeauor to extenuate or shift them of from themselues; and lastly that so many ar impatient |f. 6v| Of reproofe, and so [any] furius at the being told of what they do. What haue Ahab, Ieroboam, Domitian and a 1000 others purchas'd [by] with their Egregious Wickednes, but a lasting Infamy. (Wicked men like Tallow Candles, tho they may burn fairly for a while, euer going out in snuff.)[8] And what has all their Proud and Stately monuments seru'd for, but to keep aliue the [mer membrance] <memory> of their [Shame] Infamy. A Strange thing, that men shud be so ambitious of the Suruiuing of those Names, which (like their Bodys) must either <be buried in Oblivion> to the Graue or stink ↑aboue ground.↓ 6. It is a very trublesom and Perplexing quality: howeuer the world be pleas'd to think <conceit> otherwise. It is very wel worth the noting to obserue into what a multiplicity of Slauerys they run themselues, that wil not endure the liht and easy Yoake of Vertu.[9] [Tis somwhat Strange to me, that men shud] Tis [illeg.] easyer to be Subject to one Vertu then to |f. 7| Many Vices. And tis a Maxime amongst Statesmen, that <a> Monarchy, (tho de[ne]generated into Tyranny) is yet les Intollerable then an Anarchy.[10] Tis somwhat Strange to me, that men shud fancy so much of Trouble and so little of Deliht in Vertu, when those Ancient Sages that this World cud not then Parallel, tho but Purblind in matters of the other life, and yet go on vpon all the Difficultys of Vertu, and despize /trample vpon/ all the Plesures of Vice, to react[11] that quiet Settlednes and Content of Mind, which they beleeued to be the greatest happines vpon Erth, and a fruit that gros no where but vpon the Tree of Vertu. And [indeed] sure it seems les Troublesom to be the Slaue of [ones] a man's Passions then their Master.[12] That Guilt is a Perplexing thing most men's Knoledg wil make it vnnecessary to proue, and we may euidently see it in the Despaire of those Miserable wretches whom the Consciusnes of their own Crimes driues to saue the hangman a labor by making away themselues. Surely Guiltines is euer anxius and ferfull: and so |f. 7v| Much the more, because the wicked man has no secure <safe> Retreat to retire /withdraw/ to; specially in Aducrsity, when his empty Consolations, like [Phisicians

[7] RB used the same image in the *Aret.* (bk. 1, ch. 2 and bk. 2, ch. 6).

[8] This image was used in the *Aret.* (bk. 2, ch. 4).

[9] A paraphrase of Matt. 11:30.

[10] This maxim, however traditional, surely had vivid meaning to RB in the late 1640s. Numerous letters and passages in *Occ. Refl.* indicated his worries about disorder.

[11] "React" means "to drive back, to reflect" (OED).

[12] A proverb also used in bk. 1, ch. 2.

at the Point lice when a m] fisicians when a man is ready to expire, then leaue him, when he has most need of them. Then that Conscience that was silenc't /dumb/ before, begins to roare like an [Erth quake,] Lyon, and all the Furys make that Soul, the Stage where on they act their vtmost furys /parts/ and bring hel into it before they bring it into hell. [And certinly, as] That mouing hell, the Sting of Conscience,[13] dos antedate men's Torments, and carry along with it a horror, that [can] like heat and Cold, can not wel be perceu'd but by those that haue felt it /feele it./ 7. It is of all Qualitys the most Destructive: both to the Publick and to the Particular. The former is Euident in that Vertu is the Cement of humane Society, without which they wud <suddenly> confound themselues into a Chaos. And therfor we see, that those very Macchiavels that ar the most passionate Louers of Vice, cannot themselues subsist without seemingly hating it; and |f. 8| Oftentimes punishing in others what themselues affect /practize./[14]

So [dest dest] ruinous ar vices, and so inconsistent with themselues, that were they not restrayn'd in by Law or Vertu, eu'n the most Vitius must necessarily Proue destructive to one another. If no man moderated his Choler, what a Slauhterhowse wud the World be; if no man suppress'd his Lust, who cud without Iealousy enjoy a Wife; and if none regulated his Power, where were safety to be found. So that eu'n the Vitius themselues must be beholding to Vertu for their Security and Subsistance. And as for the Latter.[15] How many Rich men has Prodigality tauht the way to the Hospitall? How many great men has Ambition exalted to the Gallows /a Scaffold?/[16] How many rash men has Temerity entitled to the guilt of their owne Murder? How many witty men has Vain-glory expoz'd to the Derision /lafter/ of the Wiser? How many Rich men has Covetusness enslau'd to a perpetual Poverty? |f. 8v| How many Sound men has Intemperance pepled with Diseases like /as many Diseases as/ an Hospitall? And how many famous men has Ingratitude or Teachery branded with an Euerlasting Infamy? But most of all how many Precius <Immortal> Soules has it [pl] plunged into euerlasting and vnauoydable Misery: and how many Soules and Bodys has it destroy'd together, by those horrors of Conscience, that ar so much worse /mor intense/ then Deth <it self> that they <men> /many/ haue souht out Deth <it self> as a Remedy to eas them [from] of those Torments? ↑Sin is a recoyling Poyson: it turns violently bac vpon those that comit it. And it may be truly said of euery wicked man that he is Felo de se, A Murderer of himselfe.↓ [8.] And that which makes the ruin /Destruction/ the mor insupportable, is, that we cannot lay the blame of it vpon others, since it is of our own Procuring; and euery

---

[13] All of these proverbs were also used in the *Aret.* (bk. 2, ch. 6).

[14] Hypocrisy is treated at length in the *Aret.* (bk. 2, ch. 4).

[15] This transitional phrase refers to the seventh claim above that Sin is "of all Qualitys the most Destructive: both to the Publick and to the Particular. The former is Euident . . ."

[16] A trope used in the *Aret.* (bk. 2, ch. 4).

Sinner, Samson like, puls down vpon himself, that howse /that Punishment/ whose fall dos Crush him. ↑Nothing is so much a man's own as his Sinne.↓ And sure we may very safely beleeue Sin to be very Destructive, since God makes it the only Cause of all Destructions. 8. It is a [mo] very deceitfull Quality. For it cuzens vs of our Selues, and robs vs of <al> our [all] Dignity heere |f. 9| And Happines hereafter. It steales in to the Mind, and by the fals optic /glass/ of the Sensuall Appetite, making vs mistake Plesure for Happines or Specius Vices for reall Vertus, it makes vs turn traytors to our Selues and becom gilty of our own vnhappiness. Ther is (almost) Nothing more offends vs then to be deceiued <tho but in a (very) trifle>: that arguing an Inferioryty of Iudgment in the Deceiu'd; which we ar extreamely displeased to find, and very vnwilling to confess. And the more Important the thing we ar deceiu'd in, is; the greater Indignation we conceiue at /against/ the Deceit. And lastly if it be a Frend or one that shud loue vs that deceiues vs, we yet the more deeply ressent so hih an Injury. How flaming therfor shud our Anger be agenst (the Deceits of) Sin; whereby we ar not only Deceiued, and that in /about/ the most Transcendent Good our Nature is capable of, Happiness;[17] but that by those that have [most] the greatest obligation to loue vs, our selves: specially since therby we become guilty of the abhorred vn-worthines of deceiuing |f. 9v| Our best and Deerest frends, our Selues. 9. Sin is a Quality, [des] not only Destructiue to the Authors, but Destructiuely infectius to those they most desire to oblige, their Frends and Acquaintance. For Sin is Euil, not only in the Act, but the Example, and oftentimes in imitated Persons, more in th'Example then the Act. I that but ruin /[m] dam/ my Self by the commission of a Sin, may <perchance> ruin Thousands by it's Seduction. I Sin, another Sin's by my Example, a third to imitate him; and so Sin [spreads it] (which of al Diseases is the most catching and [communit] infexius) spreads it self in infinitum; leauing me the Adam of all that sinful Progeny, and making me [gi] capable of sinning in my Coffin, and gilty (perhaps) of another's deth, whole Ages after I am ded my Selfe.[18] Shal he that lends a man a Wepon to commit a Murder be gilty by the Law of man; and he that furnishes him with a bloody Mind (without which he wud neuer have made vse of that Weapon) be guiltless /Innocent/ by the Law of Conscience? |f. 10| Howeuer few haue consider'd it, yet many whose Consciences were tender enuf to Sinfulnes /Wickedness/ in it's ful Dimensions, haue found it, the most sinking and Perplexing of their Afflictions, to think what shal become of thos men that their Ill examples haue seduced: and many haue been [more] <lesse> troubled /anxius/ for their owne sins, then for other men's Sins: because tho their <own> Repentant Teares may drown their own (sinful) Issue; yet who can tel whether a whol

[17] A point made at length in the *Aret.* (bk. 2, ch. 8).

[18] Such imagery was common in contemporary casuistry.

Deluge of Teares wil reach the Off-spring of that Issue.[19]

10. And Lastly. Vice is a quality that is often times punished with seuere Iudgments in this Life, and [eu] always (if vnrepented of) in the Life to com. For the former, Theres not <scarce> a Book in the whole Bible, that is not big with Thunder against the Wicked, eu'n in this Life; or affords vs not som Notable [President] <Example> of the Execution of his Iustice against them that haue persisted to Prouoke it. And eu'n humane Historys ar fruitful in the Presidents of his Iudgments vpon Notorius Offenders; and when such men haue been found out by <any> remarquable Reuenge[s], |f. 10v| The very Hethen cud attribut it to the Iustice of the Gods. And very confident I am that if men wud but take the Paines a little more searchingly /narrowly/ to obserue the Dispensations of Prouidence [in] <about> particular Familys and Persons, they wud not need to turn ouer Ancient Chronicles to find Examples of this Nature, which (throu a Negligence injurius both to God and to themselues) they vsually (let) pass by without taking Notice of.[20] And tho indeed this Rule admits often times of exceptions (God reseruing som men's Total Share of Punishment for <to> the other World) yet [often times] <eu'n heer> those Temporal Iudgments ar <[alw]> not <always> escaped that ar delay'd: for oftentimes God giues Sinners leasure to repent in; which if neglected, he then makes them smart for his forbearance as wel as their Sin, and his Iustice, like an vninterrupted Ston, the longer it has been in the fall, with the more violence it crushes what it lihts [v] /when it is fallen./[21] But suppose a man totally escape [that] God's [Iud Re] Vengeance in this life, yet is it but forborn, not forgiuen; for (to com to the Latter) |f. 11| He shal receiue for <in lieu of> it in the other, a [n] <ful> Accumulation of all that is Euil, and a total Priuation of whatsoeuer may be cald Good. Hel being a Torment insupportable and yet vnauoidable, Interminable and yet intollerable: infinit <great> as the Iustice that is offended, and immortal as the Soule that has offended. The boldest /horridst/ Fictions of the Poets about their Tartara[22] shal proue truths there, where men shall spend whole Ages in forging causes /grounds/ of Apprehension, and yet be miserable beyond their Feares. For hel is a Deth that can neuer be painted to the Life, and a wretchednes beyond /aboue/ Hyperbole<s>.

---

[19] Cf. the lengthy digression on repentance in *Swearing* 6.17-19.

[20] RB's contemporary references to Providence, esp. in *Philaretus*, stressed miraculous deliverances rather than punishments; his discussion here highlighted the other manifestation of Providence in human affairs. In HP 26/8/1 is Dury's proposal, "A Designe for Registring of Illustrious Providences," which described a way of determining whether an incident of special providence had occurred and, if so, how it should be registered for others' benefit. RB considered how to read the decrees of Providence in *Occ. Refl.* 2.418-19.

[21] RB used the same image to make a different point in the *Aret.* (bk. 2, ch. 4).

[22] In Homer and Hesiod's *Theogony*, Tartarus was a place beneath Hades reserved for punishing the enemies of the gods.

Hauing thus inquir'd into the Nature and Danger of the Diseas, let vs now Proceed to the Remedys; which ar either Preuenting or Curatiue; the former whereof we shal discourse of in this Sexion, and conclude the Latter with the next.

Now the Antidotes against Sin ar comprised in the following Directions.

1. Resist the very Beginnings of Sin, and beware of Tampring with it <them>. |f. 11v| The greatest Euils, for the most part, grow out of Contemtible Beginnings, and ar there esily supprest.[23] But such is the Supinenes of most men, that they neglect to resist these Euils til they ar grown too great to be resisted. Sin is a Lyon, which if yow kil not while he is a Whelp, wil kil yow when he coms to be old. Meet with Sin in the very first Suggestions; fiht with it in your Thouhts;[24] as the [Prudent] Valiant Gouernor Disputes the very Outworkes with the Enemy; and the Prudent Statesman blasts the very [Buds of] Blossoms of Sedition to secure himself from the Apprehension of it's Fruits. To let a Tempta- tion /Enemy/ grow great to fame the Conquest, in this Warfar is not commenda- ble:[25] the Imprudence of letting the Enemy grow so great derogating more from <the Esteem of> a man's Prudence, then the Fortune of being Victorius can ad to that of his Valor. In a word, To tread betimes the Cocatrice Eg is the Way to keep it from |f. 12| Breaking out into a Serpent.[26] 2. Beware of Tampering with Sin. There are many People that wil euer be [lear] enquiring into the secre[a]t Practices of Villany, without any Intentions to reform them; tho indeed without any purpose to make vse of them. But let such remember, that the Desire of Knoledg of Good and Euil was the first gap that let Vice into the World. That those things ar happily Ignor'd that ar not without Danger known: and certinly many that haue desir'd the Knoledg of Euil but out of Curiosity of the Vnder- standing, haue been by that knoledg seduced to their Embracing, to the Peruert- ing of their Wils.[27] In this Case alone, Ignorans it self is comendabl: and truly, for those that mean not to reform it; the safest way is to kno no more of Vice, then is necessary to auoid it.[28] Others again there ar, that loue to be talking with the Temter about Sin, [tho p] and hear his Reasons for it, tho perhaps without any purpose to commit. But I shal desire these men to consider, That the

---

[23] RB's ten antidotes are followed by his refutation of twelve common self-deceptions about sin. The twelve self-deceptions are very similar to the fourteen pleas for sin refuted in *Swearing* 6.4-20. The list rehearsed many of the common arguments in works of practical piety.

[24] Cf. "Doctrine of Thinking" below.

[25] Cf. the response of Alexander the Great to Porus above: "At last I haue met with an Enemy worthy of my Self."

[26] C496, "Kill the cockatrice in the egg."

[27] For later remarks on unnecessary or dangerous curiosity, see *Style* 2.294; *Occ. Refl.* 2.447; and *Reconcileableness* 4.155. For RB's temptations about magic, see Hunter, "Alchemy."

[28] Cf. RB's visit to a brothel (Maddison 40); for his discussion of ignorance, see the *Aret.* (bk. 2, ch. 3).

Tempter [being] must be answered with Denyals and not with Arguments <Sillogisms>: for being incomparably the |f. 13| Better Logician of the two; wil wrangle /dispute/ yow <at last> into whatsoeuer he desires, especially hauing so potent an aduocate within yow as the flesh. Besides that kind of [Incoura] Cowardize is a<n> [kind] Incouragement to him to reiterat his Solicitations; The Louer thinks himself half way into his Mistresse's hart, if he has once got free accesse to her Eare; and the French Prouerb tels vs that, Ville qui parlemente est a demy-rendüe.

The Town that Treats is half deliuered vp.[29]

Besides that it is is very easy to be obserued that the Deuil [dos but] with the Resolution of not-consenting dos but (as it were) bribe vs to giue him a quiet hearing; confident that if he once gets entrance into the howse /Mind/ he wil not only regaine that Bribe, but force vs [to] besides to the Committing of that (very) Sin that he pleded for, and we rejected. Lastly, there is a Third sort of Peple that [stint] wil needs (forsooth) regulate their Sinfulness; giuing themselues a Dispensation to go thus far in Sin, limited with a Resolution to go /proceed/ no further. But I shal request these Pepl only to consider how od <a thing> it is, To think to keep <or deserve> a Mediocrity in that, whose very Essence consists in hauing None. /in Immediocrity./ |f. 13^{v}|

3. Thos Vices in Particular ar the most heedfully to be auoided, to which we ar Inclin'd. (And that Inclination may be easily [affor] discerned by the Plesure they afford vs in the Committing, and the Difficulty we find in the resisting them.) Tis a very hard matter to deny the requests of those Suitors that haue within vs so Persuading an Orator as our own Nature to plead for them. And the Watch can neuer be too strict or narrow against that Enemy that has frends and Intelligence within the Towne. ↑But the greater the Difficulty, the greater Shud be the Watchfulnes, and wil be the Glory.↓[30] Tis as Easy and a Common thing to abstaine from those Vices that we value not /care not for./ But when outward allurements (to Sin) ar seconded by Inward Perswasions; and the Revolting Citizens joyn with the [Forrain] <Inuading> Enemy;[31] then to make good the Place, and for the Loue of Vertu to surmount both others and one's Self, is an Axion

[29] The French source has not been identified, but RB's version was also an English proverb: V14, "A city that parleys is near won"; C402, "Cities are taken by the ears"; and C122, "A Castle that parleys and a woman that hears will both yield."

[30] Cf. Tilley. This is RB's variant, one used again below.

[31] Works of religious piety frequently used martial metaphors—the master trope of spiritual warfare requires such metaphors—but such language certainly had particular reverberations in the late 1640s and recurs often in these works: e.g., "So that Inclinate is little better Excuse for Vice, then an Eloquent Orat<ion>or for Revolt is of Rebellion" (f. 23^{v}). For RB, the connection between sin and rebellion was clear; each was the cause and the effect of the other.

worthy the Thankes of Vertu and the hihest Complement <yow> can put vpon her. Bewar therfor of those Vices that thy Nature welcoms, for there is no Enemy like a seeming Frend.

4. Fly Idlenes (which the Ancients iustly Christned, The Mother of Vices)[32] and rather do any thing that is not Bad, then nothing.[33] For there is so [ch an] Actiue and |f. 14| Restles <a> Principle in the Soul, that somthing it wil be doing; and if yow set it not vpon <somthing> of Good, it wil set it self vpon somthing of Euill; and like men vnus'd to want, if they want employment, wil turn Cut-throats or Steale. And truly what the Poet said of Loue, (Et in vacuo Pectore regnat Amor,)[34] we may iustly say of Vice; that it reignes most in Emty brests; since 'tis certin many Vices com to dwel in vs, meerly (cheefly, ne detur Vacuum.)[35] For <And> certinly the Soul had rather do any thing then Nothing, and like Water, if it haue no motion, corrupts; and becoms fruitful in Nothing but Frogs and Toades, and such like loathsom Creatures.[36] There is scarce any thing neerer of kin to Doing Ill, then Doing nothing; nor any greater Discouragement to the Deuill, then to see that a Man is not at leasur to be Wicked. /commit Sin./ To be short (for we shal [haue] elsewhere <haue> occasion to resume this Theam)[37] Whither Idlenes be a Moral Sin or no, I wil not now stand to dispute; but sure it makes the Mind like the Materia Prima of the Filosofers,[38] which tho (as such) it haue no form, is capable (successiuely) of the Reception of all formes; for iust so the Idle Soule, tho as such it were not Vitius <sinful>; yet as such it be coms susceptible of all Vices <Sins> /any Vice./ |f. 15|

5. Carefully auoid the Occasions of Vices (particularly those whereunto one is enclin'd:) and especially Euil Company. Hence that Saying of the Moralists, Vitare Peccate est, vitare occasiones Peccandi: Tis to auoid Sins to auoid the Occasions of Sinning.[39] The Nazarites that were forbidden the vse of Wine, were likewise forbidden that of Grapes (Numb. 6,3.) lest the Eating of the one, shud tempt /seduce/ to the Drinking of the other. Let not him then /therefore/

---

[32] I13 and D547; the proverb is used in the *Aret.* (bk 2, ch. 4) and discussed at length in "Of Time and Idleness." RB's discussion of idleness is hardly original—cf. Burton's discussion (*Anatomy* 2.2.4). We should also compare RB's arguments with Thomas Sprat's, who argued that experiments were an antidote for idleness (*History* 341-42).

[33] RB used the same proverb in "Of Time and Idleness."

[34] Ovid, *Amores* 1.1.26. RB also used the quote in "Of Time and Idleness."

[35] RB later rejected this argument in physics, but he used it often in his ethical writings: cf. *Fluidity and Firmness* 1.409, *Exp. Hist. of Cold* 2.499, and *Vulgar Notion* 5.227-29.

[36] For Browne's discussion of the generation of frogs by corruption, see *Pseud. Epidemica* 1.212-13; RB considered the schoolmen's teaching on the topic disgusting (*Orig. of Forms* 3.5) and discussed the mysteries of generation in *Exc. of Theol.* 4.18.

[37] Cf. "Of Time and Idleness."

[38] Cf. *Scep. Chym.* 1.506. RB used a variant of this sentence as the opening sentence in "Of Time and Idleness."

[39] Cf. Alsted 1250.

that is giu'n to Women, affect the Company of Temting Butys, Naked Pictures, and the like: nor him that ouerualues Wine frequent the Tauern. For certinly, (according to the Maxim of the Filosofers) Objecta mouent Sensus, the Presence of the Object awakens in vs many Desires /appetites/ that before were <fairly> laid asleepe.[40] And the Prouerb is no Lyar, that tels vs that Occasion makes the Theefe.[41] But aboue all beware of Euil Company (specially that which sympathizes with yow in your Inclinations to the Self-same Vices) it being almost as rare for a man to liue vninfected in a Pest-howse, as vntainted in such Company. ↑But of this (hauing elswhere discourst on it alredy)[42] I shal only for the Present [tel] desire the Reader to consider, that the↓ |f. 15v| Lest that yow can fear from it is an abatement [illeg.] in your Zeal to Vertu, and Detestation of Vice. For where all ar Bad, men grow asham'd of being Good; and we ar easily brouht to hate and fear that less, that we see frequently acted by those we loue. And tho Vertu perhaps may preserue vs from allowing [illeg.] /affecting/ it; yet Familiarity makes vs at lest, not detest it.

6. To Reflect often vpon the Buty of Vertu and the Difformity of Vice; with the Rewards the one is to expect, and the Punishments the other is to endure. For Vertu grows dul without the <spurs of the> Hope of Honor and Reward; and Vice grows hedstrong without the Curbs of Fear and Punishment.[43] Tho the Loue of Vertu did not egge vs on to the Pursuit of [Vertuus] <Good> Axions, yet at lest me thinks the expectation of Reward shud incite vs: and tho the Hatred of Vice did not dissuade from the [illeg.] acting of bad ones, yet the Apprehension of Punishment shud deter vs. And tho it be true, that tis but a Lazy Vertu that needs these kind of Whips, and an vnruly |f. 16| Mind that needs these Bits to restraine it; yet since 'tis the Vnhappines of the Age, and the Deprauednes of Mankind, that an Immixedness in Vertu or a mind wholly vnbyas't by Self-respect, is no less a Prodigy then a Blac Swan,[44] we must be forc't to allow many these Considerations, tho not as [illeg.] Causes <of>, yet at lest as Inducements to their Axions: for it is less Ill to be Innocent /do good/ for wrong Ends then not at all. Now amongst the (other) Euidences of Vertu's Excellency aboue Vice, it wil proue none of the lest; that Vertu vsually presents her self to vs [er] circled with all the Dangers and Inconveniences that may

---

[40] A common tag, but cf. Alsted 1244.

[41] O71.

[42] The perils of bad company is a recurrent theme in the *Aret.* (bk. 2, ch. 4), *Style* (2.295), *Occ. Refl.* (2.364, 420-24), and contemporary correspondence (1.xliii). For a later view, see *Greatness of Mind* 5.559. The theme was discussed in Robert Bolton's *General Directions for a Comfortable Walking with God* (1638) 73-80.

[43] This sentence is used in the *Aret.* (bk. 2, ch. 4).

[44] Cf. Browne's treatment of black swans: ". . . flying Horses, black Swans, Hydrae's, Centaur's, Harpies, and Satyres . . . are monstrosities, rarities, or else Poeticall fancies, whose shadowed moralities requite their substantiall falsities" (*Pseud. Epidemica* 1.417).

discourage vs in the attemt of obtaining her; she tels vs that the Way is Thorny to her Pallace, and our Sauior tels vs that the Crosse must be the Burden and the Badge of his Disciples; and that men shall Persecute them to that heiht for his Sake as to think their liues a sacrifice more acceptable then Hecatombs vnto the Gods: so confident is Vertu of her own [Val] Worth and Loueliness, that she thinks (and accepts of none that ar not of the same opinion) that the |f. 16v| Vndergoing of all these Difficultys is but an easy Purchase of the happiness of her fauor. Whereas Vice on the Contrary, dos almost neuer show her self [but mas] in her Natiue Colors, but maskt with [Buty,] Plesure, Riches <honor> [and the like,] ↑or whatsoeuer we loue best↓ and vnder <that> [no other] notion <only> is [euer] courted by vs. Thus the Deuill [w] (Matt. 4) when he tempted our Sauior to Sin, giues him a flattering Suruey of all the Kingdoms of the Erth and the Glory thereof; that is, seuer'd from the Miserys; as knowing Sin to be a hooke very vnlikely to be swallow'd vnles [couer'd] hidden in /which/ a Bait.[45] Where it is not vnobseruable, that God vsually tels vs first what we shal do and then what we shal haue, whereas the Deuil inuerting that Method, vses to brag of what we shal haue before he wil let vs kno what we shal do: to sho vs that God's commands ar in themselues so reasonable that reward it self must be a thing of an Inferior aime /consequence/ whereas the Deuil neuer dares venture the Proposal of his til he has first cast dust in our eyes by the largeness of his Promises: the one holds forth the Reward |f. 17| as <but> a Consequent of the thing don, [but] and the other as a Bribe to [in] seduce men to do it.

7. Meditate frequently vpon the Quatuor Nouissima, the Foure last things, Deth, Iudgment, Heu'n and Hell. Certinly we shud make vse of our Thouhts agenst the Deuil since he makes so great vse of them against vs: and begin there our Resistance where he vses to begin his Asalts. For thouhts ar like Ordinance: if we turn them against him we destroy him; but if we suffer him to turn them against vs, he destroys vs. Let therefore the Graue be often in thy Thouhts before thy Body be in the Grave. Let the Meditation of the last Iudgment so friht thee in this life, that [it] thou maist haue no cause to feare it in the next. Let thy thouhts antedate thy [hap] Felicity, and be thy (constant) Harbingers in Heu'n. And (lastly) Descend often times into Hell by Contemplation that thou maist neuer descend thither by condemnation.[46] But aboue all spend many of thy thouhts vpon the Transitorines of <Sin and> Life; the Certinty of Deth with the Incertinty of the houre, and the Euerlastingnes /infinity/ of Eternity.[47] How can he dote vpon the Sensuality of |f. 17v| Sin, that duly considers that such ar (incertin and) fading Plesure, shal be ended by Deth, and Punished with Eternity of Torments. Sin [being] like the Drug (simple) the Fisitians cal Agarac that has at first

[45] Matt. 4:8-11.

[46] Cf. "The Dayly Reflection."

[47] Cf. Bayly, *The Practice of Piety* (1642) 184ff.

a sweet [relish] <tast> but which ends in a bitter rellish;[48] the Bitternes of the Punishment incomparably outweihing the sweetnes of the Enjoyment. The [Th] Meditation of Deth is one of the best Rules of Life; moderating our Delihts /ioys, plesures/ with Feare, and sweetning our Miserys with hope: and by teaching vs what we shal be, teaching vs what we shud be. Since we ar sure Deth Wil com, let vs be Prepared for it; and since we kno not When it wil com, let vs be Still prepared for it. This transitory life is but the Dressing Chamber /Lobby/ of Eternity;[49] wherein whatsoeuer clothes we put on /weare/ we shal wear for euer. O let vs not therefor incur for an Ending Plesure an Endles Torment; but rather let vs so reflect vpon Life, Deth, and Eternity; that a Vertuus life may lead vs to a good Deth, and that (vsher vs in) to a Happy Eternity and <or> Eternal Happiness.

8. Haue a Particular care of the conseruation of thy Good Name, and Shame. |f. 18| Next Conscience they ar our gretest good: and of Fame, next Vertu, we shud haue the greatest Care.[50] [illeg.] Shame is amongst the Goods of the Soule that which the hart is amongst the Members of the Body, that which [dys last] expires the last. ↑For Impudens [it] arms and steels the brest agenst all relenting impressions, and makes Vice like an Anuil which the hammer of Reprehension dos not break but hardens.↓ And indeed it is so neer a kin to Vertu that it confesses Vice to be bad; and forbids, if not vitius intents, at lest criminal /enormous/ Actions. What are the maine cause of the most part of those Actions the Vulgar esteems Vertuus, but the Desire of Honor, and Shame, that haue <had the Power to> provoke them to those Attemts, [and] that the Loue of Vertu cud not; and restraine them from the Perpetration of those Crimes that the Vglines /hatred/ of Vice was vnable to prevent. And how many a Woman had been actually dishonest had not she fear'd more the Shame <disgrace> of being so then the Sin. And certinly Vertu may thank the thirst of Glory /Reputation/ for many of those Glittering Actions the Vulgar so admires; and Innocence is beholding to the fear of Infamy for the greatest part of her retainers /traine./ Folly it self is good for somthing (said a Modern wiseman)[51] and since it is so let vs make the best vse of it we can in the cherishing of these Airy causes, since experience speaks them the Producers of such real Effects. |f. 18v| Vertu is seldom irrecallably banisht from that hart where shame and the Loue of honor do remaine: for they argue a Reluctancy in Vitius axions proceeding from a contrary Principle,

---

[48] Agaric is a genus of fungi "growing upon trees; of which P. officinalis, chiefly found on the Larch, the 'Female Agarick ' of old writers, was renowned as a cathartic, and with P. fomentarius, and igniarius, 'Male Agarick' used as a styptic, as tinder, and in dyeing" (*OED*).

[49] Cf. the *Aret*. (bk. 2, ch. 1) and the other works cited there.

[50] Cf. the *Aret*. (bk. 2, ch. 4).

[51] Probably a reference to Erasmus's *The Praise of Folly* (1511). RB owned at least ten works by Erasmus, though this famous work is not among them.

which keepes footing for Vertu in the Soule, and preserues aliue some Embers of Goodness that may in time be blown vp into a flame. But a Brazen Face, vsually, either is made by a Brazen hart, or makes it.

9. Endeuor to discouer and obserue the Wiles and Methods of the Tempter in laboring to seduce thee, and be carefull to defeate /preuent/ them.[52] Tis an Error that I haue obserued not more common then Dangerus /hurtful/ to fancy a kind of Omnipotence in the Deuil, as if he cud sway the Soule which way he listed; or at lest to beleeue such an vnsearchable /vnscrutable/ depth of craftines in his Desseins, that it is scarcely /little/ les then an Impossibility either to discouer or auoid them. An error that has been extreamly prejudicial to mankind, not only by occasioning our own needles apprehensions to betray vs to /throuh/ a [Panick] kind of Panic Feare; but also by wholly discouraging vs from the search and Observation of those |f. 19| Snares and Methods of the Temter whose Discouery wud extreamly conduce to their Resisting and Auoiding. For tho I wil not deny but that the Diuels being of Intellectuals so suttle, and withal so numerus, that we read of no lesse then a Legion garrison'd in one man[53] [yet am I] it wil be Impossible for any one man to find out all the Particular Contriuances of their Temtations that these malitius Spirits fit to the Dispositions of euery seuerall man: yet very confident I am that it is possible for a rational Man to pick out of the Scripture and his own Reason and Experience, both the General Policys vpon which Satan bilds his Kingdom, and the Methods that he vses of course with that Party in his Endeuors to seduce him to particular Sins. For the Deuils Knoledg being [not In] finite (since his Essence is so too) and man's Will being [w] totally priuiledg'd from Violence or Coaction /constraint/[54] it wil necessarily follow that the Deuil can work vpon the Minds of men but as a very great Statesman or cunning Politician may do: only he has som aduantages aboue them (which this is no fit Place to treat of) which he knows how to improue to the vttermost. And therefor, I wud |f. 19v| aduise euery one that desires to make Vertu his Bisness, not only to imprint in his Mind a Generall Idea of the Tempters Proceedings, but also in particular to trace him <in> his priuate Methods of Seducing to thy self: obseruing diligently [w] what occasions he commonly makes the Rises of his temtings to such and such a Sin, and then what Processes

[52] The curiosity of *Philaretus* led him "to those Wild Mountaines where the First & Cheefest of the Carthusian Abbeys dos stand seated; where the Deuil taking aduantage of that deepe, rauing Melancholy, so sad a Place; his humor, & the st[r]ange storys & Pictures he found there of Bruno the Father /Patriark/ of that order, suggested such strange & hideous thoughts, & such distracting Doubts of some of the Fundamentals of Christianity /Religion;/ that tho his lookes did little betray his Thoughts, nothing but the Forbiddenesse of Selfe-dispatch, hindred his acting it" (Maddison 35). Burton noted that Carthusian friars were especially vulnerable to religious melancholy (1.220, 245-46).

[53] Cf. Mark 5:9 or Luke 8:30.

[54] Cf. Alsted 1242 and the *Aret.* (bk. 2, ch. 3); for a later view, see *Exc. of Theol.* 4.19.

he vses in the Prosecution of that Temtation /Desein./ and with what Particular Policys he carrys it on according to the Seueral Circumstances he has to work vpon: for my own experience assures me both of the Possibility of the thing[s] and of it's aduantage /vtility/, these Projects grounded vpon craft, being for the most part like Mines carry'd vnder ground; which once discouer'd seldom take effect /where the Discouery vsually defeats the Design /Effect./.

10. <And> Lastly. Consider how friuolus the Objections that continue men in their Sins. All men ar naturally [asham'd of Vice, and none wud willingly own it: but yet ar far more vnwilling to leaue it: and therefore wud fa] inclin'd to detest Vice in it selfe, but yet doat vpon |f. 20| Those Pleasures which without it they cannot enjoy; and so resolue to restraine the thing, but [sl] endeuor to shift of the imputation of the Vice: and tho oftentimes their Excuses ar as weake as a man that's dying of a Consumtion, yet [in im] wil they, in imitation of our first Parents rather sow Figleaues together to couer their Nakednes then leaue it altogether vnueyl'd.[55] These Foxholes of theirs it is our Present bisnes to stop vp, that we may thereby repaire /remember/ the notable neglect of the Moralists in this Particular; who either leaue wholly vn-answered the Objections made for Vertu (which [of] we haue elsewhere cleared) or at lest remoue not the Excuses made by the Vitius; tho they haue therein skipt ouer a more necessary [Trea] Discourse then perhaps they ar aware of: for few men ar so void of humanity as to iustify Vice in it selfe; but whilst being vnwilling to own it and yet more vnwilling to leaue it, they had much rather employ their labor to extenuate the thing then |f. 20v| To forsake it: and so to [illeg.] reclaime a vitius Soule, without the Defeating of these Excuses, is little less difficult then to make an entire conquest of a Kingdome, [on] without euer taking the Enemys fortresses, or Places of Retreat; or to catch a Rabbet without stopping <vp> the Burrohs she vses to creep in at. Now these Excuses tho but too too numerus, ar <all, or convertible> reducible to these 12 heds,[56] for a Sinner may say

1.) This Sin is Vsual and vniuersall, or Practis'd by the most. To which I answer, 1. That no vnjust Custom of man, can antiquate the iust Law of God: neither wud an Erthly Iudge acquit a Theefe [for] that had rob'd on Salisbury Plain, for saying <that> men haue vs'd to rob there: for we must liue by good Precepts, not bad examples. 2. If the General Practice cud nullify the Nature of a Sin; there were no Vice that miht not think it self wrong'd by that Title; [the S] for the Characters of Nations wil speak the Spanish Proud, the French Lecherous, the Italian Reuengefull, the |f. 21| Dutch-man a Drunkard, the Moore

[55] Cf. the metaphor of fig-leaves for self-deception in *Swearing* 6.4 and 12.

[56] These twelve arguments are very similar to the fourteen arguments deployed in *Swearing*, where he focussed on a particular sin. In August 1646, Hartlib's *The Parliaments Reformation* proposed workhouses for the children of the ungodly poor. He advocated rules against swearing, filthy talking, cursed speeches, and ill behavior against anyone (6).

trecherous; and in a word, that there is scarce a Nation where some Vice or other is not in fashion, nor scarce a Vice that has not the Practice of som Nation <People> or other to authorize it. 3. That as in Good Actions the Number and Vnion of the Persons procures a more fauorable acceptation and return of their Endeuors, so in Bad ones, the [vniuersality] <multitudes> of the Sinners prouokes and has tens the [illeg.] Punishment of the Sin. For vniuersal Sins pul down vniuersal Iudgments; because the more the Dunghils [and] the greater is the Stink; and he [has] is the les excusable that [f] runs himself into a Danger he has so much occasion to beware of. 4. It 'tis ridiculus not to fear a Disease because tis Epidemicall. To a Iudicius mind the Peoples [illeg.] <liking of a thing> (in Morality) wil rather proue a Discouragement then an Inuitation, for he wil be very apt to suspect the Goodness of that Practice that so many fools and knaues approue of.

2.) Tis a little Sin in it selfe and greater in others then in me: To which I shal only adde to what we haue already <elsewhere> answered,[57] 1. That no Sin is little, as the only thing that debars vs the fruition of the |f. 21v| Greatest Good: [because and we see that [Sandes] tho Sands be of the smallest size of Bodys, and only bigger then Atomes, yet heapes of them may sink the vastest Carrack that sayles vpon the Ocean.] ↑I remember it was the Saying of a Lady (whom if she were not my Sister I [wud] durst pronounce aboue Flattery,) that it was a ridiculus thing that because a Sin was little therefore I shud loose my Soule for't.↓[58] 2. That not to be so wicked as another is but a very mean kind of Goodness; when a man needs a foyle to set him of; and like a gloworm neuer shines but in the Dark.[59] Tis but a Poor Buty not to be as vgly as a Fury: and truly I think if yow felt the Erthquake of an Ague in your Bones /ioynts/ yow wud scarce think your self in helth, because another lay <redy to> giuing vp the Ghost. 3. That we ar too Partial <iustly> to decide the Precedency betwixt our own Fauts and those of others; on both which we [loo] vsually look throu a very Deceitful Optik; Self-loue that contracts the one, and Enuy that multiplys the other. This made the Wisdom of his Father endeuor to [illeg.] bend vs towards the Contrary extreame, by telling so often of the Moats only that ar in our Brothers Ey, but of

---

[57] Cf. the *Aret.* (bk. 2, ch. 6) and *Swearing*.

[58] The sister was almost certainly his sister Katharine, whose remarkable life is sympathetically sketched by Fraser, *The Weaker Vessel* 131-34. Her friendships with Hartlib, Dury, Waller, and Milton were well established before RB returned from Geneva (Webster 64-78); her admirers were as diverse as Waller, Burnet, and Milton. RB frequently quoted a sister's wise counsel, and by dedicating *Occ. Refl.* to her as Sophronia, RB is stressing either the Greek word for temperance (sōphrosunē) or wisdom (phronēsis). For other views of his sisters, see Mendelson, *The Mental World of Stuart Women* and Mary Prior, ed. *Women in English Society, 1500-1800* (London 1985).

[59] In "Of Beauty," Bacon described virtue as "like a Rich Stone, best plaine set"; in *The Advancement of Learning* he continued the comparison: "Virtue, being a transcendent gem, is better set without much gold or ornament."

the Beams that ar in our own.[60] And indeed not without a great deal of reason, |f. 22| For most men vse [th] Sins as little Curs do vs, they bark at Strangers, but not so much as moue the tong /fawn vpon/ against home-dwellers.

3.) It brings me som Benefit or makes me auoid som Inconuenience: for which, to what I haue elsewhere discours'd I shal only ad by way of answer, that 1. There ar very few Vices that this Plea <if good> wud not justify. 2. Tis the greater glory to ouercom a Sin, seconded with all these aduantages: and indeed, except in such Cases Vertu is scarcely commendable: because tis in man's Nature to affect it were it not for these Inconueniences. 3. That men that admit Sin vpon these Considerations, do oftentimes (by a just iudgment of God) falle short of those very Ends for which they admitted it: and (if <al> things wer rihtly considered) tho they do reach them, loose a greater Benefit then <that> they [illeg.] striue for /can get/ and run into a greater Inconuenience then they endeuor to auoid. 4. That we ar very apt to [be] deceiue[d] <our selues> in the Iudging of those Necessitys that men think may enforce vs to Sin; and <frequently> take them [oftentimes], not as Motiues but Excuses, in our sinfull Axions: |f. 22v| and in stead of Sinning to auoid Inconueniences, we oftentimes forge Inconueniency to excuse our Sins.

4.) But I did it throu Ignorance, not knoing it a Sin; To which I answer that Ignorance indeed, iustly so called dos [wash] excuse a Fault;[61] but yet remember, 1. That that Ignorance that can serue for an Apology must be vnprocur'd, fr<om> which that which we purchase by our own neglect is very distant. For many men wil not [lern the] be instructed in the Paths of Vertu lest they shud be oblig'd to tread them: and resolue obstinately <to> ignore what is Good, lest the Knoledg <idea> of it shud endebt /engage/ them to the Acting <it> /action./ But truly this kind of Studyed Ignorance is so far from excusing a Fault that it is one: and the Sins that throu it we comit, tho don Ignorantly, cannot be truly said to be committed throu Ignorance but <throu> Neglect which was the Cause of that Ignorance. And Ignorance [illeg.] is neuer the true Cause of a Fault, when a fault is the cause of that Ignorance. |f. 23| 2. That many men pretend an Ignorance that they haue not, that they may Sin more quietly, they [haue kno] ar not blind but [on] wilfully shut their Eys; they haue knoledg enuf of the sinfulnes of many Acts they commit; but either refuse to consult it, or gag <silence> it: and they hear not their Conscience exclaim agenst those Axions, meerly because they stop it's mouth or their <own> Eares. Therefore the French Prouerb says that the worst deafnes is of those that wil not hear;[62] and I remember a Modern Poet, being reproached by a Sister of mine for acting against his Iudgment answer'd

---

[60] Matt. 7:3-5 or Luke 6:41-42.

[61] Cf. the analysis in the *Aret.* (bk. 2, ch. 3).

[62] The French source has not been identified, but RB's version was also an English proverb (H296).

her, By my Troth Madam I neuer go against my Iudgment, but I haue got a trick to make that my Iudgment that I haue a mind to.[63] These People do not Sin because they Ignore; but they [wi] ar resolu'd to Ignore that they may Sin: tho truly in this Case I think the Excuse [almo] perhaps worse <as bad> then the very fault.

5.) But I haue so strong an Inclination to such a Vice, that tis impossible for me to refraine, and 'tis not so much I that Sin as <my> Natur. To which I answer that 1. Tho Natural inclination may indeed giue vs a Propensity to such |f. 23v| and such Vices, yet indeed it can but Perswade, <sollicit> not Constraine vs to offend. For Nature giues euery man's Reason a Power to rule his Passions and his Inclinations, which cannot be wrestled from it, without he betray himself and becom accessary to his own Deposing. If Vitius Inclinations were Irresistible, certinly the Laws were very vnjust to punish that Done whose doing cud not (possibly) be auoided.[64] So that Inclinatc is little better Excuse for Vice, then an Eloquent Orat<ion>or for Revolt is of Rebellion. 2. Tis oftentimes the weaknes of Reason that giues strength to our Inclinations and our own Irresoluednes that makes their Power <so> formidable. Besides, that granting it were not so, yet he that thinks to be Vertuus without thwarting his sensual Inclinations; thinks to ascend a Riuer without striuing against the Stream. And in cases of this Nature, the glory of the Victory equals the Difficulty of the Ascent.[65] 3. If Inclination excus'd Vice, there wud be few wicked men in the World: Inclination being the Grand Guide to Vice, which few men wud care for but to comply with their Inclinations. |f. 24|

6.) O but I commit this sin meerly throu heedlesnes, and <when I> do it [but] I do not think on't. To which I answer, 1. That the Excuse is little better then the fault: as if one shud excuse his horse's Stumbling by saying that he neuer minds his way. How heedful ar we of any thing that concerns our corruptible Bodys or transitory States; and truly those that ar so with the neglect of what concerns their Immortal Soules, either beleeue <consider> not they haue any, or deserue to haue none. 2. That tis sign Sin is no stranger when [he] <it> can [go] in and out without being taken notice of. Take heed thou be not like the Toade that is not sensible of his Poyson, because he is all Poyson;[66] and that [the] Fisitians reckon it amongst <with> the worst of Symtomes, when the Patient voids excrements without perceiuing it.[67]

---

[63] The poet was probably Edmund Waller, a family friend, and the sister Lady Ranelagh. For her spirited complaint about his gallant language, see her undated letter to RB (6.521-22).

[64] A point made in the *Aret.* (bk. 2, ch. 3); cf. Nich. Eth. III.v.7.

[65] RB used a variant of this proverb earlier in this work: "The greater the difficulty, the greater the glory."

[66] T360, a proverb used above.

[67] A variant perhaps of "an ill bird fouls its own nest" (B377), but given RB's medical interests, it also has a more literal meaning. RB often invoked medical terms to talk about "diagnosing" and

7.) O but I hate the Vice in my own Nature as much as any man, and do it only not to distast the Company. To which I answer, 1. That Other men's faults excuse not <those we comit> ours, no more then their diseases cure <extenuate> those we [resent] <suffer>. 2. Why shud the company plead more earnestly for Vertu then thou for Vertu; or thou be more oblig'd |f. 24v| to Embrace their Euil then they thy Good? ↑If al thy Companions shud leap into the Sea, or throu themselues down hed-long from a Precipice, wud thou bear them Company in their madnes?↓ 3. That he that dares not be singular in Vitius Company, is a Slaue in General to all vices, and must somtimes be forc't euen to contrary Vices, according to different Inclinations of the Companys he lihts vpon. Besides that, that which pleases one Company[on] wil perhaps disgust another. 4. That if Company must needs be comply'd with, I had rather comply most with my deerest, neerest and most constant Companions, my Reason and my Conscience:[68] for we think him little better then mad that wil offend /injure/ an intimate frend to please a Stranger. ↑Neuer loos therefor the Company of God and Angels for that of men /Sinners/ and since thy Dignity and happines consists more in Reason then Society /fellowship/ be sure that to gaine the Title of [illeg.] a good Companion thou neuer forfeit that of a good man.↓ 5. That howeuer the World be pleas'd to think otherwise, [tis] he is morally more faulty that sins for Company then he that dos it out of Inclination: (because there is in the former les Temtation, which alwayes aggrauates the Sin:) for in the one I offend to please others, in the latter to please my self; in the former my Inclination leads me, in the latter I force it to do Ill; <lastly> in the former I can lay part of the blame vpon Nature; <whereas> in the latter I must take it all |f. 25| /Wholly/ to my Self. Sure I wud neuer offend for another man's Pleasure if /when/ I wud not do it for my owne. 6. That if the Company be thy reall frends indeed, they wil neuer (make it their) Desire that thou shudst Sin for them; and if they be not, they do not deserue that thou shudst [f] grant it.

8.) O but tho I aknoledg it a faut yet Custom has so chain'd me to my Sin that I cannot now possibly forsake it tho I faine wud. To which I answer that a Bad custom is indeed one of the Worst things of the World, and a Yoak somtimes very difficult to be shaken of.[69] But [cons] pray take this along with yow too, 1. That Custom in Euil lessens not the Guilt; for what for being once don was Euil cannot by the Repetition of that Euil acquire a Goodness /becom good./ And therefor our Iudges that but burn men in the hand for the first theft /faut/ hang them for the Second. And indeed to [illeg.] Plead custom for continuance

"treating" the disease of sin.

[68] RB's definition of good companions included reason and conscience. He did not mention Arist.'s lengthy discussion of friendship (Nich. Eth. VIII-IX).

[69] Custom or habit is a second nature (C932); cf. the discussion of custom in *Occ. Refl.* 2.450, *Reconcileableness* 4.164, and *Swearing* 6.20.

in Sin, is as if a Malefactor shud excuse himself to his Iudg for his last robbery, because he had been so long vs'd to kill and steal that [w] he was now vnable /resolu'd not/ to forsake |f. 25v| the (long-continued) Profession. 2. Since the Power of Custom flowes /springs/ from the reiteration of the same Acts, it wil follow, that the longer /further/ a man proceeds in the repetition of those Acts, the greater wil the Difficulty of [for] shaking of that Custome proue; and by consequent the [sooner we begin to abrogate an Euil <singular> Custom the more easy shal we find it's abrogation] longer we continue an Euil Custom the more Difficult wil it be to free our self from it's Tyrrany. 3. The Difficulty is oftentimes much less then what we imagine, for we ar <very> apt to persuade [to] our selues to the Impossibility of the [Att] Success, to free [our] /excuse/ our selues from the Trouble of the Attemt. Tis not oftentimes the Difficulty that we feare, but our Feares that make the Difficulty. But grant it as great as yow your self can fancy; who knos not [but] that Delay augments and quicknes lessens it; for (as is before imply'd,) The sooner we begin to abrogate a sinfull |f. 26| Custom, the more easy shal we find it's abrogation. Many Diseases ar easily remedy'd in their begins,[70] that in processe of Time grow /com/ to mock the skill of the Fisitian. 4. Custom is so bad a Plea for Continuance in Sin, that it shud be one of the powerfulst motiues in the world to forsake it: since the Customary Sinner must not only beware of future Sins, but redeeme those that /what/ are past. ↑And since thou hast been so long Euill tis more then time thou shudst now begin to be good.↓ And indeed to Sin agen because one has sin'd once, is (me thinks) one of the hihest peeces of Injustice in the World; for what is that but to offend God <meerly> because he has been offended.

9.) O but I haue as honest a hart as the proudest of them tho I haue not the Vanity to make a Show of it. ↑Neither am I so bad as I seem.↓ To which I answer, 1. That your own Bare affirmation is but a weake Euidence of your Vertu; and it must not be among Infidels that a man's Tong gains him a Vertuus Esteem when his Actions <life> ar Silent ↑or Witnes the Contrary. The Fisitian wil hardly [beleeue] <take it illeg.> a man's word that he is wel, when a [conc] croud of bad Symtoms proclaims his Distemper.↓ 2. That Vertu is not a meere Speculatiue or Metafisicall quality, but a Practical Habitude, that can neither be generated /produc't/ but by actions, nor subsist without them. ↑Logick teaches men to reason wel, Rhetorick to speake wel, [and] Geometry to mesure well, but [the] Vertu teaches men to Do wel.↓ Our Sauior bids yow (Matt. 5,16) Let your Liht so shine before men that they may see your Good Works, and glorify your father which is in heauen. |f. 26v|

↑And in the 12 of Mat. 33. he makes the Fruit Christen the Tree Good or Bad. Be not deceiued: Vertu is like life, it is not where it has no Operations; and

---

[70] The *OED* notes that this usage of "begins" is rare and obsolete, citing only Spenser's use (1596).

that God that made both the Body and the Soule (the Outward and the Inward man) wilbe honor'd in both.↓ |f. 27| And indeed Vertu is like a Fire, wheresoeuer it is tru and not painted, it must be actiue; and like the flame of a Candle; if yow giue it not vent /smother it/ yow kil it. /extinguish or put it out./ 3. That as for those that plead [illeg.] their Inward Detestation to iustify their outward Faults, [besides they] to omit the mischeefe they do by their example; it is so far from excusing that it aggrauates their Faults; since those Sins other men commit out of complyance with their Appetites, these men (in spite of their opposing Iudgments) make it so great a Gallantry as to affect and put it on.

10.) O but I do Good now and then; and am free enuf from Vices. To which I answer, 1. That the Doing a little Good and no more, wil but aggrauate your offences, and serue but for your greater Condemnation. 2. That <bare> Innocence is but a beggerly Vertu; and were a quality more fit to commend a Lyon or a Tyger then a Man. If Doing no hurt were the gretest Excellency, the Stone that lys in the bottom of the Sea may lay claime to a greater share of it then the Innocentest man liuing. The Gardner will not suffer in his |f. 27v| Orchard a Tree that beares no fruit, tho it fal not on his hed. Vertu is a quality Posityue, not negatiue (as our Sauior tels vs Matt, 7,17, that Euery Good tree bringeth forth good Fruit) and certinly the End of man's Creation being not <so much> a Bare Abstinence from Euil, as a<n> [Do] Actual doing of good, a Meer harmlesnes wil neuer enable him to reach it. And therefore our Redeemer, [p] (Matt 25.) punishes the vnfruitfull Seruant, not for hauing wasted his Talent, but for not hauing improou'd it.[71] And what may be feard [by] for these Negatiue Christians, the Baptist tels vs (Matt 3,10) where he makes fruitlesnes quite enuf to entitle a Tree to the Ax <hatchet> and to the Fire.

11.) Wel, I confess my Actions to be blameable, but I mean to repent ere long, and begin my Reformation vpon such a Solemn day.[72] To which I answer, 1. That if Vertu be Felicity yow cannot be more injurius to Your self then by [sus] deferring your Repentance to suspend your Happiness. And indeed a man

---

[71] Matt. 25:14-30.

[72] The dangers of a death-bed repentance were stressed in such works as Henry Hammond's *Of a Late, or, a Death-Bed Repentance* (1645) and many other works. Ussher's refusal of the the sacrament to Edward Herbert, Lord Herbert of Cherbury, is recounted in Aubrey's life of Ussher. In his "Ephemerides" (1648), Hartlib recorded that "Lord Herbert De Veritate sicken't and dyed the 4 and 5 of August. Hee fore-told his owne death that hee should dye about such an houre which hee also did. The Primat of Ireland was twice with him," attributing the information to Georg Rudolph Weckherlin. Some days later he attributed the following information to RB: "Lord Herbert said to the Primat when hee asked him about Christ I beleeve so much as I can. Hee told him if hee did not revoke some of his writing (for hee had caused only 5 copies of his Atheistical Papers) hee should never see God. Speaking about forgivenes of sins against which hee had spoken it seemes afore hee said that hee confessed himself to bee a great sinner, which was all. Hee sent for the Primat to receive the sacrament from him but hee denied to give it him." For a broader view of death-bed repentance, see McAdoo, *The Structure of Caroline Moral Theology*, ch. 5.

that has an Orthodox beleef concerning Vertu can hardly conceiue a more Irrationall Resolution. |f. 28| He that [illeg.] knos how the Impatience of Louers lengthens M<oments>inits into Ages [when] til the Arriual <dawning> of the Marriage day, wil be very apt to beleeue, that either these delayers care not for Vertu or deserue not that Vertu shud care for them. 2. That Present Sins ar certinly committed, but the Future Repentance is vncertin to be performed. Tis ridiculus to be wicked for the Present that yow may be good <in the future>; to be a Rogue now because yow mean to turn honest hereafter. ↑For <And> certinly he that [resolues] leads a wicked life now vpon the Score of leading a good one afterwards, must needs be a foole either for adhering to the First or reuolting to the Second.↓ The same Causes that make yow deferre your amendment now; may haue the like Power vpon yow hereafter: or tho they ceaze, ar vsually succeeded by others: [and] for [illeg.] the verity of which obseruation I appeale to the Consciences of my Readers: for indeed he that wil delay his Repentance [for one] vpon occasions, shal seldom want occasions of such delay. ↑And of thinking that som few further Acts of Procrastination may be as safe as the many former haue been.↓ And truly (methinks) to admit a Present wickednes vpon the hope of a future Amendment; is but to surfet [now] <to day> because one is to take Fisic a month hence. 3. That Deferring of Reformation |f. 28v| Remoues vs euery day further and further from it. For Vice is an Habitude, and we all know that euery act strengthnes the Habitude. When our Bodys ar Diseased, we presently post away Messenger vpon Messenger to <for> the Physitian, but we loose that care when our Soules ar concerned: as if Delay that so much endangers the one, [cud] were a Cure /souerin/ for the other: or a Progression in wandring did facilitate a Return into the right way. The [mor] longer a man runs on in the Vsurers debt, the harder it is to get out on't. And Sins are like young Trees, The longer yow let them grow, the more Difficult is their Felling.

↑That tho yow shud not <perhaps> want Time of Repentance; yet yow may perhaps <then> want a Disposition to it. Neither ar we certin that God [illeg.] <is bound to> accept vs when we com, that refus'd to come when he cal'd. /at his Call./ To Day (not to Morro) if yow wil heare his Vojce, harden not your harts, (Ps. 95,7.) and (Esay 63,10) They rebelled and vexed his Holy Spirit, and therefore he was turned to be their Enemy and he fouht against them. And (Gen. 5,3) God tels vs that his Spirit shall not always striue with Flesh: and we kno that the Talent was [wi] taken away from that Seruant that made not vse on't. And in Effect all God's Promises ar made To nought[73] of Repentance. For he (as says the Father) that Promis'd Pardon to the Repenter, did not promise Repentance to the Sinner. Beware therefor of Procrastination, since thou art sure neither of leasure to Repent in nor Repentance to make vse of that Leasure.

---

72 For remedies, "sovereign" means efficacious or potent in a superlative degree (*OED*).

4. That (as a Sister of mine told me) ↑vpon this Subiect, the things that we ground our present sins vpon shud be the greatest Dissuasiue in the World from them, which is, that They ar to be repented of /for:/ /that we must <shall> repent them/. Sure we must [haue stru very str] beleeue the Importunity of those Pure Spirits that desire our Company, to be extreamely greate, if they will not be driuen away by our frequent Repulses and Denyals.↓ 5. That whereas most men [illeg.] put of their Repentance til the first day of the Year month, week, [or] their birth-day, or som such other [ne obseruable] <notable> Time, that their Reformation may be dated from som obseruable day;[74] this is meerly a Delusion of the Deuil to toll men on in the way of Destruction; |f. 29| and indeed only fit to [cheate] foole Children with: ↑and such as wud neuer preuaile with a Louer to defer his Mistresse's Embraces:↓ wherefore I will neuer suspend my happines for such needles <childish> Puntilio's; but if I cannot make my Repentance remarkable by the Day, I wil make the Day remarkable to me by my Repentance.

12.) Well but my Repentance ↑in my Old-age at furthest↓ vpon my Deth-bed shall make amends for all; and Repentance is one of those things that can neuer be don too late so they be don at all. To which I answer, 1. That as there is nothing more certin then Deth, so is there nothing more contingent then the Manner of it. How many haue been snatch't out of the World by sudden accidents; and how many lost their Reasons long before their Liues: in either of such Cases Repentance [wa] cud not be thout of. And a thousand wayes has deth to surprize <vs>, and not giue vs leas<u>re to take Repentance along with vs into the other World. How ful of good Resolutions is the Deuil's Mansion: and how many for hauing too long |f. 29v| Put of their Repentance heer haue been fain to [perfect] <finish> it in Hell. Repent therefor timely, lest thou be forced to repent eternaly <for not hauing Repented>. 2. That granting thee vpon thy Deth-bed leisure of Repentance, yet is that Time of all others the most vnlikely for it, [not] as wel because of the Inward horror of an Ill-led Life, and those approaching Flames it has deseru'd, as of those [Cor] Bodily Disturbances, and Diuersions that vsually meet vs vpon the Deth-bed; as stupyfying or enraging Payns; Dulnes or Numnes of Spirits and Sence; and the Hurry of Worldly Bisness then to be composed and set in order. So that one had had reason to say that Repentance [was] <is> a very easy taske, if he that is disabled for all things else is strong enuf for that. 3. That Deth-bed Repentance is as Vncomfortable as it is vnlikely. To omit that one's Frends cannot be [satisfy'd] ascertin'd of it's Sincerity: euen [in] a man's self in this Case is oftentimes either [illeg.] destructiuely deluded, or at lest perplext with |f. 30| vnspeakable Agonys and Anxietys of [mind] Spirit.

[74] RB several times marked his birthday (25 January, the conversion of St. Paul) as an occasion for reviewing his progress on various projects: cf. BP 36.85-86 and BP 22.31-36. He also noted the need for a special prayer to mark that date (BP 37.156v).

For (not to name the affrihting /horrid/ Prospect a Wicked Life presents vs with at it's Period;) how easy it is for a Wearines of this Life and Desire of the next to be mistaken for tru Conversion; and those Good Resolues to be vnsincere, that being caus'd but by Apprehension of approaching Deth, wud ceaze with, <their Motiue> as the Resolutions, not of the man but of the Disease? ↑(Such a man looses his feare of Dying and of sinning both together.)↓ [illeg.] since he neuer [desi] resolues to leaue the World til the World leaues him. 4. ↑That tis extreamely Dangerous to rely vpon it, and one of the hihest Degrees of Prouocation we can offer vp to God: as if he had so much mercy that he had no Iustice, and either cud not see thy Fauts, or durst not punish them. But the Parable of the Ten Virgins (Matt 25) may plainly tech vs that Mercy, like Swallows, haue certin seasons when they may be found and beyond /after/ which twere in vaine to expect them:[75] and that tho the Doore of Pardon /mercy/ be indeed very late open, yet when once it is shut tis bootles to knocke.

And truly if we wil but take the Paines to look on their Ends that haue taken this Course, we shall find that thousands haue <bin> miscarri'd <shipract> for one that has made a Sauing Voyage. Which truly tho I were neuer so sure [of] to make yet wud I not for the Pleasures sin cud bestow vpon me [sus] debar my self [so long] from liuing like a man and acting towards the Ends of my Creation. ↑5. And indeed God is very little beholding to them that com to him meerly because they cannot otherwise scape the Clutches of the Deuill. Men now adays make God's Seruice like an hospital to which men <they> repair not til they ar (vndon and <or>) Decrepit.↓↓ That, as for putting of <adiourning> Repentance til Old-age <to grey haires>, Tis Impudence to present God with the Lees /Dregs/ of our Liues, when the Deuill has drunk vp all the Wine: and madnes to think he wil accept of the Dry Bones when his Enemy has suck't out all the marrow. God euer required the First Fruits for his oblations, and the May of Age /youth/ in his Sacrifices; All those that were Lame or Blind, or otherwise Defectiue [were] (all Difformity being repugnant to his most perfect Nature,) were forbidden his Altars: as he himself tels vs in the Profet (Mal. 1.8.) If ye offer the Blind for sacrifice is it not Euill. And if ye offer the Lame and Sick, is it not Euill. Offer it now to the Gouernor, wil he be |f. 30v| Pleased with thee or accept thy Person sayth the Lord of hosts? And therefore the Wise-man, aduises thee (Eccl. 12,1.) to Remember now thy Creator in the Days of thy Youth, while the Euil days com not, nor the Years draw nih, when thou shalt say, I haue no pleasur in them. And certinly if [the best] (according to the Rule) the best be due vnto the best; the flower of our Dayes and choisest of our Parts will not be (found) to good for the most Excellent and Perfectest of Essences; and they wil hardly be excus'd [who] in their Dealings with God, that of Som ancient

[75] Matt. 25:1-12.

Idolaters to their Ceres, who offer'd her (in sacrifice) not the honey but the wax only of their Bees, and the Refuse and coursest (Portions) of their Fleeces. And if this be so, then how presumtuus may we safely presume them, that thinke God will be glad to take the Deuils Leauings, that [looke to receaue] <expect> God's wages for hauing done the Deuil's work; and that think that after they haue gallop't all their lifetime in the <hih or direct> way to hell, they shal meet with heu'n at their Iourney's End. Certinly men must haue very mean Opinions of God, to thinke him that <whose age> is vnfit for <skorn> any other Seruice, to be good enuf for his. 6. That to repent vpon one's Deth-bed is a Resolution |f. 31| [that contradicts it self, it being Ridiculus to resolue[s] not to begin to liue well til we haue no more [of] <make an End> to liue at all, and ↑extreamely vnreasonable↓ that the last Minit of our Life, shud be the first (Minit of our Living wel] whereof the very Foundation is contrary to the Performance; and (as one has it wittily) the Condition of all a man's Good life, a Presumtion that he shal not liue. Sure tis very Ridiculus for a man to resolue to liue well vpon no other Consideration but because the Time is com when he thinks he shal dy.[76] That being but to begin to sow in Haruest when we shud be ready to reape. And certinly it is extreamely vnreasonable, that The last minit of our Life, shud be the first (minit) of our liuing well. |f. 32|

Thus farr of the Antidotes to preuent Vice, now to the Purges that are to Cure or Expel it; and those ar principally 2, Self-examination and Repentance; whereof the one serues to (find out and) Apprehend a Sin, and the other to Execute it.[77]

1. Self-examination therefore is a [serues] <Diligent> and strict Enquiry after a man's own Faults. This Practice is the Scout of the Soule in the Spirituall Warfare, that brings it Intelligence of the Posture and Forces of the Enemy, and discouers his Embuscado's to it.[78] And therefore there is [no practice] <scarce any thing> that more disquiets Sin, more discourages the Deuill, or ouht to be more readily embrac't by all those that resolue not to let Vice haue a Peaceable dominion ouer them. Wherefore the Apostle [bids] <comands> the Corinthians (2 Cor. 13,5) to Examine themselues and to Proue their own Selues; and in the 1 Cor. 11,31. he tels vs that If we would Iudge our Selues we shud not be iudged. And indeed methinks tis ridiculus, to [be so] <be so> careful to looke <for> Fleas in our Beds and neglect <to look for> Faults in our Axions /liues/ [and to be so carefull of to weed our gardens and yet neglect the Weeding of our

---

[76] Paraphrased from Henry Hammond's *Of a Late, or, a Death-Bed Repentance* (1645) 27.

[77] RB described at length his method of self-examination in "Dayly Reflection"; in *Swearing*, he listed six steps for curing the sin.

[78] While the concept and tradition of spiritual warfare invited such figurative language, we should also recall that Marcombes provided formal instruction in fortification (Maddison 30), the value of which RB later doubted (*Usefulness* 3.426).

minds.][79] Now this Self-examination[s] ouht to be performed, 1. Frequently, that tho sin may perchance [ly] lodg in the Soul as a Passenger, yet it may neuer dwel there as a Citizen.[80] 2. Diligently and |f. 32v| Strictly, that no Vice may Scape so narrow an Enquiry. And in this Case, Consciences ar like lookin-glasses, Those ar best that discouer /hide not/ the Smallest Difformitys /blemishes/. 3. Impartially, considering Sin not as our own but as Sin; which to attain to, we must in the First place be very suspitius of our Selues, and always beleeue more faults then we see, because we vsually see fewer then ther are: and in the next, first consider the [De] Vnhamsomnes of Sin in others, and then apply it to the Parallell fauts <that we> our selues committ: for without the first we are commonly so much our own Flatters, that we shud neuer discouer our own Vices in their Tru dimensions but in those of others, where Self-loue darkens not the Ey of Iudgment: our Sins being like our Faces which we seldom see but by Reflection:[81] and as for the other, tis but a Wilful blindnes /madness/ to beleeue that that can be handsom in vs which is so misbecomming in others: or that our Axions can be exemt from the Censure that ar sharers in the Sin that prouokes it. /draws it on./ This Practice of Self-examination if sincerely and constantly performed, is of greater necessity and vse then most men ar aware of and <for> beleeue it, tis foolish to haue a greater care to weed one's Garden then one's Soule,[82] |f. 33| and He that truly hates Vice, hates it in no man more then in himself. 2. True Repentance is a certin Sorrow for a past fault, with a firm /radicated/ Resolution against it's committing for <in> the future. It is commonly listed amongst meer Christian Vertus,[83] tho [it may not] not vntruly /vnfitly/ [be] think it a branch of Morall Iustice, as the onely way of Reparation left to satisfy the Iniur'd Deity, or [wron] a man's own wrong'd Soule, for the offences committed against them. It's necessity is euident from the number and frequency of our Faults; and truly twere fit euery Sinner shud [g] always mind that Sentence of our Sauior (Luke the 13,3.) that Except ye Repent ye shal all likewise perish. Repentance is the Soap of the Soule that scoures out all it's Spots; and <or> like an vnualuable Powder I haue try'd, that is both a Purge and an Antidote, both Curing Diseases already contracted and arming vs against future.[84] But it's Vtilitys (both great and Numerus) ar extream liuely Emblem'd by an admirable liquor a great Filosofer lately show'd me the Experiment of; whereof a few drops instil'd into a great vessel of the most stinking water that runs in the kennell, not

---

[79] For a similar guide to self-scrutiny, cf. "Dayly Reflection" f. 282.

[80] The same point is made in the same language in "Dayly Reflection" f. 271v.

[81] Cf. the *Aret.* (bk. 2, ch. 4).

[82] RB deleted a similar version of this phrase a few sentences above.

[83] For further discussion of repentance, cf. the *Aret.* (bk. 2, ch. 1, 3, 4) and *Swearing* 6.17.

[84] Hartlib's "Ephemerides" (1649) referred often to Lady Kent's powder, citing the views of RB and Lady Ranelagh. Elizabeth Grey, Countess of Kent, wrote *A Choice Manual of Rare and Select Secrets*, an extremely popular collection of medical receipts. RB owned the second edition (1653).

onely frees it presently from all <[offensiue]> [ill] il tast and smell, and so restores it to it's [illeg.] former Purity and Clearnes; but secures it for euer from future corruption; and not onely so, but frees those very lees that carri'd that Putrefaction, |f. 33v| From all offensiue Sent.[85] This <Emblem> I hope dos sufficiently apply itself. ↑Let the Degree /Intensity/ of thy Sorro /Greef/ be answerable to the Criminusnes of thy offence.↓ Now true Repentance must at least consist of 2 Ingredients; a Happy sorrow for Sin and a radicated resolution agenst it. 1. The motiue of this Sorro must be Detestation of the Sin, not the Sence of the Paine we suffer for it; which ouht to be but the Rise not the Motiue /cause/ of our Repentance: and therfor those that are truly penitent ar more sensible of the Fault then the Rod; and of the Cause then the Effect of God's Displesure. ↑For that which is to be repented of is a Faut which [Punishment] <illeg.> is not in it self; tho it [hau] vsually haue one for it's Cause.↓ He that repents meerly out of Feare or Paine is not grieu'd for his Own Sins but at <for> God's Iustice, and parts with his Vices not as with an Enemy but as with a Ransom. And indeed Resolutions taken vp meerly vpon these [gro] Considerations, seldom outliue their motiues: so that we see most men resume their Vices with their helth, and relapse into the Diseases of the Soule as they recouer from <of> those of the Body. 2. There must be not only an vnfeined Sorrow for Sins past but a firm and sincere resolution neuer to fall into them for the Time to com. Repentance like Ianus, shud be double-fac't; whereof the one shud look [behind vs w] backward with a weeping Ey, and the other forward with a vigilant Ey; the one to be bewail faults [that are Past], |f. 34| and the other to Preuent Future. For true Repentance and the Design of Sinning wil neuer be reconcil'd together: and indeed, Repentance without amendment of Life, is like pumping (in a ship) without euer stopping the Leake. Repent therefore what thou hast don, and neuer do again what thou hast repented; for the best <noblest> Sacrifice we can offer vp for our Sins, is to offer vp our Sins for a Sacrifice.

---

[85] RB referred to this experiment or to a very similar one in *Specific Medicines* 5.93. I am grateful to R. E. W. Maddison for this pointing out this parallel. Between 1645-48 Hartlib received several enquiries and reports on this topic, notably a letter from Benjamin Worsley dated 8 May 1648 (HP 71/15/1-2) about "The Cure of stincking water." Worsley was probably the great philosopher.

Of Piety

|f. 38|

Piety is a Vertu that teaches vs the Tru Worship of God.[1] We intend not here to treate of Piety as it is a Christian Vertu described and Prescribed in the holy Scriptures: but as it is a Morall Vertu which the Hethen themselues by the Meere liht of Nature haue confest to be so, and Registred in their Writings: wherein tho Aristotle in his Ethicks have been extremely barren, yet Socrates, Plato, Seneca, the Stoicks, and the Pythagorians, haue in a great Measure supplyed <illeg.> that Defect <want>.[2] And that Piety is a Morall Vertu will not onely appeare by the Excesses that it moderates, but also by the [Testimo] (almost) |f. 38v| Vniuersall Consent of those who [borrowed] <illeg.> their Opinions onely [vpon] <from> the Light of Nature, whence Plato said that The Hihest Vertu amongst Men was Piety towards God;[3] and the Roman Orator calls it The Foundation or [Ground] <Basis> of all the Vertus.[4] ↑Plato in Epimonide Hic tibi propositus sit finis vt Dei cultu, and vitæ puritate optatum tandem exitum consequare.[5]

Idem 4 de legibus monet Deum nobis esse debere maximè mensuram omnium rerum.[6] Cicero, Off. Prima Deis immortalibus debemus officia.[7] Idem 1. De naturâ Deo Præstans Dei Natura hominum Pietate colitur, cùm et æterna sit & beatissima.↓[8]

II. Now all Piety consists in 2 Particulars: the Knoledge of God and That is Worship. ↑According to that of Seneca Primus deorum Cultus est, Deos credere; de inde reddere illis majestatem suam; reddere bonitatem; scire illos esse qui præsident; qui vniuersaui suâ temperant, qui humani generis tutelam ger-

---

[1] This essay is taken from MS 196. As in the *Aret.*, RB defined and illustrated the concept before considering the vices of defect and excess that opposed piety. In *Philaretus* RB referred to the essays as part of a projected work, *The Christian Gentleman* (Maddison 33).

[2] RB presented some of these views in the *Aret.* (bk. 2, ch. 4). Alsted's chapter on piety (1264-67) provided most of the sources for RB's discussion.

[3] Cf. *Laws* 4.717B and *Crito* 51C.

[4] Cicero, *Pro Plancio* 12.49.

[5] Plato, *Epinomis* 980B. "Plato in the Epinomis 'Here may the goal be proposed to you that you at last obtain [your] hoped for dessert through respect for God and through the purity of [your] life.'"

[6] Plato, *Laws* 4.716C. "Likewise in [book] four concerning laws he advises that God ought to be for us especially the measure of all things."

[7] Cicero, *De Officiis* 1.160: "our first duty is to the immortal gods."

[8] Cicero, *De Natura Deorum* (Cambridge, Mass. 1933), trans. H. Rackham, 1.45.11-12: "since the exalted nature of the gods, being both eternal and supremely blessed, would receive man's pious worship."

unt.↓[9] The Former <of these> is a Præuious and Necessary Disposition vnto the Latter. For since that Seruice that [mu] is acceptable, must be suitable to the Nature and Will of him to whom it is presented; how can a man (but by accident) [W] honor with a lik't Worship that God whose Nature and Wisdom he ignores. Hence our Sauior ( ) tels vs that This is Life Eternall to know the one True God and him that he hath sent, Iesus Christ.[10] But tis Knoledge, if it be confin'd to the Brain, and display not it self out at the Hands, is insufficient: for the very Deuils themselues Know God and yet are not by that Knoledg |f. 39| Induc't to Serue but only to Tremble. Knoledge and Practise are so essentiall to Piety, that if either of them be defectiue tis but a maim'd Vertu /Piety./ We must both Know what we shud Practice and Practize what we know: [without the Former Religion wants] if the Former be missing Religion is without an Ey, and if the Latter, she wants a Hand.[11]

III. The Knoledg of God is Threefold: Inborn, which all men bring into the World with them: Acquisite, which they acquire by improuing their Natural Reason, out of the Contemplation of the Creatures and their own Consciences, and Infus'd, <Mixt> for which they are totally beholding to Diuine Revelation.[12] The First is euident in all Nations, the second is cheefly eminent in Filosofers; |f. 39v| the latter is a peculiar Prerogatiue of those that profess the true Religion. For Religion (in the General) is nothing else but [the] <men's> Beleefe or Opinion [men haue] concerning God and [m] diuine Matters.

IV. Now amongst that great Variety of Religions that are cry'd vp in the World; This seems the safest Tuch-stone to try the best: Namely, That Religion is the Best that giues [God] <the Deity> most glory, and most [dignifys] <accomplisheth> Perfects and felicitates the Rational Creature.[13] For all the Intention of God in Creating Man was no other, then To manifest his Glory and communicate his goodness (to him). Nor can so infinite and all-sufficient a Perfection be reasonably presum'd to descend to lower /other/ Ends. And vpon this Touchstone if [any] we shall take the Paines to rub the Epidemicall Religions

---

[9] Seneca, *Epistulae Morales*, trans. Richard M. Gummere (Cambridge, Mass. 1925), 95.50.1-2. "The first way to worship the gods is to believe in the gods; the next to acknowledge their majesty, to acknowledge their goodness without which there is no majesty. Also, to know that they are supreme commanders in the universe, controlling all things by their power and acting as guardians of the human race." RB omitted the concluding clause: "even though they are sometimes unmindful of the individual." Cf. Alsted 1266.

[10] John 17:3.

[11] Regarding the *Aret.*, RB wrote Marcombes that his purpose was to move the ethics from the brain to the breast, from the school to the house (1.xxxiv); see also *Occ. Refl.* 2.460.

[12] Cf. the distinction in the *Aret.* (bk. 2, ch. 4) among natural, infused, and intellectual virtue.

[13] RB's interest in other religions dates from his stay in Florence (Maddison 40), but it was fueled by his trips to Amsterdam, where he visited in 1648 with Menasseh ben Israel (4.375 and 5.183). For other references to this rabbi, see 2.18, 280, 301; 5.172; and 6.7. See also Yosef Kaplan, Henry Méchoulan, and Richard H. Popkin, *Menasseh ben Israel and his World* (Leiden 1989).

that now reigne |f. 40| In the World; we shall find them all som way or other either [in Whole] <Totally> or in Part, to be either derogatory to God's Glory, [and] <or> rob man of his Dignity and Happiness. [But <of this taske I willingly [I] leaue to the Diuines for feare of encroaching vpon their Borders.]

V. Altho the learned haue lent vs three Furnaces[14] (as it were) to purify and spiritualize our <dull and grosse> Conceptions of God (Namely, The way of Negation, whereby we strip him of all kind of Imperfections and Defects; the Way of Causality, whereby we attribute <to> him <as to> the supreame Cause all the Most perfect Effects; and the Way of Eminency, whereby all that we see of Excellent in the Creatures we attribute to God in the hihest and most Eminent Degree, that is, in a Degree suitable to his Nature) yet [y] certinly his Nature dos so infinitely transcend our Capacity, that a Nutshel can as wel comprehend [the Sea] the Ocean [of the <narrow> Thimble of our Reason] |f. 40v| as our shallo Reason fathom the Depth of that Vnsearchable Nature, who is so truly said in the Scripture (1 Tim. 1:16) to Inhabit an Inaccessible Liht, that we must needs confess that the Sublimest and most Refin'd Notions we can possibly shape of God, [fall] are infinitely beneath the <more Infinite> Perfections of his Essence, ↑(whose Definition is to haue none).↓[15] Heere therefore there is more Vse of Faith then Reason to beleeue what we cannot comprehend when what we cannot comprehend is Infinite. And the Best way will be to frame the lest vnderualuing Conception of the Deity that we can; and heartily to Desire Ability (power) to frame Nobler. Aboue all let vs be carefull to [make] entertaine Thouhts of God in the Abstract not the Concrete; conceiuing him a Diffused Goodnes without Qua[n]lity and an Incomprehensible Greatnes without Quantity. ↑Heere refer the story of Simonides his asking stil more and more to Define God.↓[16] But the more nice Consideration of these things I leaue to the Diuines for feare of encroaching vpon their Profession. |f. 41|

VI. God thus knowne must in the next place be religiously ador'd. For 'tis but an vnhappy and Condemning Knoledge, to kno the Good we shud do, vnless we also do the Good we haue knowne. And there are 3 things in God, which [will] shud specially encline vs to his Seruice. His Excellency /Eminent

---

[14] While the figurative meaning of furnace is quite clear, RB was keenly involved in setting up his own furnace (6.39). Hartlib was very interested in the chemical experiments of George Starkey (or Stirke) after the latter arrived in London in 1650. In "Newton's *Clavis* as Starkey's *Key*," *Isis* 78 (1987) 564-74, William Newman discusses an early letter from George Starkey to RB (Boyle Lett. 6.99-100), an item not listed by Maddison. It can be dated about April-May 1651 and includes comments on Worsley and the Hartlib circle. Starkey came to London from Cambridge, Massachusetts, ca. 1650. See also Ronald Sterne Wilkinson, "The Hartlib Papers and Seventeenth-Century Chemistry: II," *Ambix* 17 (1970) 85-110.

[15] For later reflections on divine attributes, cf. *High Veneration* (5.132, 144, 146) and *Exc. of Theol.* (4.14, 21-22).

[16] Cf. Cicero, *De Natura Deorum* 1.62. RB repeated the anecdote in *Seraphic Love* 1.265.

Perfection/ his Iustice and his Goodnese. For the First Since all things less Perfect are made for the Seruice of those that enjoy a hiher /greater/ Perfection, as the Body for the Soule; the Earth for Plants, they for Beasts, and these for man, and amongst Men themselues, those of the Feminine Gender to Serue those of the Nobler Sex; why shud man disturbe this so rationall Order in things by denying his Seruice to his Creator: who being the Cheefest Good, and the most Excellent and Compleat of Essences, deserues an Adoration Suitable to the <infinite> Perfection of his Nature. And certinly as tis not onely iust ↑but Profitable↓ that the Reasonable Faculty of the Soule shud comand the Sensitiue, [but also very profitable] ↑and a Discreet Father an vnruly Childe,↓ |f. 41v| So it is not onely Reasonable but also vastly aduantagious for Ignorant and Froward Man to obey and submit [resigne/ himselue to the Wise conduct of a God, whose Goodness is no less Infinit then his Power. Whence Epicurus himself, tho he vainly beleeu'd the Gods but Idle /vnactiue/ Spectators of our Humane Vicissitudes; yet [profest] <acknoledg'd> (if we may beleeue Tully) such an Excellency in their Nature, as shud alone be sufficient to oblige the Wiseman to adore it:[17] In the Next place his Iustice will challenge our Worship; for if we pay such [pro] seruices and such Profound Respects to Magistrates, that do Iustice but in one Citty or Angle of the World; how much more are they due to that God, who distributes both rewards and Punishment thorough the whole Vniuerse, and that in so much more excellent a Way, that no offence can be so Secret as to scape his Ey, nor no Offendor so powerfull as to resist his Arme. And therefore the Hethen orator had a greate [of] deale of Reason to say, that Piety was but |f. 42| A kind of Iustice to the Gods;[18] (namely, as a Returne of theirs to vs.) And then his Goodnesse shud inuite vs to his Seruice: for since he made, preserues and gouernes both vs and all things; (and, as the Apostle [so] tels vs, (Acts. 17.28.) In him we liue and moue and haue our Being) shal we not out of a Principle of Thankfulness be willing to serue so great a Benefactor. Sure Gratitude as well as Iustice dos oblige vs to it. To which I shal onely ad one Motiue more, (that perhaps many will consider more then all the [other] <rest, or 3> which is our owne Interest. For since we allow the Industry of Subjects to get themselues well lookt on by those Princes that gouerne the Countrys /Places/ where they liue;[19] Why shud we not be equally ambitius of the Fauor of that God, who holding in his hands the Reins (as it were) of the World and the Disposall of all Things can and dos oftentimes (as a Heathen Author takes notice) [direct and contriue and] ↑by

---

[17] Cicero questioned Epicurus's piety in *De Natura Deorum* 1.123.

[18] Cicero, *De Finibus* 3.22.73; see also Alsted 1266, where he cited *De Natura Deorum; Chr. Virtuoso* 6.730; and *Seraphic Love* 1.281.

[19] This point is stressed in Cork's "True Remembrances," an edition of which, according to Hartlib, RB wanted to publish. Canny discusses the facts and fictions of the "True Remembrances" in ch. 1-3.

a secret and Wise Contriuance↓ direct the most casuall Accidents to the Good of those that feare him.[20] But the |f. 42v| Apostle, (Rom. 8.28) <and> speaking vpon Knoledge too) makes the Assertion far more Generall, for Wee Know (says hee) that All things work together for good to them that loue God. [With] How execrable has Impiety made the Names of Herod, Nero, and Caligula; and how has Religion perfum'd the Memory of Moses, Dauid, and the great Constantine. Certinly sincere Piety puts a man vnder the Protection <Conduct> of God's Grace in this World and brings him to the Fruition of his Glory in the Next; according to that of the (same) Chapter ( )[21] that Piety has the Promises of this life and that which is to come.

VII. Now as for the Seruice or Worship of God it selfe, the Whole Substance of it Consists in this one[ly] Point, To make our Selues like him that we adore. So that in effect to be Pious is nothing but to be a Good Copyist, I meane of those Actions of God that |f. 43| are Imitable by vs not those he dos (as the Creation and Diuers others) by the Prerogatiue of his Essence. Hence in the 4th Commandement the Seuenth day's Repose is enforc't vpon vs from God's Example, who rested that Day from all his Workes. Hence (Leu. 11.44.) He commands vs to be Holy because He is Holy: which command is reiterated by our Sauior (Matt. 5.48.) Be ye therefore Perfect euen as our Father which is in Heu'n is Perfect.[22] So that as God dos Good to all and Injury to none, so shud we do also; and shud make his Goodness both the [Ambition] /Aime/ and the Pattern of ours. But to say somthing of more Particular, the Worship of God may be diuided into Immediate and Mediate, the Former is payd immediately to himself, the Latter is our liuing vertuusly (for his sake) with men, as that redounds to his Glory. And that Former is distinguished into |f. 43v| Inward and Outward.

VIII. The Internal Seruice of God, is that which is paid him by the Soule of Man; and is that which he cheefly delights in and expects, as that which is most suitable to his Nature. For as our Sauior diuinely teaches vs, (Iohn 4.24.) God is a Spirit and they that worship him must worship him in Spirit and in Truth. Now this Spiritual Adoration is (generally amongst all Nations) made vp of these 3 Dutys, Loue, Feare, and Trust: For we must loue God because he is so infinitely Good; Feare him, because he is no lesse Powerfull and Iust; and hauing don this, we may Confidently Trust in him because he is Both.

IX. We ought to loue God because he is both the Best of Essences and the Souuerain Good: and whatsouever we [ha] are or haue of Good, is but the Communication of his Goodness to vs. But for a God so many ways |f. 44| Louely we must not content our selues with an Ordinary Loue: if the Amorists tell vs tru, that their Mistresses inspire a Passion [proportionable] <answerable> to the

---

[20] Cf. Seneca, *De Providentia* and Cicero, *De Natura Deorum* 2.73-153.

[21] Rom. 8:38-39.

[22] A point also made in the *Aret.* (bk. 2, ch. 4).

Excellencys they discouer in them;[23] and the Passion be to be proportion'd to the Object; with how rais'd and excellent <eminent> a Passion ought we to loue such infinite Perfections. The 2 Grand Loadstones of Loue concurre in a Degree transcendent as his Essence in the Deity: Perfections in himselfe, and Affection towards vs: the one deserues our Passion, the other encourages it: he being equally Louely in himselfe and loueing to vs. Nor need we heere feare our Loue shud passe beyond it's limits; for such is the Merit of the Object, that that very Extreamity that vsually makes Loue degenerate into a Vice, here sublimes /refines/ it into a Vertu. Not but that excess in this Loue wud be Vitius, but that God is so infinitely Perfect, that this Loue cannot admit of an excesse. And certinly [did] had we in this [Wo] Life a knowledge of God equall to that we hope for in the next, he wud so |f. 45| Monopolize our Affections, that our Soules wud neuer permit themselues to be diuerted to an ignobler loue; and it wud cure our Dotage vpon the transitory Goods of this World, as the sight of Helen wud his Passion that courted a Blacamore /kitchinwench/ meerely because he had neuer seen a greater Buty.[24]

X. The Feare or Reuerence we ought to haue of God is a Certin awfull Apprehension of offending him, arising out of the Consideration of his Omniscience that descrys our most close and Secret Faults; the Purity of his Nature which detests all kind of Sin, as contrary to it selfe; and his Iustice which wil not let wickednes escape vnpunish't; which back't by his Omnipotence, makes the Vengeance he decrees, vnauoydable. Hence it is that Vsually in the Scripture All Religion is [vsually] (by Synecdoche) exprest by the Feare of which is therefore by the Wisest of men ( ) called the Beginning of Wisedome:[25] and honored with such Elogiums in the Scripture. But heere it is to be noted |f. 45v| That the Cheefe motiue of this so comended Feare is not so much God's Iustice as his Goodnesse: (which distinguishes the slauish Feare of the Punishment from the Filial one of the Offence:) for we ouht not onely to feare God because he can punish, but we ought to feare to offend him for feare of offending him: and <one's> goodness is so fearefull of offending another; that the Good man is oftentimes no les afeard to [haue] offend God's Goodness, then for hauing offended his Iustice. This Noble Feare of God once growne vp to it's full Pitch, [deuoures] dos drowne all tother Feares, which loose themselues in it as the Riuers do in the Sea. Whence our sauior (Matt. 10.28.) Cures the Feare of Being kild in the Body by prescribing the Feare of him whose Anger reaches to the Deth of the Soule. He need not feare other things much that feares God much; for Feare which vsually destroys Courage, here turns into it: by Placing our

[23] Cf. *Style* 2.316.

[24] For other references, either literal or figurative, to Africans, see *Experimental History of Colours* 1.715 and 717; *Style* 2.289; *Specific Medicines* 5.82; and *Swearing* 6.11.

[25] Ps. 111:10.

Apprehension so wholly vpon one that it has (almost) none left for the rest. ↑See Ps. 46.2. Ps. 118.6. Pr. 14.26. and 29.25. Hosea 3,5. &c.↓ |f. 46|

XI. The Trust we are to repose in God is a Confidence that he will haue a care of vs and Protect vs from all Euill, as long as we endeuor by pursuing Lawfull Courses to deserue it: and that He will either Preserue vs from Euill or Turn /conuert/ that Euill to our Good. This Trismegistus, Plutarch and diuers of the Gentile Philosofers haue abundantly testify'd.[26] And this the holy Scriptures also witnesse, whence God is so frequently termed by the Saints their Buckler, their Sheld, the Rock of their Saluation, their strong Tower, and [all the] set out with all the greatest Epithetes of Assurance. The Ey of the Lord (says the Psalmist) is vpon them that feare him: vpon them that hope in his Mercy; to deliuer their Soule from Deth, and to keepe them aliue in Famin (Ps. 33. 18,19) and (Ps. 34.7.) The Angel of the Lord encampeth about them that Feare him, and deliuereth them and (Ps. 18.30) God is called a Buckler to all them that trust in him: |f. 46v| and (Ps. 125.1.) We are assured that They that trust in the Lord shall be as mount Sion that cannot be moued but abideth for Euer. And the whole 37 Ps. is thronged with Expressions of the like Nature. But tis heere to be obseru'd that God [requires] <expects> no ordinary trust at our hands: his Goodness and his Power, so much transcending the Common, require a Confidence suitable to the greatnesse /strength/ of it's motiues: and the better to persuade vs to it we may consider, that God vsually proportions his Protection to the [Trust] Confidence men repose in it: he is infinitely trusty when infinitely trusted; and there can be no stronger motiue to the Deity to releeue vs beyond our Hopes, then to trust in his Goodnes in spite of our Feares.

XII. Thus far of the Internall Worship of the Deity, the Externall is that [which] wherein the Body is vsed as an Instrument to express the Affections of the Mind. |f. 47| [And] For tho God being a Spirit, dos primarily require a Spirituall seruice; yet dos he also expect the Outward, both as an Expression of and helpe to, the Inward. <That> God, that created both the Body and the Soule will be glorifyd in both. [Our Adoration must be Spirituall because the Adored is a Spirit; but it must also be with the Body because the Adorers weare Flesh.] The [Adora] outward Worship without the Inward is but the Shaddow and the Carcase of Adoration: My Son giue me thy hart. (Pr. 23.26.) But withall we must not forget that Precept of our Sauior, (Matt. 5.16) Let your Light so shine &c. He that (Esay. 29.13) condemnes the Iewes for [Lips] drawing neere vnto him with their Mouth when their hart is remoued far from him; is the same that comands vs (Rom 12.1) To present our Bodys a Liuing Sacrifice vnto God which is our Reasonable seruice. What therefore God hath [en] joyned let no man diuide. He that worships not God |f. 47v| Inwardly forgets that God is a

[26] Cf. Cicero's extensive discussion of providence in *De Natura Deorum*, bks. 2-3.

Spirit; and he that dos it not outwardly, that Himself is a man. And certinly the Soule and Body ought not to be seuerd in the seruice that are sharers in the Wages. The King's Daughter is all Glorious within, (but) Her Clothing is of wrouht gold (Ps. 45.13.) Now the Principall Acts of this Externall Adoration are reckned 2, Prayer and Thankesgiuing: the one draws down Blessings from heu'n, and the other [returns] <sends vp> Prayses to it.

XIII. Prayer is Man's Petition to God, or that Speech wherein men Beg those things of their Maker that are vseful or necessary for them. The strange Power and Efficacy of Prayer tis not heere a fit Placc to insist vpon: (perhaps elsewhere in a Particular Treatise of Prayer the Reader may find it)[27] but certinly the very Heathen acknoledgd it to be so great, that Epictetus cud say, that if A man [rig] |f. 48| Did (as he ought) cal vpon God, he wud giue him Angels for his Counsellors.[28] Now he that wil make a succesfull <acceptable> Prayer, must Necessarily; 1. Ask iust and Expedient things: (for who puts vp to God an injust Petition, denys himselfe: whence Socrates said Wittily, that he did (without specifying) simply beg of God what was God, since God knew [Go] best what Good things were.)[29] 2. Consider attentiuely [h] what he says: (for how can he expect that God shud heed him that heeds not himselfe.) 3. Pray with Ernestnes and with the hart: (feruency being the feathers that wing our Prayers to make them pierce the skies; without which they wud tire <fall> by the way: God is a Spirit and heares onely the language of the Spirit: the bare Sound reaches not to Heu'n; and God heeres it not vnless it be to punish it.) 4. With Humility both inward and outward (The Sawcy Beggar inuites his own Denyal.) |f. 48v| 5. With Confidence <Faith>: (There is scarce any thing more contrary to the Nature of a Good Prayer then Distrust: of the [Doub] Distrustfull man saith St. Iames (Iam. 1.7) Let not that man Think that he shall receiue any thing of the Lord. And let not the Doubter doubt to be Deny'd.)

XIV. To Prayer is reduc't also Deprecation; whereby we petition the Deity for the Pardon of our Sins, and either to withhold his Imminent <pendent> or withdraw his Present Iudgments from vs. Hence Ouid

> Flectits iratus Voce rogante Deus,
> Prayers th'incensed Deity appease.[30]

But here we must obserue not only to beg the Remouall of our Plagues but principally to sue for the Pardon of those sins that caus'd them: otherwise either the Effect will not ceaze while the Cause continues; or if God do grant our Request,

---

[27] If RB wrote a treatise on prayer, it has not survived.

[28] Probably Epictetus, *Discourses* 1.16.15-21.

[29] Source unknown.

[30] Ovid, *Ars amatoria* 1.442. "Flectits" should read "flectitur."

it will be |f. 49| but in Anger (a Grant much worse then a Denyall) he may take away the Punishment but not the Iudgment <curse> and [ref] ceaze to correct because he meanes to destroy: as Masters oftentimes [refuse] <forbeare> to beate those Seruants that they resolue to turn away. The Gentiles in their more solemn Deprecations vs'd the Immolation of Sacrifices; [and] to suffer as it were by Proxy, ↑the Punishment of their Faults.↓ And by the Deth of Beasts, to confesse themselues Guilty of the like Punishment. Nature Indeed had taught them that sin was not to be clensed but with Blood: but alas they ignor'd that all those bleeding Lambs were but Types and [Sh] Emblems of that Immaculate Lamb that taketh away the Sins of the World; whose Deth shud bestow Life vpon the World, making an Atonement for the Iniquitys of Mankind: and whose sacred blood shud wash away the staines of the soule instead of that clotted blood of Bullocks and of Goats, to which it was as impossible to purify the soule as it was to easy to defile the Body. |f. 50|

XV. Thanksgiuing is a Part of God's Worship, whereby we return him Prayse & Thanks for all the Fauors he confers vpon vs. Epictetus his expressions herein are very Noble,[31] but he must yet giue [Pla] the Precedency to the Kingly Profet, who seems to employ his Breth to no other vse then to celebrate the Prayses of his Maker: the Examples are so obuious in the Salms and elsewhere, that I shall not need to specify. And certinly if we consider that we owe not only all that we haue, [to Go] to our Creator; we shal find a great deale of Iustice in the Psalmist's Resolution (Ps. 145.2) I will praise thy Name for euer and euer. Sure God's Fauors are very little worth if they are not worth thankes: and we must bee ingrateful in a high Extreame, if we deny Prayses to that God, whose Goodnes makes the vtmost of what we can do to be so due to Iustive, as scarce leaues vs a Possibility to exercize eu'n our Gratitude; [but] and extenuates <lessens> all our seruices into bare and |f. 50v| Defective Dutys. Shal the Hethen for far lesse obligations, crush the Altars with Hecatombs, and shall for greter Mercys be sparing of the Calues of our Lips, and redeem that expensive way of Sacrificing with that which the Apostle (Heb. 13.15) comands vnder the Title of the Sacrifice of Praise![32] Neither is this Thansgiuing onely an acknoledgment of Past Mercys, but a Procurer of Future: God Sowes Benefits, and looks to reape Prayses; where he finds a good Encrease, he casts in good store of seed, and giues there frequent occasions of praysing him, where he finds himselfe prays'd when he giues occasion: whereas he that shos himself vnthanfull for the first fauor, renders himself vnworthy of a second. But this Prayse to [be] <make it selfe> acceptable requires a Concurrence of the Soule and the Body: if the mouth only praise God, tis but lip-seruice: Thanksgiuing being a Spiritual kind of Sacrifice rather prouokes then Pleases, if it be not [per] offer'd by the Spirit.

[31] Epictetus, *Discourses* 1.16.15-21. Cf. Alsted 1265.

[32] Cf. Alsted 1265.

|f. 51r| Wherefore says the great [Artist] Craftsmaster at Prayses, (Ps. 86.12) I will praise thee o Lord my God with all my hart. And indeed the [onely] <best> harmony the Deity delights in, is, when the Tong is the Organs <Trumpet>, and is plaid vpon by the hart. Oh how [iustly ought] constant an Obligation haue we to sing Anthems to that God; whose goodnes to vs is so Strangely contriu'd; that those very Prayses which may seem to bring vs out of his Debt, engage vs more deeply in it: for tis none of the least fauors for which we ought to praise him, that he has giuen vs a hart to prayse him for his fauors.

XVI. Thus far of the seruice of God; whereby his Will is performed, remaines one Duty to treate of when his Will has been disobey'd: and that is Repentance, the grand Reconciler betwixt God and man, and the onely way to appeaze the offended Deity. ↑But of the Nature and parts of this Repentance already.↓ That the Heathen held this a Part of Diuine Worship, |f. 51v| may be easily gathered both out of many Testimonys extant on their Writings; and the fam'd Example of the Niniuites, (recorded in Ionas) whose Actions euidently witnesse in them both a Beleefe that the glowing fire of Diuine Fury was quenchable by penitent Tears; and a Hope to rake vp those Embers that were going to kindle into a Flame, in the penitent Ashe wherein they bury'd themselues during their 3-days Fast.[33] To Solemnize their Repentance they also vsed sacrifices, and with the [Deth of] Blood of [Bull] Heifers and of Rams thought to quench the Anger of their injur'd Gods. But tis very vnlikely that the Deity shud be pleased with the Destruction of those harmless Animals it self took pleasure to Creature: nor [that] can that be a Deity that has either appetite to need their sacrifices, or stomacke to disgest them. The sacrifice that is acceptable to that supreame Power, is not |f. 52r| to butcher [these[<our> Innocent Beasts that neuer offended him, but our Beastly Affections that Rebel against, and deface his Image, Reason.[34] The Immolation that the Deity requires, is not (that) of the Beasts we haue, but of the Beasts we are. And if this Repentance haue all the Requisites that God expects, his Goodnesse oftentimes makes it the occasion of a Neerer and Stricter [vn] Comunion betwixt himself and the Soule then was before: as bones once broken if <afterwards> well set, acquire a stronger Vnion then they had when they were whole.[35]

XVII. Hitherto of the more Immediate seruice of God, rests the more Mediate, or remote, that is rendered to him by our Vertuus Behauior towards men, as Vertu tends to his Glory. Of this says our Sauior, ( ) Let your Liht so shine &c.[36] And certinly there can be no greater seruice to God [then] nor hiher expression of our Zeale to him, then to make his Will the Square of our [Action]

---

33 Jon. 3:1-10.

34 Cf. *Usefulness* 2.63 and *Swearing* 6.13.

35 RB reviewed the claims for the accelerated healing of broken bones in *Usefulness* 2.194-95.

36 Matt. 5:16.

Lifes, and coppy out his Axions in ours. |f. 52v| Alas the Deity enjoying so perfect and supreame [endeauor] a Happines cannot receaue the least Addition of Felicity by all our vtmost services: but appoints our Fellow-creatures his Receiuers (and Substitutes) to whom whatsoeuer Good we do he reputes don vnto himselfe, as the kindnes we show to a man's Children or his seruants, is interpreted a Seruice to their Father or their Master. My Goodness (says Dauid) extendeth not to thee, But to the Saints that are in the Earth &c (Ps. 16.2,3) As on the other side tis no sleight Disseruice that is don to God by [a] iniustice to men: since we cannot debase our selues below our owne Dignity without defacing and wronging his Image; which prouokes him, as a Father whips /chides/ the Child he loues for falling, tho himself only feel the smart of the Fall. And since the End of God in our Creation was to communicate his Goodness to [his] vs; we can not but offend him when we |f. 53r| Necessitate him to withhold and restraine that Bounty, by making our selues vnworthy and incapable of receiuing it. So great is God's loue to man kind, that his very Anger proceeds from his Loue and Nothing incenses him agenst Mortals, but that they will not giue him leaue (if I may so speake) without wronging his Iustice, to make them happy. Wherefor the sacrifice that is acceptable to the Deity, is not to Sacrifice our Cattel to him but our Vices. To which purpose I remember a handsom answer of a Sister of mine; who when one told her that the Seuerity of her Vertu had frihted such and such young Gallants from talking loosely in her Company; presently made answer, That she thought her self very hihly oblig'd to them: for she tooke for a far les honor that they [illeg.] shud keep of their Hats to her then their Vices.[37]

XVIII. Thus far of Piety in it selfe. The Vices opposite thereunto are in Excesse, Superstition, in Defect, Impiety.[38] |f. 53v|

XIX. They are calld Superstitius, that are in a perpetuall and Anxious apprehension of the Deity, which fearing all ways to be angry with them, they endeuor to appease and gaine its fauor; by the too strict and Nice Obseruation of outward ceremonyes, or adding to God's Worship vncomanded seruices.[39] People, that as our Sauior describes the Farisees (Matt. 23.23) Pay Tithe of Mint and Cumin, and omit the weightier matters of the Law, Iudgment, Mercy, Faith. Like the hypocriticall Iewes (Iohn 18.28) that made Conscience to enter a Pagan's house, but scrupled not to do the Deuils Worke, in murdering the Lord of Life.

---

[37] Cf. *Swearing* 6.17, *Style* 2.305, and Lady Ranelagh's letter about Waller (6.521).

[38] Alsted 1264.

[39] RB recalled that in Rome he "cud not chuse but smile, to see a Young Churchman after the seruice ended, vpon his knees carefully with his feet sweepe into his handkercheefe the Dust his holynesse's (Gowty) feet, had by treading on it consecrated, as if it had been some Miraculous Relique" (Maddison 42). RB thought the College of Cardinals looked like "Common Fryers," his codeword for superstition and hypocrisy.

An vsuall Companion of Superstition is Idolatry: when men will see what they worship; and adore that for their Maker which themselues made. This was so grosse [that] amongst the Ancient hethen, that [no less then 30000 Gods] they might haue muster'd vp their |f. 54r| Deitys by Legions (a good Author affirms they had 30000)[40] and conquer a Kingdom with an Army of Men les numerous then was that of their Gods. Such were also the Inhabitants of an American Iland (newly conuerted by a Protestant marchand who ador'd a wooden Bell, [to] to whose seruice were dedicated, onely the 2 Eldest women in the whole Island, Fit Priests for such a Deity.[41] To omit the ancient Romans, that cud brooke all Religions but the Christian (as indeed all Colors agree well enuf in the Darke.) Now as for superstition, me thinks tis od, that we shud Confess God to be infinitely wise, and yet not allow him wise enuf to chuse his owne Worship; (a fauor seruants deny not to their Masters amongst vs) and that we shud think to make our [selues] <Seruice> more acceptable to God by adding to his Will, when the onely thing that delights him in them is their suitablenes to his Will. Hence Samuel tels Saule (1 Sam. 15.22.) that Obedience is better then Sacrifice: and our Sauior |f. 54v| speaking of the Iewes, (Matt. 15.9) says, that, In vaine [do] they <do> worship me, teaching for Doctrines the Comandements of Men.

XX. Impiety is a Word of a very large signification, being oftentimes taken for [any] all things that are contrary to any Vertu: but in this Place we onely meane by it, that Particular Vice, that is [oppos] the Defectiue extreame in the Worship of the Deity. And vnder this Notion, it comprehends. 1. Atheists either grosse, such as simply deny God in his Essence, or those that deny him by Consequence, stripping him of those Prerogatiues that are Essentiall to the Deity;[42] for the simplicity of God being so perfect, that his Attributes are him self (according to the Maxime of the Diuines, Quicquid in Deo est, Deus est, What soeuer is in God, is God); he that Denys the One is conceiued also to deny the Other.[43] As he that denys a Piece of mony to be Yellow, [or] <and> Malleable, or <so> heauier then Iron <Siluer> denys it by consequence to be |f. 55r| Gold. Of that Former bestiall kind of Atheists, I beleeue the World affords but very few, and am confident that there are farr more Atheists in Thesis then in

[40] Cf. Alsted 1265.

[41] RB had a life-long interest in missionary work among the Indians. Jacob surveys RB's support for such projects (148-55).

[42] This is RB's earliest reference to atheism. For later discussions, see *Usefulness* (2.55); *Style* (2.253, 278); *Occ. Refl.* (2.347, 427); *Continuation of New Exp.* (3.274); *Vulgar Notion* (5.158, 163, 192); *Chr. Virtuoso* (5.514-15, 534); *Greatness of Mind* (5.550); and his correspondence (6.58, 59, 445, 448, 450, 514, 516). In a very late inventory of boxes in RB's home (17 September 1691), he referred to "14. A folio Pastbord case, writt upon Papers relating to ye Causes of Atheism" (BP 36.122v).

[43] That awareness of God's attributes should lead to veneration is an argument developed in *High Veneration* (5.132ff, 144-46) and *Exc. of Theol.* (4.14, 21-22).

Opinion, and ten out of Van<it>y for one that is so out of Beleefe. For the beleefe that there is a Deity, is so naturally ingrauen in the harts of men, that tho there be nothing that [men] gos more against men's stomacks then to submit themselues to a Superior; yet in this Case men are carried so strongly against that Inclination, that they will rather worship a Serpent or a Stone for a Deity then haue <serue> none at all. ↑(Hence [said] that Ancient Filosofer pronounced him vnworthy of Arguments but one to be confuted with blows and fagots that deny'd the Existence of a Deity.[44] Nor dos [the illeg.] the vniversall consent of Nations onely, but that of Natures also, assert this truth: The World and all the Creatures in it vnanimously conspiring to proclaime the Essence and Glory of their Maker.↓ If [God] the existence of God be but a Fiction those that beleeue it none are as safe from the Imagin'd Fury as are the Atheists. But if there be really such a thing as a God, what may not the others feare.[45] Certinly, if we will take the Paines to consider, we shall find that the most part of these Atheists ↑(the Wickednes of their Liues considered)↓ do but speake as they wish, and affirm that there is no god, because it |f. 55v| Were good for them there were None. And as for that Grand Objection <Argument> they so much build vpon: the sad multitude of contrary Religions, certinly it makes very little to their purpose; since the particular Religions disagree amongst themselues, yet they all agree agenst them: and tho they dissent in euery thing else, yet they all concur in acknoledging a God. 2. Machiauillians; of whom already.[46] 3. Profane Persons. Such as are not Atheists in their Opinions but in ther Liues. And vse to Scoffe at Religion, and call those Puritans, and nice, squeamish Fooles that profess it.[47] ↑In this work then the Atheists, that their Knoledge, (like that of the Deuill) serues but to render them inexcusable: it being [far] a Less sin not to confess the God we prouoke, then to prouoke the God we confesse. As he deserues a gentler punishment that offends the King beleeuing him a Common man /under the notion of &c/ then he that injures him notwithstanding the Knoledg that he is a King.↓ Such was that Filosofer (Hermelaus) Barbarous who complain'd that reading of the Bible had lost him his Latine:[48] and that Traueller (who shall heere be nameless) that hauing enjoy'd a Nun in the Forenoon and a Whore in the Afternoone, brag'd at night, that [in one day] he had |f. 56r| Cuckolded both God and the Deuill <in one Day.>[49] But of these more in a fitter

---

[44] I have found no specific source for this observation.

[45] RB's statement anticipated Pascal's "wager" about the existence of God.

[46] RB has scattered references to Machiavellians in the *Aret.* and *Style*, but his reference here is otherwise obscure.

[47] Cork used 'Puritan' derisively. Before leaving Ireland, Mary Boyle was "stead-fastly set against being a puritan" (Canny 34-35; Mendelson 80).

[48] For this anecdote about Hermolaus, see Ada Adler, ed., *Suidae Lexicon* 1.416. Cf. Alsted 1265.

[49] This claim may be Tom Killigrew's (*II Lismore* 4.235). But such braggadocio was also fea-

Chapter.) 4. Lastly. The gross and wilfully Ignorant: That shut their Eyes against the light for feare they shud see themselues out of the way: and are resolued not to know their Duty, for feare their Consciences shud press them to perform it. But these People shud consider that twill neuer pas for an Apology with God that we Did not his Will because he did not kno it, if we refus'd to kno it that we might not be oblig'd to do it.[50] We do not onely whip that Schooleboy that Copys out scuruily the Example that is giuen him, but we vse the like Punishment for him that wil not come to Schoole to take the Example he shud coppy. Ignorance dos not excuse a Fault when it is one.

XXI. Thus haue we presented yow with a ruf Draught of Piety: such as cud be delineated by the Dim [light] |f. 56v| Twilight of Nature: <to> which many things might haue been added, but that this Discourse being calculated for no particular Religion, was to insist onely /cheefly/ [but] vpon those dutys that are common to [(al most)] all. That the Liht of reason (as to Piety) might haue been improued to a much hiher pitch then euer the most cry'd vp Gentiles did, I am very willing to confess: and that diuers of the hethen Filosophers, had very noble sparkes and glympses of this Light, I will not [also] <likewise> deny: prouided it be granted on the other side, that they were but meere Darkness, or at best but [faint] obscure Shaddowes in Comparaison of the bright Sun shine of the Gospell. For certinly many of the Filosofers were doutfull of his Essence, all <most of them> Ignorant of his Nature. Hence <oftentimes> they that in the Singular Number cal'd the Deity, God, wud [oft] instantly (as it were) forget themselues, and all in a breth, giue him that plurall Name, |f. 57r| The Gods; as incertin which of the 2 were most agreable to his [illeg.] Nature. Hence the Diuinest of the Filosofers (Plato in Cratylo) conscious of his owne and [other's blind] the blindness of Filosofy, in this Particular, introduces Socrates swearing, That if they wud ingeniously confess the Truth, they knew nothing, neither of the Gods nor of their Names.[51] And the Christian Stoick (Seneca) pronounces that God dwels in euery body, but yet tis incertin who that God is.[52] Nor was their Worship <of God> much better then their Knoledg: the Delphic Oracle [aske] being consulted to kno which way God shud be worshipt, made answer, Ciuitatis more, according to the Custom of our Dwelling Place: but it being replyd that the Customs of the Citty are subject to frequent Changes, it added, Optimum esse sectandum, that the best must be follow'd.[53] It seems then that those that had recourse to the Oracle were before ignorant of the manner of seruing God: nor were they |f. 57v| by this Answer a Iot the Wiser, the Oracle indeed telling them

---

tured in Mateo Aleman's *The rogue, or the life of Guzman de Allafarache* (1622), which RB owned.

[50] Cf. the discussion of ignorance in the *Aret.* (bk. 2, ch. 3).

[51] Cf. *Cratylus* 397.

[52] Seneca, *Epistulae Morales* 41.1.

[53] Cf. Alsted 1265.

in generall termes that they shud do what was best, but giuing them no particular Instructions of what was Best to Doo. Suitable to this [K] imperfect conception of God, were their Performances to him. They acknoledg'd indeed God to be Omnipotent and Wise, but scarce any considered him as their Particular Benefactor. They fear'd him, not as a louing father, but a Reuengfull Iudge. Their <Vertuus> Actions were directed not to his Glory but their owne, or at best but to gaine a certin Tranquillity of Mind which they always considered more then his Fauor. Their Rule of his Worship with them, was their own Reason, not his Will: and [they] ↑the best of them↓ were apt to murmure at the <Iustice of the> Gods whensoeuer they saw vnfortunate Vertu or Lucky wickedness. They pray'd with a Hope as incertin |f. 58r| as the Notion they had of the Deity they implor'd: and their Repentance was rather a Punishment inflicted by their Anger'd Conscience then a[n Ilumination] <Sacrifice> to appease the injur'd Deity. These Considerations I thought conuenient for this Place, that we may see how high (or rather how low) the wings of naturall Reason will [lift] carry vs towards Heu'n: that seeing with such slender helps the Filosofers cud raise themselues to such a Pitch as many of them did;[54] we might be asham'd of our Improficiency (in Piety) that haue the ods of Diuinity to boot: that we might quicken our Thankfullnes to God for the Gifts of so cleare a Liht, and carefull to improue it, lest the Hethen rise vp in iudgment against vs, that kept their way better by [the dim li] Starlight; then we do at Noone Day: and that seeing how [owle-eyd] purblind the Wisest men are by Nature in the Misterys of [the Seruice] Salvation, |f. 58v| and those things that concern their euerlasting happinesse, we may confesse with the Apostle (1 Cor. 2.14) that The Natural man receiueth not the things of the spirit of God, for they are foolishness vnto him: neither can he kno them, because they are spiritually discerned: and [how] what need we haue of the spirit of truth that will guide vs into all Truth. (Iohn 16.13.) It thus acknoledges that No man knoweth the Father save the son, and he to whomsoeuer the Son will reueale him: [we may with Z] we may cry out (but in a [better] ↑more spirituall↓ sence) with [Filip] that Apostle, (Iohn 14.8) Lord show vs the Father: ↑This is Life Eternall to kno thee the onely tru God and Iesus Christ whom thow has sent (Io. 17.3) and that↓ and with the Kingly Profet, (Ps. 119.18) Open thou mine Eyes, that I may behold wondrows things out of thy Law.

[54] This passage is RB's earliest discussion of the limitations of Reason, a topic to which he often returned (cf. *Vulgar Notion* 5.174). In early 1647 Worsley, Hall, and Hartlib corresponded about "whether the Scriptures be an adequate Iudge in physicall controversies" (HP 36/6/1-3).

The Doctrine of Thinking

|f. 4|

Amongst that great Variety of Employments which I haue fancy'd to take vp my thoughts with, I haue scarce found any more noble nor more worthy of them then the Contemplation of themselues.[1] Tis tru that [it is a Scrutiny somewhat] the Diuing into their Nature is a Scrutiny of no small Difficulty, our Thoughts being of the Number of those things that are much more Easily comprehended then expresed: and like the greatest part of men, are no where more ignorant then they are at home. Wherefore leauing <to leasurd [Schoo] hermits> the Nice and Perplext speculations [to them that haue both |f. 5| Lerning and Leasure to insist vpon them,] I shall [roundly] content my self to fall onely vpon the Practicall Part of the Doctrine of thoughts, which consists in their [Relu orderi] Regulation [only] and Improuing; induc't therevnto by [illeg.] a throng of President in Naturall things, wherein we are very Ready in the Vses of many things, of which we totally <altogether> ignore the Nature. Neither let any man be discouraged by the Vulgar mistake, that [fancy] beleeue Thoughts so bootlesse and so vnruly that they haue made [it] <them> the Hyperbole of freedom: since tho indeed our Thoughts do not perhaps admit that Strictness of restraint, that awes our speaches and our Actions: yet that they will admit of some reasonable Rule, this whole Discourse will (I hope) [bring] <put> out of question. And truly (me thinks) that to maintaine that those fountaines of all we do, Our Thoughts, shud haue no channell, is to do like the |f. 5^{v}| Flatterers of Tyrants, that persuade them, that they that giue the Law to all the World, are exempt from it [th] /shud [obey] <be without it> regard none/ themselues. I shall therefore for the Present make my Thoughts there owne Theame, and cast my Obseruations vpon this Subject into the following Directions.

---

[1] This essay is found in MS 197. Ff. 1-3 are blank. The MS consists of small sheets pasted to larger sheets and then bound. RB's own title for the MS is illegible, and so I have supplied the title, "The Doctrine of Thinking." In "Of Time and Idleness" he refers to a work as his "doctrine of thinking" (BP 14.17^{v}). In the inventory of his writings made on 25 January 1650, he referred to several essays that might be included under this title (see Table 1). On f. 3^{v} he wrote a barely legible epigraph: "[illeg.] wud rather [ex] perplex then Instruct most those I heere desire to informe." The importance of regulating one's thoughts was stressed in "Dayly Reflection" as well as in "Of Sin" and the *Aret*. RB's influence on John Locke is well examined in Peter Alexander's *Ideas, Qualities and Corpuscles: Locke and Boyle on the External World* (Cambridge 1985). RB recognized the importance and the difficulty of scrutinizing how the mind worked and contented himself here with practical advice.

Direction

1.) Think often. I haue seldom compared the Benefits of Meditation with the sliht [most] men make of it, without concluding it one of the Arch-Policys of the Deuill to endeauor by all kind of Meanes to bring that into Disesteeme, whose Practice he cannot but foresee so destructiue to his Designes. And this Conjecture will easily appeare not to be |f. 6| vngrounded, if we do but take a survey [of] both of the Pleasure and the Profit it affords vs. And for the First, Certinly it's owne Greatness is an obstacle to it's Comprehension: for from whence haue all the Sciences of the World been deduced but out of our owne Thoughts: 'tis from them that they pump whatsoeuer they haue written of handsom, that are Authors and not Copyists. /Transcribers./ And tho we may learn most things [by] out of Books, where did they learn them that first compoz'd those books. We haue bread indeed from the Bakers but the Baker must be beholding to the Plowman for the Corn that makes it. The Pythagoreans whose [Sect] Fame in Filosofy has suruiued such a Multitude of successiue |f. 7| Succeeding Ages, tooke a Course to deserue the Reputation they had acquir'd; by [silencing] <bridling> the Tong, and [giuing the Reins to] <spurring> the Thoughts. Had all men been as carelesse of Thinking as most men are, the World might til it's Dotage haue [bin] embrac't the Errors of it's Infancy; and for a More Cleare liht of things <we> might haue stayd till the last great Fire. Alas if men haue been able to [light vpon] <descry> so many Truths and vnmaske so many Mistakes, when they do [but as it] scarce more then take Notice of those onely Errors that ly in their Way, and but stumble <(as it were)> vpon the Truths <they find> how [much] many do yow think will their Discouerys liht vpon, when those same Searching Sir Francis Drakes of Knoledge (our Thoughts) that before were but Trauellers (Passengers) in the Mind, shall grow to be Inhabitants?

The Experiments of this I haue |f. 8| lately Seen in those I haue had the Happiness to be acquainted with of the Filosoficall Colledge:[2] who all confess themselues to be beholding for [most p] the better part of their rare and New-coynd Notions to the Diligence and Intelligence of their Thoughts. And sure most men are guilty of his mistake [that lookt] searcht <ransackt> all the Corners of the House for the Gloue he had vpon <in> his hand: like many Book Fisitians, that trouble the Indies for those exoticke (and vsually sophisticated) Drugges against Popular Diseases, when they might rather [more pr] simple <for> more Preualent against those sicknesses in their own Gardens.[3] But he that

---

[2] For discussions of the Invisible College, see Webster 57-67; Maddison 67-72; Jacob 28-37; and Canny 142-43. RB's comment about the "Great Filosofer" who had found a way to sanitize foul water is another comment on the workings of this group ("Of Sin" ff. 33-33^{v}).

[3] This passage is slightly garbled, but the meaning is clear. For a later expression of this same position, see *Simple Medicines* 5.111.

will not yet beleeue the Strange Efficacy of pursued Thoughts, which way soeuer they apply themselues; let him but consider our newfashiond Plays and our Modern Romances:[4] <that> what perfection they haue been capable to giue so meane[r] and barren a Theame as Loue; and if Rauing can fly so high, to how lofty a Pitch Meditation may soare, and I am confident he shall meet no other Remedy [of] <to cure> his vnbeleefe.[5] |f. 8v| And then for the Pleasure of Thinking, certinly tis very little Inferior to the Benefit: the Thoughts like the Katerers of the Mind trauelling through the whole Vniuerse of things to bring vs in all the Variety of Delights. Nay it workes Impossibilitys for our Content, for it recalls Time, reuiuing and giuing a Present existence /being/ to our past Delights, and anticipating our Future Happines with the Liuely Company of the Pleasing Ideas of those lou'd Objects. Nor are we heere forc't to be beholding to outward Goods for our Enjoyment of them: no, our Plesures are within vs, [bounded] that admit no Limits but what we are pleased to giue them: and can furnish vs out a Feast without troubling either the [Butcher] <shambles> or the Cooke. These kind of Pleasures [mo] take most with the Soule, because most suitable to her Nature: for shee being but a kind of Prisoner in this Carkas, neuer receaues Delights so pure and vntroubled, as those that are free from the Disturbances she receaues [by] <from> the Dull Comerce of the Body. And to this Purpose we reade of diuers Solitary Friers that haue so lost themselues in the Delights of |f. 9| Contemplation, as for diuers meales together to forget to giue hungry <half starued> Nature the least part of her due, scorning to be diuerted from those Nobler Contentments, by those meane Pleasures of the Mouth and Belly which it shall be a part of our Happiness one day to want.

I haue knowne the Time that were I permitted to name the Sin I wud be priuiledgd in, my Choice shud haue pitcht vpon the Liberty of Thinking what I listed: which alone shud [bring be] <make me tast> the Sweets of all the Rest: and that perhaps in the most Pleasing <taking> Dresse: for the Fruition of sinfull Pleasures always falls short of the happiness of the Imagination: which represents vs those delihts in their most [perf cha] perfect and most charming Ideas, seuer'd from the Inconueniences, and stript of all those Euils that vsually attend their Enjoyment.[6] He that can conceiue a Strong Imagination to be but a Waking Dreame, and has euer felt how Sensible are the Delights our Dreames do

[4] For contemporary attitudes toward the theatre, see Jonas Barish, *The Antitheatrical Prejudice* (Berkeley 1981) and Martin Butler, *Theatre and Crisis* (Cambridge 1984).

[5] RB wrote "vnbeleefe" in such a way that it filled most of the line. "Right thinking" was a kind of meditating, and thus thoughts should be governed by the same systematic procedures recommended for daily meditation. In *Philaretus*, RB illustrated the dangerous connection between raving, literature, and melancholy (17). Like Burton, RB found that algebra was a useful curative (*Anatomy* 2.95; "Doctrine of Thinking," and Maddison 17-18). For a later use of "raving," see *Vulgar Notion* 5.175.

[6] Cf. the *Aret.* (bk. 2, ch. 4).

sometimes afford vs, will [need to great Entreaty] <be easily persuaded> to assent to this Truth. And indeed I am |f. 10| Afraid, that as to <for> them that ar much Conuersant with their owne Thoughts, I must make it much more my Taske to Moderate the Greatnes of the Pleasure of Thinking, then to proue it.

2.) Think not Sinfull Thoughts. He that thinkes that a Thought cannot be a Sin, sins in that Thought. And that [very] scuruy Prouerbe that Thoughts are Free,[7] (which the Vulgar make a kind of Magna Charta for the Liberty or rather licentiusnes of Thinking) is as false as [what] <the Thouts> it countenances are vaine, if it be vnderstood of thc Permitted not the Vsurped Liberty: and giues our Thoughts as full an Immunity from the Commandements of God as they haue from the Laws of men. But because [this Truth] I feare this Truth will proue somwhat too censorious a Guest to be easily [admit] <readily entertained> we shall make way for it's admittance by the <ample> Recommendations both of Scripture and of Reason. |f. 11| As for the first, We shall not <long> doubt that thoughts may be sinfull, if we consider, that They defile the Man, (Matt. 15, 19) that ↑[That] they are an Abhomination to the Lord, (Pr. 15.26.)↓ Christ himself Rebukes the Farisees for them, Matt 9,4. that They are to be Repented of, Esay 55,7. Are capable of Pardon, and so conclude Offences, Acts 8,22, which certinly they are in so high a Degree that our Sauior, Matt 15.19 giues them the Van of Murder, Adultery, Fornication, Theft, False-witness and Blasphemy. And therefore [tho tis ve] which is very obseruable [that] in the 6 of Genesis when God resolues to drowne the World and wash away the Sinners with their Sins tho the Wicked <Monsters> of that Age were doubtlesly no les [vil] Giants in their Vices then their Statures, yet the maine <only> Cause that [is there specifyd <(v. 5)> to] had the Power to [wri force] prouoke so fatall <heui> and so vniuersall a Iudgment /Destiny/ is in the 5 verse specifyd to be, [the Wickednes of the Thoughts and Imagination] that euery Imagination of the thoughts of man's hart was onely Euill [and that] continually. |f. 12| Nor dos Reason les strongly assert the Sinfulnes of Thoughts: for they being the First Motioners of (wel neere) all the Euils in vs; and the Springs whereof our Actions are but the Streames, cannot be Innocents, when their Effects are Guilty. Wicked Thoughts, are the Eue's of the Soule <Mind> that sho it the Forbidden Fruit, tell it tis Louely to the Ey, delightfull <sweet> to the Tast, put it into the Mouth and persuade him to eat it.

[The Soule has very seldom comitted Adult] Bad Thoughts are those Sins in the Seed which euill Actions are in the Eare: Thoughts being but Internall Actions and Actions but Externall <actuated> Thoughts. And certinly the Soule has very seldom playd the whore with any Object but Vitius Thoughts have been the Pandars <Procurers>; and therefore in the 55 Esay and the 7 The Thoughts

---

[7] Cf. T244.

are made as it were the starting post of Repentance, [w fr] whence the vprighteus man must set forth that intends <designs> [to] <a> Return to the Lord.

Now amongst that great Multiplicity of Sinfull Thoughts, there are 2 Kinds that are very Eminent |f. 13| and of a Large Extent, which we shall Christen Speculatiue Wickedness and Intentionall Euills, [of] <into> whose Nature and Branches, tho a[n exact hand] <more particular> enquiry be not of the Design of this Discourse, yet [tis] twill not be perhaps amisse to take Notice, that Speculatiue Wickedness is that which (for example) in a Letcher builds a Baudy-howse, peoples it with a Charming Venus <temting ladys>, prouides a Pimp, [that] takes hold of an Opportunity, brings them <the Lady and his Master> together, and makes him enjoy her with the hihest gustos of sensuality, and all this in the Imagination; by Ideas of our own Framing, which oftentimes affect [no] <little> less then the Reall Embraces that we burn for. And this kind of Sinning has a Cozen German that we may call Memoratiue Wickedness; ↑(Which is a kind of Chewing the Cud after the committing of a Sin.)↓ when men do as it were put forth a Second Edition of the Same Sin, and conjure vp their past Delihts to make them act their Parts agen, as the Sick Drunkard that pledges <drinks> more helths with his Thoughts then euer he did with his Mouth ↑(making himself at once both the Drinker, the Drawer and the Wine.)↓ But sure these kind of Sins are not so triuiall as men wud make them |f. 14| for [no] besides their Frequency and vndiscernedness (whereby they easily grow habituall and hardly curable) they haue this of particular malignity, that they can be committed in the Absence of the Object, and a man may this way be drunk without Wine, and Wench without a Whore.[8] Neither is the Pleasing Memory of our Past Faults more Innocent; for euery Time we reuiue those Delights <Sins>, we repeat them, since we cannot sincerely repent the Doing of those Things that we take a Pleasure to think done: nor can he reasonably be suppos'd by bare Conscience to be bar'd from the Committing of those things for which he applauds himself when they are committed: Approbation being but a kind of late <after> consent. And these same After-sins [are r] do often times continue in the very Impotency of sinning otherwise; as the diseased Old man <dotard> whom Vices haue deserted rather then he them, will repeate the Dissoluteness of his Wilder Age, emptying whole Cellars and lying with whole Serralio's in his Thoughts, when perhaps he miht be fudled with as much Wine, as |f. 15| men in burning feauers dare drink aqua vitæ and haue needed Marrow and Eringo roots aboue these 20 yeares.[9] And sure whilst the <a> Delight in remembring Sin remaines [wi] in

---

[8] RB returned to an attack on the reasoning behind sin: the belief that some sins were small, a topic also discussed in the *Aret.* (bk. 2, ch. 6) and in "Of Sin."

[9] Eryngo is "the candied root of the Sea Holly (*Eryngium maritimum*), formerly used as a sweetmeat, and regarded as an aphrodisiac" (*OED*). Aqua vitæ includes any ardent spirits or unrectified alcohol.

spite of the Impotency of Committing it, the same Euill is Acted and the Scene <Stage> only chang'd <alter'd> (I meane transferd from the Bed or the Tauerne to the Braine.) For God as well in Vices as in Vertus takes the Will for the Deed:[10] and those that haue lost the Power of offending without the Desire <loue>, [tho they] abstaine <indeed> from the Act, but not at all from the sin. As for Intentionall Euils (which less properly belong to this Place [which] <that shud> handle[)] but the Meditatiue Faculty of the Soule) the Lawes of Men themselues haue in som Cases pronounc't them Criminall, as iudging rightly, that the bad Intention (by example of murdering a King) proceeded from their owne Wickedness, and the Nonexecution meerly from the Almighty's Goodness, who is too narrow a Searcher of Hearts, not to condemne Murder [in] as well in the Will as in the Hand:[11] As the Scriptures |f. 16| do most frequently wittness. And indeed Thoughts <Intents> (or Sins in the Nest,) are but callow Actions, and Actions but fledg'd Thoughts <Intents>. Neither will the Vulgar excuse satisfy, that [tho] a man <oftentimes> takes delight in thinking of those Sins which Tortures shud not force him really to commit; for besides that 'tis very difficult to keep the Streames clean that flow from a Polluted fountain: besides the perpetuall entercourse betwixt the Braine and the hart, and the potent <powerful> influence that has vpon the other.[12] Besides that we conceiue a far les horror of the outward acting of those sins that we haue been vs'd to commit within; besides all these, I say, dayly Experience is but too sad a Witness that many that entertaine sins in their Thoughts with [a] <very> strong Resolues to confine them to the Braine, haue easily afterwards been temted to grant them a Loding in the hart. Like many of those that [we f] <we see> run mad for the loue of those butys that at first they went to visit out of meere Curiosity. But if all this cannot preuaile, [do but con] <I must refer yow |f. 17| [Consider] <to> that [Excellent] <dredfull> Genealogy <extant> in St Iames 1,14,15, But euery man (says he) is temted when he is drawne away of his owne Lust and entised; then when Lust hath Conceiued it Bringeth forth Sin, and Sin, when it is finished, bringeth forth Deth.

3) Abstaine from vaine Thoughts. I must not [heere] <in this place> insist vpon the Vanity that [may be] is incident to the manner of our Thinking, since that will fall vnder seuerall and distinct heads heereafter: but onely vpon that Vanity that is vsuall in the Choice of the Subject or Theame of our Thoughts; which we heere call Vnprofitable, to discriminate those Vaine Thoughts we handle heere from those sinfull ones we haue tuch't vpon already. Tho perhaps, that Vnprofitable Thoughts, if too long dwelt vpon, are not without som small

[10] Cf. *Theodora* 5.291.

[11] RB touched on this theme in the *Aret*. (bk. 2, ch. 1 and 3).

[12] Cf. the letter to Marcombes, where RB discussed the movement in his *Ethics* from the brain to the breast (1.xxxiv).

/mixture/ <slice, tast> of Sinfulness, were a task of no greate Difficulty to proue. Now the most remarkable Vanity in the Text (if I may so term it) of our Thoughts; is, when we [make] <faine> a supposition [of a] and then in our Thoughts descant vpon it, and Imagine |f. 18| Actions and Successes suitable to it's Nature. Thus the Absent <fond> Louer, he fancys himself in his Mistresse's Presence, makes <pronounces> her set speeches of the greatness <excess> of his Passion, puts [fauorable] <kind> answers into her Mouth, and <places> smiles [into] <vpon> her Face, and hugs himself [with] <in> this Imaginary Happiness, with little less content then he wud reape from the Reality of her Affection.[13] Thus the Ambitious Fauorite, in his Fancy erects himself a Throne, seats himself in it, and creates a Thousand Fauning Courtiers that with their supple knees, pay <doe> homage to his greatnesse. Thus the vaine Female, that like a Peacock's <illeg.> Traine, is esteem'd onely for the Color, tricks her self <vp> in her Imagination with all that Dress or Clothes or Art can contribute of most exquisite to the Ornament of Nature and then assembles in a Trice those Gallants she most desires to be lou'd by, appeares to him [in] with those Irresistible aduantages, that [captiuate her Freedoms and] <make them all her Idolators:> and then acts a Triumph in her self worthy such a Conquest, and resents a Reall Pleasure from the Thought of their Imaginary Paines. Thus the self conceited <poet> Scholler, composes a Peece suitable <not> to his [Desires] Abilitys but his Desires, Reads it to all those of whom he ambitions the Esteeme, and with extasies of Ioy conceits the Admiration of the wondring /rauisht/ hearers at euery Periode. |f. 19| Thus he whose [Fortu] <Estate> fals short of his Desires, carues himself out a Fortune of 10000 pound a Yeare, [and then bus th] with which, heere he builds a stately howse; there, he railes in a [goodly] <wel stord> Parke, heere he digs a [spacious] <swarming> Fish-pond, and there he plants a Fruitfull orchard. This Place he designes for a warren, and this other for a Garden, which he embroiders <amel> with all the rarest Flowers our owne or forraine Climats can afford.[14] And thus we fancy to our selues, <the> Conditions, <we most affect> and then busy our Thoughts how to dispose of them and <to> behaue our selues in them.[15] (And therefore I esteeme this one of the surest Tuch-stones of our

[13] For contrasting examples of such texts, see "Joseph's Mistress" below and another early piece, "To my Mistress" (BP 37.164-65), which is dated 2 May 1645.

[14] At Lismore, Canny argued, "Cork sought to reshape the surrounding landscape in imitation of the surrounds of an English lordly mansion. The importance which this assumed for Cork can be gauged from the fact that the development and stocking of a deer park, the selection and grafting of fruit trees, the making of fish ponds, the development of a stud, the erection of eyries, the contraction of a rabbit warren . . . all assume as much importance in Cork's correspondence as the clearing of forests, the building of castles, towns and fortifications or the development of iron smelting or the erection of religious and educational foundations: they all contributed . . . to shaping the countryside—especially that adjacent to Lismore—after the English fashion" (Canny 72).

[15] For RB's disappointment over the breakage of his furnace and his subsequent loss of "fine

Inclinations, to obserue vpon what objects our Thoughts do the most frequently and voluntarily liht /pitch or, dwell/[16] since according to that of our sauior ( )[17] where our Treasure is, there will our hart be also. The Vanity then of Thoughts that we wud heere Restraine, is their Vnprofitableness, which is most conspicuus in those thoughts that are built vpon, [vnlikely or] impossible, vnlikely or vseless suppositions <hypotheses>, (which is) commonly cald Rauing which is nothing but a Play or a Romance personated <acted> in the Braine /Imagination./[18] But yet this kind of Thinking, so it be neither too long, too frequent nor at times vnseasonable, is not (perhaps) absolutely to be condemn'd. |f. 20| For certinly, if it be permitted to vs to spend oftentimes diuers of our [Thoug] Words and of our Actions in <for> our Recreation, I know not why we [may not] shud be forbidden that Liberty in our Thoughts; specially when they ar much more free from Inconueniences then the other, and can oftentimes sweeten and diuert our Cares in the Absence of all other Recreations, and somtimes too in our Impotency to make vse of them tho to be come by. Neither see I any Reason why it shud not be equally Lawfull to Think Playes and Romances, or to Read or see them. Neither are we oblig'd to belieue so precise an vselesness in all those Thouhts that descant vpon Imaginary Hypotheses as the more Censorious Affirm, since certinly they often excercise both the Wit and Iudgment very much; as is euident by the Practice of the Schooles, where tis vsuall to giue Themes to discourse on and arguments to maintaine, that haue neither Truth nor existence in Nature. Not <Besides> to mention the Necessity that iustifys this Way of Thinking, which it is Impossible to be without, and tho it twere in our power to suppresse all such kind of Thoughts, yet the Mind that by their [vn] pleasing Variety feeles an vnspeakable Refreshment, wud by a continuall standing bent, grow so melancholy, so dull and so discontented, that the aduantage[s] |f. 21| of <wholly> laying them [whol] downe, wud [som g] soone be outweigh'd by those <the necessity> of their Resuminge. But to deliuer ingeniously my Opinion of this kind of Thinking, tho I beleeue that to [many] <some diuers> spirits with the <fore> mention'd limitation[s] it may <lawfully enuf> be permitted, yet if we must <needs> determine the matter in the Generall, I must confess that I think I may truly say of Raueing to most men, what a Fisitian said of eating Mushroms to a weake stomack, that tho in som sort it might be allow'd, yet it cud not be conceded without so many Cautions and Modifications that he thought <twas> it not onely more safe, but (perhaps) more easy, to abstaine <not

---

experiments, and castles in the air," see his letter to Lady Ranelagh on 6 March 1647 (1.xxxvi-xxxvii).

[16] RB discussed this theme at several points in the *Aret.*, and it is a common topic in works of contemporary moral psychology, esp. Wright, Dyke, and Fenner.

[17] Matt. 6:21. RB inadvertently omitted the citation, a mistake repeated a few pages later.

[18] Cf. Maddison 24 for a parallel view of this topic.

to meddle with> from the Thing then precisely to obserue <ty ones self, or, be bound> them.[19] And because most haue those that are gifted with actiue Fancys, very seldom haue the least regard to those Conditions that excuse Rauing, and so make themselues gilty of it in it's most inexcusable <criminall> signification, we shall desire such to take the paines <seriously> to consider, 1. What an Emty happiness it is thus Cameleon-like to feed vpon the Aire, <and Indian-> like [the Old Heathen,] <fall downe to, or worship> adore Idols of their owne making. And since [those that] all [men] Persons of more raysed Spirits, haue euer esteem'd the beggerly goods of this World but the |f. 22| shadows (and Apparitions) of tru Ones, How meane and low must their Ambition be, that Place <seek> so much Felicity in the Shadow's of those Goods <Shaddos?> that are themselues but so <such>. 2. That these kind of Extrauagancys are not vsually so innocent and so exemt from Danger as they are beleeu'd. For besides that in many they serue extreamely to feed their Vanity and Self-conceit, and besides that they <may> argue [a blameworthy] no very Christian Impatience at the Condition God has been pleas'd to think fittest for vs, and a Sawcy [atten] <Desire> to be our own Caruers of a better by ways that he [allows] <prescribes> not; besides all this, I say, <these thoughts do often serue to> chaine vs [vp too much] to the World, and heihten too much our Passions for erthly things, by representing to vs in their Ideas a Louelines /Contentment/ [that] far beyond [any] that that [may] can be found in their Originals. 3. That they that are most giuen to Raueing, being generally such as are endow'd with the [strongest] acti-u'st <nimblest> and most working Braines, <they> will haue the more to answer for if they misemploy those Parts; since our Sauior teches vs ( )[20] that our Returns of <our> Seruice will be expected Proportionable to the abilitys we receaue. 4. And that [we must] in Rauing we must not onely consider the Mis-pending our Thoughts, but that also of our Time: so that tho now and then the <bare> loss of |f. 23| the one might perhaps be <as> excusable, yet <as so much sleepe> it looses it's Innocence, by the Necessity of <it's> being attended by the squandring away <wasting> of the other. And truly as we do not only condemn him that diuides his money to Tapsters, Murderers, and whores, but <do the like to> him also that lays out too much of it vpon Trifles, so must we not onely [censure] <blame> them that spend their thoughts vpon sinfull Speculations, [so] but inuolue those also in the same censure that wast too many of their pretious thougths in Idle and vnprofitable Raueings. Now because I haue frequently obserued that they that indeuor to improue their thouhts to some good vse, neuer loose more of them then in those Interuals or (as I may so call them) Parentheses of [seriousnes] /Bisnes/ which they think not long enuf to perfect and so to short

[19] Cf. general advice in the *Aret.* (bk. 2, ch. 4). RB's approach to this problem is typical of the reasoning found in cases of conscience.

[20] RB inadvertently omitted the citation, Matt. 25:14-30, the parable of the talents.

to begin any thing of serious in, I shall <not think it amiss> to propose the 6 kinds of Employment <half a dozen expedients> I vse to set my Thoughts awork vpon in those shreds of Time, [as] 1. of which the First is, to recall to mind any thing I haue almost forgotten, or repeate any thing I desire to retaine more firmly in my Memory.[21] The 2 is to consider and Reflect vpon any Late [Accident or] Passage or accident I tooke notice of and extract some vse or other out of it. The 3 is |f. 24| To delineate in my Fancy <braine> or draw a Modell of any short Discourse <Treatise> I haue to make or any Letter of Importance, I haue to write. The 4 is, To [resolue] make Resolues concerning the more particular Managing and continuing of my owne Bisness, and if need be, consigne them to my Table-booke. The 5 is, To compose <(in my braine)> any [short] <little> discourse, whose length may be suitable to that of my leasure, as a letter, an Essay, a Coppy of Verses, or [li] the like. And the Last is, To entertaine my [sel] Thoughts with som short and deuout soliloquy or Ejaculation, or else in the composure of som Occasionall Meditation, which latter I most of all fancy for this purpose, tho I [make] vse to busy my thoughts about any of the Former Objects, seuerally, or [mo] together, as the Toy takes me, [think bel] esteeming it much better to let my Fancy please it selfe in the Choice of any, then displease my Reason <Iudgment> by an vseless Raueing.[22] In order to whose Cure, I shall annex the ensuing Considerations.

As 1. To conceiue all your Thoughts [na] lying naked to the all seeing Ey of God; who makes it one of his cheefe attributes to |f. 25| Try the Reins and the heart, (Ier. 11.20) that who by his Word, is a Discerner of the Thoughts and intents of the Hart, (Heb 4, 12) [and who] from whom No thought can be with-held, (Iob 42.2) <May> and who, as the Psalmist tels vs, Vnderstands our Thoughts afar of (Ps. 139.2.) ↑Fancy him always seeing, as he dos in The Prophet (Ier. 4,14) How long Shall thy vaine thoughts lodge within thee?↓ Imagine thy self always in the [si] sight of that God, [whose Omnipresence is vnauoidable; and] whose Omniscience can diue into the secret closets of thy Hart[s], and see thy darkest Thoughts as cleerly as the Sun; and this Persuasion, will (as the Prophet [ter] speakes, Ps. 119, 61) make thy hart stand in Aw, and this Thought[s] compose all the Rest. For if the Presence of an Erthly Father can awe his Children, from [gamesom] <their vsuall> wantonness, how much more shud

[21] RB recorded contradictory assessments of his own memory (cf. 1.xlix, 1.xxxviii, 1.xv, and Maddison 15) and was very interested in schemes for improving memory. His amanuensis, Robin Bacon, thought RB had a very good memory (BL Add. MS 4229, f. 66), but in the *Scep. Chym.* 1.511, RB noted the proverb that "good wits have bad memories." For the importance of memory systems, cf. *Occ. Refl.* 2.334. Hartlib had given John Beale a MS by Caleb Morley on the subject (6.330-39), and Beale wrote about the subject several times (e.g., 6.325) in the 1660s.

[22] In "Dayly Reflection," RB described in great detail his method of meditation and contemplation. His writing of "occasional meditations" emerged from his desire to use time wisely and to suppress raving.

our Respect of the (vnauoidable) Omnipresence of a Heu'nly Father [lay a like] haue the like Power to restrain our Thoughts. 2. To pitch vpon som such Course of Life as will take vp the Thoughts, and [giue] allow them but little Time to raue. There being nothing that more befrends Raueing then Idleness, |f. 26| [Especially if attended with Solitude. For the Thoughts being most busy when we are Idle, are extreamely apt to find themselues a Vaine Employment when we want a serious one; and if this want of Bisness] For the one sets our Idle Thoughts a working (who vse to be most busy when we are least so) and the other, continues <feeds> them in that Vanity by leauing them no objects to diuert them from that Trifling Employment. Which [is] <may be> the Reason why Poets and amorists that [delight] so much affect the Society of their Rauing Thoughts, so loue those Places that sequester them from all other Company.[23] 3. To weigh the [Incon] vanity and Inconueniences of Rauing as we haue already inuentory'd them; which certinly are such that <oftentimes> whilst we <wast time in> [m] thinking what we wud do in another Condition, <at lest> we neglect what we shud do in our owne. 4. To practice (now and then) those studys that haue the Power to fix the Thoughts, by obliging them to an Attention inconsistent with the least of Distractions, such as are Geometricall Speculations, the Extractions of the Square and Cubick Roots, with those other more Difficult and laborious Operations of Arithmetick and Algebra, to whose Efficacy in this |f. 27| Particular, not onely Reason but my owne Experience will permit me to giue a very large Commendation.[24] For tho it shud seem the Fixednes of the Mind belong not to the Matter, but the Manner of our Thinking; yet certinly it is extreamely <very> aduantagious to both since (besides that it giues the Mind both a kind of Soberness and an Employment) the Thoughts seldom [run] <go> a gadding, but in the pursuite of <to steale the> these Seducing Objects. ↑As to keepe Scholars hard <close> to their Bookes <study> in Summer [hin] contributes to keep them <from> robbing of Orchards; because they vse to play the Truant <seldom truant it>, but for such kind of Desseins.↓[25] 5. To auoid the Occasions of Rauing, amongst which the most actiue are [Come] the Reading of Comedys and of Romances. For they, (for the most part,) being but Printed Rauings, haue a Strange Power in rousing <starting> [their Fellows in our Thoughts;] Thoughts of their owne Nature [with]in our Fancys. They are a Kind of Decoy-thoughts, that toll all our wandring Imaginations, to the Subject they dwell vpon. And sure these kind of Bookes /writings/ furnish a man with so many Theames [of and] and Presidents of Rauing, that he must be no Remisse

---

[23] RB linked solitude, love of poetry, and raving in his *Philaretus* and explained why he burned his own poetry when he reached his majority (Maddison 20-21). At the end of his life RB left himself a memorandum to burn documents associated with *Theodora* (BP 36.116).

[24] Cf. *Philaretus* (Maddison 17-18), where the wording is very similar.

[25] Cf. RB's own "robbing" of an orchard (Maddison 6).

Master of his owne Thoughts that can keep [them] <himself> from [running after those delightfull Ideas.] <thinking a Dozen Romances for one he reades.> 6. And because the Thoughts of man are of so actiue and restless a Nature, that like the Spheares, they will be perpetually in Motion; and will do any thing rather then Nothing |f. 28| therefore the safest way to hinder our Thoughts from ouerflowing to those objects [we] they shud not approach, is to dig them Channels many and deepe enuf for them all to flow <run> in. I meane to entertaine our Thoughts <(as often as it proues needfull)> with som thing or other that has a Mixture both of profitt and Deliht, as well to satisfy as benefitt [th] them. I cannot but wonder men shud take [th] so much Pleasure to spend their whole Thoughts vpon vnprofitable Objects, when there is so great a variety of those that do no less content then they do Instruct. Like those Indian Caciques[26] who in <contemning> an enuy'd affluence of all [those Goods we are most] <the World calls goode, are couetous> greedy of; [are ambitius of vnderualue those Treasures for the Purchase of] <nothing but counterfet beads,> Glasses, [beads] painted whistles and such other Childish gugaws, that we that kno their value, count <rate, esteem> but trifles. Of these kind of Pleasing Meditations, that yeld an equall satisfaction to the Fancy and the Reason, I dessein in another Place a particular Discourse, (because I am) confident that to the Ignorance or Neglect of these may be imputed [all the Esteem men giue the other] <[most part haue for]> the greatest <best> part of the esteem men's vanity has giuen the Other.[27] 7. Lastly; If all this will not Do, Both Pray and Striue against it. Prayer being |f. 29| A spirituall Enemy, must be [ouercom] <subdu'd> by Weapons suitable to it's Nature. But the Truth on't is, that <(in most men)> [such] so absolute a Conquest [is (in most men)] in this Life is rather to be hop't <wish't> then look't <hop't> for, these Idle Thoughts ([being amongst] <part of> our Rags of Mortality,) being like the Nayles of our Toes and Fingers [and] that tho neuer so often cut will neuer leaue growing till we leaue liuing. But the best of it is, that tho in spite of vs these foolish Thoughts will make a Thorou-fare of the Mind, [we are] they are not guilty, that permit them not to Lodge there; (Ier. 4.14. How long shall thy vaine Thoughts LODGE within thee!) [He that Raues against his Will receiues theeues into his Howse, is not gilty of giuing that Entertainment <because> they take <it>.] ↑[Eui] Rauings [that] force an Entrance into the Minde; [make vs not most guilty of their] When theeues breake open a man's

[26] A cacique was a native chief or prince of the aborigines in the West Indies and adjacent parts of America (*OED*). In "Of Felicity," an essay in *Horæ Vacivæ* (1646), Hall wrote that "They can set a true estimation of those sublunarie things, that others are contented to overbuy, more Sottish then the Barbarous Indians to exchange Gold for Glasse: more greedy then Atalanta, loose themselves to stoope for a golden Apple" (27). For similar language, cf. *Swearing* 6.25.

[27] RB could refer to several surviving works: "Dayly Reflection" or *Occ. Refl.* are obvious possibilities.

Howse, he is not condemn'd for giuing them [entertainment] <harbor>, because they haue no other then what they force; nor dos he [so much] <properly> giue them Entertainment, but they take it.↓[28] The Soule may to these Thoughts be a High-way, to these wandring Thoughts but an In it must not. Tis in this Case as when a Virgin's <Woman's> honor is attempted, if she yeeld not, she Ouercoms; for if he forcibly enjoy, 'tis no more an Adultery but a Rape.[29] For there is [out] this Difference betwixt [the] <our> Combats <battles> with our outward Enemys, and those we fight against our |f. 30| Lusts, that in these Latter, the Victory depends on our Resistance, <Endeuors,> and not on our Successe <Euents>. Persist therefore Constantly in so Gallant a Defence, and whensoeuer the Multitude of your Enemys shall begin to dismay yow, deriue a fresh Courage /Respite/ from that euer-to-be-considered Passage of the Apostle (2 Cor. 10, 4,5) For the Weapons of our Warfarr are not Carnall but Mighty through God, to the pulling down of strong-holds; Casting down Imaginations, and EUERY high thing that exalteth it self against the Knoledge of God, and bringing into Captiuity EUERY Thought to the Obedience of Christ.

4.) Begin your Meditations with a Petition to God for his blessing vpon them. A Precept to whose Neglect I dare confidently ascribe the greatest part of that want of Excellency and Vsefulness we see in the Printed Copys of our <most men's> Thoughts. For whilst men (who of themselues are not able so much as to thinke a good Thought) will confide wholly in their owne skill in Meditation, and scarce vouthsafe God to be a bare Spectator <looker on> in their Thoughts; tis no wonder |f. 31| if he giue not them a wholsom wisedom, that scorne to beg it at his hands, and that their productions haue so little of Diuine, that neuer car'd for a hiher assistance then that of Man. This, tho blameworthy in all, is most Criminall in our Schoole-diuines, [who /that/ vse to treat of God's Nature and his Word, without caring for his spirit that is the One and did endite the other, and with the Dim owle-liht of humane Reason, think to pry into his Nature that ( ) is said to Inhabit] that thinke to [vnderst] diue into the Deepe Mysterys of the World without the [his] Illumination <of that Spirit> that endited it; and by <with> the dim Spectacles of their own Enquirys, to pry into his vnconceiu'd Essence /Nature,/ that (1 Tim. 6.16) Inhabits an Innaccessible Light, and like the Bright Planet that rules the Day, is neuer discouerable but by those very beams himself is pleasd to lend vs. ↑But we must not presume <expect> that God will so prostitute his Fauors as to think vs worthy to receaue them whilst we do not think them worth the asking for. /or, As to thrust <them> vpon those that esteem <think> them not <so much as> worth the asking for./↓ Shall the Heathen say, A Ioue Principium, and their very Poets themselues (a generation seldom gilty of more religion then they need,) not dare to begin a

[28] Cf. the *Aret.* (bk. 2, ch. 3) and *Exc. of Theol.* 4.19.

[29] Cf. the discussion of the will in the *Aret.* (bk. 2, ch. 3).

Fiction without the Invocation of their Imaginary Deitys, and shall a Christian in his most serious Thoughts forget such a Necessary Peece of Devotion! Neither do |f. 32| I belieue it a grounded Nicety to think we ought not to looke for any particular blessing vpon those Meditations that do not precisely belong to Diuinity. God (that in the 65 of Esay and the 16 is called the God of Truth,) is both the Souerain Truth and the Author of all Truths; ↑(Ps. 36.9 In thy liht shall we see light!)↓ <the honor of> whose Discouery is cheefly due to him, whence St Iames [informs] assures vs (Iam. 1,17) that Euery good Gift and euery perfect Gift is from aboue and cometh down from the Father of Lights; and the Hethen Orator himself cud say that Nemo vir Magnus sine afflatu Diuino.[30] The Deuill on the other side is sayd to be the Father of Lys (Iohn 8.44.) as an vtter Enemy to all Truth, ↑(which he always attemts either to Disguise, peruert or obscure.)↓ [to] of which sure God is not [as] to be conceiu'd a less vniuersall Fauorer then he is an Opponent. Besides that if <since> we may confidently inuocate and expect God's blessing vpon our Endeuors in our Temporall <Secular> Callings, why may [be] we not hope for the like fauor vpon these Endeuors, that are both more Noble in themselues and haue a neerer Relation to his Seruice. The Apostle St Iames (Iam. 1,5) giues vs [no] both a Precept and a Promise (both to oblige and Encourage vs to this Duty) in these Words, |f. 33| If any of yow lack Wisdom let him ask of God, (that giueth to all men Liberally, and vpbraideth not) and it shall be giu'n him. Let vs therefore <make our> humble and feruent <ernest[ly]> addresses [our selues] to that God <of Truth> that is able to do exceeding aboundantly aboue all that we ask or think (Ephes. 3,20) that he wud be gratiously pleas'd to giue vs his Spirit of Truth to guide vs into all Truth, (Iohn 16.13) and whensoeuer we meane to spend a Considerable Portion of Time with our own Thoughts, let the Prologue of our Meditations be that heu'nly <sweet, deuout> Epilogue of the 19th Salm, Let the Words of my Mouth and the Meditation of my hart be acceptable in thy Sight, O Lord my Strength and my Redeemer.[31]

5.) Before thou beginneth to Meditate, lay downe a Modell of thy Meditation. Tis a receau'd Custom amongst the skilfullest Architects, neuer to lay the Foundation of any Building of Importance, till in an Epitome or Model of the Whole Edifice, they haue exposed to their View and Consideration, all |f. 34| the Parts that make it vp, with their Simmetry; and left themselues a liberty to [to alt] with an Incosiderable cost, to alter that in the Type, which cud not be corrected in the Building it selfe, without Defacing perhaps, the whole frame of the Structure.[32] Truly methinkes this is a Practice wel worth the Coppying by those,

---

[30] Cicero, *De Natura Deorum* 2.66, 67; Alsted 1250; and Jam. 1:17. RB used the same quote in the *Aret.* (bk. 2, ch. 7).

[31] Ps. 19:14.

[32] Cf. the other references to architecture in the *Aret.* (bk. 2, ch. 1).

that beleeue they ought to [les] be no less Carefull, of the Construction <Piles,> of their Thoughts, then those of their Masons <stones>. I wud therefore when-soeuer I enter in to any longwinded Meditation, contract it first into a Modell: and tho I know these maps of our meditations admit of as infinite a Variety as the meditations themselues; yet in the Generall, the method I shud most approue of; is to diuide this Modelling of our Thoughts into 1. An Establishment of the Scope or Drifts (if need be) of the present Meditation; 2. A Branching it into |f. 35| the Principal Parts (or seuerall Theames) of which it is to consist. I say the Principall or more Generall Parts; because the Subdiuision of those Branches into shootes and Twigs /Leaues/ wud but breed confusion in the first Draught of the Modell; and therefore I reserue them till /for/ the particular Consideration of those boughes that need them. [3.] Like Cookes that first carue a Capon in to Wings and Legs, &c, before they proceed to mince each Member in to Bits. 3. A marshalling these Principall Branches, if they be any thing to one another, into that Order, in which 'tis fittest for them to present themselues to our Consideration: which is a Point not to be Neglected, (whereof more hereafter.) These 3 Acts make vp a Good Moddel; tho in some Subjects, the 1 and the 2 com often to be complicated or confounded. And [he that] these Models well made, are of much greater Vse, |f. 36| then at first sight they promise, not only in seruing for a Compass to steer our Thoughts <by>; (whence it is that many that neglect them in their Meditations, may be said rather to light vpon Truths then to Discouer them) but also in doing the Duty of a Mastif to barke at those that shud not be admitted; and so facilitating the Practice of the ensuing Precept, which commands vs to

6.) Exclude Heterogeneas from thy Meditation. Iudgment <discerning> (the Touchstone of the Soul) [mus] shud do that in thoughts; that Heat is said to do in the Body; Congregare Homogenea, et Heterogenea disgregare. Vnite /assemble/ things of a Sympathizing, and dissociate those of a repugning Nature. Now the Heterogeneas that must be heere remou'd, are either Too many things at once or Things not to the Purpose. The First of these is incident enuf to nimble Fancys; tho they may |f. 37| [Consider,] <apprehend his Fate> that [he that] <for hauing> hunted 2 hares at once, <cud> catch[t] Neither; and I remember an <the> Italian Prouerbe (not more Common then Oraculus) that tells vs, that Chi troppo abbraccia, poco stringe: he that grasps too much holds fast too little.[33] And questionless it falls out oftentimes; that those <Thoughts> that Vnited were able to ouertake one or few Truths; being weakned by Distraction, faint and tyre in the Pursuit of Many. The Brooke that is swift and Deep enuf to turne [driue] <turne> one Mill with Ease; fork't into a Double Channell to [d] driue 2 <will> proue [oftenti] perhaps too shallo /vnable/ to Turn either. But the Second Tribe

[33] Though fluent in Italian (*Style* 2.312), RB also owned Giovanni Torriano's *Select Italian Proverbs* (Cambridge 1649). Hall used the same proverb in *Horæ Vacivæ* 71.

of these Heterogeneas, (or wandring, Gipsey thoughts) are no less Epi[ck]demicall to Men then destructiue to orderly Meditations:[34] making the Conuersations <Entertainments> of the Thoughts with the Objects like those of the Courtiers in the [Presence] Chamber, where no sooner a Conuersation [of] is begun, but som body or other that either wants or seekes Company, steps in to interrupt it, or at least to Byass it from it's former line /course./ And indeed (such is the Weakeness of our |f. 38| Nature and the Deuil's diligence /craft/) there is nothing, as more Dangerous so more vsuall, /ordinary/ then when our Thoughts are very attentiue in the Consideration of som particular Object for som vagabond interuening Fancy to interrupt their Progress and seduce them [f] from the prosecution of their First Dessein. Like Children that sent to schoole, if they liht vpon a Birds nest <see a Game of football,> or some Truant by the Way, are easily temted from the Remembrance of their first Errant,[35] and either wholly forget to go to schoole, or arriue there too late. This Wandringness of Mind is, very much both our Fault and our Hindrance, and therefore ought carefully to improue, both the Way formerly hinted for the fixing our Thoughts, and any other expedient that has but the least Tendency to so great a Good. Twas euer the Policy of the Deuill, when he sees vs zealously employed either in Praying, hearing, or any heu'nly Meditation, to endeuor to distract vs by the offer /Tender/ of some Interuening Thought, that besides the [P] Nouelty or |f. 39| Pleasingness, [that] may peraduenture haue something of Piety it self in it [t] and ought to be at another time both Welcom and entertain'd. Like Fisitians that when they cannot Dry vp /exhaust/ an Humor; procure a Reuulsion; But in this Case, as in Diet presently after hauing swallowd a Purge, we must not only [lo] <looke> how good a Thing is, but how seasonable. Atalanta was censur'd for stooping eu'n to Bals of Gold; when the taking of them vp [cau] occasion'd <endanger'd> the Losse of the Race.[36] Those Thoughts that are Good in themselues, fork that Nature in relation to vs, when they diuert vs from the prosecution of better; (and therefore ought to be excluded, tho not for their Quality yet for their Time.) Let vs therefore hedge in our Meditations and set a Porter at the Gate: to examine and keep /bolt/ out all <vnbidden, vninuited> wayfaring /trauelling/ Thoughts, that are strangers to the Present scope; and offer to intrude vpon our Priuacys: We see in Frontier Garrisons, the Drawbridge is not let downe euen to Frends, if they require Admission at an vndue houre. But |f. 40| somewhat to mitigate the seuerity of this Maxime, I thinke it Necessary to sweeten it with this following Caution: which is, That in Case when we are Meditating vpon any Subject; there com a Cross vs a Thought (or more) that if it be not presently improu'd, is likely to /be lost/ fly <escape> our Memorys; and if then laid hold on, can

[34] Cf. "Dayly Reflection" f. 272.

[35] "Errant" is a variant spelling of "errand" (*OED*).

[36] Ovid, *Metamorphoses* 10.681ff.

(aduantagiously) [m] recompence [the] what we loose for it's sake; in that Case, I say, it is not only lawfull but Expedient to quit the Entertainment of our Former Thoughts, to welcom this New com Guest. For we oftentimes find, [that Triuiall and vulgar siz'd Tho] (so strange, and, to vs, so extrauagant, are the secret alliances of Things)[37] that Triuiall, [low] and vulgar-siz'd <lowe> Thoughts, (like Hazel switches that are said to help Metallists to the Discouery of Mines)[38] haue hinted Notions to vs, [that] of infinitely greater <more> Value then themselues; and which, like Opportunity it's painted Bald behind,[39] if they be not intercepted /arrested/ in their Passage, are but fruitelessely pursu'd <in their flight>.[40] |f. 41| Now vpon these Terms [not] to neglect such Prizes vpon the Pretence of constancy in the Prosecution of our first Voyage, were to <be> like the Cock in the Fable, who was so greedy in scraping vp a few moldy graines of rotten Corn, that he scorn'd to take Notice of a Pearle. Here <to> leaue our first Thoughts, for more sublime, is <only> to alter, not their Nature but their Object; that like him that hunting of a Hare, chances to rouze a Stagge, by whose Pursuit he changes, not his Sport but his Game.

7.) Let thy Meditation be continued and not by Iumps. There is a twofold Interruption of our Thoughts; the one by Interuening Fancys, that hurry them away from their first Purpose, and make them do what the Filosofers hold Impossible for Accidents, migrare de Subjecto in Subiectum, skip from one subject to another,[41] so strangely, that [I] after Recollection I haue oftentimes admired by what imperceptible and Extrauagant Wayes my Meditations shud so widely wander from their first Theame; and concluded that the Way of a Swallow |f. 42| in the Aire is not more Pathlesse, nor that of a fox't fish in the sea more vntraceable. But of this, enuf already. The second [of] Kind of Parenthesis in Thinking, is made by Dessein (as the other was by Negligence) when after hauing made som Progress in our Thoughts, we adiourn their Prosecution till another time. Now this Suspension <(if not Disjoynting)> of his thoughts dos very much Retard the Thinker. For besides, that the Motions of the Mind like those of a Coa[r]ch or Rouling Stones, are much more Easily continu'd then

---

[37] RB's belief in the "secret alliance of Things" and "Connexions of Truths" underlay much of his later writing in both natural and moral philosophy. He did not doubt the efficacy of "sympathetic magic" (cf. *Usefulness* 2.115 and *Cert. Phys. Essays* 1.346). In the latter work he argued that the medicinal power of the paeony root was related to the time at which it was harvested (1.347). Birch quoted with approval Shaw's assessment that RB was benignly sceptical toward sympathetic magic (1.cxlvii).

[38] Cf. Thomas, *Decline* 266, 280, 289, 362, and 796.

[39] The source may be Phaedrus's *Aesop's Fables* (#40), but cf. T311. Bacon used the same image in "Of Delays."

[40] RB echoed two proverbs: L518, "Praise is the shadow of virtue" and L479, "Love/woman/honor, like a shadow/crocodile/death flies one following and pursues one fleeing."

[41] For a discussion of accidents and essences as schoolmen saw them, see *Orig. of Forms* 3.16.

begun;[42] and besides that the Thoughts being once put (as it were) into a Posture (or Straine) of Meditating, are as much fitter to be Then improu'd that way, then at another Time, as Iron is more obsequious to the hammer when Red [fire] hot; then when growne Cold againe: besides all this, I say, there are Connexions of Truths that link them betwixt Themselues, and certin Dependances one vpon another <[of (which (to omit seuerall]> |f. 43| All present to our minds when we (abruptly) breake of our Meditations; of which (to omit seuerall Circumstances, Hard, and yet Deseruing to be remembred) it is <almost> impossible not to forget some part, when we com <afterwards> to Resume them. So that (me thinks) he that [hauing] sets his Thoughts on <a> working vpon some Subject, and then [Defer] Delays it's Pursuit till another season, is not vnlike that Fantasticall Cooke, who was wont to take his Pot from of the Fire [as soone] when once the Water began to Boyle.[43] Neuerthelesse this generall Rule is to be qualify'd with this [Limitation] <Reseruation>: that in Case, either better Thoughts (as in the Former Article) diuert vs from the Prosecution of these: or that we find (not Feigne) our selues, by reason of Wearinesse vnfit to prosecute the[s] Present Theame: or that our <vrgent> Occasions call vs away; in all these Cases, we are permitted (without being beholding to his holyness) to giue our selues a Dispensation from the Rigor of this Precept.

---

[42] Cf. the *Aret.* (bk. 2, ch. 4).

[43] Source unknown.

The Dayly Reflection

|f. 269|

To render this Discourse lesse Tedious then Vsefull,[1] I shall decline the accustom'd Formality of a Preface; to addresse my selfe immediately to the Theame I am to [handle] <conuerse with>; that my Title calls the Dayly Reflection: by which I here vnderstand, A Quotidian and serious Obseruation of and Reflection vpon what has occur'd to one of most Considerable the foregoing Day.

To proceed Orderly in what we haue to deliuer vpon <the handling of> this Subject; there are three seueralls, that will successiuely challenge our Attention: we being in this Selfe-examination to enquire;

1. Why
2. When It is to be performed; [or if yow]
3. How [illeg.] Or if yow will, The Motiues, the Season, and the Manner of the Duty: each of which we will cast into a Peculiar Section.

The First Section.

And [th] for the First of these, so many Benefitts <Vses> consequent <deriuable from> to this Practise, disclose themselues; that I am likely to be |f. 269v| Much more troubled, how to select and order, [them] then how to instance <discouer> them: and therefore to auoid Confusions, we shall content our selues to obserue, that tho the Benfitts that streame from this Duty do reach and cherish almost all [Christian] <heu'nly> Graces; yet they flow in greater Channels. [too]

In the first Place to our Integrity;[2] a Vertu that refuses all Toleration to the very least or Dearest Sin: and permits not the Soule to deale with our Vices, as Saul did with the Amalekites, when he kild all the most Inconsiderable of the People and destroy'd the Refuse of the Cattell; but preseru'd the King of Amaleck and the fattest of the Beasts aliue; but obliges [/enjoynes/] it to [deal] roote them out with as vnreserued and impartiall a Destruction; as was enjoyned to the same Saul, in the Words <tenor> of his Commission which run thus, ↑1 Sam.

---

[1] This essay is found in BP 7.269-87. It does not have much similarity to the "Discourse Touching Occasional Meditations" that served as the preface to *Occ. Refl.* In BP 35.172-73, Boyle entitled an earlier version of this MS, "The | Dayly | REFLECTOR | To my Lady RANALAUGH." For John Dury's method of meditation, see HP/26/4. For modern studies from quite different perspectives, see Isabel G. MacCaffrey, "The Meditation Example," *ELH* 32 (1965) 388-407; Barbara K. Lewalski, *Protestant Poetics and the Seventeenth-Century Religious Lyric* (Princeton 1979); and Michael A. West, ed., *The Psychology of Meditation* (Oxford 1987).

[2] In the *Aret.* (bk. 2, ch. 6), RB discussed the importance of integrity, sincerity, and perseverance.

15.3.↓ Now go and smite Amalek and vtterly destroy all that they haue and spare them not; but slay both Man and Woman, infant and suckling ox and sheep, Camel and Asse. For the frequent Enquirys the Soule makes into her owne Actions, render it extreamely difficult for the least Vice, [to] long to lurke vndescry'd: and when 'tis once discouer'd; the Clamours of our Conscience proue so constant and persecute vs so often by the suddennesse of their Returnes; that [we find] it becoms lesse Troublesome <for vs> to renounce those (petty) sins; then (always) to endure those (tedious) Reproaches. And then, when we find it a lesse Trouble to suppresse /exile, banish/ then to Tolerate /entertaine/ our Faults; who wud not prefer <be so mad of> Innocence with Quiet, before Guilt with the Contrary Inconuenience. |f. 270|

In the next Place, to our Syncerity. For certinly when the Soule is accustom'd euery Night to throw of those Vizors that disguise her to the World, (and oftentimes to her very Selfe) and considers that she is in the Presence of that God whose Eyes [dis] pierce [as] <more> clearly the most intricate and obscure Angles /Corners/ of the Hart, [as] <then> ours do thorough the most Transparent Christall; it cannot but <strongly> Arm her against that Temtation of Priuacy in Sin, that conceales it not from him, <his sight> who is both best able and most concern'd to punish it: and proue a [st] powerfull Dissuasiue from all vnholynesses <that may Displease a Holy Deity> to represent her selfe to be ey'd by him, whose Sanctity and his Omniscience make any thing of Vncleane, so vnconcealable from his Search and so repugnant <detested, abhoring> to his Nature. ↑A Purity resembling his, to whom we endeauor to conform our selues.↓ To omit, that vpon the same score that Soldiers and Louers act more handsomly when their Princes and their Mistrisses looke on; the Consideration of God's being Witnesse of our whole Deportments, ought to inspire vs with Desseins, worthy so Diuine /glorious/ a Spectator. ↑'Tis the Prescription of God himselfe to the Father of the Faithfull (Gen. 17,1.) Walke before me and be thou perfect. There being no way more compendious to be Perfect, then to behaue our selues as in his Presence whose is onely and comprizes all Perfection.↓ And in effect, 'tis more happy to be [cred] resented then Easy to be credited /beleeu'd/ how much the Dayly appeareance before the Tribunall of our owne Conscience alone, dos contribute to the Establishment <and Encrease> of Syncerity. For these <many> Secret Sins, that like Screetchowles [fre] affect the Darke; and loue not to appeare where they may be seene, seldome frequent those Soules, where they are vsually expos'd vnto the Ey of Consicence: and banish themselues from those Places where they perceiue themselues to be taken notice of.[3] [And then] This <pious> Practise makes vs contract a Habitude of Paying a iust Reuerence to our selues: and then this Habitude makes vs lesse Feare to haue

[3] Cf. *Aret.*, f. 137ᵛ.

Witnesses of our Actions, then to do Actions that need <to> feare a Witnesse.

In the third place, to our Humility, |f. 270v| For by this Rigorous Examen of our Selues, we shall apprehend [so great] such a Multitude of [Sins] Faults and of Infirmitys; that might otherwise haue pass'd <scap'd> Vndiscerned; that [we] <the very Perfectest> shall [take] <find> that Expression of the Psalmist; that ↑Ps. 40.12.↓ Our Iniquitys are more then the Haires of our Hed, not an humble <bold> Hyperbole, but a Modest Truth. And then, <if> on the other side we do but examine our holyest and exactest Actions, by their Conformity to that Rule and Pattern, to which an exquisite <perfect> Correspondence, can alone make <entitle> them merit <deserue> the Attribute of Good; we shall find our very best Performances [so] vitiated <inquinated> with so much Frailty and so many Imperfections; that shall be [f] necessitated to acknoledge but too much Iustice in that Confesion of the Prophet, in which he [sayes,] <avowes> that ↑Esay. 64.6.↓ All our Righteousnesses are as filthy Rags: and shall find our selues in greater Danger of Despaire then Pride. And truly the very best of our [Pers] Actions, consider'd in themselues, resemble <are like> that Mysterious Image described in the Prophet ↑Dan. 2. 31, 32, 33.↓ Daniel in which to the Gold and Syluer of the Head and Breasts, were vnited /concorporated/ the Brasse, the Iron, and the Clay of the Inferior Members: and where the greater Part by much, was that of the more ignoble Materialls. I am very apt to beleeue that the Ignorance of our Selues is so vnseuer'd a Concomitant of [euery] <all the> Causes of Pride, that neither of them wud be preualent without it. For the more heinous faults of other men, by [p] entitling vs to a Comparatiue Meritt /Piety/ do no more inuest vs with an Essentiall Sanctity; then the Ribbe of a ship is made /becoms/ really <absolute> strait, by being compared to a Ramshorne. |f. 271| And a more intimate Knoledge of our selues will discouer in the Vertuousest and Wisest of vs, so many Defects, so many Faylings, and so many Weakenesses; that perhaps it will be no Presumtion to Hope, that [to] <in> the Conscionable Practisers of this Duty, Pride /that haughty Trespasse/ will become, almost as great a[n Impossibility] <wonder> as it is <wud be> a Sin.

In the Fourth Place, to our Charity: and this Aduantage is vsually deriued from the former <precedent>. For the sense and Consideration of our owne Wickedness and Frailtys; dos very effectually dispose vs to compassionate those of others. And our constant Experience, how hard <difficult> a thing it is, entirely to subdue our Imperfections; induces vs to looke vpon many of the Faylings of our Neighbors; rather as Effects /consequences/ of the Weakeness of Humanity /our Nature/ then Testimonys of their Faultynesse. /malice/ To these fauorable sentiments our Reflection also leads vs by another Motiue, for when we seriously perpend how frequent and how vast are God's Forgiuenesses to vs; we cannot but conclude <find> our selues vncapable of Admiring and acknowledging that Goodnesse as we ought, vnlesse by endeauoring to imitate it in our Pardons and Indulgence to the faults of others for his sake: we cannot but esteem him (in the Gospell) that after being acquitted <forgiu'n> of a Debt of 10 thousand Talents, refuses to respite the Payment of one poore hundred Pence, (most richly) worthy of his Destiny:[4] and shall find so much Reason for the Disposition I require that if we shall be apt to beleeue, it will <must> loose the Title of Charity to assume that of Iustice. |f. 271v| In effect, there is scarce any more certin Antidote against Vncharitablenesse, then the true Knoledge of our Selues: since that will discloze to vs so many Imperfections; that we shall [d] no more, either find it strange that men shud dissent from our Opinions; or aggrauate the Injurys <displeasures> we receiue, by a flattring Opinion of vnusuall Merit, in the Person they are offred to: which (two) I take <conceiue> to be maine Motiues / / of Vncharitablenesse /most guilty of the Want of Charity./

In the Fifth Place, to a certin exquisite Temper and Disposition of Soule, which some haue (aptly enuf) Christn'd Heu'nly-mindednesse.[5] For the faythfull Practise of this Reflection dos very much facilitate Repentance, by making it ouertake Faults, before Custom and Neglect has hatch't them into Vices: and allowes them not the least Pretence to the Title of Prescription. (In such a spirit [illeg. line] Sin may baite indeed, but lodges not all Night; for (as if the Sun carryed them away with [t] him,) they euery night deuest their Clothes and Faults together: so that to such Minds, a Sin[s] is like that Feauor Physitians call Ephemeris, that seldome is lastinger to outliue the Day the fit first takes men in.)[6] This preuents all that Brawninesse of Conscience, that is generally contracted, by vnrepented Habitudes of ill: which is so Dangerous, that it vsually either produces a Security that feares /scruples at/ no Offence, or concludes in a Despaire that hopes for no forgiuenesse. The Soule, thus pure from all those [loathed] <hideous> spots which make Gods holy Spirit loath the Residence, is soone inhabited by that blessed Guest /Spirit/ |f. 272| And (by Degrees) contracts with it a holy Familiarity, so full of rauishing Transports and Ioyes; that this (inexplicable) conversation like the Employment of the Saints in heau'n, becoms at once our Duty and our Happinesse.[7] [(In our Communion with God, [our] men's Felicity dos consist in the other /next/ Life, and would do so in this, could we be bless'd with an vninterrupted Fruition of it: but since the Frailtys and Distractions of our Earthly Condition, render that Blessing rather the Object of our [B] Wishes then our Hopes; at least let vs assigne some Portion of those houres /that <all> Time/ that God has lent vs, to entertaine and to Enjoy his

4 Matt. 18:21-35.

5 For a similar discussion, see the *Aret.*, f. 230.

6 For analysis of the relevant medical literature, see W. F. Bynum and V. Nutton, *Theories of Fever from Antiquity to the Enlightenment*, *Medical History*, Supplement No. 1 (London 1981); ch. 2, Don Bates, "Thomas Willis and the fevers literature of the seventeenth century" 45-70.

7 Cf. "Doctrine of Thinking" f. 37. RB owned Henry Ainsworth's *Communion of Saints with God, Angels, and One Another in this Life* (1628) and Henry Lawrence's *Our Communion and Warres with Angels* (Amsterdam? 1646), but many other theological works also addressed this topic.

Friendship./]

This is a Coniunction <our Conjunction with God> /commerce/ highly resembling that of the Needle with the Loadstone (by which the [Minerall] Stone acquires no new quality /vertu/ but all the Aduantages do accrue vnto the [illeg.] Steele.)[8] This holy Conuersation insensibly models the Soule into a Conformity to him we conuerse with, and snatches /inuites/ Heau'n to this side of the Graue: by producing those hopes (or rather[s] Assurances) of <the immutability of our happines in> God's fauor; those Confidences, (nay) those Intimacys, those languishing Transports, those zealous [Ex] Sallyes; and those ore-ioying Extasyes, and all those / / Symtomes of a heau'nly Loue; which do create such <inexpressible> Ioyes, ↑that I dare <must> /will/ not vndertake <pretend, attempt> to describe them, for feare of being beleeu'd neuer to haue resented them.↓ that to hope /attempt/ to describe <expresse> them, is a<n> (strong) Argument of <a man's> not /neuer/ hauing resented them.[9]

In the last Place, to Knowledge and Wisdome both Humane and Spirituall. For (first) the Repetition of what we learn greatly contributes /conduces/ to secure our Acquists from (the Danger of) Obliuion. And (then) our Reflections on what we haue obseru'd, improoues it into consequences /new Axioms/ and Vses; that otherwise would haue been bury'd in Neglect. The Same Consideration that [induces] moues |f. 272v| Statesmen to consel Princes to study most the Historys of their owne and Neighbour states;[10] induces me to aduise all men to study cheeflyest their owne Actions, and theirs they are to conuerse with: for as Princes are most concern'd in the one, <(as most relating to their owne Conditions)> so are Particulars /all men/ in the other: there being a certin resemblance <conformity> betwixt the Past and [Present] Future Passages of the same man's life, which makes the one the best and Perfectest Instructor of the other. The liues of Ancient Heros do much lesse instruct ours, then a iust contemplation of our owne, because of the Disparity both betwixt Times and Persons: which dos create so greate Difference in Ciuil Affaires, that [what] <the same Action which> formerly was cry'd vp for Gallantry or Prudence, now often passes vnder a <quite> Contrary notion. Besides, that many <materiall> Circumstances of their Carriage the omissions of hystory has conceald from vs; ↑and how many <grosse> mistakes the Ignorance of the True Motiues and Circumstances dos occasion, <in the tru Estimate of Actions> he must not be a Macchiauel that ignores.↓ whereas those of owne Actions and theirs we are intimate with; being all discloz'd <naked> vnto vs, and reflected on whilst their Ideas are yet recent

---

[8] For other symbolic uses of the lodestone, see the index entry for "lodestone."

[9] On this point, cf. *Seraphic Love* 1.290 and *Theodora* 5.311.

[10] Some of Cork's proudest possesions were the works of RB's grandfather, Sir Geoffrey Fenton. Among other works, Fenton translated *The History of Guicciardin* (1579), a history of the wars in Italy.

and all the Passages <lineaments> /Circumstances/ remaine frely impressed /grauen/ in the memory; giue vs the [man] meanes of making <drawing> much more certin and rationall as well as more concerning and more applicatiue <relatiue> (Maximes and) Deductions. The true Conduct of our selues is to be gathered out of the study of our Selues. This Dayly [Experi] Reflection dispenses Experience from the Lawes of Time, and ripens their Iudgment <Wisdome> whilst their Age is Greene: for what men Commonly stile [Prudence] Experience is nothing else but a certin Dexterity of conduct, resulting from the Remembrance and Consideration of [the] Occasions suitably circumstanced, and the Examples of men's Prudence or miscarriages in them, with the Documents and /Rules/ Instructions those Passages haue afforded. Which being so, it is consonant to Reason as wel as verify'd by [Experience,] numerous Presidents; that he who makes it his constant Practise, both to obserue attentiuely [the] the considerable Passages /Transactions/ <he is conuersant in /with/> that occurre to him, and not content to treasure them in [th] his Memory drawes them out /deduces them/ into <those> Consequences, and mints /coynes/ them into <those> Axioms they are capable of affoording, [wi] must very much anticipate Experience /Prudence/ and [needs not] may weare gray haires vpon his Braine before any haire at all vpon his Chin.[11] For in effect, Experience Consists, not in the multitude of years but in that of Obseruations, /Experience is the result, not of Yeares but of Obseruations./ Thus this Admirable ↑Examen makes <renders> a man <become> both the Teacher, the Scholler and the Booke of his owne selfe.↓ |f. 273| But (Dear Sister) because Distastfulnesse to our depraued Nature has been euer held a Property of Vertuus Practises; least this extolld Reflection shud, by [wanting] being readily embrac't by all men, be suspected of not deseruing to be so by the Best (men) I find my selfe oblig'd to mention and Remoue a couple of Obiections that (generally) forbid <interpose best betwixt men's Practise> the Banns betwixt most men and this Duty.

The first Inconuenience attributed to it, is, the Expence of Time it necessarily requires.[12] But Time, like Mony, is neuer well employ'd but when 'tis spent: and when 'tis spent in pious Exercises, it is not wasted <lost> but lay'd out; and howres so employ'd are as little to be regretted as Plowmen, do their seede, which they part with to regaine multiply'd; since no Employment of our Time can be more aduantageous, then that which assures vs of a happy Eternity: and the best vse we can employ Time to, is to purchase vs a Felicity when it shall be

---

[11] In *Occ. Refl.* 2.366, RB discussed the sands of time and his own beardless chin (Easter 1648); for a similar remark about John Hall, cf. BW 1.xl.

[12] The removal of objections was a standard feature of such works as Bayly's *Practice of Piety*, works of casuistry, and works of devotion so heavily represented in RB's library. For an extended list of objections and ways to remove them, see *Swearing* 6.4-20.

no more /which it (selfe) cannot End./[13] Besides, that there is no such large Portion of Time [exacted <challenged>] <requisite for> by this Duty: A quarter of an Hower (or halfe at most) constantly allotted and thriftily contriu'd is as much as it's (Performance) dos exact. How many are there that cannot (forsooth) find a few moments for God's seruice and their owne /Soule's/ that can find whole Dayes and Nights, for carding, Dicing, [Wenchi] Drinking, and (perhaps) worse Employments: by which they not onely squander away <pretious> Time, but misuse it to bespeake themselues (a) Wretchednesse, <misery> when Time shall loose it selfe into /be swallow'd vp of/ Eternity. [I wil] Pray heau'n, [that] these men [ref thinke] grudge lesse to spend time then to spend it well, and [resen] like [so] those vncharitable Prodigals that are miserable (only) in their Alms, they do not then alone esteeme Time scarce, when it is to be employ'd in his seruice that lent it them. 'Tis our Communion and Conuersation with God, that makes men (perfectly) happy in the next life, and twould do so in this, could we be bless'd with a Constant and vndisturb'd Fruition of it: but [since] <if> the inuincible Frailtys of our Nature, and the necessary Distractions [of] that attend our Trauelling Condition, make <render> |f. 273[v]| So supreame a Blessing (which euer to possess <resent> creates the <our> Ioyes in Heu'n) a fitter object for our Wishes then our Hopes; at least let vs not grudge some little portion of our Time to Entertaine and [conuerse with] <to enioy> that God, to whom we owe it all: specially since that [holy] <sacred> Conuersation when duly cultiuated, dos produce such Ioyes, as are inferior to none, but those they lead to /are Prologues to./[14]

But there is another Consideration, that tho seldomer the Pretence is much oftner the Cause that Diuerts men from the Practise of this Examen. And that is, that this serious Shriuing of our Selues, (to those that are conscious to their owne Guilt) by lighting a Candle to the bottome of the hart, discouers Nastinesses, that they are loath to see, and awakes the Conscience against those <many> Sins that they are vnwilling to desert. Thus we haue knowne some fantasticke Ladyes, who hauing lost their [Bo] former Buty by the Rudenesse of the small,[15] do at first apprehend to cast their Eyes vpon a Looking-Glasse, for feare of Discouering their owne Difformity. But, rather then to permit a Wound to be search't, to let it rankle /fester/ by neglect, into an immedicable Hurt; is a peece of Madnesse that wud be laf't at in a very Bedlam. Ladyes, that are the most displeas'd that their Glasses shud present them Pictures of themselues vnsuitable to their Desires; are not <yet> so nice, as when they are told that something is disorder'd in their Dresse, or their face stain'd with some vnhandsome spot; to decline, for feare fo discouering what is amisse, the Meanes /possibility/ of

[13] RB made the same points in "Of Time and Idleness."

[14] Cf. RB on self-conversation in BP 37.291.

[15] Probably a reference to small-pox.

repairing <remoouing> it. If the Great Searcher of hearts, be (as the Prophet speakes of him) ↑Habbakkuk 1.13.↓ Of purer eyes then to behold Euill; and cannot looke on Iniquity; how can men hope, that God can discern without Anger, what themselues cannot |f. 274| Looke on without Shame: and why shud they not Feare to cherish qualitys so hideous, that they cannot behold them without horror! Shud the Egyptians, when the Frogs pester'd their houses, haue rather elected entirely to desert <forgoe> all the Conueniences [and (Aduantages)] of Habitation, [rather] then to rid /free/ their Residences, of that noysom <loath'd> vermine that infested them; who would not esteem them as arrant fooles as they were Sinners?[16] And yet that Folly is inferior to theirs, who [had rath] chuse to forgo all the Contentments /Satisfactions/ and aduantages that Result from men's Conversation with their owne Thoughts, rather then part with those Defilements /toyes/ that render them equally vncapable and vnworthy of that Happinesse. Nor is the Trouble <Difficulty> of pacyfying our Consciences, and renewing our League with Heu'n, so great as the Deuil would haue vs imagine, and our owne Feares (brib'd by our slouth) suggest. Those Clamors of the [Clam] Conscience that precede conuersion are but like the Crowing of the Cocke whilst yet the starre's <Niht's> raigne lasts, which tho a Sound somewhat harsh in it selfe, is yet extreamely welcom in consideration of that which it foreruns; since as the one dos aduertise /assure/ vs of the approach of the Day; so the other [is a signe] <presages> that the Glorious Sun of righteousnesse is arizing vpon the Horizon of our Soules with Healing in his Wings.

As therefore in Lutes <Musicke>, altho the (slackned) strings make but a Iarring and vnpleasing [sourd/] noyse, vntill the Instrument be tun'd, the Lutanist is not by that diuerted from the Pursuit of a melody (harmony) whose Delights abundantly [rep] recompence that short Trouble which was the Prologue to them: so neither shud Christians for feare of the first Expostulations of angry Conscience, decline a <happy> reconciliation with it; that will produce such Ioyes; [th] as will oblige vs to blesse the Teares Repentance /that Fz/ cost vs: and which will not be qualify'd with any other Sorrow, then that we shall resent for hauing tasted |f. 274v| Them no sooner /for permitting our Obstinancy to depriue vs so long of so high a Satisfaction. <contentment>/ The Joy that attends man's Reconciliation with his Maker, is emblem'd in the ↑Luke 15.↓ Gospel, <Parable> by the Musicke and the Reuels that welcom'd the repenting Prodigal Son's return vnto his Father.[17] There ↑Ibidem.↓ our Sauior tels vs, that There is Ioy in the Presence of the Angels of God, over one Sinner that repenteth.[18] If then those blessed spirits, whose Felicity /happines/ seemes incapable of accession, find it encreas'd by a Conuersion in which their Charity alone concernes

[16] Exo. 8:2.
[17] Luke 15:24.
[18] Luke 15:10.

them; how great a Ioy [th] must that be which the sinner himselfe resents In a change, whose sweets he possesses /enioyes/ by personall /appropriated/ Fruition not bare Sympathy. ↑I can compare our Combats with our Sins to nothinge fitlyer then to Samson's with his Lyon, who whilst aliue roar'd against and molested him, but being dead, he found his Carcasse full of Honey-combs: for so, tho the Being / / of our Sins incessantly affright vs, yet when kil'd by sincere Repentance they afford Ioyes aduantagiously repaying the trouble of the Conquest.↓[19] And certinly, if once our Vices fall within the Notion of Enemys, it will be as cleare in reason as agreable to experience, that to ouercome them must be <much> more satisfactory /a hiher Satisfaction/ then to obey them; and that lesse Delights are created by committing [them] then by Subduing them: Sins being like Mayden-heads, that neuer giue so much Pleasure as when parted with. And as Moses, the first time that by God's ↑Ex. 4, 6,7.↓ Command he put his hand into his Bosome, he [tooke it out <pull'd>] tooke it out as white as Snow with leprosie; but the next time he put it there againe, he drew it thence perfectly Sound /recouer'd <[restor'd]>/. So Sinners that haue long forgotten <both> to do good [workes] and to take notice of the Ill they act, <do> when they begin to turne their eyes inward vpon themselues discouer there a hideous Leprosy of Sins and Faults that dos at first affright them; but then /afterwards/ the (faythfull) Repetition of the Same Duty, restores them to a Condition not inferior to that which preceded their Apostasy.

These ↑Ibidem.↓ I conceiue to be the grand Dissuasiues which the Deuill employes to make men Strangers to [this Dut] Self-conuersation: but the Inducement which makes the Diuell himselfe so much it's Enemy, |f. 275| Is that it /this duty/ is a branch [of] /Kind/ of Consideration: a quality /practise,/ that he as much detests /abhorres/ as we neglect; as being equally destructiue to what is His Dessein<s>, and aduantageous to what should be our's. Yow haue too rententiue /good/ a Memory (Dear Sister) to [reta] forget /not to retaine <remember>/ a Story my Father often vs'd to tell, how hauing employ'd a Footman into Bohemia expressely about Bisnesse of Concernment, and permitted him to performe another triuiall Errand (to serue for a <specius> Pretence to the [ot] former) he loyter'd so long by the Way that [he abs] at his returne to Lismore, [being] his Lord requiring an account of his Success, he gaue him an exact one of the Triuiall Errand of his Iourney; but being demanded one of the Important one, he then remembers that he had cleane, /quite <absolutely>/ forgotten it. This Story has very often presented it selfe to my Fancy; for methinkes euery one I see is <personates> (by his inconsideratenesse) this Footman; and acts his <in greate> ouersights. For God sends vs in to this World that by seruing him in this life, we may secure our selues of an immortall happinesse in the next: and

[19] Jud. 14:9.

[f] (in the meane time) for our better accomodation in this Pilgrimage, allowes vs Recreations, and moderate endeauors to purchase transitory Goods: but forgetfull /wretched/ we, mindlesse of the grand End and Dessein of our Creation, God's seruice, [b] entirely busy our selues in the Fruition of these fleeting Pleasures, and the Cares of these /our/ lesser Concernments, till we are call'd to an account by Death, and then at the End of our Liues we begin to remember that we haue forgot the Businesse of them. Poore Mortals, that come into the World they remember not Why, liue in the World they consider not How, and go out of the World they know not Whither.[20] <I am confident> this Quick-sand / / of Inconsideration has cast away more Sinners, then all those hideous Rockes (of notorious Crimes,) that are so fam'd for Shipwracking of Soules. ↑{like} Beasts that chewed not the Cud we |are| vncleane by the Law. Leuit. 11,7.↓

It has euer been one of the greatest and most successfull Policys of the old Tempter (as I show in [my] a Treatise, Of the Strategems of the Deuill)[21] by keeping in a perpetuall /continuall/ Hurrey, so to [diu] busy our Cares <thouhts> about the Accessary /Incidents/ of Life, as to diuert vs wholly from the Thoughts of the Bisnes /Errand/ of our Liues, or at least to put of /defer/ those Thoughts so long, till at last they serue rather to beget Despaire then Amendment. <Conuersion> For certinly the Condition that most men are fool'd into and liue in, is so vaine and so vnworthy, that they could neuer be preuail'd with to endure it if they would but allow themselues the leasure to consider it. The [Honors and] Happinesse and Delights this [and delu] Empty World dos delude vs with, being iust like those we vse to tast in Dreames, which we enjoy no longer then whilst we are <lye> asleepe, and <but> disappeare as soone as our Reason dos return to the Exercise <performe> of it's Function. <accustom'd proper> ↑which we then only {see} when we make no vse /vse not/ our eyes.↓ |f. 275v| Which Opinion, (to omit other Reasons that suggest it) I am much confirm'd in, by this Consideration, that I haue euer obseru'd that Sicknesse or any other Great affliction, dos vsually produce, (eu'n in their greediest courters <passionatest louers>) a hih Disesteem and Disrelish of the Vanityes of the World, tho formerly neuer so eagerly pursu'd or fondly doated on. The <leading> Cause of this Greate Change I haue euer esteem'd to be, that Sicknesse by rowzing vp the Conscience, obliges /forces/ vs to consider, and consequently to Despize, those trifling vanitys, [tha] we forfeit heau'n for: since otherwise, the Priuation of a Good making vs prize it more; the Losse of these transitory [thi] Pleasures /things/ we doted on, shud encrease <augment> our Value of them; and their [Want] Absence, keene <spurre, stimulate> our Desire of reinioying them. Nor can our Libertines iustly

[20] Source unknown.

[21] No MS of this title has survived. RB made a similar point in the *Aret.* (bk. 2, ch. 4). Cf. Jacobus Acontius's *Satanæ Strategemata* as *Satans Stratagems, or the devils Cabinet-Council Discovered* (1648), a project for which Dury and Thomas Goodwin were responsible (Webster 34).

attribute this Effect to sick men's feare of Death as they contemn'd the world rather [as] because to loue <doate on> it was sinfull in /danger to/ a Dying then vnworthy of a liuing /wise/ man: since not onely [forlorne /] Desperate and forlorne Diseases, but tooth-akes, and any outward affliction <we resent> that concernes not Life, and least not to the Graue, [pro] (so it be greate enuf but to oblige vs to consider) produce[s] the same Effect.

↑[And by this we is no illeg.] And by this we may iudge of the Importance of consideration[s] since such sharpe /harsh/ Motiues <Inducements> as Afflictions, are both thought necessary /requisite/ and employ'd /made vse of/ to [induce] constraine vs to it.↓ I find in the Euangelical Profet, that when God begins to reckon vp the Sins of the [Iew rebellio] obdurate Iewes, (to iustify those Iudgments that they did prouoke,) he premises (as the cause of all, ↑Esay. 1.3.↓ The Oxe knoweth his owner and the Asse his master's crib: but Israel doth not not know, my People doth not Consider: ranking Inconsideration with Ignorance (as indeed it is but Ignorance for the Time,) and he that refuses to consider, with the Dullest of Beasts. Suitably to which [t] in the same Booke, the Diuine Author of it complaining of the Brutishnesse of his People, expreses his Resentment in these Termes, ↑Esay. 44.19.↓ And none considereth in his Heart, neither is there Knowledge or vnderstanding to say &c. So Elihu ↑Iob. 34,17.↓ declaring the iust and Terrible Iudgments of God vpon the Wicked, addes, Because they turned back from him, and would not consider any of his Wayes. Consonant to this are those Expressions of God in Ezekiall, ↑Ezek. 18,14.↓ Now lo, if he beget a Son that seeth all his father's sins which he hath don, and considereth, and doth not such like, &c. And in the Progresse of the same Chapter ↑vers, the 28.↓ Because he considereth and turneth way from all his Transgressions that he hath committed, he shall surely liue, he shall not dye. And thus in Hosea speaking of the Impenitence of his People (which made them vnfit Obiects and incapable of mercy) he sayth, ↑Hosea, 7,2.↓ And they consider not in their hearts that I remember all their wickednesse, &c. Thus in the first of Haggai, God twice commands the Iewes to ↑Haggai 1,5,7.↓ Consider their wayes. Let men therefore euer imagine that they heare God saying as he dos in the cloze of the 50th Psalme, ↑Ps. 50,22.↓ Now consider this ye that forget God, least I teare yow in peeces, and there be none to deliuer. |f. 276| Let me therefore, for forgetfull Mortals take vp that Wish of the 2 and 30th of Deuteronomy, ↑Deut. 32,29.↓ O that they were wise, that they vnderstood this; that they would consider their latter End.[22] But [alas, most men] it has euer been the Deuil's Dessein and his Endeauor, to render consideration as odious to vs as it is destructiue to his Ends vpon vs; that hauing spent our Liues without considering to what Purposes they were lent vs, we may leape (as it were) hoodwink't into an

[22] RB has used "consider" sixteen times in this passage, evidently following the concordance quite closely.

Eternity we (neuer thought on and) are vtterly vnprepar'd for; and in it be euerlastingly vnhappy. Most men on the other side are so obsequious to the least suggestions /temptations/ of this Nature and are so willing to busy their thoughts vpon any Employment that may diuert <deliuer> them from that hatefull thing cald Considering; that it is now growne not onely neglected but despiz'd and laught at; and the vsefullest employment of Wit and Reason, is held an Argument of the want of them. They had rather liue at Randome, then take the paines to examine whither or no they do soe: /erre in then consider what they do/ their Bodyes are oftentimes carry'd to the Graue before /sooner then/ their thoughts: they more resent a Sicknesse because it obliges them to consider, then out of the Consideration of it Paines or Danger, and if I not apprehend to be accus'd rather of a homely then a False comparaison /expression/ I shoud affirme that many of them <are so vnconcern'd in their owne Actions that they seeme> Act meerly as they spit, I meane without thinking <deliberating, considering> of it before or reflecting on it afterwards; in a word there is nothing (except Vertu,) to which they are greater strangers then to themselues.

But truly most men liue after such a Rate, that we must cease to wonder they are so vnwilling to [be] <grow> acquainted with themselues, for as soone as they come to know themselues they fright themselues. (Alas) The Vanitys the World presents vs are so tempting /alluring/ and our Natures so treacherous, that for those whom their Condition and relation /constraines / obliges/ to be conuersant with [these glitters] them, it is extreamely difficult to haue them so [of] much the Objects of our Senses, without hauing them at length <tho by vnheeded steps> too much those of our Affections, if frequent and timely Reflections on their Emptinesse and Danger, forbid not the banes betwixt our hearts and them, before our Desires are growne too eager /violent/ to obey our Reasons. Then too [the fond] Our Iudgments are easily [sed] deluded by the Currant Opinions of the Times and Places that we liue in; which from a bare Conniuence at, or [Cor] Prudent complyance with /Conformity to/ it insensibly passes, not only to beleeue /approue/ but to applaud; and last of all heedlesnesse, by vnperceiu'd degrees hatches our Failings into Habitudes; and Sin (that has this of Tyrannous in it's Nature, to deriue a Right /title/ from it's owne Vsurpations) |f. 276v| becoms almost incurable before it is perceiu'd: then Shame and Custome, make[s] vs thinke rather how to excuse our Vices then how to [f relinquish] abandon them: such is the foolish Pride that reignes within vs, that we had rather by obstinacy persist in our past faults, then by amendment / / tacitly avow /confesse/ them: as if to Repeat Faults when once acknowledg'd to be such, ought to produce lesse Blushes then the Failings that preceded that confession: as if the same Guilt that merits Shame in the first vnfit Acts, did loose that Property in succeeding ones, and Faults that deserue Censure in <for> themselues, [shu] were chang'd into Vertus by the Accession /Aggrandisement/ of that other Fault call'd obstinacy.

Now often remembring vs that we are but Pilgrims in this World and Citizens of a better; proportions our Concernments and our aymes to those Relations: weaning vs from those transitory Pleasures, that may make vs forfeit our Title to euerlasting ones; and making vs much more carefull of the <great> End and Errand /Bisness/ of Life then those things that are at best but the Conueniences /Accessarys/ and Accomodations of Life. This Practise makes vs as strictly examine our owne Actions as we would do those our Enemys; and take a suruay of our owne Deportments /carriage/ [that] after which we need not feare [the Examen of] another's: it withdrawes our Desires from trifles to place [them] /addresse/ them to <on> more congruous objects; and vnconcerns <our Affections> [vs] in the World, ere they haue leasure /time/ to take deepe rooting there. Then for the vnexamin'd opinions of the Vulgar, that Cry vp things (meerly) because they are cry'd vp, and rate them rather by their Esteem then their value; Considering teaches vs <both> to vse them, and at the same time Pitty or laf at them: to reach our ends with other men's opinions; but frame our Creed solely of our owne: ↑A ladder to our Ends, but not an Article <Pillar> of our Creed.↓ and deale with such opinions as Diuines do with the ingenious fictions of the <ancient> Poets, which they Employ indeed, but Beleeue not. For my part (Dear Sister) I must confesse that when in my solitary retirements I do sometimes deuest myselfe of all sublunary Relations; and with abstracted thoughts looke <behold> on the Intrigue and Passages of the world, with the same temper <eyes> that I haue don on Playes, (I meane only to [deli] please and to informe my selfe, without being otherwise concern'd either in the miscarriages of Actors or the Euents of things;) I little misse /I do not much regret the Absence of/ Blacfryars;[23] the whole World being but a spacious /vast/ stage /scene/ where there's perpetually <dayly> acted, Comy-tragedys, (to me) no lesse diuerting, and incomparably more Instructiue. And it is <tis in this> heere perhaps as 'tis in other <lesser> Playes, where altho some weare Kings, and others are calld |f. 277| Lords and weare rich Clothes; and haue perchance both bigger Titles and far brighter <gawdyer> suits, then many that but looke on in the Boxes; yet the Spectators haue a greater share of the Pleasure of the Play /Tis Certin/ then the [(very)] Actors. In Effect there are some persons that take as much deliht to contemplate and laf at the Vanitys of the World, as others do to hunt or to enjoy them. And truly he that [with] shall take the paines to strip what men's desires so greedily /eagerly/ pursue; of those borrow'd ornaments (or Disguizes rather) that vse to [set] dazle and to cheat our sight; and with a Penetrating ey will pierce and pry into their conceald /retir'd <inward>/ or Essentiall Propertys; shall perceiue, that not only this Empty Pageantry and these Glittering Trifles the fonder world adores; but most of those more solemne and more likely Goods, that they

[23] The public theatres were closed in 1642.

that passe for wise so much affect; are all but vary'd and disguized Folly: the Obiects of our Pursuits being (for the most part) soe Vnsatisfying; and the contentment they Promise being so defeatingly disproportionate to that they giue, ↑and by consequent so vnworthy of a wiseman's serious Passion,↓ that we may iustly Pitty their Ambitions, that aspire but to Scepters, Schollership or Faces. For me, that neuer thought the World but a greate Bedlam, peopled with fooles and Knaues <knaues and Mad men>; I cannot consider it without at once ressenting the differing /contrasting/ Passions of both those Ancient Sages; for at the same time that Heraclitus his Teares ouerflow my Eyes to behold so much Wickednesse /misery,/ Democritus his Fits of Lafter seize me /Smiles dimple my cheekes,/ to looke on so much Folly /Madnesse./[24] ↑I could <heere> very willingly pursue [this su] so copious <amply> a subiect↓ but ↑that my Thoughts being at present engaged vnto another,↓ I feare I haue <already> so farre digress'd from my Theame, that I shal perhaps be held /thought/ Inconsiderate eu'n in treating of Consideration:[25] but when I remember that (eu'n) Market people's Charity will oblige them to ride a little out their owne way, to direct a wandring <errant> Traueller into his; (and yet they are not censur'd <shamed> but thank't for it) I shall not be much troubled to haue been lesse obedient to the Lawes of Method if this Excursion bring any body to be more obsequious to those of God. Nor shall I much regret to be esteem'd an Inconsiderate Writer, so I preuaile with my Readers to grow Considerate Liuers.

The Second Section

To proceed now to the time of this Reflection, we are first to consider what Portion of Time is <dayly> to be allotted to this Exercise, and next vpon what part of this Day it is to be assign'd.

The former of these [place] we can as little place positiue <[and vnalterable]> limits to, as Temperance and |f. 277v| Liberality can exactly and vnalterably define the Quantitys of our meate and drinke, and the value of our Gifts: which depend vpon [such] a multiplicity of (oftentimes) disagreeing Circumstances; that they [beco] admit not of precise <particular> and vnuary'd Rules. But as in Temperance, the number of our Cups tho not namedly prescrib'd, is to be deduc't from our Constitution, and those other considerations that circumstantiate our Mirth, so heere, we must determine the time we employ in Reflection, employ in on the one side by the number or paucity of obseruables that deserue our thoughts; and on the other by the Presence or Want <Absence> of Distractions, and the fitnesse or indisposednesse of our Minds to this exercice: which

[24] Heraclitus was known as 'the weeping philosopher'; Juvenal stressed Democritus's laughter at the world. Both epithets were commonplaces.

[25] Such wordplay was unusual for RB.

somtimes will require halfe an hower, [for] often A quarter will suffice; sometimes it will exact more then the former, and at other times lesse then the latter will serue the turne.[26] It being far lesse materiall how much time was spent in this Reflection, as how wel it is perform'd.

Then for the season of the Day vpon which this Portion of time is to be assign'd: it ought (if possible) to be constantly the same. Vnder the Old Testament, God commanded the Dayly sacrifices to be offered constantly Morning and Euening; and vnder the New he requires the seuenth Day to be constantly reseru'd for and employed in his Publick seruice /worship./ And in effect, as both Fisick and experience teach vs, when we regularly obserue set houres for meales; our stomacks do conforme themselues therevnto, and perform their functions more [ex] vigorously /exactly/ at those houres, then if we either anticipated, or forgot /let them slip/ them: so <find we> in the Exercices of the mind, the thoughts accustom'd to set times of acting, do then fall to it more disposedly, <and with much more alacrity> then the Distractions vsually consequent to an irregular and vnorderly Employment of them dos permit.[27] But what part of the Day is the fittest for our Reflection, if the [thing] /point/ we are cheefly to determine. The Disciples of Pythagoras antiently declar'd in fauor of the Euening; which time they strictly chose to walke out once a day and giue one another a [illeg.] <mutuall and> particular account of their Proficiency or Failings in the Progresse /   / of Vertu and of Knowledge.[28] And it seems the Preference of that season for this Purpose, was as old as Isaac, who when he first met his Mistris was ↑Gen. 24,63.↓ walking out into the field to meditate [at] in the Evening.

For my part I haue still esteem'd the night the properest time for this Reflection, (and therefore I [dedicate to it] <practise> somtimes during my vndrese; [and sometimes] <but commonly> dedicate to it some [time] leasure betwixt my being abed <going to> and falling asleep. And that for |f. 278|

---

[26] RB mentioned Bishop Joseph Hall in the preface to *Occ. Refl.* (2.327 and 332-33) but noted that he wrote his meditations before reading Hall's *Arte of Divine Meditation* (1606). (RB owned two other volumes by Hall.) RB's sister Mary meditated for two hours each day after her conversion in 1647 (Mendelson 94-95). For a broader perspective, Mary's own account is useful: T. C. Croker, ed. *Some Specialities in the Life of Mary, Countess of Warwick* (1848).

[27] For RB's scheduled prayers, see BP 37.156^{v}: "A long Morning Prayer. A shorter Morning Prayer. A Prayer for the Evening Longer and Shorter. A Prayer in Travell. A Prayer on Sunday. Morning, Evening. A Prayer on a Fast Day. A Prayer in Sicknesse. A Prayer before Fisick. A Prayer on the first of May. A Prayer on the 25th of January. A Thanksgiving after the Sacrament. Divers Graces. A Prayer before the Sacrament." January 25 was his birthday; May 1, RB told Burnet, was the day he was thrown from a horse, which led to serious health problems (cf. BL Add. MS 4229, f. 60). Evelyn recalled that in the mornings RB had private devotions and then pursued philosophic studies and worked in his laboratory (Maddison 187). RB owned two copies of Thomas Goodwyn's *The Returne of Prayers* (1636, 1641), which resolved the case of how to discern the answer to prayers. Goodwyn emphasized behavior before, during, and after prayer.

[28] Perhaps Laërtius, *Life of Pythagoras* 8.15-21.

Diuerse Reasons; as (First) because then the Period of the Day and end (Close) of Action being arriu'd; we can then more conueniently then at any other time, as it were Muster (vp) all those obseruables of the foregoing day, which are to be the obiects of our Thoughts /Reflections./ Next because not onely that season is freest from visits and [suc] such like Disturbances and Interruptions;[29] but the Darknesse of the Night not distracting the Soule by the (various) Obiects of the outward senses; dos as it were concenter her within her selfe, and [there] <so> by restraining invigorate / / her operations <Functions>. And certinly the multitude of outward obiects that incessantly sollicit the Soule to gad and wander after them, do so debauch (and diuert) her from her Employments, that ‘tis no wonder if according to the Arabian Prouerbe that bids vs Shut the Windowes that the Light may come in;[30] the Soule [discernes] (like owles that see best <most> in the darke) discernes best when the Body's Eyes are cloz'd, and bestowes most attention vpon her owne Acts, when her selfe is the sole obiect of that attention. Afterwards /[next] then/ because the reading or meditating any thing before sleepe <dos, as experience witnesses,> stampe[s] deeper impresses of it in the memory /mind/ because that the immediately subsequent sleepe, hinders those [freq newest /latest/] <freshest> Images, /Lineaments/ to be suddenly effac't or obliterated by any new ones, till these latest haue had time to fix /root/ and settle there. Which peraduenture also is the cause <reason> why our Dreames vsually are much ally'd /of kinne/ to those Thoughts or Discourses we haue been very earnest in to bedward /before sleepe seizes vs/ whence we may deriue a new benefit to this season of Reflection, which is the Influence it may haue on our Dreames.[31] To all this we may adde that sleepe being but a Short Death (which mou'd the Spartans to place the sister's statues still together)[32] and oftentimes the Prologue of a lasting one; [the] vpon the same consideration <reason> that a modern wit sayd that sleep look't so like Death, he durst not venture himselfe with it without saying his Prayers,[33] we may iustly feare to trust our

[29] For RB's view of social visits, cf. “Of Time and Idleness” (f. 16^{v}) and two early letters to Lady Ranelagh (1.xxvii and 6.49). He apparently wrote to Marcombes while someone was visiting him (BW 1.xxxiv).

[30] Source unknown. In *Style*, RB referred to Theodoricus Hackspan, *Fides et Leges Mohammedis* (1646), which included selections from the Koran.

[31] In the *Aret.*, RB noted that among the symptoms of acquired virtue were “Chast and vntroubled Dreames: because it argues, wel regulated Affections, when the horse gos on his way /behaues himself/ quietly, tho his Rider be asleepe” (f. 230).

[32] The metaphor of sleep as a short death is a commonplace, but since he quoted Browne's *Religio Medici* (1643) in the next clause, RB might also have recalled the poem printed on the previous page in Browne: *“Sleepe is a death, O make me try, / By sleeping what it is to die. / And as gently lay my head / On my Grave, as now my bed”* (ii.§12, p. 72).

[33] Browne, *Religio Medici* ii.§12, p. 71. Because death so resembles sleep, Browne dared “not trust it without [his] prayers, and an halfe adiew unto the world, and take [his] farewell in a Colloquy with God.” RB's library included a 1682 edition of *Religio Medici*.

selfes with /to/ it till we haue leuell'd [al] our accounts with God: since those, whose Conscience is not more gasping then their Bodyes, vse still to take a Care to euen scores with heu'n, when they approach their End. Both this Reflection and this season of it are prescribed by Dauid to his opposers [in the] where he sayes to them, ↑Ps. 4, 4.↓ Stand in awe and sin not: Commune with your owne hart vpon your bed &c. And practised by himselfe as appeares by that expression of his in the <book of> Psalmes, I will blesse the Lord who hath giuen me Counsel; My reins[34] also instruct me in the night seasons: and doubtlesse he that can truly say wih the |f. 278^{v}| Spouse in the Canticles ↑Cant. 3,1.↓ By night on my bed I sought him whom my soul loueth: [shall] if he perform that Duty as he ought, shall not haue long occasion <cause, reason> to sigh out the rest /make an end/ of the Verse, I sought him but I found him not. But where as it may be pretended against the fitnesse of the night season to reflect in, that it <this Practice> looses vs too much sleepe, <and so creates a trouble> it will be answered, that so triuiall an inconuenience is aduantageously repay'd by the alleadg'd Aduantages; and that this Practise [robs /impedes] <abridges> so little <encroach on> our Necessary rest, that a short Custome will quickly take of any harshnesse we may at first find in it. (And truly to a person of my humor that thinke those [l] Moments clearly gain'd, that I redeem from sleepe; the shortning /paring/ of that <Deth> is look't on [/consider'd/] rather as a motiue to my Choice / / then a Dissuasiue from it.[35] Howeuer tho the Considerations I haue mention'd; make me most fancy that Elation they haue led me to: yet do I not esteem the being made in the darke /night/ so essential a Property of our Reflection, that they to whom the posture <aspects> of Circumstances render that season inconuenient, may not constantly employ another: or that he that has ty'd himself to any one in particular may not (for a time) dispense with himselfe vpon occasion: for these setled howers, and all those orderly Circumstances of Actions /Dutys/ that belong not properly to their nature; being established <attended to> but for conueniency may safely and innocently be declin'd or alter'd when the Motiue /End/ of their Establishment <constructing> becoms that of their Change.

---

[34] In Biblical usage, the reins are the seat of affections and feelings; other contemporary uses defined it as the kidneys or loins.

[35] Cf. "Of Time and Idleness," f. 16^{v}. By 1653 William Petty and Broghill worried about RB's excessive reading. Petty noted that RB could "draw more knowledge and satisfaction from two hours of [his] own meditation, than from twelve hours endurance of other men's loquacity. For when [RB meditated], it is always upon something that [he is] not yet clear in (and a little armour will serve, being put upon the right place)" (6.138).

The Third Section

And now we are arriu'd at the last part of this Discourse, which must instruct vs to perform well, what we haue hitherto so highly commended if it be well perform'd. To render therefore [this] our Reflection both acceptable to God and Profitable to our selues, it must be condition'd with these 4 Propertys; and be perform'd Willingly, Attentiuely, Reflectingly, and Constantly.

The Former of these Attributes is exacted in our Reflection, vpon the Score of being a Necessary qualification in all Acts of Devotion. ↑For [a] Good Performances without a Good Intent, may indeed make the Act Good but not the Agent.↓[36] [And] <But> that the Will is the principall thing that God requires in his Seruice, is a truth acknowledg'd that it's euincing [can] <will> not here be necessary: and therefore I shall no longer back at this Point then will suffice, to answer to the Doubt whether it be lawfull and Expedient, to <tye themselues (as many do)> |f. 279| To Assigne <consecrate> dayly such and <or> so much time to [su] Meditation or the like deuout Employments, by /with/ the solemne engagement of an Oath; That as I dare not Condemne it as vnlawfull, so I cannot commend /approue/ it as Conuenient.[37] For the vowes of that Nature about <things or> Circumstances indifferent be not (perhaps) absolutely sinfull, yet certainly these Passages of [th] Scripture seeme <much> to frowne on them as infringers of our Christian Liberty; And truly, we, whose Frailtys render [vs] it <so> impossible for vs to auoid stumbling at those blockes <that> God's [precise] Law precisely <positiuely> and expresly has prohibited; shud not methinks, <our selues> purposely augment the impossibility of our owne Innocence by creating those omissions, sins, by our vowes, which are not so in their nature. ↑To omit the (not improbable) opinion of some Diuines, who vnderstand that rigid Passage in the of Matt.[38] Sweare not at all &c. to Promissory Oaths, as relating to the foregoing words, where that kind of oaths is mention'd.↓ Specially since the Diuel is euer most actiue to diuert vs from [Dutys] Pious Exercices, when our Engagements are the greatest to performe them; and the Forbiddennesse of things has vsually the Property of encreasing men's Desires. [I would not haue Christians] Tis true that to those [Vowes invigorate their Weakenesse] that possesse but a faint Perseuerance, <these Vowes invigorate> [by turning]

[36] Cf. the *Aret.* (bk. 2, ch. 6).

[37] The question of oaths was hotly debated by Dury and others during the 1640s. RB framed the issue as an opportunity for casuistry and the resolving of a doubt or scruple. He never altered his reluctance to take oaths. In 1680 RB declined the presidency of the Royal Society and wrote to Hooke about his "great (and perhaps peculiar) tenderness in point of oaths" (BW 1.cxix). For useful discussion, see Hunter's "Alchemy."

[38] Matt. 5:33-37; see also *Swearing* 6.26, where RB wrote that he did not justify "that plausible error of our modern *Anabaptists*, that indiscriminately condemn all oaths as absolutely and indispensably prohibited and absolutely abolished by the gospel."

their Resolues <by turning them> into Dutys: but then they are not so much to be approoued for that Aduantage <turning our Resolues into Dutys> as to be dislik't for turning our Omissions into Sins: I would not haue Christians owe their Constancy to our Reflection to any other motiue then it's owne Excellence; nor enslaue themselues by Engagements, that lessen the Gallantry <merit> of their Perseuerance, and create a Guilt<iness> in their Neglects.

The second Attribute we haue required in our Examen /Reflection/ is Attention, which ought both to Precede, to Accompany, and to Follow it. An Antecedaneous Attention is very necessary to prepare Materialls for our thoughts /Reflections/ and truly they that dayly Looke on things without taking notice of them, and make those Passages that are conuersant [to] with their Senses, strangers to their Obseruation, may easily be Children at the Age of Methusaleh,[39] altho their Heedlessness be in this more culpable then that of Beasts or Infants, that |f. 279v| the latter can father vpon their Want[s] of Reason, what the former owe entirely to their Neglect of it. Wherefore I haue euer approu'd and often practis'd their Custom, that after any considerable Portion of time spent either in Study or in Conuersation, vse to [employ] <improoue> the next conuenient Pawses that succeed those Employments, to [ruminate and] recollect what their Bookes or their Company haue afforded or suggested (to) them of most obseruable. And indeed since both Reading and Discoursing haue been so iustly compared to the Eating <Ingesting> of the Soule, and Ruminating /Reflecting/ to it's Concoction; me thinkes we that [seldom] spend <not> aboue 2 howres of the Day to feed our selues, and employ all the Residue of the [D] twenty-foure, to concoct and to disgest what (during that short [ti] space) our stomackes haue receiu'd; shud at least allow our selues to Inuert the Proportion, and make the time employ'd in Reading or Conuersing, pay Tithe to that assign'd to Recollection. |f. 280|

There is next in our Reflection required a Concomitant Attention, which forbids vs to perform it, only as many People go to heare a sermon vpon Sundays, not to do it but to haue it done.[40] No, let [vs the] <vs by> our Attention in this Duty [/examen/] expresse our Concernment <how much we ar concern'd> in the things it conuerses with; and by a due consideration of the Importance of this Examen fit our selues for it's more exquisite Performance. Nor will it suffice that Attention both Precede and Accompany our Reflection; but it must also be subsequent vnto it, to take Notice of it's success[es]. For it has euer been one of the greatest strategemes of the Deuill, to make vs consider Practises of this nature, meerly as <vnder the notion of> Taskes, and not as Meanes of improouement; and make sinners perform Dutys, as children vse to take Fisick, rather to obey their Parents, not to regaine their Health. Now by this fond mistake we

---

[39] Gen. 5:21-27.

[40] In Table 1, note essay #15. A Censure of some Preachers & Hearers of Sermons.

wrong our selues, not only by rendring our Performances vncomfortable, (by cheating our selues of the contentment of 'better' expectation's) but we also make them oftentimes vnprofitable <too>; for whilst we looke vpon Pious Prescriptions only as Taskes and not as Meanes of Grace, by looking no farther, we think our whole Duty [satisfy'd /performed/] <accomplish't> in the Act; and loose the Benefit <aduantage> of [Improouement] <the Proficiency they [wo] might afford> by not aspiring <intending> to it.

The Third and principal Property, that (at [the] our entrance into this Section) we haue required in our Examen, is, that it be perform'd Reflectiuely; in order to which, both our Memorys, our Reasons and our Consciences, must all 3 act their Parts. But because their Dutys are hugely complicated in the Examen it selfe, we will not seuer them in our Discourses of it; but mold all our Aduices on that Theame, into the following Directions.

1. The first is, to recall orderly to mind, |f. 280v| Whateuer new obseruables in <any kind of> Knowledge, either your Study or Conuersation has afforded or your owne Thoughts suggested yow, the foregoing Day. The memory may be [commanded] <enioyn'd> to make this Restitution either in the order their Seniority /Priority/ <came [in] thither in> giues them, or that which their Considerablenesse assignes them in your Esteem. Those that deserue a permanent station and a more setled Residence in your memory; ought by a frequenter Repetition to be more secur'd from Obliuion. To which End it were highly conducible to keepe a kind of written Diary, to preserue Choicer obseruations and Collections from Vanishing. Of which (Dear Sister) your Comands may exact of me a Draught /Modell/ which I remember I once inuented, and, for a time, made vse of; [in] <by> which, [w] (if I mistake not) without any tedious nicety of subdivisions, particulars may be so contriu'd, <marshall'd> as to auoid the Inconuenience of Bulke without incurring that of Confusednesse.[41]

2. Secondly, Consider what good (things) yow haue don that Day; for so either their Paucyty wil produce blushes in yow for your [Re] Vnprofitablenesse and create desires of redeeming those omissions; or the Applauses of your conscience[s] (for your numerous good actions) wil both confirm your vertuous habitudes; and [heigh] (like Ionathan's Hony, that so [enliuen'd] <reuiu'd> him in his [P] Chase /Pursuit/ of the Philistims)[42] heighten your Zeale against those spirituall Aduersarys, whose ouerthrow is [a] recompenc'd /attended/ with so great suauitys. ↑And tho <if> (as Moses when he conuers't with the People wore a Vaile [ouer] <vpon> his face (Gen. 34.)[43] yow [dis] maske your actions vnto men, at least, [as the same, Mose] imitate the same Moses his vnualing himselfe [befo] when he [w] treated with the Lord, by throwing off all Disguises

[41] His diary has not survived.

[42] 1 Sam. 14:24-30.

[43] Exo. 34:33.

when yow make[s] your Court to Heu'n, and your Appearance before God.↓ And at such seasons as your kinder <applauding> Conscience, shall (as it will sometimes) proue not only liberall but <almost> profuse in her Rewards; be carefull to improue those fauor'd interuals to the making of [ho pi] vertuus <pious> and handsom Resolutions; and remember in your faintings and your Doubts, the temper of our [Soule] <Mind spirit> at the establishing of those Resolues; and make vse of those Opportunitys, to treasure vp such a stocke of Ioy, /Comfort/ as may enable your Piety to subsist during the Absence of the /ordinary/ vsuall reuenues of sensible consolations[44] |f. 281| As the Israelites were commanded to reserue of that Double Portion of Manna they gathered on the sixth day of the weeke, that what they then lay'd vp might serue to sustaine them when there fell none on the seauenth.[45] Also let any more illustrius Benefit perceiu'd by <hauing> waited on God's ordinances, make yow more Diligent and constant in your attendance on them: but haue a <mighty> care withall, lest your Pride vpon <of> your Improouements, turn not this Pretious Manna into Wormes: the surest Protector against which Danger is strictly to examine our [best] Seruices; for then the best of them will appeare so defectuous, that we shall rather find our selues fauor'd /oblig'd/ by their acceptation, then meriters by their Performance. Besides, that (indeed) Ordinances, ought not so much to make vs proud for their being profited by as to humble vs for their beeing needed: for as the <most> successfull Operations of Fisick in purging euill humors, do yet argue som vnsoundnesse or Infirmity <in the Body> so [eu] the very greatest Proficiency we can deriue from [the] Preaching the Sacraments, and other such helps of Grace, [argue] imply [some] an Imperfection in the Soule; and therefore in heu'n, where we shall be fully Perfect, these ordinances shall [cease] <be no more.> This Manna ceases when the spirituall Israëll, enters the heu'nly Canaan. Nor (eu'n in the Wildernesse) did manna fall on the Sabbath, because that sacred Rest (perhaps) typyfy'd that Eternall one in heu'n, where Christ / / shall be All in All.

Thirdly, Consider what sins thou hast that day committed; and looke on them in the most aggrauating Circumstances that belong to them, and are likely to produce a Detestation of them. But let not that suruey end before your Repentance begins; as soone as yow haue discry'd your Sins, drowne them in your Teares; and chuse rather <now> to [shed] <weepe> a little Water then euer to endure a quenchlesse Fire. [To Facili] In order to this, it is highly necessary [betimes] to oppose Sin betimes, and [vse] |f. 281[v]| decline all delayes in interrupting it's Prescriptions. The Soule with all knowne Faults must liue at greater distance, then [the] God did with the Iewes, eu'n when the Prophet complaines,

[44] The importance of a good conscience and the danger of a guilty conscience were stressed in the *Aret.* (e.g., f. 113) as well as in many works of popular divinity.

[45] Exo. 16:5.

that he was ↑Ier. 14, 8.↓ As a stranger in the Land, and as a Way-faring man that turneth aside to tarry for a night. For as we [must not (in obedience to the A ought no] shud not ↑Eph. 4, 26↓ Let the Sun go downe vpon our Wrath, so ought we not to let it Rise vpon our Impenitence: and since [Deth] <Sleepe> is always so resembling vnto Death, and so frequently it's Prologue, [the] that we know not when we [ly do] enter our beds, whither euer we shall rise out of them aliue, the only safe way is euery euening so to cleare scores with heu'n; that yow need not care tho yow do not. And surely tho Sin may sometimes baite [at] <on> the best soule, yet to [let him] entertaine and let it quietly repose there all night, is hugely hazardous and almost Desperate: there being no Bedfellow more dangerous then <vnrepented> Sin, nor any thing more vnsafe then to let that sleep with [th] yow, that [is capable to] <may> condemn yow if yow neuer wake vntill the <dredfull Clap of the> Archangels trumpet [yo] rowse yow vp.[46] In order to the Preuention of which Danger it will be requisite watchfully to [ob] (examine and) obserue, the Pretenses of the Deuill in our Passions, and not to be too fond nor too indulgent in our Constructions of their Intendments / / for as [we reade in] the sacred story dos record that the Rechab and Baanah the seruants of Ishbosheth (Saul's sonne;) [entring] <came in> into their Master's house /Pallace/ but ↑2. Sam. 4, 6.↓ |f. 282| As tho they would haue fetched wheate, but employ'd their Admission to the murder of their Lord; so oftentimes [do] our Passions, vnder the Pretence of barely satisfying the Necessitys of Naturall <Appetences> make vse of the opportunitys obtain'd vpon that score, to the subuersion of their <iust> Souuerain, Reason. Nor let the seeming[nesse] Pettynesse of any Fault, and the Infinitenesse of your Sauior's [persuade] <Mercy entice> yow to leaue any Sin vnmolested: since against so <such> greate a a Goodnesse, no Trespasse can be small; and least of all the Basenesse / / of presuming the contrary of this Truth. For certinly in this particular Consciences are like [Glass] Looking-glasses:[47] one of their greatest Perfections is faythfully to discouer the[ir] least Imperfections [t] of those that consult them. But further to secure our Piety, it will be hugely conducible to take notice of our first Coolings and Refrigerations towards Vertue; and remember that our Sauior himselfe makes it [the Crime of] <his quarrel to> the Ephesian Angel, that he had ↑Reuel. 2,4.↓ Left his First Loue. [Vpon th] And surely Apostasy dos not [always] <vsually> so boystrously attempt <our> Piety, like those nimble and violent Diseases that make it but one Act, to summon and to hurry vs to the Graue, but for the most part dos first disclose it's approaches by some fainting and languishing Distastes; which is so perillous a symptome, that it requires, a speedy bringing the syncerity of <our> performances to the test; and that we should carefully examine whither or no the

[46] RB used the sleep-death comparison on f. 278 above; Philaretus used similar language to describe his religious conversion (Maddison 32).

[47] For a similar discussion, see "Of Sin" f. 32.

Fruit <syncerity> of Vertu be not all drop't /faln/ of; tho the Leaues of a Faire outside still hang vpon the Tree. For as we see in Boats, [tho] when the Watermen approach the Staires they are to land at, tho they take in those oares that made the vessel moue, it yet persists in motion, in vigor of that, the oares had first imparted; so in religious Practises, [Good Customs are oftentimes for a while carry'd on,] we are often [carry] times for a while carry'd on to perseuere in our first Performances in vertue of [those] Good Customes [we owe to] <produc't by> our first Zeale, eu'n after that [first] Zeale [has] <has> quite [departed] forsaken vs. It will be therefore highly important, vpon occasion, to examine whither we owe |f. 282^{v}| Our Performances to what we haue been, or to what still we are; that [in] <vpon Discouery of> the former of these Cases, we may by a sudden Returne to our First Loue, both preuent our Coldnesses to Vertu from degenerating into [Enmity] <Auersion>; and make our selues as well capable of the Merit /Recording/ of our Reflection, as we vndergoe the Trouble of performing it.

Fourthly. Yow must not only consider the Good and Euill yow haue don, but the principall Circumstances that haue [attended b] promoted both, specially those <coniunctures of> accidents [that whose coniuncture] <that most> frequently do produce Euil or Good Effects, that yow may studiously decline the Former, and with an equall industry [procure] fauor the latter. Yow must examine whither in the Company yow keepe, yow are like a sparke of Fire in a Barrell of Gunpowder that conuerts euery cornel of it into it's owne Nature, or like those [th] Brookes that run into the Sea <by ([a mi] their mixture with it's brackish waues)> and loose all their owne Sweetnesse [(by mingling with it's waues)] without imparting that quality to the ocean.[48] But especially obserue the strategems of the Deuil in his Temp[ta]tings of yow; [by] after what manner he makes his first Approaches, and by what steps he [conti] proceeds in his Progresse, in the Mistery of Iniquity. For certinly tis one of the greatest suttletys of the Deuill to persuade vs that we cannot vnweaue his suttletys: since nothing can more [contribute] <conduce> to <the> making <of> his Conquests easy, then our Beleefe that his Reaches are inscrutable, and can not be describ'd. And indeed <lazy> we <do> in part contribute as much as may be, to so [ru] dangerous a cheate, being apt to be deceiu'd and glad of an Excuse, to father vpon the Impossibility of our succes the cause /guilt/ of our Neglects. But we should rather consider that the Deuill being but a Rationall and Finite Creature cannot necessitate or constraine, but only bend and inflect our Wills; otherwise there wud be very little vse of, and as little truth [th] in that Exhortation of Iames, ↑Iam. 4,7.↓ Resist the diuell and he will flee from yow. And tho it cannot be indeed deny'd, that his Facility to communicate any impressions and [con] infusions to vs; his

48 For a similar image, cf. *Aret.*, f. 214^{v}.

great skilfulnesse in our Dispositions, and dexterity of varying and fitting his Temptations to them, ioyn'd to those other Aduantages he [is] |f. 283| Possesses, make it no easy taske to track each seuerall [Proiect] <Plot [Proiect]> through all it's winding Intricacys, yet certainly they that shall seriously perpend all the Circumstances of his Temptations to the First and second Adam, and shall carefully obserue the Methode of those Addresses /suggestions/ to themselues, which his more frequent of them has (as it were) trodden /beaten/ into Pathes; shall be able to discouer enuf of his Strategems to Defeat /disappoint/ many of them: according to that of the Apostle, ↑2. Cor. 2,11.↓ We are not ignorant of his Deuices. How much the Knowledge of the Discipline and desseins of our Enemy may contribute to the regulating <improouement> and the successe of ours; I thinke euery Body cannot but acknowledge. And truly we should be able to vnriddle much of the mistery of Iniquity; if Loue were but as [Diligent] <industrious> as Enuy, and if proportioning our Care to our Concernment, we would blush, [th] not to be as [co] watchfull for our owne Preseruation, as the Deuil is to procvure our Ruine. Now the most vsuall Cheate the Deuill employs, is to represent vs forbidden Pleasures dres't in encreas'd Delights, and in those <only> qualiltys that may render them the obiects of Desire: as when the [tempted] serpent tempted the Woman's seed, the Text relates, that he tooke vp our Sauior ↑Matt. 4,8.↓ Into an exceeding high mountain (no vnfit Emblems of Expectation) and shewed him all the Kingdomes of the World and The Glory[49] of them, that is The Glory seuer'd from those conceal'd cares and <vnknown> Inconueniences, which discloz'd might (possibly) make men esteem them a fitter obiect for Patience then Ambition. Now the Properest Antidote [fo] against this Poyson is [made] <extracted [prepar'd]> out of the Poyson it selfe (as the principall Ingredient of Treacle is the Flesh of Vipers.)[50] for when we once haue been seduc't to the enjoyment of vnlawfull Pleasures, and haue found vpon triall the vast Disproportion betwixt their Promises and their Exhibitions, let vs carefully preserue those Notions our Experience and our Repentance haue form'd of them; and when soeuer we find our selues sollicited to the Repetition of our past <former> Faults, let vs but recall those solider Ideas, and but beleeue rather the vnseducing <vnerring> [Depositions] <Attestations> of our *owne* Experience, then the [Flattering] <[che] faithlesse> Promises of our [{] false Enemy or our blind /rais'd/ Desires, and we are safe. For so vnsatisfying and so empty are these meane, beggerly, criminall Delights, and so much, tho they flatter our Hopes do they discontent our |f. 283v| Tryals, that we should neuer be seduc't to relapse

[49] "The Glory" is written in letters 2X larger than usual.

[50] The *OED* notes that the original sense of treacle is "a medical compound, orig. a kind of salve, composed of many ingredients, formely in repute as an alexipharmic against and antitode to venomous bites, poisons generally, and malignant diseases." RB defined the term on f. 286; see also "Time and Idleness."

into sinfull Pleasures, [in] did we but see them when we are tempted to them, what they will appeare when we haue once enioy'd them. Thus may our Vertue (like the Gyant Antæus in the Fable)[51] be inuigorated by our falls, since culpable Fruitions thus improu'd, by <hauing> deluded our expectation / / disabuse our Desires. ↑But if sometimes (for sometimes it may happen) the Deuill proues better then his Promise in sensuall Delight; be sure then to distrust him most of all; there being then no meane betwixt our Diffidence and Ruine. For he neuer dos men the Kindnesse of Jael to Sisera, <(Iudg. 4, 19,20,21.)> to whom when he desir'd but Water she presented /brought/ Milke, but with the like Dessein of more securely afterwards oppressing [them,] /destroying/ them. If therefore yow receiue (from a suttler then Jael) like Complements with Sisera, beware yow partake not also of his Destiny.↓

Fifthly. In order to the more facile performance of all these Prescriptions, it would be extreamely expedient /conducing/ when Opportunitys permit and occasion requires, frequently and seriously to examine and catechize our selues; by asking our selues a reason <or an account> both of the Opinions we embrace, and the Actions we frequent; whether concerning this world [alone,] <only> or <else> relating to the World to come. ↑Or rather fancying /supposing/ that some Pious and iudicious Person, [exacts] <requires> of vs an account of what we Beleeue and Act, after he has obiected against them whatsoeuer our Thoughts can suggest.↓ This Practise alone I must confesse [my self] that I esteeme more auailable to the Improouement both of [our] men's Abilitys and their Conduct /Piety/ then [whole Librarys of Bookes.] <a> voluminous [Bookes,] Library. For first, by accustoming our selues to giue a reason of euery thing we either assert or Do, we insensibly accustom our selues to maintaine no opinion, nor [illeg.] practise any thing (we are concern'd in) we cannot giue a reason for. <Iust> as Grammarians by long examining [what] <euery word> they speake by the rules of their Art, at last acquire the skill of expressing themselues readily according to those Rules eu'n whilst they think not of <mind not> them. In the next Place, either we shall find our selues able to giue a rationall account of our Opinions and Carriages, [or we (and that in] or we shall not.[52] In the former case, we shall hugely encrease [our] <the> satisfation of our being in the Right by our more certain Knowledge that we are so. It teaches vs both more groundedly and more readily to iustify our sentiments and Practises, by promting vs with the same Considerations, that haue oblig'd /induc't <mou'd>/ vs to embrace them. And vpon the same score they [mig] <very> much facilitate our persuading of others;

---

[51] Apollodorus, *Bibliotheca* 2.115.

[52] Philaretus observed that "'twas not a greater happyness to inherit a good Religion; then 'twas a Fault to haue it only by inheritance; & thinke it the best because 'tis generally embrac't; rather then embrace it because we know it to be the best. That tho we cannot often Give a Reason for /of/ What we beleeue; we shud be euer able to giue a Reason Why we beleeuve it" (Maddison 35).

as indeed why shud those Arguments that [are] <we think> insufficient [in] to convince others, haue that influence vpon [me] vs?[53] |f. 284| Then, in the Latter of these Cases, this Practise will discloze to vs our owne Ignorance (and questionlesse the first step to Knowledge is to know that we want it)[54] and by that Information render vs, both lesse Peremptory in asserting our owne Opinions, and more Charitable in our Censures of those of others, by proportioning <first> our Confidence to our Euidence, and then our [Zeale] <Fiercenesse> to that Confidence.[55] And surely he that shall impartially and vnbyass'tly [ex] consider, how vast /large/ a Portion of Knowledge is yet Problematicke, [cannot but find it vnreasonable in most thin] how little of Truth we are groundedly and thoroughly [convinc't of] <satisfy'd> our selues, and how much lesse of it we are able clearly and vndeniably to demonstrate vnto others, will think the Points not few in which 'twere very vnreasonable to passe harsh Censure vpon all Dissenters. It has often been obseru'd, that they haue the most of Fierceness in their Opinions that haue [fewest] <the least of> Argument for them.[56] And truly I [am] dare confidently impute, many of those rash quarrels and those deadly Fewds which <now adays> Distances and Dissents in matters of Religion do [day] so fatally [produce] <create,> solely to men's not [exam] seriously examining whither they can [bring] <produce> as cleare Arguments <Euidence> for all the Tenets they Professe, as they require of ther Aduersarys for them which they oppose; for [sur] <certinly> were not this Practise <Duty> so neglected, we shud in diuers Articles (not Fundamentall), <find> so much of Probability on both sides, and <or> so little more then Probability on either; that we would rather wonder that we haue hit vpon the Truth, then that others haue mis<taken>s't it; and thinke our selues oblig'd to let the former much more busy our Gratitude then the latter our admiration.[57]

Sixthly; to reflect not only [but] vpon our own Actions and their Euents, but also vpon those of others; especially of those Person, in whom our [illeg.] <seuerall> Relations, do any way more peculiarly concern vs. |f. 284^{v}| For as the Ey beholds not it selfe Directly, but in a Glasse, so certinly we are the fittest iudges of our owne Actions, when we looke vpon them in the Person of another. Since then deuesting them of Relations, we consider them barely as Actions;

[53] Cf. Browne, *Religio Medici*: "the Rhetoricke wherewith I perswade another cannot perswade my selfe" (i.§55, p. 52).

[54] Cf. *Aret.*, f. 58^{v}.

[55] Among the major points of Acontius's *Satans Stratagems, or the devils Cabinet-Council Discovered* (1648) were the need to avoid unnecessary controversy (18) and the importance of gentleness is dealing with opponents: the author noted that in "*every Controversy* [*there was*] *a double Combate, between us and our dissenting opposite, and between us and* Sathan" (p. 35).

[56] Cf. the "Remoras of Truth" (Table 5).

[57] See Shapiro, *Probability and Certainty*, ch. 3. Browne made a similar point in *Religio Medici* i.§6, pp. 6-7.

when [as] otherwise we vse to consider them as Ours; and then our [selfe Loue] <Reason> brib'd by our owne Concernments, is <vsually> by the Treachery of Selfe-loue betray'd [to] into a Verdict, much more suitable to what we Do think of our selues, then to what we should thinke of our Actions.[58] Like those fond mothers that dote vpon their owne Children (because Theirs) tho otherwise neuer so noted for Deformity. This makes [the] <our> Moralists with reason say, that to giue a true Estimate of Actions, we must consider them Abstractedly, not as they stand enclozed /encompassed/ with Relations. Thus the Prophet (in the book of ↑1 Kings 20. 39,40.)↓ by <a> suppos'd Relation, made wicked Ahab condemn in a third Person an Action which imputed <in> to himselfe he would probably haue Excus'd. Let vs therefore frequently reflect, on the Actions of others, and hauing consider'd whither we esteem them worthy of Commendation or of Blame, let vs thinke [fit] it [our Duty] iust to imitate what we think fit to Prayse, and (on the other side,) beleeue that to merit <require> our Auersion <Declining> that deserues our Censure; for selfe loue without <strangely> blinding vs cannot persuade vs, that the Being our's aduantageously [varys] changes the Nature of a Fault, and that others will not disapproue in vs what we dislike in others. We must not only by [the] Reflecting vpon the Deportments of others [learne informe] <acquaint> our selues both [of] <with> the Interests and Dispositions of men, and the Motiues and Conduct of Affaires; but by the Consideration of Euents, make those Rockes against <on> which others haue been cast away, serue vs for Sea-markes to steere our Course by; and [by] from their Miscarriages or Successe, learne to correct the frequent Errors in those Vulgar |f. 285| Axioms (commonly as little question'd as many of them deserue to be rely'd on) in Ciuill Knoledge that are vsually grounded vpon too few Particulars not to be found very fallacious in Many. For certinly tho the Inconueniences in which our Errors do actually inuolue vs, be very powerfull Dissuasiues from Relapses; yet doutlesse his Destiny is much to be preferr'd, whom [by] other men's [Misery] Follys haue made Wise and Carefull; and whom their Misfortunes haue instructed to shunne those Errors that haue produc't them. It being much more Happy and Discreet, to be so by the Misery and Experience of others [men] then our owne, and to [purchse] <learne> at a lesse Rate then that of our owne Disasters, the Truth of the reuerse of that saying of Aristotle, He that regards few things, determines easily.[59] ↑There ly hid in the Bosome of all humane actions, certin secret Axioms and Principles of Wisdom, the skill of whose extracting were possibly worth that of making the so [fa] coueted Elixir. [/the] And there are certain Hints in most of those to discerning Eyes (as Plants do to Physitians by their signatures reueale their Propertys;) that discloze [the] much of what

[58] RB owned Daniel Rogers's *Naaman the Syrian his Disease and Cvre* (1642), which analyzed the "spirituall Leprosie of Sinne and Selfe-love" in a treatise of about 900 pages.

[59] Source unknown.

they conceale.[60] Concerning this great Art, I shall not [refuse (Dear Sister)] <vpon command refuse (Dear Sister)> to acquaint yow with my Thoughts: but for the present I shall only giue this generall Aduice; to frame [A M] Rules and Maximes vpon the Axions of People acknowledg'd skilfull in their owne Professions, when neither our Reason nor experience persuade vs to the contrary.↓ Nor ought we simply to consider the Actions of those we conuerse with, and the [Euents] <Issues [and Successes]> of their Enterprises; but <Obserue both> as there is a hand of God appearing in them, and as they are [swa] byass't by a Prouidence, whose [Prudent] <wise> Dispensations and vnreseru'd [Management] <Disposall> of all things; dos so perfectly <(to sedulous and sanctify'd Eyes)> exclude Fortune from so much as sharing in the Gouernment <management> of things / / that they must be as blind as that false Deity is say'd to be, that dare ascribe Euents to Her.[61] Let the Contemplation both of God's Care of his Children and his Iudgements vpon his Enemys, either correct our sinfull or confirme vs in our vertuus <good> Habitudes. 'Tis an Vnspeakable comfort to obserue how oftentimes God[s] contriues the humors and Interests of his worst Enemys to the Aduantage and Protection of his Children, and (as he ↑1 Kings. 17, 4,6.↓ fed the Prophet Elijah by Rauens,) makes the very wickedde[n]st both cherish and support that Innocence, they naturally hate, and (vnrestrain'd by [priuate Considerations) wud] <peculiar respectes)> wud greedily persecute, <[Destroy]> and willingly destroy. Mark the Perfect man (sayes the Psalmist) ↑Ps. 37,37.↓ and behold the Vpright, for the End of that Man is Peace. |f. 285v| And truly as in Comedies, how tragicall soeuer the former do appeare, yet the Last Scene [rewards] dos recompence all <Trauerses and> Troubles by a fortunate Period; so in the liues of Iust men, tho the Progresse of their Dayes, be [<but> an <vninterrupted> [continu'd] succession of <Afflictions and> Crosses, yet they conclude happily enuf to make the desperatest and most forlorne sinner wish with / / ↑Numb. 23.10.↓ Balaam. Let me dye the Death of the Righteous, and let my last End be like His. On the other side, obserue how G O D behaues himselfe towards the Wicked; how not onely their Ioyes are Fleeting and seldome vndisturb'd by Feares or Remorse, but the things they are oftentimes enuy'd for as Blessings are but disguized and mistaken Iudgments: Deliuerances themselues prouing but Repreeues, which but suspend to aggrauate their Miserys. As the <captiue> King of ↑Gen. the 14 and 19 chpts↓[62] Sodom when

[60] Cf. Browne, *Religio Medici* i.§16, p. 15, for similar concepts and language. In *High Veneration* 5.147, RB discussed the creatures as signatures of God, but the topic was extensively discussed in Hartlib's "Ephermerides" (1648). RB's references to creation as God's hieroglyphics (*Occ. Refl.* 2.349) or God's stenography (*Usefulness* 2.63) reflect the same outlook.

[61] RB's concern with Providence is a dominant theme in the *Aret.* (bk. 2, ch. 4); for similar views of Fortune and Providence, cf. Browne, *Religio Medici* i.§16-17, pp. 15-18.

[62] Gen. 14:1-24 and 19:1-29.

rescu'd by Abraham [from the] <out of his Victor's> hands [of] was but reseru'd to perish by that hideous storme / / of Fire that <afterwards> destroy'd his Execrable Cuntry. But especially in the Reprobate let vs obserue their End. For (like [wo] woods / / that beare no fruite whilst they florish and yet shine when they are rotten,)[63] there are many Persons whose liues were wholely vseless, that proue instructiue [after th] when they once are Dead. Consider a Dying greate man, one of those Illustrious Executioners <Hangmen comonly> (cal'd Conquerors) that had so little rest in the world and gaue so little to it; when he once comes to dye, ↑Ps. 146, 4↓ His breath (says the Psalmist) goeth forth, he returneth to his Earth; in that very Day his Thoughts perish.[64] Wherefore according to the Counsell of a<n> [Person] <inspired Author> very well vers'd in [this] the Theame he treates of, ↑Ps. 37, 1,2.↓ Fret not thy selfe because of euill doers, neither be thou enuious against the workers of Iniquity. For they shall soone be cut downe like the grasse and wither as the greene herbe. [But] <And> when we see such conspicuous iudgments, <let> the [Terror of] Apprehension of prouoking like Curses by like [Misde] Transgressions, repulse any Temptation, |f. 286| Their seeming Prosperity might attemt for to create. Let the <wicked's exemplary> Fall [of the Wicked] protect vs from the [Infection] <Contagion> of their Presidents. And as Vipers tho extreamely venemous whilst aliue, yet kild proue the best antidotes against the Bites /Poyson/ of Vipers (their Flesh being the Principall Ingredient that enters the Composition of Treacle)[65] so the Consideration of the Ruine of wicked men, dos most powerfully preserue vs from the Infection of their Example; when the horror of their Deaths frights vs from the Imitation of their Liues. Where it is very obseruable how he oftentimes takes the Wicked in their owne Snare, and employes no other then their own Proiects to the Contriuer's [fu] Destruction /subuersion/. As of the Exhalations the (reeking) Earth (it selfe) sends forth, he formes those fatall <destructiue> Thunderbolts, that he employs to punish our /it's/ Rebellions, and ruine the proudest Fabrickes it can boast.[66] Nor will it be vnfit (vpon occasion,) to inuite our Soules

[63] In *Style*, RB used the same comparison to criticize wits (2.303-04), but see also BW 3.157 and 3.651.

[64] As with many of RB's potentially political comments, this sentence and the next one have very general application but may also address contemporary issues. Who was the executioner of Charles I? On 20 June 1649 George Thomason received a copy of the *Confession of Richard Brandon, the executioner of Charles I, on his deathbed* (E.561[14]); there was a response on 3 July 1649 (669.f.14[51]). Later, on the cover of E.430(2), Thomason identified William Walker of Darnal as the executioner. Clearly, the topic interested readers. Boyle's reaction to the king's execution has not survived. On 11 May 1649 Dury reported to Worsley that the Prince of Anhalt had drawn one conclusion from the execution: princes must not be tyrants (Boyle Lett. 7.2^{v}).

[65] See the note on treacle above (f. 283).

[66] In *Hist. of Air*, RB recalled an experience with lightning near Geneva and described the odor "produced by the thunder" (5.636).

to looke abroad in the Termes of the Psalmist ↑Ps. 46,8.↓ Come, behold the Workes of the Lord, what desolations he hath made in the Earth. For when we see and seriously consider the Ruine of th[os]e [Conditions] most Establish't Conditions /Fortunes/ the World dos pretend to; and find the Subuersions of what fond Mortals most rely on, as frequent as men fancy them vnlikely; we cannot but be inform'd of the Transitorinesse of all that Felicity that is built but vpon Transitory Obiects; and [the sad Fall of] those adored Greatnesses will by their Fall crush all that value [th] our Folly and their Glittering apparances / / [illeg.] may haue giuen vs for them: by teaching vs how vnfit they are to be the <sole> Obiects of our Ambition, that can so suddenly become those of our Compassion /Pitty./[67] My Pen could dwell an Age vpon this Theame, but hauing reseru'd [a] the fuller Prosecution of it to Peculiar Discourses,[68] least further Instances might proue as tedious to be inserted / / as vsefull to be obseru'd; I shall conclude this Point with this one Generall Direction; which is, |f. 286v| Still to endeuour through all the fleeting Variety and perpetuall Vicissitudes of Sublunary Euents, to discerne the Workings <Character> of that adorable Prouidence to whose wise Conduct they are all assigned; <committed> and which may in them as easily be discern'd, inspite of the /Differences / / of the Persons and Actions that reflect it; as in a cloudlesse Day gazing vpon a Riuer, we can long behold the selfe same vnchang'd Image of the Bright Planet that disperses light /creates the Day/ tho the Drops that do reflect /repz/ it, being in [too] perpetuall Motion, and still successiuely alter'd and renew'd, can not be for 2 moments the selfe-same, those swiftly gliding Streames incessantly chasing <pursuing> and flying from each other.[69]

Within these 6 directions I conceiue the Method of a[ll] fuller and [more] deliberate Reflection to be compriz'd: but when our Indispos'dnesse or our Hast, forbids the Practise of so leisurely a[n Exam] Reflection / / those halfe a dozen mention'd heads may be conueniently enuf <contracted and> reduc't to halfe that Number: if in the first Place we remember what Good done the foregoing Day, merits our Conscience's Applause; in the next, what Sin or Indiscretion (either of Omission or of Act) we haue that day been guilty of; and if, in the last Place, we recall to mind, what thing considerable [we] (either from our selues or others)

---

[67] On 6 March 1647 RB wrote Lady Ranelagh about his bitter disappointment over the breakage of his furnace and the loss of "fine experiments, and castles in the air," an experience that taught him "how brittle that happiness is, that we build upon earth" (1.xxxvi-xxxvii). To Philaretus, after the outbreak of the rebellion in Ireland, Lismore Castle served "only for an Instance & a Lecture, of the Instability of that Happinesse, that is built upon the incertin Possession of such fleeting Goods, as it selfe was" (Maddison 3).

[68] It is not clear whether RB referred to works already written or works that he intended to write.

[69] In *Occ. Refl.* the narrator explained how Philaretus had saved him from giddiness caused by looking attentively on a rapid stream (2.426-27).

we haue that day learn't that we knew not before. I say, What thing Considerable; for I am extreamely out of charity with those memorys now so much in Fashion, which are stuff't with almost nothing else then what deserues to be excluded thence, and [which] whose <fond> owners, by lodging in them nothing but <storys,> Songs, Iests, Sonnets, and such like empty Trifles are very carefull to giue men cause to compare their Memorys to Iet, which attracts nought but Strawes, Dust, Feather, [and] <or> such lighter Trash. Whereas (methinkes) a Wise-man's memory should resemble Quicksiluer, [in] which (as both Chimists and my owne Experience assure me) none but the Noblest of all Metalls, Gold, has weight enuf /Power/ to sinke into.[70]

The Last great Property we first required in our Reflection is, Constancy or Persistence, which is the / / that reapes what has been sowed by our first Endeauors. Nor ought it to discourage young Beginners, that their Improuement by the helpe of this Practise, [dos] |f. 287| Oft-times seemes not at first to answer those large Prayses we haue ascrib'd vnto it; for this Practise is none of those nimble chymicke Remedys, whose Operations are resented almost before themselues be taken /swallow'd/ or apply'd, but like a Good Diet, which to be vs'd successfully must be vs'd long: and whose aduantages are as well late ere they be perceiu'd as long ere they<(r Influence)> be forfeited. <decay lost>[71] But to auoid mistakes it will not be vnnecessary to declare, that in each single Day's Examen, I do not at all require, that euery particular Article of our former Method be [p] seuerally and punctually insisted on. I will not exact from men more then I can expect. And so some of our Directions (I mean those <that> best [suited] fit the present Circumstances) be [em] made vse of at one time, and [fo or] some of them at another; it is not necessary that all of them be practis'd still at once. They being mention'd here, but as [wise] Physitians when they prescribe a Diet, <to valetudinary /sickly/ persons> vse to specify sundry sorts of meats, not to lay an obligation vpon the Patient to eate them all each meale, but that that variety might supply /afford/ them with Choice, to suite with [th] seuerall Occasions. And truly this ouertasking of our selues in matters of Deuotion (where Alacrity and the Manner are <much> more consider'd then the Performances themselues) has often vntimely crush't many a hopefull but too-forward Zeale. Nor has the persuading men to it been obseru'd by me amongst the least frequent and succesfull strategeming of the old [Tem] (suttle) Tempter, who; (like [Trauellers / /] <those> that [when they] finding themselues vnable to hold in their Horses, ride them full speed ouer plow'd Grounds and Ditches, to run them of their legs) when he cannot curbe in men's <[acti] busy> Deuotions

---

[70] RB conducted many such experiments. For specific accounts, see *History of Fluidity* 1.394 and *Specific Medicines* 5.86-87; in 1668 Oldenburg wrote to RB about current experiments intended to fill the pores of gold with mercury (6.268).

[71] RB considered the importance of diet in *Usefulness* 2.103-13.

to a lazy supinenesse, ruines their mettle by it's [selfe] owne freenesse, spurring them <euer> till [they] by ouer straining they tyre downright at last. In effect, when we [taske] <engage> our selues [aboue those Abilitys,] to taskes greater then we can cheerfully performe, either the Deuill (vsually) persuades vs by the impossibility of long Continuing those Performances, wholly to abrogate the Custome of them; or else at least we find Perseuerance so tedious and vncomfortable, that we content our selues, and hope /thinke/ to content God with that bare, heartlesse, customary Act, which [in] <to> his Purer Eyes, appeares the Carkasse only of Deuotion.[72] ↑And as in the Conquest of [Can] the land of Canaan, from the first Towne the People of Israëll sack't; they deriu'd no other Profit nor aduantage, then the Destruction of God's and their Enemys; [but in] (all being offer'd either by the sword or to the Tabernacle an offering to God) but in their next Expedition (against Ai) the [Spoile] Booty was their owne;[73] so in our Spirituall Warfare, against our Vices and our Passions, [from] our first Victors will possibly afford vs no other Emolument /nor Benefit/ then the Destruction <Weakning> of so many Aduersarys /Enemys/ but from the Prosecution of that warre, we shall deriue such satisfactions and such aduantages, that Canaan after the Destruction of those gyants /Monsters/ the sons of Anak,<ites> prou'd a Land flowing with milke and hony; so the Soule, freed from the vsurping Tiranny of monstruous affections growes <shows it selfe> fertile in all <sorts of> Pure and innocent Delights. (figur'd /emblem'd by milke and hony.)↓ |f. 287[v]| And certinly as there is scarce any thing better then a [Good] Custome, <of doing Good> so is there scarce any thing Worse, then [a] <doing> Good (Things) meerly out of Custome. Wherefore, for busy'd or vnleasur'd Persons, the safest (and, possibly the most expedient) way is vsually to employ that shorter and contracted Method, mention'd at the [End] <Bottome> of [the] our last [Ins] Direction; and when both Time shall permitt and Occasion require, then to make vse of such of the other Instructions, as shall be found /thought/ [most] <the> fittest furtherers of Enquiry, into those Particulars, that exact a fuller or <and> more fixt Reflection. But as on the one side I freely disapproue that rash ill-husbanding of [our] <men's> Forwardnesse, <zeale> that often makes it Dropticke; (I meane, first makes it swell excessiuely, and <then soon> after Dy) since the Indiscreet [Precipitancy] <ouerstraining> of our Zeale, is but like <our> Breth to opening Buds of Rozes, which makes them appeare indeed the [sooner] <quicklyer> /earlyer/ blowne, but makes them wither much the sooner too: so on the other side, I like not vpon Triuiall excuses /   / to intermitt a Custom engag'd to by <on> mature deliberation; but had rather twice very much abridge my Reflection, then once totally omitt it. For besides that our Nature is so prone to Failings /Ill/ that [it] ‘tis almost as apt to abuse <illeg.

[72] A point made several times in the *Aret.* (e.g., f. 184).

[73] The reference is to the destruction of Jericho (Jos. 6:24) and Ai (Jos. 7:2-8:29).

Vertu's> [the] least indulgences [of] as vntam'd <ramage> / / Hawkes; who could they get loose but for one single Day wud by that one Day's <liberty> relapse into more Wildnesse, then could be vntaught them by a Weeke's looking to: besides this I say; <the> Totall Discontinuance[s] of [any] good Customes, do very much danger (as being very apt to degenerate into) a Finall one: and at least, <tis acknoledg'd that> in Habitudes <(especially)> of Good frequently interrupted by Cessations; the Trouble of Renewing [them,] dos much surpasse that of Continuing them. Wherefore according to the Exhortation of the Apostle ↑Gal. 6.9.↓ Let vs not be weary in well-doing, for in due time we shall reape, if we faint not: And as we should End our Dayly Reflections themselues, so let vs now conclude this <our> Treatise of them with the Petition of that Man of God whose equall is as difficult to be found as the Place of his Buriall <Entomb-ment> /as his Sepulcher/ Lord, ↑Psalm. 90.12.↓ So teach vs to number our Dayes that we may apply our harts vnto Wisdom. Amen and Amen.

FINIS.

Of Time and Idleness

|f. 15|

Idleness is to Vices, what the Materia Prima of the Filosofers is to Formes;[1] it is None, in Particular, but yet (‘tis that which) makes Things susceptible /capable/ of All. /any./ But this, (by the Way) is to be vnderstood [of] onely of <in> the most Charitable <and indulgent> or rather Partiall Acception of Idlenesse. ↑Sure Idlenesse was thought no Petty sin by him, that (Ex. 16.49) listeth the abundance of it amongst the Three Capitall (and prouoking) iniquitys of Sodom it selfe. Vnlesse that Extrauagant speech (Ex 5,17) [be vnderstoo] haue rather a Politick then a Theological /morall/ meaning; I shud think Pharaoh as much blinded in his Iudgment as hardned in his hart, when he tels the People, Ye are Idle, ye are Idle, therefore ye say, Let vs go and do sacrifice to the LORD. See Pr. 19.15. and Pr. 31.27↓ For those that beleeue sins of Omission as well as of Commission, will easily beleeue, that man being Created for the Glory of his Maker, he dos not onely fall short of that Dessein of his Creation, that is seduced in his Way to it; but he also that stubbornly refuses to Trauell towards it. And [therefore] <in effect> we find in the Gospell, that not onely the Wicked Steward; but he that but hid his Talent in a Napkin, was condemn'd to utter Darknesse.[2] The Buriall of the Talent being Crime enuf in the Trustee, when the end of the Trust<or> was it's Improuement. And therefore as in <the Disposall of> Mony, they are not only censur'd for vitius, that lauish it vpon, Assassins, Wenches and Flatterers; but they are also condemn'd, that (securing rather then Possessing it) by a Niggardly Closefistednesse [lock] <hoord> it vp from those Vses, for which alone it is, both Ordain'd and Desirable: so in the stewarding of Time; we may as Iustly censure it's Nonemployment |f. 15v| As it's Mispending: and the Idle man, by an Extrauagant kind of Profuseness, (which makes him Lauish Time by the very Not vsing it) makes himselfe gilty of a Prodigality by so much worse then that of Mony, by how much what that squanders away is more Precious and the losses it occasions more Irrecoverable.[3] ↑Good God! how easy /temting, Inuiting/ is the Road to hell, when eu'n [the] by sitting still one may trauell [/arriue/] thither. And how little Paines is required to arriue at Perdition, when not onely the Doing Ill, but the Doing Nothing will

---

[1] This essay is taken from BP 14.15-23. RB discussed idleness in many other contexts. For example, he used almost the same sentence in “Of Sin” f. 14. The second essay in John Hall's *Horæ Vacivæ* (1646) was “Of Time,” but the topic was discussed in many contemporary works of moral philosophy, essays, and sermons. RB mentioned this essay in an inventory completed on his twenty-third birthday (see Table 1).

[2] Cf. Matt. 25:14-30.

[3] In “Dayly Reflection,” RB noted that “Time, like Mony, is neuer well employ'd but when ‘tis spent: and when ‘tis spent in pious Exercises, it is not wasted <lost> but lay'd out” (f. 273).

serue the Turn.↓

Now the principall Cut-purses that cheate vs of our Time and foment our Idlenes, may be conueniently enuf marshal'd /muster'd, rang'd/ vnder the Colors of, First, [Gaming] Rauing;[4] when the Thouhts like a blind man's Arrows, fly at Rouers, not leuel'd at any Certin Marke. This kind of Idleness is extreamely incident to stirring and nimble Fancys: whom (because of its insinuating sweetnesse) vnperceiuedly it robs of a huge Deale of Time. And whereas it may be objected that both this and som of the ensuing [kind] <Tribes> of Idlenesse are wrong'd in that Title, because they are a Doing of somthing; it may be iustly replyed; that Idleness is not properly an [la] absolute Cessation from all Action, but <rather> an Action not to the Purpose; or a Cessation from what shud be done; and therefore those Employments <(as Rauing)> that cannot be precisely cal'd Idlenes because of the Actiuity of their Nature will yet deserue that Name, in respect of their Irrelation to the Duty /End/ of the Agent: and so may a |f. 16| Rauer be as properly cal'd Idle, as a schooleboy that whilst he shud be conning of his Lesson, is playing at Cat. Secondly, Gaming; where the very Winner is sure to loose, what all his Gaines can neuer purchase, Time. Alas! how many Times has the setting sun left those at Cards, whom [at] his Rising [he] has [found] <presented him> in the selfe same Posture. ↑To whom I may but too iustly put that question of our sauior, (Matt. 20.6) Why stand ye heere all the day idle.↓ How many haue we that [neuer study but how to Play: It] <liue> as if they thought their Time /Life/ like their Light Gold;[5] good for nothing but to be play'd away. Durst I venture to alleadg [my own] any Actions of mine for Examples to others; I wud tell the Reader, that eu'n whilst I was not conuinc't of the vnlawfulnesse of Play; /Dicing/ ↑The Consideration of it's affinity to Idleness made me↓ [I] still refrain['d] to vse <practice> it, but when I was vnder the Fisitians hands; so that I vs'd Gaming but as other sick Persons vse Posset drinke, To make <helpe> my Fisick <to> work the better.[6] Thirdly. [Thir] Hunting, Hawking, shooting, and all other Recreations whatsoeuer, when their Immoderate Length or Frequency, makes them too Prodigall of Time. A Fault Epidemicall in those men, <(honorable Butchers! <caterers>)> that wast the greatest part of their owne Lifes in shortning that of a <harmlesse> Partridge or a Deere.[7] Persons, who seeme to ambition no other Excellency then that of their Greyhounds; who are good for nothing but to kill a [som] cowardly Rabbet or som

---

[4] RB's critique of "raving" is consistent with his treatment of it above.

[5] "Light gold," a term RB repeated a few lines later, was counterfeit money. For Marcombes's painful experience with light gold, see *II Lismore* 4.96-97.

[6] This example illustrates RB's reasoning about lawful recreation. For Cork's use of gambling, see Canny 73-74.

[7] RB was more alarmed by the waste of human time than the loss of animal life, but for a broader view of RB and the animal soul, see Malcolm Oster, "The 'Beame of Diuinity': Animal Suffering in the Early Thought of Robert Boyle," *BJHS* 22 (1989) 151-80.

silly hare: and that conuerse amongst Beasts, till (as the Poets fable of Acteon) they becom as arrant Beasts as those they pursue.[8] To this Tribe is reducible the [was] ouermuch Reading of Playes and Romances: which (to omitt the whole Croud of it's other Inconueniences:) is in a very high degree (especially in actiue Fancys) both the Tinder /bellows/ and the Fewell of that Rauing we haue formerly condemn'd.[9] |f. 16v| Fourthly, sleeping, (and lying in bed.) Which when Moderate, is, I must confesse, A Necessary Idlenesse; but when Excessiue, seems but a voluntary Deth. Which I think insufferable in those who most vse it, whose Labor, (being nothing but to eat and Drink and Play) [cud] dos least of all either need or authorize so long a Rest; if their sleeping from their waking did not cheefly differ, but in the Posture of their Eylids.[10] I remember that being 'tother day in a Company where one <of them> that compos'd it, after hauing spent 10 houres in his bed, was loudly complaining that he had been 14 without sleep. Why Sir, replyes a Gentleman that stood by, What wil yow do when yow com to Heu'n. And indeed for my owne Part, I haue often [con] look't vpon it as none of the least Priuiledges we shall enjoy in the other life, a perfect immunity from that slauery of sleepe, which I haue euer esteem'd one of the Badges /and Parts/ of that Infirmity we are subject to in this.[11] It being very sensible to me, to see my selfe necessitated, hauing but <so short> a span of life heere to [spend] <wast> the Third (if not the half) of that in that vnprofitable (tho not vnnecessary) sleeping, which my Opinion [persu] represents to me to be but a kind of dying by Fits. Fifthly, Designlesse and vninstructiue Visits: which are made onely as sick <idle> Persons vse to play at Tables, to <get> rid of the Time.[12] I say Designelesse; because I |f. 17| Know the Wisest may be somtimes oblig'd to emty Vninstructiue Visits, where yet the End legitimates the Meanes. Tho I must confess I haue neuer thought it one of the least Vnhappinesses /miserys/ of Greatnesse, to be forc't to make and to receaue these sencelesse Visits; specially since the springing vp /whelping/ of a <certin> Generation <of wast times> amongst vs, whose Idleness is Infectious; who not knowing to do with their owne Time, presume others haue as little to do with theirs: and then [one] <that> Tyrannicall <thing cal'd> Custome <(in the disguise of Ciuility)> forsooth must oblige me to wast <loose> my Time with euery Coxcombe that wants employment for his; and not onely to suffer /endure/ but to Return his Visits. Sixthly. That friuolous and vselesse <vnprofitable> Conuersation [be] neither [Profit]

---

[8] Cf. Ovid, *Metamorphoses* 3.138ff.

[9] Yet another objection to reading plays and romances.

[10] For other remarks about sleeping, see "Dayly Reflection" f. 278v.

[11] RB offered many different descriptions of the afterlife: cf. *Seraphic Love* (1.288, 290-91), *Theodora* (5.294), and *Greatness of Mind* (5.555, 557).

[12] Throughout his life RB complained about visitors and the custom of visiting, this passage perhaps being the most spirited: cf. two early letters to Lady Ranelagh (1.xxvii and 6.49); *Reflections upon a Theological Distinction* 5.541; and, late in life, his visiting rules (1.cxxix).

Beneficiall nor Delightfull either to the Speaker or the Hearer: which, if the Threatning against Idle Words, admit of a litterall Interpretation, will one Day make multitudes wish it their Happiness to haue been born Dumb /speechlesse/.[13] Of this Kind is your so epidemicall Almanac-Discourse, where (for want of other [matter] <entertainment> the <help of the> wether is so often implored to Consume the time: and where the Clouds and the Wind vsually make the Theames of Discourses as Emty as Themselues. ↑This kind of Tatling, being like the Trick of Crafty Alewiues /Tapsters/ that fill vp all the neck of the Iug with Froth; not to giue yow Drink but Compleat /[fill] <make> vp/ the Measure.↓ Of the same Nature also is your Gossip-talke: of the Diseases that then raigne (of which that very Idlenesse, tho left out, is oftentimes the most hurtfull) of such a Woman's being brought to Bed; and of the (Imaginary) likenesse, betwtixt the (Monkyfac't) Child, and the (supposed) Father.[14] In the same [lis] Inuentary may be Iustly inserted the Repetiting <telling> |f. 17^v| of Idle, fantasticall Dreames that are not worth the Hearing; and a Million of other such friuolous and fruitless kinds of Chattings; that (did not a Constrain'd vse, enure and brawne their Eare to it) wud no less turne a wiseman's stomack then the being tost in a storme at sea, or the being Drencht with a whole Pound of infus'd Antimony.[15] But after all this there yet remaines vnspoken of the Last and (perhaps) the greatest Cankerworme /Moth, Glutton/ of Time of all the Rest, which is, the [the] Losse of those Interuals [and (as it were Parentheses)] of Time, which interuene like Enterludes in Playes, betweene the more serious /Acts/ Bisness of our Liues.[16] These Parentheses of Leasure, tho because of the shortness of each one single, they are commonly trifled away vnregarded: yet in the summe totall of a man's life, amount to a much vaster <more considerable> Proportion of it, then is imagin'd; aduantagiously recompencing [in] <with> their frequency and their number what may be Defectiue in their Length /Bulke./ The Neglect of these Remnants of Time, is [m] very incident to those very Persons that highlyest value it. But these lauish away their shreds of Time as Gamesters play

---

[13] For the danger of idle words, see Matt. 12:36; for the danger of idle conversation and bad company, cf. *Occ. Refl.* (2.420, 424, 426), *Swearing* (6.23), and "Of Sin." Alsted also had a section on conversation (1331-34), "De Civilitate."

[14] Keith Thomas extensively discusses each of these topics: for the significance of monstrous births, see *Decline* 104ff; the popularity of almanacs, 347-56; for dreams, 152-53. In 1664 Oldenburg reported to RB that because the daughter of the queen of France was shaped like a Moor, the king had banished Moors, dwarfs, and monkeys. Apparently the queen had seen a little Moor (6.178). For other remarks on monstrous births, cf. 6.165ff and, more philosophically, *Vulgar Notion* (5.201, 220, 226). RB's major target is gossip.

[15] Marcombes reported to Cork (4 March 1635) that the "Sea . . . hath soe well phisick'd [Roger and Lewis Boyle] for a good while, that they shall not shortly have any need of more purging" (*II Lismore* 3.239). RB considered the effects of antimony in *Simple Medicines* 5.118-20.

[16] RB developed this point at length in his "Doctrine of Thinking" and "Dayly Reflection."

away their Light Gold, <counterfet mony> not with Designe to Loose, but for want of knowing [what] <any> other vse ↑it may be↓ ['tis] good for. The best Remedy therefore I know for this Inconuenience, is to show a way, how by a handsom contriuance, these vnregarded scraps of Time, may be improued to some Profitable vse: concerning which I haue already deliuered my poore opinion in my Discourse of Thinking. |f. 18| To which for the present I shall onely adde, That the Excellency and Irrecouerableness of Time considered: there is no part of it so small as to deserue <iustify> a Wise man's Contempt <neglect>: it's shortest Periods; being considerable, for their Nature, tho not for their Length.

Now the Remedys of Idleness I conceiue to be in the first Place to consider, the Preciousness of Time: ↑[A thing so delicate that it]↓ that is wasted not onely by the Misemploying it but by the not medling with it at all. Like Camfire (an Experiment both Strange and True) that not onely consumes by being cast into the Fire: but vanishes but onely let alone in the open Aire.[17] Nor is Time of the Nature of all other goods: whose losses admit of a Reparation: No; Time has Eyes to see it's way forwards, but no Eares to be cald back by. It knows not the Krab's Pace, to go Backwards. <[Regression]> ↑Nor has it (as the Sun has) any Tropicks, [sh] from whence (at it's Arriuall there) it begins a Regression.↓ It is Irrecouerable and Vnrecallable. How chary ought we therefore to be of so delicate /nice/ a Good; that is so Easy to be lost and so impossible to be Regain'd. And indeed a Good, that was Design'd, not for Possession but for vse, required such a Flying /Vanishing/ nature. ↑I like that Theban Captain who [visiting] finding a sleeping Centry, and hauing kild him in that Posture, reply'd to those that ask't a Reason of that Cruelty; I onely left him as I found him.↓[18] Therefore Procrastination is [for Idle] an Excuse for Idleness not more common then it is Impertinent. Since Time is lauish't as well by the keeping as the vsing. Nor is it of the Nature of Mony; where a Man may (perhaps) <by his Industry> out of the last Remnant, redintegrate the whole stock. No. Time like inspir'd Graces /infus'd qualitys/ may be employ'd but cannot be bought. Like the Drips of Raine; if they be not Intercepted in their Passage, 'tis in vaine to run after them: and indeed of all the Tenses: the Certinty of the |f. 18v| Præterit's being Gone <Past> and the Vncertinty of the Future's Arriuall, leauing vs the onely Present to call our owne. And that too if we had a Mind to subtilize, may perchance be prou'd no Time (but an Instant /Moment/) but I had rather allow it to be <let it passe for> what it is thought, then loose it in wrangling (about) what it is. Twud next be considered; how meane and vnworthy Idlenesse is for a Man. 'Tis a Fault that

---

[17] For references to RB's experiments with camphor, see 1.96, 1.136, 1.388, 1.433, 1.478, 1.481, 1.636, 1.711, 1.723, 3.279, 3.581, 3.749, 4.313, 4.334, 4.498, 4.553, and 5.104.

[18] Sextus Julius Frontinus, *Stratagems*, trans. Mary B. McElwain (Cambridge, Mass. 1941), 3.12.2-3. Browne used the same anecdote in *Religio Medici* ii.§12, p. 71, though he attributed the execution to Themistocles.

[they] those Great Spirits that haue ornamented Mankind were neuer <seldome> Guilty of. And in Effect Fame and Immortality inhabit the Top of a very lofty Mountain and of a steepe Ascent.[19] There's no Climing thither but by Labor and Industry: it may indeed be somtimes arriu'd at by Crooked Paths; but is neuer reach't without som Trauelling: so that he shall no more get thither that still sleepes at the Bottom of it, then he that Turns his Back vpon it. To which we may adde, the Danger it exposes vs to. For what the Poet sayd of Loue, may be [very] with a greate Deale of Iustice apply'd to Vice

Et in vacuo Pectore regnat Amor.
Vice Tyrannizes in the empty brest.[20]

Which is but the Inne where (whilst the Roomes are emty) the lewdest Passengers; may alight and becom guests; or like Vninhabited Lands in America, the spoile /Prey/ of the First Discouerer. Certinly the Idle man is in this the most inexcusable of All men, that whereas all other sinners can Father their Sins vpon the Deuill, the Deuill can father many of his vpon him: for he vsurps the Deuils office and Tempts his Temter to Tempt him. ↑Tho Idleness were granted to be no sinne Essentially; yet certinly it is a very greate one Endangeringly /occasionally/ and as much more to be shun'd <declin'd> then many Actual Faults; as the rushing inconsiderately to <in> the battle vnarm'd, is [then som sli] less Perillous then som slight Cut vpon the Fingers. And in effect [we find that] the holy Ghost has recorded (2 Sam. 11.2) that Dauid, a man after God's owne hart, and one that had been proofe both against the Allurements of smiling and the terrors of frowning accidents: when once the Temter had surpriz'd him in such an idle, lazy, posture of Ease, as to spend the Afternoone vpon his Bed, and the Euening vpon the roofe of his house, he easily seduc't him to a Crime, little less heinous then his Piety was eminent.↓ |f. 19| Good God! How little is Time beholding to Mankind: most men take no other Care for it, then our Young Brothers vse to do for their Creditors;[21] (I meane) How to be rid of them. Nay most of our young Gallants; neuer study but How to Play; and like Prodigalls that spend their Mony to buy Wax and Parchment to seale away their Estates; they squander away one Part of their Time, in Contriuing <thinking> how to squander away the Rest.[22]

---

[19] For heroic spirits, see the *Aret.* (bk. 2, ch. 7).

[20] Ovid, *Amores* 1.1.26. RB used the same quote in "Of Sin."

[21] Regarding Lewis Boyle's debts, see his letter to his father (27 December 1638, *II Lismore* 3.277). Marcombes wrote Cork (14 July 1641) that Frank and RB "are not enclined to any vice that I know, and yow need not feare that they should runne in debt; for I haue exclaimed soe often and soe much against that vice, that they doe hate it now as much as I" (*II Lismore* 4.202). Much to Cork's chagrin, several of RB's siblings and in-laws were chronic debtors. According to Marcombes, Tom Killigrew bragged about defrauding merchants (*II Lismore* 4.235).

[22] On 20 December 1641 Marcombes defended himself to Cork against the intrigues of Eliza-

And all this (forsooth) vnder the truthlesse [Color] <Pretence> of Recreation; which certinly (in the generally) they [ought] <haue> lest [to Pretend] <lest right> who that most vse. I see all men make it their Bisness how to Passe away the Time: but I will som of them wud think lesse how to passe away the Time, and consider more how the Time Passes them away. ↑Men liue as if they were the Proprietors /Lords/ not the stewards of Time.↓ For my part it is one of the lest of my Cares how to Passe away my Time, and one of the greatest how to Employ: for I am sure the Time will passe away but too fast without my Care; but will not (perhaps) be well employ'd without my Industry. ↑[As] <If> Filosofers say that the Fire will rather descend then leaue a Vacuum in Nature; 'tis no wonder if Temtations ascend, and the greatest quit their Places rather then permit one in the Mind.↓[23] Others do not more wish to goad /spurre/ on Time, then I, that it were Clog'd; and cud my wishes, (as the Poets fabled of Proteus) change themselues /assume/ into what shapes they pleas'd, I shud metamorphose them into Cizers to Clip the Wings of Time. Which certinly if it were saleable, and I Rich, there is no thing vnder Vertu that I wud purchase at a Dearer Rate. Sure 'tis the Ignorance of what we Ignore and how much we may Know; that makes vs thus puzzled how to Dispose of |f. 19v| Our leisure howres. Otherwise it were Impossible that Man, that is born to know so much Truth, and Do so much Good, shud find a Tediousness in that Time, of which he might with a thousand times more Iustice bewayle the Fugacity. Vita Breuis, Ars longa, says the Long-liu'd Hippocrates:[24] and, the Iust complaint of the Shortnesse of our Life præfaces his Aphorismes, who has left vs the best Instructions /Directions/ to Prolong it. Alas, Time is not lent vs by God, as Rattles <Cards> are giuen to Children, only to be Playd with. No; Life is a serious Thing; and tho it be [generally beleeu'd] <the People's Faith /Creed/> that an Idle frolick humor, ads as much to our Days as it takes away from our Cares; yet certinly, they do not so much lengthen their Yeares [then] as they shorten their Liues; that are more carefull how to spend their Time then how to Employ it. We are all in this Life

---

beth Boyle, wife of Francis Boyle and sister of Tom Killigrew. In a lengthy letter, Marcombes complained about Frank's miseducation at Eton: "if [Frank] had been Longer att Eatton he had Learned there to drinke with other deboice scholers, as I haue been informed by Mr Robert, which is y^{e} finest gentleman of y^{e} wordle [=world]; he had alsoe thaken an ill habitude (which perhaps was not little fomented by y^{e} actions and discourses of y^{e} afore named Gentleman) to thinke that the greatest Glory of a Gentleman did consist in expending foolishly his money and in vanitys, neuer spaking of any other thing but what he should doe when he should once Commaund his state; how many dogs he should keepe; how many horses; how many fine bands, sutes and rubans, and how freely he would play and keepe Company with good followes, etc." (*II Lismore* 4.234). The similarity between Marcombes's views and RB's is hardly coincidental.

[23] A variation on the tag, "Nature abhors a vacuum." For later discussion of the topic, cf. *Fluidity and Firmness* 1.409, *Exp. Hist. of Cold* 2.499, and *Vulgar Notion* 5.227.

[24] Hippocrates, *Aphorisms* 1.1, a tag also used in the *Aret.* (bk. 1, ch. 2). For a Paracelsian commentary on this proverb, cf. *Usefulness* 2.152-53.

Probationers for Eternity. And as Polityque Masters will somtimes deale with a suspected Seruant; let fall (by a dissembled Negligence) some [trifling] siluer spoone or other Trifling Peece of Plate; to sift whither or no it were safe trusting them with the whole Cup-board.[25] So God dos in this Life commit Time to our Custody to see <try> how we are likely to behaue our selues shud he trust vs with Eternity. But as our Sauior tels vs (Luke 16.10,11) He that is vnjust in the least is vniust also in Much &c. So beleeue it, God will neuer trust him with Eternity that giues him no better an Account of his Time. |f. 20| Now the 2 best Exorcists I know to Dispossess vs of that Grand Beel-zebub of Idlenesse <(that rust of the Mind)> is in the First Place a Calling [Suiting] (either in Church or state) suiting our Inclinations and our Quality.[26] ↑Vertu /Grace/ is like fire, it's very Essence <so> consists in it's Actiuity that if yow but stifle /smother/ it's Motion yow Destroy it's Nature /being/.↓ For the Apostles Comand (by which he endeuors to ouercome /subdue/ Idlenesse as Generals vse to take those Places that are vnforceable by storme, I meane, by staruing it) [and God's owne Interuention, I] That if any would not Worke Neither should he Eate)[27] and God's owne Injunction, <to all Mankind> In the Sweat of thy Brows shalt thou eat thy bread; lay vpon all men a (strict) /and perhaps indispensible/ Obligation to Labor either with the Body or the Mind.[28] Neither indeed is it reasonable that those Drones shud participate of the Benefits of Society, that will contribute nothing (that is theirs) to it's Good. But hauing handled this Particular fully enuf in another Discourse,[29] I shall insist no longer vpon it in this; but passe to [the] my second Exorcist of Idlenesse; which is, That euery Person that is likely to haue <any> vacant houres from serious Employments; shud lern som indifferent skill, in [som manuall] Limming, Turning, Watch-making, Gardening, or som manuall Vocation, or other. I know this will be spurn'd at by all our Gallants as a Proposition fit to be made rather to blue Aprons then to skarlet Cloakes. But sure it is not so much below a gentleman to do somthing, as it is below both a Man and a Christian to be Idle. Nor [dos the] can the one so much sully our hands, as the other dos our Minds. Methinks they that are not |f. 20v| Asham'd to

---

25 In 1646 RB wrote to Marcombes about the knavery of his steward: "The roguery of *Tom. Murray* gave me a great deal of trouble to discover and prevent; but I thence reaped the benefit of making further discoveries into œconomical knowledge, than ever otherwise I should have done. I turned him away last year, to let him know, that I could do my business very well without him; but now, having attained to a knowledge of my own small fortune beyond the possibility of being cheated, I am likely to make use of him again, to shew my father's servants, that I wish no hurt to the man, but to the knave" (1.xxxiii).

26 For RB's discussion of vocation, see the *Aret.* (bk. 2, ch. 4 and 7) and the "Doctrine of Thinking."

27 2 Thes. 3:10.

28 Gen. 3:19.

29 Cf. the *Aret.* (bk. 2, ch. 4).

stoope to take vp a Dropt sixpence lest they shud loose it; shud haue no lesse Considerations for that Time, whereof they shall one day be brought to giue by so much a stricter account then of their Mony; by how much the Thing entrusted is more precious. Shud I instance the Presidents that the Inspir'd [leaues tender] <volum holds forth> to our Transcription, we shud find all the Patriarkes shepheards: Gideon, that had Seruants enuf to cull out 10 that durst oppose the Religion then in request, Threshing of Barley; Saul, then the son of a Mighty Man, and afterwards a Mightyer man himself, [run] ouerrunning Countrys in pursuit of his Father's Asses; Sara, whose husband had 300 seruants able to beare Armes; and Thamar, the louely Daughter of the most Victorious Prince [that] the World till then had heard of:[30] both skild and both Practitioners in Cookery: [th] St Paul, (that vessell of Election) a Tentmaker; most of the Apostles [Fi] Fishermen. Not to say any thing of our blessed Sauior himselfe, who in the Dayes of his Flesh, whilst he took vpon him the Forme of a seruant, did perchance (following <inevitably to> his supposed Father's profession) [help f] <squared> Timber to build houses, that had himselfe built the Worlde.[31] But to proceed to more secular and more Approaching Instances; I find that that great and victorious Almanzor, the Conqueror, both of Spaine and a large Share of |f. 21| the Terrestriall <sublunary> World;[32] (he that spoke more Tongues then euer were heard at their Confusion <building of> in Babel) found leisure in the croud /midst/ of all his victorys and his speculations, not onely to make Coats of Male, but to be come his Craftsmaster in the Trade. And [the] many of the Turkish Emperours <sultans> (that sure did not for want; haue taken pleasure to sweeten the /King-craft/ Trade of Ruling Kingdomes, with the Exercice of som (more diuerting) Manuall Profession. /handycraft./ I cud instance in diuers of our owne gentry and nobility whose Example I haue beleeu'd so [worthy of] <highly deseruing> my Imitation; that I haue oftentimes; when I haue found my selfe fit for Nothing else, vs'd a spade in a Garden, saw'd or Cleft Wood, Graffed Trees; and diuers such other things, in Pursuance of a Principle of mine, that comands me to consider not so much what ([in] those [things]) <Employments make me> do; as what the being busy'd in them keeps me from Doing: and to beleeue, that to do Any thing (that is vndecent or vnuertuus) is better then to do Nothing.[33] But I shall rather chuse to alledge the greatest and fairest Ornaments of the sweeter sex, (the Ladys;) who will not oftentimes disdaine to spend whole Afternoones; in the Contri[tion]uing of their soft silk into those storys, that their softer Lookes [haue] peraduenture <haue> occasion'd; and [to] vse to [wo] perce

---

[30] Jud. 6:11, 1 Sam. 9:3, Gen. 14:14, and 2 Sam. 13. Thamar (or Tamar) was a daughter of David.

[31] Acts 18:3 and Mark 6:3.

[32] RB also used this example in the *Aret.* (bk. 2, ch. 4).

[33] RB used the same proverb in "Of Sin."

<wound> their Holand[34] as often with their Needles, as they do our harts with the more Penetrating <irresistible needle lihtning> beames of their Eys. |f. 21v| ('Tis) strange that our Gallants shud onely in their Vanitys think their Mistresses worthy of their Imitation. Not that I wud haue a Gentleman make a Trade his Bisness but that [Recreation] (to omit the [Vic] extrauagant Vicissitudes of worldly Conditions; which may make [Peop] the Greatest need som Knoledge not onely for an Ornament but for a Subsistance; as these Times haue but too sadly /fully/ [dem] euinc'd.)[35] I wud haue him vse sometimes [(when he findes himself] Recreations that may not be altogether so barren and vnprofitable as many of those that are now adays cry'd vp: and by this Meanes haue an honest, delightful and vsefull way to passe those Leisure houres; which many, for want of other Employments, spend in the Worst (of them.) Certinly those that despize this neglect /despize/ a very securing <valid fortifying> Antidote against <to staue of> the Temtations of the Deuill, who oftentimes despaires to find admittance into a Mind; that is already Full /throng'd, taken-vp/ [wi] of other Desseins: and is so far from assenting to his [Eu] Wicked Motions; that it is not at leasure so much as to giue eare /heare/ his seducing Persuasions. ↑Temtations are best ouercome as the Parthians did their Enemys, by flying. There is not so much Valor in succesfully <fortunately> Resisting them; as Rashness in needlesly expecting <inuiting> them; and Wisdom in prudently Declining them. Beleeue it, if thou once condiscend to argue with the Deuill, (the Perfidiousness of thy owne Corruptions considered;) heel proue the better <nimbler> Logician /sophister/ of the 2.[36] That which the Psalmist (Ps. 58.5.) <[in an]]> makes the simile of a Wicked man in another Case, may in this becom the Embleme /Comparison/ of a good one: to be, Like the Deaf Adder that stoppeth her Ear, and will not hearken to the Voice of the Charmer. For the Certinly, the Deuils Allurements <Temtations>, are much safelyer [repuls'd] <answer'd> by stopping <bolting> of the Eare, then by opening the Mouth.↓ [To which I shall ad,] We see the Bird vpon the Wing scapes the Fouler's Aime, when she that perches oftentimes becomes his Prey. |f. 22| To which I must adde, that the Pleasingest /best/ Way to Pass ones time well is to Employ it so. For as when [w] men are very attentiuely /ernestly/ considering some <one> Object; a world of others may passe by vnregarded:[37] so to those [that are] whose Thoughts are very

---

[34] Holland is a kind of linen (*OED*).

[35] This remark comments not only on RB's financial situation but on the circumstances of others in the Hartlib circle. A major theme of the group was to pursue both "lucriferous" and "fructiferous" experiments. Maddison's discussion of the Durys' financial straits is pertinent (69); Webster analyzes the issue in detail (ch. 5).

[36] Cf. Jacobus Acontius's *Satanæ Strategemata* (1648).

[37] On 31 August 1649, RB wrote to Lady Ranelagh that despite illness he was entertained by his furnace: "*Vulcan* has so transported and bewitched me, that as the delights I taste in it, make me fancy my laboratory a kind of Elysium, so, as if the threshold of it possessed the quality the poets

seriously taken vp with som Bisnesse or another; [It] the Houres steale by vndiscernedly: and such People yow shall heare often Complaine that they want Time, neuer that it lyes vpon their hands. On the other side there is nothing [more] <so> tedious or so tyring as an Idle man is to himselfe: (as indeed I haue been very seldom more weary of Doing any thing, then I haue been of Doing nothing) whereas the sun's Pace to a busy'd Person, appeares as swift /nimble/ as an Impatient Louer makes it in his Wishes. And truly insted of (with many others,) Anticipating <or doting> [by ri] in my desires the [App] Arriuall of the Night; [(were it not] I cud wish (were it not vncharitable to the Antipodes) that Ioshua's Miracle were more frequent; when his <Prayers> gaue the Sun a full stop in his Careere; and oblig'd him to a Visit to (the Horizon of) Gibeon, 24 houres longer, then his Naturall Ciuility <vsuall Courtship> wud haue permitted. ↑But I kno not how, 'tis either the Fault or the Vnhappiness of Greatnesse; to Create it a Basenesse to haue an Employment; and so because their Plenty excuses them from the Need of any Employment, the want of that need makes them make their Recreation their Bisnesse. Which (Recreation) is indeed allowable as a [Par] refreshing Parenthesis of like. But when that (Parenthesis) is too long, it marres the sense /Discourse/ and the Truth is, that that Recreation that is not iustyfy'd by a (Necessity) Vicissitude and Alternation of Busyness, is but Idlenes flatter'd with /disguis'd in/ a more ciuill <excusing> Appellation.↓ I cud tell yow of their Opinion that hold no Diuersion allowable but as it either Conduces to, or Results from Action. And of the Practise of some very Eminent and [rather] <truly> Admirable men I haue the Honor to be acquainted with; that (if we may Credit [them] <what they say)> find that Recreation in the |f. 22v| Variety of [their] Employments, that we seeke in their Suspension /Cessation./[38] But these sublime Examples, I will (for the present) forbeare to insist on, because methinks I heare men muttering /pretending/ that (like the Miracles of our Sauior) they are fitter fo[u]r our Wonder then our Imitation. Onely I must adde, that since the Angels are Christned with a Name that Originally signifyes Messengers; and are elsewhere in the Scriptures Termed Ministring spirits; (as indeed they always consider more the[r] Master then their Errand; and whom they Obey, then whom they serue) I see no Reason, why we shud think that Employedness a Derogation [from] to vs, from whence those blessed and seraphick spirits, deriue their most Glorious Titles of honor. And since our first Father [him] eu'n in Paradise it selfe, had Handywork enjoyn'd him in that Comand hee receau'd to till that Ground of which he was compos'd <taken>;[39] I

---

ascribed to that *Lethe* their fictions made men taste of, before their entrance into those feats of bliss, I there forget my standish and my books . . ." (1.xlv).

[38] As in his "Doctrine of Thinking," this passage refers to RB's admiration for the work of the Invisible College.

[39] Gen. 2:7. RB draws on the Hebrew etymology of Adam ("red earth") and angel ("messen-

see not why we his Posterity in our delapidated and Decay'd <faln, deprest/ Condition, shud thinke a Corperiall Employment either a Burden or an [vnnecessary] <needless> skreene betwixt vs and Temtations: when God himself gaue <bestow'd [prescrib'd]> it Adam, both as a Part of his Deliht [eu'n] in Paradise (it selfe) and prescrib'd it him to preserue <as the fittest meanes> his Integrity in the very state of Innocence. |f. 23| To hasten to a Period /Conclusion/ [Arist] In the husbanding and Management of Time, Aristotles Rules of Mediocrity seem (almost) vnnecessary;[40] there being heere but one Extreame[l] to be shun'd /auoyded/ which is that of Prodigality /Excesse/ since Auarice in <of> Time, is either Commendable or Impossible. Tis <onely> the Improuement of Time, ↑(which like the Viper, whose flesh [makes Treacle, is /becoms/ it's owne Antidote)] prepar'd becoms an Antidote against it's [owne Poyson,] selfe.)↓[41] that can secure our Memorys from the Iniurys of Time; [and] disarms <blunts> him of his All-destroying scythe, and knocks out his Iron Teeth.[42] But they that make Idleness the Companion /Darling/ of their Liues, must Expect Obliuion, /obscureness, forgetfulness/ to Digge their Graues. ↑If I cud be of the vnthankful [M] humor of those Filosofers that cal'd Nature Stepmother;[43] I shud do her that Iniury vpon no score so much, as that hauing giuen vs [an] so strong an Inclination to know all kinds of Truths and tast all kinds of Good; she [shall] has confin'd vs to so narrow a Terme for the Discouery of the one and the Fruition of the other: and certinly Deth wud be fear'd by good men, rather for what it hinders vs to pursue then what it depriues vs of; if by finishing our Pursuits, it did not put vs into Possession of what <the Goods> we long for.↓

ger").

[40] Cf. Nich. Eth. II.ix.1-9 and the *Aret.* (bk. 2, ch. 5).

[41] RB often referred to this antidote: see *Usefulness* 2.85 and Letters (6.477, 496, and 499).

[42] RB used a similar image in the *Aret.* (bk. 2, ch. 4).

[43] Hall used the same image in *Horæ Vacivæ* (1646): "He seem'd to carry Reason along with him, who called Nature Step-mother, in that she gives us so small a portion of time" (15).

Boyle's Library

Previously known only as a volume of seventeenth-century theological notes, MS 23 is a partial catalogue of Boyle's library, compiled by John Warr the Younger not long before (or shortly after) Boyle's death in 1691. (The latest book was *A letter from Leghorn, March the twenty foureh* [sic] [London 1691]).[1] Warr's authorship of this catalogue is easily proven. On f. 16 the compiler listed this item: "Tachensius his Hippocrates Chymicus Englished by my Father (1677)." This note accomplishes three things. It identified the compiler of this list; it identified John Warr the Elder as the previously anonymous translator ("J. W.") of *O. Tachenius his Hippocrates Chymicus, discovering the ancient foundation of the late Viperine salt with his clavis thereunto annexed* (London 1677; Wing T98, not T89 as listed in Wing); and it explains why a manuscript translation of Tachenius survives among Boyle's papers (BP 32). That volume was probably a private translation, performed by someone to whom Boyle entrusted his own chemical papers (Maddison 203). Beyond any question, the compiler of MS 23 was John Warr the Younger, a long-time servant of Robert Boyle and one of the executors of his will.

Warr's catalog offers a great deal of new information about Boyle's library, a topic on which little has been written for almost forty years. In 1949 D. McKie noted a contemporary's observation that Boyle's estate had "330 fols., 801 qtos. and 2440 Oct and 12., most well bound."[2] A year later Maddison drew on Hooke's diary and other sources to chronicle the sad dispersal of Boyle's scientific books among the bookstalls in Moorfields and their later conflation with the books of Sylvanus Morgan, the sale catalogue of which made precise ownership impossible to determine.[3] Books owned by Boyle are quite scarce: I have examined only one such volume, the Wellcome Institute's copy of Joannes Sancto Nazario, *De peste libri tres* (1538). The volume was previously owned by Dr. Thomas Sydenham, Boyle's friend and neighbor in Pall Mall, who died in 1689.

MS 23 provided a shelflist of books in several rooms of Boyle's house in Pall Mall. Warr apparently purchased some of the books before the sale of books, for he indicated prices for some of the volumes and totalled the prices at

---

[1] In BP 36.87, RB referred to a "list of my Writings from War." From the handwriting and the other items on the list (his will, legacies to servants, and memorials for his executors), I would place the MS among Boyle's last writings.

[2] *Nature* 163 (1949) 627.

[3] *Nature* 165 (1950) 981. The sale of Warr's library created a similar problem as we can see from the sale catalogue, *A catalogue of Mr. John Warre, Secretary to the Honourable Robert Boyle, Esq: deceas'd, and of another Gentleman* (15 May 1717; BL shelfmark 821.e.4[8]).

several points; as one of Boyle's executors, he was responsible for selling the books.[4] Although he recorded the number of folios, quartos, and duodecimos, his inventory accounts for fewer than 700 volumes of the 3,500 volumes noted by McKie. I do not have sufficient space to discuss Warr's responsibilities to Boyle's estate or to present the actual shelflist, which casts interesting light on the arrangement of books in particular rooms—e.g., volumes in the room of Thomas Smith, the apothecary who lived with Boyle; books that had been loaned to various people, including Warr's father; or pamphlets that had been bound together. Nor will I discuss what the contents of the library suggest about Boyle's interests and outlook. I will discuss these issues in a future publication.

If Warr was the compiler, whose books has he catalogued? The question is important because he listed the contents only of some rooms in Boyle's house, and it is not certain, as Michael Hunter has noted in private correspondence, that the books in those rooms belonged to Boyle rather than to his servants. Warr identified six (or possibly seven) rooms in two residences: the closet of Warr's room on Brewer Street (f. 9^v), the shelves in Thomas Smith's bedroom (f. 10^v), Warr's room in Boyle's house (f. 14), the closet in the lower room in Brewer Street (f. 22), the upper closet in Brewer Street (f. 22), Warr's room in Boyle's house (f. 26), Warr's chamber at Boyle's house (f. 32), Warr's room at Boyle's house (f. 36), the garret closet in Brewer Street (f. 48), and the upper back closet in Brewer Street (f. 56). Warr did not include in this manuscript the bedrooms of Boyle or of Lady Ranelagh, though we know from Evelyn that Boyle had a great number of books in his bed chamber. The reference to Thomas Smith's room indicates that one of the homes was Boyle's residence at Pall Mall. The information about Brewer Street may refer to another private residence maintained by Boyle.

Evelyn recalled that in order to escape from company at Pall Mall "now and then [Boyle] repaired to a private lodging in another quarter of the town" (Maddison 187). If this lodging was on Brewer Street, it would have been appropriate for Warr to include rooms in that residence. I do not believe that Warr lived on Brewer Street because of several parenthetical comments. When he listed the contents of "the closet of the Back Garret in Brewer Street (in folio)," he noted that two of the three volumes of Foxe's *Acts and monuments* (1641) were in his "upper closet at home" (f. 9). This comment makes sense only if Brewer Street was not his residence. Among many books in his room at his master's, he noted that a few volumes were "at home": Theophilus Gale's *Covrt of the gentiles* (1677) and Samuel Annesley's *The morning exercise at Cripplegate*. If the books in Boyle's house belonged to Warr, it would be odd

[4] Maddison reviews Warr's dispute with the co-executors of Boyle's estate (206-08) and concludes that Warr, "in whom Robert Boyle had shown so much confidence, completely neglected to establish trusts for [Boyle's] charitable scheme" (217).

for him to include volumes in Smith's room. Even if we assumed that the books in these rooms belonged to Boyle's servants and not to him, we have learned something about the kinds of servants Boyle selected and the kinds of books kept in the house where he lived for the last three decades of his life. But I believe that other evidence points to Boyle's ownership.

In his summary for these ten rooms, Warr indicated that 63 quartos were to be "S" and 90 quartos were to be "K." I assume that "S" meant "Sell" or "Sold" and that "K" meant "Keep" or "Kept." Further, I assume that "K" meant kept by Warr, who was purchasing some volumes from Boyle's estate (or perhaps acquiring without purchasing), and that "S" indicated volumes that were to be sold.[5] Certainly, "K" and "S" could stand for other words; but considering the date of the inventory, its careful arithmetic, and its selection from various rooms, I believe that Warr's catalogue was created as part of his responsibilities either to Boyle or to Boyle's estate.

We should recall John Evelyn's description of Boyle's library and bed-chamber.

> Glasses, pots, chemical and mathematical instruments, books and bundles of papers, did so fill and crowd his bed-chamber, that there was but just room for a few chairs; so as his whole equipage was very philosophical without formality. There were yet other rooms, and a small library (and as you know had Descartes), as learning more from men, real experiments, and in his laboratory (which was ample and well furnished), than from books.
>
> Maddison 187

Some of the volumes listed by Warr are of special interest: a copy of *Style* (1661), which Warr noted was "interleaved" and perhaps suggested Boyle's interest in a second edition of the work. Of the thirteen volumes with gilt bindings, four are works by Boyle. (For volumes written by Boyle, Warr always referred to the author as "Mr Boyle.")

In the present account of Boyle's library, I have alphabetized the volumes by author. In addition, I have supplemented Warr's information in several ways. First, Warr was not terribly precise about authorship: for example, Heinrich Buenting's *Itinerarium totius sacræ Scripturæ, or, the travells of the patriarchs* (1636) was identified only by its subtitle and date of publication: "the travells of the patriarchs (1636)." Where possible, I have provided correct information about authorship as well as place and date of publication. Square brackets indicate Warr's listing; angle brackets indicate my additions to or emendations of the

---

[5] In his will, Boyle forgave Warr's £50 debt (Maddison 260) and bequeathed £40 and his "wearing Apparrell and Linnen" (Maddison 262); in a later codicil, Boyle provided an annual sum of £40 while Warr was executing the will (Maddison 280). It is possible that volumes marked "K" were additional gifts.

entry. I have silently modernized the places of publication, transliterated Greek letters to Roman, and provided STC and Wing numbers. (I have also noted more than thirty entries where Warr's attribution or publication data conflict with information in Wing or STC.) I have included in quotation marks some of Warr's comments (e.g., gilt bindings, number of copies owned, irregularities of the title pages, etc.), but I have not indicated the books' prices, the room and residence where they were kept, or their location on the shelf. For anonymous works, I have not indicated whether Warr classified the author as anonymous or simply failed to provide an author. Finally, unless otherwise indicated, London was the place of publication.

1. *Account of proceedings at Guild Hall* (Sept 28, 1682).
2. *Address and advice of the peers* (1679).
3. Agrippa, Cornelius. *Vanity of arts and sciences* (1676). Wing A790.
4. Ainsworth, <Henry>. *An arrow against idolatrie* (1640). Wing A223.
5. <Ainsworth, Henry>. *Communion of saints with God, angels, and one another in this life* (1628). STC lists three different editions or issues printed in 1628.
6. Ainsworth, William. *Medulla Bibliorum* [Marrow of the Bible] (1652). Wing A818.
7. <Aleman, Mateo>. *<The rogue, or the> life of Guzman <de Allafarache>* (1622). STC 288.
8. Alleine, Joseph. *An alarme to unconverted sinners* (1673). Wing A961a.
9. Alleine, Richard. *Vindicæ pietatis* (1664). Wing A1004.
10. <Alleine, Richard> [R. A.]. *<A> rebuke to backsliders* (1684). Wing A1000.
11. Allen, Richard. *Instructions about heart worke* (1684). Wing A995.
12. Alsop, <Vincent>. *Of scandal and Christian liberty* (1683). Wing lists only 1680.
13. Alsted, Johann. *Compendium <lexici philosphici> grammatica Latina* (Herborn 1613).
14. Alsted, Johann. *Methodus <sacrosanctæ> theologiæ* (Frankfurt 1614).
15. Alsted, Johann. *Definitiones theologicæ* (Frankfurt 1626).
16. Alsted, Johann. *<Synopsis theologiæ . . . locorum communium theologicorum> Loci communes theologici* (Frankfurt 1630).
17. Alvarus, <Emmanuel>. *<De institutione grammatica>* [Latina grammar] (Antwerp 1675).
18. Ames, William. *Coronis ad collationem Hagiensem* [sive adversus remonstran . . .] (1630). STC 553.
19. Ames, William. *Medulla theologiæ* (1630). STC 557.
20. Ames, <William>. *Marrow of <sacred> divinity* (1642). Wing A3000.
21. Ames, William. *Marrow of <sacred> divinity* (<1642 or 1643>). Wing

A3000 or A3001.

22. Ames, William. <. . . *magni theologi . . . philosophemata*> [Philosophemata] (Leiden 1643).

23. Ames, <William>. *Lectiones in omnes psalmes Davidis* (1647). Wing A2999.

24. Ames, William. <*De conscientia et . . . casibus*> [De casibus conscientia] (Amsterdam 1670).

25. Amyraldus, <Moses>. *Treatise of religions* (1660). Wing A3037.

26. Amyraldus, Moses. *De libero hominis arbitrio disputatio* (Saumur 1667).

27. <Andrews, Lancelot>. *Pattern of catechistical doctrine* (1630). STC 603.

28. *An essay for reconciling differences among Christians* (1678). Warr noted that the volume was "(Dr. Worsley's)." Did he mean that Boyle bought the work at Worsley's sale (13 May 1678), or that this was a work written by Worsley? Worsley died in 1677 and left no known publications. Cf. an anonymous 13-page anonymous pamphlet (dated 13 July 1678): *Christian unity exhorted to: being a few words in tender love to all professing of Christianity in Old England, the Land of my Nativity. Wherein the differences between profession and possesion of that which is really the substance of true religion, is clearly manifested* (Wing C3950). Another possibility is John Nalson's *The project of peace, or, unity of faith and government, the only expedient to procure peace both foreign and domestique* (1678) Wing N113; I have found no title that matches Warr's description more closely than these two.

29. <Annesley, Samuel>. <*A*> *supplement to the morning exercise at Cripplegate* (1676). "2nd edition, gilt back." Wing lists 1661, 1664, 1671, and 1677.

30. <Annesley, Samuel>. <*The*> *morning exercise* <*at Cripplegate*> [against popery] (1676), five vols. "One of them is at home." Wing lists 1661, 1664, 1671, and 1677.

31. <Anon.> *Assemblies confession of faith examined* (1651). Wing C5786A. The author is probably Henry Parker.

32. Anon. "Old (Latine) grammar" (n.p., n.d.). Perhaps another copy of William Lily's *Grammar*, which went through numerous editions (see below).

33. Anon. <*A confession of faith, put forth by the elders* [Baptized believers confession of faith] (1677). Wing C5794.

34. Anon. <*An orthodox creed*: *or, a protestant*> *confession of faith* (1679). Wing O503.

35. Anon. <*An*> *apology for God's worship* [and worshippers] (1683). Wing A3543A. Warr attributed the work to "Ralphson," but I have not

confirmed this attribution.

36. Anon. *A Christians journall* (1684). Wing C3956.
37. Anon. *A congratulatory letter of thanks from North Allerton* (1681). Wing C5818.
38. Anon. *A dialogue between two burgesses* (<1681>). Wing D1339
39. Anon. *A dictionarie of English and Latine* (1623). STC 6831.
40. Anon. *A discourse of episcopacy* (n.p., n.d.). Without author, date, or place of publication, it is impossible to identify the work.
41. Anon. *A guide to English juries* (1682). Wing G2184D.
42. Anon. *A remonstrance concerning the present troubles* (1640). STC 20880.
43. Anon. *An answer to a letter written by a member of Parliament* (1679). Wing A3320.
44. Anon. *Character of an unjust judge* (1681). Wing C2015.
45. Anon. *<England's happiness in a lineal succession; and the deplorable miseries which ever attended doubtful titles to the crown, historically demonstrated . . .>* [Warrs between the houses of Yorke and Lancaster] (1685). Wing E2978.
46. Anon. Several narratives &c bound in a thick volume (1679). Many narratives about the Popish Plot were published in 1679, including Robert Jennison, *The narrative of Robert Jennison*; William Bedloe, *A narrative and impartial discovery of the horrid Popish Plot*; Anon., *A just narrative of the hellish new counter-plots;* Anon., *A narrative of the sessions*; and Titus Oates, *A true narrative.* For another entry related to the Popish Plot, cf. #546.
47. Anon. *The merchants dayly companion* (1684). Wing P57.
48. <Anon.> *<The> grounds <and principles> of* [Christian] *religion.* Wing lists 1646, 1648, 1649, 1650, 1662, 1667, 1678, 1682, and 1687.
49. <Anon>.*<A full and true relation of His Excellency the Pope's nuncio making his publick entry at Windsor on Sunday the third of the instant* [Nuncio's entry] (<1687>). Wing F2318B.
50. <Anon.> *Rhetor familiaris* (Paris 1663). "gilt back" This work has not been identified.
51. Aristotle. *Organon* (Basel <1543>).
52. Aristotle. *Rhetorick* [English'd] (1686). Wing A3695.
53. <Arnauld, Antoine>. *Ars cogitandi* (1674). Wing A3725.
54. Asellius, <Gaspar>. *Dissertatio de venis lacteis pecquati experimenta nova anatomica* (Paris 1651).
55. Augustine. *Flores Augustini ex civitate dei excerpti* (Lyons 1580).
56. <Augustine>. *Sancti aurelii Augustini <. . .> operum* (Paris 1683), tomes 1, 3, 4, 5.
57. Augustine. *Confessions* (Douai 1616).

58. <B., C.>. *An address to the honourable city of London* (1681). Wing B40.
59. <B., H.> *A true copy of a letter (intercepted) going for Holland.* (<1680>). Wing B80.
60. Bacchanellus, <Johannes>. *De consensu medicorum* (Leiden 1572).
61. <Bacon, James>. *A plaine and profitable catechisme* (Oxford 1660). Wing B344.
62. <Bacon, Nathaniel>. *<A relation of the fearful estate of> Francis Spira* (1668). Wing lists editions in 1649, 1653, 1657, 1665, 1672, 1675, 1678, 1681, 1683, and 1688.
63. Balduinus, <Fridericus>. *Tractatus de casibus conscientia* (Frankfurt 1654).
64. Ball, John. *<A treatise> of divine meditation* (1660). Wing B576.
65. Ball, John. *Treatise of the covenant of grace* (1645). Wing B579.
66. <Ball, John>. *<The power of godliness . . . whereunto are annexed distinct treatises 1. Of the affections. 2. Of the spiritual combate. 3. Of the government of the tongue . . .>* [Combat of the tongue and the five senses for superiority] (1657). Wing B561.
67. Bamfield, <Francis>. *The Lords free prisoner* (1683). Wing B626.
68. <Banks, Jonathan>. *<Janua clavis, or Lily's> [Syntax explained]* (1679). Wing B668B.
69. Barbette, <Paul>. *<Opera chirurgico-anatomica>* [Chiurgia] (Leiden 1672).
70. Barbette, <Paul>. *<Thesaurus chirurgiæ>* [Chyurgical and anatomical works] (1672). Wing B699.
71. Barrow, Isaac. *Lectiones mathematica* (1683). Wing lists 1684 and 1685.
72. Bartholin, <Thomas>. *<De pulmonum substantia et motu diatribe>* [De pulmonibus diatribe] (Copenhagen 1663).
73. Basil, <Saint>. *Magni opera <omnia>* [Græco-Latina] (Paris 1618).
74. Bauderon, <Brice>. *Praxis* [medicinæ] (Paris 1620).
75. Baudius, Dominicus. *Epistolæ . . . orationes* (Amsterdam 1662).
76. Baxter, <Richard>. *<The> one thing necessary* (1685). Wing B1336.
77. Baxter, <Richard>. *Methodus theologicæ Christianæ* (1681). Wing B1308.
78. Baynes, <Paul>. *<An entire commentary upon . . . Ephesians>* [Comment on the first of the Ephesians] (1643). Wing B1549.
79. Becmanus, <Johann>. *Notitia dignitatum illustrium* (Frankfurt and Leipzig 1685).
80. Béguin, <Jean>. *Tyrocinium chymicus* (Amsterdam 1669).
81. Benn, <William>. *Soul-prosperity* (1683). Wing B1880.
82. Berchetus, <Tussanus>. *Catechisme* (Greeke-Latine) (Hanau 1628).
83. <Bertramus, presbyter> [Bertram]. *The book of Bertram* [On the

sacrament] (1686). Wing B2049.

84. Bethel, Slingsby. *Vindication of Slingsby Bethel* (1681). Wing B2078.

85. Beverley, <Thomas>. *Principles of Protestant truth and peace* (1683). Wing B2188A.

86. *Bible* "in 12mo bound in red Turky leather" (n.p., n.d.). As we consider Boyle's Bibles, we should also note John Bridges's poetic edition and the 'Puritan' Bible with notes by John Canne.

87. *Bible* (French) (1687). two copies. Wing B2707a.

88. *Bible* (French) (1687). Wing B2707a.

89. *French Bible* "in blew Turky leather gilt back" (n.p., n.d.)

90. *Bible* (Greek testament) (1633). STC 2798.

91. *Bible* (Greek testament) (Cologne 1609).

92. *Bible* (Greeke new testament) (Utrecht 1675).

93. *Bible* (Irish old testament) (1685). There is also a second copy "with a Title Page." Wing B2711.

94. *Bible* (Old testament) (1674). "in blew Turkey leather gilt."

95. *Bible* (Old testament) (1676). "in blew Turky leather." Wing B2675 or B2676.

96. *Bible. With Common Prayer, apocrypha and concordance* (1627).

97. Binchius, Johannes. *Mellificium theologicum* (Amsterdam 1666).

98. <Blount, Thomas>. *<A law dictionary, interpreting difficult and obscure words and terms in common or statute, ancient or modern lawes>* [Dictionary interpreting hard words] (1670). Wing B3340.

99. Boe, <Francisis de le>. *Opera medica* (Amsterdam 1679).

100. Bolton, <Samuel>. *<True> bounds of Christian freedom* (<1645 or 1656>).

101. Bolton, Robert. *General directions for a comfortable walking with God* (1638). STC 3254.

102. Bonet, <Théophile>. *<Medecine efficace et operative>* [Cautiones &c. medicinales] (Geneva 1668). No collective title page. The publication, 1668-70, was a 4-vol. collection.

103. Bonet, <Théophile>. *Mercurius compitalitius* (Geneva 1682).

104. Bonham, <Josias>. *The churches glory* (1674). Wing B3592.

105. Borrichius, Olaus. *Hermetis ægyptiorum & chemicorum sapientia . . .* (Copenhagen 1674).

106. Boyle, Robert. *<A continuation of nevv experiments>* [New experiments physico-mechanical and his defense against Linus and Hobbs] (Oxford 1662 and 1682). Wing B3934 and B3935. Warr always designated Boyle as "Mr Boyle."

107. Boyle, Robert. *<Some considerations touching the> excellency of theology* (1674). "gilt back" Wing B3955.

108. Boyle, Robert. *<Some considerations touching the> style of holy*

scriptures (1661). “interleaved” Wing B4025.

109. Boyle, Robert. <*Some considerations touching the*> *usefulness of experimental philosophy* (Oxford 1664). Wing B4030.
110. Boyle, Robert. <*The*> *ærial noctiluca* (1680). Wing B3925.
111. Boyle, Robert. *Continuation of experiments* (1682). Wing B3934. “2d part.” Warr noted that it was bound with two other items.
112. Boyle, Robert. *Continuation of nevv experiments* (Oxford 1669). Wing B3935. “first part.” Warr noted that eight other items were bound with it.
113. Boyle, Robert. *Discourse of things above reason* (1681). Wing B3944.
114. Boyle, Robert. *Experimentorum novorum* (1680). “gilt back.” Wing B3965.
115. Boyle, Robert. *Final causes* (1688). “gilt back” Wing B3965.
116. Boyle, Robert. *Memoirs for the natural history of humane blood* (1684). “gilt back.” Wing B393.
117. Boyle, Robert. *Physiological essays* (1669). Wing B3930.
118. Boyle, Robert. *Sceptical chymist* “2nd ed” (Oxford 1680). Wing B4022.
119. Brabourne, <Theophilus>. <*A confutation of the Dutch-Arminian tenent*> [Confutation of universal redemption] (1651). Wing B4089.
120. Brandmullerus, <Joannes>. *Conciones funebres . . . Joanne Brandmullero* (Basel 1576).
121. <Bridges, John>. <*Sacro-sanctum novum testamentum*> [New testament in latine verse Joanno episcopum Oxonienses] (1604). STC 3735.
122. Browne, <Richard>. *Prosodia pharmacopæidior* (1685). Wing B5141.
123. <Browne, Sir Thomas>. *Religio medici* (1682). “8th ed.” Wing B5178.
124. <Browne, William>. <*A compendious and accurate treatise of recoveries*> [A treatise of fines and recoveries] (1678). Wing B5081.
125. Bruele, Gualtherus. *Praxis medicinæ* (Antwerp 1581). This work was bound in vellum, Warr noted, along with Galen's *Epitome* and Bruele's *Praxis Medicinæ*.
126. Bruele, Gualtherus. *Praxis medicinæ theorica* (Leiden 1612).
127. Brugis, <Thomas>. <*Vade mecum*: *or*, *a*> *companion for a chyurgion* (1670). Wing lists 1652, 1653, 1657, 1679, and 1689.
128. Bruno, <Giordano>. *Artificium perorandi* (Frankfurt 1612).
129. Bucanus <Guilelmus>. *Institutiones theologicæ* (Geneva 1617).
130. <Buenting, Heinrich>. <*Itinerarium totius sacræ Scripturæ*, *or*, *the*> *travells of the patriarchs* (1636). STC 4020.
131. Bunyan, <John>. *Grace abounding to the chiefe of sinners* (1680). Wing B5525.
132. Bunyan, John. *Pilgrims progress* “in 2 vols (1 and 2 part), 3rd edit.” (1682 and 1683). The 1682 edition is Wing B5567 or B5568; the 1683 edition B5569. The “3rd edit.” is incorrect.

133. Bunyan, John. *Pilgrims progress* (1684). Wing B5570.
134. Burgess, <Anthony>. *<A treatise> of original sin* (1659). Wing lists 1658.
135. Burgess, Anthony. *<Vindiciæ legis: or, a vindication>* [of the moral law] (1647). Wing B5667.
136. Burgess, Anthony. *The true doctrine of iustification* (1655). Wing B5665.
137. Burnet, <Thomas>. *Thesaurus medicinæ practicæ* (1673). Wing B5959.
138. Burroughes, Jeremiah. *<The rare jewel> of Christian contentment* (1649). Wing B6103.
139. Burroughes, Jeremiah. *<An> exposition . . . of Hosea* (1652). Wing B6069.
140. Burroughes, Jeremiah. *Gospel conversation* (1650). Wing lists 1648, 1653, and 1654.
141. Burthogge, <Richard>. *Cavsa dei, or an apology for God* (1675). Wing B6149.
142. Burton, Robert. *<Anatomy of> melancholy* (1676). Wing B6184
143. Calepinus, Ambrosius. *Dictionarium undecim linguarum* (Basel 1605).
144. Calepinus, Ambrosius. *Linguarum novem dictionarium* (Leiden n.d.).
145. Calvin, <Jean>. *Catechismus ecclesia genevensis* (1572). STC 4377.
146. Calvin, <Jean>. *<Institutionis christianæ religionis . . . epitome>* [Epitome institutionum &c calvini] (1584). STC 4428.
147. <Calvin, Jean>. *Aphorismi doctrinæ Christianæ* (Herborn 1626).
148. Calvin, <Jean>. *Institutions* (1634). STC 4425.
149. Calvin, Jean>. *Aphorismi doctrinæ Christianæ <. . . per Johann Piscator>* (n.p. 1650).
150. Canne, <John>. *Bible with marginal notes* (<Amsterdam?> 1664). Wing B2271.
151. Capoa, <Leonardo di>. *<The> uncertainty of the art of physick* (1684). Wing C481.
152. Cardano, <Girolamo>. *Commentaria in aphorismes Hippocratis* (Padua 1653).
153. Care, Henry. *<Draconica; or, an abstract>* [Abstract of the penal lawes] (1687). Wing C510.
154. <Care, Henry>. *English liberties* (1682). Wing C517.
155. Carleton, <George>. *<Consensus ecclesiæ catholicæ contra Tridentos>* [Ecclesia catholica consensu contra tridentinos] (1613). STC 4631.
156. Cartwright, <Thomas>. *<A confutation of the Rhemists translation>* [Annotations on the Rhemish testament] ([London] 1618) STC 4709.
157. Cartwright, Thomas. *Harmonia evangelica* (Leiden 1647).
158. Caryl, <Joseph>. *Exposition upon the 15th, 16th, and 17th chapters of Job* (1653). Wing C765A.
159. Caryl, <Joseph>. *The moderator* [in matters of religion] (1652). Wing

C780B.

160. <Castellensis, Hadrianus> [Adrianus]. *De sermone Latino et modis Latine loquendi* (Cologne 1522).

161. Caussin, <Nicholas>. <*Tragœdiæ sacræ*> [Tragœdia sacred] (Paris n.d.). There were editions in 1620 and 1629.

162. Chaloner, Edward. <*Credo ecclesiam sanctum catholicam*> [The authority universality & visibility of the Church] (1625). STC 4934.

163. Chamberlain, Robert. *The accomptants guide* (1679). Wing C1812.

164. Chamier, <Daniel>. *Contractus* (Geneva 1643).

165. Chamier, <Daniel>. *Corpus theologicum sive loci communes* (Geneva 1653).

166. <Chappuzeau, Samuel>. *History of jewels* (1674). Wing lists 1671.

167. Charas, <Moise>. <*New*> *experiments upon vipers* (1670). Wing C2037.

168. Charas, <Moise>. <*The*> *royal pharmicopœa* (1678). Wing C2040.

169. Charleton, Walter. *Natural history of the passions* (1659). Warr has conflated two works by Charleton: *Natural history of the passions* (1674), Wing C3684A, and *Natural history of nutrition* (1659), Wing C3684.

170. Charnock, <Stephen>. *A discourse* [*Treatise*] *of divine providence* (1680). Wing C3708.

171. Charnock, <Stephen>. *Works* (1682). [Both "first" and "second" are deleted.] If this is vol. 1, it appeared in 1684; no volume appeared in 1682.

172. Charnock, <Stephen>. *Works* (1684). "second vol." Wing C3705.

173. <Chasteignier de la Rochepozay, Henri Louis> [Castane]. *Distionctionum philosophicarum* <*synopsis*> (Oxford 1657). Wing C3729.

174. Chytræus, <David>. *In genesis enarratio* (Wittenberg 1568).

175. Cicero. *Quæstiones Tusculanæ* (1574). STC 5314.5.

176. Cicero. *Offices* (Antwerp 1603). "in 24mo."

177. Cicero. *Orations* (Hanau 1603). "second vol."

178. Cicero. <*De officiis*> [Tullies offices] (1669). Wing C4293.

179. Cicero. *Familiar epistles translated* (1671). Wing C4306.

180. Cicero. "one part of Cicero's *Phrases*" (n.p., n.d.). Perhaps Thomas Drax, *Callipeia*: *or a rich storehouse of . . . phrases . . . out of . . . Tully* (1616) or Manutius's *Phrases Latinæ*, of which Boyle had two copies.

181. Cicero. "another part of Cicero's *Phrases*."

182. Cicero. *Opera omnis* (1681). "2nd vol." Wing C4286. Warr noted that "one volume of Cicero's workes is lent my Father."

183. Cicero. *Three books touching the nature of the gods* (1683). Wing C4323.

184. Clark, <John>. *Dux grammaticus* [et oratoribus] (1657). Wing lists 1664.

185. Clark, <John>. *Phraseologia puerilis* <Anglo-Latina> (1655).

"interleaved" Wing C4474.

186. Clarkson, <David>. *<No evidence for diocesan churches>* [Against diocesan churches and bishops] (1681). Wing C4574.

187. Clarkson, <David>. *<The practical divinity of the Papists>* [Against popery] (1676). Wing C4575.

188. Claude, <Jean>. *<An historical> defence of the reformation* (1683). Wing C4593.

189. Cocker, <Edward>. *Arithmetick* (1685). Wing C4822.

190. Cocker, <Edward>. *Decimal arithmetick* (1685). Wing C4833.

191. <Cocker, Edward>. *<The young clerk's tutor enlarged>* [Young clerkes guide "10th impression"] (1659). Wing C4861. If this is the 10th impression, the date must be 1682. The first edition appeared in 1662.

192. <Cocker, Edward>. *<The> young clerks tutor* (1670). "6th edition." Wing C4859.

193. <Cocker, Edward>. *Young clerkes <tutor> [companion]* (<1672>). Wing notes editions in 1662 1663, 1664, 1668, 1670 (6th edition), 1675 (8th edition), 1680 (9th edition), and 1682 (10th edition).

194. *<Codex medicamentarius seu> pharmacopœa Parisiensis* (Paris 1645).

195. <Coles, Elisha>. *<A> dictionary <English-Latin>* (1679). Wing C5068

196. Columbus, <Matthæus>. *<De re anatomica libri XV>* [Anatome] (Frankfurt 1593).

197. Comenius, <Johann Amos>. *Janua linguarum reserata* (Leiden 1643).

198. Comenius, <Johann Amos>. *<Vestibulum>* [Linguæ latinæ vestibulum] (1647). Wing C5531.

199. Comenius, <Johann Amos>. *Janua linguarum reserata* (1647). Wing C5513.

200. Comenius, <Johann Amos>. *Janua linguarum* (1656). Wing lists 1665, 1670, and 1674.

201. Comenius, <Johann Amos>. *Schola ludus sive encyclopedia viva* (1664). Wing C5530.

202. Comenius, <Johann Amos>. *Orbis sensualium pictus* (1667). Wing lists 1659, 1672, and 1685.

203. Comenius, <Johann Amos>. *Janua linguarum trilinguis* (1670). Wing C5519.

204. *Commons address to the King* (1680).

205. Cooper, Thomas. *<Thesaurus linguæ Romane & Britannicæ>* [Dictionary] (1573). STC 5686.

206. Cotton, <John>. [Treatise of] *The covenant of grace* (1671). Wing C6467.

207. <Courcelles, Etienne de> [Curcellai]. *Opera theologica* (Amsterdam 1675).

208. Coxe, Nehemiah. *<A> discourse of the covenants* [On the covenants &c.]

(1681). Wing C6717. Boyle owned five copies.

209. Craaneen, Theodorus. *Praxis medica reformata* (Middleburg 1686).

210. Cradock, Walter. *Divine drops* (1650). Wing C6757.

211. Cradock, Walter. *Gospel-libertie* (1648). Wing C6762.

212. Cradock, Walter. *Gospel-holinesse* (1651). Wing C6760.

213. <Cranmer, Thomas>. *Reformatio legum eccesiasticarum* [ex authoritate regis henrici 8vi & edward 6ti] (1641). Wing C6828.

214. Crisp, Tobias. *Christ alone exalted* (1646), "2nd and 3rd volumes." Wing has 1643 and 1648 for vols. 2 and 3.

215. Crisp, Tobias. *Christ alone exalted* (two sermons) (1683). Wing has 1643, 1644, and 1690.

216. Crisp, Tobias. *Christ alone exalted* (1643). Wing C6955.

217. <Crouch, Nathaniel>. *The English empire in America* (1685). Wing C7319.

218. Crucius, Jacobus. *Suada delphica, sive orationes 69 varii argumenti* (Amsterdam 1675).

219. Culpeper, <Nicholas>. *<Physick>* [*Medicine*] *for the poor* (1662). Wing lists 1656 and 1670.

220. Culpeper, <Nicholas>. *Directory for midwives* (1652). Wing lists 1651, 1653, 1656, 1660, 1671, 1675, and 1681.

221. Culpeper, <Nicholas>. *English physitian enlarged* (1661). Wing C7504.

222. Culpeper, <Nicholas>. *Directory for midwives enlarged* (1666). Wing lists 1651, 1653, 1656, 1660, 1671, 1675, and 1681.

223. Culpeper, <Nicholas>. *His last legacy* (1676). Wing C7521A.

224. <Culpeper, Nicholas>. *<Pharacopœia Londiniensis, or, the new> London dispensatory* (1669). Wing lists 1653, 1654, 1655, 1656, 1659, 1661, 1667, 1672, 1675, 1679, and 1683.

225. Culverwel, Nathaniel. *<An elegant and learned discourse>* [Discourse of the light of nature] (1652). Wing C7569.

226. Cuperus, Franciscus. *Arcana atheismi revelata* (Rotterdam 1676).

227. Curtius, <Rufus> Quintus. *<De rebus gestis Alexandri Magni>* (Amsterdam 1633).

228. Daille, <Jean>. *<A treatise concerning the> right use of the fathers* (1675). Wing D119.

229. D'Anvers, <Henry>. *<A treatise of laying on of hands>* [Treatise of baptism] (1674). Wing D236.

230. Davenant, <John>. *<Dissertationes duæ>* [De morte christi and de predestinatione &c.] (Cambridge 1650). Wing D317.

231. <Davenant, John> [Bishop of Salisbury]. *Animadversions <written by>* [on a treatise entituled Gods love to mankind] (1641). Wing D314.

232. Dekkers, <Frederik>. *Exercitationes <medicæ practicæ> circa medendi methodum* (Leiden and Amsterdam 1673).

233. Dekkers, <Frederik>. *Praxis Barbettiana* (Leiden 1669).
234. Dell, William. *<Several> sermons and discovrses of* (1652). Wing D929.
235. De Laun, <Thomas>. *The present state of London* (1681). Wing D894.
236. Dickson, <David>. *Therapeutica sacra* (1656). Wing D1406.
237. Diemerbroeck, <Isbrandus de>. *Anatome corporis humani* (Utrecht 1672).
238. Digby, Sir Kenelm. *Choyce and experimental receipts* [Recipes in physick and chuirgery] (1668). Wing D1423. Two copies.
239. Diodati, Giovanni. *<Pious> annotations* [on the Bible] (1643). Wing D1510. Boyle probably attended Diodati's church while living in Geneva (Maddison 29).
240. *Directorium politicum studii linguarum* (1662). This work has not been identified.
241. Dodoens, <Rembert>. *Praxis <artis> medicæ* (Amsterdam 1640).
242. Dorney, <Henry>. *Divine contemplations* (1684). Wing D1930.
243. Drelincourt, <Charles>. *<The> Protestant's selfe-defence* (1685). Wing D2161.
244. Du Moulin, <Pierre>. *Contentment of mind* (1678). Wing does not list this edition, but a copy is found in the British Library.
245. Du Moulin, Pierre. *<The> buckler of <the> faith* (1631). STC 7315.
246. Du Moulin, Pierre. *<The> elements of logick* (1624). STC 7323.
247. Du Moulin, Pierre. *<The> accomplishment of <the> prophecies* (Oxford 1613). STC 7306.
248. Du-Gard, <William>. *Græcæ grammatica* [rudimentum] (1654). Wing D2466.
249. *Ecclesia<rum> Belgica<rum> confessio . . . et catechisis* (Leiden 1623).
250. Eobanus, <Helius>. *Exempla memorabilia* [of Andrew Eborensen] (Paris 1590). This work has not been identified.
251. Erasmus, Desiderius. *<Paraphrasis, seu potius epitome>* [Epitome Erasmus in eleg<antias> L<aurentius> Valla] (Freiburg 1531).
252. Erasmus, Desiderius. *Epistolæ familiares* (Antwerp 1545).
253. Erasmus, Desiderius. *Apophthegmata* (Antwerp 1554).
254. Erasmus, Desiderius. *Enchiridion militis Christiani* (Leiden 1641).
255. Erasmus, Desiderius. *Adagiorum . . . epitome* (Amsterdam 1649).
256. Erasmus, Desiderius. *Colloquia* (n.p., n.d.). "wants title." There were many editions of this work.
257. Erasmus, Desiderius. *De copia verborum* (1668). Wing E3197B.
258. Erasmus, Desiderius. *De ratione conscribendi epistolas* (Amsterdam 1670).
259. Erasmus, Desiderius. *Colloquies in English* (1671). Wing E3190.

260. Erasmus, Desiderius. *Familiarum colloqui* [Familiares colloquendi formulæ] (1678). Wing lists editions in 1649, 1652, 1657, 1673, 1677, 1681, and 1686.
261. Essex, <Arthur Capel>, earl of. *His speech &c.* (<1681>). Wing E3304, E3305, or E3306.
262. Fabricius Ab Aquapendente, Hieronymus. *Opera chiurgica* (Frankfurt 1620).
263. Faldo, <John>. *<Quakerism no Christianity>* [Against the Quakers] (1675). Wing F301.
264. Farnaby, <Thomas>. *Phrases* [oratorica] *elegantiores* (1638). STC 10708.
265. Farnaby, <Thomas>. *Systema grammaticvm* (1641). Wing F464.
266. Farnaby, <Thomas>. *Florilegium* [epigrammatum græcorum] (1671). Wing F301.
267. Farnaby, <Thomas>. *Phrases oratoriæ* (1658). Wing F462.
268. <Feguernekinus, Isaac>. *Enchiridion locorum communium theologicorum* (1591). STC 10748.
269. Fenner, William. *Treatise of the affections* (1642). Wing F707.
270. Fenner, William. *<A> divine message to the elect soule* (1676). Wing F689B.
271. <Ferguson, Robert> [R. F.]. *<A sober enquiry into the nature, measure, and principle>* [Discourse] of moral vertue [and grace] (1673). Wing F760.
272. Ferguson, <Robert>. *<The> interest of reason in religion* (1675). Wing F740.
273. Fernel, <Jean>. *De naturali parte medicinæ* (Paris 1542).
274. Fernel, <Jean>. *<Universa medicina . . . methodus generalis curandum>* [Methodus medendi] (Leiden 1571).
275. Fernel, <Jean>. *Methodus medendi* (n.p., n.d.).
276. Fernel, <Jean>. *Methodus medendi* (Frankfurt 1574).
277. Ferri, <Pauli>. *Scholastici orthodoxi specimen* (Neostadt 1616).
278. Field, Richard. *Of the church* (Oxford 1628). STC 10858.
279. Finch, Henry. [Of the] *Law* (1627). STC 10871.
280. Finett, Sir John. <Some choice> *observations touching forraigne ambassadors* (1656). Wing (F948) lists only a 1658 edition.
281. <Fisher, Edward>. *Marrow of modern divinity* (1646). Wing F997.
282. Fisher, <Samuel>. *Christianismus redivivus* (1655). Wing F1049
283. <Fisher, Edward>. *Marrow of modern divinity* (1656). Wing lists 1645, 1646, 1647, 1650, 1651, and 1658.
284. <Flaminius, Marcus Antonius>. *The scholars vade mecum* (1674). Wing F1132A.
285. Flavel, John. *<The> touchstone of sincerity* (1679). Wing F1200.

286. Flavel, John. <*The*> *method of grace* (1681). Wing F1169.
287. Flavel, John. <*Two treatises*> [Treatises of fear and the righteous mans refuge &c] (1682). Wing F1204.
288. Flavel, <John>. <*Pneumatologia*> [treatise of the soul of man] (1685). Wing F1176.
289. Flavel, John. <*The*> *balm of the covenant* (1688). Wing F1157.
290. <Fleming, Robert>. *The fulfilling of the Scripture* (1681). Wing F1267.
291. Florus. *Rerum à Romanis gestarvm* [History (Latin)] (Oxford 1650). Wing F1371.
292. Foulis, <Henry>. <*The*> *history of Romish treasons* (1681). Wing F1640
293. Foxe, John. <*Acts and monuments*> [Booke of martyrs in 3 volumes] (1641). Wing F2035. "2 of the volumes in my upper closet at home." There were two copies of this edition.
294. Fuchs, <Leonhard>. *Medicina compendium* (Basel 1541).
295. Fuchs, <Leonhard>. *Institutiones medicinæ* (Lyons 1560).
296. Fuchs, <Leonhard>. *Institutiones medicinæ* (n.p., n.d.). "imperfect" Editions include Lyons (1555, 1560, 1583) and Basel (1618).
297. <Fuller, Thomas>. *Ephemeris parliamentaria* (<1654>). Wing F2422
298. Gale, Theophilus. *Covrt of the Gentiles* (Oxford 1672), 2 vols. Wing G137.
299. Gale, Theophilus. *Covrt of the gentiles* (1677), 3rd and 4th parts. Wing G141 and G142. "Another volume of the same Authors 1 and 2d part (at home)."
300. Gale, Theophilus. *Idea theologiæ* [(in Latine)] (1673). Wing G145.
301. Gale, Thomas. <*Certain workes of*> *chirurgerie* (1563). STC 11529.
302. Galen. *Epitome Galeni operum* (Basel 1551).
303. Galen. *De* <*simplicium*> *medicamentorum facultatibus* (Antwerp n.d.). This work was bound in vellum along with Galen's *Epitome* and Bruele's *Praxis Medicinæ* (see above).
304. Galen. *Epitomes Galeni operum sectio tertiæ* (n.p., n.d.). There were many such epitomes and compendia.
305. Gaussenus, <Stephanus>. <. . . *quatuor dissertationes theologicæ*> [De ratione studii theologici] (Utrecht 1678).
306. Gautruche, <Pierre>. *Mathematica* <*totius*> [institutio] (Cambridge 1668). Wing G382.
307. Gautruche, <Pierre>. <*The poetical*> *history* [of the heathen gods] (1683). Wing G387A.
308. <Geneva catechism>. *Rudimenta fidei Christianæ* (Greeke et Latine) (<Geneva> 1565).
309. <Gibson, Thomas>. *The anatomy of humane bodies epitomized* (1682). Wing G672.
310. <Gildas>. *The epistle of Gildas* (1638). STC 11895.

311. <Gillespie, George>. *<The ark of the covenant opened: or,> a treatise of the covenant of redemption* (1677). Wing G744A.
312. Godwyn, <Thomas>. *<Moses and Aaron. Civil & ecclesiastical rites used by the Hebrewes>* [Jewish and romane antiquity] (1634). STC 11951.
313. <Goodwyn, John>. *<Eirenomachia . . . the agreement and distance of the brethren>* [The agreement and distance between the Arminians and others about election] (1652). Wing G1164.
314. Goodwyn, Thomas. *<The> returne of prayers* (1636). STC 12040.
315. Goodwyn, Thomas. *<The> returne of prayers* (1641). Wing G1253A.
316. Goodwyn, Thomas. *Christ set forth* [triumph of faith &c.] (1645). Wing G1234.
317. Goodwyn, Thomas. *<Certaine> select cases* [resolved by Thomas Goodwyn] (1647). Wing lists 1651 (Wing G1229).
318. Goodwyn, Thomas. *<A discourse> of the punishment of sin in Hell* (1680). Wing G1239.
319. Goodwyn, Thomas. *<The works of . . .> on the Ephesians* (1681). Wing G1219. "Lent Mr Norket [illeg.] in the Strand." I have not identified this figure, who borrowed this volume and Goodwyn's *Works* in January, 1688.
320. Goodwyn, Thomas. *Works* (1683). Wing G1220. One vol. "is lent Mr Norket in January 1687/8."
321. Gordon, <Alexander>. *Tyrocinium linguæ Latinæ* (1664). Wing G1276.
322. Gouldman, <Francis>. *<A compendious> Dictionary* (Cambridge 1674). Wing G1445.
323. <Gowan, Thomas>. *Ars sciendi sive logica & nova methodo disposita* (1681). Wing G1457A.
324. Graaf, <Regnerus de>. *De virorum organis generationi servientibus, de clysteribus et de usu syphonis in anatomia* (Leiden 1668).
325. Granger, <Thomas>. *Syntagma grammaticum, <or an easie, and methodicall explanation of Lillies Grammar>* (1616). STC 12183.
326. Grantham, <Thomas>. *Christianismus <primitivus>* [redivivus] (1678). Wing G1528.
327. *Greeke Grammar* (1656). Three Greek grammars were published in London that year: Tussanus Berchetus, *Versia et notæ ad Stephani catechismum græcum*; James Shirley, *Introductorium anglo-latino-græcum*; and William Dugard, *Rudimenta græcæ linguæ.*
328. *Greeke grammar* (1653). Possibly Charles Hooke, *Novum testamentum: omnia difficiliorum vocabulorum themata quæ in G. Pasoris lexico grammatice resolvuntur* (1653).
329. Greenhill, William. *Exposition of the 5 first chapters of Ezekiel* (1645). Wing G1851.

330. Grew, <Nehemiah>. <*Mvsæum regalis societatis*> [Rarities of the Royal Society] (1681). Wing G1952.
331. <Grey, Elizabeth, Countess of Kent>. <*A choice manual of rare and select secrets*> [Select secrets in physick and chirurgery] (1653). "2nd edition" Wing K311.
332. Grosse, Alexander. <*A*> *fiery pillar of heavenly truth* (1644). Wing G2071.
333. <Guainerius, Antonius> [Faventinus]. *Practica medicinalis* (Lyons 1554).
334. Guibert, <Philibert>. *Medici officiosi* (Paris 1649).
335. Gurnall, <William>. <*The*> *Christian armour* (1679). Wing G2257A.
336. *Habeus Corpus Act*. The Habeus Corpus act was passed 21 May 1679.
337. Hale, Sir Matthew. *Contemplations moral and divine* (1676). "gilt back" Wing H225.
338. <Hall, John> [Cooke]. *Select observations on English bodies* (1657). Wing H356. Warr attributed this to Cooke.
339. Hall, Joseph. <*Susurrium cum Deo*> [Soliloquies] (1659). Wing H421.
340. Hall, Joseph. <*The remedy of discontentment*> [Of contentation] 4th edition (1684). Wing H405.
341. Hammond, Henry. <*A*> *practicall catechisme* (Oxford 1645). Wing H581.
342. Hammond, Henry. <*CHARIS KAI EIRENE; or, A*> *pacifick discourse* (1660). Wing H519.
343. Harington, <Sir> John. <*A*> *briefe view of the state of the Church of England* (1653). Wing H770.
344. Harris, Robert [of Hanwell]. *Workes* (1635). STC 12816.
345. Harris, Robert. <*The way to true happinesse*> [Treatise of the new covenant] (1632). STC 12855.
346. Harris, Walter. <*Pharmacologia anti-empirica*: *or a*> *rational discourse of remedies* (1683). Wing H885.
347. Hartmann, <Georgius>. *Praxis chymiatrica* (Leiden 1663).
348. Harvey, <Gideon>. *Family physician* (1676). Wing H1064.
349. Harvey, Gideon. <*A new discourse of the small pox*> [Of the small-pox malignant feavers and scurvy] (1685). Wing H1074.
350. <Head, Richard>. *The English rogue* (1680), 2 vols. Wing H1248cA or H1251.
351. Heereboord, Adrianus. <. . .> *Logica* (Leiden 1658).
352. Heurnius, <Joannes>. *Praxis medicinæ* <*nova ratio*> (Leiden 1590).
353. Heurnius, <Joannes>. *Praxis medicinæ* (n.p., n.d.). "old and wants title page."
354. Hewes, <John>. <*A perfect*> *survey of the English tongue according the use* [*and analogy*] *of the Latine* (1624). STC 13260.

355. Heylin, <Peter>. *Cosmographie* (1682). Wing H1696.
356. <Hickeringill, Edmund>. *<The> history of whiggism* (1682). Wing H1809.
357. Hickman, <Henry>. *<Historia quinq-articularis exarticulata>* [History of the Arminians] (1673). Wing H1909.
358. Hicks, <Thomas>. *<Three dialogues>* [Dialogues between a Christian and a Quaker] (1679). Wing H1927.
359. Hilton, <John> [Captain]. *<The English Guzman: or, Captain Hilton's memoirs, the grand informer>* [Memoirs of the English Guzman] (<1683>). This is a single sheet and thus is not in Wing.
360. Hippocrates. *Aphorismi Hippocratis* (Greek and Latine) (Leiden n.d.).
361. Hippocrates. *Hippocrates contractus* (Edinburgh 1685). Wing H2073. Warr attributed this to Burnet (Thomas Burnet, M.D.).
362. Hippocrates. *Opera omnia* (Frankfurt 1624).
363. Hodges, Thomas. *<A> Scripture-catechisme* (Oxford 1658). Wing H2318.
364. Hofmann, Caspar. *Institutiones medicæ* (Leiden 1645).
365. Hofmann, Caspar. *Pro veritate opellæ tres* (Paris 1647).
366. Hollerius, <Jacobus>. *<De morborum curatione>* [Methodus curande mortos] "wants title and preface"
367. Holyoke, <Thomas>. *<A large> dictionary* (1677). Wing H2535.
368. Hoole, <Charles>. *<The common accidence>* [Examination of the accidence] (1683). Wing H2678.
369. Horace. *Odes in English* (1636). The STC lists 1625, 1631, 1635, and 1638.
370. Horace. *Poemata* (1637). STC 13796.
371. Horne, <Thomas>. *<Cheirogogia sive manuductio in ædem Palladis, qua utilissima methodus authores>* [De usu authoris] (1687). Wing H2812.
372. Hornius, Georgius. *Arca mosis* (Leiden and Rotterdam 1668).
373. <How, William>. *Phytologia Britannica* (1650). Wing H2956.
374. Howe, <John>. *<Of thoughtfulnes>* [Thoughtfullness for the morrow] (1681). Wing H3034.
375. Huet, <Pierre>. *De interpretatione* (Hague 1683).
376. Hughes, <George>. *<Aphorisms, or select propositions of the Scripture shortly determining the> doctrine of the sabbath* (1670). Wing H3306.
377. Huisc, John. *<Florilogium phrasicon>* [Phrases] (1659). Wing H3353.
378. <Huish, Anthony>. *Priscianus embryo* [et nascens] (<1670>). Wing H3357.
379. <Huish, Anthony>. *Priscianus ephebus* (1669). Wing H3356A.
380. <Hunfrey, John> [J. H.]. *Obligation of human lawes* (1671). Wing

H3696.

381. Jackson, Thomas. <*A*> *treatise of the divine essence and attributes* (1628). STC 14318.
382. Jewel, John. *Works* (1609). STC 14579.
383. Joel, Franciscus. *Opera medica* (Amsterdam 1663).
384. Johnson, <William>. *Lexicon chymicum.* Wing lists editions published in London in 1652, 1657, and 1660.
385. Jones, <James>. *Modesty and faithfulness* [in opposition to envy and rashness] (1683). Wing J957.
386. <Jones, James>. *A token of Christian love* (<1683>). Wing J960.
387. <Jones, James>. <*A*> *plea for liberty of conscience* (<1684>). Wing J959.
388. <Jones, James>. <*The*> *grand case of subjection to the higher powers* (<1684>). Wing J956A.
389. <Jones, James>. *Nonconformity not inconsistent with loyalty* (<1684>). Wing J958.
390. Joubert, <Laurent>. *Medicinæ practicæ* (Lyons 1575).
391. Justinianus. <*Corpus juris civilis*> [Institutiones] (Amsterdam 1664).
392. Juvenal. *Junii Juvenalis et Auli Persii Flacci satyræ* (1620). STC 14891.
393. <Keach, Benjamin> [B. K.]. <*The*> *travels of true godliness* (1683). Wing K9.
394. Keble, <Joseph>. *Statutes at large* (1681). Wing E923F. Wing misprints the date as 1611.
395. <Kerhuel, Jean de>. *Idea eloquentia &c.* (1673). Wing K346A.
396. Kiffin, <William>. *Of right to church communion* (1681). Wing K425.
397. Kimedoncius, <Jacobus>. *De redemptione generis humani* (Heidelberg 1592).
398. *Kings message and Commons address* (1680).
399. Knolles, <Richard>. <*The*> *Turkish history* [in two volumes] (1687). Wing K702.
400. Knollys, Hanserd. *The world that now is* [and the world to come] (1681). Wing K726.
401. Kyper, <Albertus>. *Medicinam rite discendi et exercendi methodus* (Leiden 1643).
402. Langston, <John>. *Lusus poeticus* <*Latino-Anglicanus*> (1675). Wing L411.
403. Larkin, <Edward>. <*Speculum patrum*: *a*> *looking-glass of the fathers* (1659). Wing L444.
404. <Laurens, André>. <*Historia anatomica humani corporis*> [Anatomica] (Frankfurt n.d.)
405. Lawrence, <Henry>. <*Our*> *communion* <*and warres*> *with angels* (<Amsterdam?> 1646). Wing L665.

406. Le Fèvre, <Nicholas>. *<A> compleat body of chymistry* (1670). Wing L926.
407. Le Grand, Antoine. *Institutio philosophiæ* (1675). Wing L955.
408. Le Mort, <Jacob>. *Compendium chymicum* (Leiden 1682).
409. Leigh, Edward. *Treatise of divinity* (1647). Wing L1012.
410. Leusden, <Jan>. *Compendium Græcum novi testamenti* (Utrecht 1677).
411. Lewis, <Mark>. *<Institutio grammaticæ pueriles>* [Grammar] (1670). Wing L1843.
412. Lewis, <Mark>. *<An essay to facilitate the education of youth>* [Essay &c]. (1674). Wing L1842.
413. Lewis, <Mark>. *Vestibulum technicum* (1675). Wing L1850.
414. Lightfoot, <John>. *<The> harmony <chronicle and order> of the old testament* (1647). Wing L2056.
415. Lightfoot, <John>. *<The> harmony of the foure evangelists* (1650). Wing L2060.
416. Lipsius, <Justus>. *Epistolæ selectæ* (n.p. 1613).
417. <Lister, Martin>. *De fontibus medicatis Angliæ* (1684). Wing L2519.
418. <Lloyd, Richard>. *<The Latine grammar>* Latine grammar and construing booke (1669). Wing has 1653 and 1659.
419. <Locke, John>. *<Graphautarkeia, or, the Scriptures sufficiency practically demonstrated>* [Scripture's selfe-evidence] (1667). This date is probably a slip for 1676 (Wing L2746B). Wing lists editions in 1676 and 1684 (Wing L2746C), not 1667: but it is surprising that on f. 53 Warr also wrote 1667 for the date of the other copy in the library.
420. *London petition*. This work has not been identified.
421. Loss, <Friedrich>. *<Observationum medicinalium>* [Observationes medicinales] (1672). Wing L3080B.
422. Love, <John>. *<Geodæsia: or, the art> of surveying* (1688). Wing L3191.
423. Lovell, Robert. *<. . . A> compleat herball* (Oxford 1665). Wing L3244.
424. Lower, <Richard>. *<Tractus> de corde* [and de motu sanguinis] (1669). Wing L3310.
425. Lubin, <Eilhard>. *Clavis Græcæ lingvæ* (1662). Wing L3386A.
426. Lucretius. *De rerum naturâ* (Leiden 1597).
427. Lukin, <Henry>. *<An> introduction to the <Holy> Scripture* (1669). Wing L3476.
428. <Lusignano, Steffano>. *The history of the war of Cyprus* (1687). Wing L3503A.
429. Luther, <Martin>. *<Special and> chosen sermons* (1581). STC 16994
430. Luther, Martin. *<A> commentarie vpon fiftene Psalmes* (1577). STC 16975.
431. Luther, Martin. *<A commentarie . . . vpon the epistle to>* [On] *the*

Galatians (1635). STC 16974.

432. Luther, Martin. *Colloquia mensalia* (1652). Wing L3510.
433. Luther, Martin. *Loci communes* [theologici] (1651). Wing L3512.
434. Lyford, <William>. *<Principles of faith and good conscience>* [Catechisme] (1642). Wing L3552.
435. Lyser, <Michæl>. *Culter anatomicus* (Copenhagen 1653).
436. <M., W.> *A letter from Leghorn* (1691). Wing M95a. Full title is "A letter from Leghorn, March the twenty foureh [sic]". *This volume is the latest work listed in this manuscript.*
437. Maccov, <Johannes>. <. . .> *distinctiones et regulæ* [theologicæ] (Oxford 1656). Wing M118.
438. Manning, <William>. *Catholick religion* (1686). Wing M491.
439. Manton, <Thomas>. *Sermons <preached by>* (1678). Wing M536.
440. Manton, <Thomas>. *Several discourses* [&c] (1685). Wing M537.
441. Manutius, <Aldus>. *<Puræ> Latine <linguæ> phrases* (Cologne 1575).
442. Manutius, <Pauli>. *<Paul Manuti in M.T. Ciceronis orationum volumen secundum commentarius>* [Commentaries in Ciceronis epistolas familiares] (Frankfurt 1580). "in two volumes"
443. Manutius, Aldus Pius. *Phrases Latinæ* (imperfect).
444. Manutius, Pauli. *Epistolæ <familiares>* (<Geneva> 1616).
445. Marius, <John>. *Advice concerning bills of exchange* (1670). Wing M605.
446. Mason, Francis. *Vindica ecclesiæ Anglicanæ* (1638). STC 17599
447. Mauriceau, <Francois>. *<The> diseases of women with child* (1672). Wing M1371B.
448. May, <Thomas>. *<A breviary of the> history of the Parliament of England* (1655). Wing M1396.
449. Mede, Joseph. *<The> key of the revelation* (1643). Wing M1600.
450. Melanchthon, <Phillip>. *Loci communes <rerum theologicarum>* [theologici] (Wittenberg 1535).
451. Mercurialis, <Hieronymus>. *In <omnes> Hippocratis aphorismos, prælectiones patavinæ* (Lyons 1621).
452. Meriton, <George>. *<A> guide for constables* (1679). "6th edition" Wing M1796.
453. Meriton, <George>. *Nomenclatura clericalis <or, the young clerk's vocabulary>* (1685). Wing M1807.
454. Merret, <Christopher>. *Pinax rerum naturalium* [britanicorum] (1667). Wing M1839.
455. <Mesuré, Fortuné>. [Fortunatus] *Fidelis de relationibus medicorum* (Leipzig 1674).
456. <Midgley, Robert>. *<A new> treatise of natural philosophy freed from the intricacies of the schools* (1687). Wing M1995.

457. Miège, <Guy>. *English and French dictionary* (1685). Wing M2027.
458. Milton, John. *<Considerations touching the likeliest means to remove hirelings>* [Means to remove hirelings out of the church] (1659). Wing M2101.
459. Milton, John. *Accedence commenc't grammar* (1669). Wing M2088.
460. Milton, John. *Artis logicæ* (1672). Wing M2093.
461. Milton, John. *Literæ pseudo-senatus Anglicani, Cromwellii* [&c.] (1676). Wing M2128 or M2129.
462. Minsheu, <John>. *<The guide into tongues>* [Dictionary of several languages] (n.p., n.d.). Several editions of this polyglot dictionary were printed in London after 1617. Warr noted that this vol. was "lent my father."
463. <Mitchell, William>. *<A sober ansvvere>* [Sober answer to the friendly debate] (1669). Wing has only 1671, Wing M2294.
464. Moellenbrock, <Valentin Andreas>. *Medulla totius praxeos medicæ aphoristica* (<Erfurt> 1656).
465. Molinos, <Miguel de>. *<The> spiritual guide* (1688). Wing M2387.
466. Montaigne, Michel. *Essayes* (1682). Wing has 1685-86 in 3 volumes (Wing M2479).
467. Monteage, <Stephen>. *Debtor and creditor* [made easy] (1682). Wing M2488.
468. More, Henry. *Enchiridion ethicum* (1668). Wing M2652.
469. Morellus, Petrus. *Methodus præscribendi formulas remediorum* (Amsterdam 1665).
470. <Morley, Christopher Love>. *Collectanea chymica Leidensis* (Leiden 1684).
471. Mornay, <Philippe de>. *<A> treatise of the church* (1606). STC 18162.
472. Mornay, <Philippe de>. *<The> mysterie of iniquitie* (1612). STC 18147.
473. Mornay, <Philippe de>. *<A woorke concerning the trewness>* [Of the truth] *of the Christian religion* (1617). STC 18152.
474. Moxon, <Joseph>. *<Mathematicks made easie>* [Mathematical dictionary] (1679). Wing M3006.
475. <Mucklow, William>. *Liberty of conscience asserted* [and vindicated] (1682). Wing lists 1673 and 1674.
476. Nardi, <Giovanni>. *Lactis physica analysis* <Florence 1634>.
477. *Narrative of the proceedings of the Ecclesiastical Court* (1683). "2 of them" These works have not been identified.
478. Needham, <Walter>. *Disquisitio anatomica* [de forniculo &c] (1667). Wing N411.
479. <Newman, Samuel>. [Cambridge] *Concordance* (Cambridge 1682). Wing N927.
480. Newton, John. *<An> introduction to the art of logick* (1678). Wing

N1064.

481. Nizoliuis, <Marius>. *<Appartus Latinæ locutions . . .> sive thesaurus Ciceronianus* (Lyons 1608).
482. *Noble peers speech* (Sept 28, 1682). "3 of them." Perhaps the trials of Essex, Russell, and Sidney.
483. *Nomenclatura reformata* (1663). I have have not found a precise match for this title. Wing N1222A is *Nomenclatura vestibularis*: *or*, *a further improvement of . . . Comenius* (1662); two works by Paulus Jasz-Berejyi, *Institutionum grammaticorum* (1663) and *Fax nova linguæ Latinæ* (1663) are also possible.
484. Norton, John. *<The> orthodox evangelist* (1657). Wing N1320.
485. <Noye, Sir William>. *<The> compleat <lawyer>* [attorney and solicitor] (1681). Wing lists 1651, 1661, 1665, 1670, and 1674.
486. Orrery, Earl of. *<A treatise of the> art of warr* (1677). Wing O499. There is no evidence that Boyle owned copies of his brother's plays or romances.
487. Osborne, Francis. *Works* (1682). "eighth edition" Wing O506.
488. <Osborne, Francis>. *Fathers advice to his son* (1683). Wing lists editions of the *Works*, which contains *Advice*, in 1673, 1682, and 1689; *Advice* was published separately in 1656 and 1658.
489. Osiander, <Lucas>. *<A manuell or briefe volume of controversies of religion>* [Manual of controversies] (1606). STC 18880.
490. Ovid. *<. . . operum>* [Works] (Amsterdam 1664).
491. Owen, John. *<A> display of Arminianisme* (1643). Wing O811.
492. Owen, John. *<Vindiciæ evangelicæ or the mystery>* [Against Biddle the Socinian] (Oxford 1655). Wing O823.
493. Owen, John. *<Of the> mortification of sinne in beleevers* (Oxford <1656, 1658, or 1668>).
494. Owen, John. *<A brief> instruction in the worship of God* (1667). Wing O721.
495. Owen, John. *<A brief declaration and vindication of the . . . Trinity>* [Doctrine of the trinity vindicated] (1669). Wing O718.
496. Owen, <John>. *<The> reason of faith* (1677). Wing O801.
497. Owen, John. *<The> doctrine of justification <by faith>* (1677). Wing O739. (two copies)
498. Owen, John. *<. . . or, the causes, waies, and means> of understanding the mind of God* (1678). Wing O809.
499. Owen, <John>. *<PHRONEMA TOU PNEUMATOU, or the grace and duty> of spiritual mindedness* (1681). Wing O792.
500. Owen, John. *<A discourse of the work of the Holy Spirit>* [Of the work of the spirit in prayer] (1682). Wing O738.
501. <Pagitt, Ephraim>. *Christianographie* (1636). STC 19111.

502. <Parival, Jean Nicolas de>. *<The> historie of this iron age* (1659). Wing P361.
503. Parkinson, John. *<Theatrum botanicum: the theater of plants>* [Herbal] (1640). STC 19302.
504. Pasor, George. *Lexicon <Græco-Latinum>* (1650). Wing P650.
505. Penn, <William>. *<The speech of>* [Pens Speech] (<1687>). Wing P1327A or P1373
506. Perdulcis, <Bartholomæus>. *Universa medicina* (Paris 1630).
507. Perkins, <William>. *Works* (1616), first vol. C19651 The early *Works* were collections of pamphlets printed at various times.
508. Perkins, <William>. *Works* (Cambridge 1613). third vol. C19650
509. Petrus, Lombard. *Sententiarum* (Louvain 1552).
510. Petto, <Samuel>. *<The> difference between the old and new covenant* (1674). Wing P1896.
511. Phalaris. *Supplementa ad grammatica* (1652). This work has not been identified. In his first edition Wing notes a "Phalaris revived (1659), and refers the reader to "B., A." but there is no entry for that author; in the revised edition, there is no entry for "Phalaris revived."
512. *Pharmacopœia Hagiensis* (Hague 1659).
513. *Pharmacopœia Bruxellensis* (Brussels 1641).
514. <Pierce, Thomas>. *Pacificatorium orthodoxæ theologiæ corpusculum* (1683). Wing P2187.
515. Piscator, <Johann>. *Analysis logica evangelii secundum <Matthæum>* (1594). STC 19948.
516. *Plain dealing* (n.p., n.d.). At least five works with this title appeared between 1640 and 1691: authors included Mr. Johnson (1691, Wing J769), Thomas Lechford (1642, Wing L810), Nathaniel Homes (1642, Wing H2572), Edward Harrison (1649, Wing H889), and Samuel Richardson (1656, Wing R1412).
517. Plat, <Sir Hugh>. *<The> garden of Eden* (1653). Wing P2384 or P2385.
518. Platerus, Felix. *Praxeos medicæ* (Basel 1625).
519. Plato. *Platonis opera tralatione Marsilii Ficini* (Lyons 1548).
520. Plutarch. *Plutarch's morals translated* (1684). Wing P2642.
521. Plutarch. *Vitarum Plutarchi epitome* (n.p. 1608).
522. Polhill, <Edward>. *<The divine will considered>* [Of the divine will &c.] (1673). Wing P2753.
523. Polhill, <Edward>. *Precious faith* (1675). Wing P2755.
524. Polhill, <Edward>. *<Speculum theologiæ>* [View of divine truths] (1678). Wing P2757.
525. Polhill, <Edward>. *<Christus in corde: or the mystical union>* [Mystical union between Christ and beleevers] (1680). Wing S2751.
526. Polhill, <Edward>. *<Armatvra Dei: or, a preparation>* [Preparation for

suffering] (1682). Wing P2750.

527. Polhill, <Edward>. *<The Samaritan, shewing>* [Portraiturc of a suffering Christian] (1685). Wing lists 1682 (Wing S2756).

528. <Polyander, Johannes>. *Synopsis purioris theologiæ* (Amsterdam 1658).

529. <Pomey, François Antoine>. *Indiculus universalis* (1679). Wing P2791.

530. <Pontanus, Jacobus> [Pontanus]. *Progymnasmatum Latinitatis liber primus & secundus* (Frankfurt 1630).

531. Poole, <Matthew>. *Dialogue between a popish priest* [and a protestant] (1680). Wing P2852.

532. Poole, <Matthew>. *Synopsis criticorum* (London, 1669, 1671, 1673, 1674, 1676). "in five volumes" Wing P2853.

533. Possel, <Johann>. *<Familiarum colloqiorum>* [Colloquia familiaria] (1656). Wing P3017A.

534. <Powell, Thomas>. *<Humane industry>* [History of manual arts] (1661). Wing P3072.

535. Preston, John. *<Life eternall or, a treatise> of the divine essence and attributes* (1631). STC 20231.

536. Preston, John. *<A> liveles life* (1633). STC 20235.

537. Preston, John. *The saints dayly exercise* (n.p., n.d.). "wants title page" Wing lists London editions of 1629, 1630, 1631, 1632, 1633, 1634, and 1635.

538. <Preston, John>. *<An> abridgment of Dr Preston's vvorks* (1658). Wing P3299.

539. Primerosius, <Jacobus>. *Ars pharmaceutica* (Amsterdam 1651).

540. Primerosius, <Jacobus>. *Enchiridion medicum* (Amsterdam 1654).

541. *Primmer* (n.p., n.d.) This author or work has not been identified.

542. Primrose, <James>. [Of] *Popular errours* (1651). Wing P3476.

543. *Proceedings against Whitfield & Smalbones* (n.p., n.d.).

544. *Proceedings at Guildhall London* (n.p., n.d.).

545. *Proceedings betwixt the two houses about the tryal of the lords* (n.p., n.d.). Probably the trials of Essex, Russell, and Sidney. Russell was executed on 21 July 1683.

546. *Proceedings of Parliament relating to the Popish Plot* (1679).

547. Prynne, <William>. *<A breviate of the life of William Laud>* [Briefe of the life of the archbishop of Canterbury (Laud)] (1644). Wing P3904.

548. <Puteanus, Erycius>. *<Suada Attica, sive orationum se lectarum syntagma>* [Orations] (Oxford 1640). STC 20518.

549. Quintilian. *Declamations* [in English] (1686). Wing Q224. A second copy is in gilt back.

550. <Ranchin, Guillaume>. *<A> review of the council of Trent* (Oxford 1638). STC 20667.

551. <Ravesteini, Adriani> [Castellio]. *Lexicon medicum græco-latinum*

(Toulouse 1669).

552. Ravisius, Johannes [Textoris]. <*Epithetorum Joann. Rauisii Textoris epitome*> [Epitheta] (1626). STC 20764.

553. *Reasons for passing the bill of exclusion* (1681).

554. *Reasons for the indict<ment> of the Duke of York* (n.p., n.d.). In 1680 the Duke of York and the Duchess of Portsmouth were indicted for being Popish recusants.

555. Reed, <?>. *Of chirurgery* (n.p., n.d.). There are many possible works by John Read (or Reed), a late 16th-century surgeon, or Alexander Read (or Reid), a 17th-century surgeon.

556. Regius, <Henricus>. *Medicina & praxis medica* (Frankfurt 1668).

557. Riverius, Lazarus. *Observationes medicæ* (Hague 1656).

558. Riverius, Lazarus. *Praxis medica* (Hague 1664).

559. Robertson, <William>. <*A*> *gate* <*or door*> *to the holy tongue* [opened English] (1653). Wing R1612.

560. Robertson, <William>. *Phraseologia generalis* (Cambridge 1681). Wing R1616.

561. Robinson, <Sir Thomas>. <*A special*> *booke of entries* (1684). Wing R1717.

562. <Robinson, Hugh>. <*Scholæ Wintoniensis phrases*> [Winchester Phrases] <(1658)>. Wing R1682 "wants only title page."

563. <Robinson, Hugh>. *Antiquæ historiæ synopsis* (Oxford 1660). Wing R1681.

564. Roborough, Henry. *Doctrine of justification cleared and vindicated* (1650). Wing R1736.

565. <Rogers, Daniel> [D. R.]. *A practicall catechisme* (1633). STC 21167

566. Rogers, <Daniel>. <*Naaman the Syrian his disease and cvre*> [History of Naaman the Syrian] (1642). Wing R1799.

567. Rorario, <Girolamo>. *Quod animalia bruta ratione utantur melius homine* (Amsterdam 1654).

568. Ross, Alexander. <*PANSEBEIA; or A*> *view of* <*all*> *religions* (1658). Wing R1973.

569. Rous, <Francis>. <*Treatises and meditations*> [Works] (1657). Wing R2030 or R2031.

570. <Royal College of Physicians>. *Pharmacopœia Londoniensis* (1668). Wing R2116.

571. Russell, <William, Lord>. *Lord Russell's speech* (July 21, 1683). Wing R2356.

572. Rutherford, Samuel. *Influences of the life of grace* (1659). Wing R2380.

573. <S., T.> *The perplexed prince* (<1682?>) Wing S174.

574. <S., W.> *Matchiavel Junior* (1683). Wing S197.

575. <Sacchi, Bartholomæus de> [Platina]. *De vitis pontificio* (<Cologne>

1664).

576. Sallust. *Historia* (Cambridge 1665). Wing S405.

577. Saltmarsh, <John>. [Of] *Free grace* (1646). Wing S485.

578. <Sanchez, Francisco>. *Francisci sanctii minverva cum animadversiones . . . Gasparis Scioppi* (Amsterdam 1664).

579. Sanctorius, <Santorius>. *<De> medicina statica* (1663). Wing lists only 1676.

580. Scapula, <Joannes>. *Lexicon* (n.p., n.d.). "wants only title page." There were many editions after 1580.

581. Scarlett, John. *<The> stile of exchanges* (1682). Wing S827.

582. Scheiner, Christopher. *<Oculus hoc est; fundamentum oculum>* [Fundamentum opticum] (1652). Wing S858.

583. Schoppe, Caspar. *De arte critica commentarius* (Amsterdam 1662).

584. Schoppe, Caspar. *Grammatica philosophica* (Amsterdam 1664).

585. <Scott, Robert>. *<Catalogus librorum ex variis Europæ>* [Catalog of Mr Scots bookes] (1674). Wing S2078.

586. Scudder, Henry. *<The> Christians dayly walke* (1637). STC 22120.

587. <Scultetus, Joannes> [Hadrianus, <Petrus>]. *<CHEIROPLOTHEKE> armamentarium <chirurgicum>* [medico-chymicum] (Rouen 1651).

588. Selveccero, <Perhaps Selve, Lazareda> Mich. *Carmen peraphrasticum in epistolas D. Petri* (Jena 1647).

589. Seneca, <Lucius Annæus>. *Senecæ operum.* tomus secundus (Cologne 1543) "in two volumes."

590. Sennertus, <Daniel>. *<Epitome> institutionum medicinæ* (Amsterdam 1653).

591. *Sententia sævo-medicæ* (Hamburg 1640). I have not identified this work, but it is possible that Warr has referred to James Primerose, *Animadversiones in Iohannis Wallai . . . cui additaest, ejusdem de usu Lienis adversus medicos recentiores sententia* (Amsterdam 1640). Boyle had two other books by that author.

592. *Several parcels of Votes of the House of Commons* (1680). Possibilities include Wing E2544, *A coppy of the Journall-book of the House of Commons* (1680); Wing E2545, *The debates in the honorourable House of Commons* (1680); and Wing E2746, *A true and perfect collection of all messages, addresses &c. from the House of Commons* (1680).

593. Shaw, <Samuel>. *<Grammatica Anglo-Romana>* [Syncritical grammar] (1687). Wing S3035.

594. Sibbes, <Richard>. *<The> bruised reede, and smoaking flax* (1631). STC 22480.

595. Sibbes, <Richard>. *<Bowels opened, or, a discovery of the love, union, and communion betwixt Christ and the Church>* [On the 4th 5th and

6th of the Canticles] (1639). STC 22476.

596. Skippon, <Philip> [Major General]. *<A salve for every sore>* [Collection of promises] (1643). Wing S3951.

597. Smetius, <Heinrich>. *Prosodia* (1635). STC 22649.

598. <Smith, John> [J. S.]. *<The> horological dialogues* (1675). Wing H4105.

599. Smith, <Samuel>. *Aditus ad logicam* (Oxford 1649). Wing S4194.

600. Speed, <John>. *<A clowd> [cloud] of witnesses* [&c.] (1628). STC 23033.

601. Speed, <John>. *<The theatre of the empire of Great Britaine>* [Maps] (1611). STC 23041.

602. Speed, <John>. *<The genealogies recorded in the sacred Scripture* [History] (1632). STC 23039.

603. <Spencer, Thomas>. [T. S.] *Logick unfolded* (1656). Wing S4962.

604. <Spenser, Edmund>. *Spencer redivivus* (1687). Wing S4969.

605. Spicelii, *Pius literati homines secessus* (Augsberg 1669). This work has not been identified.

606. Spurstowe, William. *<The wels of salvation opened>* [Rules for the right use of the promises] (1655). Wing S5100.

607. Stahl, Daniel. *<Regulæ philosophicæ>* [Axioms] (Oxford 1663). Wing S5167.

608. Stanhorst, <Nicholas>. *Officina chymica Londinensis* (1685). Wing S5254.

609. Stedman, <Rowland>. *Sober singularity* (1668). Wing S5376.

610. Steno, <Nicolaus>. *<Dissertatio> de cerebri anatome* (Leiden 1671).

611. <Stephens, Edward>. *Observations upon a treatise of humane reason* (1675). Wing S5430. Two copies.

612. <Stephens, Philip and William Browne>. *<Catalogus horti botanici Oxoniensis>* [Catalogue of the Oxford physick garden] (Oxford 1658). Wing S5454.

613. Stockwood, <John>. *Disputatiuncularum grammaticalium* (1619). STC 23279.

614. Strong, William. *<A treatise shewing the> subordination of the will of man* [to the will of God] (1657). Wing S6008.

615. Strong, William. *Discourse of the two covenants* (1678). Wing S600.

616. <Strong, William>. *A discourse of the two covenants* (1673). "gilt back" Wing lists only 1678 for this work.

617. *Sure guide to the Latine tongue* (1678). Wing lists no *Sure guide to the Latine tongue*, but cf. P. Cogneau, *Guide to the French tongue* (1658), Wing C4893; anon., *The English guide to the Latin tongue* (1675), Wing E3087; or Elisha Coles, *Easy method of learning Latin* (1677).

618. Swinnock, George. *<The> sinners last sentence* [to eternal punishment] (1675). Wing S6281.
619. Sydenham, Thomas. *Opera <universa>* [omnia medica] (1685). Wing S6304.
620. Tachenius, Otto. *<. . .> his Hippocrates Chymicus* (1677). Wing T98 (Wing erroneously has T89). "Englished by my Father." See John Warr [J.W.], *O. Tachenius his Hippocrates Chymicus, discovering the ancient foundation of the late Viperine salt with his clavis thereunto annexed* (1677). The MS of this translation is BP 32.
621. Tacquet, <Andrea>. *Elementa geometriæ* (Antwerp 1672).
622. Taylor, Jeremy. *<The rvle and exercises of holy living>* [Holy living and holy dying] (1674). Wing S378.
623. Terence. "translated after Dr. Webbs Method" (1629). STC notes Webb's translations of *Andria* (STC 23896) and *Eunuchus* (STC 23898) in 1629.
624. Terence. *<Terence in English. Fabulæ . . . Anglicæ>* [in Latine and English] (1641). Wing T751.
625. Terence. *<P. Terentius a M. A. Mureto emendatus>* (1669). Wing T738.
626. Terence. *Terence* [cum notis marginalibus] (Rotterdam 1670).
627. <Torriano, Giovanni>. *<Select> Italian proverbs* (Cambridge 1649). Wing T1932.
628. Torsellino, <Horatius>. *De particulis Latinæ orationis* (Leipzig 1682).
629. Torsellino, <Orazio>. *Sententiæ Ciceronis Demosthenis* (Antwerp 1567).
630. Torsellino, <Orazio>. *De particulis Latinæ orationis* (Rouen 1662).
631. Trincavellius, <Victor>. *Consilia medica* (Basel 1587).
632. <Truman, Joseph>. *A discourse of natural and moral impotency* (1671). Wing T3138.
633. Tully, <Thomas>. *<Præcipuorum theologiæ>* [Enchiridion theologicum] (Oxford 1683). Wing T3249.
634. Turretinus, Franciscus. *Institutio theologicæ elencticæ* (Geneva 1680), "3 vols. gilt back."
635. Turrianus, <Franciscus>. *Ad repetita <F.> Turriani <. . .> sophismata <de Ecclesia>* (Morges 1580).
636. Twisse, <William>. *Vindicæ gratiæ* (Amsterdam 1632).
637. *Tyrorum erudiendi methodus* (1680). This work has not been identified.
638. Ulstadt, <Philip>. *<Cælum philosophorum seu> de secretis natura* (n.p., n.d.). There were many editions after 1526.
639. <Ursinus, Zacharias> [Parry]. *<The> summe of <the> Christian religion* (Oxford 1587). STC 24532. Two copies.
640. Ursinus, Zacharias. *<The> summe of <the> Christian religion* (1633). STC 24539.
641. <Ursinus, Zacharias> [Parrye]. *<A collection of certaine learned*

discourses> [Explanation of Ursinus catechisme (in Latine)]. (n.p. 1608). STC lists editions published in Oxford in 1600 and 1613.

642. Ussher, James. <*A body of divinitie*> [Summe of Christian religion or body of divinity] (1645). Wing U151.
643. Ussher, James. <*The*> *principles of Christian religion* (1653). Wing U205.
644. Valdés, Juan de. *Divine considerations* (Cambridge 1646). Wing V22.
645. Veil, <Charles Marie de>. <*A literal explanation*> [Explication of the acts of the apostles] (1685). Wing V179. Two copies.
646. Velleius Paterculus, <Marcus>. <*Historiæ Romanæ*> [cum notis variorum] (Leiden 1668).
647. <Vermigli, Pietro Martire> [Martyris, Petri]. *Loci communes theologica* (1576). STC 24667.
648. Vernon, <John>. <*The*> *compleat compting house* (1683). Wing V250.
649. Veslingius, Joannes. *Syntagma anatomicum* [cum commentariis Gerardi Blassis] (Amsterdam 1666).
650. Viger, François. *De præcipius Græcæ* [dictionis idiosismis] (1647). Wing V374.
651. Virgil. (n.p., n.d.) "wants only title page."
652. Virgil. *Opera* (Amsterdam 1650).
653. Vives, <Juan Luiz>. <*Linguæ Latinæ exercitatio*> [Exercitatio linguæ Latinæ] (1667). Wing V667. Wing lists 1657 and 1674.
654. Vossius, <Gerardus> [Johann]. *Institutiones oratoriæ* (Frankfurt 1617).
655. Vossius, <Gerardus>. *Grammatica latina* (Leiden 1644).
656. Vossius, <Gerardus>. *Rhetorices contractæ* (Amsterdam 1666).
657. <Wade, John> [J. W.]. *Redemption of time* (1683). Wing W178.
658. <Walker, Obadiah>. <*Of*> *education* <*especially*> *of young gentlemen* (Oxford 1673). Wing W399.
659. Walker, <William>. <*A treatise of English*> *particles* (1676). "6th edition" Wing W446.
660. Walker, <William>. <*A treatise of English particles*> [Anglicisms Latiniz'd] (1655). Wing W441.
661. Walker, <William>. <*Idiomatalogia*> [Idiomes] (1670). Wing W424.
662. Walker, <William>. <*Parœmiologia Anglo-Latina*> [Phraseologia Anglo-Latina with a collection of English and Latine proverbs] (1672). Wing W431.
663. Walker, <William>. <*Some*> *improvements to the art of teaching* (1669). Wing W436.
664. Walker, <William>. <*Some*> *improvements of the art of teaching* (1683). Wing W438.
665. <Walker, William>. <*An explanation of the rules of the royal grammar* (1670) or *English examples* (1683). [Examples for understanding

grammar] (1678).

666. <Walker, William>. *Idiomatologia* [Idiosismi verborum &c.] "two volumes" Wing lists editions in 1670, 1673, 1680, 1685, and 1690.

667. Wallis, John. <. . . *Operum mathematicorum pars altera*> [Opera mathematica, 2 vols.] (Oxford 1657). Wing W599.

668. Wallis, John. <*A*> *treatise of algebra* (1685). Wing W613.

669. Wase, Christopher. <*Dictionarium minus*: *a compendious dictionary*> [Dictionary] (1683). Wing lists 1662 and 1675.

670. Warton, Anthony. <*CHONEUTERION TES ZION*> *Refinement of Zion* (1657). Wing W987.

671. <Wase, Christopher>. <*Methodi practicæ specimen. An essay of*> a practical grammar (1682). Wing W1021.

672. <Watt, George>. <*Tythes no Gospel ordinance*> [Temporalities and tythes not due &c. by any Gospel rule (1672). Wing lists 1673.

673. Webbe, <Joseph>. *Pueriles confabulatiunculæ* . . . (1627). STC 25170.5 "after Dr. Webbs Method"

674. <Webbe, Joseph>. <*Pueriles confabulatiunculæ, or childrens* <*talke*: *claused and drawne into lessons, after the method of Dr Webbe*> [Lessons and exercises out of Cicero ad Atticum after Dr Webbs Method] (1627). This work is probably a second copy of the vol. cited above.

675. Wecker, <Hanss Jacob>. *Antidotarium special* (Basel 1588).

676. Weidenfeld, Johann <Seger de>. *De secretis adeptorum* (1684). Wing W1252.

677. <Weldon, Sir Anthony>. <*The*> *court* <*and character*> *of King James* (1650). Wing W1272.

678. Wendelin, <Marcus Frederik>. *Christianicæ theologicæ* (Amsterdam 1657).

679. West, <Edward>. *Discourse of the perfect man* (1679). Wing D1378.

680. Westminster assembly of divines. *Assemblies confession of faith; longer and shorter catechisme* (<1647 and 1648>). There were several editions.

681. <Westminster School>. <*An*> *English introduction to the Latin tongue* (1659). Wing W3090A.

682. White, John. <*A*> *commentary on the three first chapters of . . . Genesis* (1656). Wing W1775.

683. Wigand, <Johann>. <*Syntagma, seu corpus*> [*de doctrina Christi &c* two vols.] (Basel 1568).

684. Wilkins, John. <*A discourse*> *of the gift of prayer* (1674). Wing W2182A.

685. Wilkins, John. <*Of the principles*> [Principles of natural religion and his funeral sermon] (1683). Wing W2206.

686. Willet, <Andrew>. *Synopsis papismi* (1600). STC 25698
687. Willis, <Thomas>. *Pharmaceutice rationalis* (Oxford 1674). Wing W2844.
688. Willis, <Thomas>. *Works* (with plates) (1684). In 1684 Willis published *An essay of the pathology of the brain* (Wing W2836A) and *Pharmaceutice rationalis* (Wing W2851), both of which had plates. The remaining medical works were published in 1681.
689. <Wilson, John>. *<The scriptures genuine interpreter asserted>* [The Scriptures sufficiency practically demonstrated] (1678). Wing W2903.
690. Wilson, Joseph>. *Nehushtan*: *<or, a sober and peaceable discourse>* [&c.] (1668). Wing W292.
691. <Wilson, Thomas>. *<Judicium discretionis*: *or a just and necessary apology, for the peoples>* [apology for a] *judgment of private discretion* (1667). Wing W2946.
692. Wilson, <Thomas>. *<A> Christian dictionary* (1678). Wing W2945.
693. Wingate, <Edmund>. *<The> body of the common law* (1662). Wing W3008.
694. <Wirdig, Sebastian>. *Nova medicina spirituum* (Hamburg 1673).
695. Wiseman, <Richard>. *<Several chirurgicall treatises>* [Wiseman's chirurgery] (1676). Wing W3107.
696. Witty, <Robert>. *Fons Scarburgensis* (1678). Wing W3227.
697. Wolleb, <John>. *Compendium theologicæ* (1647). Wing W3258.
698. <Yearwood, Randolph>. *The penitent murderer* (<1657>). Wing Y23.
699. Zanchius, <Hieronymus>. *De religione <Christiana fides>* [Christianâ] (<Neustadt an her Haardt 1585>

Appendix A: Joseph's Mistress

Textual Notes

Index

Appendix A: Joseph's Mistresse

|f. 2^{v}|

Joseph [to] his Mistresse

Dearest Joseph,[1]

After hauing giuen yow so many powerfull Testimonys of a Passion, great as the Merits that haue rais'd it, and vnalterable <and [more] vncapable both of Addition and of Change> then the Decrees of Fate: [no longer think it presumtion for my Loue to Demand those Assurances of Yours, that yow cannot with Ingratitude Deny] ↑[thinke it lawfull for me to Demand <expect> to [Demand] those Assurances of your Loue without Presumtion; that I know yow cannot <longer> deny without Ingratitude.] I shall now expect those Assurances of your Loue from your Iustice /Gratitude/ that before /till now/ I cud hope for but from your Inclination.↓ And tho I hope that in the Expressions of the heiht of my Affections, my Actions haue preuented my Tong; yet if for all this yow shud do me the Iniury to entertaine the least doubt of it; I am Confident that scruple will be easily remou'd;[2] if yow will but consider how much I trample vpon the vsuall Bashfulness of my sex, and all those restraints that oblige other women to the Concealement of their Passions, to make yow a Discouery of mine. Had I but the least part of as much Vanity as I haue Loue; I might tell yow, that yow haue now Reason to bless your Fortune that brings her in the Posture of a suppliant to yow, to whom the Proudest Knees of the Egyptian Court are hourely bended; and proffers yow those Fauors; of whom so much as a Hope is |f. 3| Deny'd to all their Numerous sighs and their long Seruices. Let not that dull Vertu that always opposes it self to our Happiness, depriue yow of a greater Pleasure, then any [it] she is able to bestow: but if yow needs will be so squeamish and so nice to be accessary to your own Deceiuing, remember that Gratitude is a Vertu too as well as Chastity; and by so much the greater, by how much it's Contrary is more detested. Consider Ioseph, that [it] my fauor is the onely thing that can support <establish> yow in the Condition yow now are in the Family of my Lord, and

---

[1] This selection is taken from BP 14.1-13, "Scripture Obseruations." Some observations were dated, the earliest 7 March 1647 (f. 7) and the latest 26 May 1647 (f. 13). Two of them, "Vpon his being caru'd to at a Feast" (f. 9) and "Vpon his Making of a Fire" (f. 10^{v}), were printed in substantially revised form in *Occ. Refl.* 2.385 and 383. The reflections illustrate his reading of and meditation on the Old Testament. RB's lengthy analysis and justification of meditation (*Occ. Refl.* 3.323-59) developed from his earlier essays, "Doctrine of Thinking" and "Dayly Reflection." For this meditation, the source is Gen. 39:7-23. In the *Aret.*, Alsted, and the moralists, Joseph exemplifies successful resistance to temptation; in this selection RB presented the seducer's arguments, not Joseph's refutation of them.

[2] The removal of scruples was an important constituent in "cases of conscience."

that by Doing your self the seruice I <now> beg of yow; yow will oblige me to riuet yow so strongly to the Dignity yow now hold, that ↑the change of my Affection will [be] not be a greater Impossibility then the Ebbing <[loss of that]> of his Fauor.↓ 'Twill be out of the Power of Fortune and the Destinys themselues to remoue yow. Thorough what Throngs of Difficultys and Dangers do men pursu Aduancement <Promotion>: but when the Way to certin Greatness is [st] carpetted with Delihts, who wud not [thi] pronounce him a Mad-man that shud Decline to tread it. Sure, cud hony cure Diseases, we shud [think] <lodge> his rather in his Braine then in his Humors, that wud procrastinate his Recouery. See how fortune it self seems to contribute to our Happiness, by befrending vs with an Opportunity so inuiting to those Delights, whose Name yow must expect rather from my Blushes then my [Words] <Tongue>. There we will in the Fruition of each other enjoy Delihts that the Gods themselues might envy; and that were infinitely below what they are, if they did as much transcend the reach of our Expressions. Neither ought it to lessen their Value in our Esteem, that they are |f. 3v| Censur'd by those dull phlegmatick Dotards; that wud cheat others of the Pleasures of that fruition they are past themselues: <out of> enuy[ing] <that> others <shud enioy> that Happiness their owne Impotence makes them vncapable of, and ambition to haue Companions in their Misery. Consider, Ioseph that so faire an opportunity were able to raise <create> Desires where there were none, since now the Gods themselues [wud] must change these Wals to Eys and this Obscurity to Lightsom beames, to be spectators of those Delights that are the only Company we haue heere to apprehend. The extreame [Affecti] Confidence that my husband reposes both in yow and in me will <altogether> free vs from his least suspition. And the future repetition of our stoln sweets, will meet with no more Difficulty <other Obstacles> then will iust serve to heihten the Extasys of their Fruition and raise Desires for their Renewing. But remember, Ioseph, that tho I am a Louer yet I am a Woman, ↑and if deny'd the Satisfaction I demand and Proffer, may be prouok't to make yow [suf] Endure the Punishment of that Adultery, whereof yow haue so [discourted] cruelly refus'd the Plesure.↓ And therefore beware <take heed> of wronging <my> Patience beyond it's Sufferance; lest my mock't Loue de[ne]generate into a Hatred great as was it selfe [which will neuer find Rest but in your Ruine] ↑since that <very> Passion /antagonist/ that euery where else /in all other cases/ opposes it's effects; will heere contribute to it's Violence.↓ Lastly, consider, ô my Dearest Ioseph, of how great an Importance the sentence yow are now to pronounce, is to my Happines and Life. Tho my Face (howeuer priz'd by others) merit not your Loue, yet my Hart, (for the sake of your owne Image so deeply stampt vpon it) at least deserues your Pitty. O let not your Tong bely your Lookes, and make it self guilty of [a greater] <more> Cruelty then they promise sweetness. Let not that Loue, that vses to [pro] beget it's like, produce it's Contrary, now I'm concern'd; |f. 4| [and] Reward not her that lou's yow best with the

Punishment we reserue for our worst Enemys: but remember, that tis in your Power to make me happy with a Fauor, that shall bring no less contentment to yow the Giuer, then to me that shall receiue it. ↑And that I value not halfe so much for the Delihts I shall posesse my self as I do for the Plesure it will bestow on yow.↓ Let then your Inclination conspire with my Fortune, to make me what yow vse to call me, your mistress: and tho vpon that score, I may Comand what I haue chosen to entreat, yet I am willing to [choose] <take> the milder way <straine> to reach my /Ends/ Desires, that I may be beholding <seem endebted> for <owe> your Kindness, [to the thanfulness <Goodnesse> of your Nature, not the Wretchedness of your Condition.] to the Obligingness of your Nature <Mind> not the Vnhappiness of your Condition.[3]

Suppose that by this Freedom I slight the Rules /fetters/ of that dull sneaking thing /Vertu/ that the deluded World cals Modesty. Tho there cud be an excesse in the Adoration <Loue> of Ioseph; and tho the Gods did not sufficiently authorize my Passion, when the Charmes they haue giu'n yow make it impossible for [yow] <me> to Resist: yet certinly yow haue reason not onely to forgiue but to applaud /reward/ a Crime, which my sole Passion for yow has [forc't] <oblig'd> me to commit: and to [co] measure the Greatness of my Affection by that of the Considerations it [makes] <forces> me to desert: and to beleeue, that she will easily resigne all <of> her things to your Disposall, that dare sacrifice her very Vertu it selfe to your Contentment. ↑Why shud these empty Names /sounds/ of Husband and of Wife depriue vs of those Ioyes for which alone that dull Relation was invented? Tis the Vnion of the Harts, not the Ioyning of the hands, that dos Essentiat Marriage: which all those Formall Ceremonys, do [not] not constitute but Declare. Since then 'tis not the Priest but the Consent makes Marriage; the Wedding of our Bodys without that of our Affections, is but a Lawfull Rape; and either of the Parties may vntie that knot with as much Iustice as their Fathers vs'd gold to compell vnion.↓[4]

---

[3] RB left several blank lines between this paragraph and the one before it. The following paragraph continued the text in a different ink, one that is now badly faded.

[4] This final sentence is very difficult to read because of the condition of the MS, and the last five words are a conjectural reading. Cork's negotiations for his children's marriages provide Canny with exceptionally interesting material (ch. 5) about the grounds for matrimony; see esp. tables 2 and 3 (88-89) for the ages at which marriage contracts had been negotiated. Conspicuously unhappy marriages among RB's siblings include those of Lady Ranelagh and Lady Goring. RB's visit to Lettice Goring in 1636 was very distressing, according to Robert Carew, because of Lettice's melancholy. "[My] masters did comfort her as much as they could," he noted, "but her languishing heart could not receive much comfort, soe that it made them cry often to looke vppon her" (*II Lismore* 3.268).

Textual Notes

Page 3

L. 14 is a Felicity.] is a Felicity

Page 5

L. 5 Chapter [2] II.] Chapter II.

L. 7 Of False Felicitys.] Of False Felicitys

L. 7 RB placed the Roman numerals in the margins, but I have placed them in the body of the paragraphs.

L. 16 nce] once

L. 17 those Good] those Goods

Page 6

L. 1 The copyist began by mistakenly transcribing this paragraph—from "The Epicureans . . ." to "to many in our times,"—and then deleting it. The spelling and punctuation differ markedly from RB's.

L. 6 3] 3.

L. 9 satisfie,] satisfie;

L. 11 6. and] 6. And

L. 14 that solitude is] solitude that is

L. 15 Neitheir] Neither
This refutation of the Epicureans continues with a lengthy insertion from f. 60^{v}.

L. 28 RB added the following parenthetical direction to ensure correct placement: "(For the 3rd Chapter, see it at the End of the 1 Booke foregoing.)"

L. 29 RB returned to f. 55^{v}.

Page 7

L. 3 Passions which] Passions, which

L. 4 selfe) selfe,
The copyist has not indicated where the first parenthesis should have been, so I have eliminated the latter.

L. 5 RB resumed the transcription after this sentence.

L. 10 4:] 4.

L. 11 diuer] diuers

L. 12 Stength,] Strength,

L. 24 The copyist resumed the transcription after this sentence.

L. 26 but: 1] but 1.

L. 27 Quench itt,] Quench itt.

L. 34 To with wee] To wit, wee

L. 36 beleueued.] beleeued.

Page 8

L. 2 Iudgments.] Iudgments,

L. 5 fortune,] fortune.

L. 8 RB resumed the transcription after this sentence.

L. 12 Corrupts.] Corrupts

L. 13 RB did not indicate where this marginal insertion should be placed, but in style and content it fits here.

L. 24 duers] diuers

Page 9

L. 25 CSpeculations,] Speculations,

Page 10

L. 2 Fancy most that] Fancy most, that

Page 11

L. 9 Ff. 61^{v}-63 are blank.

L. 15 of Moral Vertu.] of Moral Vertu

Page 12

L. 6 RB made this lengthy deletion by drawing a single line through nearly a half-page of the MS. The final version of the sentence thus reads: ". . . contenting our selues for the Present with a Necessary Question; namely whether the Subiect . . ."

L. 14 wchich] which

Page 13

L. 12 Hat,] Hate,

Page 13 (continued)

L. 32 This insertion is found on f. 84.

Page 14

L. 2 (mediante sensu) For] (mediante sensu). For

L. 34 These Affection] These Affections

Page 15

L. 3 Opinion] Opinion.

L. 20 re[spe]gard of reall] regard of reall

L. 23 the Faculty; then it worketh;] the Faculty) then it worketh,

Page 16

L. 6 The copyist resumed the transcription after this sentence.

L. 8 the # Sheepe.] the Sheepe.
It is not clear what the hash mark signifies.

L. 10 (one the contrarie)] (on the contrarie)

L. 23 RB resumed the transcription.

Page 17

L. 7 Because this paragraph is so lengthy, I have provided a break at this point.

L. 7 multi[pli]tude] multitude

L. 9 Namely because 1. Because ther] Namely because 1. ther

L. 24 Me[sure]sure.)] Mesure.)

Page 18

L. 7 Studity] Stupidity

L. 16 RB wrote "Aboue them," the last words on the page, in exceptionally large letters, filling the space usually devoted to two full lines.

L. 21 (or honestum) Profitable,] (or honestum), Profitable,

L. 22 (Commonly] Commonly
In the next several pages RB often failed to provide matched sets of parentheses.

L. 25 Amor Concupiscentiæ; a loue] Amor Concupiscentiæ, a loue

L. 29 Seruants to their Seruants:] Seruants to their Masters:
RB inadvertently repeated "Seruants."

Page 19

L. 7 Desire.] Desire.)

L. 12 God.] Good.

L. 21 thing] think

L. 25 obstruction] obstructing

L. 34 them been guilty] them have been guilty

L. 39 (And] And

Page 20

L. 13 (For] For

L. 15 some[thi]what] somewhat

Page 21

L. 5 (This Passion,] This Passion,

L. 7 RB deleted this sentence and the next two paragraphs by drawing a large "X" through them. Both of the deleted paragraphs had an "O" placed in the margin at the beginning of the paragraph, perhaps an abbreviation for "Omit."

L. 15 This insertion comes from f. 79.

L. 15 bloods;] blood;

L. 17 In the margin RB wrote, "The Discourse thus included shud be transfer'd to Number ," omitting the target. Since he seldom used brackets in this MS, I assume that the bracketed sentences on ff. 78^{v}-79 were meant to be kept together. For the sake of clarity, I have changed his square brackets to braces. But it is not clear where RB intended to place this passage. While several passages in this book are plausible, its present position is also appropriate, and thus I have left it here.

L. 21 ret[ribution]urn] return

L. 26 shul] shud

Page 22

L. 17 those Persons, they both those persons they] those Persons, they both

L. 32 This lengthy addition is in RB's hand but in a different ink from the one used in the preceding passage. The insertion comes from f. 84.

Page 23

L. 3 Gration] Gradation

L. 11 too blame] to blame

L. 19 The text continues on f. 81.

Page 24

L. 8 The copyist transcribed the next few sentences.

L. 14 # seruants] seruants,
It is unclear what the copyist meant by the hash mark.

L. 14 RB resumed the transcription.

L. 17 A[nd]s] As

L. 19 & As] And as

L. 31 Brun] Brunt

L. 32 wether; they] wether, they

Page 25

L. 4 by Distracti[ng]on;] Distraction;

L. 10 satter] scatter

L. 13 objects. (so] objects (so

L. 25 temperatus)] temperatus,

Page 27

L. 8 and Paine.] and Paine

Page 30

L. 25 [Plesure must needs be a Good; and that God himself enjoys] Though this clause was deleted, RB failed to provide either a substitute for it or to emend the passage. Since the sentence continues with a phrase that grammatically completes the sentence—"a Plesur as infinite as his Essence"—I have emended this passage by restoring the deletion.

Page 31

L. 5 Pre[cedency]<eminence>] Preeminence

L. 23 RB included a caret both before and after "have," so "indeed" might have been placed in either spot.

Page 33

L. 2 F. 92 is blank.

L. 8 Of Moral Actions.] Of Moral Actions

L. 8 [Of the Principles] Of Moral Actions.] Of Moral Actions.

L. 10 ithe Efficient] the Efficient

L. 24 we se] we see

Page 35

L. 1 prope] propose

L. 31 seldon] seldom

L. 38 Ease, I and] Ease, and

Page 36

L. 8 (or Forc'd)] (or Forc'd),

L. 12 [and] I] [and]

L. 15 from at] from an

L. 25 RB mistakenly placed "or out of" before "with."

L. 32 cause it] cause is

L. 36 eiter] either

Page 37

L. 5 if forc'd] is forc'd

Page 38

L. 13 besides] Besides

L. 24 Circunstances] Circumstances

L. 29 Prudence.] Prudence.)

Page 39

L. 5 thou] throu

L. 14 on] one

L. 25 namly,] namely,

L. 26 to Vn-affected,] to be Vn-affected,

L. 32 and find[ing]s] and finds

Page 40

L. 10 s[eeming]<pecious>] specious

L. 38 Drunke?] Drunke,

Page 41

L. 20 those Iniury] those Iniurys

Page 42

L. 22 them; be] them; we

L. 29 Sea or no] Sea or no,

Page 44

L. 15 Coherenc[y]<e>] Coherence

L. 19 Wherefore the] Wherefore

Page 45

L. 2 Ff. 110-11 are blank.

L. 6 Chapter IIII] Chapter IIII.

L. 8 of Moral Vertu.] of Moral Vertu

Page 46

L. 26 F. 114^{v} is blank.

L. 27 Decologue,] Decalogue,

L. 30 whose] those

Page 47

L. 15 Synteris] Synteresis

L. 17 F. E.] For Example,

L. 23 Con[s]c[ience]lusion,] Conclusion,

Page 49

L. 17 liht as Feare:] liht as Ayre:

Page 50

L. 12 RB used upper-case letters to mark the beginning of this section.

Page 51

L. 18 foll[illeg.]y] folly

L. 28 do not] do yow not

L. 33 7] 10
RB offers ten points, not seven, and he circles each of the numerals in the series. Instead of circling the numbers, I have placed periods after each numeral.

L. 35 Arguments)] Arguments;

Page 54

L. 4 Testament.] Testament.)

L. 6 3618)] 3618,

L. 25 Fisitian, but] Fisitian, is but

Page 55

L. 26 Discourse;)] Discourse;

Page 56

L. 21 Gratitude.] Gratitude?

L. 22 hevnly] heu'nly

L. 23 purchase in] purchase an

Page 58

L. 7 s[ingle] <elect>] select

L. 14 Strong,] Strong?

L. 16 wel-voic't,] wel-voic't?

L. 17 but man] But man

Page 59

L. 5 antipate] anticipate

L. 17 Hupocrites,] Hypocrites,

Page 60

L. 7 offend vs;] offend vs,

L. 38 as the Body is more Excellent then the Soule.] as the Soule is more Excellent then the Body.
RB inadvertently reversed the order of elements in his comparison. I have restored what he surely meant.

L. 39 <And> Since] <And> since

Page 61

L. 17 speaking,] speaking,)

L. 25 tels vs.] tels vs

L. 27 Workes.)] Workes.

Page 62

L. 23 ;] |thing|
RB left space for a word. Since the material in this section has no parallel in MS 192, my conjecture of "thing" is based on the grammatical requirements of the passage. For similar usage, see the examples under "seisin"

Page 62 (continued)
(*OED* 1.b).
L. 36 <2.> Pet. 3.13)] (<2.> Pet. 3.13)
L. 37 In this marginal insertion, RB used lower-case letters to signal the series of six biblical passages explicated later in this passage. For the sake of clarity and consistency, I have placed periods after each of the letters, RB using a period only after item "d," both in this list and in the discussion.

Page 63
L. 14 to Permanent,] so Permanent,
L. 17 fauing] hauing
L. 27 6] 8
RB presented eight objections, not six.

Page 64
L. 20 stong] strong
L. 22 Godness] Goodness
L. 26 No signal indicated the placement of this marginal insertion, but since it is written alongside this passage and since its content is pertinent, I have inserted it here.

Page 65
L. 27 my] by

Page 66
L. 13 in those Morality;] in Morality;
L. 15 gowe.] gowne.
L. 21 Affections. [being] like] Affections, [being] like

Page 67
L. 2 himsel] himself
L. 7 regarder] regarded
L. 12 to bound to] bound to
L. 18 7.] 8.
L. 28 <that> that] that

Page 68
L. 8 to into, or] to go into, or
L. 19 causesly] causlesly
L. 33 Melancholy humors.] Melancholy humors,

Page 69
L. 2 to diuerted] to be diuerted
L. 11 Thing then in] Thing but in

Page 71
L. 12 what] What
L. 26 that [can] needs] and [can] needs
L. 34 [happy,] or rich either] [happy,] rich either

Page 73
L. 21 a Qualitys] a Quality
L. 30 but shos him] but Vertu shos

Page 75
L. 6 Paines dos Fade,] Paines doe Fade,
L. 12 obserues)] obserues
L. 28 abridge, vs:] abridge vs:

Page 76
L. 20 the Way these] the Way; these

Page 77
L. 20 Superscript "°" before "som" and superscript "o" after "good"
L. 33 Acquisition Vertu;] Acquisition of Vertu;

Page 78
L. 6 self-guiltines)] self-guiltines
It is not clear where RB intended to begin the parentheses.
L. 9 There is no signal for placing this marginal insertion, but since it is written alongside this passage and since its content is pertinent to RB's point, I have placed it here.
L. 9 /Appetite/] /Appetite/.
L. 10 19.20 &c.)] 19.20 &c.
L. 16 Repution,] Reputation,

Page 79
L. 8 Young men neuer] Young men ar neuer

Page 80
L. 3 There is no signal for placing this marginal insertion, but since it is written alongside this passage and since its content is pertinent to RB's point, I have inserted it here.

Page 81
L. 19 commend[ation]ed] commended
L. 30 Cudged] Cudgel

Page 83
L. 4 ar] our
L. 8 There is no signal for placing this marginal insertion, but since it is written alongside this passage and since its content is pertinent to RB's point, I have inserted it here.
L. 12 kind] kind of
L. 34 ha[d]uing] hauing

Page 85
L. 18 3 Tim. 5,8] 1 Tim. 5,8

Page 86
L. 2 neither ar] Neither ar

Page 87
L. 36 Braines overwrites Browes

Page 88
L. 4 /warres/ making] /warres/, making
L. 8 himsel] himself
L. 15 vpon looking-glasses] vpon looking-glasses,
L. 16 RB's insertion ("and in Sum . . .") was placed before the phrase, "courting of Ladys . . ."; it makes more sense grammatically for it to be placed after it.
L. 18 vn-[necessary]vsefull] vn-vsefull
L. 28 were any] were any)

Page 89
L. 19 it we] it were

Page 91
L. 4 Work[es]<ing.>] Working.
L. 7 F. 230^{v} contains notes on geometry, the next leaf has been torn from the MS, and so the text continues on f. 231.
L. 15 vsufulness] vsfulness
L. 18 venter] venture

Page 92
L. 1 X. But to auoid] But to auoid The "X." is a "flag," not a numeral. The paragraph that follows is a formal transition to chapter five.

Page 93
L. 8 of Morall Vertu.] of Morall Vertu
L. 23 me in] be in
L. 28 The MS has had a page removed at this point.
L. 28 Qualy] Quality
L. 30 nor a externall] nor an externall

Page 94
L. 3 these Action,] these Actions,
L. 23 Ignorant Constrain'd,] Ignorant, Constrain'd,
L. 29 Many Vertu] Many Vertus
L. 36 other.] other.)
L. 37 Peope] People

Page 95
L. 8 (whose] whose
L. 11 This full-page passage on f. 127^{v} was written in the same ink as the two marginal insertions immediately above it on this page, an ink different from that of the surrounding pages. RB also began the passage much lower on the page than when he merely continued the previous passage. The material on f. 127^{v}

Page 95 (continued)

does not follow logically or syntactically from the material on f. 127; but the material does fit with and extend the discussion of means that RB had just initiated. In addition, f. 127 ended with the words “Such is,” and f. 128 began with an inadvertent repetition of those words. For these reasons I have moved these paragraphs to this position.

L. 30 The MS returns to the middle of f. 126^{v}.

Page 96

L. 19 Two lines have been thoroughly deleted.

Page 97

L. 32 riht-ly-informed] rihtly-informed

Page 99

L. 11 Fragily,] Fragility,

L. 34 (cap. 2) 26)] (cap. 2,26)

Page 101

L. 2 F. 134^{v} is blank.

L. 8 of Morall Vertu.] of Morall Vertu

L. 20 of the Vertus; but] of the Vertus;) but

Page 102

L. 20 no necessary] so necessary

L. 33 it all of,] it all,

L. 34 mot-ley-minded] motley-minded

Page 103

L. 2 Haue but] Has but

L. 10 but; if] but if

Page 104

L. 4 Secret Sins at] Secret Sins ar at

L. 34 a Gangrenes.] a Gangrene.

Page 105

L. 3 lest Sins the one,] lest Sins in the one,

L. 9 l<esser>ittle] little

L. 20 nonly] only

Page 106

L. 5 ac[q]knoledgment] acknoledgment

L. 13 Superscript “$^{\circ}$” after “thou” and superscript “o” after “Deliht”

L. 30 that wil a] or a

L. 30 This insertion comes from f. 141^{v}.

Page 107

L. 29 This lengthy marginal insertion has no indication where it was to be placed. The context suggests that it belonged here, but it might also be placed just before the sentence beginning, “And why shud it not . . .”

L. 32 a Action] an Action

Page 108

L. 15 /Sacrz/] /Sacrednes/

Page 109

L. 3 This lengthy insertion comes from f. 169. RB signalled the source of the insertion thus: “turn onward till yow com to this Mark.”

L. 27 This insertion comes from f. 170^{v}.

L. 34 The MS continues on f. 169^{v}.

Page 110

L. 8 Parts;] Parts;)

L. 14 /Paz/] /Parent/

L. 31 Singulary] Singularity

L. 32 to good] to be good

Page 111

L. 5 This insertion comes from f. 173^{v}.

L. 19 The MS returns to f. 171^{v}.

L. 30 villany est;] villanyes;

Page 112

L. 16 full turn prinz] full turn principall
It is not certain what RB intended by "prinz."

L. 34 /worrz/] /worthy/

L. 35 /endz/] /endeuvor/

Page 113

L. 2 he eate] he eates

L. 19 /consz/] /consequences/

L. 26 this an] this is an

Page 114

L. 15 (our Sauior, Matt 6,2)] (our Sauior, Matt 6,2,

L. 36 Nothing more] Nothing is more

Page 115

L. 5 of /weknes/ of] of /weknes/

L. 13 qality] quality

L. 20 Qality] Quality

L. 21 Qality] Quality

L. 31 out out a little] out of a little

L. 35 Ch.)] Chapter)

Page 116

L. 9 thefore] therfore

L. 23 sweetnes] sweetens

Page 117

L. 13 Goliahs.] Goliaths.

L. 15 Comenda but] Comendable but
This marginal insertion comes from f. 179^{v}.

L. 21 This second insertion comes from f. 177^{v}.
RB signalled this insertion thus: "turn 2 leaues bac and look [illeg.] this Mark."

L. 34 St] Saint

Page 118

L. 13 Ephes. 6; 10,11,12.] Ephes. 6,10,11,12.

L. 29 qualitity] quality

L. 30 make a] makes a

L. 32 they first] the first

L. 33 Place For] Place, For

Page 119

L. 8 /consz/] /consider/

L. 14 /herz/] /hereafter/

L. 14 Temptation grow] Temptation grows

Page 120

L. 5 Just below this insertion is a very short passage of shorthand that I have been unable to decipher.

L. 8 /Desz/] /Desuetude/

L. 13 that hou] that thou

L. 14 Compz] Companion

L. 16 Felicity/] Felicity,

Page 121

L. 10 seldom know] seldom known

L. 11 Remedy.] Remedy; and

L. 12 RB did not signal the placement of this insertion, but in style and content it is appropriate here.

L. 16 Liberalal] Liberal

L. 17 Loue, Reu. 2,4.)] Loue, (Reu. 2,4.)

L. 23 This insertion is not formally signalled to be placed here, but in style and content it is appropriate to this passage.

L. 34 which it is rewarded.] which is rewarded.

Page 122

L. 5 /that Prz/] /that Promise/

Page 123

L. 2 F. 186 is blank. The MS now returns to f. 144; ff. 142-143 are blank.

L. 9 Heroick Vertu.] Heroick Vertu

L. 32 then other som] then others

Page 124

L. 9 demoninatio] denominatio

L. 37 out that] out of that

Page 126
L. 16 Perijt is] Perijt est

Page 127
L. 11 (matter) of] (matter of)

Page 128
L. 10 Interualls; or Pauses;] Interualls, or Pauses;
L. 22 [t]his Cupiditys,] his Cupiditys,
L. 24 they both persists] they both persist
L. 26 Continet] Continent

Page 129
L. 2 will all] with all

Page 131
L. 9 Vertu. Yet] Vertu, yet
L. 36 Magnamity] Magnanimity

Page 132
L. 18 of the Emperours.] of the Emperours,

Page 133
L. 1 S[upreame] <ouueraine>] Soueraine
L. 9 B[arbar]rutality] Brutality
L. 10 Beast.)] Beast.

Page 135
L. 7 Vertus Contrarys.] Vertus Contrarys
L. 7 Ff. 158^{v} and 159 are blank. RB inadvertently omitted a title for this chapter, so I have provided one by using a key phrase from the first sentence.
L. 17 This insertion was not signalled, but it was written alongside the deleted passage in the same ink used to delete the previous sentence. Its content is appropriate here.
L. 20 Vulgar mistakes] Vulgar mistake

Page 136
L. 3 Ys] Eys
L. 22 After deleting the subject of this sentence—most likely a word like "men"—RB failed to provide a substitute. I have therefore emended this passage to read, "For when men desist from doing Good . . ."
L. 32 Defence is one's] Defence of one's
L. 37 Habide] Habitude

Page 137
L. 5 that Middle that] that Middle
L. 36 not one 9] not onely 9

Page 138
L. 25 M[iddle]eane;] Meane;
L. 29 I, and] and
L. 31 This reference to Matthew is written in an ink different from the ink used in the rest of this passage, indicating RB's return to this MS some time after its original transcription.
L. 36 giuen] giuing

Page 139
L. 10 demonstated] demonstrated
L. 23 Lust, Impudency,] Lust, Impudency;
L. 30 calc[cal]ulated] calculated
L. 32 Vi[tius]ce,] Vice,

Page 140
L. 5 ar required, the lesser,] ar required; the lesser,
L. 21 Will,:] Will,
L. 21 Affections.] Affections,
L. 23 RB noted in the margin, "This shud haue been the first of the Occasioners." Since this note was to himself, I have not included it in the text or moved its referent to the first position in the next paragraph.
L. 29 folling trust] failing trust

Page 140 (continued)

L. 39 Superscript "°" before "wilful" and superscript "o" before "knowne"

Page 141

L. 16 F. 168 is blank.

Page 143

L. 24 /sunk down)] /sunk down/

L. 24 B<rutes>ests] Brutes

L. 25 as it contrary] as it is contrary

L. 32 RB did not indicate where this marginal insertion was to be placed, but it is placed alongside this passage and is compatible with its content.

Page 144

L. 2 b[ecause]y] by

L. 5 RB did not indicate where this marginal insertion was to be placed, but it is placed alongside this passage and is compatible with its content.

L. 7 forth Sin] forth Sin;

L. 9 the Primum Ens and)] the Primum Ens and

L. 9 This insertion continues onto f. 5^v.

L. 12 A small mark above "Hatred" indicates that either "Hate" or "Hatred" could be used.

L. 15 /Ess/] /Essences/

L. 17 Neuer Good.] Neuer Good,

L. 25 as other Euils as] other Euils as

L. 27 odious,] odious

L. 28 for sure] For sure

L. 33 Self-respectes] Self-respecte

Page 145

L. 14 burid] buried

L. 14 stink.] stink

L. 23 Purbling] Purblind

L. 26 beleeued to the] beleeued to be the

L. 34 /witz/] /withdraw/

Page 146

L. 7 per<con>ceu'd] perceu'd

L. 9 the Partz] the Particular.

L. 16 must necessary] must necessarily

L. 21 In the next few sentences I have silently changed periods to question marks where RB was inconsistent in his punctuation.

L. 31 intz/] intense/

L. 33 RB did not indicate where this marginal insertion was to be placed, but it is inserted beside this passage and is compatible with its content.

L. 37 Punishment)] Punishment/

Page 147

L. 2 RB did not indicate where this marginal insertion was to be placed, but it is placed alongside this passage and is compatible with its content.

L. 10 (that] that

L. 15 Deceitful of] Deceits of

L. 18 loue vs] loue vs,

L. 29 (perhaps) another's] (perhaps) of another's

L. 33 to them Sinfulness] to Sinfulness

L. 37 for their other] for other

Page 148

L. 27 RB used an "O" to stand for "able" in the last three adjectives.

L. 30 /grz/] /grounds/

Page 149

L. 15 /Enz/] /Enemy/

Page 150

L. 2 F. 12^v is blank.

L. 13 were] were)

L. 16 (very] (very)

L. 20 Essenz] Essence

L. 21 consist] consists

L. 30 value not /care not for/] value not /care not for./

Page 150 (continued)
L. 32 joynes] joyn
L. 34 can be put] can put

Page 151
L. 3 no Enemy to] no Enemy like
L. 5 (For] For
L. 8 like, men] like men
L. 12 (cheefz/ ne detz Vacuum.] (cheefly, ne detur Vacuum.)
L. 22 F. 14^{v} is blank.

Page 152
L. 5 asleepe.)] asleepe.
L. 10 The] the
L. 27 Self-respects,] Self-respect,

Page 153
L. 26 Ordinance] Ordinance:
L. 33 by con[si]demnation.] by condemnation.
L. 35 /infz/] /infinity/

Page 154
L. 7 /Lobz/] /Lobby/
L. 8 After "Eternity," RB filled the remainder of the line with a squiggly line whose meaning is not evident.
L. 19 it so] it is so
L. 32 Effects] Effects.
L. 33 banisht that] banisht from that

Page 155
L. 10 manking,] mankind,
L. 16 After "man" RB left unfilled a set of parentheses, probably reserving space for a scriptural citation.

Page 156
L. 4 /vtz/] /vtility/,
L. 16 /remz/] /remember/
L. 27 convz] convertible

Page 158
L. 6 justify;] justify.
L. 35 (Therefore] Therefore

Page 159
L. 11 himself.] himself
L. 20 Ascemt.] Ascent.

Page 160
L. 1 I but I] O but I
L. 3 <extz>] <extenuate>
L. 11 Besides that that] Besides that, that
L. 14 we thing] we think
L. 17 /fellz/] /fellowship/
L. 17 besure] be sure
L. 24 I must take /ingz/] I must take It is unclear what the expanded form of "ingz" should be.
L. 29 has chain'd me to my that] has so chain'd me to my Sin that

Page 161
L. 4 springs/] /springs/
L. 4 reitation] reiteration
L. 19 Customamary] Customary
L. 21 This insertion comes from f. 25^{v}.
L. 25 I but I] O but I
L. 25 proudest on them] proudest of them
L. 29 Silent.] Silent
L. 36 grorify] glorify
L. 38 This insertion comes from f. 26^{v}.
L. 39 Be not deceiued] Be not deceiued:

Page 162
L. 2 F. 26^{v} is devoted entirely to insertions for placement elsewhere in the text.
L. 24 quilte] quite

Page 163
L. 5 no that] not that
L. 7 may be good;] may be good
L. 28 This insertion is signalled by the phrase, "turn 2 leaues bac til yow come to this Marque," and is found on f. 26^{v}.
L. 33 Gen. 5,3)] (Gen. 5,3)
L. 36 To not] To nought

Page 163 (continued)

L. 36 Repz] Repentance

Page 164

L. 1 5.] 4. In this complex sequence of insertions, RB misnumbered both this point and the next one.

L. 4 repent them/ ____] repent them/.

L. 6 RB wrote a 6 over a 4, but with the re-arrangement of material, it is actually point 5.

L. 39 For (no] For (not

Page 165

L. 2 it for] it is for

L. 8 This insertion comes from ff. 29^{v}-.30^{v}.

L. 23 The text now returns to the middle of f. 30.

L. 28 Sacrifrices;] Sacrifices;

L. 40 sacrifrice)] sacrifice)

Page 166

L. 16 things] thinks

L. 19 F. 31^{v} is blank.

L. 21 2.] 2,

L. 29 Peacable] Peaceable

Page 167

L. 1 1] 1.

L. 3 Strictly. That] Strictly, that

L. 6 /blemishes/] /blemishes/.

L. 32 ad[uance]mirable liquor] admirable liquor

Page 168

L. 6 RB did not indicate where this marginal insertion is to be placed, but it is placed alongside this passage and is compatible with its content.

L. 8 must the] must be the

L. 28 Ff. 34^{v}-37^{v} are blank.

Page 169

L. 20 The insertion continues on f. 39.

Page 170

L. 4 Wis] Wisdom

L. 5 RB left space for the citation but provided only the ( ).

L. 18 the Second in cheefly eminent in] the Second is cheefly eminent in

L. 27 goodness. (to him)] goodness (to him).

Page 171

L. 8 Defects,] Defects;

L. 9 Effects,] Effects;

L. 17 Essence.] Essence,

L. 18 none)] none).

L. 32 /Em. Perf/] /Eminent Perfection/

Page 172

L. 2 /gr/] [greater]

L. 14 /vnactz/] /vnactiue/

L. 24] RB set off this first line with a short squiggly line.

L. 24 to vs.] to vs.)

L. 26 Acts. 17.28.)] (Acts. 17.28.)

L. 27 not out a] not out of a

L. 30 which our] which is our

L. 31 of Subject] of Subjects

Page 173

L. 2 (Rom. 8.28/] (Rom. 8.28)

L. 9 ( )] RB did not indicate which verses he intended. He wrote "Chapter" over "Apostle."

L. 12 Point To] Point, To

L. 20 So shud do also;] So shud we do also;

Page 174

L. 12 F. 44^{v} is blank.

L. 15 meerely he] meerely because he

L. 33 drownes] drowne

Page 175

L. 23 there can no] there can be no

L. 38 what] What

Page 176

L. 17 things a<w>re.)] things were.)
L. 27 That, let] And let
L. 27 Deny'd.] Deny'd.)
L. 29 witthod] withhold

Page 177

L. 2 no the] not the
L. 13 Gods,] Goats,
L. 13 imposs.] impossible
L. 14 F. 49^{v} is blank.
L. 33 Prayses,] Prayses;

Page 178

L. 35 ( )] RB left the parentheses unfilled.

Page 180

L. 3 This so grosse] This was so grosse
L. 4 Authors] Author
L. 7 marhand] marchand
L. 9 Island. Fit] Island, Fit
L. 26 Deo est, Deus est,)] Deo est, Deus est,
L. 27 is God)] is God);

Page 181

L. 6 (Hence] Hence
L. 29 Barbarous)] Barbarous
L. 34 Chapter.)] Chapter.

Page 182

L. 22 instant] instantly

Page 183

L. 11 impor'd:] implor'd:
L. 27 (Iohn 16.13. It] (Iohn 16.13.) It
L. 27 acknoledging] acknoledges
L. 31 This insertion on f. 58^{v} is at the top of the margin, but it is not clear where RB intended to place it.
L. 33 Ff. 59 and 59^{v} are blank.

Page 186

L. 10 A pencilled line is in the margin to the end of this page.
L. 16 succe<eeding>ssiue] successiue
L. 16 F. 6^{v} is blank except for three illegible lines written by someone other than RB, who writes "the world might haue beene as full of simpplisity as it [illeg.] wass since it began and at." This is not the handwriting of the amanuensis in MS 195, and I have been unable to identify the author.
L. 28 F. 7^{v} is blank. Because RB's first point was so lengthy, I have provided a paragraph break at this point, "The Experiments of this."
L. 35 Drugges)] Drugges

Page 187

L. 13 no our] no, our
L. 14 plasd] pleased
L. 25 Because this paragraph was so lengthy, I have provided a break at this point.
L. 28 A pencilled line is in the margin to the end of this page.

Page 188

L. 2 F. 9^{v} is blank.
L. 13 make may for] make way for
L. 14 F. 10^{v} is blank except for one insertion signalled from f. 11.
L. 16 Matt. 15, 19)] (Matt. 15, 19)
L. 16 Pr. 15, 26)] (Pr. 15.26)
L. 20 Thelf] Theft,
L. 21 obseruable)] obseruable
L. 23 Ages] Age
L. 23 doubtesly] doubtlesly
L. 28 F. 11^{v} is blank.
L. 30 (welneere)] (wel neere)
L. 37 A pencilled line is in the margin for the last two lines.
L. 40 Repence,] Repentance,
L. 40 the[y must]] the

Page 189

L. 4 F. 12^{v} is blank except for two insertions signalled from f. 12.
L. 10 <the L and his M>] <the Lady and his Master>

Page 189 (continued)

- L. 14 Which is] (Which is This insertion comes from f. 12^{v}.
- L. 19 Dr<inker>unkard,] Drinker,
- L. 19 This insertion comes from f. 12^{v}.
- L. 19 the kind] these kind
- L. 26 re<peat>act them,] repeat them,
- L. 29 late-<after> consent.] late <after> consent.
- L. 34 F. 14^{v} is blank.
- L. 35 has needed] have needed

Page 190

- L. 3 Braine.] Braine.)
- L. 12 F. 15^{v} is blank.
- L. 24 <those> those] of those
- L. 25 But all this] But if all this
- L. 26 F. 16^{v} is blank.
- L. 28 and entised] and entised
- L. 35 dis<criminate>tinguish] discriminate
- L. 36 haue tuch] haue tuch't
- L. 38 a[re] task] a task

Pagc 191

- L. 4 F. 17^{v} is blank.
- L. 14 ex[cellent]quisite] exquisite
- L. 22 heares] hearers
- L. 22 F. 18^{v} is blank.
- L. 25 howse,] howse;
- L. 26 orchard,] orchard.
- L. 29 fance] fancy

Page 192

- L. 8 Braine /Imagination/] Braine /Imagination./
- L. 8 not] nor
- L. 9 (perhaps] (perhaps)
- L. 9 F. 19^{v} is blank.
- L. 17 precise[ness]] precise
- L. 26 F. 20^{v} is blank.

Page 193

- L. 9 F. 21^{v} is blank.
- L. 16 Condition has been] Condition God has been
- L. 28 F. 22^{v} is blank.
- L. 36 obserue] obserued
- L. 38 /Bisnes)] /Bisnes/

Page 194

- L. 7 F. 23^{v} is blank.
- L. 18 These two lines have a pencilled marker in the margin.
- L. 21 Because this paragraph was so lengthy, I have provided a break at this point.
- L. 22 F. 24^{v} is blank except for an insertion signalled from f. 25.
- L. 23 b who (by] who by
- L. 27 This insertion comes from f. 25.
- L. 29 secrets closets] secret closets
- L. 32 Erthy Father] Erthly Father
- L. 34 (vnauoibable)] (vnauoidable)

Page 195

- L. 4 F. 25^{v} is blank.
- L. 18 least of Distraction,] least of Distractions,
- L. 20 F. 26^{v} is blank except for an insertion signalled from f. 27.
- L. 27 This inscrtion comcs from f. 26^{v}.

Page 196

- L. 5 F. 27^{v} is blank.
- L. 8 needfull>] needfull)>
- L. 22 F. 28^{v} is blank except for an insertion signalled from f. 29.
- L. 26 for.] for,
- L. 28 A pencilled line is in the margin to the end of this page.
- L. 30 (Ier. 4.14.) How] (Ier. 4.14. How
- L. 33 Entr<ance>y] Entrance
- L. 34 into the Minde] into the Minde;
- L. 34 This insertion comes from f. 28^{v}.

Page 197

- L. 6 forc<ibly>edly] forcibly
- L. 8 F. 29^{v} is blank.
- L. 9 These first two lines have a pencilled X in their margin.
- L. 14 EUery] EUERY
- L. 17 A pencilled line is in the margin of this sentence.
- L. 20 Thoughs.] Thoughts.

Page 197 (continued)

L. 23 F. 30^{v} is blank except for an insertion signalled from f. 31.
L. 29 ( )] It is not clear what passage RB intended.
L. 32 /Nature,] /Nature,/
L. 33 A pencilled line is in the margin to the end of the sentence.
L. 35 This insertion is found on f. 30^{v}.

Page 198

L. 3 F. 31^{v} is blank except for two insertions signalled from f. 32.
L. 5 16)] 16
L. 7 This insertion comes from f. 31^{v}.
L. 8 "Euery" is written in letters 2X larger than the other letters.
L. 10 There is a pencil mark in the margin from this point to the beginning of the last sentence on the page.
L. 12 This insertion comes from f. 31^{v}.
L. 14 Oppo<nent>ser.] Opponent.
L. 18 (I 1,5)] (Iam. 1,5)
L. 19 F. 31^{v} is blank.
L. 33 F. 33^{v} is blank.

Page 199

L. 7 F. 34^{v} is blank.
L. 8 consist.)] consist.
L. 10 shootest] shootes
L. 13 Bits.)] Bits.
L. 14 any thing of to] any thing to
L. 19 F. 35^{v} is blank.
L. 20 (whe[ch]nce] (whence
L. 25 A pencilled line is in the margin to the end of this page.
L. 27 to do in Body;] to do in the Body;
L. 31 F. 36^{v} is blank.

Page 200

L. 3 Pencil mark to the end of the page in margin.
L. 6 line /course/] line /course./
L. 7 F. 37^{v} is blank.
L. 7 craft/] craft/)
L. 12 ca Game] see a Game
L. 14 shcoolc,] schoolc,
L. 15 There is a pencil mark beside this sentence, "This Wandring-ness. . ."
L. 17 Twas been euer] Twas euer
L. 20 F. 38^{v} is blank.
L. 27 forkt] fork
L. 34 F. 39^{v} is blank.

Page 201

L. 6 A pencilled line is in the margin to the end of this page.
L. 10 F. 40^{v} is blank.
L. 14 A pencil mark is in the margin of this sentence.
L. 17 All of point seven has a pencil mark in its margin.
L. 20 Accidents)] Accidents,
L. 24 F. 41^{v} is blank.
L. 24 Pencil mark for this sentence.
L. 29 Re<tard>pulse] Retard

Page 202

L. 2 Meditati<ng>on,] Meditating, A pencil mark is in the margin from "Meditation" to "Colde againe."
L. 6 F. 42^{v} is blank.

Page 203

L. 15 RB provided a brace large enough to encompass all three points.
L. 26 Channels, [too]] Channels. [too]

Page 204

L. 17 th<at>e] that
L. 24 RB did not signal where to place this insertion; in the MS it is parallel to this sentence.
L. 28 RB did not signal where to place this insertion; in the MS it is parallel to this sentence.

Page 205

L. 8 examine and] examine our
L. 18 was<were>] were

Page 205 (continued)

L. 19 the Brasse the Iron] the Brasse, the Iron,

L. 26 abundanly] abundantly

L. 29 obliges] oblige

L. 29 /that Fz/] It is not clear what the expanded form should be.

Page 206

L. 4 that it] that if

L. 11 RB did not provide an alternate reading but left space for one.

L. 20 is seldome is] seldome is

L. 22 vn<repented>controuled] vnrepented

L. 24 From "Despaire" to "forgiuenesse," RB wrote in letters twice as large and bold as in the surrounding text.

L. 24 Soule thus] Soule, thus

L. 24 [o]fr<om>] from

L. 28 com[munion]<versat>ion,] conversation

L. 31 vn<disturbed>interrupted] vninterrupted

Page 207

L. 4 but) all] but all

L. 5 Steele. This] Steele.) This

L. 5 Con[iunction]<uersation>] Conuersation

L. 6 [we] conuerses] we conuerse

L. 10 RB did not provide an alternate reading but left space for one.

L. 16 (first] (first)

L. 33 Circunstances] Circumstances

Page 208

L. 22 Teacher] Teacher,

L. 23 (D. S.)] (Dear Sister)

L. 27 (generally] (generally)

L. 28 Banes] Banns RB used an obsolete spelling.

Page 209

L. 27 owne) Guilt)] owne Guilt)

L. 27 dis<couers>clozes] discouers

L. 37 vn<handsome>seemly] vnhandsome

Page 210

L. 12 Com<versation>merce] Conversation

Page 211

L. 4 RB did not signal where to place this insertion; in the MS it is parallel to this sentence.

L. 6 RB did not provide an alternate reading but left space for one.

L. 16 <[restor'd]>/] <[restor'd]>/.

L. 21 Apostasy./] Apostasy.

L. 24 it.] it

Page 212

L. 3 gr<and>eat] grand

L. 9 This Quick-sand] this Quicksand

L. 9 RB did not provide an alternate reading but left space for one.

L. 12 RB did not signal where to place this insertion; in the MS it is parallel to this sentence. I have provided the words in curly braces because the MS is indecipherable where it has been bound.

L. 13 Because this paragraph was so lengthy, I have provided a break at this point.

L. 17 /de<fer>lay/] /defer/

L. 26 RB did not signal where to place this insertion; in the MS it is parallel to this sentence. I have provided the words in curly braces because the MS is indecipherable in its margins.

L. 36 /Absence, keene/] Absence, keene

Page 213

L. 4 toot-akes,] tooth-akes,

L. 7 Because this paragraph was so lengthy, I have provided a break at this point.

L. 15 Ignoratice] Ignorance

L. 22 Ezek. 18,14,] Ezek. 18,14.

Page 213 (continued)

L. 34 (Wish] Wish

Page 214

L. 13 vn-[seem] concern'd] vnconcern'd

L. 17 Because this paragraph was so lengthy, I have provided a break at this point.

L. 34 to our excuse our] to excuse our

L. 36 RB did not provide an alternate reading but left space for one.

L. 41 /Aggrz/] /Aggrandisement/

Page 215

L. 1 Now due considering by often remembring] Now often remembring The first part of the sentence is badly garbled. Because this paragraph was so lengthy, I have provided a break at this point.

L. 16 RB did not signal where to place this insertion; in the MS it is parallel to this sentence.

L. 31 /Tz Cz/] It is not clear what the expanded form should be.

Page 216

L. 10 Wickednesse /misery/] Wickednesse /misery,/

L. 12 RB did not signal where to place this insertion; in the MS it is parallel to this sentence, and it fits grammatically with the next sentence.

L. 12 But] but

L. 31 multiplicy] multiplicity

L. 35 m[ay]ust] must

Page 217

L. 13 antipated,] anticipated,

L. 21 RB did not provide an alternate reading but left space for one.

L. 25 Because this paragraph was so lengthy, I have provided a break at this point.

L. 27 (falling) asleep.)] falling asleep.

Page 218

L. 4 Thoughts /Reflections/] Thoughts /Reflections./

L. 8 RB did not provide an alternate reading but left space for one.

L. 10 RB placed a caret between "her" and "Employments," bu provided no insertion.

L. 19 /obliterated] obliterated

Page 219

L. 13 Prz] Practice

L. 18 find in it] find in it.

L. 20 RB did not provide an alternate reading but left space for one.

Page 220

L. 10 RB did not signal where to place this insertion; in the MS it is parallel to this sentence.

L. 13 ba??] back The MS is damaged for the last two letters in "back."

L. 20 RB provided an "insertion" signal—most certainly a list of Biblical citations—but did not provide the citations in the margin or at any other place in this MS.

L. 26 RB did not signal where to place this insertion; in the MS it is parallel to this sentence.

L. 27 RB did not provide an alternate reading but has left space for one.

Page 221

L. 2 to approued] to be approued

L. 7 /Rz/] /Reflection/

L. 10 /Rx/] /Reflections/

L. 22 /Rz/] /Reflecting/

L. 23 Re<sidue>[mainder]] Residue

L. 31 Concerment] Concernment

Page 222

L. 8 Third (and] Third and

L. 18 /Pz/] /Priority/

L. 34 /attz/] /attended/

Page 222 (continued)
L. 36 RB did not signal where to place this insertion; in the MS it is parallel to this sentence.

Page 223
L. 7 /Comfz/] /Comfort/
L. 28 RB did not provide an alternate reading but has left space for one.

Page 224
L. 16 RB did not provide an alternate reading but has left space for one.
L. 17 re<cord>late] record
L. 24 Infinite[mercy]<nesse>] Infinitenesse
L. 26 RB did not provide an alternate reading but left space for one.
L. 27 The MS is damaged after glasses; I have provided the punctuation.
L. 36 Dis<tastes>gusts;] Distastes;

Page 225
L. 5 imp[rest]<arted>; imparted; The MS is damaged after imparted; I have provided the punctuation.
L. 14 /Recz/] /Recording/
L. 19 do <that most> frequently produce] <that most> frequently do produce
L. 22 corne] cornel
L. 31 and not be] and can not be
L. 32 on parts,] in part

Page 226
L. 23 dis[couer'd]<cloz'd>] discloz'd
L. 32 RB wrote "owne" in italic script.

Page 227
L. 4 RB did not provide an alternate reading but left space for one.
L. 8 <Iudg. 4, 19,20,21.)> (to] <(Iudg. 4, 19,20,21.)> to
L. 26 <Iust> As] <Iust> as
L. 29 </mind not> them./] <mind not> them.
L. 32 [vast]<huge>ly] hugely

Page 228
L. 6 others.] others,

Page 229
L. 9 1 Kings 20. 39,40. Kings)] 1 Kings 20. 39,40.)
L. 23 Errors |illeg.| those] Errors in those The MS is damaged.
L. 26 fall<acious>ible] fallacious
L. 37 in most of those <there are certin hints>] in most of those
L. 38 Propertys;) discloze] Propertys;) that discloze

Page 230
L. 12 RB did not provide an alternate reading but left space for one.
L. 23 At the top of this page RB wrote "signor sr."
L. 25 Iust them,] Iust men,
L. 28 RB did not provide an alternate reading but left space for one.
L. 29 RB used very large letters for "G O D"
L. 32 Superscript "o" before "disguized" and superscript "o" before "mistaken"

Page 231
L. 2 RB did not provide an alternate reading but left space for one.
L. 4 RB did not provide an alternate reading but left space for one.
L. 18 pr[eserue]<otect>] protect
L. 26 /subz/] /subuersion/.

Page 232
L. 8 RB did not provide an alternate reading but left space for one.
L. 13 RB did not provide an alternate reading but left space for one.
L. 14 Generall Directed;] Generall Direction;
L. 18 /Diffz/ /] /Differences / / RB did not provide an alternate reading but left space for one.

Page 232 (continued)

L. 21 /repz/] It is not clear what word RB intended.

L. 27 RB did not provide an alternate reading but left space for one.

L. 32 reall] recall

Page 233

L. 3 with almost with nothing] with almost nothing

L. 12 RB did not provide an alternate reading but left space for one.

L. 35 RB did not provide an alternate reading but left space for one.

Page 234

L. 10 RB did not signal where to place this insertion; in the MS it was placed in the margin between f. 286^{v} and f. 287 and ran the length of the page.

L. 12 Tabernacle)] Tabernacle

L. 20 The passage continues on f. 287^{v}.

L. 33 </ouerstraining>] <ouerstrain-ing>

L. 36 RB did not provide an alternate reading but left space for one.

Page 235

L. 1 RB did not provide an alternate reading but left space for one.

L. 10 (as we] as we

Page 237

L. 9 RB has not indicated where this lengthy insertion was to be placed. The two sentences fill the left-hand margin of the page.

Page 238

L. 20 RB did not signal where this insertion should be placed, but the insertion is parallel to this passage.

L. 30 Superscript "°" before "Length" and superscript "o" before Frequency

Page 239

L. 21 sleeping)] sleeping,

L. 31 of Ciuility>] of Ciuility)>

L. 32 that want] that wants

Page 240

L. 4 /speechlesse/] /speechlesse/.

L. 6 the Wind are] the Wind

L. 12 brough] brought

L. 21 Inueruals] Interuals

Page 241

L. 16 Eyes over Eares

L. 17 (Nor has it] Nor has it

L. 24 RB did not indicate where this addition was to be placed, but it is parallel to this passage.

L. 25 Procrastion] Procrastination

Page 242

L. 20 <delin'd>] <declin'd>

L. 24 that been] that had been

Page 243

L. 3 to that] who that
This sentence is somewhat garbled, but RB probably meant that people who have the most time for recreation have the least right to use that time.

L. 5 if the were] if they were RB did not indicate where this addition was to be placed, but it is parallel to this passage.

L. 10 RB has not indicated where this lengthy insertion was to be placed, but it is parallel to this sentence.

Page 244

L. 2 with suspected Seruant;] with a suspected Seruant;

L. 12 RB has not indicated where this insertion was to be placed, but it is parallel to this sentence.

L. 22 Superscript "°" before "insist" and superscript "o" before "vpon"

Page 244 (continued)

L. 23 Per[th]son] Person

Page 245

L. 7 request)] request,

L. 9 Asses:] Asses;

L. 9 300 seruant] 300 seruants

L. 15 profession;] profession)

L. 23 (that sure] that sure
RB did not provide the end parenthesis several times on this page.

L. 26 (I haue] I haue

L. 30 ([in] those [things])] [in] those [things]

L. 31 in th[ose things]<em>] in them

Page 246

L. 2 lihthing>] lihtning>

L. 10 (as many] as many

L. 17 secuding] seducing

L. 18 are to best] are best

L. 25 /Compz/] /Comparison/

Page 247

L. 22 (and] and

L. 23 (that;] that

Page 248

L. 17 RB did not indicate where this insertion was to be placed.

L. 18 hauing vs giuen] hauing giuen

Page 283

L. 10 I shall now [no longer] [no longer
Since RB repeated "I shall now" after this lengthy and complex deletion, I have omitted the phrase here.

L. 20 restraint] restraints

L. 26 "Numerous sighs" was written in substantially larger letters than the surrounding words.

Page 284

L. 4 'twill] 'Twill

L. 10 our self] it self

L. 19 ambiti[us]<on>] ambition

L. 20 opportunable] opportunity

Page 285

L. 5 con[cur]<spire>] conspire

L. 13 /V/] /Vertu/

L. 22 RB did not indicate where this insertion was to be placed.

Index

— D —

— U —

— V —

— W —

— Y —

— Z —

An associate professor of English at The Pennsylvania State University, *John T. Harwood* teaches courses in rhetoric and literature and holds a half-time appointment in the Center for Academic Computing. He is the author of two other volumes published by the Southern Illinois University Press: *Critics, Values, and Restoration Comedy* (1982) and *The Rhetorics of Thomas Hobbes and Bernard Lamy* (1986).

His current research examines the relationship between print culture and the emergence and diffusion of the New Philosophy.